TRACTS AND PAMPHLETS

BY

RICHARD STEELE

THE

Political Writings

OF

Sir *Richard Steele.*

Mala Opinio, Bene parta, delectat. Sen.

LONDON:

Printed for *J. T.* and Sold by *Owen Lloyd* near the
Church in the *Temple,* and *J. Brown* at the *Black
Swan,* without *Temple-Bar.* **1715.**

TRACTS AND PAMPHLETS

BY

RICHARD STEELE

EDITED WITH NOTES AND COMMENTARY

BY

RAE BLANCHARD

BALTIMORE

THE JOHNS HOPKINS PRESS

1944

The publication of this volume has been aided by a grant from the American Council of Learned Societies from a fund provided by the Carnegie Corporation of New York.

LONDON: HUMPHREY MILFORD
OXFORD UNIVERSITY PRESS

PRINTED IN THE UNITED STATES OF AMERICA
BY J. H. FURST COMPANY, BALTIMORE, MARYLAND

The PREFACE

Steele's plays and major periodicals have been reprinted in modern times. But the miscellaneous tracts and pamphlets, which in his own day ran into many editions and made his name famous, must now be sought out in antiquarian book shops and, one here, one there, in university libraries. To bring them all together for rereading is the purpose of this collected edition.

Only one of the thirty-three pieces included has been reprinted in a modern edition.[1] None of the others has been issued in any form since the eighteenth century. Early in his career Steele himself collected eight of them in *The Political Writings of Sir Richard Steele* (1715); and he incorporated two others in collected periodicals (1714, 1719).[2] Then towards the end of the century, a great admirer of his, Dr. John Nichols, London printer and editor, reissued twelve more, to supplement the collection of 1715, in several miscellaneous volumes which today are as scarce as Steele's original editions.[3] Of the remaining ten of the thirty-three, four—rare and little known—exist only as Steele first issued them; and two have not appeared in print before.[4]

[1] *The Christian Hero*, ed. Rae Blanchard (Oxford University Press, 1932).

[2] *The Political Writings of Sir Richard Steele* (1715) contains: *The Englishman's Thanks to the Duke of Marlborough; A Letter to Sir Miles Warton Concerning Occasional Peers; The Guardian of August the 7th, 1713; The Importance of Dunkirk Consider'd; The French Faith Represented in the Present State of Dunkirk; The Crisis; A Letter to a Member . . . Concerning the Bill for Preventing the Growth of Schism; Mr. Steele's Apology for Himself and His Writings.*
The collected *Englishman* (1714) contains *Englishman*, No. 57, which was first issued as a separate pamphlet; and *The Plebeian* was collected in 1719.

[3] (1) *The Lover and Reader to Which are Prefix'd the Whig Examiner . . .* (1789) contains *Medley*, No. 23. (2) *Town Talk, The Fish Pool . . .* (1789) contains *Town Talk*, No. 5; *A Letter to a Member Concerning the Condemn'd Lords; Speech for the Septennial Bill; An Account of the Fish Pool; The Plebeian* (also reissued by Steele in 1719); *A Letter to the Earl of Oxford Concerning the Bill of Peerage; The Spinster: In defence of the Woollen Manufactures.* (3) *The Town Talk, The Fish Pool . . . A New Edition* (1790) contains also *A Letter from the Earl of Mar to the King.* (4) *The Theatre . . . with The Anti-Theatre* (1791) contains *The Crisis of Property; A Nation A Family; The State of the Case; Pasquin*, Nos. 46 and 51.

[4] This group of ten includes the following: *The British Subject's Answer to*

vii

The intention is that every tract and every short piece of writing in pamphlet form known certainly to be Steele's should have a place here.[5] This does not mean, however, that the list is complete and final; for without any doubt at all, papers and pamphlets published anonymously remain unidentified as his. Taking refuge in anonymity was not habitual with Steele; but even so, nearly half of the known tracts were first issued without his name, and a few of these, for one reason or another, never directly acknowledged. So very certainly there are others still to be found. Moreover, the bulk is suspiciously small for a journalist so ingrained, with convictions and a sense of responsibility to the public so strong. Probably there were few crises or paper battles between 1700 and 1725 when, as publicist or propagandist, Steele could resist speaking out in a pamphlet, even when he had at hand for use one of his half-dozen periodicals.[6] It is not conceivable, for example, that he could remain silent when his friend Dr. Hoadly was engaged in the Bangorian Controversy; yet no contribution of his is known.

the Pretender's Declaration; The Joint and Humble Address of the Tories and Whigs; The Antidote in a Letter to the Free-Thinker; The Antidote No. II; two of Steele's parliamentary speeches; The Romish Ecclesiastical History; and An Account of the State of the Roman Catholick Religion (prefatory matter). The unpublished pamphlets are [Greatness Among the Moderns] and Isaack Bickerstaffe Esq. to Pasquin.

[5] Excluded, of course, are unauthorized tracts with Steele's name on the title page as an advertisement, such as: Curll's publication, Sir Richard Steele's Account of Mr. Desaguliers' new-invented Chimneys (1716), which has in it a few sentences from Town Talk, No. 3; Memoirs of . . . Thomas, Late Marquess of Wharton . . . To which is added His Lordship's Character by Sir Richard Steele (1715), containing the Dedication of Spectator, V; and The Court of Honour . . . with Some Observations by Sir Richard Steele (1720) containing a quotation from The Theatre, No. 19.

In quite another category is The Ladies Library. Written by a Lady. Published by Mr. Steele (3 vols., 1714), which was translated into several foreign languages and had many English editions during the eighteenth century. With regret, it is excluded because of its length and the uncertainty of Steele's contributions to the compilation. It does contain, however, besides the Dedications and a little-known and attractive Preface which are certainly his several connecting links which are probably from his pen.

[6] These are so well-known that a list of them given here may seem gratuitous. It is a reminder, however, of Steele's unflagging journalism during a decade of his career:

The Tatler (1709-10); The Spectator (1711-12); The Guardian (1713); The Englishman (first series, 1713-14); The Englishman (second series, 1715); The Lover (1714); The Reader (1714); Town Talk (1715-16); The Theatre (1720).

Tracts have been ascribed to Steele, now and again, which lie in a doubtful realm. A list of the more important of them is given in the *Appendix*. Several of these ascriptions have been demonstrated erroneous, and others are generally held to be so. But inquiring scholars may yet find convincing evidence that some among them are from his pen.

A bibliography and textual notes for each item included are given at the back of the book, the bibliography containing a description of the various editions and translations and a partial census of copies. The editor has made it a practice, within a limited experience of course, to handle and examine as many copies as possible in the various libraries in this country and the British Isles where the work has been carried on. In some cases, however, the existence of a copy has been confirmed only by a statement in the Union Catalogue at the Library of Congress. Copies used for the reproduction of the text are marked with an asterisk. Facsimiles of twenty-four title pages—those which were obtainable—are included.

The basic principle applied in establishing a text has been to find the edition or issue which represents Steele's final word. For the ten which he himself collected that was a simple matter, although the earlier editions have been collated with the final form to determine any significant alterations. Another ten, which exist only in first editions, are given as they stand except for corrections which he authorized in *errata*. The folio issue has been used for papers separately contributed to periodicals, in one instance collated with the collected form. For the half-dozen uncollected tracts existing in several editions or issues, collation was used to determine which seems to be nearest what Steele intended finally to say. Lists of *errata* are found in five, and these corrections have been incorporated. The existence of autograph manuscripts for three has made it possible to study his habits and methods of composition. To the statement concerning the text of each one are added, when they occur, the variant readings.

A brief introduction placed before each tract outlines the occasion and the general background for it and answers the obvious questions of date, authorship, and interpretation. A detailed analysis is not attempted of Steele's ideas and ethics, his contribution to Whig journalism, his range and scope as a pamphleteer, his methods, and the effects of his propaganda, although such a study might be very revealing in a reappraisal of his genius. Assembled here are the basic materials for it. A complete analysis, however, would cover also the political essays of the periodicals.

Although his reputation as a man of letters is secure in the dramas and essays, the Steele of public life has been for some reason underrated or even forgotten. Perhaps he has been overshadowed by other publicists of his time. It may be true that his tracts are not so informed as Defoe's, so polished as Addison's, or so powerfully reasoned as Swift's. Yet if success can be measured by circulation, answering tracts for and against, and controversies stirred up, they hit their mark effectively. Perhaps he has been dismissed as an irresponsible, a whimsical, a flibbertigibbet, not to be taken very seriously. Whatever the reason, it is generally forgotten that during fourteen crucial years for Great Britain, Steele was a member of parliament, for a decade—before ill-health prevented—a conscientious, working member, as can be seen by reading the *Journals of the Commons*; that he took a turn of three years at editing the *Gazette* under the Godolphin Ministry; that he was for six or seven years on the forfeited estates commission; that he directed the journalistic Whig front, both before the Hanoverian accession and afterwards when the legality of the King's title was now and again contested by rebels.

A closer study than has ever been made would reveal the thread of unity in his political tracts to be passionate adherence to the doctrine of the Revolution of 1688—the Protestant Succession, religious toleration, civil rights and liberties, a spirit of opposition to exorbitant power in any part of the constitution. His Whiggism was downright in matters of trade, foreign policy, the church, and the dynasty. Tory absolutist doctrines and Francophil Jacobitism in any guise were always his targets. Yet political considerations never came before loyalty to national interests as he understood them. He was never a slavish placeman, and his partizanship has been exaggerated. It is surprising to find how often he acted as an opposition Whig or an independent, calmly, with an absence of illusion, taking the penalties for adherence to his convictions.

His views on church and state are those of a moderate; and his expression of them is marked, in the main, by conciliation, mildness of tone, absence of personal abuse. Harshness and vindictive recriminations always seemed to him not only un-Christian but also lacking in political wisdom. He himself never held a grudge very long for political or personal injuries. His inexhaustible courage is exhibited by more than one tract. Fearless and persistent writing on behalf of his principles brought him disgrace: once, expulsion from the House for service to his party; again, at the hands of his party, threatened expulsion and the actual loss of his post at Drury Lane.

Many of these tracts are pervaded by an old-fashioned eloquence; in places, it is only fair to admit, their style is turgid. And the diction, phrasing, and form often suggest the modes of the preceding century rather than those of Steele's own. At their worst, several have an omnibus quality. But the buoyancy, liveliness, and earnest altruism in all of them make amends, in part, for imperfections of form. There is no doubt that Steele's own public was kindled. And, on the whole, they make rather thoughtful reading even now, after two centuries have gone by.

I began assembling the materials for this book several years ago in the British Isles, where the resources of various libraries—but chiefly those of the British Museum—were drawn upon; and I have finished it, here at home, in the Goucher College Library and other libraries of Baltimore and in the Library of Congress at Washington. The summer of 1941 I spent somewhat farther afield, at the University of Texas, which now holds the unusual Steele collection made by George A. Aitken, the English scholar. To the librarians of these institutions and of all others mentioned in the *Bibliographies,* I am very grateful. Librarians are almost the best friends that research students have. It is a pleasure to make public acknowledgement to the Library of Harvard University for permission to use the manuscript, *Isaack Bickerstaffe Esq. to Pasquin*; to the Library of Yale University for the use of the rare pamphlet, *The Englishman's Thanks to the Duke of Marlborough*; and to Professor Sherburn for his copy of *The British Subject's Answer* from his fine collection of Steele. I am especially indebted to Professor William T. Morgan of Indiana University, who examined portions of the book and made valuable suggestions that I have endeavored to follow. Two other persons, among the many who have shared their knowledge, patience, and skill, I should like to mention by name—Mr. Chester Reather, of Baltimore, who made the photographs, and Miss Jean Webster, my student, who helped with the clerical work. Finally, my hearty thanks are given to those groups of persons whose cooperation has made possible the publication of the book—the Johns Hopkins Press, the Modern Language Association of America, the American Council of Learned Societies, and the Carnegie Corporation of New York.

R. B.

1 August 1943
Goucher College
Baltimore, Maryland

The CONTENTS

FACSIMILES OF TITLE PAGES, &c.

xvii

The Christian Hero (April, 1701)

This tract in 1701, Steele's first prose work, was written when he was on active duty in and near London as an Ensign of the Guards. It was addressed to "Men of Wit and Gallantry," but particularly to his fellow soldiers, and was dedicated to his colonel, Lord Cutts, one of Marlborough's most able generals. In purpose and content it is related to the moral essay, the manual of piety, and the reforming tract issued in such vast numbers at the turn of the century. That Steele's first object of reform was himself he confessed some years later: he wrote it "with a design principally to fix upon his own Mind a strong Impression of Virtue and Religion." For a time he did not publish it (the summer of 1699 was the date of its inception); but "This secret Admonition was too Weak; he therefore Printed the Book with his Name, in hopes that a standing Testimony against Himself might . . . make him ashamed of Understanding and seeming to feel what was Virtuous and living so quite contrary a Life" (*Apology*, 1714).

The general theme is the superiority as a moral guide of the Christian religion over pagan philosophy. Steele placed himself with the moralists who deprecated neo-Stoicism. Despite "the Pompous Look Elegant Pens" had given pagan heroes, he hoped to prove that the early Christians were the "most truly Gallant and Heroick that ever appeared to Mankind." In the first chapter the lives of Cato, Caesar, and Brutus are recounted to demonstrate that their philosophy failed them in times of crises. The second has an account of the heroic elements in the life of Christ. The third eulogizes the precepts and conduct of the early Christians, especially St. Paul. The fourth endeavors to show the value of religious motives to all men aspiring to greatness and ends with a tribute to King William, a modern hero.

Steele himself thought well of this tract and gave to it more revisory attention than to any other of his prose writings. Twenty editions of it before the end of the century are testimony of its popularity with contemporary readers. Modern readers value it chiefly, perhaps, as the first expression of some of the ideas elaborated in *The Tatler* and *The Spectator*, for it is seen that the moral theory outlined here is his starting point for two decades of writing. But regarded in the light of Steele's life and his achievement, the sincerity and grace of his first tract make their own appeal. Textual notes on p. 636.

1

THE
Chriſtian Hero:

AN
ARGUMENT

Proving that no

PRINCIPLES

BUT THOSE OF

RELIGION

Are Sufficient to make a

GREAT MAN.

——*Fragili quærens illidere dentem*
Offendet ſolido——*Ho.*

The THIRD EDITION.

LONDON:

Printed for *Jacob Tonſon*, within *Gray's-Inn Gate*,
next *Gray's-Inn-Lane.* 1710.

3

To the Right Honourable the

LORD *CUTTS*,

Colonel *of His Majesty's* Cold-Stream *Regiment of Guards,* &c.

My Lord,

THE Address of the following Papers is so very much Due
to your Lordship, that they are but a mere Report of what
has past upon my Guard to my Commander, for they were Writ
upon Duty, when the Mind was perfectly Disengag'd and at
Leisure in the Silent Watch of the Night, to run over the Busy
Dream of the Day; and the Vigilance which Obliges us to
suppose an Enemy always near us, has Awaken'd a Sense that
there is a Restless and Subtle one which constantly attends our
Steps, and meditates our Ruin.

Thoughts of this Nature, a Man may with Freedom Acknowledge to Your Lordship, who have ever been so far from
running into the Fashionable Vice of Exploding Religion, that
your Early Valour first appear'd against the Profess'd Enemies
of Christianity; and *Buda* had Transmitted you to late Posterity,
but that you your self have Obliterated your Part in that
Glorious Scene by the fresher Memory of you, at *Limerick*
and *Namure.*

With one honest purpose of Life, and constant Service of
one Interest, and one Cause, in what Country have you not
Fought? in what Field have you not Bled? but I know I here
Offend you, nor will you allow Warmth in Commendation to
be like a Friend; but if, my Lord, to speak you Generous,
Honest and Brave be not so, I do assure you 'tis the only thing
I'll ever do in common with your Enemies.

I said your Enemies, but if there are any who have Ignorance
or Malice enough to be such, their little Hates must be lost in
the Distinction the better World allow you, and that Country
(whose Discerning is refin'd by a Learned and Elegant Uni-

versity) has done you so great an Honour, in making you Unanimously their Representative in Parliament, that they who would Oppose your Reputation, do but confess they are Unacquainted with what passes in the World, and Strangers to the Residence of Knowledge and Virtue.

'Twas there you receiv'd those Rudiments of Honour, which have render'd your Life Conspicuous enough to make you appear a worthy Descendant of an Ancient and Distinguish'd Family, which has Serv'd the Crown in the most Eminent Stations, and been equally Favourites of their Country; 'twas there you Receiv'd[1] those Impressions which Inspire that true Use of your Being, which so justly divides your Time, between Labour and Diversion, that the one does but Recreate for the other, and which give a generous Contempt of both, when they come[2] in Competition with the Service of that Country which you Love, and that God whom you Worship.

Go on, my Lord, thus to Contemn, and thus to Enjoy Life; and if some great *English* Day does not call for that Sacrifice, which you are always ready to Offer, may you in a Mature Age go to Sleep with your Ancestors, in Expectation not of an Imaginary Fame, but a Real Immortality.[3]

As for the Present I now make you, if you'll Accept it with your usual Goodness and Affection to me, I shall Entertain no further Hopes; for as your Favour is my Fortune, so your Approbation is my Fame,

I am,

MY LORD,

Your Lordship's

Tower-Guard,
March 23. 1701.

Most Obedient, most Faithful

and most Humble Servant,

RICHARD STEELE.

PREFACE.

THE World is divided between two sorts of People, the Men of Wit and the Men of Business, and these have it wholly in their Power; but however Mighty the latter may esteem themselves, they have much the less share in the Government of Mankind, and till they can keep the others out of Company as well as Employment, they will have an almost Irresistible Dominion over us: For their Imagination is so very quick and lively, that in all they enjoy or possess, they have a Relish highly Superior to that of slower Men; which fine Sense of things they can communicate to others in so prevailing a manner, that they give and take away what Impressions they please; for while the Man of Wit speaks, he bestows upon his Hearers, by an apt Representation of his Thoughts, all the Happiness and Pleasure of being such as he is, and quickens our heavier Life into Joys we should never of our selves have tasted, so that we are for our own sakes his Slaves and Followers: But indeed they generally use this charming Force with the utmost Tyranny, and as 'tis too much in their Power, misplace our Love, our Hatred, our Desires and Aversions, on improper Objects; so that when we are left to our selves, we find Truth discolour'd to us, and they of Faculties above us have wrapt things, in their own nature of a dark and horrid Aspect, in so bright a Disguise, that they have stamp'd a kind of Praise and Gallantry on some Vices, and half persuaded us that a Whore may be still a Beauty, and an Adulterer no Villain.

These Ills are supported by the Arbitrary Sway of Legislative Ridicule, while by, I know not what Pedantry of good Breeding, Conversation is confin'd to Indifferent, Low, or perhaps Vitious Subjects; and all that is Serious, Good or Great, almost Banished the World: For in Imitation of those we have mentioned, there daily arise so many Pretenders to do Mischief, that what seem'd at first but a Conspiracy, is now a general Insurrection against Virtue; and when they who really have Wit lead the way it is hardly to be prevented, but that they must be followed by a

7

Crowd who would be such, and make what shift they can to appear so, by helping one Defect with another, and supplying want of Wit with want of Grace, and want of Reputation with want of Shame.

Thus are Men hurry'd away in the Prosecution of mean and sensual Desires, and instead of Employing their Passions in the service of Life, they spend their Life in the service of their Passions; yet tho' 'tis a Truth very little receiv'd, that Virtue is its own Reward, 'tis surely an undeniable one, that Vice is its own Punishment; for when we have giv'n our Appetites a loose Rein, we are immediately precipitated by 'em into unbounded and endless Wishes, while we repine at our Fortune, if its Narrowness curbs 'em, tho' the Gratification of 'em were a Kindness, like the Indulgence of a Man's Thirst in a Dropsy; but this Distemper of Mind is never to be remedied, till Men will more unreservedly attempt the Work, and will resolve to value themselves rather upon a strong Reason to allay their Passions, than a fine Imagination to raise 'em.

For if we best Judge of things when we are not actually engag'd or concern'd in 'em, every Man's own Experience must inform him, that both the Pleasures we follow, and the Sorrows we shun, are in Nature very different from what we conceive 'em, when we observe that past Enjoyments are Anxious, past Sufferings pleasing in the Reflection; and since the Memory of the one makes us apprehend our Strength, the other our Weakness, it is an Argument of a trivial Mind to prefer the Satisfactions that lead to Inquietude before Pains that lead to Tranquility.

But if that consists (as it certainly does) in the Mind's enjoyment of Truth, the most vexatious Circumstance of its Anguish, is that of being in Doubt; from which Men will find but a very short Relief, if they draw it from the Collections or Observations of sedentary Men, who have been call'd Wise for proposing Rules of active Life, which they cannot be supposed to understand: For between the Arrogant and Fanatick Indolence of some, and the false and pleasurable Felicity of others (which are equally Chimæras) a Man is so utterly divided, that the Happiness of Philosophers appears as Fantastisk as the Misery of Lovers.

We shall not, 'tis hop'd, be understood by saying this, to

Imagine that there is a sufficient Force in the short following Essay,[5] to stem the Universal and Destructive Torrent of Error and Pleasure; it is sufficient if we can stand without being carry'd away with it, and we shall very willingly resign the Glory of an Opposition, if we can enjoy the Safety of a Defence; and as it was at first attempted to disengage my own Mind from deceiving Appearances, so it can be publish'd for no other end, but to set others a thinking with the same Inclination: Which whoever will please to do, will make a much better Argument for his own private Use, than any body else can for Him: For ill Habits of the Mind, no more than those of the Body,[6] are to be cur'd by the Patient's Approbation of the Medicine, except He'll resolve to take it; and if my Fellow-Soldiers (to whose Service more especially I would direct any Thoughts I were capable of) would form to themselves, (if any do not) a constant Reason of their Actions, they would find themselves better prepar'd for all the Vicissitudes they are to meet with, when instead of the Changeable Heat of mere Courage and Blood, they acted upon the firm Motives of Duty, Valour, and Constancy of Soul.

For (however they are dis-esteem'd by some Unthinking, not to say, Ungrateful Men) to Profess Arms, is to Profess being ready to Die for others; nor is it an Ordinary Struggle between Reason, Sense, and Passion, that can raise Men to a calm and ready Negligence of Life, and animate 'em to Assault without Fear, Pursue without Cruelty, and Stab without Hatred.[7]

But Virtuous Principles must infallibly be not only better than any other We can Embrace, to Warm us to great Attempts,[8] but also to make Our Days in their Ordinary Passage slide away Agreeably: For as nothing is more daring than Truth, so there is nothing more Chearful than Innocence;[9] and indeed I need not have been beholden to the Experience of a various Life to have been convinc'd, that true Happiness is not to be found but where I at present place it;[10] For I was long ago inform'd where only it was to be had,[11] by the Reverend Dr. *Ellis*, my ever Honour'd Tutor; which Great Obligation I could not but Mention, tho' my Gratitude to Him is perhaps an Accusation of my self, who shall appear to have so little Profited by the Institution of so Solid and Excellent a Writer, tho' he is above the Temptation of (what is always in his Power) being Famous.

The Christian Hero :

O R,

No Principles but those of

RELIGION

SUFFICIENT

To make a Great Man.

I T is certainly the most useful Task we can possibly Undertake, to rescue our Minds from the Prejudice with which a false and unreasonable Fondness of our selves has enslaved us. But the Examination of our own Bosoms is so ungrateful an Exercise, that we are forc'd upon a Thousand little Arts, to lull our Selves into an imperfect Tranquility, which we might obtain sincere and uninterrupted, if we had Courage enough to look at the ghastly Part of our Condition: But we are still Flatterers to our selves, and Hypocrites the wrong way, by chusing, instead of the solid Satisfaction of Innocence and Truth, the returning Pangs of Conscience, and working out our Damnation as we are taught to do our Happiness, *with Fear and Trembling.*

But this Misfortune we owe, as we do most others, to an unjust Education, by which we are inspir'd with an Ambition of acquiring such Modes and Accomplishments, as rather enable us to give Pleasure and Entertainment to others, than Satisfaction and Quiet to our selves: So Phantastical are we as to dress for a Ball when we are to set out on a Journey, and upon Change of Weather, are justly derided, not pitied by the Beholders. How then shall we prepare for the unaccountable

Road of Life, when we know not how long or how short it will prove, or what Accidents we shall meet in our Passage? Can we take any thing with us that can make us chearful, ready and prepar'd for all Occasions, and can support us against all Encounters? Yes, we may (if we would receive it) a Confidence in God. Yet, lest this be impos'd upon Men by a blind force of Custom, or the Artifice of such Persons whose Interest perhaps it may be to obtrude upon our Mirth, and our Gaiety, and give us a melancholy Prospect [12] (as some Men would persuade us) [13] to maintain themselves in the Luxury they deny us; let us not be frighted from the liberal use of our Senses, or meanly resign our present Opinions, 'till we are con-vinc'd from our own Reflection also, that there is something in that Opinion which can make us less insolent in Joy, less depress'd in Adversity, than the Methods we are already en-gag'd [14] in. And indeed the chief Cause of Irresolution in either State, must proceed from the want of an adæquate Motive to our Actions, that can render Men Dauntless and Invincible both to Pleasure and Pain.

It were not then, methinks, an useless Enquiry to search into the Reason that we are so willing to arm our selves against the Assaults of Delight and Sorrow, rather with the Dictates of Morality than those of Religion; and how it has obtain'd, that when we say a thing was done like an old *Roman*, we have a generous and sublime Idea, that warms and kindles in us, to-gether with a certain Self-disdain, a desire of Imitation; when, on the other side, to say, 'twas like a Primitive Christian, chills Ambition, and seldom rises to more than the cold approbation of a Duty that perhaps a Man wishes he were not oblig'd to. Or, in a word, why is it that the Heathen struts, and the Christian sneaks in our Imagination: If it be as *Machiavil* says, that Religion throws our Minds below noble and hazardous Pursuits, then its Followers are Slaves and Cowards; but if it gives a more hardy and aspiring Genius than the World before knew, then He, and All our fine Observers, who have been pleas'd to give us only Heathen Portraitures, to say no worse, have robb'd their Pens of Characters the most truly Gallant and Heroick that ever appear'd to Mankind.

About the time the World receiv'd the best News it ever

heard, The Men whose Actions and Fortunes are most pomp-
ously array'd in Story, had just acted or were then performing
their Parts, as if it had been the Design of Providence to pre-
possess at that time, after a more singular manner than ordinary,
the Minds of Men, with the Trappings and Furniture of Glory
and Riches, to heighten the Virtue and Magnanimity of those
who were to oppose 'em all, by passing through Wants, Miseries
and Disgraces; and indeed the shining Actions of these illustrious Men do yet glare so much in our Faces, that we lose our
Way by following a false Fire, which well consider'd is but a
delusive Vapour of the Earth, when we might enjoy the leading
constant Light of Heav'n.

To make therefore a just Judgment in our Conduct, let us
consider two or three of the most eminent Heathen, and observe
whether they, or we, are better appointed for the hard and weary
March of human Life; for which Examination we will not look
into the Closets of Men of Reflection and Retirement, but into
the Practice and Resolution of those of Action and Enterprize.
There were never Persons more conspicuously of this latter
sort, than those concern'd in the Fortunes and Death of *Cæsar*;
and since the Pulse of Man then beat at the highest, we will
think it sufficient to our Purpose carefully to review Him, and
Them, as they March by us, and if we can see any apparent
Defect in their Armour, find out some way to mend it in our
own. But it will require all our Patience, by taking notice of
the minutest Things, to come at (what is absolutely necessary
to us) the Recesses of their Hearts, and Folds of their Tempers.

Sallust has transmitted to us two very great, but very different
Personages, *Cæsar* and *Cato*, and plac'd them together in the
most judicious Manner for appearing to advantage, by the
alternate Light and Shade of each other: *Cæsar*'s Bounty, Magnificence, Popular and Sumptuous Entertainments stole an universal Affection; *Cato*'s Parsimony, Integrity, Austere and Rigid
Behaviour commanded as universal Reverence: None could do
an ungentile thing before *Cæsar*, none a loose one before *Cato*:
To one 'twas Recommendation enough to be Miserable, to the
other to be Good: To *Cæsar* all Faults were pardonable, to
Cato none: One gave, oblig'd, pity'd and succour'd indiffer-
ently; t'other blam'd, oppos'd, and condemn'd impartially:

Cæsar was the Refuge of the Unhappy, *Cato* the Bane of the Wicked: *Cato* had rather be, than seem Good; *Cæsar* was careless of either, but as it serv'd his Interests: *Cato*'s Sword was the Sword of Justice, *Cæsar*'s that of Ambition: *Cæsar* had an excellent common Sense and right Judgment of Occasion, Time and Place; the other blunt Man understood not Application, knew how to be in the Right, but was generally so, out of Season: *Cæsar*'s Manner made even his Vice charming, *Cato*'s even [15] his Virtue disagreeable: *Cæsar* insinuated Ill, *Cato* intruded Good: *Cæsar* in his Sayings, his Actions and his Writings was the first and happiest of all Men: In his Discourse he had a constant Wit and right Reason; in his Actions, Gallantry and Success; in his Writings, every thing that any Author can pretend to, and one which perhaps no Man else ever had; he mentions himself with a good Grace. Thus it was very natural for *Cæsar*, adorn'd with every Art, Master of every necessary Quality, either for Use or Ornament, with a steady and well-plac'd Industry to out-run *Cato*, and all like him, who had none and desir'd none, but (an ever weak Party) the Good for his Friends.

Now this sort of Men were *Cæsar* and *Cato*, and by these Arts they arriv'd [16] at that height, which has left one's Name proverbial for a Noble and Princely Nature, t'other's for an Unmov'd and Inexorable Honesty: Yet, without following 'em thro' all the handsome Incidents and Passages of Life, we may know 'em well enough in Miniature, by beholding 'em only in their manner of Dying: For in those last Minutes, the Soul and Body both collect all their Force, either bravely to oppose the Enemy, or gracefully receive the *Conqueror*, Death.

Cæsar, by a long Tract of Successes, was now become apparent Master of his Country, but with a Security, that's natural to gallant Men, Heroically forgave the most inveterate of his Opposers: Now was He follow'd with Applause, Renown, and Acclamation: His Valour had subdued the Bodies, his Clemency the Minds of his Enemies: And how bless'd must the Earth be under his Command, who seems to court Dominion for no other end, but to indulge an insatiable Mind in the glorious Pleasures of bestowing and forgiving? This was the Figure *Cæsar* bore in the World's Opinion, but not in *Cato*'s. He was there a Tyrant in spite of the Gloss of Success and of Fortune, which could not create Appearances bright enough to dazzle his Eyes from seeing the Traitor in the Conqueror: He knew to give a Man his own as a Bounty was but a more impudent Robbery, and a Wrong improv'd by the Slavery of an Obligation: He justly and generously disdain'd that his Fellow-Citizen shou'd pretend to be his Lord; to his honest Mind a Pardon was but a more arrogant Insult, nor could he bear the Apprehension of seeing his Equal inflict upon him a *tyrannical Forgiveness*: What then must this unhappy good Man do? Whither shall oppress'd Virtue fly from Slavery? From *Slavery*? *No.* He is still Free Lord of Himself, and Master of his Passions; *Cæsar* is the Captive, He is Shackl'd, He is Chain'd, and the numerous Troops which he boasts the Companions of his Triumphs, and his Glories, are but so many Witnesses of his Shame and Confusion, to whom he has by an open Usurpation manifested his broken Faith, false Profession, and prostituted Honour. But how far this Impression of intrinsick Glory and Happiness in sincere, tho' distress'd Virtue, and the sense of a wicked Man's abject, tho' prosperous Condition (which *Cato*'s Philosophy gave Him) did avail in his afflicted Hours; the Resolution he is going to take will demonstrate.

He had now at *Utica* fresh and shocking Intelligence of the gathering Adherents to his Enemy, and could read, in his own Company, the mere Followers of Fortune in their Countenance, but observ'd it with a negligent and undaunted Air, concern'd only for the Fate of others, whose weak Pity of themselves made 'em the Objects of his Compassion also. It was visible by a thousand little officious things he did, he was resolv'd to leave this bad World: For he spent the Day, which he design'd should be his last,[17] in a certain Vanity of Goodness: He Consulted, Persuaded, and Dispatch'd all he thought necessary for the Safety of those that were about him; which Services they receiv'd from him, whose Intent they saw, with Tears, and Shame, and Admiration.

He continued the whole Evening this affected Enjoyment of his Friends Anxiety for him, which he rais'd by set Discourses, and abated, or rather confirm'd by a studied Indifference, 'till he went to Bed, where he read *Plato*'s Immortality, and Guesses at a future Life: At last he enquir'd for his Sword, on purpose mis-laid by his Son; they did not immediately bring it, which he seem'd to take no notice of, but again fell to his Book: After his Second Lecture, he again wanted his Sword: Their Hesitation in letting him have it, threw him into an unseemly Rage, and Expostulation with his Friends, whose obliging Sorrow withheld it: What has he done, what has he committed, to be betray'd into the Hands of his Enemy? Had *Cato*'s Wisdom so far left him, that he must be disarm'd, like a Slave and a Madman? What had his Son seen so indiscreet in his Father, that he was not to be trusted with himself? To all this cruel and intemperate Qustion, he was answer'd with the humblest Behaviour, tenderest Beseeching, and deepest Esteem; They implor'd his Stay amongst 'em as their Genius, their Guardian, and Benefactor; Among the rest, a fond Slave was putting in his Resistance, and his Affliction, for which he dash'd the poor Fellow's Teeth out with his Fist, and forc'd out of the Room his lamenting Friends, with Noise, and Taunt, and Tumult; a little while after had his Hand with which he struck his Servant dress'd, lay down, and was heard to Snore; but sure we may charitably enough believe, from all this unquiet Carriage, that the Sleep was dissembled, from which as soon as he awak'd, he Stabb'd himself, and fell on the Floor; His Fall alarm'd his wretched Dependants, whose help he resisted by tearing open his own Bowels, and rushing out of Life with Fury, Rage and Indignation.

This was the applauded Exit of that Noble *Roman*, who is said with a superior and invincible Constancy to have eluded the Partiality of Fortune, and escap'd the Incursion upon the Liberty of his Country: It seems then, had he liv'd, his own had been lost, and his calling himself still Free, and *Cæsar* the Usurper, a Bond-man and Slave, were but mere Words; for his Opinion of things was in reality Stunn'd by Success, and he dy'd Disappointed of the Imaginary Self-Existence his own Set of Thoughts had promis'd him, by an Action below the Precepts of his Philosophy, and the Constancy of his Life.

Thus did *Cato* leave the World, for which indeed he was very unfit, in the Hands of the most Skilful Man in it, who at his entrance on its Empire excell'd his past Glorious Life, by using with so much Temper and Moderation what he had purchas'd with so much Bloodshed and Violence: But we must leave, at present, this busie and *Incessant* Mind to the Meditation of Levelling inaccessible Mountains, Checking the Course of the Ocean,[18] and correcting the Periods of Time: We must leave him employ'd in Modeling the Universe (now his own) in the secure Enjoyment of a Life hitherto led in Illustrious Hazards, and now every way safe, but where 'tis its Beauty to lye open, to the Treachery of his Friends.

Among the many Pretenders to that Character was *Cassius*, an able and experienc'd Soldier, bound to him by no less an Obligation, than the giving him Life and Quarter in Battel; He was of a Dark, Sullen and *Involv'd* Spirit, quick to receive, but slow to discover a Distaste; His Anger never flew into his Face, but descended to his Heart, which rankled, and prey'd upon it self, and could not admit [19] of Composure, either from Religion or Philosophy; but being a perfect *Epicurean*, and fancying there were none, or if any, only Lazy and Supine Deities, must necessarily Terminate his Hopes and Fears in himself, and from his own Arm expect all the Good and Evil of which his Life was capable: This Man, in his Temper uneasie, and piqu'd by a certain Partiality of *Cæsar*'s to his Disadvantage, could not satisfie a Sedate Bloody Humour by any less Reparation than his Ruin; and having [20] a revengeful Biass of Mind, a short Memory of Kindnesses, and an indelible Resentment of Wrongs, resolv'd to cancel an odious Benefit, by a pleasing Injury: To this Determination he was prompted by the worst *only Good* Quality a Man can have, an undaunted Courage, which fermented in Him a restless and *Gnawing* Meditation of his *Enemy's, that is, his Benefactor's Death*; A Thought befitting the Greatness of his Ambition, and the Largeness of his pernicious Capacity; His Capacity which consisted in a skilful Dissimulation of his Faults; for being full of those Vices which nearly approach, and easily assume the Resemblance of Virtue, and seldom throw a Man into visible and obvious Follies, he so well accommodated his ill Qualities to the good ones of those with whom he Convers'd, that he was very well with the best Men by a Similitude of their Manners; His Avarice obtain'd the Frugal; his Spleen, and Disrelish of Joy, the Sober and Abstinent; His Envy, and Hatred of Superiors, the Asserters of

Publick Liberty: This considerable Wretch skilfully warm'd and urg'd some of his own Temper, whom he knew ready for any great Mischief, to pull down the Overgrown *Cæsar*, and ensnar'd others by the specious Pretence of a sincere Love to his Country, to meet all Hazards for her Recovery; These illustrious Ruffians, who were indeed Men of the most Weight, and the boldest Spirits of the *Roman Empire*, design'd to dispatch him in the Eye of all the World, in open Senate; but neither their Quality or Accomplishments were great enough to support 'em in so Nefarious an Attempt, without there could be an Expedient thought of, to give it a more sacred Esteem, than any of their Characters could inspire: 'Twas therefore necessary to make *Marcus Brutus* of the Conspiracy.

This Gentleman possess'd the very Bosom of *Cæsar*, who having had a Notorious Intrigue with his Mother, was believ'd to have thought him his Son; but whether that, or an Admiration of his Virtue, was the cause of his Fondness, He had so tender a regard for him, that at the Battel of *Pharsalia* he gave it in Orders to the whole Army, if he would not take Quarter to let him escape: He was, like *Cæsar*, addicted to Letters and Arms, and tho' not equal to him in his *Capacity for either*, above him in the use of both. He never drew his Sword but with a design to serve his Country, nor ever Read with any other purpose but to subdue his Passions, so that he had from Books rather an habit of Life than a Faculty of Speech; in his Thoughts as well as Actions he was a strict Follower of Honesty and Justice; all he said, as well as all he did, seem'd to flow from a publick and unbiass'd Spirit: He had no occasion for the Powers of Eloquence to be able to persuade, for all Men knew 'twas their Interest to be of his Mind; and he had before he spoke that first Point, the [21] good will of his Audience, for every Man's Love of himself made him a Lover of *Brutus*. He had this Eminence without the least taint of Vanity, and a great Fame seem'd not so much the Pursuit, as the Consequence of his Actions: Thus should he do a thing which might be liable to Exception, Men would be more apt to suspect their own Judgment than his Integrity, and believe whatever was the Cause of the Action, it must be a good one since it mov'd him: And tho' a perfect Love of Mankind was the Spring of all he acted, that

Human Temper never threw him into Facility, but since he knew an ungrounded Compassion to one Man might be a Cruelty to another, mere Distresses without Justice to plead for 'em could never prevail upon him, but, all Gentle as he was, he was impregnable to the most repeated Importunity, even that of his own good Nature.

Such was the Renown'd *Brutus*, and one would think a Man who had no ill Ambition to satisfie, no loose Passions to indulge, but whose Life was a Regular, Easie, and Sedate Motion, should be in little Temptation of falling into a Plot; but ill Men, where they cannot meet a convenient Vice, can make use of a Virtue to a base purpose.

He was Lineally Descended from the famous *Brutus*, that extinguish'd the *Tarquins*, whose Debauches and Cruelties made a Regal Name in *Rome* as justly odious, as that of the *Bruti* venerable for the Extirpation of it; [22] and *Cæsar* had very lately, in the midst of an absolute and unlimited Power, betray'd a Fantastick Ambition of being call'd King, which render'd him Obnoxious to the Malice of the Conspirators and the Virtue of *Brutus*. This was the Place where the Magnanimity of that Patriot seem'd most accessible, for 'twas obvious, that He who wanted nothing else to spur him to Glorious Attempts, must be also Animated by the Memory of Illustrious Ancestors, and not like narrow and degenerate Spirits, be satisfied with the Fantask of Honour deriv'd from others, from whom, without a Similitude of Virtue, 'tis an unhappy distinction to descend.

Yet however hopeful this Handle appear'd, they could not so abruptly attempt upon his awful Character, as immediately to propose the Murder to him, without some distant Preparation of Mind to receive it. There were therefore these Words frequently dropt in his way, from unknown Hands: Thou art no longer *Brutus*; Thou art asleep, *Brutus*; and the like; by which Artifice he grew very Thoughtful and busie with himself, about the purpose of these Advertisements; One of such Moments *Cassius* took hold of, and opened to him the great Design for the Liberty of his Country from *Cæsar*'s Usurpation: There needed no more to make him do a thing, but his Belief that 'twas Just; He soon consented that [23] *Cæsar* deserv'd to Die, and since he did, to Die by his Hand: Gaining this Personage, made all ripe for Execution, and *Cassius* possess'd a full Satisfaction, in that he had engag'd a Man in the Attempt, who in the Eyes of the People, instead of being sully'd by it, would stamp a Justice and Authority upon the Action; whose confirm'd Reputation was sufficient to expiate a Murder, and consecrate an Assassination.

Yet tho' his Justice made him readily consent to *Cæsar's* Death, his Gratitude upon Reflection shook his Resolution to Act in it; all which Conflict with himself we cannot view without the Incident of *Porcia's* Story.

This Lady observ'd her Husband fall on a sudden from an easie, placid and fond, into a troubled, short and distracted Behaviour; she saw his Mind too much employ'd for the conjugal Endearments, and kind Tendernesses, in which she was usually happy, yet upon this Observation grew neither Jealous or Sullen, but mourn'd his Silence of his Affliction to her with as deep a Silence: This Lady, I say, this noble *Roman* Wife turn'd all her Suspicion upon her self, and modestly believ'd 'twas [24] her Incapacity for bearing so great a Secret, as that which discompos'd the stedfast *Brutus*, made him conceal from her an Affliction, which she thought she had a Title to participate; and therefore resolv'd to know of her self, whether his Secrecy was a Wrong to her before she would think it so; to make this Experiment, she gave her self a deep Stab in the Thigh, and thought if she could bear that Torture, she could also that of a Secret; the Anguish and Concealment of her Wound threw her into a Fever, in that condition she thus spoke to her Husband.

" I, *Brutus*, being the Daughter of *Cato*, was given to you in Marriage, not like a Concubine, to partake only of the common Civilities of Bed and Board, but to bear a Part in all your good and all your evil Fortunes; and for my part, when I look on you, I find no Reason to repent this Match; But from Me, what Evidence of my Love, what Satisfaction can you receive, if I may not share with you in your most hidden Griefs, nor be admitted to any of your Counsels, that require Secrecy and Trust; I know very well, that Women seem to be of too weak a Nature to be trusted with Secrets, but certainly, *Brutus*, a Virtuous Birth and Education, and a Conversation with the

Good and Honourable, are of some force to the forming our
Manners and strengthning our Natural Weakness; and I can
boast that I am the Daughter of *Cato*, and the Wife of *Brutus*.
In which two great Titles, tho' before I put too little Confidence,
yet now I have try'd my self, I find that even against Grief and
Pain I am Invincible." [a]

She then told him what she had done, but it is [25] not easie
to represent the kind Admiration such a Discourse must give
a Husband, and the sweet Transport that was drawn from their
mutual Affliction, is too delicate a touch of Mind to be understood but by a *Brutus* and a *Porcia*. Yet tho' he was not too
Wise to be tender to his Wife, when he had unbosom'd himself,
in spite of this last Action, and a thousand nameless things,
that occur'd to his Memory to soften him, he left his Illustrious
Heroin in her Pains and her Sorrows, to pursue his publick
Resolutions. But he is gone, and she can burst into those Tears
which the Awe of his Virtue had made her smother; for how
alas shall the Heart of Woman receive so harsh a Virtue, as
to gratifie her Husband's Will, by consenting to his Ruin? How
shall she struggle with her own Weakness and his Honour?
But while she lay in his Bosom she learn'd all the Gallantry of
it, and when she ponders his Immortal Fame, his Generous
Justice, and *Roman* Resolution, her Mind enlarges into a Greatness, which surmounts her Sex, and her Affection: When she
views him in the conspicuous part of Life, she can bear, nay
Triumph in his Loss; but when she reflects and remembers their
Tenderer Hours, thus would he Look, thus would he Talk, such
was his Gesture, Mein, the Mirth, the Gaiety of the Man she
Lov'd (which Instances are more intimate Objects of Affection,
than Mens greater Qualities) then she is all Woman, she resigns
the great but laments the agreeable Man; Can then my *Brutus*
leave me? Can he leave these longing Arms for Fame? She
has no just Notion of any higher Being to support her wretched
Condition, but however her Female Infirmity made her languish,
she has still Constancy enough to keep a Secret that concerns
her Husband's Reputation, tho' she melts away in Tears, and
pines into Death in Contemplation of her Sufferings.

Such must have been the Soliloquy of this Memorable Wife,

---

[a] *Vid.* Mr. Duke's *Translation of the Life of* Brutus. [Steele's note]

who has left behind her an everlasting Argument, how far a
Generous Treatment can make that tender Sex go even beyond
the Resolution of Man, when we allow that they are by Nature
form'd to Pity, Love and Fear, and we with an Impulse to
Ambition, Danger and Adventure.

The World bore a Gloom and heavy Presage of *Cæsar's*
approaching Fate. 'Tis said Wild Beasts came into the most
frequented Parts of the City, Apparitions in the Streets, unusual
Illuminations in the Skies, and inauspicious Sacrifices damp'd
the Hearts of all Men, but the Assassins, who with an incredible
Calm of Mind expected the opportunity of Satiating their
Vengeance in the Blood of the Usurper; yet was not *Cassius*
himself wholly unconcern'd, for tho' he was as great an Atheist
as any among Us can pretend to be, he had the Weakness and
Superstition at that time, to invoke a Statue of *Pompey* for his
Assistance. It is as [26] observable, that *Cæsar*, the Evening before
his Fate, in a Supper-conversation (at one of his Murderers
Houses) on the subject of Death, pronounc'd a sudden one to
be the most desirable, and a little shogg'd with reiterated ill
Omens, and touch'd with the foreboding Dreams and Frights of
a tender Wife, resolv'd to forbear going to the Senate on the
Morning appointed for his *Execution*; which Difficulty *D.
Brutus* undertook to get over; a Gentleman so superlatively
excellent that way, that he could not only upon such an occasion
appear Compos'd, but also in very good Humour; this *sneering*
Ruffian rallied away his Fears, and with a very good Mein
conducted his Friend to his Murder.

When he came into the Senate, they rose to him, and with a
pretended joint Petition for a Banish'd Man, the Assassins
press'd about him, as soon as he was Seated: He severally
check'd their Importunity, but while they were thus imploy'd,
one of 'em gave the Sign by throwing his Robe over his Neck,
another oppress'd with the Grandeur of the Attempt, made at
him an irresolute Pass: He briskly oppos'd the Villain, and
call'd him so; They all rush'd on him with drawn Ponyards,
still he resisted 'till he saw *Brutus* coming on, then with a generous and disdainful Resignation, yielded to the stroke of a
Pardon'd, Oblig'd and Rewarded Friend. But there are in
England a Race of Men, who have this Action in the most

profess'd Veneration, and who speciously miscall the Rancour, Malice and Hatred of all Happier and Higher than themselves, (which they have in common with *Cassius*) Gallantry of Mind, Disdain of Servitude, and Passion for publick Good, which they pretend to with *Brutus*; and [27] thus qualified with Ill, set up for Faction, Business, and Enmity to Kings. But 'tis to be hop'd these Men only run round 'till they're giddy, and when all things turn too, fancy themselves Authors of the Motion about 'em, and so take their Vertigo for their Force; for sure they have a futile Pretence to a good publick Spirit, who have an ill private one.

But there lies the Mighty *Cæsar*, an Eternal Instance how much too Generous and too Believing those unhappy Princes are, who depend upon the tie of Mens Obligations to 'em, without having their Opinions on their side; for nothing hinders a Man's walking by the Principles of his Soul, but an Opportunity to exert 'em; when that occurs, the secret Enemy throws off his Mask and draws his Dagger.

Yet Reflections of this nature are somewhat foreign to our Purpose, we must therefore follow these bloody Men, to a Fate as violent as they gave their Benefactor; for 'twas in Providence to frustrate their Counsels, by turning that Virtue to their Ruin, which they had ensnared for their Protection. The fearless *Brutus* had too much Clemency, to make this Blow safe by the Execution of the nearest Adherents to *Cæsar*; His Safety consisted in his unbiass'd Mind and undaunted Resolution, which would not let him stoop to the taking away [28] any Life, below that of the Greatest of Mankind.

However this Injury was repair'd to *Cæsar*, for he was voted a God in the very Place where he ceas'd to be a Man, which had been a good saving Clause, cou'd they have persuaded his Successor *Octavius* also, to have been contented with *Omnipotence*; but the young *Scholar* was so much enamour'd with this World, that he left his *Book* to disturb and rule it; and to compass his End, took upon him the hopeful Resolution of sparing no Man, from a Reflection perhaps that his Uncle was Ruin'd by Mercy in his Victories.

But it is [29] not our Business, to fall into an Historical Account of the various Occurrences, which happen'd in the War between the *Cæsarian* Army and that of the Conspirators, any farther than it is necessary [30] for judging how far the Principles they walk'd by were useful to 'em in their greatest Extremities: As *Brutus* one Evening sate Pensive and Revolving, the Passages of Life, and the Memory of *Cæsar*, occurr'd to him, now perhaps not as a Traitor, a Tyrant, or Usurper, but as one he Lov'd, and Murder'd; an Apparition appear'd (or he thought appear'd to him) which told him he was his Evil Genius and would meet him at *Philippi*, to which he calmly answer'd, *I'll meet thee there*: But he communicated a sad Impression which [31] this made upon him to *Cassius*, who in an *Epicurean* manner gave him a Superficial Comfort, by Discourses of the Illusions, our Fancies our Dreams and our Sorrows Imprint upon the Mind, and make an imaginary a real Torment. Yet the Night before the Fatal Battel, he enquir'd (in case of a Defeat) his Resolution as to Flight and Death. To which *Brutus*:

"When I was Young, *Cassius*, and unskilful in Affairs, I was Engag'd I know not how into an Opinion of Philosophy, which made me accuse *Cato* for killing himself, as thinking it an Irreligious Act against the Gods, nor any way Valiant amongst Men, not to submit to Divine Providence, nor be able fearlessly to receive and undergo whatever shall happen; but to fly from it: But now in the midst of Dangers I am quite of another Mind, for if Providence shall not dispose what I now Undertake according to our Wishes, I resolve to try no farther Hopes, nor make any more Preparations for War, but will Die contented with my Fortune, for I already have given up my Life to the Service of my Country on the *Ides* of *March*, and all the time that I Lived since, has been with Liberty and Honour." [a]

However Gallant this Speech may seem at first Sight, it is upon Reflection a very mean one; for he urges no manner of Reason for his Desertion of the noble Principle of Resignation to the Divine Will, but his Dangers and Distresses; which indeed is no more than if he had plainly Confess'd, that all the Schemes we can form to our selves in a Compos'd and Prosperous Condition, when we come to be oppress'd with Calamities, vanish from us, and are but the Effects of luxuriant Ease and good

[a] *Vid.* Mr. Duke's *Translation of the Life of* Brutus. Plut. [Steele's note]

Humour, and [32] languish and die away with 'em: But to make this a fair deduction from his Discourse, let us Impartially (but with Tenderness and Pity) look at him in his last Pangs: At the Battel of *Philippi*, *Brutus* Commanded the Right, *Cassius* the Left of the Line: The first broke the opposite Wing of the Enemy, the second was himself forc'd. But by a Failure in their Orders and Intelligence, each was Ignorant of the other's Fortune; *Brutus* follow'd his Blow, and his Heat drove him too far before he thought of *Cassius*, whom at last, with a strong Detachment, he returns to Relieve. His Friend Retreated [33] to a rising Ground, to View and Bewail the Fate of their Cause, and Commanded an Officer to observe that Body marching towards him: The Gentleman soon found 'em Friends, and confidently Rid in amongst 'em; they as kindly enclos'd him to enquire News: Upon seeing this, the miserable *Cassius* concluded him taken by the Enemy, and giving all for lost, retir'd into a Tent, where he was by his own order Kill'd by a Servant.

Here *Brutus*, whom neither the Fondness of an excellent Wife, Obligations to a generous Friend, or a Message from the Dead cou'd Divert from meeting all Encounters, sinks and falls into the most extream Despair.

He, with some others that escap'd the Pursuit, retir'd to a Thicket of a Wood, where also finding they were trac'd, 'twas propos'd still to Fly: But he, after having express'd [34] a Satisfaction (but a false one, since he could not live with it) in his Integrity, which he preferr'd to the Successes of his Enemies, ran upon his Sword, and transfix'd that great Heart with a superfluous Blow, which sure was before Stabb'd with the killing Reflection upon *Et tu Brute?*

Here let us throw a Veil over this mistaken Great Man, and if possible cover him from Human Sight for ever, that his seduc'd and *Ambiguous* Virtue may be no more Prophan'd, as an Umbrage to the Counsels of Perjur'd Friends, Sacrilegious Regicides, and implacable Desperadoes.

Now the use we make of these Reflections, is, that since we have seen the mighty *Cæsar* himself fall into Superstition at the Thought of his Exit, since *Cato*'s firm Constancy, *Brutus* his [35] generous Zeal, and *Cassius* his [36] steady Malice, all ended in the same Dereliction of themselves, and Despondence at last, we

may justly conclude, that whatever Law we may make to ourselves, from the Greatness of Nature or the Principles of
Philosophy [37] for the Conduct and Regulation of Life, is it self
but an Artificial Passion, by which we vainly hope to subdue
those that are Natural, and which will certainly rise or fall with
our Disappointment or Success, and we that are liable to both
are highly concern'd to be prepar'd for either: At which Perfection there is no nearer way to arrive, but by attending our
own Make, and observing by what means human Life, from its
simple and rural Happiness, swell'd into the weighty Cares
and Distractions with which it is at present Enchanted; and
from this Knowledge of our Misery, *Extract* our Satisfaction.

C H A P. II.

MAN is a Creature of so mix'd a Composure, and of a [38]
Frame so Inconsistent and Different from *Its* self, that it
easily speaks his Affinity to the highest and meanest Beings; that
is to say, he is made of Body and Soul, he is at once an *Engine*
and an *Engineer*: Tho' indeed both that Body and Soul [39] act
in many Instances separate and independent of each other: For
when he Thinks, Reasons and Concludes, he has not in all that
Work the least Assistance from his Body: His finest Fibres,
purest Blood, and highest Spirits are as brute and distant from a
Capacity of Thinking as his very Bones; and the Body is so mere
a Machine, that it Hungers, Thirsts, Tastes and Digests, without any exerted Thought of the Mind to command that Operation: Which when he observes upon himself, he may, without
deriving it from Vapour, Fume or Distemper, believe that his
Soul may as well Exist out of, as in that Body from which it
borrows nothing to make it capable of performing its most
perfect Functions. This may give him hopes, that tho' his
Trunk return to its native Dust he may not all Perish, but the
Inhabitant of it may remove to another Mansion; especially
since he knows only Mechanically that they have, not Demon-
stratively how they have, ev'n a present Union.

And since this Mind has a Consciousness and superior Reflection upon its own Being and Actions, and that Thoughts flow in upon it, from it knows not what Source, it is not Unnatural for it to conceive, that there is something of a Nature like it self, which may, Imperceptibly,[40] act upon it, and where it cannot deduce its reasonable Performances from any corporeal Beginning, draw Hopes or Fears from some Being thus capable to Impress Pleasure or Torment; which Being it cannot but suppose its Author.

But this its Author is Incomprehensible to the Soul (which he has thought fit to Imprison in Sense and Matter) but as he is pleas'd to reveal himself, and bestow upon it an Expectation of its Enlargement; yet were we to take the Account which Poetical writers give, and suppose a Creature with these Endowments wandring among other wild Animals, the Intelligent [41] Savage would not be contented with what Rapine or Craft could gain from his Brethren Beasts, but his Condition would still be as necessitous for his better Part; and his dark natural Enquiry would make him, for want of a more just Knowledge of his Creator, fall into Superstition, and believe every Fountain, Grove and Forest inhabited by some peculiar Deity, that bestow'd upon Mankind the Stream, the Shade and the Breeze.

But we are inform'd that the [42] wonderful Creator of all Things, after he had given the Rivers to Flow, the Earth to bring Forth, and the Beasts to Feed, saw and approv'd his Work, but thought a dumb Brute and Mechanick World an imperfect Creation 'till inhabited by a conscious [43] Being, whose Happiness should consist in Obedience to, and a Contemplation on him and his *Wonders.*

For this Reason Man was created with intellectual Powers and higher Faculties, who immediately beheld with Joy and Rapture, a World made for the Support and Admiration of his new Being; how came he into this happy happy State! whence the Order! the Beauty! the *Melody* of this *Living* Garden! Are the Trees Verdant? Do the Birds Sing? Do the Fountains Flow for no other reason but to Delight and Entertain him? How does he pass through the most bright and delicious Objects, and how does he *Burn* to utter himself upon the *Extatick* Motions which they give him! In such sweet Inquietude were

the first Hours of the World spent, and in this Lassitude of
Bliss and Thought our Parent fell into a profound Sleep, when
his Maker, who knew how Irksome a lonely Happiness was
to a sociable Nature, form'd out of his Side a Companion,
Woman: He awak'd, and by a secret Simpathy beheld his
Wife: He beheld his own rougher Make soften'd into Sweetness
and temper'd into Smiles: He saw a Creature (who [44] had as
'twere Heav'ns second Thought in her Formation) to whom [45]
he cou'd communicate his Conceptions,[46] on whom [47] he could
Glut his Eyes, with whom [48] he could Ravish his Heart: Over
this Consort his Strength and Wisdom claim'd, but his Affection resign'd, the Superiority: These both *Equal* and both
Superior were to live in a perfect Tranquility, and produce as
happy a Progeny: The Earth and all its Fruit were theirs, Except
only one Tree: Which light *Injunction* was all that was requir'd
of 'em as an Instance of their Obedience and Gratitude to his
Bounty, who had giv'n 'em everything else. But such was their
Vanity and Ingratitude, that they soon forgot the Dependance
suitable to a Borrow'd Being, and were deluded into an empty
hope of becoming by their Transgression like their Creator,
and (tho' just Born of the Dust) proud enough from that No-
Existence to disdain one that was Precarious: They did [49] *therefore Eat* and were Undone; they offended God, and like all
their succeeding Criminals against him, were conscious that they
did so. Innocence and Simplicity were banish'd their Bosoms,
to give way to Remorse and Conviction. Guilt and Shame are
the new Ideas they have pluck'd from the Tree of Knowledge:
Their affronted Creator pronounces upon 'em a Sentence which
they now think more supportable than the Pain of his offended
Presence, which he withdrew; and commanded Nature to give
'em no further voluntary Obedience; so that he was now to
extort from her the continuance of their wretched Condition by
Toil and Labour, and she to bring forth Heirs to it with Pangs
and Torture.

This is the Account we have from a certain neglected Book,
which is call'd, and for its genuine Excellence above all other
Books deservedly call'd THE SCRIPTURE: And methinks we
may be convinc'd of the Truth of this History of our Parents,
by the infallible Spots and Symptoms of their Hereditary Disease

in our Tempers, Pride and Ingratitude: For what is more natural to us, than by an unreasonable Self-opinion, (tho' we cannot but feel that we are but mere Creatures and not of our selves) to assume to our selves the Praise and Glory of our Capacities and Endowments! and how Lazy, how unwilling are we to *Eradicate* the deep and Inward Satisfaction of Self-admiration? However, it must be confess'd, that 'tis the most senseless and stupid of all our Infirmities, for 'till you can remember and recount to us, when that Thinking, *Throbbing* Particle within, first resolv'd to *Wear* a Body, when it spun out its Arteries, Fibres and Veins, contriv'd the warm circulating Stream that runs through 'em, when you first ventur'd to let the Heart pant; the Lungs suck Air, and at last to lanch the whole tender Machine into the hazard of Motion; 'till, I say, you can acquaint us with all this, you must kneel and fall down before him, by whom you were thus Fearfully and Wonderfully Made.

But the first Pair, now suspicious of each other, banish'd the more immediate Influence and Presence of their Almighty Protector, were liable (Naked and Distress'd as they were) to be entangled by the Thorn and the Brier, and torn by the Lion and Wolf, who have ever since been prompted to fly in the Faces of the detested Ingrates: Therefore the increasing World, for their Defence against Themselves, and other Animals, were oblig'd to go into Contracts and Policies, so that human Life (by long Gradation) ascended into an Art: The Tongue was now to Utter one thing, and the Bosom to Conceal another; and from a desire of Superiority in our deprav'd Natures, was bred that unsatisfied *Hunger* Ambition; a monstrous Excrescence of the Mind, which makes Superfluity, Riches, Honour and Distinction, but mere Necessities of Life, as if 'twere our Fate in our fallen Condition (lest a Supply of what frugal Nature desires should be obtain'd) to find out an Indigence foreign to us, which is incapable of being reliev'd, and (which to confirm our Want and Misery) increases with its Acquisitions: Under this leading Crime, are Envy, Hatred, Cruelty, Cunning, Craft and Debate, Muster'd and Arm'd; and a Battalion of Diseases, Torments and Cares, the natural Effects of those Evils, become our bosom Companions; from which no Arms can rescue, no Flight secure us but a Return to that God, in whose Protection only is our Native lost Seat of Rest and Tranquility. To which Abode since our Expulsion we cannot dare to approach, but Guilt which runs even to Succours it knows vain, makes us, with our first Parents in the same Circumstances, hide from Omnipresence: I said in the same Circumstances, for we have not only implicitly committed their Crime, as we were in them, but do also actually repeat it in our own Persons: For when a Created Being relinquishes the Power of its Creator, and instead of relying on his Conduct and Government, draws to it self an independent Model of Life, what does it but pluck from the Tree of Knowledge, and attempt a Theft of Understanding, from him who is Wisdom it self? This is a tremendous Consideration, yet is there not that Man breathing, who has any where placed his Confidence but in God, and considers seriously his own Heart, but feels its Weight, nor can the Bosom under it receive any Impression, but that of endless Despair.

But behold the Darkness disperses, and there is still Hope breaking in upon our Sorrow, by the Light of which we may again lift up our Eyes, and see our Maker: For in the midst of our deserv'd Misery, our Reconciliation is coming on through a Mediator, who [50] is perfectly unconcern'd in our Crime: [51] But tho' innocent of our Transgression, assumes that and our Nature, and, as an Atonement for us, offers his Life a Ransom, with this regard on our Part, that as it is an Expiation, it is also an Example: An Example to instruct us, that not only the first Command laid upon us was a reasonable one, but also the present Life easie and supportable, for he himself voluntarily undergoes it in its greatest Calamities: He who had all things in his Power, and wanted all things, by inforcing an abstinent use of Wealth, and patient enduring of Poverty, restores us not only to the Bliss of leading this Life with Satisfaction and Resignation to the Divine Will (which only is our true Life) but by a short Passage through a momentary Death, translates us to an happy everlasting Existence, incapable of Sorrow, Weariness or Change: To accomplish which great Revolution, our glorious Deliverer from our selves design'd to Establish his Empire, not by Conquest, but a Right much more lasting, *Arduous* and *Indisputable Conviction*; For our Slavery being Intellectual and in our own Bosoms, the Redemption must be

there also; Yet the World, Inchanted with its own imaginary
Notions of Freedom, knew not how to receive so Abstracted a
Manumission, but contemn'd the Promise of Restoration to
Life and *Liberty*, from a poor Man who himself enjoy'd none
of the Advantages which arise from those *Dear* (but *Misunder-
stood*) Appellations.

May we then without Blame approach and behold this Sacred
and Miraculous Life? How, alas! shall we Trace the Mysterious
Steps of God and Man? How consider him at once in Subjection to, and Dominion over Nature?

The most Apposite, (tho' most slow) Method of reducing
the World to its Obedience, was that our Blessed Saviour should
appear in the despicable Attire which he did, without any of
those attendant Accidents which attract the Eye, and charm the
Imagination: For the Knowledge which he was to Introduce,
being an Eternal Truth; the proper Mansion for it was in the
Reason and Judgment, into which when it had once enter'd, it
was not to be remov'd by any Impressions upon the lower
Faculties, to which it was not to be [52] beholden for a Reception.
There is not therefore one Instance in the New Testament of
Power exerted to the Destruction, tho' so many to the Preserva-
tion of Mankind: But to a degenerate Race, he that Heals, is
less valu'd than he that Kills: Confusion, Terror, Noise and
Amazement, are what only strike servile Minds; but Order,
Symmetry, silent Awe, Blessings and Peace are Allurements to
the Open, Simple, Innocent and Truly knowing; yet the very
Nation among whom the Holy *Jesus* Descended to Converse,
had (if we may so speak) in a manner [53] tir'd Heav'n with
appearing in the more Pompous Demonstrations of its Power:
They pass'd through Waves *Divided* and *Erect* for their March,
they were supernaturally Fed in a Wilderness, a Mountain shook,
and Thunder utter'd their Law; Nations were Destroy'd to gain
them Inheritance! But they soon forgot these Benefits, and upon
the least Cessation of Fear and Miracle, they deserted their
Creator, and return'd to their own Handywork Deities, who
were as senseless of their Makers, as themselves were of theirs.

Thus short-liv'd is Wonder, and thus Impotent to fix (what
we have said our Law-giver design'd) Conviction. For which
Reason our Astonishment in the New Testament is more spar-

ingly rais'd, and that only to awaken our Attention to Plain, Easie, and Obvious Truths (which support themselves when receiv'd) by the Authority of Miracle.

We Read [a] that he was led into a Wilderness, where he wonderfully bore Hunger and Want for Forty Days; in the height of which Exigence and Necessity, the Tempter came to him and Urg'd him, if he were the Son of God, to Relieve his present Misery, by turning the Stones [54] into Bread; which Attempt when he found Fruitless, and observ'd that he wou'd Use no supernatural Relief, but bear Human Nature and its Infirmities, he Attacks him [55] the most acceptable way to our *Weakness* in the Supplies of Pride and Vanity: He showed him the Kingdoms and Glory of the World, (which he had Purchased from Man by his Defection from God) and offer'd him the Dominion of 'em if he would Worship him; but our Lord Contemn'd this also, and in his Want and Poverty retir'd into a private Village; where and in the Adjacent Parts if the Necessitous Man lay in Obscurity, the merciful God did not, for he never discontinued his Visible benign Assistance, to the Relief of the Diseas'd, the Possess'd and the Tormented.

In his admirable Sermon upon the Mount,[b] he gives his Divine Precepts in so easie and familiar a manner, and which [56] are so well adapted to all the Rules of Life and right Reason, that they must needs carry throughout a self evident Authority to all that Read 'em; to those that Obey 'em, from the firm Satisfaction which they Inspire; to those that neglect 'em, from the Anxiety that naturally attends a contrary Practice; There is the whole Heart of Man discover'd by him that Made it, and all our secret Impulses to Ill, and false appearances of Good, expos'd and detected: Among other excellent Doctrines, one which methinks must be, to those who are so harden'd as to read the Divine Oracles with Unbelief, an irrefragable Argument of his Divinity: *But when thou Prayest, enter into thy Closet, and when thou hast shut thy Door, Pray to thy Father which is in Secret, and thy Father which seeth in Secret, shall reward thee Openly.*[c] Now it cannot enter into the Heart of Man, that any

[a] *Matt.* 4. [Steele's note]
[b] *Matt.* 5. [Steele's note]
[c] *Matt.* 6. 6. [Steele's note]

4

but God could be the Author of a Command so abstracted from all worldly Interests; for how absurd were it in a Being, that had not an intercourse with our Souls, or knew not their most secret Motions, to direct our Application to it self,[57] so strictly apart,[58] and out of the Observation of any Power less than Ubiquitary?

There came to him a Captain,[a] in the behalf of his Servant, grievously tormented with a Palsie: Our Lord promis'd him to come and heal him, but the Soldier (with an openness and sincerity of Mind peculiar to his Profession) who [59] could not believe in, or serve him, but with his whole Heart, told him, he knew Nature was [60] in his Power with as despotick a Subjection, as his Men were under his, begg'd him only to speak him whole, and he knew he would be so: Our Saviour extoll'd his honest, frank and unreserved Confidence, gave him a suitable Success, sending him away with this Glorious Eulogium, that he had not found such Faith, no not in *Israel*!

Thus did he bestow Mercy and Salvation upon the easie and common terms of ordinary *Friendship*, as if there needed nothing to make him, but believing he would be, their Benefactor. And, who in the least Affairs, is a Friend to him that distrusts him?

In plain and apt Parable, Similitude and Allegory, he proceeded daily to inspire and enforce the Doctrine of our Salvation; [b] but they of his Acquaintance, instead of receiving what they could not oppose, were offended at the Presumption, of being wiser than they: Is not this the Carpenter's Son, is not his Mother call'd *Mary*, his Brethren, *James*, *Joseph*, *Simon* and *Judas*? They could not raise their little Ideas above the consideration of him, in those Circumstances familiar to 'em, or conceive that he who appear'd not more Terrible or Pompous, should have any thing more Exalted than themselves; he in that Place [61] therefore would not longer [62] ineffectually exert a Power which was incapable of Conquering the Prepossession of their narrow and mean Conceptions.

Multitudes follow'd him, and brought him the Dumb, the Blind, the Sick and Maim'd; whom when their Creator had

---

[a] *Matt.* 8. [Steele's note]
[b] *Matt.* 13. 55. [Steele's note]

Touch'd, with a second Life they Saw, Spoke, Leap'd and Ran; in Affection to him, and Admiration of his Actions, the Crowd could not leave him, but waited near him Three Days, 'till they were almost as faint and helpless as others they brought for Succour: He had compassion on 'em, commanded 'em to be seated, and with Seven Loaves, and a few little Fishes, Fed four thousand Men, besides Women and Children: [a] Oh the Extatick Entertainment, when they could behold their Food immediately increase, to the Distributer's Hand, and see their God in Person, Feeding and Refreshing his Creatures: Oh Envied Happiness! But why do I say Envied, as if our Good God did not still preside over our temperate Meals, chearful Hours, and innocent Conversations.

But tho' the sacred Story is every where full of Miracles, not inferior to this, and tho' in the midst of those Acts of Divinity, he never gave the least hint of a Design to become a Secular Prince, or in a Forcible or Miraculous manner to cast off the *Roman* Yoke they were under, and restore again those disgrac'd Favourites of Heav'n, to its former Indulgence, yet had not hitherto the Apostles themselves (so *deep set* is our Natural Pride) any other than hopes of Worldly Power, Preferment, Riches and Pomp: For *Peter*, who it seems ever since he left his Net and his Skiff, Dreamt of nothing but being a great man, was utterly undone to hear our Saviour explain to 'em, upon an Accident of Ambition among 'em, that his Kingdom was not of this World; and was so scandaliz'd, that he, whom he had so long follow'd, should suffer the Ignominy, Shame and Death which he foretold, that he took him aside and said, *Be it far from thee, Lord, this shall not be unto thee:* [b] For which he suffer'd a severe Reprehension from his Master, having [63] in his View the Glory of Man, rather than that of God.

The great Change of things began to draw near, when the Lord of Nature thought fit as a Saviour and Deliverer to make his publick Entry into *Jerusalem*, with more than the Power and Joy, but none of the Ostentation and Pomp of a Triumph: He came Humble, Meek and Lowly; with an unfelt new Extasie,

[a] *Matt.* 15. [Steele's note]
[b] *Matt.* 1. 22. ![Steele's note. The correct reference, Matthew 16. 22., was given in the fourth edition.]

Multitudes strow'd his way with Garments and Olive-branches, Crying with loud Gladness and Acclamation, *Hosannah to the Son of* David, *Blessed is he that cometh in the Name of the Lord!*[a] At this Great King's Accession to his Throne, Men were not Ennobled but Sav'd; Crimes were not Remitted, but Sins Forgiven; he did not bestow Medals, Honours, Favours, but Health, Joy, Sight, Speech! The first Object the Blind ever saw, was the Author of Sight, while the Lame Ran before, and the Dumb repeated the *Hosannah*! Thus Attended, he Entred into his own House, the Sacred Temple, and by his Divine Authority Expell'd Traders and Worldlings that Prophan'd it; and thus did he, for a time, use a great and Despotick Power, to let Unbelievers understand, that 'twas not want of, but Superiority to all Worldly Dominion, that made him not exert it: But is this then the Saviour, is this the Deliverer? shall this Obscure *Nazerene* command *Israel*, and sit in the Throne of *David*? such [64] were the unpleasant Forms that ran in the Thoughts of the then Powerful in *Jerusalem*, upon the most Truly Glorious Entry that ever Prince made; for there was not one that follow'd him, who was not in his Interest; their Proud and Disdainful Hearts, which were putrified with the Love and Pride of this World, were impregnable to the Reception of so mean a Benefactor, and were now enough exasperated with Benefits to Conspire his Death: Our Lord was sensible of their Design, and prepar'd his Disciples for it, by recounting to 'em now more distinctly what should befall him; but *Peter* with an ungrounded Resolution, and in a Flush of Temper, made a Sanguine Protestation; that tho' all Men were offended in him, yet would not he be offended.[b] It was a great Article of our Saviour's Business in the World, to bring us to a Sense of our Inability, without God's Assistance, to do any thing Great or Good; he therefore told *Peter*, who thought so well of his Courage and Fidelity, that they would both fail him, and ev'n he should deny him Thrice that very Night.

But what Heart can conceive? What Tongue utter the Sequel? Who is that yonder Buffeted, Mock'd and Spurn'd? Whom do they Drag like a Felon? Whither do they carry my Lord, my

[a] *Matt.* 21. [Steele's note]
[b] *Matt.* 26. 33. [Steele's note]

King, my Saviour and my God? And will he Die to expiate those very Injuries? See where they have Nail'd the Lord and Giver of Life! How his Wounds blacken! His Body writhes, and Heart heaves with Pity, and with Agony! Oh Almighty Sufferer, look down, look down from thy Triumphant Infamy; Lo he inclines his Head to his Sacred Bosom! Hark he Groans, see he Expires! The Earth trembles, the Temple rends, the Rocks Burst, the Dead Arise; Which are the Quick? Which are the Dead? Sure Nature, all Nature is departing with her Creator.

CHAP. III.

THERE was nothing in our Saviour's own Deportment, or in the Principles He introduc'd for our Conduct, but what was so far from Opposing, that they might naturally fall in with the Statutes or Forms of any Civil Government whatever, and regarded 'em no otherwise than to make us more Obedient to 'em: Yet the Professors of this Doctrine were told they were to meet but very little Quarter, for the acceptable Service they were to do 'em, but must lay down their very lives to bring Us to a Contempt of their Grandeur in Comparison of Greater and Higher Pursuits: In order to this Great End, their Despicable Artillery were Poverty and Meekness; the consideration therefore of those Arms is no Digression from our Purpose: It is in every Body's Observation with what disadvantage a Poor Man enters upon the most Ordinary Affairs, much more disputing with the whole World, and in [65] contradiction of the Rich, that it, the Wise; For as certainly as Wealth gives Acceptance and Grace to all that its Possessor says or does, so Poverty creates Disesteem, Scorn and Prejudice to all the Undertakings of the Indigent: The Necessitous Man has neither Hands, Lips, or Understanding, for his own, or Friends use, but is in the same condition with the Sick, with this Difference only, that his is an Infection no Man will Relieve, or Assist, or if he does,

'tis seldom with so much Pity, as Contempt, and rather for the
Ostentation of the Physician, than Compassion on the Patient:
It is a Circumstance, wherein a Man finds all the Good he
deserves inaccessible, all the Ill unavoidable; and the Poor Hero
is as certainly Ragged, as the Poor Villain Hang'd: Under these
Pressures the Poor Man speaks with Hæsitation, undertakes with
Irresolution, and acts with Disappointment: He is slighted in
Mens Conversations, overlook'd in their Assemblies, and beaten
at their Doors: But from whence alas has he this Treatment?
from [66] a Creature that has only the Supply of, but [67] not an [68]
Exemption from the Wants, for which he despises him: For
such is the unaccountable Insolence of Man, that he will not see
that he who is supported, is in the same Class of natural
Necessity with him that wants a Support; and to be help'd,
implies to be indigent. In a Word, after all you can say of a
Man, conclude that he is Rich, and you have made him Friends;
nor have you utterly overthrown a Man in the World's Opinion,
'till you have said he is Poor: This is the Emphatical Expression
of Praise and Blame, for Men so stupidly forget their natural
Impotence and Want, that Riches and Poverty have taken in
our Imagination the place of Innocence and Guilt; he therefore
that has suffer'd the Contumelies, Disappointments and Miseries
which attend the Poor Man's Condition, and without running
into base, indecent or servile Arts for his redress, hath [69] return'd upon an insolent World its Scorn. He (I say) [70] has
fought a nobler Fight, Conquer'd greater Difficulties, and deserves a brighter Diadem, than ever Fortune bestow'd on the
most fonded and most gaudy of her Favourites: But to capaci-
tate ones self [71] for this hard Work, how necessary is that
Sublime and Heroick Virtue, Meekness, a Virtue which seems
the very Characteristick of a Christian, and arises from a great,
not a groveling Idea of things: For as certainly as Pride proceeds from a mean and narrow view of the little Advantages
about a Man's self, so Meekness is founded on the extended
Contemplation of the Place we bear in the Universe, and a just
Observation how little, how empty, how wavering are our
deepest Resolves and Councils; and as (to a well taught Mind)
when you've said an Haughty and Proud Man, you have spoke
a narrow Conception, little Spirit, and despicable Carriage; so

when you've said a Man's Meek and Humble, you've acquainted us, that such a Person [72] has arriv'd at the hardest Task in the World in an universal Observation round him, to be quick to see his own Faults and other Mens Virtues, and [73] at the height of pardoning every Man sooner than himself; you've also [74] given us to understand, that to treat him kindly, sincerely and respectfully, is but a mere Justice to him that's ready to do us the same Offices: This Temper of Soul keeps us always awake to a just sense of things, teaches us that we are as well akin to Worms as to Angels, and as nothing is above these, so is nothing below those: It keeps our Understanding tight [75] about us, so that all things appear to us great or little as they are in Nature, not as they are gilded or sullied by Accident and Fortune.

Meekness is to the Mind, what a good Mein is to the Body, without which, the best Limb'd and finest Complection'd Person may be very Disagreeable; and with it, a very Homely and Plain one cannot be so; for a good Air supplies the Imperfection of Feature and Shape, by throwing a certain Beauty [76] on the whole, which covers [77] the disagreeableness [78] of the Parts; it has a State and Humility peculiar to its self above all Virtues, like the Holy Scripture, its sacred Record, where the highest things are express'd in the most easie Terms, and which carries throughout a condescending Explanation, and a certain Meekness of Stile.

With this Circumstance, and this ready Virtue, the faithful Followers of a Crucify'd Master were to shape their Course to an Eternal Kingdom, and with that in Prospect to contemn the hazards and disasters of a Cruel and Impenitent Generation. Great were the Actions and Sufferings of all our Blessed Saviour's Apostles, but St. *Paul* being peculiarly sent to Us who were or are Gentiles, he methinks more particularly challenges our regard: God who [79] bestow'd upon others supernaturally the Gift of Tongues, but not of Arts, thought therefore fit to make use of him already Master in some measure [80] of both, and qualified to converse with the politer World by his Acquaintance with their Studies, Laws and Customs: But tho' he shows himself by frequent brisk Sallies and quick Interrogatories, skilful in approaching the Passions by Rhetorick, yet he is very modest in any of those Ornaments, and strikes all along at the Reason, where he never fails to convince the attentive and unprejudic'd; and tho' his Person was very despicable (which to a Stranger is almost an insuperable [81] Inconvenience) yet such was the Power of the Commanding Truth which he utter'd, and his Skill how and when to utter it, that there every where appears in his Character, either the Man of Business, the Gentleman, the Hero, the Apostle, or the Martyr; which Eminence above the other Apostles, might well be expected from his Sanguine and Undertaking Complexion, temper'd by Education, and quickened by Grace: 'Tis true indeed, he had Oppos'd in the most Outragious and Violent manner this new Faith, and was accessary to [82] the Murder of the glorious Leader of the Army of Martyrs, St. *Stephen*; but that fierce Disposition fell off with the Scales from his Eyes, and God, who ever regards the Intention, chang'd his mistaken Method of serving him, and he is now ready to promote the same Religion by his Sufferings, which before he would have Extirpated by his Persecutions. He and his Companion had made very great Progress in the Conversion both of Jews and Gentiles, but certain Unbelievers Prompted the Multitude to a Resolution at a general Assembly to Assassine 'em, but they advertis'd of it fled into *Lycaonia*, where their Actions and Eloquence were very Successful; but at *Lystra*, a certain poor Cripple (from his Mother's Womb) heard him with very particular Attention and Devotion, whom the Apostle (observing in his very Countenance his warm Contrition and Preparation of Soul to receive the Benefit) commanded to stand up, upon which he immediately Jump'd upon his Legs, and Walk'd: [a] This Miracle alarm'd the whole City, who believ'd their Gods had descended in Human Shapes: *Barnabas* was immediately *Jove*, and *Paul* his *Mercury*: The Priest of *Jupiter* now is coming to Sacrifice to 'em with Oxen and Garlands; but they ran into the Multitude; we are Men like you, are subject to the same Weakness, Infirmities, and Passions with your selves; [b] We, alas! are Impotent of the great things our selves have done; your and our Creator will no longer let you wander in the Maze and Error of your Vanities

a *Acts* 14. [Steele's note]
b *Ver.* 15. [Steele's note]

and false Notions of his Deity, but has sent us with Instances
of his Omnipotence to awake you to a Worship worthy him,
and worthy you. Oh graceful Passage to see the great Apostle
oppose his own Success! Now only his Vehemence, his Power
and his Eloquence are too feeble when they are urgent against
themselves; for with Prayers and Entreaties the Crowd could
hardly be prevail'd upon, to forbear their Adoration. But this
Applause, like all other, was but a mere Gust, for the Malice
of certain Jews follow'd 'em from *Iconium*, and quickly insinuated into the giddy Multitude, as much Rancour as they
had before Devotion; who in a Tumultuary manner Ston'd St.
Paul, and drag'd him as Dead,[83] out of the Gates of the City;
but he bore their Affronts with much less Indignation than
their Worship: Here was in a trice the highest and lowest condition, the most respectful and most insolent treatment that
Man could receive; but Christianity, which kept his Eye upon
the Cause not Effect of his Actions, (and always gives us a
transient regard to transitory things,) depress'd him when
Ador'd, exalted him when Affronted.

But these two excellent Men, tho' they had the Endearments
of Fellow Suffering, and their Friendship heightned by the yet
faster tie of Religion, could not longer accompany each other,
but upon a Dispute about taking *Mark* with 'em,[a] who it seems
had before deserted 'em, their Dissention grew to the highest
a Resentment between Generous Friends ever can, even [84] to
part and estrange 'em: But they did it without Rancour, Malice,
or perhaps Dis-esteem of each other; for God has made us,
whether we observe it at the instant of being so or not, so
much Instruments of his great and secret Purposes, that he has
given every individual Man, I know not what peculiarly his
own, which so much distinguishes him from all other Persons,
that 'tis impossible, sometimes, for two of the same generous
Resolutions, Honesty and Integrity to do well together; whether
it be that Providence has so order'd it to distribute Virtue the
more, or whatever it is, such is the frequent effect. For these
noble Personages were forc'd to take different Ways, and in
those were eminently useful in the same Cause; as you may

[a] *Acts* 15. *ver.* 39. [Steele's note]

have seen two Chymical Waters, asunder, shiningly transparent, thrown together, muddy and offensive.

The Apostle was warn'd in a [85] Vision to go into *Macedonia,* whither he and his now Companion *Silas* accordingly went: [a] At *Philippi* he commanded an Evil Spirit to depart out of a Young Woman; but her Master (to whom her distraction was a Revenue, which ceas'd by her future Inability to answer the Demands usually made to her,) with the ordinary method of hiding private Malice in publick Zeal, rais'd the Multitude upon 'em, as Disturbers of the publick Peace, and Innovators upon their Laws and Liberties: The Multitude hurry'd 'em to the Magistrates, who happening to be as wise as themselves, commanded 'em to be Stripp'd, Whipp'd, and clap'd in Gaol: The Keeper receiving very strict orders for their safe Custody, put 'em in Irons in the Dungeon; the abus'd Innocents had now no way left for their redress, but applying to their God, who when all human Arts and Forces fail, is ready for our Relief, nor did St. *Paul* on less Occasions implore præternatural Assistance; *Nec Deus intersit nisi dignus vindice Nodus Inciderit*—[b]

> *Let not a God approach the Scene,*
> *In cases for a God too mean.*

We must, to Men of Wit and Gallantry, quote out of their own Scriptures. Their Generous way of Devotion, and begging Assistance, was giving Thanks for their present Extremities: In the midst of their Sores and Chains, they Sang Hymns and Praises to their Creator: Immediately the Bolts flew, the Manacles fell off, the Doors were opened, and the Earth shook: The Gaoler awakes in Terrour, and believing all under his Custody escap'd, went to dispatch himself; but St. *Paul* calls to him, he comes and beholds his Prisoners detain'd by nothing but [86] their amazing Liberty; the Horror, Sorrow, Torture, and Despair of a Dungeon, turn'd into the Joy, the Rapture, the Hallelujah, the Extasie of an Heav'n; He fell Trembling at the Apostles Feet, resign'd himself to his Captives, and felt in himself the happy Exchange of his Liberty, for that Yoke in

[a] *Acts* 11. [Steele's note. The correct reference, Acts 16, was given in the fourth edition.]

[b] *Horace's General Epistle to Piso's Verse* 105. [Steele's note.]

which alone is [87] perfect Freedom. Early the next Morning, upon this stupendious occasion, the Magistrates sent Orders those Men might be Releas'd: But St. *Paul*, who knew he had Law on his side, and that his being a Prisoner made him not the less [88] a Gentleman and a *Roman*, scorn'd their pretended Favour, nor would regard their Message, 'till they had themselves in as publick a manner acknowledg'd their Offence, as they had committed it, which they did by attending 'em in the Gaol, and desiring in a Ceremonious manner they would leave the [89] City; upon which the Apostle accepted his Inlargement, and when he had settled what Business he had in that Town, left it and its Rulers to forget that painful Truth, which they had neither Power to gainsay, nor Ingenuity to acknowledge.[a]

His taking leave of the Chief of the *Ephesian* Churches, is hardly to be Read without Tears, where, when he had reminded 'em of his whole Blameless, Disinterested, Humble, and Laborious Carriage, he acquaints 'em with his Resolution of going to *Jerusalem* and never to return thither; he knew not, he said, what would particularly befal him there, but that in general, Afflictions, Distresses and Indignities were the Portion of his Life, which he was ready to hazard or lay down in a Cause which has a certain sweetness in it, that can make a Man embrace his Chains, and enjoy his Miseries; what could be answer'd to his gallant Declaration and Behaviour but what they did, who *All wept sore, and fell on St.* Paul*'s Neck, and Kissed him? Sorrowing most of all for the Words which he spake, that they should see his Face no more.*[b] Certain Jews of *Asia* were glad to see him again at *Jerusalem*, and inflam'd the City with their Personal Knowledge of his Carriage, to the disparagement of the Temple, and the Rites of their Nation: Upon which he had been torn to Pieces, had he not been Rescu'd by the Commanding Military Officer there; of whom (going with him as a Prisoner into the Castle) he obtain'd the Liberty of speaking to the People: They heard him with great attention, 'till he contradicted their Monopoly of God; at which they lost all Order and Patience. But Opposition was so far from dispiriting, that it did but quicken his Resolution; for his great Heart, in-

[a] *Acts* 16. [Steele's note]
[b] *Acts* 20. 38. [Steele's note]

stead of Fainting and Subsiding, rose and biggen'd in proportion to any growing Danger that[90] threatened him; however
he is carry'd to[91] his Imprisonment, but not ev'n there to be
without debate, for he is by the Commander's Order to be
Scourg'd, to which he does not Passively, or basely submit, but
asserts his *Roman* Privilege, and Exemption from such Indignities.

He was thereupon next Morning[a] brought down to a Trial
by a Council of his own Nation, where upon his very opening
his Mouth, the Chief Priest commanded him to be struck, for
which he calls him Hypocrite and false Pretender to Justice,
who could use a Man, he was to sit as Judge of, so Inhumanly;
but his good Breeding being founded upon no less a Sanction
than the Command of God, he immediately Recollects himself,
and acknowledges his Error and Disrespect to the Dignity of his
Office: Yet observing (by this treatment from the President of
the Council) the usage he was to expect, by a very skilful turn
he makes Friends in an Assembly unanimous in his Ruin, but in
that only unanimous; for *Pharisees*, in which Sect he was Bred,
composing part of the Court, he closes with their belief of a
Resurrection, and there grounded the Cruelty he had met with
among the Jews: This put 'em into so great a Flame, that to
save him he was forcibly taken away into the place from whence
he came: His[92] Enemies, gall'd to the quick at his escape, Conspir'd to Kill him, when (upon the High Priest's request) he
should be remanded to a Trial: A Nephew of the Apostle's
acquainted him with this; he was neither afraid or amaz'd at
the Intelligence, but like a Man of Business and the World,
discreetly and calmly order'd the Youth to be introduc'd to the
Captain, whom he knew answerable for the Safety of his
Prisoner: The Officer in the Night sent him with a strong
Party to *Fælix* the Governor of the Province, and directed his
Accusers to follow him thither: Before *Fælix*, one *Tertullus*, a
Mercenary Orator, baul'd an impertinent Harangue, introduc'd
with false Praise of the Judge, and clos'd with false Accusation
of the Prisoner, who with cogent plain Truths, and matter of
Fact, baffled his barbarous Eloquence, and obtain'd so good a
Sense of himself and his Innocence with the Viceroy, that he
gave him a private Audience on the subject of his Faith; but
instead of then making his Court to him, he fell upon his

[a] *Acts cap.* 23. [Steele's note]

Excellency's own darling Vices, talk'd of Righteousness, Temperance, and Judgment,[93] with its Terrors for neglect of such Duties. In those Heathen times, it seems it was usual to have Excess, Wantonness, and Gluttony, to be [94] the Practice of Courts, and the Apostle so nearly touch'd his Lordship, that he fell into a sudden Disorder before his Inferior, and dismiss'd him 'till another Season; he afterwards frequently was entertain'd by him, not without hopes of a Bribe, which was also, in very old Times, the way to the Favours of the Great.

But *Fælix* now leaving his Lieutenancy to *Festus*, this Friendless good Man was a proper Person for a Tool to his Vanity, by doing an obliging thing to the Jews, in leaving him still in Custody at his departure, and no less useful to his New Excellency to be Sacrific'd to 'em upon his Entry: For at their request to have him brought to *Jerusalem* (designing to dispatch him by the way) tho' he at first denied it, he afterwards propos'd it to the Apostle himself, to have the Issue of his Tryal there: But he handsomly evaded his base Condescention, and their as base Malice, by Appealing as a *Roman* to *Cæsar* himself, before whose Authority he also then stood: But he is still kept in Gaol in the same state, to gratifie the Jews 'till *Agrippa* the *Tetrarch* of *Galilee* came to wait on *Festus*, who (after he had been there some Days) entertain'd him with the Case of St. *Paul*, and acquainted him that he was at a loss what to do with him: He was so Odious to the Jews, that he car'd not to Enlarge him, and so Innocent in himself, that he knew not what Account to send with him to *Rome*: This mov'd *Agrippa*'s Curiosity to hear him himself; in very great Pomp, he, his Sister, and whole Retinue came to his Tryal: The Apostle made so excellent a Defence, that Mean, Wrong'd, Poor and Unfriended as he was, he was neither Ridiculous or Contemptible to that Courtly Audience, but prevail'd so far upon the Greatest and Wisest Man there, that he forc'd him to declare, *thou hast almost persuaded me to be a Christian*; it would, methinks, be a Sin not to repeat his very handsome Answer.

I would to God, that not only thou, but also all that hear me this day, were not only almost, but altogether such as I am, except these bonds.[a]

[a] *Acts* 26. *ver.* 29. [Steele's note]

His Appeal made it necessary in course of Law, that he should go to *Rome*;[a] in his Passage thither, and in the Tempest, Hunger and Shipwrack, his Constancy was not a Support to him only, but also to the whole Company; and being thrown upon a barbarous Island, he did and receiv'd mutual Offices among the Poor Savages, not yet cultivated into Ingratitude. At *Rome*, the other Prisoners were carry'd into safe Custody, but he was permitted, with a Soldier only for his Ward, to live in his own hired House, teaching the things which concern the Lord Jesus Christ, no Man forbidding him; for it was only in *Nero*'s Reign, nor had *Rome* yet arriv'd at the exquisite and refin'd Tyranny of an Inquisition. Thus we have been distinct in running through the more illustrious Passages [95] of this Consummate Life and Character, as they are plac'd in Holy Writ, and may presume, after all the Injuries we have done him, that there is not any Portraiture in the most excellent Writers of Morality, that can come up to its Native Beauty; yet was not he contented to serve his God only, by Example, but has as Eminently done it by Precept; where he pursues Vice, and urges Virtue with all the Reason, Energy and Force that either good Sense or Piety can Inspire: And not upon the airy and fleeting Foundation of the Insensibility noble Minds bear to the Assaults of Fortune; which has been the Impertinence of Heathen Moralists, and [96] among them *Seneca*.

"A good Man is not only the Friend of God, but the very Image, the Disciple, the Imitator of him, and the true Child of his Heav'nly Father: He is True to himself, and Acts with Constancy and Resolution. *Scipio*, by a cross Wind being forc'd into the Power of his Enemies, cast himself upon the Point of his Sword; and as the People were enquiring what was become of the General, the General, says *Scipio*, is very well, and so he Expir'd. A Gallant Man, is Fortunes match: His Courage Provokes and Despises those terrible Appearances, that would Enslave us; a Wise Man is out of the reach of Fortune, but not free from the Malice of it; and all Attempts upon him are no more than *Xerxes's* Arrows; they may darken the Day, but they cannot strike the Sun." [b]

---

[a] *ver.* 23. [Steele's note. The correct reference for this passage, Acts 27 and 28, was given in the fourth edition.]
[b] L'Strange's *3d p. of* Seneca's *Morals.* Epist. 26. [Steele's note]

This is *Seneca's* very Spirit, Opinion and Genius; [97] but alas, what Absurdity is here! after the Panegyrick of a Brave or Honest Man, as the Disciple and Imitator of God, this is Instanc'd in the basest Action a Man could be guilty of; a General's dispatching himself in an extream Difficulty, and Deserting his Men and his Honour; and what is this but doing a mean Action with a great Countenance? What could this Imitator of God, out of the Power of Fortune, do more in Obedience to what they call so, than Sacrificing his Life to it: But this is Bombast got into the very Soul, Fustian in thinking!

Quanto Rectius hic qui nil molitur Inepte.

How much better he?

Be ye stedfast, unmoveable, always abounding in the Works of the Lord, forasmuch as [98] *you know that your Labour is not in vain in the Lord.*[a]

Here is supporting our selves under Misfortunes, propos'd upon the reasonable terms of Reward and Punishment; and all other is Fantastick, Arrogant and Ungrounded.

The First Epistle to *Corinth* is most exquisitely adapted [99] to the present Temper of *England,* nor did ever that City (tho' proverbial of [100] it) pretend to be more refinedly pleas'd than at present *London*: But St. *Paul* more Emphatically dissuades from those embasing Satisfactions of Sense.

Meats for the Belly, and the Belly for Meats; but God shall destroy both it and them.[b]

He, methinks, throws Blush and Confusion in the Face of his Readers, when he Argues on these Subjects; for who can conceive his Body the Mansion of an immortal Spirit, capable to receive the Aspiration and Grace of an Eternal God, and at the same time, by Gluttony and Drunkenness, entertain in that place Fuel to enflame themselves into Adultery, Rage and Revenge? as if our Misery were our Study, and Chastity, Innocence and Temperance, (those easie and agreeable Companions,) were not preferable to the Convulsions of Wrath, and Tortures of Lust.

---

[a] *Cor.* 15. *ver.* 58. [Steele's note. The correct reference, 1 Cor. 15. 58., was given in the fourth edition.]

[b] *Cor.* 9. *v.* 13. [Steele's note. Corrected in the fourth edition—1 Cor. 6. 13.]

Know ye not that your Bodies are the Members of Christ,
shall I then take the Members of Christ and make them the
Members of an Harlot? [a]

How Ugly has he made *Corinna* at one Sentence? Shall I,
who am conscious that he who laid down an immaculate Body,
to cleanse me from the Filth and Stain of a Polluted one, and
know that the Holy *Jesus* has promis'd to be present to all the
Conflicts of my Soul, Banish him thence, and be Guilty of
so unnatural a Coition, as to throw that Temple into the
Embraces [101] of a Mercenary Strumpet?

But must we then desert Love and the Fair?

The Cordial Drop Heav'n in our Cup has thrown,
To make the nauseous Draught of Life go down.

No, God forbid! the Apostle allows us a vertuous Enjoyment
of our Passions; but indeed extirpates all our false Ideas of
Pleasure and Happiness in 'em; he takes Love out of its Disguise, and puts it on its own gay and becoming Dress of Innocence; and indeed it is, among other Reasons, from want of
Wit and Invention in our Modern Gallants, that the beautiful
Sex is absurdly [102] and vitiously entertain'd by 'em: For there
is in their tender Frame, native Simplicity, groundless Fear,
and little unaccountable Contradictions, upon which there might
be built Expostulations to divert a good and Intelligent young
Woman, as well as the fulsome Raptures, guilty Impressions,
senseless Deifications, and pretended Deaths that are every Day
offer'd her.

No Pen certainly ever surpass'd either the Logick or Rhetorick
of his Fifteenth Chapter: How does he intermingle Hope and
Fear, Life and Death? Our rising from our Graves is most
admirably Argued on the receiv'd Philosophy, that Corruption
precedes Generation, and the easie Instances of new Grain, new
Plants and new Trees, from the minute Particles of Seed; and
when he has Buried us, how does he move the Heart with an
Oh Death where is thy Sting! Oh Grave where is thy Victory!
We have at once all along the quickest Touches of Distress and
of Triumph. It were endless to enumerate these Excellences
and Beauties in his Writings; but since they were all in his

[a] 1 Cor. 6 v. 15. [Steele's note]

more publick and ministerial Office, let's see him in his private Life: There is nothing expresses a Man's particular Character more fully, than his Letters to his Intimate Friends; we have one of that Nature of this great Apostle to *Philemon*, which in the Modern Language would perhaps run thus.

SIR,

"IT is with the deepest Satisfaction that I every Day hear you Commended, for your Generous Behaviour to all of that Faith, in the Articles of which I had the Honour and Happiness to Initiate you; for which, tho' I might presume to an Authority to oblige your Compliance in a Request I am going to make to you, yet chuse I rather to apply my self to you as a Friend, than an Apostle; for with a Man of your Great Temper, I know I need not a more Powerful Pretence than that of my Age and Imprisonment: Yet is not my Petition for my self, but in behalf of the Bearer, your Servant *Onesimus*, who has robb'd you, and ran away from you; what he has Defrauded you of, I will be answerable for, this shall be a Demand upon me; not to say that you owe me your very self: I call'd him your Servant, but he is now also to be Regarded by you in a greater Relation, ev'n that of your Fellow-Christian; for I esteem him a Son of mine as much as your self; nay, methinks it is a certain peculiar Endearment of him to me, that I had the happiness of gaining him in my Confinement: I beseech you to receive him, and think it an Act of Providence, that he went away from you for a Season, to return more Improv'd to your Service for ever."

This Letter is the sincere Image of a Worthy, Pious, and Brave Man, and the ready Utterance of a generous Christian Temper; How handsomly does he assume, tho' a Prisoner? How humbly condescend, tho' an Apostle? Could any Request have been made, or any Person oblig'd with a better Grace? The very Criminal Servant, is no less with him than his Son and his Brother; for Christianity has that in it, which makes Men pity, not scorn the Wicked, and by a beautiful kind of Ignorance of themselves, think those Wretches their Equals; it aggravates all the Benefits and good Offices of Life, by making 'em seem Fraternal; and the Christian feels the Wants of the Miserable

5

so much his own, that it sweetens the Pain of the oblig'd, when he that gives, does it with an Air, that has neither Oppression or Superiority in it, but had rather have his Generosity appear an enlarg'd Self-Love than diffusive Bounty, and is always a Benefactor with the Mein of a Receiver.

These are the great and beauteous Parts of Life and Friendship; and what is there in all that Morality can prescribe, that can make a Man do so much as the high Ambition of pleasing his Creator, with whom the Methods of Address are as Immutable as the Favour obtain'd by 'em?

Here, methinks we could begin again upon this Amiable Picture, or shall we search Antiquity for the Period and Consummation of his Illustrious Life, to give him the Crown and Glory of Martyrdom? That were a needless Labour, for he that has been in a Battel, has to his Prince the Merit of having Dy'd there; and St. *Paul* has so often in our Narration confronted Death, that we may bestow upon him that Cœlestial Title, and dismiss him with the just Eulogy in his own spritely Expression that he *Dy'd daily.*

Now the Address and Constancy with which this great Apostle has behav'd himself in so many various Forms of Calamity, are an ample Conviction, that to make our Life one decent and consistent Action, we should have one constant Motive of Living, and that Motive a Confidence in God: For had he Breath'd on any other Cause, instead of Application to the Almighty, he must (on many Occasions which we have mention'd) have ran to the Dagger, or the Bowl of Poison: For the Heathen Virtue prescribes Death before Stripes or Imprisonment; but whatever Pompous Look, Elegant Pens may have given to the Illustrious Distress'd (as they would have us think the Persons are,[103] who to evade Miseries, have profus'd their Lives, and rush'd to Death for Relief;) If we look to the bottom of things, we shall easily observe, that 'tis not a generous Scorn of Chains, or delicate Distaste of an Impertinent Being, (which two Pretences include all the Varnish that is put upon Self-murder) but[104] it ever was, and ever will be, Pride or Cowardise, that makes Life insupportable: For, since Accidents are not in our Power, but will (in spite of all our Care and Vigilance) befall us; what remains, but that we accommodate our selves so far, as to bear 'em with the greatest Decency and handsomest Patience we are able? And indeed Resistance to what we cannot avoid, is not the Effect of a valiant Heart, but a stubborn Stomach: Which Contumacy, 'till we have quite rooted out our Pride, will always make things too little, and our Cowardise too large: For as Fear gives a false Idea of Sufferings, and Attempts, as above our Strength, tho' they are not such, so Vanity makes things despicable, and beneath us, which are rather for our Honour and Reputation; but if Men would sincerely understand that they are but Creatures, all the distinctions of Great and Little, High and Low, would be easily swallow'd up in the Contemplation of the Hopes we entertain in the Place we shall have in his Mercy, who is the Author of all things.

CHAP. IV.

BUT [105] since we have hitherto treated this Subject in Examples only, (by a View of some Eminent Heathen, by a distant Admiration of the Life of our Blessed Saviour, and a near Examination of that of his Apostle St. *Paul*,) and since the Indulgence of Mens Passions and Interests calls all things that contradict their Practice, mere Notion, and Theory: We must from [106] this Place descend from the bright Incentives of their Actions to consider Lower Life, and talk of Motives which are common to all Men, and which are the Impulses of the ordinary World, as well as of Captains, Heroes, Worthies, Lawgivers, and Saints. Which when we have perform'd, if it shall appear, that those Motives are best us'd and improv'd, when join'd with Religion; we may rest assur'd, that it is a Stable, Sober, and Practical, as well as Generous, Exalted and Heroick, Position, that True Greatness of Mind is to be maintain'd only by Christian Principles.

We will venture then to assert, that the two great Springs of Human Actions are Fame and Conscience; for tho' we usually say such a one does not value his Reputation, and such a one is a Man of no Conscience, it will perhaps be very easie to prove, that there seldom [107] lives a Person so Profligate and Abandon'd, as not to prefer either the One or the [108] Other, even to Life its self; and by the way, methinks, the quick Pleasure Men taste in the one, and as lively Smart in the other, are strong Arguments of their Immortal Nature: For such Abstracted Sufferings and Enjoyments argue our Souls too large for their present Mansions, and raise Us (ev'n while we are in these Bodies) to a Being which does not at all affect 'em, but which is wholly Spiritual and Immaterial.

So strong (as we were going to proceed) is the Passion for Fame, that it never seems utterly extinct: For not to look among the Men of the Sword, (whose whole Pay it is,) and who suffer infinite Hazards, Toils, and Miseries to enjoy it; not, I say, to dwell upon them, whose more professed Pursuit is Glory, we shall find it Intrudes also as restlessly upon those of the Quill, nay the very Authors who conceal their Names, are yet Vainer than they who publish theirs. They both indeed aim at your Applause, but the Mock-Disguise of themselves in the former, is but a more subtle Arrogance, at once to enjoy your Esteem, and the Reputation of Contemning it: Nay, not only such who would recommend themselves by Great Actions, and Liberal Arts, but ev'n the lowest of Mankind, and they who have gone out of the road, not only of Honour, but also common Honesty, have still a remaining relish for Praise and Applause. For you may frequently observe Malefactors at an Execution, ev'n in that Weight of Shame and Terror, preserve as it were a corner of their Souls for the Reception of Pity, and Dye with the sturdy Satisfaction of not appearing to bend at the Calamity, or perhaps desert their Accomplices, by the Sacrifice and Betraying of whose Lives we frequently see they might have sav'd their Own.

By which last Instance (that the basest Men have still something Punctilious to 'em) we may Observe, that the Sense of Fame and Conscience is never quite Kill'd, but that when we are come to the worst, we have only carry'd 'em into another Interest, and turn'd our Gratifications that way, only to different Objects; nor can it be imagin'd that the Love-Histories we daily hear young Fellows relate of the Favours and Fondness of

Debauch'd Women to 'em, can be all that time design'd for a Self-Accusation: No, their idle Minds have only shifted their Sense of things, and tho' they Glory in their Shame, yet still they Glory.

What then must Men do to make themselves easie in this Invincible Passion, or how shall they possess a thing that is of so Inconsistent a Nature, that if they will be Masters of it, they must shun it: For if they speak to their own Advantage, or suffer another to do it to 'em, they are equally Contemptible: Thus they spend their Lives in pursuit of *an ever absent Good*; and yet, tho' Applause must never come quite Home to 'em, they are it seems miserable, except they are conscious that they have it.

Now if every Heart lies open to it, that Heart that is most Passionate of it, must be in eternal Anxiety to attain it, though that very Love[109] frequently leads to the Loss of it: For when our utmost Bliss is plac'd in this Charming Possession of Praise, and the World's Opinion of our Accomplishments, a Flatterer needs no more in Attempts upon Mens Honesty, and Womens Chastity, but their being convinc'd their Crimes may be a Secret: So easily, alas! are both Sexes led by admiration into Contempt.

To Rectifie therefore, and Adjust our Desires in this kind, we have the other concomitant Motive of a[110] Living Conscience, or the Knowledge and Judgment of what we are doing, which in the Voyage of Life is our Ballast, as the other is our Sail: But tho' Fame and Conscience, like Judge and Criminal, are thus plac'd together in us, they will have an Understanding, and go into each others Interest, except there is a Superior Court, in which both may be Examin'd. Here was the unhappy Block on which the noble Heathen stumbled, and lost his way; for the bare Conscience of a thing's being ill, was not of Consideration enough of its self to support Men in the Anguish of Disgrace, Poverty and Imprisonment. But Success, Applause, Renown, Honour and Command had Attractions too forcible to mere Men, to be relinquish'd but with Life it self; to which Truth, the braver and higher Part of the Heathen World have Dy'd Martyrs.

The different Sects and sortings of themselves into distinct Classes of Opinion, seem to be no other than the Prosecution of this Natural Impulse to Reputation, which Class was Stoical

or *Epicurean*, or the like,[111] according to the force and bent of
their Complexions, which they mis-understood for their Conscience; and *Sallust* begins his fine Story of *Catiline*'s Conspiracy, with an acknowledgement to this Purpose, for he takes
it to be the peculiar Duty and Superiority of the Human Race
above other Animals (which he calls Prone and Obedient to
their Bellies) *Ne Vitam silentio Transeant*, not to let Life pass
away in a Lazy Silence; and further, *Is mihi Demum vivere &
frui Anima videtur qui, negotio aliquo intentus Artis, bonae
famam quaerit*: He only in his Opinion might truly be said to
Live, who being employ'd in some useful Affair, obtain'd a
Reputation in an Honest or Liberal Art. Thus this Author of
Sober and Excellent Sense, makes it the End and Happy Consummation of a well-spent Life, to arrive at a good Fame;
which makes our Assertion in the beginning of this Discourse
very Natural, *viz.* That the Heathen Virtues, which were little
else but Disguis'd or Artificial Passions, (since their Good was
in Fame) must rise or fall with Disappointment or Success.

Now our good God, who claims not an utter Extirpation, but
the Direction only of our Passions, has provided also for this
great Desire, in giving it a Scope as boundless as it self; and
since 'tis never to be Satisfy'd, hath [112] allow'd it an Aim which
may supply it with Eternal employment.

*Let your Light so shine before Men that they may see your
Good Works, and Glorifie your Father which is in Heaven.*[a]

In this Command is the whole Business of Reputation, (about
which we are so miserably Anxious) wholly rectify'd; and Fame
no longer a Turbulent, Wayward, Uneasie Pursuit, but (when
thus made a Subordinate, and Secondary Cause of Action) a
calm, easie, indifferent and untroubled Possession.

And what more glorious Ambition can the Mind of Man
have, than to consider it self actually Imploy'd in the Service
of, and in a manner[113] in Conjunction with, the Mind of the
Universe, which is for ever Busie without Toil, and Working
without Weariness.

Thus the Spirit of Man, by new Acquisitions, will daily
receive Earnests of a nobler State, and by its own enlargement

[a] *Matt.* 5. 16. [Steele's note]

better apprehend that Spirit, after whose Image it was made, which knows no confinement of Place.

This adjusted Passion will make Men truly Agreeable, substantially Famous, for when the first Intention pursues the Service of the Almighty, distinction will naturally come, the only way it ever does come, without being apparently Courted; nor will Men be Lost through a fondness of it, by affectation in the familiar Life, or Knavery in the Busie:

It is not a Stoical Rant, but a reasonable Confidence in a Man thus Arm'd, to be unmov'd at Misfortunes; let the Sea, or the People rage; let the Billows beat, the World be confus'd, the Earth be shook; 'Tis not to him a Terror, but a daily request of his to hasten the very last Day of Human Nature, that He may finish this various Being, and enjoy the Presence of his Maker in an endless Tranquility.

Thus, by taking in Fame, the Christian Religion (and no other Motive) has fortify'd our Minds on all sides, and made 'em Impregnable by any Happiness or Misery with which this World can attack it: [114] And now, if it is Impartially apparent to us, that the Christian Scheme is not only the way to Ease and Composure of Mind in unhappy Circumstances, but also the noblest Spur to honest and great Actions, what hinders, but that we be Baptiz'd, and Resolve all our perplex'd Notions of Justice, Generosity, Patience and Bravery, into that one easie and portable Virtue, Piety? Which could arm our Ancestors in this Faith with so resistless and victorious a Constancy, that by their Sufferings, their Religion, from the Outcast and Scorn of the Earth, has ascended Soveraign Thrones; and Defender of the Faith, and most Christian King, are Appellations of the Greatest Monarchs of the most refin'd Nations; nor can we enough thank the Almighty who has dispos'd us into the World, when the Christian Name bears Pomp and Authority, and not in its offensive, low and despis'd Beginnings: But alas! its State is [115] as much Militant as ever, for there are Earthly and Narrow Souls, as deeply Scandal'd at the Prosperity the Professors and Teachers of this Sacred Faith enjoy, and object to 'em the Miseries and Necessities of the Primitive Believers: Light and Superficial Men! Not seeing that Riches is a much more dangerous Dispensation than that of [116] Poverty, this we oppose as a Foe, that we run to meet as a Friend, and an Enemy does his Work more successfully in an Embrace than a Blow; but since the Necessaries, Conveniencies and Honours of Life which the Clergy enjoy, are so great an Offence to their Despisers, they are the more engag'd to hold 'em dear; for they who envy a Man for what he has, would certainly scorn him without it; when therefore they are both in good and bad Fortune irreconcilable to 'em, may they always offend with their Happiness; for it is not to be doubted, but that there are Bishops and Governors in the Church of *England*, whose decent Hospitality, Meekness, and Charity to their Brethren, will place 'em in the same Mansions with the most Heroick Poor; and convince the Mistake of their Enemies, that the Eternal Pastor has giv'n his Worldly Blessings into Hands by which he approves their Distribution; and still bestows upon us great and exemplary Spirits, that can Conquer the Difficulties and Enchantments of Wealth it self.

To follow such excellent Leaders, it will be necessary we now consider also, what may be our best Rule in that State we call our good Fortune; and enquire whether Christianity can as well become its Professors in the Enjoyments of Prosperity, as we have seen it has in the hardships of Adversity; this also we shall best know by contemplating our Natural Frame and Tendency, which Religion either assists or corrects in these Circumstances.

The Eternal God, in whom we Live, and Move, and have our Being, has Impress'd upon us all one Nature, which as an Emanation from him, who is Universal Life, presses us by Natural Society to a close Union with each other; which is, methinks, a sort of Enlargement of our very selves when we run into the Ideas, Sensations and Concerns of our Brethren: By this Force of their Make, Men are insensibly hurried into each other, and by a secret Charm we lament with the Unfortunate, and rejoice with the Glad; for it is not possible for an human Heart to be averse to any thing that is Human: But by the very Mein and Gesture of the Joyful and Distress'd we rise and fall into their Condition; and since Joy is Communicative, 'tis reasonable that Grief should be Contagious, both which are seen and felt at a look, for one Man's Eyes are Spectacles to another to Read his Heart: Those useful and honest Instruments do not only discover Objects to us, but make our selves also Transparent; for they, in spite of Dissimulation, when the Heart is full, will brighten into Gladness, and gush into Tears: From this Foundation in nature is kindled that noble Spark of Cœlestial Fire, we call Charity or Compassion, which opens our Bosoms, and extends our Arms to Embrace all Mankind, and by this it is that the Amorous Man is not more suddenly melted with Beauty, than the Compassionate with Misery.

Thus are we fram'd for mutual Kindness, good Will and Service, and therefore our Blessed Saviour has been pleased to give us (as a reiterated Abridgment of all his Law) the Command of Loving one another; and the Man that Imbibes that noble Principle is in no Danger of insolently Transgressing against his Fellow Creatures, but will certainly use all the Advantages which he has from Nature and Fortune to the Good and Welfare of others, for whose Benefit (next to the Adoration of his Maker) he knows he was Created: This Temper of Mind, when neither Polluted or Mis-led, tends to this Purpose, and the Improvement of it by Religion raises on it an exalted Superstructure, which inclines him in his Words and Actions, to be above the little Crafts and Doubles with which the World beneath him is perplex'd: He is Intrinsically possessed of what mere Morality must own to be a Fantastical Chimæra, the being wholly dis-interested in the Affairs of the Person he affects or befriends; for indeed when the Regard of our Maker is not our first Impulse and Desire in our Hopes and Purposes, it is impossible but that the Fondness of our selves and our own Interest must recurr upon us, and leaven the whole Course of our Actions: When the Fountain is Muddy it must stain the Rivulet, and the prædominant Passion gives a Tincture to all our Cares and Pleasures; so that Men ordinarily Love others out of a Tenderness to themselves, and do good Offices to receive 'em with Encrease and Usury: Nay, if we follow the best Friendship we meet with to its Sourse, and allow it to be what it sometimes really is, a passionate Inclination to serve another, without hopes or visible Possibility of receiving a Return, yet we must also allow, that there is a deep Interest to our selves (though indeed a Beautiful one) in satis-

fying that Inclination; but that good Intention is subject to be
Chang'd and Interrupted (as perhaps it was taken up) by
Accident, Mistake, or turn of Humour; but he that Loves others
for the Love of God, must be unchangeable, for the Cause of
his Benevolence to us is so; and though indeed he is not without
Self-regard in the hopes of receiving one Day an immense
Reward of all his Labour, yet since that is separate from this
World, it is to all Intents of Life, as far from the Interfering
with our Purposes, as if he had no such Expectation; and that
very Prospect in him is not of a selfish incommunicable Nature,
but is augmented and furthered by our Participation, while his
Joys are quickened and redoubled by the joint Wishes of others:
This is that Blessed State of Mind which is so excellently call'd
Singleness of Heart; which inseparable Peace and Happiness,
'tis not in the power of all the Tinsel in the World to dis-
compose; for to a Christian and knowing Mind Earth is but
Earth, though the refin'd Dirt shine into Gems, and glister
into Gold.

He that thus justly values the Wealth which Heav'n has
bestow'd upon him, cannot grow giddy in the Possession of it,
for it serves only to express a Noble and Christian Nature,
which dispenses liberally, and enjoys abstinently the Goods which
he knows he may lose and must leave: But this extensive
Magnanimity, according to the Rules of our Faith, is not to be
bestow'd on those only who are our Friends, but must reach
also to [117] our very Enemies; though [118] good Sense as well as
Religion is so utterly banish'd the World, that Men glory in
their very Passions, and pursue Trifles with the Utmost Vengeance: So little do they know that to Forgive is the most
arduous Pitch human Nature can arrive at; a Coward has often
Fought, a Coward has often Conquer'd, but *a Coward never
Forgave.* The Power of doing that flows from a Strength of
Soul conscious of its own Force, whence it draws a certain
Safety which its Enemy is not of consideration enough to Inter-
rupt; for 'tis peculiar in the Make of a brave Man to have his
Friends seem much above him, his Enemies much below him.

Yet though the neglect of our Enemies may so intense a
Forgiveness, as the Love of 'em is not to be in the least accounted
for by the force of Constitution, but is a more spiritual and

refin'd Moral introduc'd by him, who Dy'd for those that Persecuted him, yet very justly deliver'd to us, when we consider our selves as Offenders, and to be forgiven on the reasonable Terms of Forgiving; For who can ask what he will not bestow? Especially when that Gift is attended with a Redemption from the cruellest Slavery to the most acceptable Freedom: For when the Mind is in the Contemplation of Revenge, all its Thoughts must surely be Tortur'd with the Alternate Pangs of Rancour, Envy, Hatred, and Indignation: And they who profess a Sweet in the Enjoyment of it, certainly never felt the consummate Bliss of Reconciliation: At such an Instant the false Ideas we receiv'd unravel, and the Shiness, the Distrust, the secret Scorns, and all the base Satisfactions, Men had in each others Faults and Misfortunes, are dispell'd, and their Souls appear in their Native Whiteness, without the least Streak of that Malice or Distaste which sullied 'em: And perhaps those very Actions, which (when we look'd at 'em in the oblique Glance with which Hatred doth always see[119] Things) were Horrid and Odious, when observ'd with honest and open Eyes, are Beauteous and Ornamental.

But if Men are averse to us in the most violent Degree, and we can never bring 'em to an amicable Temper, then indeed we are to exert an obstinate Opposition to 'em, and never let the Malice of our Enemies have so effectual an Advantage over us, as to escape our good Will: For the neglected and despised Tenets of Religion are so Generous, and in so Transcendent and Heroick a manner disposed for publick Good, that 'tis not in a Man's power to avoid their Influence; for the Christian is as much inclin'd to your Service when your Enemy, as the moral Man when your Friend.

Now since the Dictates of Christianity are thus excellently suited to an enlarg'd Love and Ambition to serve the World, the most immediate Method of seeing to what height they would accomplish that noble Work, is taking the Liberty of observing how they would naturally Influence the Actions and Passions of such Persons, as have Power to exert all the Dictates and Impulses which are Inspir'd, either by their Inclinations or Opinions; for whatever is Acted in the narrow Path of a private Life, passes away in the same Obscurity that 'twas perform'd in; [120] while the Purposes and Conduct of Princes attract all Eyes, and employ all Tongues; in which difficult Station and Character it is not possible, but that a Man, without Religion must be more exquisitely Unhappy, than the meanest of his Vassals; for the repeated Pomp and Pageantry of Greatness must needs become in time, either Languid in the Satisfactions they give, or turn the Heads of the Powerful, so that 'tis absolutely necessary that he should have something of more inward and deep regard, to keep his Condition from being an Oppression, either to himself or others.

There were not ever before the Entrance of the Christian Name into the World, Men who have maintain'd a more re-nown'd Carriage than the two great Rivals who possess the full Fame of the present Age, and will be the Theme and Examination of the future: They are exactly formed by Nature for those Ends, to which Heav'n seems to have sent 'em amongst us: Both animated with a restless Desire of Glory, but pursue it by different Means, and with different Motives: To one it consists in an extensive undisputed Empire over his Subjects, to the other in their rational and voluntary Obedience: One's Happiness is founded in their want of Power, the others in their want of Desire to oppose him: The one enjoys the Summet of Fortune with the Luxury of a *Persian*, the other with the Moderation of a *Spartan*; one is made to Oppress, the other to relieve the Oppressed: The one is satisfied with the Pomp and Ostentation of Power to prefer and debase his Inferiors, the other delighted only with the Cause and Foundation of it, to cherish and protect 'em: To one therefore Religion is [121] but a convenient Disguise, to the other a vigorous Motive of Action.

For without such Tyes of real and solid Honour, there is no way of forming a Monarch, but after the *Machiavilian* Scheme, by which a Prince must ever seem to have all Vertues, but really to be Master of none, but is to be Liberal, Merciful and Just, only as they serve his Interests; while with the noble Art of Hypocrisie, Empire would be to be Extended, and new Con-quests be made by new Devices, by which prompt Address his Creatures might insensibly give Law in the Business of Life, by leading Men in the Entertainment of it, and making their great Monarch the Fountain of all that's delicate and refin'd,

and his Court the Model for Opinions in Pleasure, as well as
the Pattern in Dress; which might prevail so far upon an
undiscerning World as (to accomplish it for its approaching
Slavery) to make it receive a superfluous Babble for an Universal
Language.

Thus when Words and Show are apt to pass for the sub-
stantial Things they are only to express, there would need no
more to enslave a Country but to adorn a Court; for while every
Man's Vanity makes him believe himself capable of becoming
Luxury, Enjoyments are a ready Bait for Sufferings, and the
hopes of Preferment Invitations to Servitude, which Slavery
would be colour'd with all the Agreements, as they call it,
Imaginable: The noblest Arts and Artists, the finest Pens and
most elegant Minds, jointly employ'd to set it off, with the
various Embellishments of sumptuous Entertainments, charming
Assemblies and polish'd Discourses: And those apostate Abilities of Men, the ador'd Monarch might profusely and skilfully
encourage, while they flatter his Virtue, and gild his Vice at so
high a rate, that he without Scorn of the one, or Love of the
other, would alternately and occasionally use both, so that his
Bounty should support him in his Rapines, his Mercy in his
Cruelties.

Nor is it to give Things a more severe Look than is natural,
to suppose such must be the Consequences of a Prince's having
no other Pursuit than that of his own Glory; for if we consider
an Infant born into the World, and beholding it self the
mightiest Thing in it, it self the present Admiration and future
Prospect of a fawning People, who profess themselves great or
mean according to the Figure he is to make amongst 'em, what
Fancy would not be Debauch'd to believe they were but what
they professed themselves, his mere Creatures, and use 'em
as such by purchasing with their Lives a boundless Renown,
which he, for want of a more just Prospect, would place in the
number of his Slaves, and the extent of his Territories; such
undoubtedly would be the Tragical Effects of a Prince's living
with no Religion, which are not to be surpass'd by his having
a False one.

If Ambition were Spirited with Zeal, what would follow,
but that his People should be converted into an Army, whose

Swords can make Right in Power, and solve Controversie in Belief; and if Men should be Stiff-necked to the Doctrine of that visible Church, let 'em be contented with an Oar and a Chain in the midst of Stripes and Anguish, to contemplate on him, whose Yoke is Easie, and whose Burthen is Light.

With a Tyranny begun on his own Subjects, and Indignation that others draw their Breath Independent of his Frown or Smile, why should he not proceed to the seizure of the World; and if nothing but the Thirst of Sway were the Motive of his Actions, why should Treaties be other than mere Words, or solemn National Compacts be any thing but an Halt in the March of that Army, who are never to lay down their Arms, 'till all Men are reduc'd to the Necessity of Hanging their Lives on his Way-ward Will; who might Supinely, and at Leisure, expiate his own Sins by other Mens Sufferings; while he daily Meditates New Slaughter, and New Conquest.

For mere Man, when giddy with unbridled Power, is an insatiate Idol, not to be appeased with Myriads offer'd to his Pride, which may be puffed up by the Adulation of a base and prostrate World, into an Opinion that he is something more than Human, by being something less: And alas, what is there that Mortal man will not believe of himself, when Complimented with the Attributes of God? He can then conceive Thoughts of a Power as *Omnipræsent* as his: But should there be such a Foe of Mankind now upon Earth, have our Sins so far provok'd Heav'n, that we are left utterly Naked to his Fury? Is there no Power, no Leader, no Genius that can Conduct and Animate us to our Death, or our Defence? Yes, our great God never gave one to Reign by his Permission, but he gave to another also, to Reign by his Grace.

All the Circumstances of the Illustrious Life of our Prince seem to have Conspir'd to make him the Check and Bridle of Tyranny, for his Mind has been strengthen'd and confirm'd by one continued Struggle, and Heav'n has Educated him by Adversity to a quick Sense of the Distresses and Miseries of Mankind, which he was born to Redress: In just Scorn of the trivial Glories and light Ostentations of Power, that Glorious Instrument of Providence, moves like that, in a steddy, calm and silent Course, Independent either of Applause or of Calumny, which renders him, if not in a Political, yet in a Moral, a Philosophick, an Heroick, and a Christian Sense, an absolute Monarch: Who satisfied with this unchangeable, just and ample Glory, must needs turn all his Regards from himself, to the Service of others; for he begins his Enterprizes with his own share in the Success of 'em, for Integrity bears in its self its Reward, nor can that which depends not on Event ever know Disappointment.

With the undoubted Character of a glorious Captain, and (what he much more Values than the most splendid Titles) that of a sincere and honest Man, he is the Hope and Stay of *Europe*, an Universal Good not to be Engrossed by us only; for distant Potentates implore his Friendship, and injur'd Empires Court his Assistance: He rules the World, not by an Invasion of the People of the Earth, but the Address of its Princes; and if that World should be again rous'd from the Repose which his prevailing Arms have giv'n it, why should we not hope that there is an Almighty, by whose Influence the terrible Enemy that thinks himself prepar'd for Battel, may find he is but ripe for Destruction, and that there may be in the Womb of Time great Incidents, which may make the Catastrophe of a prosperous Life as Unfortunate, as the particular Scenes of it were Successful.

For there does not want a skilful Eye, and resolute Arm, to observe and grasp the Occasion: A Prince, who from a just Notion of his Duty to that Being, to whom he must be accountable, has in the service of his Fellow-Creatures, a noble contempt of Pleasures, and Patience of Labours, to whom 'tis Hæreditary to be the Guardian and Asserter of the Native Rights and Liberties of Mankind; and who, with a rational Ambition, knows how much greater 'tis to give than take away; whose every Day is productive of some great Action, in behalf of Mens Universal Liberty, which great Affection to 'em 'tis not in the Power of their very Ingratitude to alienate; he is Constant and Collected in himself, nor can their Murmurs interrupt his Toil, any more than their Dreams his Vigilance; a Prince, who never did or spoke any thing that could justly give Grief to his People, but when he mention'd his *Succession* to 'em: But what grateful Mind can bear that insupportable Reflection? No, we will with endless Adoration implore Heav'n to continue him to us, or expire in Heaps before his Pavilion, to guard his important Life, and in the Joint Cause of Heav'n and Earth, our Religion and our Liberty, destroy like Ministring Angels, or die an Army of Martyrs.

FINIS.

The Medley No. 23 (5 March 1711)

There is no doubt that Steele contributed several papers or parts of them to Arthur Maynwaring's Whiggish periodical, *The Medley* (October 1710 to August 1711); but a portion of No. 23 is all that can be attributed to him by direct external evidence. John Oldmixon, assistant to Maynwaring, who gave an account of the collaborators, stated: " The 23d Medley with that pleasant story of the Ball at Wapping, was written by Mr. Steele. . . . The comparison between Abel Roper and the Examiner, at the end of this paper is Manwaring's." (*Life and Posthumous Works of Arthur Maynwaring*, 1715).

The purpose of the *Medley*, first appearing in the feverish autumn of 1710, was, in its own words, to oppose the Tory *Examiner*, which " vilify'd the late Ministry, the *Scots* nation and the Union, the Trading and Mony'd Interest of *Great Britain*, the moderate Clergy and Laity of our Church, the Dissenters, and the whole Whig-Party . . ." (No. 34). Steele's theme in No. 23, as in several other *Medley* papers of about that time, is a defence of the late Whig Ministry, his patrons and friends, who were being vigorously attacked in retrospect by the *Examiner*, that is by Swift. The week preceding (in Nos. 28, 29), Swift had branded them as " Purloiners of the Publick " . . . " a pernicious Crew," who had drained the national wealth and conspired to destroy church and state. Steele's anonymous rejoinder combines dignity and drollery and is milder in tone than were his real feelings.

Steele and Maynwaring, who had been friends for a number of years, had been very closely associated during the previous summer and autumn when the Whig Ministry was falling; and in the midst of the excitement, in July, Steele had dedicated the first volume of the collected *Tatler* to his friend, as a mark of esteem. Maynwaring was a Whig office-holder, a Kit Cat, and a liason man between politicians and men of letters. According to one tradition it was he who suggested Steele as editor for *The Gazette*, a post he held from 1707 to 1710. Textual notes on p. 639.

6

From Monday, February 26. to Monday, March 5. 1711.

THERE are no Affections of the Mind that seem at first sight more nearly related to one another than Envy and Emulation. Yet if we consider them attentively, we shall find that there are none more different. Both indeed arise from the Comparison of our selves with those above us; but in these Comparisons, Envy repines at superiour Merit in another, Emulation bewails the want of it in ourselves. The business therefore of the envious Man is to vilify and disparage, as it is the nature of the Emulous to endeavour after those Perfections which they behold in Men more excellent than themselves. The Design of both is to place themselves upon a level with those above them: but as to this end one of them practises all the little Arts of Detraction, Defamation, and Calumny, to pull down their Superiours to their own Condition; the other makes use of Industry, Vigilance, and Application, the Instruments of an honest and active Ambition, to raise himself up to that pitch of Reputation which he admires in Men above him.

As every Passion is more useful or pernicious according to the Circumstances of the Person in whom it reigns; what makes Men of a private Character disagreeable, makes those in a publick Station pernicious. In order to equal those who have served their Country with Glory in the same Stations, they derogate from every Action that is confessedly Great, and give the worst Interpretation to every thing that can appear doubtful. Thus when they despair of rising to the Perfections of their Predecessors, they keep themselves in countenance by endeavouring to deface them.

I cannot forbear repeating on this occasion the Story of a merry Rake, who was giving an account of a Ball which he had seen at a Musick-House in *Wapping*. The Men concerned in it were made up of a Crew of Sailors and Colliers. The Colliers, who came in last, observing the Sailors, contrary to their Expectation, to be spruc'd up in their best Clothes, withdrew into another Room to wash their Faces and brush themselves; when the Head of the Colliery, who was more cunning than the rest, said to them: *Look ye, Lads, it is all fruitless pains; if you will be rul'd by me, let us go into the great Room, and justle among the Sailors for their Places: and I'll engage, tho we cannot make our selves as clean as they are, we shall quickly make them as black as our selves.*

I make a Present of this short Story to my Friend the *Examiner*, in return for his polite Simile of a Man of Quality going to a Ball with Smut upon his Forehead.

Were any such Persons as are above describ'd at the head of Affairs at any time, how happy wou'd they be in such a Tool as the *Examiner*? such an Inventor of groundless Falsehoods, such a Reviver of confuted Calumnies, who has no regard to the Dictates of Truth, nor even the Sentiments of common Humanity; that takes upon him the infamous Task of libelling and reviling every one that has done service to his Country for these ten Years, and of cherishing in the Minds of the Ignorant a Spirit of Bitterness and Prejudice. Slanderous and reproachful Libels were formerly the Weapons of the Party that was out of power, which they made use of as the Means, tho they were very base Means, to reinstate themselves. One cannot however but reflect, that Adversaries must be very formidable, and have uncommon Merit, when there is a necessity for defaming them even in their Adversity.

This kind of Ribaldry passes for Wit and Humour among the Underlings of the Party; who, when the Author is very foul-mouth'd, are taught to believe that he is very satyrical; and when he appears scurrilous in an extraordinary degree, smile upon one another, and whisper, *the Examiner is Devilish severe to day.* Thus plain Calumnies, and downright matter of Scandal without any of those nice Glances or Strokes of Wit that are admir'd in other Writers of this kind, are here receiv'd as fine Raillery and Invective. Nay I have known some so very silly, as to admire him for the boldness of his Sentiments, tho every one knows that he deserves too ill to be in Danger. 'Tis true, he himself has suggested to us, that his Paper is an *Orthodox* Libel, where he calls those of his Adversaries, *The Tolerated Papers of the Week.*

The Englishman's Thanks to the Duke of Marlborough
(January, 1712)

This anonymous public letter is Steele's first known political pamphlet, written in indignation the day after the Queen dismissed Marlborough from all his offices, including that of Captain-General (31 Dec. 1711). The Tory ministers had manoeuvered the dismissal, upon charges of peculation and accepting bribes, as a necessary step in their negotiations for peace; and they had been preparing during 1711 for its favorable effect on public opinion by a flood of anti-Marlborough propaganda in *The Examiner* and in party pamphlets— one of the most potent being Swift's *Conduct of the Allies* (27 Nov. 1711). All of these proceedings were disagreeable to Steele, who not only was in sympathy with the foreign and domestic policies of the Whigs but admired Marlborough's military achievements, his statesmanship, and his personal qualities to the point of hero worship. His old-fashioned eloquence is deeply sincere. Such treatment of Marlborough after his successful prosecution of the war with France Steele regarded as national ingratitude. The dedication of *Spectator* IV was made to Marlborough a few months later, in November, 1712, about the time when he went into voluntary exile on the continent. Both dedication and pamphlet were known to be Steele's. Textual notes on p. 639.

THE

ENGLISHMAN's

THANKS

TO THE

Duke of *Marlborough.*

L O N D O N:

Printed for *A. Baldwin*, near the *Oxford-Arms* in
Warwick-Lane. MDCCXII. *Price Twopence.*

My LORD,

IT was with the utmost Consternation I, this Day, heard Your Grace had received a Dismission from all Your Employments: And lest You should, out of the Softness which is inseparable from Natures truly Heroick, believe this a Diminution of Your Glory, I take the Liberty to express to You, as well as I can, the Sense which Mankind has of Your Merit.

That Great Genius with which God has endowed You, was raised by Him, to give the First Notion, That the Enemy was to be Conquer'd: Till You were plac'd at the Head of Armies, the Confederates seem'd contented to show *France,* That She could not overcome *Europe:* But it enter'd not into the Heart of Man, That the rest of *Europe* could Conquer *France.* When I have said this, *My Lord,* there arise in my Soul so many Instances of Your having been the Ministring Angel in the Cause of LIBERTY, that my Heart flags, as if it expected the lash of Slavery, when the Sword is taken out of His Hand, who Defended Me and all Men from it. Believe me, *Immortal Sir,* You have a slighter Loss in this Change of Your Condition, than any other Man in *England.* Your Actions have exalted You to be the Chief of Your Species; and a continued Chain of Successes resulting from Wise Counsels, have denominated You the First of Mankind in the Age which was Bless'd with Your Birth. Enjoy what it is not in the Power of Fate it self to take from You, the Memory of Your Past Actions. Past Actions make up Present Glory. It is in the Power of Mortals to be Thankless to You for Doing them; but it is not in their Power to take from You, that You have Done them. It is in the Power of Man to make Your Services Ineffectual in Consequences to Your Country; but it is not in their Power to make them Inglorious to Your Self. Be not therefore You concern'd; but let Us lament, who may suffer by Your Removal. Your Glory is augmented by Comparison of your Merit to the Reward it meets with: But the Honour of Your Country—

It is as impossible to do You Dishonour, as to recall Yester-

day: Your Character is indelible in the Book of Fame: And tho'
after a few Turbulent Years, it will be said of Us the rest of
Mankind, *They were*; it will be to the End of Time said,
MARLBOROUGH Is. *My Lord*, You are possess'd of all the
English Glory, of the whole Age in which You live; and all
who shall be transmitted to Posterity, must pass down only
memorable, as they have exerted themselves in Concert with
You, or against You, with Endless Honour as Your Friends,
Infamy as Your Enemies. The Brightest Circumstance that can
be related of the QUEEN Her Self, will be, It was SHE for
whom *MARLBOROUGH* conquer'd. Since it is Thus, *My
Lord*, if even the Glorious Edifice which Your Country decreed
should be Erected to Perpetuate Your Memory, stand Unfinish'd,
let it stand so a Monument of the Instability of Human Affairs.
Your Glory is not chang'd, because the rest of Mankind are
changeable. It is not Your Fault, that other Generals have
receiv'd a Greater Reward for Escaping Your Valour, than You
have for making them fly before it.

Had it pleas'd God that we had lost You by Your Mortality,
the Greatest Man next to You would have had the Mitigation
of his Inferior Desert, that the same Age could not produce
such another: But how will he do to avert the Eyes of Mankind,
upon all Exigencies, from looking towards You yet living?

My Noble Lord, Be convinc'd, that You cannot be Disgrac'd;
that Your Stand in Human Life is Immutable; that Your Glory
is as Impassive as the Fame of Him who Dy'd a Thousand
Years ago. Whence is it that we thus Love You, that we thus
Honour You? It is from the very Qualities, which lay You open
to the Assaults of Your Enemies. That Sweet Complacency,
that Admirable Spirit, which is so tempered for the Arts of
Common Life, makes us lose our Wonder in Love. Is that
Amiable Man, with that Easy Gesture, that Gentle Beseeching
Mein the Man Terrible in Battel, the Scourge of Tyrants? My
Lord *MARLBOROUGH*, do not think there are not Men who
can see Your several Accomplishments, Your Excellencies that
Expose You to the Possibility of being ill treated. We understand You too well not to see, and to thank You, that You
come Home, as if You had never heard the Acclamations of
the Universe. That Your Modesty and Resignation have made

Your Transcendent, Your Heroick, Your God-like Virtue capable of being blended in Society with other Men. And, My Lord, do You think we can let that Virtue be Dangerous to You, which only makes Your other Qualities not Dangerous to us? Accept, O Familiar, O Amiable, O Glorious Man, the Thanks of every Generous, every Honest Man in *Great Britain*. Go on in Your Easie Mein of Life, be contented we See You, we Admire You, we Love You the more. While You are what You cannot cease to be, that Mild Virtue is Your Armour; the Shameless Ruffian that should Attempt to Sully it, would find his Force against it as Detestable, as the Strength of a Ravisher in the Violation of Chastity; the Testimonies of a Perjur'd Man Confronting Truth, or Clamour drowning the Voice of Innocence.

I am,

My LORD,

Your Grateful Fellow-Subject,

and Faithful Friend,

SCOTO-BRITANNUS.

A Letter to Sir M.[iles] W.[arton] Concerning Occasional Peers (March, 1713)

As biographers of Steele have said nothing of Warton, a brief sketch may be useful here. Sir Michael (Miles) Warton (Wharton) (1649-1725) came from a Yorkshire family, apparently of wealth, who in the 17th century had expended both their money and their blood in the Royalist cause. For generations they had lived in Beverley. Sir Miles's father was Michael Warton, Esq., of Beverley Parks, and his mother, the Hon. Susanna Poulet, daughter of John, Third Baron Poulet of Hinton, St. George, Somerset. Sir Miles was a member of St. John's, Cambridge, and of Gray's Inn; he was knighted in 1666, at the age of 17; at various times and for many years he sat for Yorkshire boroughs. According to Luttrell's entry, he was appointed by William in May, 1689, to the commission for the admiralty, apparently at that time being Whiggishly inclined. At his death in 1725, his benefactions to various institutions in Beverley were considerable. He is buried in the Minster there. See *Alumni Cantabrigienses*; W. A. Shaw, *The Knights of England* (1906), II, 242; *Dugdale's Visitation of Yorkshire*; George Oliver, *History and Antiquities of the Town and Minster of Beverley* (1829).

Evidently Steele did not know Warton personally in 1713; and he seems not to have mentioned him elsewhere except in *Theatre* No. 11 (6 Feb. 1720), where Warton's name is merely included among other patrons to whom Steele had made dedications. The occasion for Steele's admiration is explained by Luttrell's entry on 1 Jan. 1712: " Sir Michael Wharton desired to be excused from being a peer." It will be remembered that on 31 Dec. 1711 Queen Anne had issued patents for twelve new Tory peers, whose function was to offset the Tory defection in the Lords and thus save the Ministry and the peace negotiations. In refusing to accept such a peerage, Warton doubtless had acted independently, against the influence of his kinsman Lord Poulet (4th Baron), Oxford's Tory friend, since June, 1711, Anne's High Steward, and a conspirator in this constitutional *coup d'état*. Such independence of spirit as Warton's would attract Steele; and he would thus appear a logical person to address in the pamphlet written in 1713 upon the rumor that six new peers would shortly be created to supply needed Tory votes. For at this time in the spring, as the Tory peace negotiations neared their climax, further defection of the Hanover Tories threatened the commercial clauses of the Treaties.

72

Steele argues the danger of this practice to the prerogative of the Queen, to the power of the House of Lords, to the liberties of the people, and to the maintaining of the constitution: " If Men cannot carry on the Business of the Nation without such Helps, they may as well in plain Terms tell us they cannot maintain the Constitution, but they will alter it to one which they can." His title implies that " occasional peers " might be thought as objectionable for political reasons as occasional conformers. The Tory Occasional Conformity Bill had been passed in December, 1711, at the time the new peers were created. Textual notes on p. 639.

[*A Letter to Sir M. W.*]

SIR,

I Have not the Happiness to be in the least known to you, but
have, with all *England*, Obligations to you for the Greatness
of Mind which you exerted in refusing, not long ago, to be
made a Peer of this Realm in a hasty and surreptitious Manner:
It was not so much as pretended, that the Dozen of Nobles
were then introduced for any other Purpose, but to gain a
Question of the highest Importance, no less than a Question
of Peace and War. Were the Point obtained by it never so
much conducive to our Good, the Novelty, if not obviated for
the future, cannot but tend to the apparent Danger of the
Queen and all her Subjects. It is from a Report that there are
another half dozen to be made within few Days, that I am
engaged to give you this Trouble.

You, Sir, who are adorned with more than Title, a Superiority
to it, from the Refusal of it when you thought it inconsistent with
Honour, are the properest Man to be addressed, when I consider the Danger of making Occasional Lords, and lay before
the World this fatal Novelty, as it affects the Queen's most
Excellent Majesty, the House of Peers, and the whole People
of *England*.

Honour is the Conscience of doing just and laudable Actions,
independent of the Success of those Actions. God is the
Fountain of this Honour, and animates and supports all who
are actuated by it; he is an inexhaustible Fountain, and cannot
be impaired by his Creations. But if it be not Prophane to
mention, so near after his Omnipotence, any Distinctions we
give one another here, I would proceed to say, that it is not so
with Sovereigns upon Earth, whom we phrase Fountains of
Honour. They, alas! are themselves diminished in Proportion
to what they grant out of themselves. An unguarded and lavish
Hand, in Grants of this Kind, would very soon make the
Honour, flowing from a Prince, of no Value and Consideration

to those on whom it is bestowed, and take away any Power of giving more from the Giver. To come immediately to the Point; I assert, that the numerous Creation of Peers is the greatest Wound that can be given to the Prerogative. A Peer and his Heirs are Checks in the Legislature to the Queen and Her Heirs; that part of the Legislature which is in the Queen, is apparently diminished by so much as she gives out of it, from her own into other Families. This is equally destructive with relation to the Merit of the Persons on whom Honour is conferred; if they happen to be Men who are barely unblamable, without Talents or high Qualifications, they do but crowd that illustrious Assembly, and like all other Crowds, they are serviceable and hurtful but just as they are inspired by those who have Skill to lead them. Thus the Crown is no way sure of their Concurrence any farther than by Promise of their first Vote; and they may ever after turn Patriots on the side of the People, to the constant Interruption of Affairs; for it generally happens that those who are conscious of an Inability to promote Business, give themselves a Figure, and fancy they are considerable, from the Power of retarding it. Thus much as to what regards the Queen's most Excellent Majesty.

As to the House of Peers, it is visible to any thing above a natural Fool, that the Power of each Lord is so much less considerable as it is repeated in other Persons; but the great Hardship to that Great and Awful Body, whose Privileges have so often been a Safety and Protection to the Rights of us below them, I say the great Hardship to these Noble Patriots is, that when they are prepared with the most strict Honour and Integrity to do their Duty in relation to their Prince and Country, all their Determinations may be avoided by a Sett of People brought in the Moment before they come to a Question. This has been done once, as I am credibly informed, in so frank a way, that there have been above six at a time brought into that Place, without any further Preamble than, This Gentleman's Name is so, do not call him Mr. from this time forward, but My Lord, for he is now one of you: Sit close there, *let the Gentlemen sit down*; I beg Pardon, *make way for his Lordship.*

Now when we come to consider the Introduction of *Occasional Lords with Regard to the People*, what can be more plain, than that it is doing all that is necessary to take from them both Liberty and Property at once. If there were nothing in being a Lord, but the Advantage of being received with more Distinction and Ceremony, let it be given to any who are delighted with it; they may be well pleased, and we not hurt: But the case is much otherwise; for from the very Moment a Man has a Patent, and is introduc'd into the House of Peers (tho' he was the Day before notoriously ignorant in our Laws) Men appeal to him from the Decree of all the Judges. Besides this, the Lords are perpetual Legislators, and have an hand in the repealing as well as making Laws; by which means the whole Constitution may be subverted by this one Innovation. And it is plain, that the Prince who should place so entire a Confidence in his Ministry, as to give Peerage upon their Recommendation, would enable them by that Power in the Legislature, joined to the Execution of the Regal Authority as Ministers, to give that Prince and Nation to the next Potentate who should be powerful enough to receive and maintain so vast a Present.

However well disposed Mens Minds may be, there are some things which are not to be committed to their Wills.

The whole Constitution is in Danger, if this Matter is not prevented by some future Law; and I think I have in my Head a sufficient Expedient, that can no way impair the Prerogative of the Crown, the Power of the Peers, or the Liberty of the People; and that is, that a Bill be brought in to disable any Peer to Vote in any Case, till three Years after the Date of his Patent.

You see, Noble Sir, that without giving the Matter the least Aggravation, I have shown that if this Avenue to the House of Lords is not shut, that House must be blown up by it as effectually as it might have been by the combustible Matter laid under it an Age ago by *Guido Faux.*

He that brings the Torch into the Room to fire it in the midst of the Company, differs from him who undermines it only in Point of Modesty.

It is amazing that such Care should be taken to prohibit an Occasional Conformist from being a Constable, and no Body takes it in his Head to prevent an Occasional Lord from being a Judge, nay, Legislator. I am very willing that a Good and Honourable Peace may expiate this Step, which was made in

the Eye of the World without the least Deference to a Good
and Gracious Sovereign, to an Illustrious Nobility, to a Learned
and Knowing Gentry, to a Great and Valiant People: I say,
let even this Step be forgiven for a Good Peace; but let not
that Peace receive its Sanction from the Repetition of it. If
Men cannot carry on the Business of the Nation without such
Helps, they may as well in plain Terms tell us they cannot main-
tain the Constitution, but they will alter it to one which they
can. But how is this received with so much Indifference? Why,
Men qualified for Power direct Mankind by consulting their
Interest and managing their Affections; but Pretenders to
Administration indulge the Passions of the Multitude at the
Expence of their real Interest and Advantage. It is by this latter
Method all the Anarchical Proceedings, which have of late dis-
tracted this unhappy Nation, have been tolerated. When the
Minds of Men are prejudiced, wonderful Effects may be wrought
against Common-Sense. One weak Step, in trying a Fool for
what he said in a Pulpit, with all the Pomp that could be used
to take down a more dangerous and powerful Man than ever
England yet has seen, cost the most Able Ministry that ever any
Prince was honoured with, its Being. The Judgment of the
House of Lords was by this means insulted and evaded, and
the Anarchical Fury ran so high, that *Harry Sacheverel* swell-
ing, and *Jack Huggins* laughing, marched through *England* in
a Triumph more than Military. Many extraordinary Things
which have happened since, have been brought about upon a
Maxim no deeper than *Pax bello potior, Peace is better than
War*. A great many Lyes grafted upon this unquestionable
Truth, could not but produce Wonders among all who pay
Taxes. But Arithmetick is so common an Art, that the very
common People, now their Passions are fallen, see their Case
in one Sheet of Paper call'd *A View of the Taxes, Funds, and
publick Revenues of England*. Printed for *Tim. Child* at the
White Hart at the West End of St. *Pauls.*

As for my self, what I have here suggested is from a very
honest Heart, and I have an Armour in my Integrity against all
Gainsayers. My Comfort is, that the Laws of *England* are still
in Force, and tho' what I have said may be Unacceptable, I
am sure it is not Illegal. While the Laws are in Being, I am

safe; and no Man can be safe who out-lives them; may I, whenever they expire, die with them.

I wish you the long Possession of the Honour in which your generous Behaviour has placed you in the Minds of all true *Englishmen*; and am, with great Respect,

Your most Obedient Servant

Fleetstreet   Francis Hicks.
March 5, 1713.

The Guardian of August the 7th, 1713 (No. 128)

This is the first of several pamphlets on Dunkirk contributed by Steele to the controversy on Anglo-French trade, which followed close upon the termination of the War of the Spanish Succession. The fortifications of Dunkirk, which lay across the Channel on the French coast, were a military threat to England; and the harbor, a covert for privateers, was even more menacing to British shipping.

The Treaty of Utrecht, signed the last of March, provided that within the space of five months France on her part should raze the fortifications and destroy the harbor and that England in return should reimburse France for her loss. In June, Queen Anne stated that arrangements were made to carry out these provisions. But early in July a deputy for the magistrates of Dunkirk had presented a memorial to the Queen asking that both fort and harbor be spared; and that not being heeded, on the 30th July he had addressed a printed memorial to the public begging for the preservation of the harbor.

Now the demolition of Dunkirk was considered imperative, especially by the Whigs, who still distrusted France, who looked with fear upon any port from which the Pretender might embark for England, and who were touchy upon all points related to British shipping. The French memorialist's direct appeal to the English people on the ground of mercy Steele considered dangerous and tricky propaganda. So in this *Guardian* paper, as a private subject, he exhorted the Ministry to carry out the original provisions of the treaty. And indeed the exhortation was timely, for already rumors were afloat that France was not only seeking to preserve the facilities at Dunkirk but was actually taking steps to construct a new port at the neighboring Mardyk.

As a reminder that only a few weeks earlier a Tory group with mercantile vested interests had assisted the Whig opposition in rejecting the trade clauses of the Peace Treaty with France, Steele signs himself " English Tory." For further discussion of the Dunkirk problems, see *The Importance of Dunkirk Consider'd* and *The French Faith . . . in Dunkirk*. The text of this *Guardian* pamphlet will be found on pp. 94-97. Textual notes on p. 640.

7

OEUVRES
DIVERSES
DE
Mr. RICHARD STEELE,
SUR
LES AFFAIRES
DE
LA GRANDE BRETAGNE.

Traduit de l'Anglois.

A AMSTERDAM,
Chez DAVID MORTIER, Libraire.

M. DCC. XV.

The Importance of Dunkirk Consider'd
(September, 1713)

The cry of Dunkirk was closely related to the trade policies of the Whigs, with which Steele had shown his alignment in the *Guardian of August the 7th*. The trade treaty with France, voted down by Whig opposition in June, was intended to revive Anglo-French trade by ending high protection on both sides; but it had been fought and defeated by the Whigs on the issues of industrial protection and balance of trade. In the airing of these questions, the pamphlet press was led by two periodicals: *The Mercator*, in which the arguments for free trade were marshalled for the Tory Ministry by Defoe, and *The British Merchant*, subsidized by Stanhope and Halifax and edited by Henry Martyn, presenting the Whig case for protectionism.

While Steele's pamphlets on Dunkirk were not technical in the sense of dealing with the figures and statistics of the Board of Trade, they were regarded as important support for mercantile and shipping interests; and indeed they touched at least upon practically every aspect of the dispute. Shortly after the appearance of this present tract, Defoe, not altogether in jest—for the name of *Tatler*, or *Spectator*, or *Guardian* was one to conjure with—wrote in *The Mercator* (26-29 Sept.): "To carry on this war more successfully than they have yet been able to do, they have chosen a new General. *The Guardian* is now entered into the dispute; and who shall be able to stand before the Guardian?"

In *The Importance of Dunkirk Consider'd*, Steele prints Tugghe's Memorial circulated in July and meets the arguments point by point. He quotes extracts from the pamphlets and periodicals which had attacked his *Guardian* paper, particularly *The Examiner, The Mercator, The Honour and Prerogative of the Queen's Majesty Vindicated,* and *Reasons concerning the Immediate Demolishing of Dunkirk*—somewhat on the defensive, it is true, when he protests against the accusation that he has overstepped the proper bounds in demanding the destruction of Dunkirk. Now, as he could not in August, he speaks from a new vantage, because he had recently been elected M. P. for Stockbridge, Hants., in a general election which stressed the trade issue.

In this second Dunkirk pamphlet Steele goes more fully into the reasons why England is unsafe from France while the fortifications stand and why British shipping is at a disadvantage while the harbor

83

remains intact. Possibly the technical support for his arguments was secured from the pool of Whig propaganda; but the presentation of his general arguments, the stand on the prerogative, the idealism in public service are characteristically his own. Steele's views on Dunkirk will be found also in *Guardian* Nos. 128, 168, 170; *Englishman*, Nos. 1, 18, 31, etc.; *The Crisis*; *The Apology*; and *The French Faith*. Textual notes on p. 640.

THE
IMPORTANCE
OF
DUNKIRK
CONSIDER'D:

In Defence of the

GUARDIAN

Of *August* the 7th.

IN

A LETTER to the Bailiff of *Stockbridge*.

By Mr. *STEELE*.

LONDON:

Printed for *A. Baldwin* in *Warwick-lane.* 1713.

To the Worshipful

MR. JOHN SNOW,

Bailiff of *STOCKBRIDGE.*

SIR,

According to my Promise when I took my Leave of you, I send you all the Pamphlets and Papers which have been Printed since the Dissolution of the last Parliament; among these you will find your Humble Servant no small Man, but spoken of more than once in Print: You will find I take up whole Pages in the *Examiner*, and that there is a little Pamphlet written wholly upon me, and directed to me. As you are the Magistrate of the Town wherein, of all Places in the World, it concerns me most to appear a different Man, from the Person whom these Writers represent me; I address my Vindication to you, and at the same time to the whole Borough. In the first Place I must recommend to your Perusal a printed Paper, which was publish'd in *French* on one side, and *English* on the other, and given *Gratis* in the open Streets: A Country Gentleman of my Acquaintance, who was going into *Wales* the next Day, receiv'd one of them from a Boy distributing them in *Cheapside*, and made me a Present of it. I will trouble you only with the *English*.

A most Humble Address or Memorial presented to Her Majesty the Queen of Great Britain, *by the Deputy of the Magistrates of* Dunkirk, *to Her Majesty.*

May it please your most Excellent Majesty,

THE Sieur *Tugghe*, Deputy of the Magistrates of *Dunkirk* to your Majesty, to implore your Clemency in relation to the intended Demolition of the Fortifications and Port of the said Town, had entertain'd Hopes that by the most humble Representations he had presum'd to make, touching the extreme Misery to which the said Demolition will reduce Eighteen Thousand

87

Families that make up that City, your Majesty's Mercy might have been moved, and that according to his most respectful Request, he might have obtain'd the Preservation at least of the Mole or Dikes of that Port. But he was as it were Thunderstruck by the Denunciation which My Lord Viscount *Bolingbroke* made to him, that your Majesty did not think fit to make any Alteration in the dreadful Sentence you have pronounc'd against that Town, and that 'tis your Majesty's Pleasure that Sentence should be executed in its full Extent. Tho' stunn'd by this Blow, the Sieur *Tugghe* yet presumes to approach once more your Majesty's awful Throne, being thereto encouraged by the Benefit your Majesty's Clemency pours down on all the Nations of the Earth; and with trembling to represent to your Majesty, that he does not demand that the Works that may serve either for the Attack or Defence of *Dunkirk* be preserved, either on the Landside, or towards the Sea. The unfortunate Inhabitants of *Dunkirk* are no longer concern'd for those magnificent Works, that strike Terror on all the Beholders. The Magistrates only beg the Preservation of the Mole and Dikes that form and keep up the Harbour, thereby to preserve to their People only their necessary Subsistence, by enabling them to carry on their Herring Fishing, and some other small Trade along the Coast.

" Your Majesty endued with Native Clemency and Christian Charity, of which all Nations feel the benign Influence, desires not to return Evil for Evil; nor does your Majesty admit it in your Resolutions any farther than it is indispensably necessary according to Political Views, and agreeable to the Welfare of your own Subjects. The Sieur *Tugghe* will presume to observe to your Majesty that the Preservation of the Harbour of *Dunkirk*, in the naked Condition it has been Represented, will neither be inconsistent either with the Political Views of *Great Britain*, or the Welfare and Good of the *British* Subjects, but rather Beneficial to both.

" *Dunkirk* has had the Misfortune to become the Object of *Great Britain*'s Indignation, either by the Sea Armaments the King made there, and which during the late Wars may have disturb'd the Tranquility of your Majesty's Kingdoms, and retarded the Execution of your Majesty's Projects, or by the

Privateering of its Inhabitants, which has often annoy'd and molested the Trade of your Majesty's Subjects. But in the Condition to which your Petitioner begs its Harbour to be reduc'd, that is, divested of all its Works and Fortifications, and its Mole and Dikes only preserv'd, it will never be able, whatever War (which God avert) may happen for the future, either to form any Obstacle to Your Majesty's Projects, or to disturb the Trade of your Majesty's Subjects, since in such a Condition it will be an open Town, both on the Land and Sea-side, abandon'd to the first Invader, defenceless for whomsoever shall possess it, and which any Enemy may enter by Sea and by Land, in order to burn both the Ships that might be sitting out there, and even the Town and Harbour. Thus in such a Condition *Dunkirk* neither will nor even can be opposite either to your Majesty's Political Views, or to the Welfare of Your Majesty's Subjects.

" The Preservation of the Harbour of *Dunkirk* without Works and Fortifications, may in fine be equally useful, and become even absolutely necessary, both for your Majesty's Political Views, and the Good of your Subjects.

" Your Majesty's Political Views, chiefly in Times of Peace, center all in the Increase of the Commerce of your Majesty's Subjects, and at the same time the Welfare and Interest of your Subjects lie in the Improvement of their Trade. Therefore by proving that the Preservation of the Harbour of *Dunkirk* will be not only advantageous, but also necessary for the Commerce of the Subjects of *Great Britain*, your Petitioner hopes he shall prove all that's contain'd in his Second Proposition.

" *First, Dunkirk* is become the Object of the Jealousy of the *Dutch*, and the *Dutch* have wish'd for its Destruction upon no other View, but to assume to themselves alone all the Commerce of the *Austrian* Low-Countries and of all *Germany*, being apprehensive that other Nations might share those Two Branches of Trades with them, in case the Harbour of that Town were preserv'd, because it is the only Harbour on the Coast from *Ostend* Westward, by which Commodities from foreign Countries may be brought into those Provinces, which they design to surround, as it were with a Wall of Brass, in order to secure to themselves all the Trade thereof by the *Scheld*, the *Lys*, and the *Rhine*. And as it highly concerns *Great Britain* not to be excluded from those Two Branches of Trade, so it very much concerns *Great Britain* to preserve the Harbour of *Dunkirk*, by which means alone *Great Britain* can maintain its Commerce in the said Provinces.

"*Secondly,* Supposing that your Majesty's Subjects might, in spite of the Designs of the *Dutch*, carry on their Trade in the *Austrian* Netherlands, by the Harbours of *Ostend* and *Newport,* yet they will not be able to hold it long in Competition with the *Hollanders*, both by reason of the Conveniency and less Expence which the latter will find in carrying on their Commerce by the *Scheld* and the *Lys*, and the round about way the other will be oblig'd to go. Whereas by preserving the Harbour of *Dunkirk*, the *English* would have that way Conveniencies almost equal to those the *Dutch* have; especially if your Majesty would, as you easily may, obtain from the King a free Passage Custom-free for all Commodities from *England,* from *Dunkirk* to the *Austrian* Low-Countries, by the Way of *Lisle* and *Douay.*

"*Thirdly,* If according to your Majesty's Resolution the Harbour of *Dunkirk* be fill'd up, your Majesty's Subjects will thereby be excluded not only from the Trade of the *Austrian* Netherlands, but also from that of *French Flanders, Hainault, Artois,* and Part of *Picardy*, because they will have no other Harbour on all that Coast, to import their Commodities into those Four Provinces, that of *Calais* being unserviceable to that Commerce.

"*Fourthly,* If the Demolition of the Harbour of *Dunkirk* should not discourage your Majesty's Subjects from the Trade of *French Flanders, Hainault, Artois,* and part of *Picardy*, and they should endeavour to supply it by the Harbours of *Ostend* and *Newport*; they will however undergo infinite Inconveniencies to carry on that Trade, and thereby render their Commodities unmarketable, by reason of the Expence of Carriage that will be treble, and by the treble Customs and Duties they must pay, *viz* to the House of *Austria* upon their Entrance into those Harbours, to the *Dutch* in their Passage to *Furnes, Ipres, Menin*, and other Towns in their Possession, and to the King at their Entrance into his Dominions: Whereas by entring those four Provinces by the way of *Dunkirk* the Expence for Carriage will be small, by reason of the Conveniency of Canals, and they shall only pay the single Duty of Importation to the King.

" *Fifthly*, By the Treaty of Commerce concluded between your Majesty, and his most Christian Majesty, the tariff of 1671 has been preserved in the conquered Countries. This Tariff is far more favourable than that of 1664, which is to be observed in all the other Harbours on the Western Coast of *France*, and consequently the Commerce of your Majesty's Subjects is very much concerned in the Preservation of the Harbour of *Dunkirk*, since that Harbour, will make enjoy the Benefit of that Tariff for all the Commodities they shall import there for the Consumption of the Provinces of *Flanders*, *Artois*, and *Hainault*; whereas if the same Merchandizes be imported by other Harbours, they must pay the Duties according to the Tariff of 1664.

" *Sixthly*, To confirm to your Majesty how advantageous the Harbour of *Dunkirk* is to the Trade of your Majesty's Subjects, the Sieur *Tugghe* has the Honour to present to your Majesty a List of Two Hundred and Eighteen *English* Ships, which from the $\frac{16}{27}$ th of *August*, 1712. to the $\frac{12}{28}$ th of *May*, 1713. have come into that Harbour, and unloaded their Cargoes there to the Value of above Two Millions of *French* Livres; praying at the same time your Majesty to observe first, That *France* being, during those Nine Months, in War with *Holland*, those Commodities could not be carried into the *Austrian* Provinces possess'd by the *Dutch*, and must have been vented and consumed only in the *French* Provinces of *Flanders*, *Hainault,* and *Artois*, and that in Time of Peace the said Consumption, and consequently the Trade of *England* there, will very much encrease. Secondly, That as the *Dunkirkers* could not furnish in Return or Exchange for the Commodities imported there, during those Nine Months either any Manufactures or Commodities of their own Growth, because they have none, they were obliged to pay the whole Value of the same in Money, and must ever pay for them in same manner, which is a most considerable Advantage in all sorts of Traffick.

" *Seventhly*, As it is not impossible that in process of time, there may happen some Rupture between *Great Britain* and

Holland, so *Great Britain* in such a Conjuncture, which God avert, will find it self entirely deprived of the Trade to French *Flanders, Hainault, Artois,* and, Part of *Picardy,* since at such a time it will not be in the Power of your Majesty's Subjects to carry on the said Trade by the Harbours of *Ostend* or *Newport,* not even under all the Inconveniencies and Expences to which those Two Harbours do naturally subject them, because their Commodities could not from those Two Harbours be carried into the *French* Provinces, but by going through Places possess'd by the *Dutch,* who in all likelihood would not give them free Passage. Thus in such a Conjuncture, at least the Preservation of the Harbour of *Dunkirk* would be necessary for the Trade of your Majesty's Subjects.

"*Eighthly,* The Freedom of the Port and Town of *Dunkirk,* in case your Majesty will vouchsafe to alter the severe Resolution you have taken against its Mole and Dykes, will enable your Majesty's Subjects to carry on their Commerce with more Conveniency than any other Nation in the *Austrian* Provinces of *Flanders, Hainault,* and *Brabant;* in the *French* Provinces of *Flanders, Hainault, Artois* and *Picardy;* and even in *Germany* by the Staples and Store-houses they may erect there, and which will facilitate their answering the Demands of Commodities from all those respective Countries punctually, and at proper Times and Seasons.

"*Ninthly,* Supposing that the Opposition which the Eighth and Ninth Articles of the Treaty of Commerce concluded by your Majesty with *France,* has met with in the House of Commons of Your Parliament should take place, and destroy the Arguments above alleg'd in favour of the *British* Trade by the Way of *Dunkirk,* into the *French* Provinces; yet the Reasons relating to the said Commerce by the Way of *Dunkirk,* into the *Austrian Low-Countries* and into *Germany,* by means of a free Passage, without paying any Custom or Duties, would still subsist, and may suffice to let your Majesty see, that the Preservation of that Harbour, with its bare Mole and Dikes, despoil'd of all manner of Fortifications, will not only be most beneficial and advantageous, but even absolutely necessary to the Trade of *Great Britain.*

" *Tenthly,* All such as have any tolerable Skill in Navigation know that Ships that are at Sea, can never have under the Wind too many Places of Retreat, either to shelter themselves against Storms when they happen to fall into them, or to repair their Losses and refit after they have sustained ill Weather. The Harbour of *Dunkirk* is one of those desirable Retreats for Ships that sail to, or come from the North Seas. And altho' the Coast of *England* affords many Places for Ships to put into, it may nevertheless happen oftentimes after the Demolition of the Mole and Dikes, for which the Magistrates of *Dunkirk* beg your Majesty's Mercy, that the Ships of your Subjects may be so driven and Wind-bound by bad Weather on the Coast of *Dunkirk,* that being unable to reach their own Shoar, they will in vain regret, as well as all other Nations trading to the North, that Harbour of Safety, of which they shall be deprived; and avoid a bare Commiseration of the Danger to which Seafaring Men are expos'd, ought to have preserv'd for them, according to the common Dictates of Humanity.

" Upon all these Considerations, that is, considering the small Damage which the Harbour of *Dunkirk,* despoil'd of all its Fortifications, both on the Sea and the Land-side, may cause either to your Majesty's Subjects, or to those of Your Allies; the Usefulness and Benefit which the Trade of *Great Britain* will find in the Preservation of the said Harbour in the manner above explained, And the unprofitable but ruinous Loss which the unfortunate Inhabitants of that Town will suffer by its Demolition, the Magistrates of *Dunkirk* and the Sieur *Tugghe* their Deputy presume to hope that your Majesty will graciously be pleased to recal part of Your Sentence, by causing your Thunderbolts to fall only on the Martial Works which may have incurr'd your Majesty's Displeasure, and by sparing only the Mole and Dikes, which in their naked Condition can, for the future, be no more than an Object of Pity. Nay, they shall even be an Eternal Monument of your Majesty's Glory, since by incessantly Reminding the Beholders of the dreadful Ornaments of which they shall remain despoil'd by your Majesty's Will alone, they will, at the same time, eternally preserve the Memory of your Majesty's Clemency, which shall have bestow'd them on the Tears and Groans of the Inhabitants of that Town, overwhelmed with Grief.

" 'Tis by those Tears and by those Groans, that the Magistrates and their Deputy, humbly prostrate at the Feet of your Majesty's Throne, no less Gracious than Dreadful, beg the Preservation of their Harbour, and beseech your Majesty to vouchsafe to look with Eyes of Pity on Eighteen Thousand Families, who must be reduced to wander about, if by the entire and severe Execution of your Majesty's Orders, they are forced to quit their Habitations to go and seek or rather beg their Bread.

" Let not your Majesty's ever beneficent Hand be the Instrument of their Misery and Dispersion! And let not the Inhabitants of *Dunkirk* be the only People in the World that may complain of the Rigor of a Queen whose Wisdom and Clemency is adored by all the Earth."

My Indignation at this Usage of my Queen and Country, prompted me to write a Letter to *Nestor Ironside*, Esq; which I subscribed *English Tory*.[1]

Mr. *Ironside* thereupon Prints my Letter Word for Word, and on *August* the 7th publishes it with a short Preface, as follows:

IT is usually thought, with great Justice, a very impertinent thing in a private Man to intermeddle in Matters which regard the State. But the Memorial which is mentioned in the following Letter is so daring, and so apparently designed for the most Traiterous Purpose imaginable, that I do not care what Misinterpretation I suffer, when I expose it to the Resentment of all Men who value their Country, or have any Regard to the Honour, Safety, or Glory of their Queen. It is certain there is not much Danger in delaying the Demolition of *Dunkirk* during the Life of his present most Christian Majesty, who is renowned for the most inviolable Regard to Treaties; but that pious Prince is aged, and in case of his Decease, now the Power of *France* and *Spain* is in the same Family, it is possible an Ambitious Successor (or his Ministry in a King's Minority) might dispute his being bound by the Act of his Predecessor in so weighty a Particular.

Mr. IRONSIDE,

"YOU employ your important Moments, methinks, a little too frivolously, when you consider so often little Circumstances of Dress and Behaviour, and never make mention of Matters wherein you and all your Fellow-Subjects in general are concerned. I give you now an Opportunity, not only of manifesting your Loyalty to your Queen, but your Affection to your Country, if you treat an Insolence done to them² both with the Disdain it deserves. The enclosed Printed Paper in *French* and *English* has been handed about the Town, and given *gratis* to Passengers in the Streets at Noon-Day. You see the Title of it is, *A most humble Address or Memorial, presented to her Majesty the Queen of* Great-Britain, *by the Deputy of the Magistrates of* Dunkirk. The nauseous Memorialist, with the most fulsome Flattery, tells the Queen of her Thunder, and of Wisdom and Clemency adored by all the Earth, at the same time that he attempts to undermine her Power, and escape her Wisdom, by beseeching her to do an Act which would give a well-grounded Jealousie to her People. What the Sycophant desires is, that the Mole and Dikes of *Dunkirk* may be spared; and, it seems, the Sieur *Tugghe,* for so the Petitioner is called, was Thunder-struck by the *Denunciation* (which he says) *the Lord Viscount* Bolinbroke *made to him,* That her Majesty did not think to make any Alteration in the dreadful Sentence she had pronounced against the Town. Mr. IRONSIDE I think you would do an Act worthy your general Humanity, if you would put the Sieur *Tugghe* right in this Matter, and let him know That her Majesty has pronounced no Sentence against the Town, but his most Christian Majesty has agreed that the Town and Harbour shall be Demolished.

"That the *British* Nation expect the immediate Demolition of it.

"That the very Common People know, that within two³ Months after the signing of the Peace, the Works towards the Sea were to be demolished, and within three Months after it the Works towards the Land.

"That the said Peace was signed the last of *March,* O. S.

8

"That the Parliament has been told from the Queen, that the Equivalent for it is in the Hands of the *French* King.

"That the Sieur *Tugghe* has the Impudence to ask the Queen to remit the most material Part of the Articles of Peace between Her Majesty and his Master.

"That the *British* Nation received more Damage in their Trade from the Port of *Dunkirk*, than from almost all the Ports of *France*, either in the Ocean or in the Mediterranean.

"That Fleets of above thirty Sail have come together out of *Dunkirk*, during the late War, and taken Ships of War as well as Merchant Men.

"That the Pretender sailed from thence to *Scotland*; and that it is the only Port the *French* have till you come to *Brest*, for the whole Length of St. *George*'s Channel, where any considerable Naval Armament can be made.

"That destroying the Fortifications of *Dunkirk* is an inconsiderable Advantage to *England*, in Comparison to the Advantage of destroying the Mole, Dykes and Harbour, it being the Naval Force from thence which only can hurt the *British Nation*.

"That the *British* Nation expect the immediate Demolition of *Dunkirk*

"That the *Dutch*, who suffered equally with us from those of *Dunkirk*, were, probably induced to Sign the Treaty with *France* from this Consideration, That the Town and Harbour of *Dunkirk* should be destroyed.

"That the Situation of *Dunkirk* is such, as that it may always keep Runners to observe all Ships sailing on the *Thames* and *Medway*.

"That all the Suggestions, which the Sieur *Tugghe* brings concerning the *Dutch*, are false and scandalous.

"That whether it may be advantageous to the Trade of *Holland* or not, that *Dunkirk* should be demolish'd, it is necessary for the Safety, Honour, and Liberty of *England* that it should be so.

"That when *Dunkirk* is demolished, the Power of *France*, on that side, should it ever be turned against us, will be removed several hundred Miles further off of *Great Britain* than it is at present.

"That after the Demolition there can be no considerable

Preparation made at Sea by the *French* in all the Channel but at *Brest*; and that *Great Britain* being an Island, which cannot be attacked but by a Naval Power, we may esteem *France* effectually removed by the Demolition from *Great Britain* as far as the Distance from *Dunkirk* to *Brest*.

"Pray, Mr. IRONSDE, repeat this last Particular, and put it in a different Letter, *That the Demolition of* Dunkirk *will remove* France *many hundred Miles further off from us*; and then repeat again, *That the* British *Nation expects the Demolition of* Dunkirk.

"I demand of you, as you Love and Honour your Queen and Country, that you insert this Letter, or speak, to this Purpose, your own way; for in this all Parties must agree, that however bound in Friendship one Nation is with another, it is but prudent, that, in case of a Rupture, they should be, if possible, upon equal Terms.

"Be Honest, old NESTOR, and say all this; for whatever half-witted hot Whigs may think, we all value our Estates and Liberties, and every true Man of each Party must think himself concerned that *Dunkirk* should be Demolished.

"It lies upon all who have the Honour to be in the Ministry to hasten this Matter, and not let the Credulity of an honest brave People be thus infamously abused in our open Streets.

"I cannot go on for Indignation; but pray God that our Mercy to *France* may not expose us to the Mercy of *France*.

Your Humble Servant,

English Tory.

This Letter happened to disoblige some People, and the Day before I went out of Town came out the Pamphlet, Entituled, *The Honour and Prerogative of the Queen's Majesty Vindicated and Defended against the unexampled Insolence of the Author of the* Guardian: *In a Letter from a Country Whig to Mr.* Steele. You may read the whole at your Lesiure; but the Ninth and Tenth Pages are enough for Me, and I think there is nothing else in the whole Pamphlet but Repetition of the same thing.

See how the Villain threats the best of Sovereigns, the best Mistress to him, whose Bread he has eaten, and who has kept him from a Gaol! Read it again, say they: Put it into English, *said a Neighbour of mine to me, come make the best of it! then he reads the abominable Language as follows;*

"*The* British *Nation* EXPECT, &c. *And again, The* British *Nation* EXPECT *the immediate Demolition of* Dunkirk. *And a third time, with a Tone of threatening, The* British *Nation* EXPECT *it.* See the *Guardian, August* 7, 1713.

I would fain have pleaded for you, that this was not to be understood to be spoken to or pointed at the Queen, but to the People of Dunkirk, *and I search'd the whole Paper for something to have brought you off with that way.*

But it would not do, they laugh'd at me: How could it be spoken to him, say they? his Memorial is to the Queen, and if it should be directed to Monsieur Tugghe *it would be still worse; for that would be to talk thus to him, viz. What do ye Petition the Queen for? We tell you,* The British Nation *will not suffer it, the Queen dares not do it, for the* British Nation EXPECT it be immediately Demolish'd. *This stop'd my Mouth indeed, with respect to that part of the Excuse, and then they went on with me: Come, says my Neighbour, if you cannot put it into Words, I'll do it for you.*

"*The* British *Nation* EXPECT *the immediate Demolition of* Dunkirk."

We all know Her Majesty has Possession of Dunkirk, *and tho' the Work is to be done by the* French, *Her Majesty may appoint the Day. Now, says he, read the words.*

What is it but thus?

"*Look you,* Madam, *Your Majesty had best take Care that* Dunkirk *be Demolish'd, or else,* &c."

And again;

"*Madam!* WE EXPECT, *and we would have you take Notice that we expect it, that* Dunkirk *be Demolish'd, and that immediately.*

"*Just thus an Imperious Planter at* Barbadoes *speaks to a* Negro Slave, ' Look you, Sirrah, I expect this Sugar to be ground, and look to it that it be done forthwith. 'Tis enough *to tell you I EXPECT it, or else,' &c. and then he holds up his Stick at him, Take what follows."*

The *Examiner*, in a Style quite as polite as that of this Pamphleteer, in his Paper of *August* the 21st has it thus,

" I believe I may challenge all the Nations of the World, and all the Histories of this Nation for a thousand Years past, to shew us an Instance so flagrant as what we have now before us, (*viz.*) When ever *a Subject, nay a Servant* under *a Salary,* and favoured *in Spight of ill Behaviour past,* with a considerable Employment in the Government, treated his Sovereign in such a manner as the GUARDIAN has done the Person of the Queen; *and went Unpunished.*

" If the Clemency of the Queen prevails to save such a Man; if Her Majesty thinks it below Her to resent an Injury from so contemptible a *Wretch,* by so much the rather should every Subject resent it; and shew their Duty and Respect to their Sovereign, by trampling under their Feet the very *Name* and *Memory* of the Man that can have Boldness enough *to Insult his Prince* in a Printed, *and for that reason Scandalous,* Libel, and can have INGRATITUDE enough to do it while he is eating Her Bread.

" How can any Man shew himself a faithful Subject to Her Majesty, and not resent such a piece of Conduct! to see a Subject hold up a Rod at his Prince! and openly threaten the Queen, if She does not cause *Dunkirk* to be demolished! to *threaten* Her Majesty with the Nation's Resentment if it be not forthwith entered upon, and *Command Her* to do it IMMEDIATELY; it ought to fill every faithful Subject with Abhorrence, and cause them either to shun the Man, or let him know they Detest his Behaviour.

" And yet *this Man* was never so dear to the *Whigs* as since he let them know that he durst assault his Queen; this has made him their Favourite, and one of their Authors has made his dull Panegyrick upon him already for it; while another Sett of them are endeavouring to get him chosen for the next Parliament, that he may carry on his Insult there; and obtain the *Honour,* as another of their haughty Leaders has already done, *of being expelled the House.*

"I have not Room to enlarge in this Case, as so unexampled a Piece of *Ingratitude* deserves; he has been handsomely, *only too favourably*, exposed in this very Case, by a Book just published, and which I recommend for that reason in the following Advertisement."

After this he subjoins the following Advertisement.

The Honour and Prerogative of the Queen's Majesty Vindicated and Defended against the Unexampled Insolence of the Author of the GUARDIAN: *In a Letter from a Country Whig to Mr.* Steele. *Printed for* John Morphew *near Stationers-Hall. Price* 3 d.

On the 24th following he Rallies me again thus,

"For these Reasons, saving the Trespass on Custom, the LYE might be given in the Teeth of *the Guardian*, when he Insolently tells the Queen, in his late Seditious Libel, *for such it must be accounted by every True* Britain; That the *British Nation* EXPECTS the *Immediate demolition of* Dunkirk: I say *it is not so*; the *British* Nation does not EXPECT that Her Majesty should divest Her Self of the Power which is in Her Hands, by the Possession of *Dunkirk*, to do Her Self Right, and to secure to Her Self the Performance of such Conditions from all the Princes concerned, as they have agreed to be just and ought to be performed; but which we do not find them so free to execute, as the Obligations *Britain* has laid on them has given us reason to expect.

"It might, with much more Duty to Her Majesty, and Justice to our Country, have been said, That the *British Nation* HOPES Her Majesty will not part with *Dunkirk*, nor suffer it to be demolished, till the Danger of any Foreign Power, insulting Her Subjects, *be removed*; till the Commerce, and Privileges of Her Subjects of *Great Britain*, shall be effectually secured; and till there shall be no danger of the Incroachments and Invasions of any Nation, *not* France *only*, but other Powers as well as *France*; for I must be allow'd, with *these Gentlemens Pardon*, to suppose that there are Dangers to be expected from other Powers in the World, as well as *France*, especially Dangers to our Trade; and these Dangers are the greater, by how much we find the *Whigs* forward to give up our Trading-Interest to the *Dutch*, in order to make Friends with them in their other nameless Designs against the Ministry.

" Those then who have a true Concern for the Good of *Great Britain*, would be very sorry to see *Dunkirk* put out of Her Majesty's Power, till every just Thing, which the keeping it can be a Means to secure to us, be obtain'd.

" I might be more particular, in letting the World see what these Things are which *Britain* ought to obtain from the neighbouring Powers; and which *Dunkirk* is so far a Pledge for, that it ought to remain in Her Majesty's Hands till they are obtained: But as this is preparing by another Hand, and will be set in a clearer Light, to the Confusion of the *Guardian* and all his Factious Party, I shall say no more to it here."

After this He repeats the following Advertisement.

To Morrow will be publish'd a Second Edition of *The Honour and Prerogative of the Queen's Majesty Vindicated and Defended against the Unexampled Insolence of the Author of the* GUARDIAN: *In a Letter from a Country Whig to Mr.* Steele. *Printed for* John Morphew, *near* Stationers-Hall. Price 3*d*.

You have now my Letter to the *Guardian*, with what the Writers of the Pamphlet, and the *Examiner*, have been pleased to say upon it, at one View.

In Order to my Justification, I shall show more accurately the Advantages the Nation might reap from the Demolition, which will appear by Considering what Part of our Trade has and may be annoy'd by *Dunkirk*.

The Port of *London* is allowed to carry Two Parts in Three, or Six Parts in Nine, of the Foreign Trade of *England*. We may give one Ninth to the Ports on the *South* Coasts of this Island, which *South* Coast is opposite to the *North* Coast of *France*; the Sea between which is what we call the Channel.

The *East* End of this, on our Side, is the *North* Foreland, which stands opposite to *Newport* in *France*; the *West* End, on our Side, is the Land's-End, over-against *Ushant*, or *Brest* in *France*; they allow one Ninth of the Trade to the *East* Coast washed by the *German* Ocean; and the other Ninth to the *West* Coast, which looks on the *Irish* Seas; in this Computation, it is presumed, there is not any great Disproportion, except from *Bristol*'s lying on the *West* Coast, the said *West* Coast ought to be allowed more than one Ninth.

Dunkirk is from the *South* Foreland about Thirteen Leagues, and the Course from *Dunkirk* to the Foreland *West, North-West,* to the Entrance of the River *Thames,* is *North-West* about Twenty Leagues; so that any Easterly Wind, which carries our Ships down the Channel, at the same time brings those of *Dunkirk* to meet and intercept them: The *French* have very frequently this last War reaped the Advantage of this Situation, by surprising many rich Ships, and taking others as they lay at Anchor in the *Downs*; when the *French* are dispossessed of *Dunkirk,* the dread and danger of their Men of War, of any considerable Force, will be removed as far as *Brest,* which is a hundred and twenty Leagues, or three hundred and sixty Miles; and that of their Privateers, of any Consideration, as far as St. *Malo*'s, which is seventy eight Leagues, or two hundred and thirty four Miles.

Brest lies without the Channel, under this great Incapacity to hurt us, that the same Wind which carries our Trade down the Channel prevents the Ships of *Brest* from coming into it.

The East End of the Channel which is so much exposed to *Dunkirk* is but seven Leagues broad, and gives an Enemy an Opportunity of seeing our Ships from Side to Side.

The West End of the Channel, for which the greatest Fears are from *Brest,* is twenty-eight Leagues broad, and of course, there is at that End a greater Chance of escaping the Enemy.

If Ships from *Brest* are appointed to Way-lay our Ships in the Channel, they must take the Opportunity of Westerly Winds, to come into it; and wait the coming of an Easterly Wind to carry our Ships down it; by this means they must all that time be at Sea, exposed to all Dangers for want of a Port in which to Harbour their Men of War, or return to *Brest,* which they cannot do with the Wind that brought them out.

We must add to this, that if the *French* from *Brest* should be hovering to the Eastward of *Plimouth,* they are between two Fires, from those Ships in the *Downs,* and those from *Plimouth*; and our Ships from *Portsmouth* may chase them either Way, while they are way-laid at each End of the Channel by the others, not having the Port of *Dunkirk*, or any other in the Channel, to afford them Shelter. Thus, should they be chased up the Channel by a too great Force, before they can return to *Brest*, they must either run into the *German* Ocean, and wait another Opportunity of coming down again, with the Hazard of meeting all our Men of War; or else sail *North* about *Great Britain*, which is at least 550 Leagues more than they need have sailed, with the Port of *Dunkirk* to fly to.

This Want of *Dunkirk* will expose them to the same Inconveniencies, to which the Fear of it often obliged our running Ships from the *South* Parts of the World, as well as our *East-India* Men, during the late War: To this Distress you are to add Wages, Provision, loss of Time, and the dangerous Navigation of the *North* Seas.

From hence it plainly appears, that by the Demolition of *Dunkirk*, in case of a Rupture with *France*, Six Parts in Nine of our Trade, from the Port of *London*, is 330 Miles removed from the Hazards of the last War; and tho' part of this must be exposed when it passes through the *Chopps*, or Western Entrance of the Channel, it must be considered, that this it was also liable to before, besides the Terrors of *Dunkirk*, and that this is only the Southern Trade; and all that go to *Holland*, *Hamborough*, and other Northern Countries, will be quite out of Danger.

The Ninth of our Trade on the *East* Coast, would be still safer.

From these distinct Considerations, you observe only one Ninth of the Trade on the *Irish* Seas and *Bristol* Channel, and part of the other Ninth in the Coast of the Channel (to come at which they are in danger from *Portsmouth* to *Plimouth*) is the whole of the *British* Trade, which after the Demolition of *Dunkirk* will lie open to the Assaults of the *French*. The Demolition of *Dunkirk* will in a great Measure secure seven Ninths of the Trade of *England*, from the Power of *France* at Sea, the *French* having no Port in the Channel but St. *Malo's*, which can harbour any great Ships, and that it self can receive none which exceeds 30 or 40 Guns. *Brest* lies 35 Leagues from the Lizard Point, which is the nearest Land of *England*; their Ships must have an Easterly Wind to come out, and that will serve them no farther than to the Chopps of the Channel, because it blows directly down it.

The Course to go from *Brest* to cruise off the Lizard Point in order to annoy Us, is first, *West* about 13 Leagues, and then *North* or *North* and by *East* about 30 Leagues more, except they run the Hazard of going within the Island of *Ushant* which is not practised, and therefore may be supposed Impracticable.

In the last Place, our Charge in defending our selves from such Annoyance as we formerly had from *Dunkirk*, will decrease in Proportion to the removal of the Danger.

Such is the Importance of the Demolition of *Dunkirk*, with regard to the Trade of *England* only; and in the present Conjuncture, I think we ought to have something more than the Mercy of his Most Christian Majesty, to render the forbearing such Demolition less Hazardous to our Religion and Liberty; and yet you see, how criminal a Thing it is to say, The *British* Nation EXPECT the Demolition of it.

It is evident that the Letter to the *Guardian*, subscribed *English* Tory, could have no Prospect but to do Honour and Service to Her Majesty and Her Subjects; the Sieur *Tugghe* himself acknowledges that he has received an Answer from the Queen, by Her Secretary of State, with a Negative to his Petition; upon which here appears a Memorial in Print, expostulating with Her upon that Subject, and laying before Her the Distresses of a Crowd of helpless People, whose Misfortunes are to be attributed to Her, if she shall think fit, in behalf of Her own Subjects, to insist upon the Execution of what is stipulated by Treaty: The Sieur *Tugghe* may insinuate, that it is unmerciful in the Queen to deny his Request, without being taken Notice of; but I must not defend my Sovereign's Refusal from the Imputation of Cruelty, without being said, to Insult Her Prerogative. My Adversaries argue, That it is in Her Majesty's Power to forward or delay the Demolition as she pleases; be that as it will, Do not I do as a faithful Subject, to insist that she does no Cruelty if she pleases to Demolish it?

The Sieur *Tugghe* is not contented with this Arrogance, but has so little an Opinion of our *English* Statesmen, that he pretends to instruct our Sovereign, and Her Council, in what Political Views they ought to have upon this Occasion: But least his Assertions may prevail upon that numerous part of Mankind, which has a great while taken every Thing upon Content, I shall have the Patience to run through all he gives us as Arguments for our saving *Dunkirk*, and with the same Tautology; and when He repeats the same Thing, repeat also what I have said against it. To proceed then like a Man of great Gravity and Business.

In Answer *to the* SIEUR'S First.

First, DUnkirk was the Dread of the *Dutch* Trade in time of War, but cannot be the Object of Jealousy of the *Dutch* with respect to their Trade to *Germany* and the *Austrian* Low-Countries, because *Newport* and *Graveling* (which are capable of receiving as large Ships as ever are used in that Trade by us) can supply those Countries with the same Ease; of course *Dunkirk* is not the only Harbour on this Coast useful to that Trade: As for securing the *Scheld*, that River was many Years before the two last Wars with *France* possessed by the *Dutch,* who Command the Entrance of it by Fort *Lillo*, which prevents all Foreign Ships from passing up. Nay, so far are they from permitting Foreigners, that none of their own Sea-ships, above the Bulk of Schuyts or Billanders, which we call Smacks and Hoys, are ever allowed to go beyond that Fort. Mr. *Tugghe* supposes Us to a most notorious degree Ignorant of common Geography, when he asserts that *Dunkirk* is the only Port from *Ostend* Westward, by which Commodities can be brought into the Provinces of the *Austrian* Low-Countries and *Germany*. There runs from *Calais* a Navigable River to *Graveling*, the River of *Graveling* runs to St. *Omer*; from the *East* Side of this River run two Canals, one through *Bourbough* to *Dunkirk*, the other directly to *Winoxberg*: There is a Canal from *Dunkirk* to *Furnes*, and another from *Winoxberg* to the same Place; from *Furnes* the Canal runs to *Newport*, and from thence to *Ostend* and *Bruges*; from their Canals and Rivers the Countries of French *Flanders, Hainault,* and *Picardy,* have their Water Carriage; nor is there any Carriage from *Dunkirk* to the *Rhine, Lys,* or *Scheld,* but through the same Streams, except by open Sea; so that *Ostend, Newport, Graveling,* and *Calais,* have the same Water-Carriage which *Dunkirk* has to any Inland Country, or any Place in the World. What Trade had we through *Dunkirk*, before, or during the two last Wars? We can have no Trade through *Dunkirk* (but to the *French* Territories) which we had not in the last Wars from other Harbours.

As to the Sieur's *Second*, We always carried on our Trade to the *Austrian Netherlands* through *Ostend* and *Newport*, since the *Dutch* got possession of the *Scheld*, the same Conveniency we shall have still; nor can the Port of *Dunkirk*, being left open, be any ease of Charges on our Trade, or give us a nearer Passage; neither can the Demolition in the least obstruct our Trade, because our Commodities will still pass through the same Inland Waters, which they must if they are sent through *Dunkirk*. If it is easie for Her Majesty to obtain from the King *a Free Passage Custom-Free* for all Commodities from *England,* through *Dunkirk*, to the *Austrian* Low-Counties, she may with the same ease Obtain the same through his other Ports. It will be good News to hear he makes no difficulty of granting such a Request, because by the same Rule, Her Majesty may obtain an Alteration in favour of Her Subjects in the Treaty of Commerce, which has been disapprov'd by the Parliament.

If we should at any time be prevented sending our Trade to the *Austrian* Low-Countries, any other way than through his Dominions, he will then find us under the Necessity of carrying it on this Way, and demand Toll in a manner suitable to his great Power and Force; and how shall we deny it him?

If he should grant us this Passage Custom-free, it may be bought too dear; for if we dismantle the Town, and leave the Ports undemolish'd, it is in his Power to take Possession of it again at Pleasure; and in case of another War we shall be as much annoy'd in our Trade as we were in the two last, and the Town can be easily Re-fortified; he may have a very good View in this: But really I would not have him run the Risque of it, tho' it may prove so much for his Advantage; for we all know the *Dutch* are a sly People, and if the Town should be dismantled, and the Port left open, they may come and get the Possession of it, and fortifie it again for their own Use, which I know, out of the great Concern he has for us, and the Welfare of our Trade, he would be utterly against.

As to his *Third*, It is a false Assertion to say that there is no

other Port serviceable to the Trade of French *Flanders, Hainault,*
Artois, or *Picardy,* for there are many useful to this Trade,
Ostend, Newport, Graveling, and *Calais,* whose Waters run
into the same Canals that that of *Dunkirk* does, besides
Boulogne, Estaples, St. *Valery* and *Diep*; for the Trade to
Picardy, all these Ports are capable of receiving as large Vessels
as ever we made use of in this Trade, which are from 20, 60,
or 100 Tuns at most.

As to the Sieur's *Fourth,* It is well known the Trade may be
profitably carried on by other Places than *Dunkirk*; and an
Ease of Charge for so inconsiderable a part of our Trade is not
to be mentioned, in Competition with the hazard of so great a
part as, on a Rupture with *France,* that Place can molest; the
rest of this Article is already answer'd, because other Ports can
convey our Trade to any Place that *Dunkirk* can.

As to Mr. Deputy's *Fifth,* If the Treaty of Commerce has
preserved the Tariff of 1671 in the Conquer'd Countries, it is
preserv'd to *Graveling,* and other Ports there, as well as *Dunkirk.*

As to the Sieur's *Sixth,* The Stress he lays on the List of 218
Ships which was printed in the *Mercator,* No. 29, with their
Cargoes, has no Weight in it, because those Ships might have
gone to the Neighbouring Ports; he is also unjust in arguing
from that List, that the Trade of *England* there will very much
Increase: Whoever looks over the *Mercator,* will find that their
Loading consisted chiefly of Food and Firing, the whole he
values at two Millions of *French* Livres; the Coals indeed they
may always take, as they will other Commodities that Necessity
obliges them to, and which they have not of their own Growth
or Manufacture, but a constant Market of this kind is not to
be expected; it is not to be supposed, because they took these
Quantities of Corn and Provisions of us in their late famish'd
Condition, that they will do the same when they have plentiful
Crops; and this whole Sum is but 100,000£ *Sterling,* of which
the Provisions amount to at least 3 Quarters. Their Trade to
us standing in a manner upon the Foot of a Prohibition, they
could not well pay us any otherwise than with ready Money;
but if the Treaty of Commerce should pass, and the Port of
Dunkirk remain as it is, the *Dunkirkers* will soon find Commodities to supply us with, tho' they have none of their own

Growth. Mr. *Tugghe* does not do us Justice in this part of the Memorial, because he omitted to tell us, of the Combination of Merchants, who made our People take their own Prices for our Goods, which were sold to Loss, rather than to bring them back again through the Risque of the Seas, and to run the Danger of their being Damaged, and of their Perishing. There might be other Observations made from their want of Corn, of the Advantage we might have taken of their Low Condition.

As to this Agent's *Seventh*, Mr. *Tugghe* with great Piety and Charity towards us, prays to God to avert a War between us and *Holland*, and represents a great many Dangers in it in regard to our Trade with French *Flanders, Hainault, Artois,* and *Picardy*, which is already answer'd, because other Ports can supply them as well as *Dunkirk*. Now if we should turn the other side of the Matter, I wonder what Danger the Memorialist would represent us from another War with *France*.

As to the Sieur's *Eighth*, This Article is false, as is already proved; nor do we want him to teach us our Trade to *Germany*, who would perswade us it is our Interest to Trade thither through *Dunkirk* by Land-Carriage, whose Waters have not any Correspondence with the Rivers of *Germany*, and to erect Staples and Store-Houses, which would be a good Booty for the *French* in case of a Rupture; nor can we ever carry it on so safely or cheaply through Countries possessed by *France*, as we do through *Hamburg*, and other Places, by Water Carriage.

As to his *Ninth*, He has here the Insolence to call it a *severe Resolution* in the Queen to insist on the Demolition. This is objected to in *Answer* 2. But his Assertion, that it is absolutely Necessary to the Trade of *Great Britain*, is the Reverse of our Case.

As to the Memorialist's *Tenth*, It is Necessary for all Ships to have a Lee-Port to flie to if they cannot get to Windward, or weather a Storm; but *All such as have any tolerable Skill in Navigation, know*, that our Ships keep their own Shoar abroad, as the *French* do theirs; and therefore the Port of *Dunkirk* is useless to us. I would fain know, what use our Ships had of that Port for above twenty Years last past. Mr. *Tugghe* I am sure, can tell us what *English* Ships ever refitted there, and how many ever repair'd their [4] Losses; all the World know there have been many Hundreds refitted there to annoy our own Country, and some Thousands suffer'd Losses there that were never repair'd. It is a *most desirable Port* for the Ships of *France*, but all *English* Ships have dreaded it for above twenty Years. The Publick Joy the News of its being to be Demolish'd created this Nation, is a convincing Argument, how much *they will in vain Regret, as well as all other Nations trading to the Northward, that Harbour of Safety.* It raises something more than Indignation to see a Magistrate of *Dunkirk*, sent to talk to the Queen of *Great Britain*, and dictate Rules of Humanity.

It will be a great Act of Humanity to insist upon the Demolition of that Town, which has destroyed so many Thousand of her Majesty's Subjects and their Ships.

This is all I have to say to my Foreign Enemy the Sieur *Tugghe*, and humbly recommending to his Most Christian Majesty the Care of the eighteen thousand Families, I take the liberty to repeat to him, that the *British* Nation expect the Demolition of *Dunkirk*. I am now to face about to my Domestick Foes, by whom I am accus'd of the Ingratitude of insulting my Prince, while I am eating her Bread.

Mr. *Bailiff*, It is so far otherwise, that to avoid the least Appearance of it, I did not attempt doing what proceeded from a true Grateful, and Loyal Heart, (*viz.*) the laying before her Majesty's Ministry, that the Nation had a strict Eye upon their Behaviour with relation to *Dunkirk*, before I had resigned all, which their Interposition with Her most Gracious Majesty, could take from me; I am so far from eating her Bread, with a Disinclination to her Service, that I had resigned a plentiful Income I had from her Favour, in a considerable Office and Pension, which incapacitate a Man of sitting in Parliament, to render my self more useful to Her and my Country, in the Station, with which your Borough has since honoured me.

If he is an Enemy to the Prerogative, that is satisfied with what he has already received from his Prince, and gives up all Expectations of ever receiving more, with no other View, than serving his Prince and Country in a more eminent manner than when he enjoyed Employments; if such a Man I say is an Enemy, I am an Enemy: But the Author of the Letter from the Country Whig, personates that Character so awkwardly, and the *Examiner*, without entering into the Point, treats me so outrageously, that I know not how to offer against such Adversaries, Reason and Argument, without appearing void of both. However, since it has for some time been the Fashion to run down Men of much greater Consequence than I am, with general Terms, that fall in with Prejudices and Corruptions of the People, I shall not bear in silence the Accusation of being in the least Degree undutiful to my Most Gracious Mistress, much less of assaulting Her Prerogative. These Writers shall treat me as they think fit, as I am their Brother-Scribler; but I shall not be so unconcern'd when they attack me as an Honest Man: I shall therefore inform them, that it is not in the Power of a Private and an Indifferent Man to hurt the Honour and Prerogative of the Crown, without being punish'd, if the Ministry think fit, as he deserves, by the Laws of our Country; but true and real Danger to the Queen's Honour may arise, if Persons in Authority Tolerate Men (who have no Compunction of Conscience) in abusing such Instruments of Glory and Honour to our Country as the Illustrious Duke of *Marlborough,* such wise and faithful Managers as the late Earl of *Godolphin,* such Pious, Disinterested, Generous, and Self-denying Patriots as the Bishops.

There is no Man will deny, but that it is in the Power of the Ministry to call the *Examiner* to an Account, as well as the *Flying-Post.* It is not for me to enter into the Reasons why they do not do themselves that Justice; but where is Honour, where is Government, where is Prerogative, while neither Age nor Sex, Virtue nor Innocence can have any Redress from the Assaults made upon their Reputation, which is dearer than Life? but such Injuries the *Examiner* repeats every Week with Impunity. But after I have fully answered the specious Pretension of Monsieur *Tugghe,* concerning the Trade, and Vindicated my Sovereign from his treacherous Insinuation, That it would be want of Mercy in Her to insist on the Demolition of *Dunkirk,* it is incumbent on me to come more closely to the Point with the Pamphleteer, and the *Examiner.* The former says, in his 17th Page, *Why must the Queen be attacked with such Insolence, and be told,* in terrorem, *that the People of* Great Britain *expect* Dunkirk *shall be demolished?*

The *Examiner*, as above, puts the stress of his Argument on the same words in the *Guardian*, of whom he says,

" For these Reasons, saving the Trespass on Custom, the LYE might be given in the Teeth of the *Guardian*, when he insolently tells the Queen, in his late Seditious Libel, *for such it must be accounted by every True* Britain; That the *British Nation* EXPECTS the *Immediate demolition of* Dunkirk: I say it is not so; the British Nation does *not* EXPECT that Her Majesty should divest Her self of the Power which is in her Hands, by the Possession of *Dunkirk*, to do Herself Right, and to secure to Herself the Performance of such Conditions from all the Princes concerned, as they have agreed to be just and ought to be performed; but which we do not find them so free to execute, as the Obligations *Britain* has laid on them has given us reason to expect."

Both these great Authors lay the weight of the Accusation, upon saying, the *British* Nation *expects*; you see the difference of a Man's Condition who acts under the Laws of his Country in general, from his who acts only under the Prerogative.

Here is a Treaty concluded; I am reckoned disrespectful, because I say, the Nation EXPECTS the Conditions to be complied with; he is a very loyal Man, who says, the Nation does not EXPECT it; but this wary Politician, the *Examiner*, says, *There are Dangers to be expected from other Powers in the World, as well as* France; he observes, *The Whigs forward to give up our trading Interest to the* Dutch, *in order to make Friends with them in their other nameless Designs against the Ministry.*

What has been already said to Monsieur *Tugghe*, concerning the Advantages the Dutch may reap from the Demolition, is also an Answer to the *Examiner*; All reasonable Men know, that the *Dutch* can reap no Advantage, but what must flow from their Industry, and our Negligence; but the Power of *France* cannot only rival us in Trade, but also when the King pleases (which is mentioned as a thing possible, not probable) invade us again with the Pretender, from the very same Place, whence he last set out to visit us, when we have no Troops to defend us, no Allies to succour us: When I think of these Things with Horror, from the Love I bear my Sovereign and my Country,

9

they say, I offend the Prerogative. Authors who write for the Prerogative, if they acted like Men of Honour, should be alarm'd at the improper Application of it by a Ministry, as much as by any other Acts of their Fellow-Subjects.

It is the Prerogative of the Crown to create Peers of *England,* but if in the midst of a Question in the Legislature, half a dozen new ones should march in, and by their Votes turn a Point, upon which our All might depend, would the Honour and Prerogative of the Crown be equally consulted at that Instant?

It is the Prerogative of the Crown to make Peace and War; shall the Crown therefore lay down its conquering Arms, and deliver it self up to the Vanquish'd? A Man is born with Free-will; does it therefore follow, that it is lawful to kill himself?

It is the Prerogative of the Crown to make Alliances, and act in Conjunction with their Allies; shall therefore its Armies march with them, in Confidence and Friendship, till they come to Front the Enemy, and then Face about, and leave them in the Day, in the Moment of Distress?

But it is a Folly to put Cases, which I hope will never happen among us; for if they should, the Persons who should transact any thing like any such things as I have now mentioned, would be so far from considering the Honour of the Prince, that they would diminish and blast it; and be so far from being a Support to, that they would be a Rent Charge upon the Prerogative.

The true Meaning and Use of the Prerogative is to be interpreted and understood by the Rules of the joint Welfare and Happiness of Prince and People, and all great Genius's in Business in all Nations and in all Ages, have apply'd it in this manner.

But from the Example of all Nations, who have lost their Liberty, we see that when, for the Sins of a Nation, Men of poor and narrow Conceptions, Self-interested, and without Benevolence to Mankind, have had the use of their Princes Favour and Prerogative, they think only what they may do, not what they ought to do.

All that I have at present to complain of, is, that the Defence of my Queen and Country, and of the most valuable part of our Trade, is treated as an Offence against the Honour and Prerogative of the Crown: I am heartily sorry to hear the word Prerogative introduced with so much Pomp against so inconsiderable a Man as my Self, or in the *Examiner's* words, *against so contemptible a Wretch.* If this word Prerogative comes to be used to frighten Men from speaking what they lawfully may upon publick Occurrences, it may come to pass hereafter that it may be a Refuge to indiscreet Ministers, and they may in time to come protect their Miscarriages under that aweful Word.

It would follow that whatever should be painful or disagreeable to the People, would be imputed to the Prince, whatever should be pleasing would be attributed to the Ministry. Ministers would not fail to cover their Follies, or Iniquities, under the shelter of the Prerogative. What was urged concerning *Dunkirk* in the Letter to the *Guardian,* was apparently and professedly laid before the Ministry, that they might not be unmindful of what the *British* Nation expect from them. I say again and again, if once Men are so intimidated as not to dare to offer their Thoughts upon publick Affairs, without incurring the Imputation of offending against the Prerogative of their Prince, that Prince, whatever Advantage his Ministers might make of his Prerogative, would himself have no Prerogative but that of being deceived: As for my part, I have that sincere and faithful Duty to Her Majesty, that I will never fear to attempt any thing that I am able for her Service, however her Favour may be intercepted from me. The *Examiner* accuses me of Ingratitude, as being actually under Salary, when I writ the Letter to the *Guardian*; but he is mistaken in that Particular, for I had resign'd, not only my Office in the Stampt Duties, but also my Pension as Servant to his late Royal Highness, which her Majesty hath been graciously pleased to continue to the whole Family of that Excellent Prince: I divested my self of all that I was so happy to enjoy by her Majesty's Goodness and Favour, before I would presume to write any thing, which was so apparently an Advertisement [5] to those employ'd in her service.

I have thrown away all Expectations of Preferment for the Happiness of serving in Parliament, and for the hopes of having

a Vote in the Legislature in the present Great Crisis of Affairs:
As long as I enjoy this Station (from which the *Examiner* takes
the Liberty to suggest I shall be expell'd) I shall follow no
Leader or Leaders, but Act, that is to say, Vote, according to
the Dictates of my Conscience, in the publick Service. But I
have said, *The* British *Nation Expect*: What is there in that of
Insolence and Ingratitude to a Queen and a Benefactress? Nay,
What is there in it more or less, the Premisses in my Letter
being consider'd, than the Duty of a Faithful, and a Grateful
Subject? Some of the Queen's immediate Servants are told by
their Fellow-Subject, that it lies upon all that have the Honour
to be in the Ministry to hasten the Demolition, for the sake of
the Queen, and all her faithful Subjects. What, are Majesty and
Ministry consolidated, and must the People of *Great Britain*
make no Distinction between the one and the other? We very
well know the difference, Sir, and humbly conceive, that if a
whole Ministry were Impeach'd and Condemn'd by the People
of *Great Britain* in Parliament, for any notorious Neglect of
Duty, or Breach of Trust, the Prince could not suffer by it. But
such is the Hardiness of these sort of Writers, that the Honour,
the Interest, nay, the Person, and Prerogative of the Sovereign
is communicated to, and confounded with the Ministry; and
those that by Law are accountable for all Wrongs done to the
Publick, must be screen'd and protected under the Sacred and
Incommunicable Character and Attributes of one, that by Law
can do no Wrong. But for Argument sake, I will suppose those
Words, *The* British *Nation Expects the immediate Demolition*
of Dunkirk, were address'd immediately to the Queen: With
what Propriety or Honesty of speaking, can a Man who utters
them be call'd Insolent or Ingrate? He sees and apprehends
with his own Eyes and Understanding, the imminent Danger
that attends the Delay of the Demolition of *Dunkirk*: which
perhaps others, whose greater Concern it is, do not; and the
thing not being done, by the Care of those under whose immediate Direction it is, but overlooked, (for suffering, without Ani-
madversion upon it, *Tugghe*'s Memorial published in Print, is
that or worse) after all the Obstacles that could have prevented it on the part of *France*, as Her Majesty has been
pleas'd to tell Her People, have been remov'd; an honest, tho'

a mean Man, gives Her Majesty to understand, in the best
Method he can take, and from the Sincerity of a grateful Heart,
That the British *Nation Expects the immediate Demolition of*
Dunkirk; and the Reasons he gives for such Expectations are
no less cogent, than the Preservation of Her Sacred Person, Her
Crown and Dignity, and the Safety and Welfare of the People
committed to Her Charge. He considers the Queen, in this
Case, as the Head of the Constitution of his Country: He considers himself, as a Member of the Community represented in
Parliament, whether one of the Representative Body, or no: He
knows *Britons*, by their Birth-right, are a Part of the Legislature,
and knows too, that the Executive Power is a Prerogative or
Peculiar vested in the Head of the Constitution, for the Good
of the whole; that it attends the Crown, Honour and Dignity,
and not the Will and Pleasure, or, it may be Passion of the
Prince; and as an Evidence of it, is Immortal, and ceases not,
when the Persons of our Princes are gather'd to their Fathers:
He knows too that all Treaties are made, and War and Peace
enter'd into, for the common Good: and in an Instance, respect-
ing the present Exigence, which he apprehends to be absolutely
necessary for that End; with a zealous and honest Mind, and
the warmest Concern for the fatal Consequences that may ensue
the Defect of it, tells the Mother of his Country, *That the*
British *Nation Expects the immediate Demolition of* Dunkirk:
Expects it, from the Duty they owe their Queen! from their
Care of the Preservation of Her Sacred Life, Her Crown and
Dignity! from the Honour and Justice of Her Administration!
from the Integrity of Her Councils! from the glorious Advantages of Her Arms! from the Faith and Sincerity of Her
Treaties! from the Veneration and Regard due to Her from
His Most Christian Majesty, and from the Duty they owe them-
selves and their Posterity! And is this Insolence and Ingratitude?

My Adversaries are so unjust, as they will not take the least
Notice of what led me into the necessity of writing my Letter
to the *Guardian*. They know if they stated it honestly, they
must acknowledge, that instead of what they call me, I was a
faithful Servant to the Queen, and an Honest Fellow-Subject
to the Ministry. My Lord *Bolingbroke* tells the Sieur *Tugghe*,
as a Secretary of State from the Queen, That his Request can-

not be complied with: The Sieur prints a Memorial, which is no other than an Appeal to all the weak People in *England*, against Her Severity. Nay, if the Translator has done him Justice, he has used the very Word *Severe*. This I take for the utmost Insult against the Queen, and Her Ministry; and instead of allowing my Zeal, I am publickly bereft of the Protection the Ministry should afford me, and all Honest Men, in the Performance of their Duty; and Partizans who pretend to write for them use me accordingly. I am not to be born with, even when I am for them: But I deserve well of them in this Question about *Tugghe*, or else they are not so angry, as I am, at what *Tugghe* has done against their Queen.

Good God! does this Creature, this *Tugghe*, come out of his Country, who writ that pious Letter to the Bishop of *Paris*, wherein Leavings of Fear made His Most Christian Majesty forget His Politicks, and (as if he had seen an Hand of Providence was in it, to his Favour, and our Misfortune) acknowledge he owed his very Kingdom to the *Suspension of the* English *Arms*? Does this very Potentate leave to the Burghers of *Dunkirk* to send some Body to treat about abating an Article of a Treaty, with the Glorious and Puissant Queen of *Great Britain*!

Tell it not in Gath, *nor publish it in the Streets of* Ashkelon!

We know not what is the Equivalent for *Dunkirk*, but according to the Circumstances of *France*, before the Suspension of the *English* Arms, under the gallant Duke of *Ormond*, (who would certainly have done his Duty) the *French* King has owned that the Equivalent might have been *Paris*.

When such was our Case, and such is our Case, some Men lately preferred, and grown too Delicate, would have Men of liberal Education, that know the World as well as themselves, afraid, for fear of offending them in their new Cloths, to speak when they think their Queen and Country is ill Treated.

While I am upon this Subject, I am glad to observe, that there are others who take up the same Argument; and my Servant has just now brought me a printed Half Sheet, Entituled, *A Letter to the Guardian, about* Dunkirk. With a great deal of very apt Raillery, upon the Madness of the Times, he pleasantly imagines our Language is altered of late Years, particularly in the Words *Good, Safe, Honourable, Advantageous*, England,

France, *Trade, Commerce*: He makes the *Examiner* the Mint-Master for the New Tongue, and then proceeds in a more serious and close manner to argue on the side of the *English* Tory's Letter: He speaks of the *Examiner* in these Words:

"Nor are his *new Politicks* any better than his *new Language*; he tells us, that *the keeping* Dunkirk *undemolish'd* in our Hands, is our Security against all the Princes concerned besides *France*; i. e. against the *Confederates*, as well as against *France*. It may be a Security against the *Confederates*, but while it is so, it cannot be a Security against *France*. *France* can neither apprehend nor feel any Mischief from it, whilst it is a Bridle against the Confederates. The Reason is plain, *France* has it in its Power to Demolish it when it will. The IXth Article says, *France* is to Demolish it in so many Months Time; those Months are expired, and therefore *France* can demolish it when it will: And whenever *France* apprehends any Danger from *Dunkirk undemolish'd*, it will Demolish it immediately. 'Tis therefore plainly for the Good and Interest of *France*, that *Dunkirk* is undemolish'd. *What*, do we think we have a Tool of *France*?

"Upon the whole Matter, if there were no other Reason, Argument, or Motive in the World, for the Demolition of *Dunkirk*, but the Content and Easiness of *France* in seeing it not demolished, it were sufficient to move an honest *Englishman* to *hope*, and *wish* and *pray*, that it might be immediately demolish'd and that some other Bridle might be found out to keep in the Confederates, than that which is in the *French* Dominions, and may, whenever *France* pleases (let us talk what we will) be in the *French* Hands. What if *Dunkirk* should be besieged, can the poor *British Garrison* defend it? Shall we raise an Army to recover it? *Dunkirk undemolished* may be lost, taken, betrayed, and got again into the Hands of *France*. *Dunkirk demolished* is a Fisher-Town again, and can do no harm."

This Gentleman argues *France* has a Power; but I say, what is more with all Honest Men, *France* has a Right to demolish it; and who shall resist it, when the great King of *France* has both Power and Right to demolish it. But alas! who knows how long it will be in his Majesty's Will to do it?

I cannot forbear wishing he had deposited the Money in our Hands, before our Suspension of Arms, for the Demolition. I could name proper Persons, that would have been gladly employed in that Work, and some of them are begging in our Streets.

The King at that time was low enough, if *England* has stood out, to have granted that Demand; but it is an Human Weakness not to preserve so lively a Sense of a past Benefit, as we had at the Instant of receiving it. It was thought an hard Article to desire him to Dethrone his Grandson, though he had sent him to take, what we then believ'd, another Man's Country: Suppose he should, tho' he has put it into other People's Possession, at last take Compassion of his own Town?

It has cost, to put it in its present Condition, above Six Millions; and it would go to a Man's Heart to part with what cost so dear: But he is bound by Treaty, and he must do it, if he pleases.

But as there is this Letter published on my side, there is another Pamphlet come out on the *Examiner's*. It is Entituled, *Reasons concerning the Immediate Demolishing of* Dunkirk; *being a serious Enquiry into the State and Condition of that Affair*. I like this Man better than any of the rest, for he does not give me ill Language, 'till he gives his Reasons why I deserve it. He talks very kindly thus in the fourteenth Page:

"We can hardly express how much we are beholding in this Matter to the *worthy* Mr. *Steele*, the Publisher of the *Guardian*, No 128. I will not be so unjust to him as to call him the Author: who has effectually set us right in this Matter, and has rescued the Town and Harbour of *Dunkirk* from the depreciating Arts of our Party-Men, who, it was to be fear'd, would have brought it at last so low, that we might have been made believe, the King of *France*, if we should offer to give it him again, would not accept of it.

" But the *Guardian* has taken the Courage to do Justice to the *Dunkirkers*, and of Consequence to the Ministry, in securing such a Place in the Possession of the Queen; for he has told us expressly, that to take *Dunkirk* from the *French* is removing *France* two or three hundred Miles further from us; that they have not any Port where they can fit out any Fleet 'till they come to *Brest*; that it is of the last Consequence to *Britain* that it should no more be in the *French* Power, that the Injury we have received from them is Inestimable. His Words follow:

'*That when* Dunkirk *is demolished, the Power of* France, *on that Side, should it ever be turned against us, will be removed several hundred Miles further off of* Great Britain *than it is at present.* Vide *Guardian*, No 128.'

"As this is an undoubted Testimony given to the Zeal of the Ministry, in taking hold of the present Conjuncture, to get that Important Fortress into our Hands, and is the greatest and most just Panegyrick which Mr. *Steele* ever made upon any great Action in the World; and which, no doubt, he did in Honour to the Queen, and the present Government; and that the said Mr. *Steele* has gained the just Approbation of all Her Majesty's good Subjects for so doing: so it is a fair Confutation of all those weak Things which had been advanced by a Party among us, in Prejudice of the late Negotiations; But above all, that it is an unanswerable Argument against our too soon parting with, or too hastily Demolishing this Important Place, which is of such Consequence to the Nation; and I cannot doubt, but Mr. *Steele* did it that Justice with this intent. For it is impossible a Man of his Penetration, and of his exquisite Politicks, could Argue—" He grows in Jest here at last, for he knows as well as I do, that I am no great Politician, and I know what he is, perhaps, a little better than he Thinks. But I shall treat him as the Man whom I suppose him to be, tho' he has not me, as the Man he knows me to be. This Author you see, allows me, (tho' he did not think it was in me) to have done a laudable thing towards the Ministry, in my Representation of the Great Service the Demolition of *Dunkirk* would be; *but his Anger against me is raised for the Point of Time,* Why must the Demolition be immediate? My Reasons are as follow:

First, We have no Right to keep it, but in order to the Demolition of it.

Secondly, The Time was lapsed, within which it was to be demolished.

But why did I say the *British* Nation expect it should be immediately demolished, when the *British* Parliament had

Granted Money to subsist the Garrison of Dunkirk *till next* Christmas.

This is no Argument that the *British* Parliament did not expect the immediate Demolition; but it is indeed an Argument that the Parliament had a good Confidence in the Ministry, and were unwilling to distress them: For if the Demolition had began the Day after the Parliament rose, it might honestly have been retarded by stress of Weather, and other Accidents, till a New Parliament should sit at *Christmas*; and if all things should have favoured, and the Demolition had been now perfected, my Lord High Treasurer would stand chargeable to the Nation with the Money for the Garrison to *Christmas.*

As for what he says about our Allies, and something to be expected from them, I cannot comprehend what he means; but whatever he means, and however just Demands we may have upon them, his Most Christian Majesty will not think it any Reason for delaying the Demolition of a Town in his Dominions, in the Hands of another Prince, for Reasons of State to that Prince, and not to His *French* Majesty himself.

Really this way of arguing is treating us like Children; and as for the Allies, God be their Support, and grant we may all cement again in the Day of Distress. I think all the rest of the Book consists only of Invectives upon poor Me, as Guilty of Insolence, Falsehood, Sedition, and Absurdity; which is written well enough, and would be pretty Entertainment to an ill-natured Man; but I did not think it bore a second reading.

I hope I have fully answered all Objections made by my Adversaries against the *English* Tory's Letter to the *Guardian*: But, now Mr. *Bailiff*, as there have been very unjust Representations given of me, in your Town, as that a Man of so small a Fortune as I am, must have secret Views or Supports, which could move him to leave his Employments, and lose a Crowd of Well-wishers, to subject himself, as he must know he has, not only to the Disesteem, but also the Scorn and Hatred of very many, who, before he intermeddled with the Publick, had a Partiality towards him: I answer, that I indeed have particular Views, and tho' I may be ridiculous for saying it, I hope I am animated in my Conduct, by a Grace which is as little practised as understood, and that is Charity. It is the Happiness and Comfort of all Men, who have a Regard to their Fellow-Creatures, and desire their Good-will upon a proper Foundation, that every thing which is truly Laudable, is what every Man living may attain. The greatest Merit is in having social Virtues, such as Justice and Truth exalted with Benevolence to Mankind. Great Qualifications are not Praises to the Possessor, but from the Application of them; and all that is justly Commendable among Men, is to Love and Serve them as much as it is in your Power, with a Contempt of all Advantages to your self (above the Conveniencies of Life) but as they tend to the Service of the Publick. He who has warm'd his Heart with Impressions of this kind, will find Glowings of Good-will, which will support him in the Service of his Country, against all the Calumny, Reproach, and Invective, that can be thrown upon him. He is but a poor Creature who cannot bear being odious in the Service of Virtue. Riches and Honour can administer to the Heart no Pleasure, like what an Honest Man feels when he is contending for the Interests of his Country, and the Civil Rights of his Fellow-Subjects, without which the Being of Man grows Brute, and he can never under it give to Heav'n that Worship which is called a Reasonable Sacrifice, nor support towards his Fellow-Creatures that worthy Disposition, which we call disinterested Friendship. The highest Pleasure of the Human Soul consists in this Charity, and there is no way of making it so diffusive, as by contending for Liberty.

As to laying aside the common Views, by which the mistaken World are actuated, a Man of liberal Education can easily surmount those low Considerations; and when he considers himself, from the moment he was born into this World an Immortal, tho' a changeable Being, he will form his Interests and Prospects accordingly, and not make Provision for Eternity with perishable things. When a Man has deeply planted such a Sentiment as this for the Rule of his Conduct, the Pursuits of Avarice and Ambition will become as contemptible as the Sports of Children; and there can be no Honours, no Riches, no Pleasures laid in his way, which can possibly come in Competition with the Satisfactions of an enlarged and publick Spirit.

From this Moment therefore I shall go on, with as much

Vigour and Chearfulness as I am able, to do all that is in my Power, without the least Partiality to Persons or Parties, to remove the Prejudices which *Englishman* has against *Englishman*, and reconcile wounded Brethren, so far as to behold each other's Actions, with an Inclination to approve them.

The Man who will reduce himself to this Temper, will easily perceive how far his Affections have been wrought upon and abused, from an Opposition to particular Men, to sacrifice the Interests of his Country it self.

The prostituted Pens which are employed in a quite contrary Service, will be very ready to entertain a Pretender to such Reformations, with a Recital of his own Faults and Infirmities; but I am very well prepared for such Usage, and give up my self to all nameless Authors, to be treated just as their Mirth or their Malice directs them.

It is the Disgrace of Literature, that there are such Instruments, and to good Government, that they are suffer'd: but this Mischief is gone so far in our Age, that the Pamphleteers do not only attack those whom they believe in general disaffected to their own Principles, but even such as they believe their Friends, provided they do not act with as sincere a Prejudice as themselves. Upon the least Deviation from an implicit Hatred to the opposite Party, tho' in a Case which in the nearest Concern affects their Country, all their good Qualities are turned to Ridicule; and every thing which before was valued in them, is become contemptible: Thus in one of the Papers I send you, a Gentleman, who has distinguish'd himself by a becoming Veneration, in the *House of Commons*, for the Assembly, and has ever deliver'd himself with a Regard to his own Dignity, and that of the Place he was in, is represented frivolously as a Declaimer; and a Noble Lord, who is conspicuously adorn'd with the Knowledge of Letters, and is Eminent for a lively sprightly Eloquence, rectify'd by Learning, is declared a Companion fit only for Pert Novices and Sophisters. And what is still more Monstrous than all, a third Man of Quality, for the like Offence, is told in this nice Age of proportioning Rewards to Merit and Service, that he has as much as he deserves.

But it is to be hoped, *English* Men will at last consider, and that the Ministry will see *Dunkirk* effectually Demolished.

It is as frivolous as unjust to hope to stop our Mouths, when we are concerned for so great a Point as the Business of *Dunkirk,* by Mention of the Prerogative, and urging our Safety in our Good and Gracious Queen.

By Her great Example, Religion, Piety, and all other Publick and Domestick Virtues, are kept in Countenance in a very loose and profligate Age; all the Hours of Her precious Life, which God long preserve, are divided between the Exercises of Devotion, and taking Minutes of the Sublime Affairs of Her Government.

Besides which, Her Majesty has manifested Her self the most Affectionate Wife, the most constant Friend, the most tender Mother, and has filled every Duty with a Virtue as Superiour to the rest of the World, as is Her High Condition: But I shall leave what I have to say on this Topick, to the Time when the Consequence of it will be Insignificant to me, but which I hope will do Her Honour, that is Justice, when I am no more, and the Remains of Her Sacred Person are as common Dust as mine.

But as this bright Example is in the Person of a Lady, it cannot be supposed that the general Sense of a People, the Subdivisions of Affection and Interest among Great Men (to be learn'd only by Conversation with them, even in their unguarded Leisure) can appear to Her but from the Information of such as have the Happiness and Honour to lay them before Her. Her Majesty is therefore more particularly necessitated to rely upon the Intelligence of Her Ministry, and from that very Reason their Fellow-Subjects may be the more Sollicitous for what passes beyond the ordinary Rules of Government. Thus all which they offer for our Security and implicit Reliance upon what is transacted by the Court of *England,* to wit, Her Majesty's Care and Goodness, are Arguments for exerting both our Zeal and our Gratitude; that at any time Artful Men may not take Advantage of the Security we have in Her Virtue, to indulge too much the Power of any Foreign Prince whatsoever, especially that of the most Warlike Potentate in *Europe.*

I cannot leave this Subject, without being still anxious, with relation to the Disrespect they accuse me of to my Royal Mistress. All that can be wrested to my Disadvantage, is, That the Queen is concern'd when any thing is to be imputed to Her Servants;

but I deny that, and persist in it, that it is no manner of Diminution of the Wisdom of a Prince, that he is obliged to act by the Information of others.

If I might make an abrupt Digression from great Things to small, I should on this Occasion mention a little Circumstance which happened to the late King *William*. He had a *French* Man who took care of the Gun-Dogs, whose Business it was also to charge and deliver the Piece to the King. This Minister forgot to bring out Shot into the Field, but did not think fit to let so passionate a Man and eager a Sportsman as the King know his Offence, but gave his Majesty the Gun Loaded only with Powder. When the King missed his Aim, this Impudent Cur stood Chattering, Admiring, Commending the King's Skill in Shooting, and holding up his Hands, he had never seen *Sa Majesté* miss before in his whole Life. This Circumstance was no manner of Argument to those (who afterwards found out the Fellow's Iniquity) against the King's Reputation for a Quick Eye, and Shooting very finely. I am, with Respect to the Borough, and Your self,

SIR,

Your most Humble,

and most Obedient Servant,

Richard Steele.

The Crisis (January, 1714)

It is Steele's purpose to recall—lest they be forgotten in this present crisis, the illness and decline of Queen Anne—the dynastic and religious issues and the question of civil rights which centered in the Revolution of 1688. First, he gives verbatim, in a tedious but impressive recital, the laws enacted during the past twenty-five years to extirpate the " Arbitrary Power of a Popish Prince." (1) The Declaration of Right and the Bill of Rights (1688 and 1689) declaring the rights of parliament and subject and settling the succession in a Protestant line, thus debarring for all time a Roman Catholic sovereign. The forms of the law are given as passed in both England and Scotland. (2) The required formal oaths of allegiance and abjuration. (3) The Act of Settlement (1701) in both English and Scottish forms. Anne's only son having died, this Act authorized as next in line the Protestant Princess Sophia and her issue. (4) The Act of Attainder against James Stuart the Pretender (1702), as a consequence of Louis XIV's recognition of him as king of England. (5) The Abjuration Act (1702), calling on all office holders to deny formally the Stuart theory of divine hereditary right. (6) An Act for Naturalizing Princess Sophia and her issue (1705). (7) The Regency Act (1705), bringing the settlement up to date and providing for a regency at Anne's death until the Hanoverian Succession could be consummated. (8) The Union Treaty with Scotland (1707), Articles I and II, which dealt with provisions for the Protestant Succession. (9) Certain strengthening Acts passed in 1708-9 as a result of James Stuart's recent attempted invasion of England.

In the exposition following the recital of these Acts, Steele touches upon the points raised in current discussion: the causes and conduct of the late war with France; the disadvantages and ignominies (the Whig view) of the peace treaty; the menace of a powerful House of Bourbon to the continent and to Great Britain; the various Stuart claimants in continental royal families. What he says of the religious consequences of a possible Stuart restoration would be calculated to arouse memories of the strife between Catholic James II and his parliament and people only a short thirty years ago. If the general tone of these remarks is alarmist, Steele's underlying argument is one of principle: that the liberty of the subject and the power of parliament against the power of the crown, fought for and won in 1688, are again in danger.

Uneasiness over the dynastic question was warranted in the winter of 1713-14. The pamphlet press was active, pro and con, on the themes of passive resistance and divine hereditary right. The Tory party was split on the Succession, the Jacobite wing being openly sympathetic with the exiled Catholic Stuart. A group of non-jurors were exerting a not inconsiderable influence on public opinion. The Ministry was avowedly Francophil. And the idea of a foreign, German-speaking king was not a popular concept in England or Scotland. Anne herself was said to look kindly upon her brother's claim if he would become Protestant. It was suspected, and was true, that many men in high places were playing a double game to be on the safe side in case of a Jacobite restoration (even Marlborough, if Steele had but known it). Rumors of ministerial intrigue with the exiled court were disturbing: within a month after the publication of *The Crisis*, the Ministry was formally asking James Stuart to become a member of the Anglican Church. At this juncture then, Steele stated unequivocally under his own name " without hints and innuendos " that the Protestant Succession was in danger. Courageously, if indiscreetly, he was willing, he said later, to ripen the question of the Succession upon his own head.

Steele explains in the Preface to *The Apology* that William Moore, a lawyer friend of the Inner Temple, suggested the idea of such a tract and was his collaborator and that Addison, Hoadly, the eminent low church minister, and two Whig friends—Nicholas Lechmere and Edward Minshull—had all seen the manuscript while the tract was in preparation. Without doubt, the Dedication to the Tory clergy, the Preface, and the general exposition, Steele himself was responsible for. The writing of the tract was underway in the early autumn, and the *Englishman* of 22 October invited subscriptions. The Whig leaders, the Hanover Club, and the Hanoverian agents assisted in promoting the circulation, which was country-wide, 40,000 copies, it was said, being sold. The immediate consequence for Steele was expulsion from the House of Commons. For further comment on *The Crisis* and its effect, see *Mr. Steele's Apology*, pp. 275 ff. Textual notes on p. 641.

THE
CRISIS:
OR, A
DISCOURSE

Reprefenting,

From the moft AUTHENTICK RECORDS,

The juft Caufes of the late

Happy REVOLUTION:

AND

The feveral Settlements of the Crowns of ENGLAND *and* SCOT-
LAND *on Her* MAJESTY; *and on the Demife of Her* MA-
JESTY *without Iffue, upon the Moft Illuftrious Princefs* SO-
PHIA, *Electrefs and Dutchefs Dowager of* Hanover, *and the
Heirs of Her Body being* Proteftants; *by previous Acts of both Par-
liaments of the late Kingdoms of* ENGLAND *and* SCOTLAND;
and confirmed by the Parliament of GREAT BRITAIN.

WITH SOME
SEASONABLE REMARKS
On the Danger of a
𝕻𝖔𝖕𝖎𝖘𝖍 𝕾𝖚𝖈𝖈𝖊𝖘𝖘𝖔𝖗.

Invitus ea tanquam Vulnera attingo; Sed nifi tacta tractataq;
fanari non poffunt.   *Liv.*

By *RICHARD STEELE*, Efq;

LONDON: Printed by *Sam. Buckley ;* and Sold by *Ferd. Burleigh,* in
Amen-Corner. 1714.

127

10

TO THE

CLERGY

OF THE

Church of ENGLAND.

Gentlemen,

IT is with a just Deference to Your great Power and Influence in this Kingdom, that I lay before you the following Comment upon the Laws which regard the Settlement of the Imperial Crown of *Great Britain.* My Purpose in addressing these Matters to you, is to conjure you, as Heaven has blessed you with proper Talents and Opportunities, to recommend them, in your Writings and Discourses, to your Fellow-Subjects.

In the Character of Pastors and Teachers, you have an almost irresistible Power over us of your Congregations; and by the admirable Institution of our Laws, the Tenths of our Lands, now in your Possession, are destined to become the Property of such others, as shall by Learning and Virtue qualifie themselves to succeed you. These Circumstances of Education and Fortune, place the Minds of the People, from Age to Age, under your Direction; As therefore it would be the highest Indiscretion in Ministers of State of this Kingdom, to neglect the Care of being acceptable to You in their Administration; so it would be the greatest Impiety in you, to inflame the People committed to your Charge, with Apprehensions of Danger to you and your Constitution, from Men innocent of any such Designs.

Give *me* Leave, who have in all my Words and Actions, from my Youth upwards, maintained an inviolable Respect to you and your Order, to observe to you, that all the Dissatisfactions which have been raised in the Minds of the People, owe their Rise to the Cunning of artful Men, who have introduced the Mention of you and your Interest, (which are sacred to all good Men) to cover and sanctify their own Practices upon the Affections of the People, for Ends very different from the Promotion of Religion and Virtue. Give me Leave also to take Notice, That these Suggestions have been favoured by some few unwary Men in holy Orders, who have made the Constitution of their own Country a very little Part of their Study, and yet made Obedience and Government the frequent Subjects of their Discourses.

These Men, from the pompous Ideas of Imperial Greatness, and Submission to absolute Emperors, which they imbibed in their earlier Years, have from Time to Time inadvertently uttered Notions of Power and Obedience abhorrent from the Laws of this their native Country.

I will take the further Liberty to say, That if the Acts of Parliament mentioned in the following Treatise had been from Time to Time put in a fair and clear Light, and been carefully recommended to the Perusal of young Gentlemen in Colleges, with a Preference to all other Civil Institutions whatsoever; this Kingdom had not been in its present Condition, but the Constitution would have had, in every Member the Universities have sent into the World ever since the Revolution, an Advocate for our Rights and Liberties.

There is one thing which deserves Your most serious Consideration. You have bound your selves by the strongest Engagements Religion can lay upon Men, to support that Succession which is the Subject of the following Papers; you have tied down Your Souls by an Oath to maintain it as it is settled in the House of *Hanover*; nay, you have gone much further than is usual in Cases of this Nature, as you have *personally* abjured the Pretender to this Crown, and that expressly, without any Equivocations or mental Reservations whatsoever, that is, without any possible Escapes, by which the Subtlety of temporizing Casuists might hope to elude the Force of these solemn Obligations. You know much better than I do, whether the calling God to witness to the Sincerity of our Intentions in these Cases, whether the swearing upon the holy Evangelists in the most

solemn Manner, whether the taking of an Oath before Multitudes of Fellow-Subjects and Fellow-Christians in our publick
Courts of Justice, do not lay the greatest Obligations that can
be laid on the Consciences of Men. This I am sure of, that if
the Body of a Clergy who considerately and voluntarily entered
into these Engagements, should be made use of as Instruments
and Examples to make the Nation break through them, not only
the Succession to our Crown, but the very Essence of our
Religion is in Danger. What a Triumph would it furnish to
those evil Men among us who are Enemies to Your Sacred
Order? What Occasion would it administer to Atheists and
Unbelievers, to say that Christianity is nothing else but an outward Show and Pretence among the most knowing of its Professors? What could we afterwards object to Jesuits? What
would be the Scandal brought upon our holy Church, which is
at present the Glory and Bulwark of the Reformation? How
would our present Clergy appear in the Eyes of their Posterity
and even to the Successors of their own Order, under a Government introduced and established by a Conduct so directly opposite to all the Rules of Honour and Precepts of Christianity?

As I always speak and think of your holy Order with the
utmost Deference and Respect, I do not insist upon this Subject
to insinuate that there is such a Disposition among your venerable Body, but to shew how much your own Honour and the
Interest of Religion is concerned, that there should be no Cause
given for it.

Under Colour of a Zeal towards you, Men may sometimes
act not only with Impunity but Popularity, what would render
them, without that Hypocrisy, insufferably odious to their
Fellow-Subjects.

Under this Pretence Men may presume to practise such Arts
for the Destruction and Dishonour of their Country, as it would
be impious to make use of even for its Glory and Safety: Men
may do in the highest Prosperity, what it would not be excusable to attempt under the lowest Necessity!

The Laws of our Country, the Powers of the Legislature, the
Faith of Nations, and the Honour of God, may be too weak
Considerations to bear up against the popular tho' groundless
Cry of the Church. This fatal Prepossession may shelter Men

in raising the *French* Name and Roman-Catholick Interest in *Great Britain*, and consequently in all *Europe*.

It behoves you therefore, Gentlemen, to consider, whether the Cry of the Church's Danger may not at length become a Truth: And as You are Men of Sense and Men of Honour, to exert your selves in undeceiving the Multitude, whenever their affectionate Concern for you may prove fatal to themselves.

You are surrounded by a learned, wealthy, and knowing Gentry, who can distinguish your Merit, and do Honour to your Characters. They know with what Firmness as *Englishmen,* with what Self-Denial as Prelates, with what Charity as Christians, the Lords the Bishops, Fathers of the Church, have behaved themselves in the Publick Cause: They know what Contumelies the rest of the Clergy have undergone, what Discountenance they have laboured under, what Prejudice they have suffered in their Ministry, who have adhered to the Cause of Truth: But it is certain that the Face of things is now too melancholy to bear any longer false Appearances; and common Danger has united Men, who not long ago were artfully inflamed against each other, into some Regard of their common Safety.

When the World is in this Temper, those of our Pastors, whose exemplary Lives and charitable Dispositions both adorn. and advance our holy Religion, will be the Objects of our Love and Admiration; and those who pursue the Gratifications of Pride, Ambition, and Avarice, under the sacred Character of Clergymen, will not fail to be our Contempt and Derision.

Noise and Wrath cannot always pass for Zeal; and if we see but little of the publick Spirit of *Englishmen* or the Charity of Christians in others, it is certain we can feel but little of the Pleasure of Love and Gratitude, and but faint Emotions of Respect and Veneration in our selves.

It will be an Action worthy the Ministers of the Church of *England*, to distinguish themselves for the Love of their Country; and as we have a Religion that wants no Assistance from Artifice or Enlargement of Secular Power, but is well supported by the Wisdom and Piety of its Preachers, and its own native Truth, to let Mankind see that we have a Clergy who are of the People, obedient to the same Laws, and zealous not only

of the Supremacy and Prerogative of our Princes, but of the
Liberties of their Fellow-Subjects: This will make us who are
Your Flock burn with Joy to see, and with Zeal to imitate your
Lives and Actions. It cannot be expected but that there will be,
in so great a Body, light, superficial, vain, and ambitious Men,
who being untouched with the sublime Force of the Gospel,
will think it their Interest to insinuate Jealousies between the
Clergy and Laity, in Hopes to derive from their Order a Veneration which they know they cannot deserve from their Virtue.
But while the most worthy, conspicuous, learned, and powerful
of your sacred Function are moved by the noble and generous
Incentives of doing Good to the Souls of Men, we will not
doubt of seeing by Your Ministry the Love of our Country, due
Regard for our Laws and Liberties, and Resentment for the
Abuse of Truth, revive in the Hearts of Men. And as there
are no Instruments under Heaven so capable of this great Work,
that God would make you such to this divided Nation, is the
hearty Prayer of,

Gentlemen,

Your most Dutiful,

and most Obedient

Humble Servant,

RICHARD STEELE.

PREFACE.

I Never saw an unruly Crowd of People cool by Degrees into Temper, but it gave me an Idea of the Original of Power and the Nature of Civil Institutions. One particular Man has usually in those Cases, from the Dignity of his Appearance, or other Qualities known or imagined by the Multitude, been received into sudden Favour and Authority; the Occasion of their Difference has been represented to him, and the Matter referred to his Decision.

This first Step towards acting reasonably has brought them to themselves; and when the Person, by an Appeal to whom they first were taken out of Confusion, was gone from amongst them, they have calmly taken further Measures from a Sense of their common Good.

Absolute unlimited Power in one Person seems to have been the first and natural Recourse of Mankind from Disorder and Rapine; and such a Government must be acknowledged to be better than no Government at all: But all Restrictions of Power made by Laws and [1] Participation of Sovereignty among several Persons, are apparent Improvements made upon what began in that unlimited Power. This is what seems reasonable to common Sense; and the Manner of maintaining absolute Dominion in one Person, where-ever it subsists, verifies the Observation: For the Subjection of the People to such Authority is supported only by Terrors, sudden and private Executions, and Imprisonments; and not as with happy Britons, by the Judgment, in Cases of Liberty and Property, of the Peers, and Neighbours of Men accused or prosecuted. This absolute Power in one Person, as it is generally exercised, is not indeed Government, but at best clandestine Tyranny, supported by the Confederates, or rather Favourite-Slaves of the Tyrant.

I was glad to find this natural Sense of Power confirmed in me by very great and good Men, who have made Government, and the Principles on which it is founded, their professed Study and Meditation.

134

A very celebrated Author has these Words;

The Case of Man's Nature standing as it does, some kind of Regiment the Law of Nature doth require; yet the kinds thereof being many, Nature tieth not to any one, but leaveth the Choice as a thing arbitrary. At the first, when some certain kind of Regiment was once approved, it may be that nothing was then further thought upon for the Manner of governing, but all permitted unto their Wisdom and Discretion which were to rule, till by Experience they found this for all Parts very inconvenient, so as the thing which they had devised for a Remedy did indeed but increase the Sore which it should have cured. They saw that *to live by one Man's Will became the Cause of all Mens Misery.* This constrained them to come unto Laws, wherein all Men might see their Duties before-hand, and know the Penalties of transgressing them. Men always knew that when Force and Injury was offered, they might be Defenders of themselves; they knew that howsoever Men might seek their own Commodity, yet if this were done with Injury to others, it was not to be suffered, but by all Men and by all good Means to be withstood.

Finally, They knew that no Man might in Reason take upon him to determine his own Right, and according to his own Determination proceed in Maintenance thereof, inasmuch as every Man is towards himself, and them whom he greatly affecteth, partial; and therefore that Strikes and Troubles would be endless, except they gave their common Consent all to be ordered by some whom they should agree upon.

Mr. Stanhope, *in Defence of Resistance in Cases of extream Necessity, cites this memorable Passage from* Grotius;

If the King hath one Part of the Supream Power, and the other Part is in the Senate or People; when such a King shall invade that Part that doth not belong to him, it shall be lawful to oppose a just Force to him, because his Power doth not extend so far: Which Position I hold to be true, even though the Power of making War should be vested only in the King, which must be understood to relate only to foreign War: For as for Home, it is impossible for any to have a Share of the Supream Power, and not to have likewise a Right to defend that Share.

An eminent Divine, who deserves all Honour for the Obligations he has Laid upon both Church and State by his Writings on the Subject of Government, argues against Unlimited Power thus;

The Question is, Whether the Power of the Civil Magistrate be unlimited; that is, in other Words, Whether the Nature of his Office require it to be so. But what? Is it the End of that Office that one particular Person may do what he pleaseth without Restraint? Or that Society should be made happy and secure? Who will say the former? And if the latter be the true End of it, a less Power than absolute will answer it: Nay, an absolute Power is a Power to destroy that End, and therefore inconsistent with the End it self.

These Passages I thought fit to produce by way of Preface *to the following Discourse, as carrying in them the Reason and Foundation of Government it self, and in Maintenance of what passed at the Revolution.*

I shall only beg leave to add to them one very great Living Authority, the present Lord High Chancellor of Great Britain; *who in a late famous Tryal, did openly before Queen, Lords and Commons, maintain the Lawfulness of the Revolution under the Notion of Resistance, and assert before the most solemn and august Assembly of* Europe, *that there are* extraordinary Cases, Cases of Necessity, which are implyed, though not expressed in the General Rule; *that is, which are so plain and so open to the common Sense of Mankind, that even whilst you are declaring Resistance in all Cases to be unlawful, you are of necessity understood to mean, that Resistance in some Cases is lawful. I am pleased to observe, that no one ever put the Matter so strongly, or carried it so high as this great Man did upon that Critical Occasion. At the same time he was so just to his Country, as to declare, That* such a Case undoubtedly the Revolution was, when our late unhappy Sovereign then upon the Throne, misled by evil Counsellors, endeavoured to subvert and extirpate the Protestant Religion, and the Laws and Liberties of the Kingdom.

The *CRISIS*, &c.

IT is every Man's Duty to correct the Extravagances of his Will, in order to enjoy Life as becomes a rational Being; but we cannot possess our Souls with Pleasure and Satisfaction, except we preserve to our selves that inestimable Blessing which we call Liberty. By Liberty I desire to be understood to mean, the Happiness of Mens living under Laws of their own making by their personal Consent, or that of their Representatives.

Without this, the Distinctions amongst Mankind are but gentler Degrees of Misery; for as the true Life of Man consists in conducting it according to his own just Sentiments and innocent Inclinations, his Being is degraded below that of a free Agent, which Heaven has made him, when his Affections and Passions are no longer governed by the Dictates of his own Mind, and the Interests of Humane Society, but by the arbitrary unrestrained Will of another.

Without Liberty, even Health, and Strength, and all the Advantages bestowed on us by Nature and Providence, may at the Will of a Tyrant be employed to our own Ruin, and that of our Fellow Creatures.

Liberty is essential to our Happiness, and they who resign Life it self rather than part with it, do only a prudent Action; but those who lay it down, and voluntarily expose themselves to Death, in behalf of their Friends and Country, do an heroick One. The more exalted Part of our Species are moved by such generous Impulses as these; but even the Community, the Mass of Mankind, when convinced of the Danger of their Civil Rights, are anxious of preserving to themselves that dearest of all Possessions, Liberty.

The late Kingdoms of *England* and *Scotland* have contended for it from Age to Age, with too great a Price of Blood and Treasure to be given for the Purchase of any other Blessing; but laid out Parsimoniously, when we consider they have transmitted this to their Posterity.

But since, by I know not what Fatality, we are of late grown supine, and our Anxiety for it is abated, in Proportion to the Danger to which it is every Day more exposed, by the artful and open Attacks of the Enemies of our Constitution; it is a seasonable and honest Office to look into our Circumstances, and let the Enemies of our present Establishment behold the Securities which the Laws of our Country have given those who dare assert their Liberties, and the Terrors which they have pronounced against those who dare undermine them. For, whatever is the Prospect before our Eyes, it is the Business of every honest Man to look up with a Spirit that becomes Honesty, and to do what in him lies for the Improvement of our present Condition, which nothing but our own Pusillanimity can make desperate.

The most destructive Circumstance in our Affairs seems to be, that by the long and repeated Insinuations of our Enemies, many are worn into a kind of Doubt of their own Cause, and think with Patience of what is suggested in favour of contrary Pretensions. The most obvious Method of reviving the proper Sentiments in the Minds of Men for what they ought to esteem most dear, is to shew, That our Cause has in it all the Sanctions of Honour, Truth, and Justice; and that we are, by all the Laws of God and Man, enstated in a Condition of enjoying Religion, Life, Liberty, and Property, rescued from the most imminent Danger of having them all for ever depend upon the Arbitrary Power of a Popish Prince.

We should have been chained down in this abject Condition in the Reign of the late King *James*, had not God Almighty in Mercy given us the late happy Revolution, by that glorious Instrument of his Providence the great and memorable King WILLIAM. But though this wonderful Deliverance happened as it were but Yesterday, yet such is the Inadvertency or Ingratitude of some amongst us, that they seem not only to have forgotten the Deliverer, but even the Deliverance it self. Old Men act as if they believed the Danger which then hung over their Heads was only a Dream, the wild Effects of ill-grounded imaginary Fears; and young Men, as if they had never heard from their Fathers, nor read of what passed in this Kingdom, at a Period no farther backward than the Space of Five and Twenty Years.

I flatter my self, that if the Passages which happened in those Days, the Resolutions of the Nation thereupon, and the just Provisions made from Time to Time against our falling into the same Disasters, were fairly stated and laid in one View, all indirect Arts and mean Subtleties practised to weaken our Securities would be frustrated, and vanish before the glaring Light of Law and Reason.

I shall not govern my self on this Occasion by the partial Relation of particular Persons or Parties, but by the Sense of the whole People, by the Sense of the Houses of Lords and Commons, the representative Body of the whole Nation; in whose Resolutions, according to the different State of Things, the Condition of the Kingdom, by those who had the greatest Stakes in it, has been from time to time plainly, impartially, and pathetically expressed.

I shall begin with the Act of Parliament made in *England* in the second Session of the first Year of the late King *William* and Queen *Mary*, entituled, *An Act declaring the Rights and Liberties of the Subject, and settling the Succession of the Crown.*

It carries in it the noble Resentment of a People that had been just rescued from Tyranny; and yet, that they might justify their Actions to Posterity, it recites all the particular Instances of the Tyrannical Reign in a plain and dispassionate Simplicity. The Act runs as follows.

" Whereas the Lords Spiritual and Temporal, and Commons assembled at *Westminster*, lawfully, fully, and freely representing all the Estates of the People of this Realm, did upon the 13th Day of *February*, in the Year of our Lord 1688, present unto their Majesties, then called and known by the Names and Stile of *William* and *Mary*, Prince and Princess of *Orange*, being present in their proper Persons, a certain Declaration in Writing, made by the said Lords and Commons in the Words following, *viz.*

" Whereas the late King *James* the Second, by the Assistance of divers evil Counsellors, Judges, and Ministers employed by him, did endeavour to subvert and extirpate the Protestant Religion, and the Laws and Liberties of this Kingdom;

" By assuming and exercising a Power of dispensing with and

suspending of Laws, and the Execution of Laws, without Consent of Parliament;

" By committing and prosecuting divers worthy Prelates, for humbly petitioning to be excused from concurring to the said assumed Power;

" By issuing, and causing to be executed, a Commission under the Great Seal for erecting a Court called the Court of Commissioners for Ecclesiastical Causes;

" By levying Money for, and to the Use of the Crown, by Pretence of Prerogative, for other Time, and in other Manner, than the same was granted by Parliament;

" By raising and keeping a Standing Army within this Kingdom in Time of Peace without Consent of Parliament, and quartering Soldiers contrary to Law;

" By causing several good Subjects, being Protestants, to be disarmed at the same time when Papists were both armed and employed, contrary to Law;

" By violating the Freedom of Election of Members to serve in Parliament;

" By Prosecutions in the Court of *King's-Bench* for Matters and Causes cognizable only in Parliament, and by divers other arbitrary and illegal Courses:

" And whereas of late Years partial, corrupt, and unqualified Persons have been returned and served on Juries, in Trials, and particularly divers Jurors in Trials for High Treason which were not Free-holders;

"And excessive Bail hath been required of Persons committed in criminal Cases, to elude the Benefit of the Laws made for the Liberty of the Subjects;

"And excessive Fines have been imposed,

"And illegal and cruel Punishments inflicted,

"And several Grants and Promises made of Fines and Forfeitures, before any Conviction or Judgment against the Persons upon whom the same were to be levied:

"All which are utterly and directly contrary to the known Laws, and Statutes, and Freedom of this Realm.

"And whereas the said late King *James* the IId having abdicated the Government, and the Throne being thereby vacant,

" His Highness the Prince of *Orange* (whom it hath pleased

Almighty God to make the glorious Instrument of delivering this Kingdom from Popery and Arbitrary Power) did (by the Advice of the Lords Spiritual and Temporal, and divers principal Persons of the Commons) cause Letters to be written to the Lords Spiritual and Temporal, being Protestants, and other Letters to the several Countries, Cities, Universities, Boroughs, and Cinque-Ports, for the chusing of such Persons to represent them as were of Right to be sent to Parliament, to meet and sit at *Westminster* upon the two and twentieth Day of *January*, in this Year One thousand six hundred eighty and eight, in order to such an Establishment, as that their Religion, Laws, and Liberties might not again be in Danger of being subverted, upon which Letters Elections having been accordingly made.

"And thereupon the said Lords Spiritual and Temporal, and Commons, pursuant to their respective Letters and Elections, being now assembled in a full and free Representative of this Nation, taking into their most serious Consideration the best Means for attaining the Ends aforesaid, do, in the first place, *as their Ancestors in like Cases have usually done* for the vindicating and asserting their ancient Rights and Liberties, declare,

" That the pretended Power of suspending of Laws, or the Execution of Laws, by Regal Authority, without Consent of Parliament, is illegal.

" That the pretended Power of dispensing with Laws, or the Execution of Laws by Regal Authority, as it hath been assumed and exercised of late, is illegal.

" That the Commission for erecting the late Court of Commissioners for Ecclesiastical Causes, and all other Commissions and Courts of like Nature, are illegal and pernicious.

" That levying Money for, or to the Use of the Crown, by Pretence of Prerogative, without Grant of Parliament, for longer Time or in other Manner than the same is or shall be granted, is illegal.

" That it is the Right of the Subjects to petition the King, and all Commitments and Prosecutions for such Petitioning are illegal.

" That the raising or keeping a Standing Army within the Kingdom in Time of Peace, unless it be with Consent of Parliament, is against Law.

"That the Subjects which are Protestants, may have Arms for their Defence suitable to their Conditions, and as allowed by Law.

"That Elections of Members ought to be free.

"That the Freedom of Speech and Debates, or Proceedings in Parliament, ought not to be impeached or questioned in any Court or Place out of Parliament.

"That excessive Bail ought not to be required, nor excessive Fines imposed, nor cruel and unusual Punishments inflicted.

"That Jurors ought to be duly impannel'd, and returned, and Jurors which pass upon Men in Trials for High-Treason ought to be Freeholders.

"That all Grants, and Promises of Fines, and Forfeitures of particular Persons before Conviction, are illegal and void.

"And that for Redress of all Grievances, and for the amending, strengthning, and preserving of the Laws, Parliaments ought to be held frequently.

"And they do claim, demand, and insist upon all, and singular the Premises, as their undoubted Rights and Liberties. And that no Declarations, Judgments, Doings, or Proceedings to the Prejudice of the People in any of the said Premises, ought in any wise to be drawn hereafter into Consequence or Example.

"To which Demand of their Rights, they are particularly encouraged by the Declaration of his Highness the Prince of *Orange*, as being the only Means for obtaining a full Redress and Remedy therein.

"Having therefore an entire Confidence, that his said Highness the Prince of *Orange* will perfect the Deliverance so far advanced by him, and will still preserve them from the Violation of their Rights which they have here asserted, and from all other Attempts upon their Religion, Rights and Liberties;

"The said Lords Spiritual and Temporal, and Commons assembled at *Westminster*, do Resolve,

"That *William* and *Mary*, Prince and Princess of *Orange*, be, and be declared King and Queen of *England*, *France*, and *Ireland*, and the Dominions thereunto belonging; to hold the Crown and Royal Dignity of the said Kingdoms and Dominions, to them the said Prince and Princess during their Lives, and the

Life of the Survivor of them: and that the sole and full Exercise of the Regal Power be only in, and executed by the said Prince of *Orange*, in the Names of the said Prince and Princess during their joint Lives; and after their Deceases, the said Crown and Royal Dignity of the said Kingdoms and Dominions, to be to the Heirs of the Body of the said Princess; and for Default of such Issue, to the Princess *Anne* of *Denmark*, and the Heirs of her Body; and for Default of such Issue, to the Heirs of the Body of the said Prince of *Orange*.

"And the Lords Spiritual and Temporal, and Commons, do pray the said Prince and Princess to accept the same accordingly.

"And that the Oaths hereafter mentioned be taken by all Persons, of whom the Oaths of Allegiance and Supremacy might be required by Law, instead of them; and that the said Oaths of Allegiance and Supremacy be abrogated."

"I A. B. *do sincerely promise and swear, that I will be faithful, and bear true Allegiance to their Majesties King* William *and Queen* Mary.

So help me God.

"I A. B. *do swear, that I do from my Heart abhor, detest, and abjure, as Impious and Heretical, this damnable Doctrine and Position, that Princes excommunicated or deprived by the Pope, or any Authority of the See of Rome, may be Deposed or Murdered by their Subjects, or any other whatsoever.*

"*And I do declare, that no foreign Prince, Person, Prelate, State, or Potentate, hath, or ought to have, any Jurisdiction, Power, Superiority, Preheminence or Authority, Ecclesiastical or Spiritual, within this Realm.*   So help me God.

" Upon which their said Majesties did accept the Crown, and Royal Dignity of the Kingdoms of *England*, *France* and *Ireland*, and the Dominions thereunto belonging, according to the Resolution and Desire of the said Lords and Commons contained in the said Declaration.

"And thereupon their Majesties were pleased, that the said Lords Spiritual and Temporal, and Commons, being the two Houses of Parliament, should continue to sit, and with their

11

Majesties Royal Concurrence, make effectual Provision for the
Settlement of the Religion, Laws and Liberties of this Kingdom;
so that the same for the future might not be in Danger again
of being subverted; to which the said Lords Spiritual and Temporal, and Commons did agree, and proceed to Act accordingly.

" Now in pursuance of the Premises, the said Lords Spiritual
and Temporal, and Commons in Parliament assembled, for the
ratifying, confirming, and establishing the said Declaration, and
the Articles, Clauses, Matters, and things therein contained, by
the Force of a Law made in due Form by Authority of Parliament, do pray that it may be declared and enacted, that all and
singular the Rights and Liberties asserted and claimed in the
said Declaration, are the true ancient and indubitable Rights
and Liberties of the People of this Kingdom, and so shall be
esteemed, allowed, adjudged, deemed, and taken to be; and
that all and every the Particulars aforesaid shall be firmly and
strictly holden and observed, as they are expressed in the said
Declaration; and all Officers and Ministers whatsoever, shall
serve their Majesties and their Successors according to the same
in all Times to come.

"And the said Lords Spiritual and Temporal, and Commons,
seriously considering how it hath pleased Almighty God, in his
marvellous Providence and merciful Goodness to this Nation,
to provide and preserve their said Majesties Royal Persons most
happily to Reign over us upon the Throne of their Ancestors,
for which they render unto him from the bottom of their Hearts,
their humblest Thanks and Praises, do truly, firmly, assuredly,
and in the Sincerity of their Hearts think, and do hereby *recog-
nize, acknowledge*, and *declare*, that King *James* II. having
Abdicated the Government, and their Majesties having accepted
the Crown and Royal Dignity as aforesaid, their said Majesties
did become, were, are, and of Right ought to be by the *Laws of
this Realm*, our Sovereign Liege Lord and Lady King and Queen
of *England*, *France* and *Ireland*, and the Dominions thereunto
belonging; in, and to whose Princely Persons, the Royal State,
Crown and Dignity of the said Realms, with all Honours, Stiles,
Titles, Regalities, Prerogatives, Powers, Jurisdictions and
Authorities to the same belonging and appertaining, are most
fully, rightfully, and entirely invested and incorporated, united
and annexed.

"And for preventing all Questions and Divisions in this Realm, by reason of any pretended Titles to the Crown, and for preserving a Certainty in the Succession thereof, in, and upon which the Unity, Peace, Tranquility and Safety of this Nation doth, under God, wholly consist and depend;

" The said Lords Spiritual and Temporal, and Commons, do beseech their Majesties, That it may be enacted, established and declared, that the Crown and Regal Government of the said Kingdoms and Dominions, with all and singular Premises thereunto belonging and appertaining, shall be and continue to their said Majesties, and the Survivor of them, during their Lives, and the Life of the Survivor of them; and that the entire, perfect, and full Exercise of the Regal Power and Government be only in and executed by his Majesty, in the Names of both their Majesties during their joint Lives; and after their Deceases, the said Crown and Premises shall be and remain to the Heirs of the Body of her Majesty; and for Default of such Issue, to her Royal Highness the Princess *Anne* of *Denmark*, and the Heirs of her Body; and for Default of such Issue, to the Heirs of the Body of his said Majesty. And thereunto the said Lords Spiritual and Temporal, and Commons, do in the Name of all the People aforesaid, *most humbly and faithfully submit themselves, their Heirs, and Posterities for ever.* And do faithfully promise that they will stand to, maintain, and defend their said Majesties, and also the Limitation and Succession of the Crown herein specified and contained, to the utmost of their Powers, with their Lives and Estates, against all Persons whatsoever that shall attempt any thing to the contrary.

" And whereas it hath been found by Experience, that it is inconsistent with the Safety and Welfare of this Protestant Kingdom, to be governed by a Popish Prince, or by any King or Queen marrying a Papist;

" The said Lords Spiritual and Temporal, and Commons, do further pray, That it may be enacted, that all and every Person and Persons that is, are, or *shall be reconciled to*, or shall hold Communion with the See or Church of *Rome*, or shall profess the Popish Religion, or shall marry a Papist, shall be excluded, and be for ever uncapable to inherit, possess, or enjoy the Crown and Government of this Realm, and *Ireland*, and the

Dominions thereunto belonging, or any part of the same; or to have, use, or exercise any Regal Power Authority or Jurisdiction within the same; and in all, and every such Case, or Cases, the People of these Realms shall be, and are hereby absolved of their Allegiance; and the said Crown and Government shall from time to time descend to, and be enjoyed by such Person, or Persons, being Protestants, as should have inherited and enjoyed the same, in case the said Person or Persons so reconciled, holding Communion, or Professing or Marrying as aforesaid, were naturally dead.

"And that every King and Queen of this Realm, who any time hereafter shall come to, and succeed in the Imperial Crown of this Kingdom, shall, on the first Day of the Meeting of the first Parliament, next after his or her coming to the Crown, sitting in his or her Throne in the House of Peers, in the Presence of the Lords and Commons therein assembled, or at his or her Coronation, before such Person or Persons who shall Administer the Coronation Oath to him or her, at the time of his or her taking the said Oath, (which shall first happen) make, subscribe, and audibly repeat the Declaration mentioned in the Statute made in the thirtieth Year of the Reign of King *Charles* the IId, entitled, *An Act for the more effectual preserving the King's Person and Government, by disabling Papists from sitting in either House of Parliament.* But if it shall happen, that such King or Queen, upon his or her Succession to the Crown of this Realm, shall be under the Age of twelve Years, then every such King or Queen shall make, subscribe, and audibly repeat the said Declaration at his or her Coronation, on the first Day of the meeting of the first Parliament as aforesaid, which shall first happen, after such King or Queen shall have attained the said Age of Twelve Years.

"All which their Majesties are contented, and pleased, shall be declared, enacted, and established, by Authority of this present Parliament, and shall stand, remain, and be, *the Law of this Realm for ever*; and the same are by their said Majesties, by and with the Advice and Consent of the Lords Spiritual and Temporal, and Commons in Parliament assembled, and by the Authority of the same, declared, enacted, and established accordingly.

"And be it further declared and enacted by the Authority aforesaid, that from, and after this present Session of Parliament, no Dispensation by *Non Obstante*, of or to any Statute, or part thereof, shall be allowed, but that the same shall be held void, and of no Effect, except a Dispensation be allowed of in such Statute, and except in such Cases as shall be especially provided for by one or more Bill, or Bills, to be passed, during the present Session of Parliament.

" Provided that no Charter, or Grant, or Pardon, granted before the Three and twentieth Day of *October*, in the Year of our Lord 1689, shall be any ways Impeached or Invalidated by this Act, but that the same shall be, and remain of the same Force and Effect in Law, and no other, than as if this Act had never been made."

I have recited the Act at large, that I might on the one Hand shew the just Sense the *English Nation* then had of their Deliverance, and their Gratitude to their Deliverer the glorious King *William*; and on the other Hand, avoid being censured for heaping more Miscarriages upon that unhappy Prince King *James*, than a Nation, whose Religion, Liberties, Fortunes, and Lives were just snatched from the Brink of Ruin, thought fit to charge him with. And here, that I may do Justice to the *Scots* Nation as well as to the *English*, I shall also set down, as succinctly as I can, what that brave People did in this important Juncture.

The Convention of the Lords and Commons in the Beginning of the Year 1689, came to the Resolutions in Substance as follow, (*viz.*)

" That whereas King *James* the VIIth, being a professed Papist, did assume the Royal Power, and act as King, without ever taking the Oath required by Law, whereby every King at his Accession to the Government was obliged to swear to maintain the *Protestant Religion*, and to rule the People according to the laudable Laws: And by the Advice of wicked Counsellors, did invade the fundamental Constitution of the Kingdom of *Scotland*, and altered it from a legal limited Monarchy to an arbitrary and despotick Power; and in a publick Proclamation asserted an absolute Power to annul and disable all Laws, particularly by arraigning the Laws establishing the Protestant

Religion, and exerted that Power to the Subversion of the Protestant Religion, and to the Violation of the Laws and Liberties of the Kingdom.

" By erecting publick Schools and Societies of the Jesuits, and not only allowing Mass to be publickly said, but also converting Protestant Chappels and Churches to publick Mass-houses, contrary to the express Laws against saying and hearing Mass.

" By allowing Popish Books to be printed and dispersed by a Patent to a Popish Printer, designing him Printer to His Majesty's Household, College, and Chappel, contrary to Law.

" By taking the Children of Protestant Noblemen and Gentlemen, sending them abroad to be bred Papists, and bestowing Pensions upon Priests to pervert Protestants from their Religion by Offers of Places and Preferments.

" By discharging Protestants, at the same Time he employed Papists in Places of greatest Trust both Civil and Military, &c. and intrusting the Forts and Magazines in their Hands.

" By imposing Oaths contrary to Law.

" By exacting Money without Consent of Parliament or Convention of Estates.

" By levying and keeping up a standing Army in Time of Peace, without Consent of Parliament, and maintaining them upon free Quarter.

" By employing the Officers of the Army as Judges throughout the Kingdom, by whom the Subjects were put to Death without legal Tryal, Jury, or Record.

" By imposing exorbitant Fines to the Value of the Parties Estates, exacting extravagant Bail, and disposing Fines and Forfeitures before any Process or Conviction.

" By imprisoning Persons without expressing the Reason, and delaying to bring them to Tryal.

" By causing several Persons to be prosecuted, and their Estates to be forfeited upon Stretches of old and obsolete Laws, upon weak and frivolous Pretences, and upon lame and defective Proofs; as particularly the late Earl of *Argyle*, to the Scandal of the Justice of the Nation.

" By subverting the Rights of the Royal Boroughs, the Third Estate of Parliament, imposing upon them not only Magistrates, but also the whole Town Council and Clerks, contrary to their

Liberties and express Charters, without any Pretence of Sentence, Surrender, or Consent; so that the Commissioners to Parliament being chosen by the Magistrates and Councils, the King might in Effect as well nominate the Estate of Parliament: Besides that, many of the Magistrates by him put in were Papists, and the Boroughs were forc'd to pay Money for the Letters imposing those illegal Magistrates upon them.

" By sending Letters to the chief Courts of Justice, not only ordering the Judges to stop *sine Die*, but also commanding how to proceed in Cases depending before them, contrary to the express Laws; and by changing the Nature of the Judges Patents *ad Vitam* or *Culpam*, into a Commission *de bene Placito*, to dispose them to a Compliance with arbitrary Courses, and turning them out of their Offices if they refused to comply.

" By granting personal Protections for Civil Debts contrary to Law.

"All which Miscarriages of King *James*, were utterly and directly contrary to the known Laws, Freedoms, and Statutes of the Realm of *Scotland*. Upon which Grounds and Reasons the Estates of the Kingdom of Scotland did find and declare, that the said King *James* had forfeited the Crown, and the Throne was become vacant.

" Therefore in regard His Royal Highness then Prince of *Orange*, since King of *England*, whom it hath pleased God to make the glorious Instrument of delivering these Kingdoms from Popery and arbitrary Power, by Advice of several Lords and Gentlemen of the *Scots* Nation then at *London*, did call the Estates of this Kingdom to meet upon the 14th of *March* last, in order to such an Establishment as that the Religion, Laws, and Liberties might not again be in Danger of being subverted; The said Estates being then assembled accordingly, in a full and free Representative of the Nation, did in the first Place, as *their Ancestors in like Cases had usually done* for vindicating and asserting their ancient Rights and Liberties, declare,

" That by the Law of *Scotland* no Papist could be King or Queen of the Realm, nor bear any Office therein; nor that any Protestant Successor could exercise the Regal Power, till they had sworn the Coronation Oath.

" That all Proclamations asserting an absolute Power to null and disable Laws, in order for erecting Schools and Colleges for Jesuits, converting Protestant Churches and Chappels into Mass-houses, and the allowing Mass to be said; and the allowing Popish Books to be printed and dispersed was contrary to Law.

" That the taking the Children of Noblemen, Gentlemen, and others, and keeping them abroad to be bred Papists;

" The making Funds and Donations to Popish Schools and Colleges, the bestowing Pensions on Priests, and the seducing Protestants from their Religion by Offers of Places and Preferments, was contrary to Law.

" That the disarming of Protestants, and employing Papists in the greatest Places of Trust both Civil and Military, was contrary to Law.

" That the imposing an Oath without Authority of Parliament, was contrary to Law.

" That the raising of Money without Consent of Parliament or Convention, was contrary to Law.

" That employing the Officers of the Army as Judges, was contrary to Law.

" That the imposing extraordinary Fines, &c. was contrary to Law.

" That the imprisoning of Persons without expressing the Reasons, was contrary to Law.

" That the prosecuting and seizing Men's Estates as forfeited upon Stretches of old and obsolete Laws, &c. was contrary to Law.

" That the nominating and imposing Magistrates, &c. upon Boroughs, contrary to their express Charters, was contrary to Law.

" That the sending Letters to the Courts of Justice, ordering the Judges to desist from determining of Causes, and ordering them how to proceed in Causes depending before them, &c. was contrary to Law.

" That the granting of Personal Protections, &c. was contrary to Law.

" That the forcing the Subjects to depose against themselves in capital Causes, however the Punishments were restricted, was contrary to Law.

" That the using *Torture* without Evidence, or in ordinary Crimes, was contrary to Law.

" That the sending of an Army in a warlike Manner into any Part of the Kingdom in Time of Peace, and exacting Locality and Free-Quarters, was contrary to Law.

" That the charging the Subjects with Law-Boroughs at the King's Instance, and imposing Bonds without Authority of Parliament, and the suspending Advocates for not appearing when Bonds were offered, was contrary to Law.

" That the putting Garrisons into private Houses in Time of Peace, without Authority of Parliament, was illegal.

" That the Opinions of the Lords of the Session in the two Cases following, were Illegal; (*viz.*) That the concerting the Demand of the Supply of a Fore-faulted Person, although not given, was Treason; and that Persons refusing to discover their private Thoughts in relation to Points of Treason, or other Mens Actions, are guilty of Treason.

" That the fining Husbands for their Wives withdrawing from Church, was Illegal.

" That Prelacy and Superiority of an Office in the Church above Presbyters, is, and has been a great and unsupportable Burden to this Nation, and contrary to the Inclinations of the Generality of the People ever since the Reformation, they having reformed Popery by Presbytery, and therefore ought to be abolished.

" That it is the Right and Privilege of the Subject, to protest for Remedy of Law, to the King and Parliament, against Sentences pronounced by the Lords of the Sessions, provided the same does not stop Executions of the said Sentences.

" That it is the Right of the Subject to petition the King, and that all Prosecutions and Imprisonments for such petitioning, were contrary to Law.

" Therefore for the Redress of all Grievances, and for the amending, strengthening, and preserving the Laws, they claimed that Parliaments ought to be frequently called, and allowed to sit, and Freedom of Speech and Debate allowed the Members; and further claimed, and insisted upon all, and sundry the Premises, as their undoubted Rights and Liberties; and that no Declaration, or Proceedings, to the Prejudice of the People, in any the said Premises, ought in any wise to be drawn hereafter in Example; but that all Forfeitures, Fines, Loss of Offices, Imprisonments, Banishments, Prosecutions, and rigorous Executions be considered, and the Parties redressed.

"To which Demand of their Rights, and Redress of their Grievances, they took themselves to be encouraged by the King of *England*'s Declaration for the Kingdom of *Scotland* in *October* last, as being the only Means for obtaining a full Redress and Remedy therein.

"Therefore for as much as they had an entire Confidence, that his Majesty of *England* would perfect the Deliverance, so far advanced by him, and would still preserve them from the Violation of the Rights which they had asserted, and from all other Attempts upon their Religion, Laws, and Liberties;

"The Estates of the Kingdom of *Scotland* had resolved,

"That *William* and *Mary*, King and Queen of *England*, be declared King and Queen of *Scotland*, to hold the Crown and Royal Dignity of the said Kingdom, to them the said King and Queen during their Lives, and the longer Liver of them; and that the sole and full Exercise of the Power be only in, and exercised by him the said King, in the Names of the said King and Queen, during their joint Lives; and after their Deceases, that the said Crown and Royal Dignity, be to the Heirs of the Body of the said Queen; which failing, to Princess *Anne* of *Denmark,* and the Heirs of her Body; which also failing, to the Heirs of the Body of the said *William*, King of *England*. And then prayed the said King and Queen to accept the same accordingly." Which being accepted by their Majesties, they were proclaimed King and Queen of *Scotland*, the same Day that they were Crowned King and Queen of *England*.

The above-mentioned Acts of Settlement of the respective Crowns of *England* and *Scotland* ought to be written in the Hearts of every True *Briton*, and engraven on Columns of Brass, to be erected in all the Cities and Boroughs of this Island, that Posterity may know how much their Ancestors suffered, and how much more they were in Danger of suffering, from a Popish Prince; and that they may with Gratitude reverence the Memory of their glorious Deliverer the immortal King *William*, to whom, under God, are owing whatever Rights, whether Religious or Civil, they or their latest Posterity shall enjoy.

Thus appear the Causes each Nation had for the late Revolution, and the just Reasons for limiting the Entail of their respective Crowns in the Manner abovementioned.

They at that Time doubtless hoped they should for ever be made happy in a Descent of Protestant Princes, either from the late Queen *Mary*, Princess *Anne* of *Denmark*, or the late King *William*, and therefore saw no Necessity for extending the Limitation further; but the Death of that incomparable Princess, the late Queen *Mary*, on the 28th of *December* 1694, followed by the Death of that hopeful Royal Infant the Duke of *Gloucester*, the only surviving Issue of the Princess of *Denmark*, on the 29th of *July* 1700, gave fresh Alarms to the *English* Nation.

They saw the Entail of the Crown reduced to the Lives of the late King *William* and Her present Majesty, then Princess of *Denmark*.

They saw the Hopes of a Popish Jacobite Party taking new Spirit, and beginning to revive.

They saw a long Train of Popish Princes of the Blood next in Descent after the Demises of the late King *William* and the Princess of *Denmark* without Issue; they remembered the Danger they had so lately been in from one Popish Prince, and therefore thought it high time to take all necessary Cautions to prevent the same for the future from a numerous Train of Roman Catholick Princes, all, or most of whom, were very near in Blood to a neighbouring Monarch, the most powerful Prince in *Europe*, whose Interest, as well as Inclination, might engage him to support their Pretensions with his whole Force.

This prudent Foresight gave Birth to another Act of Parliament in *England* in the 12th and 13th Years of the Reign of the late King *William*, entituled, *An Act for the further Limitation of the Crown, and better securing the Rights and Liberties of the Subject.* " By this Act the most Illustrious Princess *Sophia*, Electress and Dutchess Dowager of *Hanover*, is declared the next in Succession in the Protestant Line to the Crown of *England*, after the late King *William* and the Princess *Anne* of *Denmark*, and their respective Issue; and that from and after the Deceases of his said Majesty and the Princess *Anne* of *Denmark*, and the Heirs of their respective Bodies, the Crown should be, remain, and continue to the said Princess *Sophia*, and the Heirs of her Body, being Protestants.

"And thereunto the Lords Spiritual and Temporal, and Commons, in the Name of all the People of this Realm, did most humbly and faithfully submit themselves, their Heirs, and Posterities; and did faithfully promise, that after the Deceases of his Majesty and her Royal Highness, and the Failure of the Heirs of their respective Bodies, to stand by, maintain and defend the said Princess *Sophia*, and the Heirs of her Body, being Protestants, according to the Limitation and Succession of the Crown in this Act specified and contained, to the utmost of their Powers, with their Lives and Estates, against all Persons whatsoever that shall attempt any thing to the contrary."

In the 13th and 14th Years of the said King, two other Acts of Parliament were made; the one entitled, *An Act of Attainder of the Pretended Prince of* Wales *of High Treason*; whereby it was enacted, "That he be attainted of High Treason, and suffer Pains of Death, as a Traytor; and that if any Subject of *England* shall, within this Realm, or without, after the First of *March*, 1701, hold, entertain, or keep any Intelligence or Correspondence, in Person, or by Letters, Messages, or otherwise, with the said Pretended Prince of *Wales*, or with any Person, or Persons, employed by Him, knowing such Person to be so employed by Him, or shall by Bill of Exchange, or otherwise, remit, or pay any Sum or Sums of Mony, for the Use or Service of the said Pretended Prince of *Wales*, knowing such Mony to be for such Use or Service, such Person, so offending, being lawfully convicted, shall be taken, deemed, and adjudged guilty of High Treason, and shall suffer and forfeit as in Cases of High Treason. And where any Offence against this Act shall be committed out of this Realm, the same may be alleged, laid, enquired of, and Tryed in any County of this Kingdom of *England*."

And the other, Entitled, *An Act for the further Security of His Majesty's Person, and the Succession of the Crown in the Protestant Line, and for extinguishing the Hopes of the Pretended Prince of Wales, and all other Pretenders, and their open and secret Abettors.* "Wherein reciting the said former Acts of Settlement of the Crown, and that the *French* King, in hopes of disturbing the Peace and Repose of his Majesty, and his Kingdoms, and creating Divisions therein, had caused the Pretended Prince of *Wales* to be Proclaimed King of *England*, *Scotland*, and *Ireland*, by the Name of *James* the Third; and that the said Pretended Prince had assumed the said Title, in open Defiance of the Provisions made for the Establishment of the Title, and Succession of the Crown, by the said several Acts of Parliament: To the Intent therefore that the said Acts might be for ever inviolably preserved, and that all future Questions, and Divisions, by reason of any pretended Titles to the Crown, might be prevented, it was enacted, That all and every Person and Persons, as well Peers as Commoners, that shall bear Office Civil or Military, or receive Pay, Fee, or Wages, or have Command, or Place of Trust from his Majesty, or in the Service of his Majesty, Prince *George*, or Princess *Anne* of *Denmark*, all Ecclesiastical Persons, or Members of Colleges and Halls, of the Foundation in either University, being Eighteen Years old, all Persons teaching Pupils, all School-masters, Ushers, Preachers, and Teachers of separate Congregations, Persons that shall act as Serjeants at Law, Counsellors, Advocates, Attorneys, Sollicitors, Proctors, Clerks, or Notaries by practising as such in any Court, and all Peers and Members of the *House of Commons*, before they can Vote in their respective Houses of Parliament, should be obliged to take the Oath herein after mentioned, commonly called *The Abjuration Oath*; which Oath was expressed in the following Words.

" I A. B. *do truly and sincerely Acknowledge, Profess, Testifie and Declare, in my Conscience, before God and the World, That our Sovereign Lord King* William *is Lawful and Rightful King of this Realm, and of all other his Majesties Dominions and Countries thereunto belonging; and I do solemnly and sincerely declare, that I do believe in my Conscience, that the Person pretended to be Prince of* Wales, *during the Life of the late King* James, *and since his Decease pretending to be, and taking upon himself the Stile and Title of* King *of* England, *by the Name of* James *the Third, hath not any Right or Title whatsoever to the Crown of this Realm, or any other the Dominions thereunto belonging; and I do renounce, refuse, and abjure, any Allegiance or Obedience to him. And I do swear, that I will bear Faith, and true Allegiance to his Majesty King* William, *and Him will defend, to the utmost of my Power, against all Traiterous Conspiracies and Attempts whatsoever, which shall be made against his Person, Crown, or Dignity; and I will do my best Endeavour to disclose and make known to his Majesty, and his Successors, all Treasons and Traiterous Conspiracies, which I shall know to be against Him, or any of them; and I do faithfully promise, to the utmost of my Power, to support, maintain and defend the Limitation and Succession of the Crown, against Him, the said* James, *and all other Persons whatsover, as the same is and stands limited (by an Act, Entitled,* An Act declaring the Rights and Liberties of the Subject, and settling the Succession of the Crown) *to his Majesty, during his Majesty's Life, and after his Majesty's Decease to the Princess* Anne *of* Denmark, *and the Heirs of her Body, being Protestants, and for Default of such Issue to the Heirs of the Body of his Majesty, being Protestants; and as the same by one other Act, Entitled,* An Act for the further Limitations of the Crown, and better securing the Rights and Liberties of the Subject, *is, and stands Limited after the Decease of his Majesty, and the Princess* Anne *of* Denmark; *and for Default of Issue of the said Princess, and of his Majesty respectively, To the Princess* Sophia, *Electress and Dutchess Dowager of* Hanover, *and the Heirs of her Body, being Protestants. And all these Things I do plainly and sincerely acknowledge, and swear, according to these express Words by me spoken, and according to the plain and common Sense and Understanding of these same Words, without any Equivocation, mental Evasion, or secret Reservation whatsoever; and I do make this Recognition, Acknowledgement, Abjuration, Renunciation, and Promise, heartly, willingly, and truly, upon the true Faith of a Christian.*

So help me God.

"And it was thereby also enacted, That if any Person or Persons, at any time after the 25th Day of *March*, 1702, should compass or imagine the Death of her Royal Highness the Princess *Anne of Denmark*, or endeavour to deprive or hinder her from succeeding to the Imperial Crown of this Realm, and the Dominions and Territories thereunto belonging, after the

Demise of his Majesty, and the same maliciously, advisedly and directly shall attempt, by any Overt-Act, or Deed, every such Offence shall be adjudged High Treason, and the Offender and Offenders therein, their Abetters, Procurers, and Counsellors, and all and every their Aiders and Comforters, knowing the said Offence to be done, being thereof Convicted, or Attainted, according to the Laws and Statutes of this Realm, shall be deemed and adjudged Traitors, and shall suffer Pains of Death, and all Losses and Forfeitures, as in Cases of High Treason."

Thus our great Deliverer accomplished His Work.

He would have thought it but half done, if he had deliver'd only one Generation from Popery and Slavery; and therefore made it his whole Care, and spent the last Remains of his invaluable Life, in contriving how the most pure Religion, and the best Laws in the Universe, might be transmitted to late Posterity.

The last mentioned Acts of Parliament, are the Legacy that great Prince left the *English* Nation, infinitely more valuable than if he had, without them, left Palaces and Principalities to each of his Subjects.

The Memory of that great Benefactor to Mankind will always be dear to every *Briton*, who loves the Religion and Laws of his Country, and is an Enemy to Popery and Arbitrary Power, and to every Man who knows the Happiness of a limited Monarchy circumscribed and fenced about with the Bulwarks of Laws, which equally guard the Subject from the Invasion of the Prince, and the Prince from the Insults of the Subject.

His Vigilance was not confined to his Kingdom of *England*; the Happiness of the Kingdom of *Scotland* was equally his Care and Study. He zealously attempted to have had the Succession to the Crown of that Kingdom settled also on the House of *Hanover*, in the same manner as that of *England* was settled, and to have united both Kingdoms; but these High Benefits were reserved by Heaven to be numbered amongst the Glories of her present Majesty's Reign, a Reign attended with so many Victories obtained by her Arms Abroad, under the Conduct of her renown'd General, the Duke of *Marlborough*; and with so many Acts of Benevolence at Home, by the Advice of the best and wisest Council that ever Prince employed, that as it has excelled the Transactions of all former Ages, so it will be a lasting Pattern for the Imitation of all which shall succeed.

Her Majesty was but just seated on her Throne, when with the same Goodness towards her Subjects, in the first Year of her Reign, she gives the Royal Assent to an Act of Parliament, Entitled, *An Act for enlarging the Time for taking the Oath of Abjuration; and also for recapacitating and indemnifying such Persons as have not taken the same by the Time limited, and shall take the same by a Time to be appointed; and for the further Security of Her Majesty's Person, and the Succession of the Crown in the Protestant Line, and for extinguishing the Hopes of the Pretended Prince of Wales, and all other Pretenders, and their open and secret Abettors.*

In which, amongst other things, it is Enacted, " That if any Person or Persons, at any time after the first Day of *March* 1702, shall endeavour to deprive, or hinder any Person who shall be the next in Succession to the Crown, for the time being, according to the Limitations in an Act, Entitled, *An Act declaring the Rights and Liberties of the Subject, and settling the Succession of the Crown*; and according to another [2] Act, Entitled, *An Act for the further Limitation of the Crown, and better securing the Rights and Liberties of the Subject,* from succeeding after the Decease of her Majesty, to the Imperial Crown of this Realm, and the Dominions and Territories thereunto belonging, according to the Limitations in the beforementioned Acts, that is to say, such Issue of her Majesty's Body, as shall from time to time be next in Succession to the Crown, if it shall please God Almighty to bless her Majesty with Issue; and during the time her Majesty shall have no Issue, the Princess *Sophia*, Electress and Dutchess Dowager of *Hanover*; and after the Decease of the said Princess *Sophia*, the next in Succession to the Crown, for the time being, according to the Limitation of the said Acts; and the same, maliciously, advisedly, and directly, shall attempt by any Overt-Act, or Deed; every such Offence shall be adjudged High Treason, and the Offender or Offenders therein, their Abettors, Procurers, and Comforters, knowing the said Offence to be done, being thereof Convicted or Attainted, according to the Laws, and Statutes of this Realm, shall be deemed and adjudged Traitors, and shall suffer Pains of Death, and all Losses and Forfeitures, as in Cases of High Treason."

Her Majesty in the Fourth Year of her Reign, gave the Royal Assent to an Act, Entitled, *An Act for the Naturalization of the most Excellent Princess* Sophia, *Electress and Dutchess Dowager* of Hanover, *and the Issue of her Body*; by which it is enacted, That the said Princess *Sophia*, and the Issue of her Body, and all Persons lineally descending from her, born or hereafter to be born, be, and shall be, to all Intents and Purposes whatsoever, deemed, taken, and esteemed Natural-born Subjects of this Kingdom, as if the said Princess, and the Issue of her Body, and all Persons lineally descending from her, born, or hereafter to be born, had been born within this Realm of *England*, any Law, Statute, Matter, or Thing whatsoever to the contrary notwithstanding. With a Proviso, that every Person who shall be Naturalized by Virtue of this Act, and shall become a Papist, or profess the Popish Religion, shall not enjoy any Benefit or Advantage of a Natural-born Subject of *England*, but shall be judged [3] an Alien.

And in the Fourth and Fifth Year of her Majesty's Reign another Act passed the Royal Assent, Entitled, *An Act for the better securing her Majesty's Person and Government, and of the Succession to the Crown of* England *in the Protestant Line*; by which, amongst other things, it is Enacted, "That if any Person or Persons, from and after the 25th Day of *March* 1706, shall maliciously, advisedly and directly, by Writing or Printing, declare, maintain, and affirm, that our Sovereign Lady the Queen, that now is, is not the Lawful or Rightful Queen of these Realms; or that the Pretended Prince of *Wales*, who now stiles himself King of *England*, by the Name of *James* the Third, hath any Right or Title to the Crown of these Realms; or that any other Person, or Persons hath, or have any Right or Title to the same, otherwise than according to an Act of Parliament, made in the First Year of their late Majesties King *William* and Queen *Mary*, Entituled, *An Act declaring the Rights and Liberties of the Subject, and settling the Succession of the Crown*; and one other Act, made in the 12th Year of the Reign of his said late Majesty King *William* the Third, Entituled, *An Act for the further Limitation of the Crown, and better securing the Rights and Liberties of the Subject*:

12

" Or that the Kings or Queens of *England*, with and by the Authority of the Parliament of *England*, are not able to make Laws and Statutes of sufficient Force and Validity, to limit and bind the Crown of this Realm, and the Descent, Limitation, Inheritance and Government thereof, every such Person or Persons shall be guilty of High Treason, and being thereof Convicted and Attainted, according to the Laws and Statutes of this Realm, shall be deemed and adjudged Traitors, and shall suffer Pains of Death, and all Losses and Forfeitures as in Case of High Treason.

" And that if any Person, or Persons, shall from and after the said 25th Day of *March*, Maliciously and Directly, by Preaching, Teaching, or advised Speaking declare, maintain, and affirm, in manner as aforesaid; every such Person, or Persons, being thereof lawfully Convicted, shall incur the Danger and Penalty of *Præmunire*.

" And that the Parliament shall not be dissolved by the Death or Demise of Her Majesty, Her Heirs or Successors; but such Parliament, if sitting at the time of such Demise, may proceed to Act for six Months, and no longer, unless the same shall be sooner Prorogued, or Dissolved by such Person to whom the Crown of this Realm of *England* shall come, according to the Acts for limiting and settling the Succession abovementioned. And if the said Parliament shall be so Prorogued, then it shall meet and sit on the Day unto which it shall be Prorogued, and continue for the residue of the said six Months, unless sooner Prorogued or dissolved as aforesaid. And if there be a Parliament in Being, at the time of the Death of Her Majesty, Her Heirs, or Successors, but happens to be separated by Adjournment, or Prorogation, such Parliament shall immediately after such Demise meet, and Act for six Months, and no longer, unless the same shall be Prorogued, or dissolved, as aforesaid. And in case there is no Parliament in being, at the time of such Demise, that has met and sate, then the last preceding Parliament shall immediately convene, and sit, at *Westminster*, and be a Parliament to continue as aforesaid; but subject to be Prorogued, and Dissolved, as aforesaid.

" That the Privy-Council of Her Majesty, Her Heirs, and Successors, shall not be dissolved, by such Death or Demise, but shall continue for six Months, unless sooner determined by the next Successor;

" Nor shall any Office, Place, or Employment, Civil, or Military, become void by such Demise, but continue also for six Months, unless the Persons enjoying them shall be sooner removed, and discharged by the next Successor.

" And if her Majesty shall happen to die without Issue, the Privy-Council shall with all convenient Speed cause the next Protestant Successor, entituled to the Crown of *England*, by Virtue of the Acts abovementioned, to be openly and solemnly Proclaimed in *England*, and *Ireland*, in usual manner; and every Member thereof Wilfully Neglecting, or Refusing to cause such Proclamation to be made, shall be guilty of High Treason; and every Officer, by the Privy-Council required to make such Proclamations, wilfully Neglecting or Refusing, shall be guilty of, and suffer the Penalties of High Treason.

" And for continuing the Administration of the Government in the Name of such Protestant Successor, until Her or His Arrival in *England*, The Lord Arch-Bishop of *Canterbury*, the Lord Chancellor or Lord Keeper, Lord High Treasurer, Lord President of the Council, Lord Privy Seal, Lord High Admiral, and Lord Chief Justice of the Queen's Bench, at that time being, are thereby Appointed Lords Justices of *England*, until such Successor arrive, or determine their Authority.

" And the Person to succeed in case of Her Majesty's Death, without Issue, is impowered at any time during Her Majesty's Life, by Three Instruments under Her or His Hand and Seal, to appoint so many Natural Born Subjects of *England*, as She or He shall think fit, to be added to the above-mentioned Lords Justices, to Act with them as Lords Justices of *England*, who, or the Major part, not being fewer than Five, shall Execute the Power of Lords Justices.

" The said Three Instruments to be Transmitted into *England*, to the Resident of the Person next to Succeed, (whose Credentials shall be inroll'd in *Chancery*,) and to the Arch-Bishop of *Canterbury*, and Lord Chancellor, or Lord Keeper, close Seal'd up; and after they are so transmitted, shall be severally put into several Covers, and severally Seal'd by such Resident, Arch-Bishop, and Chancellor, or Keeper, and severally deposited in the Hands of such Resident, Arch-Bishop, and Chancellor, or Keeper. If the next Successor shall think fit to revoke, or alter such Appointment, and shall by three Writings of the same tenor, under Her or His Hand and Seal, require the said Instruments so deposited to be delivered up; then the Persons with whom deposited, their Executors, or Administrators, and every other Person, in whose Custody the said Instruments shall happen to be, shall deliver up the same accordingly. And if any of the said Persons with whom the said Instruments shall be so deposited, shall die or be removed from their respective Offices or Employments during Her Majesty's Life, such Person, or Persons, and in Case of any of their Deaths their Executors and Administrators respectively, and every other Person, in whose Custody the same shall happen to be, shall with all convenient speed, deliver such of them as shall be in his, or their Custody to the Successor, or Successors of the person or persons, so dying or removed. Which said several Instruments so Sealed up, and deposited, shall immediately after the Demise of Her Majesty without Issue, be brought before the Privy-Council, where the same shall be forthwith open'd and read, and afterwards Inroll'd in the High Court of *Chancery*.

" If the Persons with whom the said Instruments shall be deposited, or others in whose Custody the same shall be, after the Deceases of any of the said Persons, shall open the same, or wilfully Neglect or Refuse to produce them as aforesaid, such Persons shall incur the Penalties of *Præmunire*.

" And if all the said Instruments shall not be produced, before the said Privy-Council, then any one of the said Instruments, so produced, shall be as effectual to give such Authority as aforesaid, to the Persons therein named, as if all of them had been produced. And if there be not any Nomination by such Instruments, then the said Seven Officers above named, or any Five of them, are appointed to be Lords Justices of *England*. And that the Lords Justices of *England* shall not dissolve the Parliament continued and ordered to assemble and sit as aforesaid, without express Direction from such succeeding Queen or King, and are restrained and disabled from giving the Royal Assent to any Bill for the repealing or altering the Act for the Uniformity of Publick Prayers and Administration of Sacraments,

made 13 & 14. *C.* II. under the penalty of High Treason: And
that the said Lords Justices, before they act in their said Offices,
shall take the Oaths mentioned in an Act made, 1 *W.* & *M.*
entitled, *An Act for abrogating the Oaths of Allegiance and
Supremacy, and appointing other Oaths,* and also the *Abjuration-
Oath,* before the Privy Council; and all Members of both
Houses of Parliament, and every Member of the Privy Council,
and all Officers and Persons in any Offices, Places, or Employments Civil and Military, who shall be by this Act continued
as aforesaid, shall take the said Oaths, and do all other Acts
required by the Laws of this Realm, to qualify themselves to
continue in such their respective Places, Offices and Employments, within such Time and in such Manner, and under such
Penalties and Disabilities as they should or ought to do, had
they been then newly elected, appointed, constituted, or put
into such Offices, Places or Employments in the usual and
ordinary way. And that the Lords Justices shall be deemed as
Persons executing Offices of Trust within this Kingdom, and
shall do all Acts requisite by the Laws to qualifie themselves
to be and continue in their said Offices, within such time, and
in such manner, and under such Penalties and Disabilities, as
in and by the said Acts are required.

" And it is in the said Act provided, amongst other things,
That if any of the aforesaid seven Offices, other than the Office
of Lord High Treasurer of *England,* shall be in Commission
at the time of such Demise of her Majesty, that then the first
Commissioner of such respective Commission shall be one of
the Lords Justices of *England.* And if there be no Lord High
Treasurer of *England,* and the Office of Treasurer of the
Exchequer shall be in Commission, then the first in that Commission shall be one of the Lords Justices of *England.*"

I have here shewn what wonderful Concern and Care appeared,
as well in her Majesty and her Parliament, as in the late King
William and his, for settling the Succession to the Crown of
England in the Protestant Line. I come now to the Act of
Parliament for uniting the Kingdoms of *England* and *Scotland*
in one Kingdom, by the name of *Great Britain.*

This had been unsuccessfully attempted by several of her
Majesty's Predecessors, but the Glory of it was reserv'd for her

Majesty, that she might appear as great in her Councils as her Arms.

This Act is Entitled, *An Act for an Union of the two King-doms of* England *and* Scotland; and received the Royal Assent in the Fifth Year of the Reign of her Majesty. It recites, that Articles of Union were agreed on, the 22d Day of *July*, in the Fifth Year of her Majesty's Reign, by the Commissioners nomi-nated on behalf of the Kingdom of *England*, under the Great Seal of *England*, dated the 10th Day of *April* then last past, in pursuance of an Act of Parliament made in *England* in the Third Year of her Majesty's Reign, and the Commissioners nominated on the behalf of the Kingdom of *Scotland*, under the Great Seal of *Scotland*, dated the 27th Day of *February*, in the 4th Year of Her Majesty's Reign, in pursuance of the 4th Act of the 3d Session of the then present Parliament of *Scotland*, to treat of and concerning an Union of the said Kingdoms; and reciting that an Act had passed in the Parliament of *Scotland*, the 16th Day of *January*, in the 5th Year of Her Majesty's Reign, wherein it is mentioned, that the Estates of Parliament, considering the said Articles of Union of the two Kingdoms, had agreed to and approved thereof with some Additions and Explanations, and that Her Majesty had passed in the same Session of Parliament, an Act, Entitled *Act for securing of the Protestant Religion, and Presbyterian Church Government*, which was appointed to be inserted in any Act ratifying the Treaty, and expressly declared to be a Fundamental and Essential Condition of the said Treaty of Union in all times coming;

The Tenor of which Articles, as ratify'd and approved of, is at large recited in the said Act of Union. It concerns our present Purpose to mention only the first and second.

ARTICLE I.

"That the two Kingdoms of *England* and *Scotland*, shall, upon the first day of *May*, which shall be in the Year One thousand seven hundred and seven, and for ever after, be United into one Kingdom, by the Name of *Great Britain*, and that the Ensigns Armorial of the said United Kingdom be such as Her Majesty shall appoint, and the Crosses of St. *George* and St. *Andrew* be conjoyned in such manner as Her Majesty shall think fit, and used in all Flags, Banners, Standards and Ensigns, both at Sea and on Land."

ARTICLE II.

" That the Succession to the Monarchy of the United Kingdom of *Great Britain*, and of the Dominions thereto belonging, after Her most sacred Majesty, and in default of Issue of Her Majesty, be, remain, and continue to the most Excellent Princess *Sophia*, Electress and Dutchess Dowager of *Hanover*, and the Heirs of Her Body being Protestants, upon whom the Crown of *England* is settled by an Act of Parliament made in *England* in the Twelfth Year of the Reign of his late Majesty King *William* the Third, Entituled, *An Act for the further Limitation of the Crown, and better Securing the Rights and Liberties of the Subject*; and that all Papists, and Persons Marrying Papists, shall be excluded from and for ever incapable to Inherit, Possess or Enjoy the Imperial Crown of *Great Britain*, and the Dominions thereunto belonging, or any part thereof; and in every such case the Crown and Government shall from time to time descend to, and be enjoy'd by such Person being a Protestant as should have Inherited and enjoyed the same, in case such Papist, or person Marrying a Papist, was naturally Dead, according to the Provision for the Descent of the Crown of *England*, made by another Act of Parliament in *England*, in the first Year of the Reign of their late Majesties King *William* and Queen *Mary*, Entituled, *An Act declaring the Rights and Liberties of the Subject, and settling the Succession of the Crown*."

But this Point is of so great Consequence, that I must beg leave to repeat the History and Progress of it, which was thus.

Her Majesty was impower'd by two several Acts of Parliament, one of the late Kingdom of *England*, and the other of the late Kingdom of *Scotland*, to appoint Commissioners for each Kingdom, to treat of an Union of the two Kingdoms; but it was expressly provided in each Act, that the Commissioners should not treat of, or concerning the Alteration of the Worship, Discipline, or Government of the Church in either Kingdom.

The Commissioners were accordingly appointed by her Majesty, and 25 Articles were agreed upon between them, which Articles were approved, and ratified by two several Acts of Parliament of the said late Kingdoms of *England* and *Scotland*; in which said Acts each Kingdom provided for the Preservation of the Worship, Discipline and Government of its respective Church, within their respective parts of the United Kingdom of *Great Britain*, and each Act of Parliament for the Preservation of the said Churches, were agreed to be taken as a Fundamental Condition of the Union; and to be repeated, and inserted in any Act of Parliament for agreeing to the said Treaty, or Union betwixt the two Kingdoms. And it was expressly enacted in each of the said Acts, *That the said Articles and Acts should be and continue in all time coming the sure and perpetual Foundation of a compleat and entire Union of the two Kingdoms of* England *and* Scotland.

After which an Act of Parliament of the United Kingdom of *Great Britain* was passed, Entitled, *An Act for an Union of the two Kingdoms of* England *and* Scotland; wherein reciting the said 25 Articles of the Union, ratified and confirmed by the respective Acts of Parliament of the Kingdoms of *England* and *Scotland*, and inserting the said Acts of Parliament for preserving the Worship, Discipline and Government of the respective Churches of each Kingdom: It is thereby enacted, That the said Acts of Parliament of *England* and *Scotland*, for securing their respective Churches; and the said Articles of Union, so as aforesaid ratified, approved and confirmed, be, and continue in all times coming, the compleat and entire Union of the two Kingdoms of *England* and *Scotland*.

The Words, *so as aforesaid ratified, approved and confirmed*, are very material, and ought to be carefully observed, because some of the said Articles are made Entire and Absolute; and others give a Power to the Parliament of *Great Britain* to alter the same: So that these Words, *so as aforesaid ratified, approved and confirmed*, must be taken *reddendo singula singulis*, that is, such of the said Articles as express no Power to the Parliament of *Great Britain* to alter them, shall remain entire; and such as carry a Power of Alteration by the Parliament of *Great Britain* are not so sacred.

Amongst the Articles that carry no such express Power with them, is the second Article for settling the Succession of the

Crown of *Great Britain* on the House of *Hanover*; so that I
humbly offer it to every good Subject's Consideration, Whether
this Article is not as firm as the Union it self, and as the
Settlement of Episcopacy in *England*, and Presbytery in *Scotland*.

These were the sacred Terms and Stipulations made between
the two late Kingdoms of *England* and *Scotland*, and upon which
both Kingdoms, by the Legal Representatives, consented to be
dissolved and exist no longer, *but be resolved into, and United
in one Kingdom, by the Name of* Great Britain.

The Powers that made this happy Union, the Parliaments of
England and *Scotland*, have no longer a Being, and therefore
that Union, in the express Terms thereof, must remain Inviolable.
The Union would be infringed should there be any Deviation
from these Articles; and what Consequences that would have
no good Subject can think of without Horror; for as, I humbly
presume, there is no possibility of returning into the same State
as we were in before this Union, it is wild and extravagant to
suppose it can be peaceably broken. Two Warlike Nations that
should separate, after being under solemn Obligation of perpetual Union, would, like two private Men of Spirit that had
broken Friendship, have ten thousand nameless and inexplicable
Causes of Anger boiling in their Bosoms, which would render
them incapable of living quiet Neighbours, and one of them
must be brought very low, or neither of them could live in
Peace and Safety. What I mean is, that common Sense, and the
Nature of things would make one expect that nothing less than
a War could attend the Dissatisfactions of such a Rupture. It
becomes the *Englishmen* in Generosity to be more particularly
careful in preserving this Union.

For the late Kingdom of *Scotland* had as numerous a Nobility
as *England*, and the Representatives of their Commons were also
very Numerous: they have by the Articles of Union Consented
to send only Sixteen Peers, and Forty-Five Commons, to the
Parliament of *Great Britain*, which hath the same number of
Lords and Commons for *England* that were before the Union;
so that the *Scots* Representatives can make no Stand in the
Defence of all, or any of the Articles of the Union, should they
be Oppos'd by such unequal Numbers of the Lords and Commons of *England*; and therefore it is most plain, from the

Impotence in which so many Wise and Able Men of the *Scotch* Nation left themselves in these particulars, that they understood the Points of Religion in *England* and *Scotland* respectively, the Succession to the Crown of *Great Britain*, and all other Articles of the Union, were never to be controverted.

To guard and protect this Settlement of the Crown of the united Kingdom of *Great Britain* in the Protestant Line, an Act of Parliament of the United Kingdom passed in the 6th Year of her Majesty's Reign, Entituled, *An Act for the Security of her Majesty's Person and Government and of the Succession to the Crown of* Great Britain *in the Protestant Line*, by which the Provisions in the beforementioned Act, (Entitled, *An Act for the better Security of her Majesty's Person and Government, and of the Succession to the Crown of* England *in the Protestant Line*) are extended throughout the whole United Kingdom. It is in effect a Repetition of that Act, with proper Alterations for that purpose. "So that now throughout *Great Britain* this Act hath made it high Treason for any Person maliciously, advisedly, and directly, by Writing or Printing, to maintain and affirm, that our Sovereign Lady the Queen, that now is, is not the Lawful and Rightful Queen of these Realms; or that the Pretended Prince of *Wales*, who now stiles himself King of *Great Britain*, or King of *England* by the name of *James* the IIId, or King of *Scotland* by the Name of *James* the VIIIth, hath any Right or Title to the Crown of these Realms; or that any other Person or Persons hath or have any right or Title to the same, otherwise than according to an Act of Parliament made in *England*, in the first Year of the Reign of their late Majesties King *William* and Queen *Mary*, Entitled, *An Act declaring the Rights and Liberties of the Subject, and settling the Succession of the Crown*, and one other Act made in *England*, in the Twelfth Year of the Reign of his said late Majesty King *William* the IIId, Entitled, *An Act for the further Limitation of the Crown, and better securing the Rights and Liberties of the Subject*, and the Acts lately made in *England* and *Scotland*, mutually for the Union of the two Kingdoms; or that the Kings or Queens of this Realm, with and by the Authority of Parliament, are not able to make Laws and Statutes of sufficient Force and Validity to limit and bind the Crown, and the Descent, Limitation,

Inheritance, and Government thereof, every such Person or Persons shall be guilty of High Treason; and if any Person or Persons shall maliciously and directly, by Preaching, Teaching, or advised Speaking, declare, maintain, and affirm, as aforesaid, such Person or Persons shall incur the Penalty of *Præmunire*."

Thus did our Kingdom of *Great Britain* begin in the Fifth Year of her Majesty's Reign, and in the Year of our Lord 1707. And from this Great *Æra*, to which it is so easie to look back, every *Briton* may date this happy Conclusion; that all the Notions of Hereditary Right, but that of her Majesty and the Heirs of her Body, and in Default of such Issue, that of the most Illustrious Princess *Sophia*, and the Heirs of her Body, being Protestants, are at an End.

And all this hath been done in so open a manner, and in so expressive and plain terms, that one cannot but think that our Popish or *Jacobite* Party, who have been of late so bold both in Writing and Speaking against the Settlement of the Crown of *Great Britain* in the Protestant Line, and cannot possibly plead Ignorance of these things, must have some unaccountable Encouragement for their Support. But let me inform every *Briton* that loves his Queen, Religion, Laws and Liberties, it is his Duty to appear Boldly in their Defence, and detect and seize those Enemies to his Country, where-ever he finds them. What should any Man fear in so just a Cause, who acts under the Guard and Protection of the Laws of his Country, whilst his Opponents act with Halters about their Necks?

It is not material to mention the grand Suspicions of the Spurious Birth of the Pretended Prince of *Wales*; That it was talk'd with great Assurance by the Papists, that the late King *James's* Queen was big with a Son, some Months before the Pretended Birth; for they well knew a Daughter would not do their Business; That at the Time of the Pretended Birth, the Princess *Ann*, now our most gracious Queen, was at the *Bath*; That the Bishops were clapt up in the Tower; That the Women about the Queen were Papists; That the Presumptive Heir was not present; That at the Birth of the present *French* King, the next Heir, tho' a Man, was permitted to see the Queen actually Delivered; That in our Case it might have been done with much more Decency, had there been a Birth, since the next Heir was a Woman; That the late King *James*, and his Queen, owning the Pretender, is no Argument for his not being Spurious, considering the Bigotry of that Prince, and the great Influence the Clergy of the Church of *Rome* have on their Laity; That our own History informs us, that the First Queen *Mary* was prevail'd on by her Popish Priests to feign her self with Child, to exclude her Protestant Sister, the Lady Elizabeth, from the Crown of *England*; That the Imposture had been carried on, and a Birth been impos'd upon the Nation, had not King *Philip*, her Husband, wisely consider'd, that the Imposter would not only succeed to the Crown of *England*, but also to that of *Spain*, and so prevented it. I say these things are altogether insignificant, they are foreign to the purpose. Be the Pretender who he will, or whoever was his Father or Mother, it concerns not any *Briton*; he is an Attainted Person, an Enemy to our Queen and Country; and all his Aiders and Abetters are guilty of High Treason.

Now I am upon the Subject of this late Settlement of the Crown, I cannot forbear to express my Wonder, that there can be found any *Briton* weak enough to contend against a Power in their own Nation, which is practised to a much greater Degree in other States, and without the least scruple exercised, according to the Emergencies of Human Affairs. How hard is it, that *Britain* should be debar'd the Privilege of establishing its own Security, even by relinquishing only those Branches of the Royal Line which threaten it with Destruction, whilst other Nations never scruple, upon less Occasions, to go much greater Lengths. There have been even in *France* three different Races of their Kings; the first began with *Pharamond*, the second with *Charles Martell*, and the third with *Hugh Capet*; and I doubt whether if the direct Line of the Blood Royal of *France* were to be followed, it would make for the Title of his present most Christian Majesty. But to come to fresh Instances, in which *Great Britain* it self hath not been unconcerned, What Right, by the contrary Rule, could the Duke of *Savoy* have to the Kingdom of Sicily, or the Elector of *Bavaria* to that of *Sardinia*? Can *Great Britain* help to advance Men to other Thrones, and have no Power in limiting its own? Has not *Lewis* the XIVth given us fresh Instances of such Innovations in his own Family?

Or can Men think he is not in Earnest, in excluding his Grandson the King of *Spain*, and his Descendants, from the Crown of *France*; and the Dauphin and Duke of *Berry*, and their Descendants, from the Crown of *Spain*? And if such Sacred Things as Kingdoms themselves may be thus disposed of out of the Right Line, not by any Resignation that can in any equitable Sense be called voluntary, but apparently for meer Reasons of State and Ambition, certainly the *English* and *Scotch*, for Preservation of Religion, Liberty and Property, the Essential Benefits of Life, might with more Justice settle their Crown in the Protestant Line in the manner they have done, excluding all the nearer Princes of the Blood that are Papists.

When I reflect on these many solemn strong Barriers of Laws and Oaths, of Policy and Religion, of Penalties without, and Conscience within, methinks all Fear vanisheth before them. It seems a *Phantom* only that disappears with the Light; and I begin to hope it is as ridiculous and groundless, as the Artifice of some Men endeavours to represent it. But my Thoughts will not let me rest here; I ask my self, before I am aware, what are the Marks of a lasting Security? What are our Tempers and our Hearts at Home?—In what Hands is Power lodged Abroad? Are our unnatural Divisions our Strength?—Or is it nothing to us which of the Princes of *Europe* hath the longest Sword? The Powerful Hand that deals out Crowns and Kingdoms all around us, may it not in time reach out a King to us too? Are there no Pretensions to our Crown that can ever be revived?—Or are Popery and Ambition become tame and quiet Neighbours?

These uneasie Questions are enough to satisfie any *Briton*, that we can neither know our Security, nor be sensible of our Danger from any partial view of our Condition, or from Appearances on one Side only. Our *Condition* cannot be judged of, but from the Circumstances of the Affairs of *Europe* in general, as well as of *Great Britain* in particular.

That I may represent this with the more Advantage, and put every thing in its proper View, I cannot but look back on the glorious Scene some past Years presented us with, a Scene too glorious indeed to be forgotten, and yet too affecting to be remembred. Ambition, Tyranny and Oppression seemed not long ago to be just taking their leave of this part of the World, and ready to give place to Honour, Liberty and Justice. The *French* for near an Age had been always triumphant in their Encroachments on their Neighbors; from the number of their Troops, their early taking the Field, the Remissness of their Enemies, join'd with their happy manner of interpreting the Sense of their Leagues and Treaties, they had always succeeded in every thing they undertook; the long Series of their good Fortune made them arrogate to themselves the Titles of *Intrepid* and *Invincible*; but the destin'd Time came, and they were to their Costs as fully convinced of their Mistake by the Bravery of the *British* Troops, under the Conduct of her Majesty's late General, the great Duke of *Marlborough*.

As this wonderful Instrument of Providence carried in his Fortune the Fate of the *British* People, who can forbear to run over the good Events that happened under him, and the Honours paid to him; both which are recited not as they are personal to himself, but as they concern the *British* Name and Nation, which he represented.

The first thing that meets my Imagination is, the *French* Army broken, routed, flying over the Plains of *Blenheim*, and chusing rather to throw themselves headlong into the *Danube*, than face about upon their Conqueror. I see the just Honours done him by the Emperor and the whole Empire: I hear him with loud Acclamations acknowledged the Deliverer of *Europe*. He is introduced into the College of Princes, and takes Possession of the Principality of *Mindelheim*. Triumphal Columns are erected in the Plains of *Blenheim*, recording the seasonable Assistance of the *British* Arms, and the Glories of that Immortal Day.

The *British* Leader returns from the *Danube* to the *Rhine*; he and his brave Companions are the Delight of the Nations through whom they march, and are stiled their Good, their Guardian Angels.—After passing so many different Nations in a triumphant manner, he lands in his own Country, an humble unattended Subject; honouring and adorning his Nation by Privacy and Modesty at Home, much more than by the highest Triumphs and Ostentations Abroad.

The Queen and Senate pass in Religious Pomp to thank the

Almighty for Victory over the then Common Oppressor. But the Prospect does not end here; the Plains of *Ramillies* are a new Scene of Glory to the Confederate Arms; and a second happy Day ends the Bondage of many Cities!

His Most Christian Majesty conceives new Hopes from changing his Generals, and from the Conduct of *Vendosme*, promises himself to repair the Diminution of his Glory by *Villeroy*.

The Branches of his Royal Family, the Dukes of *Burgundy* and *Berry*, are to animate the Soldiery by their Presence; but *Vendosme*, *Burgundy*, and *Berry*, are not strong enough for the Genius of the Duke of *Marlborough* at *Oudenard*.

The *French* still Change their General, and *Villars* is in Command. He soon shares the same Fate with his Predecessors, by being beaten out of his Camp by an inferior Number of Troops. A Camp so strong by Nature and Art, that as none but the Duke of *Marlborough* would have attempted it, so none but that consummate Captain at the Head of his brave Countrymen could have succeeded in it. In short, methinks I see *Ostend*, *Menin*, *Lisle*, *Tournay*, *Mons*, *Aire*, *Doway*, and innumerable other Towns held impregnable, all besieged, taken and restored to their lawful Prince and Ancient Liberties.

The *English* General, during the Course of ten Campaigns, besieged no Town but what he took, attacked no Army but what he routed, and returned each Year with the Humility of a private Man.

If beating the Enemy in the Field, and being too vigilant for their Councils in Foreign Courts, were effectual Means towards ending the War, and reducing them to a Condition too low for giving fresh Disturbance to *Europe*; the Duke of *Marlborough* took just Measures; but, however unaccountable it may appear to Posterity, that General was not permitted to enjoy the Fruits of his Glorious Labour; but as *France* changed her Generals for want of Success in their Conduct, so *Britain* changes hers after an uninterrupted Series of Conquest. The Minds of the People, against all common Sense, are debauch'd with Impressions of the Duke's Affectation of prolonging the War for his own Glory; and his Adversaries attack a Reputation, which could not well be impaired without sullying the Glory of *Great Britain* it self; his Enemies were not to be softened by that

Consideration; he is dismissed, and soon after a Suspension of Arms between *Great Britain* and *France* is Proclaimed at the Head of the Armies. The *British*, in the midst of the Enemies Garrisons, withdraw themselves from their Confederates. The *French*, now no longer having the *Britons*, or their great Leader to fear, affect no more strong Garrisons and Fortify'd Camps; but attack and rout the Earl of *Albemarle* at *Denain*, and necessitate the brave Prince *Eugene* to abandon *Landrecy*, a Place of such Importance that it gave Entrance into the Heart of *France*, of which the *French* King was so sensible, that before he was recovered from his fright, he acknowledged he in a manner owed his Crown to the Suspension of Arms between him and *Great Britain*. The Suspension is followed by a Treaty of Peace at *Utrecht*. The Peace is concluded between *Great Britain* and *France*; and between *France* and the States General. The Emperor and the Empire continue the War. I shall not presume to enter into an Examination of the Articles of Peace between us and *France*; but there can be no Crime in affirming, (if it be a Truth) that the House of *Bourbon* is at this Juncture become more formidable, and bids fairer for an Universal Monarchy, and to engross the whole Trade of *Europe*, than it did before the War.

All the World knows with what Frankness the *Dutch* have been treated to deliver up *Traerbach* to the Imperialists, as an expedient for the *French* to besiege it; because, forsooth, it lay convenient for their Incursions upon the Empire. This extravagant Demand must give a melancholy Prospect to other Nations.

The most important Article between *France* and *England* is the Demolition of *Dunkirk*, which they have begun Contemptuously and Arbitrarily, their own way: The Mole and Harbour, which only are dreadful to us, are yet untouched, and just Suspicions given that they ever will be.

Landau and *Fribourg* are taken; and in case there is no intermediate Peace, *which may still be more immediately fatal to us*, Two hundred thousand *French* may be ready in the Spring to invade the Empire, and restore the Duke of *Bavaria* to his forfeited Dominions.

These Incidents happen, when the Capital of *Austria*, the *Residence* of his Imperial Majesty, is visited with the Plague.

The Male Line of that House is likely to terminate in himself; and should it please God to take him off, and no King of the *Romans* chosen, a Prince of the House of *Bourbon* would probably bid fair for the Imperial Dignity; after which Day farewell Liberty, *Europe* would be *French*.

But the Scene is not yet closed. *Portugal*, which during the War supplied to us the place of *Spain*, by sending us vast Quantities of Gold in exchange for our Woollen Manufactures, has only at present a Suspension of Arms for its Protection, which Suspension may possibly last no longer than till the *Catalonians* are reduced; and who knows but the old Pretensions of *Spain* to *Portugal* may be then revived. I mention the *Catalonians*, but who can Name the *Catalonians* without a Tear! Brave unhappy People! drawn into the War by the Encouragement of the Maritime Powers, from which only a Nation encompassed by Land by *France* and *Spain* could hope for Relief and Protection, now abandoned and exposed to the Resentment of an enraged Prince, whose Person and Interest they have always opposed; and yet still so fond of their Ancient Liberties, that tho' hemmed up in a Nook of Land by the Forces of two Crowns, and closely besieged in *Barcelona*, they chuse rather, like their Countrymen, the famous *Saguntines* of old, to perish with their Wives and Children, than live in Slavery. Did the *French* King, with a Conquering Sword in his Hand, ever abandon the least and most inconsiderable of all his Allies? No. When these very *Catalonians* had assisted him against the King of *Spain*, he did not give up his Power of Treating 'till he had made the most Honourable Conditions for them, not a single Man amongst them was then hurt either in his Person or Privileges; but now—Poor unhappy *Catalonians*, worthy of a better Fate! Good and gracious God! to whom shall be attributed the Loss of this brave People! dreadful the Doom of those who shall in thy sight be esteemed their Destroyers!

But to bring these several Facts and Circumstances home, we must observe, that the Person who seems to be the most favoured by the *French* King in the late Treaties is the Duke of *Savoy*, who is made King of *Sicily*; and considering also the enlargement of his Territories on the Continent, by Cession from the Emperor, is become the most powerful Prince in *Italy*. This

13

Prince put in his Claim to the Crown of *England*, in the Right of his Wife, a Daughter of the late Dutchess of *Orleans*, Sister to our late King *Charles* the Second, at the time of settling the Crown of *England* on the House of *Hanover*. This Prince, a Man of as great Address and Capacity as any now living, is supposed to have entred into a Secret and Strict Alliance with the House of *Bourbon*, and may therefore very well add to our fears of a Popish Successor.

Things standing thus, and the House of *Bourbon* being in the Actual Possession of *France* and *Spain*, bidding fair for the Conquest of *Germany*, or in Peace and good Understanding with it; what have *Great Britain*, and *Holland* to hope from, but the Mercy of *France?* what else have we to prevent the Pretender's being imposed on us, when *France* shall think fit; nay, in failure of one Pretender, he has in his Quiver a Succession of them; the Dutchess of *Savoy*, or Her Sons, or the Dauphin Her Grandson. *The last named cannot be many Years from the Throne of* France.

In the next place how are we disposed at Home, for the Reception of such an Attempt? The Passions of many, which were raised so high by an Impudent Suggestion of the Church's Danger, seem to have subsided into a Lethargick Unconcern for every thing else; harmless Men are ashamed to own, how grossly they have been imposed upon; and instead of resenting the Abuse, are willing to overlook it, with a certain reluctance against being moved at any thing else; least they should fall into the Mortification of being mis-led a Second time. Many who are above being blinded by popular Noise and Outcry, yet seem to think the Warmth and Zeal of a publick Spirit to be little better than a Romantick Heat of Brain. Treasonable Books lately dispersed amongst us, that have apparently struck at the Protestant Succession in the House of *Hanover*, have passed almost without Observation from the Generality of the People; Subtle Queries have been Published, about the Birth of a certain Person, which certain Person every body knows to be intended for the Pretender; The Author of the Conduct of the Allies has dared to drop Insinuations about altering the Succession; and a late Treasonable Book, on the Subject of *Hereditary Right*, has published the Will of King *Henry* the Eighth, which seems to be intended as a Pattern for the like Occasion.

The Conversion of the Pretender to our Religion, has been occasionally Reported, and Contradicted, according to the Reception it met with among the soft Fools, who give that gross Story a hearing: The unhappy Prince, whose Son the Pretender calls himself, is a memorable Instance, how much such Conversions are to be depended upon. King *James*, when Duke of *York*, for a long time professed himself a Protestant; and even not long before his Succession [4] to the Crown, several Persons had Actions brought against them for saying he was a Papist, and exorbitant Damages given and recovered; in a word, from the Practice of all Papists, that have come to Protestant Thrones, upon pretence of embracing the Reformed Religion, we have reason to believe they have Dispensations from *Rome* to personate any thing, for the Service of that Church. A Popish Prince will never think himself obliged by the most Solemn, even the Coronation Oath, to his Protestant Subjects. All Oaths are as insignificant and as soon forgotten, as the Services done by such Protestant Subjects.

King *James*, when Duke of *York* was preserved from the Bill of Exclusion by the Church of *England*, and particularly its Bishops; when he came to the Crown, the Church was soon insulted and outraged by him, and Her Prelates committed to the Tower.

Has not a Neighbouring Prince cruelly Treated and Banished his Protestant Subjects, who preserved the Crown on his Head?

Did not the Princess *Mary* promise the Men of *Suffolk*, who joined with Her against the Lady *Jane Grey*, that she would make no Alteration in the Religion Established by Her Brother, King *Edward* the Sixth? And yet as soon as she came to the Crown, by the Assistance even of *Suffolk* Men, she filled all *England*, and in a particular manner that County, with the Flames of Martyrs. The Cruelties of that Reign were such, that Multitudes of Men, Women and Children were burnt for being Zealous Professors of the Gospel of the Lord Jesus. In short, nothing less than this can be expected from a Popish Prince; both Clergy and Laity must share the same Fate, all universally must submit to the fiery Trial, or renounce their Religion. Our Bishops and Clergy must all lose their Spiritual Preferments, or submit to all Antichristian Tyranny: And should they submit to every thing, they must notwithstanding part from their Wives and Children, which, according to the Church of *Rome*, are Harlots and Spurious. The Laity, possessed of Lands that formerly belonged to the Roman Catholick Clergy, must resign their Estates, and perhaps be made accountable for the Profits received.

What can be more moving, than to reflect upon the Barbarous Cruelties of Papists beyond all Example: And these not accidental, or the sudden Effects of Passion or Provocation, but the settled Result of their Religion and their Consciences.

Above 100 000 Men, Women and Children were Murdered in the Massacre of *Ireland*. How hot and terrible were the late Persecutions of the Protestants in *France* and *Savoy*? How frequent were the Massacres of Protestants through the whole Kingdom of *France*, when they were under the Protection of the then Laws of that Country? How barbarous, in a particular manner, was the Massacre of *Paris*, at the Marriage of the King of *Navarre*, the *French* King's Grandfather, a Protestant, with the Sister of *Charles* the Ninth, where the Famous Admiral of *France*, the great *Coligny*, the glorious Asserter of the Protestant Interest, was inhumanly Murdered, and the Body of that Heroe dragged Naked about the Streets, and this by the Direction of the King himself, who had but just before most treacherously given him, from his own Mouth, Assurance of his Protection? Ten thousand Protestants, without Distinction of Quality, Age or Sex, were put to the Sword at the same time; the King of *Navarre* himself narrowly escaped this Disaster, His Mother the Queen of *Navarre* having not long before been poysoned by the same Faction.

These are some instances of what must ever be expected. No Obligations on our side, no Humanity or Natural Probity on theirs, are of any weight; their very Religion forces them, upon Pain of Damnation, to forget and cancel the former, and to extinguish all remains of the latter. Good God! To what are they reserved, who have nothing to expect but what such a Religion can afford them? It cannot therefore be too often repeated. We should consider, over and over again, that should the Chain of the Protestant Succession be once broke in upon, tho' the Pretender should be laid aside, the next of the Blood Royal is the Dutchess of *Savoy*; after her Her two Sons; after them, the present Dauphin of *France*; the next in Succession to him, the Queen of *Spain*, and her Heirs; in Default of them, the Duke of *Orleans*, and his Heirs, and most of the other Princes of the Blood of *France*, all Papists, who may be enabled to demand Preference to the House of *Hanover*; so that besides the Probability of this Kingdom's being United to, and made a Province of *France*, the train of Popish Princes is so great, that if one should not compleat the utter Extirpation of our Religion, Laws and Liberties the rest would certainly do it.

And here I cannot but add what is still of more Importance, and ought to be the most prevalent of all Arguments, that should there be the least Hopes given to a Popish Successor, the Life of her Majesty will certainly be in most imminent Danger; for there will never be wanting bloody Zealots of that Perswasion, that will think it meritorious to take away her Majesty's Life, to hasten the Accession of such a Successor to her Throne.

The only Preservation against these Terrours are the Laws beforementioned relating to the Settlement of the Imperial Crown of *Great Britain*. Thanks be to Heaven for that Settlement. The Princess *Sophia*, and the Heirs of her Body, being Protestants, are the Successors to her present Majesty upon her Demise without Issue. The Way is plain before our Eyes, guarded on the Right Hand, and on the Left, by all the Sanctions of God and Man, and by all the Ties of *Law* and *Conscience*. Let those who act under the present Settlement, and yet pretend to dispute for an Absolute Hereditary Right, quiet *themselves* with the Arguments they have borrowed from Popery, and teach their own Consciences the Art of dispensing with the most solemn Oath to this Establishment, whilst they think themselves bound only till Opportunity shall serve to introduce another. God be thanked neither we, nor our Cause, stand in need of such detestable Prevarication. Our Cause is our Happiness. Our Oaths are our Judgment and Inclination. Honour and Affection call us, without the Solemnity of an Oath, to defend such an Establishment; but with it we have every Motive that can influence the Mind of Man. The Terrors of God, added

to the Demands of our Country, oblige and constrain us to let
our Hearts and our Hands follow our Wishes and our Consciences; and out of Regard to our Queen, our Religion, our
Country, our Liberty and our Property, to maintain and assert
the Protestant Succession in the Illustrious House of *Hanover*:
It is no time to talk with Hints and Innuendos, but openly and
honestly to profess our Sentiments, before our Enemies have
compleated and put their Designs in Execution against us. As
divided a People as we are, those who are for the House of
Hanover, are infinitely superior in Number, Wealth, Courage,
and all Arts Military and Civil, to those in the contrary Interest;
besides which, we have *the Laws*, I say *the Laws* on our side.
And those who by their Practices, whatever their Professions
are, have discover'd themselves Enemies to the Constitution,
and Friends to the Pretender, cannot make a Step farther without being guilty of Treason, without standing in broad Day-
light, confessed Criminals against their injured Queen and
Country.

When the People were in a ferment, when Faction ran high,
with irresistible Prepossessions against every thing in its former
Channel, sanguine Men might conceive Hopes of leading them
their own way. But the Building erected upon that Quicksand,
the Favour of the Multiude, will sink, and be swallowed up
by that treacherous Ground on which the Foundation was laid.

It is easie to project the Subversion of a People, when Men
see them unaccountably turned for their own Destruction; but
not so easie to effect that Ruin, when they are come to themselves, and are sensibly and reasonably affected with Thoughts
for their Preservation. We cannot help it, if so many Thousands
of our brave Brethren, who laid down their Lives against the
Power of *France*, have dyed in vain; but we may value our own
Lives dearly, like honest Men. Whatever may befall the Glory
and Wealth of *Great Britain*, let us struggle to the last Drop
of our Blood for its Religion and Liberty. The Banner under
which we are to enter this Conflict, whenever we are called to
it, are the Laws mentioned in this Discourse; when we do not
keep them in Sight, we have no Colours to fly to, no Discipline
to preserve us, but are devoted, and have given our selves up
to Slaughter and Confusion.

While we act manfully under them, we have Reason to expect the Blessing and Assistance of Heaven on its own Cause, which it has so manifestly acknowledg'd to be such, by our many wonderful Deliverances, when all Humane Assistances and ordinary Means of Succour seemed irrevocably removed. We have no Pretensions to the Divine Favour, but from our firm Adherence to that Settlement, which He has, by so many Wonders and Blessings, after such great Difficulties and Misfortunes, bestowed upon us, and which we have in his Sight, and with the Invocation of his Sacred Name, after preparing our Selves at his Altar, so frequently and solemnly Sworn to defend. This plain, unperplexed, unalterable Rule for our Conduct, is visibly the Work of his Hand to a favoured People. Her Majesty's Parliamentary Title, and the Succession in the Illustrious House of *Hanover*, is the Ark of God to *Great Britain*, and, like that of Old, carries Death to the profane Hand that shall dare to touch it.

The Englishman: Being the Close of the Paper So-called No. 57 (15 February 1714)

The Englishman, Steele's periodical of 57 numbers, which ran from 6 October 1713 to 15 February 1714, had as its avowed purpose to arouse public spirit and, as he declared later, to "frustrate the Designs of Wicked Men, at that Time in Power." So although there was an occasional paper on non-political subjects, such as the adventures of Alexander Selkirk and John Rowley's astronomical machine, its drift indicated the increasing tension in public affairs. The Succession was uppermost in Steele's mind. And indirectly, or even directly with frankness, what he considered dangerous to the Protestant Succession was put before the public in papers discussing passive obedience, hereditary right, the Pretender's movements, the trade bill with France, Dunkirk, the Roman Catholic religion, and the Irish Protestants.

In this final paper, issued as a separate pamphlet over his name, Steele stated concretely and unequivocally his position on these current issues. He also took notice of the Tory attacks upon him for "being disrespectful to the Queen, meddling with Dunkirk, and writing *The Crisis*"—especially the anonymous Toby's *Character of Richard St—le* (14 Nov. 1713), which he believed to be Swift's. One main purpose of the paper seemed to be to straighten out a journalistic quarrel as to the causes for a recent run on the Bank. The Queen's serious illness at Christmas had brought the Succession sharply to mind, and the party journalists had certainly not helped to allay public nervousness. *The Examiner* and *The Post Boy* had printed rumors of the Pretender's unusual activities in Lorraine, and the Whigs had played up the enlisting of Irish Catholic soldiers for his service. The dated newspaper excerpts and the affidavits given in Steele's pamphlet are intended to exonerate the Whigs.

Steele declares frankly that his stand is squarely for Revolution principles. He is not a mere creature of the prerogative; the fact that there are bounds to his obedience makes him a better subject. Opposition to the Ministry should not be thought opposition to the prerogative; as a private subject he has a right to be heard. He does not divide the interests of the church from those of the state; they should mutually support each other. He is speaking his own convictions and is not, as someone had accused, a mercenary hireling for the Whigs. As for party differences, he believes that moderate groups in both Whig and Tory parties are trying to serve the best interests of the nation by

183

adherence to the Revolution principles. Measures advocated by high church Tories will destroy not only the state but the church itself. The "New Converts" are very cunning in crying danger to the church; and " both Parties are occasionally play'd off and their Noddles knocked against each other." This gibe was probably intended to mean the Queen's Tory minister Oxford, who was of Presbyterian origin and was supported by Presbyterian electors.

Steele ends with three points: (1) that Dunkirk should be demolished; (2) that the Pretender should be required to remove from such uncomfortably close quarters as Lorraine; (3) that there should be a clearer understanding between Anne and the Elector of Hanover. The first two of these points were main articles of business in the Whig foreign policy after George's accession; the third was considered a seditious utterance and was cited as one reason for Steele's expulsion a month later. This tract was not included in *The Political Writings* of 1715, probably because it had already been reprinted in the collected *Englishman* (June, 1714). Textual notes on p. 641.

THE
ENGLISHMAN:

Being the Clofe of the PAPER fo called.

With an EPISTLE concerning the

Whiggs, Tories, and New Converts.

-------- *Servetur ad imum*
Qualis ab incepto procefferit, & fibi conftet.   Hor.

By RICHARD STEELE, Efq;

L O N D O N:

Printed for FERD: BURLEIGH, in *Amen-Corner.* 1714.
(Price Six-Pence.)

185

The ENGLISHMAN.

February 15. 1714.

HAVING determined to lay down this Paper called the ENGLISHMAN, which has exposed me to much Hatred and Invective, I chuse, (out of the Respect and Deference I have to the Judgment of Mankind) to explain my self, with relation to the many things I have written which have given Offence, in this large Form of a Pamphlet, rather than in a single Paper.

I was once so happy in the kind Thoughts of the Generality of People of all Conditions in this Town, that I cannot without Regret look back upon the Loss of it; and indeed I should be still more concerned, had I not forfeited it for such Considerations as only are to be preferred to their good Opinion; all which Considerations I will express in the honest plain Phrase of *the Testimony of a good Conscience.* It is possible that my Zeal may have transported me to the Supererogation of concerning my self in Matters to which I was not called by any particular Authority or Charge upon me to do more than another Man: But this Objection will lie against all Men who exert themselves for the common Good, without Regard to their own Fame or Fortune; and since I am apparently very much the worse in both these Respects for the Warmth which I have expressed in what I think the Cause of Truth, I hope all Men of Honour who differ from me will let a sincere Self-Denial expiate an offensive Zeal.

I do not know that I ought to retract any Sentiment which I have heretofore advanced; but still insist that what I have done flowed from no other Cause but Zeal for the Honour of the Queen, the Safety of the Constitution, and the Happiness of the People; all which have been concerned in the Points which

I have touched upon in the GUARDIAN, and the Paper which is a professed *Sequel* of it called the ENGLISHMAN.

THAT which moved in me a Indignation not to be suppressed, was the licentious Abuse of great and good Men who had served their Country with Honour and Success. I thought what Favour I had obtained by being the Author of an instructive Way of representing the Manners of Men, and describing Vices and Virtues in a Stile that might fall in with their ordinary Entertainments, could not be more worthily employed, improved, or lost, than in Defence of such Men, and of the Constitution it self, which they had supported.

WHEN the Subjects of Peace and War were all the Conversation in Town, I took upon me to be as concerned as I thought I had a Right to be, and speak my Sentiments with the Freedom of an English Gentleman.

THIS Behaviour brought upon me the Invectives of many unknown Authors, each of whom has writ against me with as much Violence as if I had been personally his most inveterate Enemy; for they have been succinct enough in what concerned the Argument, but have largely dwelt upon the Author they writ against, in the Articles of Birth, Education, and Fortune.

IN Compliance to the Prepossessions of others, rather than as I think it a Matter of any Consideration my self, I assert and declare (that no nice Man of my Acquaintance may think himself polluted by conversing with me) whoever talks with me is speaking to a Gentleman born.

I shall not say any more about the Monosyllable *Steele*, but proceed to take my Leave, and defend my self as the GUARDIAN and ENGLISHMAN.

THE most prevailing Insinuation against me under those Characters, is, that I have discovered in them a seditious, turbulent and disloyal Spirit; this is frequently hinted by that Destroyer of all things, the *Examiner*. If empty Words are all that are required to make up the Virtue we express by the Word Loyalty, I must own that he and his Friends are the best Subjects that ever either King or Queen were blessed with. Their Addresses are full of unlimited Loyalty and Rants against those that talk of any Laws or Bounds to their Obedience; they are so far from admitting any Limitation, that they will allow no Subject, not even a Lord Chief Justice, any Right of judging where those Limitations should be fixed. The Name of a Patriot is an Offence to them; they are, they pretend, meer Creatures of the Prerogative, or Servants who desire no higher Honour than that of doing all that they are bid. But as neither true Loyalty, nor any other Virtue, consists in Pretences, but good Works and Actions, I will abide by my old Point, and maintain that the Queen hath better Subjects and truer Friends than they are.

TO state this Matter, as much as may be even to the *Examiner's* Mind, I will not say one word of the Nation's Right: It is a Sin with him for the Nation to expect any thing, even though it be promised from the Throne. I will say nothing about the Terms of Peace, and Trade, and the State of *Europe*, they may be more offensive to his Patience; but I will suppose Loyalty to be only what it should be very much, a Love and Zeal to the Queen's Person, Honour, Interest and Safety: And even on these Heads, it is visible that their Zeal hath been shamefully to their own Interests and Places, and that her Honour, and Interest, and Love of her People, hath been sacrificed to a Scandal.

TO pass by the blackening and ridiculing all the noblest Parts of her Reign, the inhuman Usage of her old Servants, and the last insolent Jest the *Examiner* made on the Report of her Death, and his sudden Triumph and Joy, even while the Life of the Queen was yet doubtful: To pass all these, and many a real Injury besides, I will only ask whether it be for the Queen's Honour and Interst, to have one Half of her People's Affections alienated from her, by studied Provocations? The doing that, is the constant Tendency of the *Examiner*'s Writings, and of too many of his Friends. Because those whom they are pleased to call *Whigs*, are too honest to join in insidious Addresses, that sacrifice our Laws, and all that is dear to us, to a Prince's Will; and may sometimes complain if they think an Evil Minister uses his Power to break their Rights; they treat them as Men that are the Queen's Enemies, and are to have no Part in her Favour: They Brow-beat them as impudent, if they offer to approach Her Throne to desire any Part in her good Graces, see *Examiner* Numb. 36. " *Such*, saith he, is the *Nicety of this Juncture, That even our Friends are ready to revolt, as imagining that the Faction which they hate and oppose, must be in the Right, because not yet reduced by those, whose only Safety is in the other's Ruin.*" And this is all they mean by their high Flights of Loyalty. If her Majesty in great Complaisance to them, will throw off one Half of the People as Enemies that have no Right to any Favour that is worth having, and lend them her Name, and Purse, and Power, to keep those hated People under, or else ruin them; then they in Requittal will stand by her, in distributing all Places and Preferments among themselves: And so will the worst Sect we have amongst us, and the worse they are, the higher they will strain their unlimited Loyalty in Sacrifices of the Nation's Rights. But if God spares the good Queen's Life, from such secret Attempts as we have too much Reason to fear, I doubt not but to see her judge rightly of such Pretences. Though Flattery carries Witchcraft, yet when she shall see that these Men, instead of supporting her Government with their Interest, cannot carry their Elections, but by representing all others as under her Displeasure; when she shall see that they over-bear the Rights of Corporations by the impertinent Interposition of her Power and Name; when she shall see that those large Bodies of Men which the *Examiner* and others expose and exasperate, as Men whom the Queen hates, are so loth to be alienated from their Hope in her, that their being actually cast from all Preferments and Places, hath not made them guilty of one seditious, or even undutiful Action. When she shall see that those noisy Men who embarrass the Nation in every Question, with calling out the *Church*, are but like the Weathercocks and Clappers of the Steeple; and that the sober, and laborious, and peaceable Churchmen, are its real Support and Pillars. When a little more time shall bring out things that begin to appear pretty plain already: Then the Queen will shew selfish Men who would engross her Favour, that she will be Mother of all her People; and as in spite of these Mens studied Provocations, she hath their Hearts and Affections, so she will rule with equal Justice towards all. If the Nation will be so wise as to lay aside Parties and Party-Quarrels, she will have no need to keep them up, but employ all Men according as the Law makes them qualified, and their Virtues and Parts make them fit. But if several Interests, and Opinions, and Humours, shall still continue our Parties (as the *Examiner's* Violence and Partiality hath done more to sharpen them, than to take off their Edge) then she will let all see, that her Crown is not to be sunk down to be a Partizan of either Side, so as to take these to be her Friends, and the other Enemies; but that she is over both, and will use either in their Turns, according as they are fittest for the Service she hath for them at that time. And for those who shall dare to insult and exasperate the other as Enemies, they are Syco-phants instead of Friends, and rob her of her best Treasures, which is the Love of all Her People. Wise and moderate Ministers therefore, that have studied the true Interest of the Crown, and not their own, though they might desire to be so much of a Piece as to have their Counsels steady, yet aimed not at Ruin and Extirpations, but left such Marks of Favour in proper and safe Places, that none of the Subjects might think themselves rejected as Enemies, while they kept themselves dutiful. And since the whole Strain of the *Examiner's* Policy is the Reverse of this, though he and his Abettors may deceive for a Time, by calling it Friendship and Loyalty, it is but like the killing Love that the Men of *Judah* shewed to *David*, when (for their own Interests) they alienated Ten Tribes from him at a time: For if they might have no Part or Portion in *David*, they thought it could not be desirable for them to be his Subjects.

ALL this Folly and Contradiction is covered by the general Profession of Zeal for the Church; and many Churchmen, I include many even of the Clergy, have been carried away with the Cry. But let our Senses be never so much deafned with the Cry of the Church, or dazzled with the gilded Pretences of some Politicians, nothing can prove the Clergy more to be Men of Conscience, or truly Loyal, than a strict, nay a scrupulous Ad-herence to the most solemn Oaths they have so often taken, both of Allegiance to the present Establishment, and Abjuration of the *Pretender*; and at the same time Lovers of our Country, than a prudent Zeal for its Rights and Liberties. Such plain and open dealing is exactly agreeable to the Simplicity of the

14

Gospel: As the very Reverse of this, must be, a Declaration for the *Hanover* Family, and yet the asserting of the Hereditary Right; the owning of the Establishment both in the late and present glorious Reigns, and an arraigning of the Revolution; and such like mysterious and inconsistent Behaviour, which naturally tends to amuse and perplex the Minds of the Laity, and make them think very dubiously of their Teachers. Which Conduct is much more reconcileable to the Equivocation of Jesuits, and the Contradictions of the Romish Perswasion, than the obvious Truth and Honesty of the Reformed Religion, especially that purest and best part of it, the Church of *England*. I insist the more upon these Revolution-Principles (as they are scornfully called now-a-days) not only because there never was more need of them than at this Time, but because the best and greatest Part of the Clergy (especially those placed in eminent Stations) have in all Ages, so far as relates to our Nation, and as far as my small Reading informs me, been ready and hearty Assertors of the Privileges and Properties of the People; and why the whole Body should not be so now, is past my Comprehension. With all Submission to better Judgments, I am so far from dividing the Interests of the Church from that of the State, or thinking the just Power of the one inconsistent with the Wealth and Liberty of the other, that I subscribe entirely to the Opinion of the most famous Historian and Statesman, the Earl of *Clarendon*, who thinks the Branches of them to be so interwoven one with the other, that neither can subsist separately. I consider the Church and State as united in just such a Political, as the Soul and Body is in a Natural Constitution; and that the Life, as well as the Health of the whole, depends upon the UNION and Vigour of these their essential Parts. Though the Original and Nature of these distinctly taken, be as different as Heaven and Earth, Spirit and Matter, and their Faculties and Operations by Consequence are as different; yet it hath so pleased the great God, who is the Founder of all Governments, as well as the Creator of all Compositions, so to castigate and remit their FORMS (to speak in the Language of the *Aristotelian* Philosophy) as that their Influences and Effects, whether good or bad, shall be reciprocal and mutual both upon themselves and others. As then the Strength and

Vigour of the Body doth reach even to the Soul (as noble and as pure as it is, both in its Nature and Extraction) and makes the choicest Faculties of the latter, the Reason, the Memory, and the Fancy, more lively, and ready, and active; and as the Languor and Sickness of the former, makes the Operations of the other droop and decay; so the Prosperity and flourishing Condition of the State, casteth a Beauty and a Glory upon the Church, notwithstanding its heavenly Institution; and the Poverty and mouldering Condition of that, doth proportionably waste and incumber this. And (to look through the other End of the Glass) as the Soul, when it has its due Command over the Body, doth communicate a secret but inimitable Lustre and Grace to its homely Consort, (for as the Wisest Man in the World saith, *Wisdom makes the Face of a Man to shine*) and by the admirable Use and Fitness of its Dictates, such as Temperance, Chastity, Meekness, Labour, and the like, doth vastly conduce to its Health, Ease, and long Life; and as the more rebellious and stubborn the Body is to the gentle Government of the Soul, the more it procures to it self both outward and inward Mischiefs of Diseases and evil Accidents; so when the Church is thoroughly fixed in, and united to the State, and sheds its pure and heavenly Influences upon it, the more amiable and venerable the latter becomes by the Practice of all Moral and Christian Virtues; and the more untractable to, and negligent of its excellent and sublime Precepts the People are, the more they degenerate into Atheism, Prophaneness, Debauchery, and all manner of Vice, and hasten with speed to their own Ruin: For as the same *Solomon* observes, *As Righteousness exalteth a Nation, so Sin is a Reproach to any People.* Upon the whole, the nice Proportion and Harmony of each, is the finishing Stroke of both.

Alterius sic
Altera poscit Opem Res, & conjurat amicè.

I have enlarged the more upon this Head, because (since the *Examiner* and Oracles of Policy have opened themselves) many Clergymen are for giving unreasonable Preferences of the Church to the State, and advance such Notions for the securing the former, as (if put in Practice) will infallibly destroy the whole.

I appeal to all the World, whether the *Examiner* and his Friends have not all along discovered such to be their Loyalty; and I defy any Man to accuse me, even in the least unguarded Expression, to have betrayed a Disregard to the Constitution either in Church or State, as I have described them to be allied, and mutually supported by each other. But if any Body has Leisure enough to read *The Honour and Prerogative of the Queen's Majesty vindicated—The Importance of the* GUARDIAN—*The Reasons concerning the immediate Demolishing of* Dunkirk.—They will see the Offences I have committed, and the Resentment of the Authors upon them at large. But a very notable Piece, called *Toby's Character of Mr. St—le*, will let the Reader into the whole Occasion of former Anger, and the Encrease of my Sins against some People. What I have writ about *Dunkirk* provokes the Author to say thus:

" *You may imagine, Sir, perhaps, I wrong the* Demolisher *in my Interpretation of this Passage, especially if we consider him as one who professes, that the* highest Pleasure of an human Soul consists in Charity. As to laying aside, *says he,* those common Views, by which the mistaken World are actuated, a Man of liberal *Education* can easily surmount those low Considerations; and when he considers himself from the Moment he was born into the World as an Immortal, though a Changeable Being; he will form his Interests and Prospects accordingly, and not make Provision for Eternity with perishable Things. When a Man has planted such a Sentiment as this for the Rule of his Conduct, the Pursuits of Avarice and Ambition will be as contemptible as the Sports of Children; and there can be no Honours, no Riches, no Pleasures, which can possibly come in Competition with the Satisfactions of an enlarged and publick Spirit.

" *Was Mr.* St—le *the Person he here would represent himself, I would allow the Sense he puts upon his own Words. This is such a Gift of Virtue and Philosophy which a Man of* Liberal Education *can hardly ever arrive to, how easily soever he may surmount* those low Considerations, *and is never perhaps to be found in any Person, much less in one who bestows it upon himself. I wish indeed I could find any one who would give him this Character: I have hunted every where, I have conversed*

with his Companions *and* Creditors, *with his Friends and Enemies, and I must confess I never yet met the Man who had so
good an Opinion of his Veracity, as to believe him in Trifles
and Matters of the least Importance.*

" *You may blame me, perhaps, for reminding our Author of
his Debts; and I should justly think my self blameable, were
they not the Effects of his Luxury, his Vanity, and Ambition,
and not of Accident or Misfortune. I could easily excuse and
pity a Man for being* poor, *but not when he labours* by his
Vices *to undo himself. Not when he endeavours to make a*
Figure, *or become a* Senator, *at the Expence of his Creditors.*
Some Civilians *look upon such* Chymists, *who are Searchers
only of the* Philosopher's Stone, *as unfit to be tolerated in any
Community, because they reduce not only themselves and Families to Beggary, but several other People; and certainly Spend-
thrifts and Projectors of any Sort are equally pernicious, and are
so far from having any Spice of* publick Spirit, *so much boasted
of by some, that they are useless Members to the Government
they live under, and a Nuisance to the Publick. Where is the*
publick Spirit *of such a Man who will be bribed to recommend*
a Barber, a Buffoon, *or a* Perfumer *to the World, to carry on
Intrigues which a Man of Honour would blush to hear of, and
to* Pimp *in Print? Where is his Charity and* Benevolence to
Mankind, *who is squandering away a handsome Competency
among the* Illegitimate, *who is running into every body's Debt,
and paying no body? Where is his* Disinterest, *who votes for
more than double an Equivalent of the* Stamp-Office? Are the
Pursuits of Avarice and Ambition contemptible to such an one?
And is this laying aside the common Views by which the mistaken World are actuated?

" *Pardon me,* Sir, *however merry I have been, I can contain
no longer*: Publick Spirit, Charity, Benevolence to Mankind,
and Disinterest, *are Virtues known to our* Mushroom Patriot
*by Name only; and it raises the Contempt and Indignation of
every honest Man, to hear a Person of the vilest Principles, and
the most mercenary Hireling, who ever prostituted his Pen in
the Defence of any Faction, giving himself such an Air of
Sanctity and Virtue? A Man of such a* publick and enlarged
Spirit *is as well qualified as any* Judas *of them all to betray his*

Friend, his Benefactress, or his Sovereign, if you bait with a Bribe considerable enough to reach his Conscience: And he may very well be careless what Ideas *are affixed to the Letters of his Name, when it is impossible for the worst to sully him.*

"*I have dwelt the longer,* Sir, *upon Mr.* St—le's *Character, because it seems to be the main Argument at present*; Dunkirk is now demolishing, *and the* Importance *of no Consideration.*"

I would forgive *Toby* ten times more than this unjust Railing against me, if he could make out there is so much done in the Demolition, that the Importance of *Dunkirk* is of no Consideration to the *English. Toby* is mistaken; at this Day it is in a more dangerous Condition as to *England*, than it was when I writ about the Importance of it. For I insisted upon the Demolition of the Mole and Harbour, and instead of that, they have (as exactly as if Mr. *Tugghe's* Memorial had been the Direction in this Case) demolished the Works, and left the Harbour, its Sluices, and all its Accesses that concern us, our Safety, and our Trade, in good Condition. That is, they have destroyed the Works in Possession of the *British* Garrison, to make that Garrison useless, and put off the Demolition of the Harbour till Time shall serve. *Toby* has insulted me for being concerned at such Usage of my Queen and Country, and speaks me well qualified for any ill Purpose, if I am bribed high enough for a Betrayer. I think I know the Author of this, and to shew him I know no Revenge but in the Method of heaping Coals on his Head by Benefits, I forbear giving him what he deserves; for no other Reason, but that I know his Sensibility of Reproach is such, as that he would be unable to bear Life it self under half the ill language he has given me. But in his 21st Page he forewarns the World against the CRISIS.

"*I see,* Sir, *in the Advertisements that Mr.* St—le *is about to publish, by Subscription,* a Treatise justifying the Revolution, and in favour of the *Hanover* Succession. *I could wish his Subscribers would weigh the Consequence of such an Undertaking, or the Government suppress it. I know no greater Injury that can be done to that* Illustrious House, *than by employing such a* Pen *in their Service: And it may be accounted a peculiar Happiness of Her Majesty and the present Ministry, that Mr.* St—le *has been* hired *to write against them. A Man who is so good a* Lawyer, *and knows the Constitution of* Great Britain *so very well, as to tell us that,* as a Member and in the House, he is accountable to no Man, but the greatest Man in *England* is accountable to him, *cannot chuse but descant very prettily upon Subjects as require all the Nicety of the Common and Civil Law.*"

THIS Book is since come out, and I am ready to receive all that shall be said in Abuse of me for printing it, with great Satisfaction, from the Good it has done in laying before my Countrymen their present Condition, and the Rules the Laws have prescribed by which they ought to walk in this great Conjuncture of the Affairs of *Europe.*

BUT as I am leaving off this diurnal Quarrel, I will not omit to take Notice of the *Examiner's* charging upon the *Whigs* the late Rumours during the Queen's Indisposition; which put so many Persons concerned in the Funds into Apprehension, and endangered the publick Credit. I shall point out from whence the most frightful of those Rumours had their Rise, and to whose Account the propagating them ought to be placed; if the Reader have Patience to attend to so long a Story.

THE *Examiner* of *Feb.* 5. has the following Passages.

"THE *Faction,* whose Property in that *Name* grows every Day stronger, have given us a late Instance of their Conduct in the free Dispensation of *Fears* and *Jealousies,* which shews their present Temper to great Advantage, and lets us at once into all the Secret of their Management.—They considered, that it was impossible to regain the Favour and Affections of the People, (after a *Series* of so many fatal Experiments as this Nation hath had of their Conduct) unless they could level the *New Ministry* with the *Old*; and persuade their Countrymen that, tho' they had escap'd Ruin by a *Faction,* they were still in Danger of *Popery* and the *Pretender.* And because they knew very well that *plain Lying,* their last and only Game, would give but a short and faint Diversion, and never do them any solid and durable Service; therefore they were obliged to clamour upon some Grounds or other, and find out a Colour, tho' a very slight one, for their Uneasiness. *Ireland* had afforded them an Incident or two, which drew their Eyes and Hopes that Way.—One *Murphy* deposes before Mr. Alderman *Quin*, of the City of *Dublin*, That he had been *Inlisted* by one *Roch*, a Merchant, in the *French King's* Service (as was pretended) in the Company commanded by Sir *Andrew Lee*; but was promis'd that he should be transported to *France*, and thence march to *Lorrain*, where he should *see the Young K.* and, if he behav'd well, *return soon after* with Preferment. He farther swears; That one Mrs. *Catharine Lucas* is concern'd with *Roch* in the Inlisting of Men; That *two Ships* lie there to take the Men on Board; and that he was told by one of the Inlisted Persons, that they had already raised *Fifty*. This *Affidavit* thus Cook'd and Contriv'd, instead of being transmitted to the *Council* or *Secretaries of State*, is sent over to the *Printer* of the *Crisis*, and *Writer* of the *Daily Courant*, who presently publishes and disperses it as a Piece of extraordinary News; and for fear his common Readers should miss the Jest, *prints* the Words (*see the Young K.*) and (*soon return*) in a different Character; in order to fix the Hint upon them, and bespeak their more particular Notice and Observation. The Consequence is, that the *Coffee-Houses* are presently in an Uproar; the *Party* takes the Alarm; every *Post* carries some dismal and deplorable Addition into the Country; new Lyes are sent to the Press; the *Crisis* sells; the *Snow-ball* gathers as it goes.——The *Englishman* sighs and groans at Sight of an *Old Bull* of Pope *Pius*, and a *Paragraph* in the *Post-Boy*; Stocks fall; the *publick Credit* is at a Stand; the *Queen* is said to be dangerously Ill; the *Ministry* are revil'd; the *Whigs* gain a Day of Clamour to themselves——If this were the last Medley of Lyes these People intended to furnish; or if upon tracing and detecting the first diminutive Story, that gave occasion to all the other Clamours of the *Week*, they would engage to retract their Errors, would promise to amend their *Tongues* for the future, and do Penance by being Quiet and Easy; it would be worth the Government's While to enquire into, and examine strictly, the Contents of the *Original Affidavit*, by summoning the several Parties concerned in it, and sift this whole Affair to the Bottom, which carries with it all the visible Marks of *Imposture*, notwithstanding we should grant, that *Murphy* has sworn nothing but strict Fact and Truth. This however I aver, that *Lee*, and *Roch*, and *Lucas*, and their *Fifty Men*, tho' the *Pretender* were to Head them in Person, are not half so Formidable and Dangerous to the State, as those *Factious Incendiaries*, who have grafted so many other horrible Clamours upon this foolish Incident——."

TO all this I offer the following Answer.

IF the Government should think fit to trace the Rumours (which the *Examiner*, wisely consulting his own and his Friends Interest, says is not worth their while) that gradually raised the Apprehensions of the Publick, and caused the *Run* upon the *Bank*, 'tis believed they would find the principal Facts to stand in the following Order.

I. THE *Examiner* of *Friday, January* 8. gave the following Passage.

" *ACCORDING to the best Advices sent us by the* Whigs *and their Oracles, the* Demise *of the* Crown *happened upon* Thursday the 24*th of* December, *being* Christmas-Eve, *at Four of the* Clock *in the* Morning, *in the Year* One Thousand Seven Hundred *and* Thirteen. *All Ages, Sexes, Ranks, and Orders of Men, at first hearing of the ill News, were affected with the deepest Sorrow, and a general* Panick *ran through the whole Kingdom. For a long time we were distracted and inconsolable; in the utmost Horrour and Confusion upon the most excellent Queen, who then became immortal. But these black Clouds were soon dispersed, our Fears and Jealousies vanished, and we revived from a deplorable State of Grief and Misery, at the first joyful Tidings of the* happy Accession of Her *Most Sacred Majesty Queen* ANNE *the Second (whom* GOD *long preserve) to the Throne of Her Ancestors; the Nature of our Monarchy being such, that immediately after the Death of the Person in Possession, the Crown, by Right of Inheritance, descends to the next Heir, without any previous Formalities and Conditions, or admitting so much as the least Vacancy or Interregnum."*

IN these Terms, which no other Writer durst have used, did this Loyalist speak of the dangerous Fit of Illness which seized the Queen on the 24th of *December.* And as he professes, and is believed by the generality of his Readers, to write for the Ministry, and to be acquainted with their real Sentiments, 'twas impossible for any Man, who is concerned for the settled Constitution and Religion of *England*, to read this Passage in a Paper of such a Character, without seeing through the thin Cloud in which the oraculous Author has wrapped himself, and taking just Alarm: For he discovers his true Meaning, by drolling in so forced a Strain, on a Subject so serious, for a Pretence only to bring in at last a cold Witticism drawn from *the Nature of our Monarchy*.

II. LET it be supposed the News of Her Majesty's Danger on the 24th of *December*, could be so long as seven Days in getting to the Court of *France*; and then let it be considered, whether the following Intimation from *Paris* in the Advices of their 12th of *January*, (which is our 1st) of a Sea-Armament and Land-Forces for a Descent, was meerly accidental, or a Report devised by our new Friends, as proper to be immediately given out upon News so unexpected by them.

POST-BOY, Jan. 12. "*Paris, Jan.* 12. N. S. M. *du Casse* will set out forthwith for *Toulon*, in order to command the Squadron against *Barcelona*. The King is equipping 14 Men of War in divers Ports of this Kingdom, besides Frigates and Bomb-Vessels; which being to join M. *du Casse*, it is thought there is some *greater Design* upon the Anvil, than the Reduction of *Majorca* and *Barcelona*; the rather, because they are to take 12 or 14000 Land-Forces on board, with a prodigious Quantity of Ammunition and Provisions."

THE *Daily Courant* of *Jan.* 11. gave the same Passage from the same *Paris Letter*.

THE *Post-Boy* of *Jan.* 19. entertained the Publick with the following explanatory Paragraph.

BREST, Jan. 11. N. S. "The Equipment of 8 Men of War is continued. It is said, that with the Ships that are fitting out in the Harbours of the Ocean, they will make a Squadron of 15 Men of War, besides Frigates, Bomb-Vessels, and Fireships; but whither bound, or upon what Expedition, is yet a Secret."

THERE was not a Syllable of this in the *Daily Courant*.

AGAIN, the *Post-Boy* of *Jan.* 23, gave this further Explanation.

"*PARIS, Jan.* 8, N. S. They report it at Court for a Certainty, That the King of *Sweden* has resolved to return home by Sea; and, that the King's Ships that are fitting out at *Brest,* and those the English have equipp'd at *Portsmouth,* are to go together to the *Archipelago,* to take his Swedish Majesty on board at *Salonica,* in order to transport him to *Stockholm.* This, however, is *certain,* That our Sea-Armament is made in *concert* with *England*; and *not unlikely,* to carry the King of *Sweden* into his own Dominions."

THE *Daily Courant* had not a Word of this neither.

NOW were the Writer of the *Daily Courant* called upon for the first *Paris* News of the 12th of Jan. N. S. he would shew that he translated it from the original Letter, which is known to come from the Office at *Paris,* called the *Bureau d'Addresse*; which Letter he might prove is avowedly and openly sent duly hither twice a Week, by the same Hands that send over the *Paris Gazette.* And so if *Abel Roper* were asked whence he had the other two Paragraphs, it is presumed he could give as reasonable an Account.

IT may be objected, that *Abel Roper* in his *Post-Boy* of *February* 2, has retracted all, by concluding his *Hague* Article with these Words: "We have no Advice of any Fleet fitting out on the Coast of *France,* nor of any Motion of Troops in that Kingdom, but by some particular Letters from *London.*"

BUT it must be considered, that *Abel* is a Politician, and says this only *ad populum,* after it was found that the *Paris* Articles (which we will not say were originally calculated for encouraging the Pretender's Friends, when the Queen's Life was in Danger) gave too great an Alarm to all true Englishmen. He therefore roundly denies all that he himself had been so diligent to collect from his *Paris* Correspondence, and calls off the Attention of his Readers from *France* to our own Country; and then the *Examiner* steps in, and throws all upon the Whigs.

UPON the whole therefore, taking it for granted, according to *Abel's* and the *Examiner's* last Affirmation, that the late

Fears and Jealousies were founded upon groundless Rumours, and that there is really no Sea-Armament on the Coast of *France* nor any Troops in Motion to go on board; it is, however, plain we were beholden for those Rumours, either to our new Friends on the other Side of the Water, or to *Abel's* Directors here; perhaps to both, (for indeed *Abel's* third Paragraph from *Paris* will not pass with every one for a literal Translation only:) It is plain what the Intention was, had not God in Mercy restored the Queen to a State of Health, and thereby dissipated the Storm that was gathering over our Heads. And it is plain what this Nation is to expect, whenever Her Majesty's invaluable Life shall again be in Danger.

ALL these Rumours from *France* were previous to the Insertion of *Murphy's* Affidavit in the *Daily Courant*; nor have I heard that the Directors of the Bank made particular Mention of that Affidavit, when they waited upon the Lord T—r to acquaint him with their Apprehensions: And yet one would imagine by reading the *Examiner*, that this Affidavit had led the Van, was the most capital Rumour; and that the *Post-Boy* had only contributed some small Paragraph not worth mentioning. *Abel* (poor Innocent) did nothing; the Writer of the *Daily Courant*, since he became Printer of the *Crisis*, has done all; and the *Examiner* very solemnly avers, "That *Lee* and *Roch*, and *Lucas*, and their Fifty Men, though the Pretender were to head them in Person, are not half so formidable and dangerous to the State, as those factious Incendiaries, who have grafted so many other horrible Clamours upon this *foolish Incident*."

AS to that Affidavit, the *Examiner* says very truly, that the Writer of the *Courant* thought it an *extraordinary Piece of News:* He could not think otherwise, for these Reasons.

I. 'Tis extraordinary in its own Nature.

II. It appeared the more extraordinary to him, because in a former *Courant* he had inserted from the *printed Votes* of the Commons of *Ireland* of almost a Month before, this that follows:

" *Dec.* 22. The House being informed, That several Natives of this Kingdom were listed in the *French* King's Service, and were on board a Ship, of which one *Hays* is Captain; *Tho. Price* was called in and examined, and then withdrew.

"*ORDERED*, That the said *Tho. Price* do attend the Lord Chief Justice of the Queen's Bench, to give Information about that Matter."

TO conclude, it were to be wished that this Affair were less extraordinary than the following Pieces shew it to be.

By the Grand Jury of the County of Dublin.

"WE the Grand Jury of the said County do present, That whereas upon Examination on Oath, returned to us this present Quarter Session, and on the personal Knowledge of several of our Fellow Grand Jurors and other Persons, it appears, That great Numbers of young lusty Fellows, all *Irish Papists*, were listed, and have been sent since last *Michaelmas* into *France,* on Assurances given them that they shall soon return home with their Lawful King *James* the Third, as they are pleased to stile the *Pretender*. And it likewise appearing to us as aforesaid, that the same Methods are taken in almost every County in this Kingdom; and at this time that one *James Roch*, a considerable Popish Merchant in *Dublin*, Expends great Sums of Money in listing and engaging her Majesty's natural born Subjects to withdraw their Allegiance from her Majesty, by entering into the Service of the Person who pretends to take upon him the Title of King of *Great Britain* and *Ireland*: We do present the said Practices highly dangerous to her Majesty's Government and Authority in this Kingdom, and to the Protestant Interest thereof. And we have Reason to fear, if an immediate Stop be not put to the Methods now taken for transporting great Numbers of the Popish Youth of this Kingdom into the Service of the *Pretender*, the Protestant Interest of this Kingdom may in time be very much distress'd thereby: Wherefore we humbly make it our Request to the Honourable Bench, That they would lay the same before his Grace the Lord Lieutenant of this Kingdom, and humbly desire his Grace's Seasonable Interposition in preventing the same."

Com. Civit. Waterford.

The Deposition of Michael Letry Killotteran *in the Liberties of the said City, taken before us this 26th Day of January,* 1713-14.

"THE Deponent being duly sworn on the Holy Evangelist, deposeth and saith, that being at *Knockenalden* in the said County Yesterday, there he met one *Toby Butler*, who listed this Deponent in the Service of the Pretender, and was to go on board a Ship that was at the *Little Island*; and that when the said *Letry* was on board, that the said *Butler* said he would give him Three Pounds eight Shillings and eight Pence, and when he was landed in *France* that he should have Cloaths and Arms. When he first listed him, he, the said *Butler* said it was for *Newfoundland*, but immediately afterwards he said it was to go to *France* to serve the Pretender, and bid him for his Life not to tell any Body of it; and declared to this Deponent, that he had fourteen listed for the same Service, and that he would bring them all over here in a Year's time. And when this Deponent said to him, if he would list any, or had no English, he, the said *Butler*, replied, Damn the English, for I am going to root them out. He further deposes that the said *Butler* declared to him, that when he was arrived in *France,* that this Deponent should have four Pounds Advance-Money, and four Pence a Day more than any French Soldier had. And further deposes, That he is credibly informed by several Associates, that there are Forty Officers that have Commissions from the Pretender, arrived lately from *France*, and that they are raising of Men in all Parts of the Kingdom; and further saith not."

Jurat coram Nobis 26	*Mich. Letry* his Mark †
die Jan. 1713.	*Copia vera.*
Francis Barker, Mayor.	*Attested . per*
Richard Christmas	*Fra. Barker*, Mayor.

DUBLIN.

By the Lord Lieutenant and Council of Ireland, *A Proclamation.*

"WHEREAS *William Letry* and *Michael Letry* have given in Examinations upon Oath, before the Mayor of *Waterford* and another Justice of the Peace, That *Toby Butler*, a Lieutenant in the Regiment of Mr. *Butler*, commonly called Lord *Gallmoy*, did actually inlist them the said *William* and *Michael Letry* to serve the Pretender in the said Lord *Gallmoy's* Regiment, and told them, That he had inlisted 14 Men more for the same Purpose. We therefore having resolved to put a Stop to the said traiterous Practices, and to bring the Actors therein to condign Punishment, do by this our Proclamation strictly charge and command Her Majesty's Justices of the Peace, Magistrates, Sheriffs, and all other Her Majesty's Ministers of Justice, to use their utmost Endeavours to discover, take, and apprehend the said *Toby Butler* and his Accomplices, and all such as shall knowingly harbour, receive, or relieve them, or any of them, in order that they may be brought to speedy Justice. And for the Encouragement of such as shall first apprehend the said *Toby Butler*, we do hereby publish and declare, That such Person or Persons who shall apprehend and take the said *Toby Butler*, so as he be brought to Justice, shall have and receive as a Reward the Sum of 200£. And we hereby command and require the several Officers of her Majesty's Revenue in the several Ports in this Kingdom, and all Mayors, Sheriffs, Justices of the Peace, and other Magistrates, to use their utmost Care and Diligence to prevent the said *Toby Butler*, and all such Persons as he hath inlisted as aforesaid, and all such other Persons as shall hereafter be inlisted for the said Service, from going out of this Kingdom. And for the more effectual preventing of Persons being inlisted for the said Service, we hereby strictly prohibit and forbid all Persons whatsoever to entertain or list any of her Majesty's Subjects in this Kingdom in the Service of any foreign Prince or State whatsoever, without Authority or Leave from Her Majesty, or the chief Governour or Governours of this Kingdom for the Time being, as they will answer the contrary at their utmost Peril. And we do hereby declare, that any Person who has been or shall be inlisted or entertained for the Service of the Pretender, and shall discover the Person who inlisted him, before any Justice of the Peace, the first Discoverer of every Person so inlisting, shall have his Pardon for the same; and if the Person who inlisted him shall be apprehended and convicted thereof, then such first Discoverer shall have and receive the Reward of 50£. for his Service."

> *Given at the Council-Chamber in* Dublin the 2d *Day of* February, 1713.

THESE Facts and Passages sufficiently prove, how instrumental that ingenious Writer Mr. *Roper*, and that modest Author the *Examiner*, who conceals his Name, have been in rousing the World out of its late Lethargy, and alarming those who were insensible to all the Regards of Honour, Religion, and Liberty, to take care of what they valued much more, their *Cash*. Self-Interest, which inclines the Minds of Men as strongly as Gravity does Bodies, made every Man look about him; and when the Word was given, for Reasons best known to these Authors, that French Ships were preparing for secret Designs, every Man's Love of his Money (in spite of the Confidence they ought to repose in his Most Christian Majesty's disclaiming the Pretender) made him apprehensive there might be a Visit intended to *Great Britain*. Before this, Men could sit down satisfied, and never consider that it is Nonsense to profess the Support of a Protestant Church, by Steps which cannot but introduce Popery. Before this, you might declaim in favour of the Hereditary Right, and be understood to intend it for the Benefit of the House of *Hanover*. Before this, you might in Discourse give up every profitable Branch of our Commerce, and be received as a Person that understood and promoted the National Credit.

THIS is not all, for before this Run upon the Bank, a Man was thought to argue very well, that would say, for the better Consumption and Exportation of the *British* Manufactures, and Maintenance of our poor Manufacturers, it was absolutely necessary to give both *Spains* to the friendly House of *Bourbon:* But lest a Great Monarch should be tempted by Ambition to use that Trust for his own, rather than our Interest, it would be expedient to keep a Check upon him, by dismissing all our Allies. For our further Security within our selves, and to prevent all Invasions of Liberty and Property, one might very lately have said, the Dignity and Authority of Parliaments could not be better strengthened, than by placing a Despotick Power in the Sovereign.

WE have so little Publick Spirit amongst us, that these things passed like Mathematical Truths, till each Man grew afraid for his own Pocket.

A Man who was uneasy, before this Accident, for the Publick Welfare, and has observed nothing since that puts us in a better Condition; a Man, I say, who from only hearing the News contradicted, that the Pretender was a coming, cannot infer that he may not still come, ought to be excused for writing as I have and do, to raise in his Fellow-Subjects a just Concern for those Civil and Religious Rights which they at present enjoy above all other Nations.

BUT as Fear for themselves, rather than Love to others, is what will most probably affect a degenerate and inglorious Generation, I shall here take the Liberty to refer them to the 33d Page of the *CRISIS.*

I must confess it is a most irksome and painful Work to be ever entertaining one's self with these melancholy Considerations; and therefore for the future I will strive to make my self as easy as I can, and consult (like other People) my own Quiet and Happiness.

TO shew my Reader that I am resolved to look upon things in a less dismal View for the future, I shall conclude this present Writing with a Letter I lately writ in answer to a Friend of mine at Court, who, I believe, out of Kindness to me, gave me some Admonitions and Reproaches upon the Subject of what I had lately published.

15

To Mr. ———— at Windsor.

SIR,

"YOU are extreamly offended at my late Writings, which you are pleas'd to call *unwarrantable*, and give the old Addition to what is offensive to Courtiers, That it is disrespectful to the Queen. I have so much Respect to our Friendship, that I shall explain my self on the Articles wherewith you charge me: First, Meddling with *Dunkirk*, and, Secondly, Writing the *Crisis*. I am sorry there is so good an Excuse for the first, as there is at this time; the main Argument against me, *to wit*, That it was in the Queen's Hands, is vanished: Time has made good what I said, and destroyed what was answered by my Adversaries. The Queen's Garrison is exposed, by levelling the Works, to the Mercy of the *French*, and the Mole and Harbour, which were first to be demolished, stand as they did, the Terrour of the *British* Nation. Thus, Sir, as the Interest of Her Majesty and Her people are inseparable, I think I have behaved my self like a dutiful Subject, in complaining of this open Violation of Her Treaty in the most important Article of it.

"NOW, *Sir*, as to the *Crisis*, what is there said, is founded upon Acts of Parliament therein recited, and Consideration of the present State of *Europe*, with relation to the Power of *France*, and the Interests of the Pretender to Her Majesty's Dominions. You are so much a Courtier, as to say this also is disrespectful to Her Majesty, and an Insinuation that I could prescribe Rules to them for their own Safety and Honour, better than any thing of which they themselves are capable. I will not be silent, for fear of the Imputation of Arrogance, where the Thing speaks it self so apparently as in this Case; and I assert, that you Courtiers fail in your Duty to the Queen, when you pretend to guard Her Authority by Acts, which, in themselves, are destructive of it. Do you believe, *Sir*, it is not possible for any Man in *England* to take off from himself the Imputation of favouring the Pretender? If he does not think it worth his while, he must strengthen that Imputation of Course; and though he means no such thing in his Heart, as to promote his

Interests, the forbearing or deferring to give undeniable Evidences of his honest Intentions in this great Point, is such a Neglect of Mankind, such a Violation of the Tranquillity of his Country, and all that is dear to every good Man, that I cannot see how a Man can think himself capable of making an Atonement.

" IT is in vain for Men, who have no other than the general Good of their Country at Heart, to attempt the Cure of the ill Consequences which this careless and insolent Behaviour of you Courtiers has upon the Minds of the People. It is impossible to make them believe, without the Help of the Clergy, that when Men called *Whigs* are not in Power, any thing can be in danger but the Church.

" NOW, *Sir*, you have hinted that you spoke to me with the more Freedom, because you say you have seen me eat the Queen's Bread at a Table at Court.

" WHILE I did so, I believe you never heard me explain my self, with relation to Her Honour, Safety and Government, but on the Foundation which I have since made my self so obnoxious to you Courtiers, by defending.

" NOW, my dear old Friend, as you have shewed your self very much and very little a Courtier in yours to me, by treating me without your usual Gentleness, and without respect to Queen or Country betraying your self a very supple Gentleman with relation to the Queen's Upper Servants; I shall, on the side of my Queen and Country, be as free with your fine People, as you have been with me for their Sakes.

" YOU talk, Sir, very much of *Whig* and *Tory*, and call me one of them; but I tell you, whether I am one or other, (for I protest I do not know which I ought to be called, till those Terms are explained by the Rule of the present Establishment in Church and State) your upper Courtiers have nothing to do with the Matter. You say they are for the Church; shall we judge of it by their Education, or their Lives? No Man living will deny but there are *Whigs* and *Tories*, or *Tories* and *Whigs* (for I know not which to name first of these terrible People) that are pious Observers of the Ordinances of the Church, and

Laws of the Realm; and the best Men of all Parties ought, in all Reason and Charity, to be the Persons by whose Conduct we should judge of their Principles who follow them.

"ACCORDING to this, what are your Leaders, but what I used in private Conversation to call them, the new Converts? For neither as *Whigs* or *Tories* have they been, so much as in their Education, Church-men; and purely for having no self-interested Designs towards their own Salvation, but leaving their old bleak Barns and Conventicles for warm Houses and magnificent Churches, and skillfully dealing on Church Prefer-ments among Clergymen who have as little Superstition as themselves, they very gravely, and without laughing out while they are doing it, kick the *Whigs* wherever they meet them, and during the very Act of kicking them, tell the patient Ani-mals it is for their Resistance. If any one who has formerly been a Friend to Passive Obedience, comes in for a present Basting with the *Whigs*, the new Converts use him accordingly; witness my Lord you know who. Thus from the good Skill of the new Converts, and the Indulgence which the Clergy are pleased to give them as Babes of Grace, both Parties are occasionally play'd off, and their Noddles knocked against each other, when either pretends to be sawcy; I say the new Converts, when they please, set them to Loggerheads against each other, by naming the By-word *Church*; and those Clergy who are Confessors to the new Converts, because they know themselves capable of Employments in the State, but the new Converts not capable of Employment in the Church, keep up the Humour, to the great Mortification of ambitious *Whigs* and *Tories*, and the no less Diversion of those of each Party, who mean by Zeal for the Church, the Care of Honesty, Virtue, and Religion, and by the Care of the State, the Preservation of Prerogative, Liberty, and Property.

"YOU must know the new Converts are to me the very pleasantest Fellows that ever this Nation produced. Tho' there is no such thing professed in our Church as a downright Indul-gence in any written Form, yet all thinking Men agree they have a plenary Indulgence virtually given, received, and under-stood, by which they may in any thing that does not impeach or waste the Power of the Church, promise and disappoint, say and unsay, swear and forswear, lie and betray, (besides gratifying the natural Demands of Flesh and Blood by way of Whoring and Drinking) without the least Damage to their Sanctity, or Reputation as Lay-Brothers.

"IT was a shrewd Question put by an old Churchman who stood upon Terms t'other Day with a new Convert in a little Matter that concerned his Soul: 'Why if you don't, says the new Convert, the Whigs must come in; but, said the Churchman, *but if they do not shall I come in?*' The new Convert turned his Head another way, and looking upon a Picture in the Room, confessed that *Rubens* was an excellent Painter.

"You and I, *Jack*, know one another very well; I always told you you had a Genius for a Courtier, and I always owned to you I had not.

"I would not by saying this have you think I do not understand a Courtier, when he is a Man of Honour, to be the greatest Character in human Life: When a Man enjoys the Favour of his Prince with a Resolution to enjoy it no longer than it is consistent with the joint Interest of his Sovereign and his Country, he is a great and worthy Character: But if a Man should enjoy the good Fortune of succeeding at Court, with no other View than to sacrifice both his Sovereign and People to his own Avarice and Ambition, there is no Man, but one who would use the same Power the same Way, will bear with such Proceedings. I assure you, dear *Jack*, when I first found out such an Allay in you, as makes you of so malleable a Constitution that you may be worked into any Form an Artificer pleases, I foresaw I should not enjoy your Favour much longer.

"I cannot call you indeed a direct new Convert, but I can very justly say you are a Favourer of the new Converts. When this Appellation runs in my Head, and I must confess I am mightily delighted with it, I cannot but reflect upon the different Fate of those who are new Converts in *France*, and those who are such in *Great Britain*: In *France* they are upon the least Surmise persecuted and dragooned; in *England* caressed, courted, and preferred.

"BUT to answer your last Question, wherein you would

know what a Malecontent desires for his Satisfaction? All that I ask, or rather wish, is, First, The Demolition of the Harbour of *Dunkirk*. 2dly, That *Great Britain* and *France* would heartily join against the exorbitant Power of the Duke of *Lorrain*, and force the Pretender from his Asylum at *Bar le Duc*. And because I would be perfectly impartial, and take off the groundless Suspicion which *Toby* has raised against me, of having from another Hand double the Income of my resigned Place in the Stamp-Office, I wish, Thirdly, That his Electoral Highness of Hanover would be so grateful to signify to all the World, the perfect good Understanding he has with the Court of *England*, in as plain Terms as Her Majesty was pleased to declare She had with that House on Her Part. This last Circumstance, dear *Jack*, would be very pleasing to all us who are Churchmen, because if the Elector should be any ways disobliged, I am confident Her Majesty has given no Cause for it; and I cannot but attribute any Misunderstanding, if such there should be, to the Artifice of some new Converts, who, for ought I know, may still be Presbyterians in their Hearts."

I am, notwithstanding our Difference in these Matters,

Dear Jack,

Very much your humble Servant,

RICHARD STEELE.

Mr. Steele's Speech upon the Proposal of Sir Thomas Hanmer for Speaker of the House of Commons (February, 1714)

When parliament met on 16 February 1714, Steele took his seat as a member for Stockbridge, Hants, and made his first speech in support of the motion that Sir Thomas Hanmer be elected Speaker. His reference in no uncertain terms to the free-trade, Anglo-French commercial treaty antagonized the Tory House; and he was ridiculed for his words " rise up to do him honor," interpreted to mean a compliment to himself.

Hanmer was the leader of the " Hanover Tories " in the House, a group of about fifty, whose defection had made possible the defeat in June, 1713, of the trade clauses in the Peace Treaty. He was a wealthy landowner, a high churchman, an October Clubman, in short a strong and influential Tory in all save trade and the Succession; but in these questions he was on the Whig side. His stand for protectionism, particularly for the woollen and silk manufactures and the port wine trade, and his antipathy to Jacobitism, which he considered hostile to the business interests of England, greatly endeared him to the Whig party.

The letters exchanged between the two men when Steele was expelled a few weeks later are given in *The Correspondence of Steele*, ed. Blanchard (1941), pp. 89-93. Textual notes on p. 642.

Mr. Steele's Speech upon . . . Sir Thomas Hanmer.

(February, 1714)

At the Close of the last Session of Parliament, her Majesty was graciously pleased to Declare from the Throne, that the late Rejected Bill of Commerce between *Great Britain* and *France*, should be offered to this House.

That Declaration was certainly made, that every Gentleman who should have the Honour to be returned hither, might make himself Master of that Important Question.

It is Demonstration that was a most Pernicious Bill, and no Man can have so great a Merit to this Nation at this time, as his, by whose Weight and Authority that Pernicious Bill was thrown out.

I rise up to do him Honour in some measure, and distinguish my self, by saying, *I wish him our Speaker for that his Inestimable Service to his Country.*

Finis.

The Romish Ecclesiastical History of Late Years
(May, 1714)

The framework of this tract is a document purporting to describe a canonization in 1712 by Pope Clement XI; and there are five lengthy Appendixes, the miscellaneous matter of which is analyzed in the Preface. Although tradition has it that Steele was responsible only for the Dedication, there can be no doubt that in addition to planning and editing the tract, he wrote the Dedication, the Preface, the introductory paragraphs, and the various other passages which are given here. These passages, which are interpolations in the main narrative of the document, are speeches supposed to be made to the Pope by Cardinal Gualterio, explaining politics and church affairs in Great Britain. The last interpolation (not included here), on doctrinal matters and the " New Converts," was apparently the work of a collaborator.

The whole thing is frankly propaganda at a critical juncture when there seemed to be a real danger of restoring the Catholic James Edward to the throne. No secret was made of Oxford's having asked him to renounce Catholicism, and his conversion was rumored. During past months there was known to have been considerable activity among papal and Jacobite agents in Great Britain and on the continent: the abbé Gaultier, an agent of the French government in England; the Marquise de Torcy, French foreign minister in London; Cardinal Gualterio, the Papal Nuncio at Paris, in close touch with Louis XIV and spiritual adviser to the Pretender—all these were names well-known to the English public. Steele is writing as a soldier in the cause— in this tract to make threatened dangers more vivid to his readers.

What is said is directed as much against Anglican Jacobites as against Roman Catholics. The purpose is not " to Expose only the *Romish* Clergy, but also such as are unworthy to be of the Number of our own; and that for the same Reason." Steele is speaking, of course, of nonjurors (Dr. Hickes is mentioned) and those high church men who were actively asserting the doctrines of passive obedience and divine hereditary right and were openly or covertly partizans for the Pretender. " Any power, affected by Clergymen," Steele says, " above what the Laws of our Country allow them or Independent of the Sovereignty of it, is to me *Popery*." His real concern is the danger lying in wait for a constitutional monarchy in the encroachment of a church—either Anglican or Roman—upon civil rights. The temper is not that of a bigot, and there is no suggestion here of persecution of the English Catholics.

215

Toleration of their purely religious beliefs is not implied; but Steele was in accord with the liberal Whigs, who, in the reign of George I, sought to remove Catholic disabilities (Letter to Lady Steele 10 April 1717).

The dedication to Lord Finch is in part a gesture of appreciation to the Earl of Nottingham, Finch's father, the old high church Tory, who was now leading the opposition in the Lords to the Schism Bill, a piece of reactionary legislation restricting dissent on behalf of the Church. Always resolute in his zeal for the Church (the Occasional Conformity Bill of 1711, for example, had been championed by him), Nottingham was nevertheless loyal to the Hanoverian Succession and was not one of the high churchmen playing a double game on the dynastic issue. Lord Finch was also being thanked by Steele on his own account. He had been among those who had defended Steele at his trial in the Tory Commons in March against the charge of seditious writing. Textual notes on p. 642.

THE

Romish Ecclesiastical

HISTORY

OF

LATE YEARS.

BY

RICHARD STEELE, Esq;

Suis & ipsa Roma Viribus ruit.

Hor.

LONDON:

Printed for J. ROBERTS, near the
Oxford-Arms in *Warwick-Lane.*
M DCC XIV.

TO THE

Right HONOURABLE

THE

Lord *FINCH*.

MY LORD,

THIS First Part of a Narration, to which I have given the Title of a *Romish Ecclesiastical History*, is only an Account of some Collateral and Contemporary Circumstances, and Secret Passages, join'd to an Account of the Ceremony of the last Inauguration of Saints, by his Holiness the Pope.

It displays the Utmost Abuse of Christianity, and that to the most Fantastical Degree. After the See of *Rome* has usurped the Dominion over the whole Earth, it goes on to Dispose of Heaven also, and to Name the Inhabitants of those Blessed Mansions. These She employs to receive the Importunities of Mortals, before they come at the Almighty. Is this for His Ease who is All-Sufficient, for His Information who is Omniscient? Gross! Prophane! Ridiculous!

This Account gives us a lively Idea of the Pageantry used in that Church, to strike the Imaginations of the Vulgar; and needs only to be repeated, to give every Serious Man an Abhorrence, as well as Contempt of their Idolatry. I take the Liberty to Address it to Your LORDSHIP, in regard that You are by Birth, and Imitation of Your Predecessors, obliged to exert a Firm and Unshaken Zeal to our Church, which is reformed from such Absurdities, and retains every Thing that is Consistent with Gravity, Good Sense, True Religion, Virtue and Piety. Descriptions wherein Men, dedicated to the Service of God, bear a Part, are never to be made to the Derogation of such his Servants, except in Cases wherein they apparently abuse that Respect which the Laity have for them, as Conductors to a better Life, to serve their own Power, Vanity, and Ambition in this. When that happens to be the Case, it is our Business to Obviate such Injuries in the First Attempts of Imposing them on Mankind. For we neglect our Duty to Heaven, when we permit its Interests to be prostituted to Ends unworthy. For this Reason, I dare acknowledge that any Power, affected by Clergymen, above what the Laws of our Country allow them, or Independent of the Sovereignty of it, is to me *Popery*. I cannot think the Endeavour at Temporal Power from the Service at the Altar, a less Guilt, than building a false Superstructure upon that Foundation, which only can be laid for Spiritual, and Holy Purposes.

Your Noble FATHER has in all his Actions maintained so unbyassed an Affection to the Church of *England*, that to His Zeal, more than to that of any other Man, it owes the Inhibition, That any who Dissent from Her shall bear Office in these Realms. None can desire more, who do not think it reasonable that they should also be excluded from Property, and deprived of Life it self for Non-Conformity.

I have often asserted, that they who affect professing their Zeal for the Church on all Occasions, reduced themselves to an Absurdity, and betrayed the Weakness of their Cause, when they ranked his LORDSHIP among those whom they call *Whigs*. By this One Circumstance they acknowledge, it is not Care of Religion, I say, it is not Respect to Religion, or to the Persons of Clergymen, but joyning in a Combination with the least known for Vertue and Piety among them; and adding the Cry of the *Church* to their Common Projects for Power and Domination, which constitutes those (whom they call) Churchmen.

Your LORDSHIP has too good a Discerning to want that these Things should be pointed to You, and it is to the Frank Spirit of Men of Your Age and Abilities among the Nobility and Gentry, we must owe the Amendment of such Inveterate Evils.

I Congratulate Your LORDSHIP upon the Early Conspicuous Figure You make in the Business of the Nation; and doubt not, but You will every Year of Your Life give New Testimonies of Your being a True Son of the Church of *England*, and an Exemplary Patriot to Your Country.

The Noble Motive which First produced Your Natural Eloquence, was what should be the Great Purpose of that Charming Force in all who are blessed with it, the Protection of the Oppressed; and I doubt not, but Your future Conduct will be agreeable to the Manner of Your setting out, to the Nobility of Your BIRTH, the Dignity of Your own Good Sense, and the Service of Mankind in all their True Interests both Religious and Civil.

This ADDRESS is made to You, in Acknowledgment of late Favours to me; and to desire the Continuance of Your Good Opinion and Friendship.

         I am,

           MY LORD,

               Your Lordship's most Obliged,

                    Most Obedient,

                    And most Humble Servant,

                        Richard Steele.

THE
PREFACE.

THE following Leaves are professedly design'd to expose the Prophanation of True Religion, by the Artifices of the Church of *Rome*; and the Ambition of all Men, in other Communities, who make a False Zeal for Religion, their Tool, to work their Way to such Ends as Religion most abhors.

As a *Poem* begins with some Business of Importance, and engages the Reader's Curiosity, to know the Cause which brought the Heroes of the Fable into the Incidents first presented to him; so does this History, for the like Reason, take its Rise from the Consummation of Religious Imposture, a Canonization of Saints.

It is possible, future Parts of this Work may let us into the several Gradations, by which the Pontificate, from less Deceits, grew up into this undisguiz'd and open Oppression, upon all Common Sense. In the mean time, whoever will read that Admirable Scheme, and System of Christian Morality, the *Sermon on the Mount*, wherein there is nothing urged, but from the Force of Reason and Natural Justice, will be amazed to see the pretended Followers of the Sacred Person, (who declar'd himself at that Time) move by Arts which are directly Opposite to his Institution. He will be under very much Temptation, from an impartial View of what our Saviour commands us to Shun, and the Bishop of *Rome* has from time to time Pursued, to Pronounce that Prelate, *The Antichrist*.

After the Account of the *Canonization*, I have, in the *Appendix* to this Little Piece, added Matters, which I think may highly conduce to the Service of the *Protestant* World. As, in *Numb. I.* A List of Societies, made up of Persons of each Sex, not only stol'n from our Nation against our known Laws, and superstitiously immured, to the Loss of People; but also others, of Great Merit, and Excellent Talents, initiated and improved in all the Arts and Sciences, with an obstinate

222

Prejudice to employ them to the Subversion of the Present Constitution of their Country: These Produce as regularly, as our Universities Supply our Church and State with Defendants, Constant Adversaries against them. We may add to this, (which, upon Reflexion, will not appear a Trifle) that in their Nurseries are educated accomplish'd Women, who can use the Charms of their Sex, for the Promotion of their Church, and can Shine in Courts and Conversations, with Arts much superior (and vitiously used with Absolution) to those of our *Protestant* Ladies; whose Highest Good Character and Praise, are confin'd to the Cares and Interests of Their Own Families.

In *Numb. II.* are set down the Fees of his Holiness's *Chancery*; by which, the Reader will find, the Power of the Keys, is a Scriptore full of Cash.

Numb. III. is a Bull of the Pope's in 1357, given to the then King of *France*; whereby the Princes of that Nation have receiv'd an Hereditary Right, to Cheat all the rest of Mankind; and from which the Reader cannot but make to himself the following Inferences.

1. 'Tis plain here, that no King of *France* need stand to any Oath, any longer than it is for his Interest; if He can get a Confessor, to Commute for the Breach thereof.

2. He can't fail of such a Confessor; since it is at his Choice, to take what Presbyter he pleases, out of the whole Body of the Clergy, for his Confessor.

3. That the greater Bigot he is to the Papal Authority, with more Ease to his own Conscience, he may trample upon the most Sacred Oaths, and most Solemn Covenants.

4. That the Dissolving the Principal Band of Human Society and Government (Oaths) is an easy Consequence of the Doctrine of a Fulness of Power, (wherever that be thought to be lodged) to Absolve from Crimes committed, and to dispense with God's Laws.

5. That to Grant such a Power, before the Oath is taken, is a sore Temptation to Take the Oath with a Design of Breaking it.

6. That there is no possible Security, in any Treaty, with Persons who think themselves thus Privileged.

16

Numb. IV. is a Translation of a Pope's Speech, in Approbation of the Murderer of a King. The Oration is vehement; and the Successor of St. *Peter* differs very much from Him, who writ the *Epistles*, which are in the Hand of every *Protestant*; whom I would desire to judge of that Speech, by the Rule of the following Verses, in the Second Chapter of the First Epistle General of his Pretended Predecessor.

> *Submit your selves to every Ordinance of Man, for the Lord's Sake; whether it be to the King, as Supreme, or unto Governors, as unto them that are sent by him, for the Punishment of Evil-doers, and for the Praise of them that do well. For so is the Will of God, that with Well-doing ye may put to Silence the Ignorance of foolish Men. As free, and not using your Liberty for a Cloak of Maliciousness, but as the Servants of God. Honour all Men. Love the Brotherhood. Fear God. Honour the King.*

These Words, I think, are spoken with a Calm and Disinterested Spirit; and cannot, without being shamelessly wrested, be made injurious to Civil Right.

Numb. V. leads to a Collection of Tenets and Positions, which destroy the Tranquillity of Civil and Domestick Life.

In Consequence of such Principles and Positions, the most Execrable Conspiracies have been form'd, and Murders committed. *Arden, Somervile, Parry, Squire, Lopez,* and others, attempted at several times the Life of Queen *Elizabeth*: *Faux, Garnet, Catesby,* and their Fellow-Conspirators, that of King *James* the First, the *Nobility,* and Chief of the *Gentry* at once. King *Henry* the IIId of *France* was murder'd by *Jaques Clement*; *Henry* the IVth, by *Ravillac*; and Don *Carlos,* the Son of *Philip* the IId of *Spain,* by the Monks of St. *Jerome.* Not to mention Later Acts of the Disciples of such a Master, the Pretended Successor of the Blessed Apostle St. *Peter,* who left this indispensable Precept with his Followers,—*But let none of you suffer as a Murderer, or as a Thief, or as an Evil-doer, or as a Busy-Body in other Men's Matters. I Pet. iv. 15.*

I propose these Advertisements, rather as Preservatives to our selves, than Motives to inflame Men against the Persons of *Roman Catholicks.* There are, I doubt not, many among them, who are as much Enemies to the Pope's Usurpations upon Civil Rights, as in other Communions, Wise and Thinking Men, are wary of being deluded by the Artifices of Ambitious Clergymen in their own Church. Such Honest *Papists*, are not intended to be mark'd out for Observation, but to their Advantage: And, to be free, it is not intended by this Work, to Expose only the *Romish* Clergy, but also such as are unworthy to be of the Number of our own; and that for the same Reason, Because they advance Tenets, destructive of the True Interest of Human Society.

It cannot well be imagined how the Cardinal *Gualtieri* should be so much Master of some *Rash* and *Pernicious* Assertions of our *English* Divines, except we may suppose, that the *Missionaries* are watchful amongst Us, to have translated into *Italian*, or *French*, a Pamphlet call'd, *A New Catechism, with Dr. Hick's 39 Articles*: In which, the Reader may find the Main of what the Cardinal brings out at the Masquerade, relating to the Advancement of Ecclesiastical Power. Now I am on this Subject, to bring it home to our selves, I shall take the Liberty to recommend the *Englishman, Numb. 6.* wherein, I think, the Epistle of *Theophilus Deacon*, touches happily enough the present Circumstances of our *Clergy*, and the Behaviour of the *Laity* towards them; but will not forbear to recite from thence the following Paragraph.

" I cannot on this Occasion enough applaud a very Excellent Treatise, called, *The 13th Chapter to the* Romans, *vindicated from the abusive Senses put upon it*: *By a Curate of* Salop. That Ingenious Author falls into this Expedient to examine the Pretensions of forming Schemes of Power from the Authority of the Scripture: He supposes all the different Forms of Government, which are now in the World, had been in Being when the 13th Chapter, so Fruitful of Politicks, was written; and unanswerably proves, that the said Chapter would have disturbed not One of them: Nay, so far from it, that it would have made the Subject of any One of these Governments so much the better Subject to that State, whatever it should be, by becoming a Christian. When the Curate has cleared this Point, he has this close, plain, honest, and comfortable Doctrine. He shews us, that the 13th Chapter to the *Romans, requires of no People, any* more Submission *to the Higher Powers, than* the Laws of their several Countries *require: That it exacts* no other Obedience *than the* Laws *exact: That it forbids* no other Resistance, *than the* Laws *of that Country forbid: And that it* damns *no Man, for making such* Resistance, *as the* Laws *of his Country allow him to make, be it more or less. And after all this, says the Honest Curate, I have the Presumption to say, that there is not a better Subject in all the* Queen's *Dominions than I am: I tell my People that She is* the Lord's Anointed; *that She possesses the Throne, as well by* the Act of Settlement, *as by* an Hereditary Right, *as being the Daughter of King* James; *the Title, and the Hopes of the* Pretender *(be they what they will) having been extinguished by an* Act of Parliament; *so that no Body can or ought to come between the* Crown *and* Her. *I shew them moreover, that to preserve the* Protestant Religion *(which would be utterly subverted, should any* Papist *come to Reign over us)* an Act of Parliament *has quite cut off the* Hereditary Right *of more than* Twenty *several People, (all of them* Papists*) to settle the* Crown *upon the* House of Hanover, *and given to them (as long as they continue* Protestants*) an* Hereditary Right *also. I tell the people also, that Government is* the Ordinance of God, *so Beneficial to the World, that, without it, they could not live in Peace, nor have any Property, nor enjoy any good Thing of this Life; nor call either House or Land, or Meat or Drink, or Cloathing,* their own; *but that every Thing would be taken from them, by such as were Cunninger, or Stronger than they: And that they cannot Love or Thank God sufficiently for such a Blessing, as secures all others to them."*

Whoever the *Curate* is, this Work may give him Comfort, and Pleasure in *Articulo Mortis*; he deserves to be had in everlasting Remembrance for this Honest Acknowledgment, in an Age wherein Slavish and Destructive Doctrines are preached up in his Name, *whose Yoke is easy, and whose Burden is light.* But the Truth is, if Men can bring their Fellow Subjects to believe they themselves are Independent of the Sovereignty; and that the same Sovereign has an unlimited Power over all others; they are in a very good way of passing their Time very agreeably, and driving, fleecing, and devouring Us their Flock, as they think fit. But it is the Duty of every Honest Man who professes himself (though unworthy) a Christian, to vindicate that Character from such Guilt and Imposture; and oblige all who wou'd make their Fortunes by Sacrificing the Liberty of their Country, to search other Writings than the Holy Scriptures for Arguments to support their Iniquity. Fury and Nonsense mingled in a Pulpit, with good Lungs, and Haughty Gesture, will pass upon the Vulgar: But must disparage the Order with all Good and Reasonable Men. Heav'n be thanked, we have Great and Learned Divines, whose Exemplary Vertue disappoints, and atones for the Mischiefs, which wicked superficial Creatures, crept into their Order, endeavour to bring upon us. But say they, there are Enemies to the Church, who make it their Business to lessen the Reputation of Clergymen. If there are Men who delight in reviling, and disparaging the Clergy, must they return that Language? Should a Virtuous Woman hear she was abused at *Billingsgate*, and instead of neglecting such vile Offenders, take Coach immediately; call for the Scolds who had traduced her, and in Defence of her Reputation, return the very Terms in which she was Abused; what Figure wou'd a Lady of so tender and impatient Reputation make; or what would the Standers-by think of her Innocence and Purity?

All I contend for, and will contend for to my last Breath, is, That the Clergy have nothing to say to us concerning Government, but as other Men have it, from the Laws themselves: And while they are pleased to be with Relation to their Fortunes, on the same Foot with us, and Stand and Fall with us like Brethren, as *Protestants* and *Englishmen*, May God Avenge the Injury done to his Ministers, upon him who shall meditate any Thing to their Disadvantage, in the most minute Circumstance.

THE

Ecclesiastical History

OF

Late YEARS.

I HAVE long consider'd the State of these Realms, with Relation to the Unhappy Divisions and Animosities among the Subjects of them, with great Concern; and have sincerely thought, I could lay down Life it self, to cool their Rage, and reconcile their Differences; but have found, it is impossible, by any Thing of which I am capable, even to obtain a Patient Hearing from any, but those already of the same Opinion with my self. For this Reason, I have determin'd to carry it as merrily as the best of them, and indulge my self in Good Days, while they last.

If some merry Fellows, who have the best Opportunities of Knowing, do not believe there is any Danger approaching; why should not we be as Gay as they are? And if they think there is, why should not we Innocent Men be in as good Humour before it happens, as they are, who are bringing it to pass upon themselves and their Country? I speak of the *Jacobites*, and the Friends of the *Pretender* to Her Majesty's Dominions.

To take off the Chagrin which Dabbling in Politicks naturally brings upon People, I receiv'd some Papers into my Hands, which I had directed a Capable Person to Translate into *English*; which is the Second Language it has been turned into, since it was first publish'd to the World. It was some Months ago put into my Custody, as a great Curiosity in *High-Dutch*, and a Thing very fit to fall under my Consideration, in the Character under which I then writ. I have been highly delighted with it; and shall be very well pleas'd, if the Thoughts which rose in

my Mind upon Reading it, may be as diverting to the rest of
my Countrymen, as they were to my self. I shall set them down
in the same artless manner that they occurr'd; so that, I hope,
what is wanting in Elegance and Stile, will be made up in
Plainness and Truth.

The Title-Page, which is almost as long as any other in the
Book, is as follows.

> A *Particular Relation of the Canonization of St.* Pius V.
> *Late Pope, of the* Dominican *Order*; St. Andrew Avellino,
> *of the Order of the* Theatines *Regular*; St. Felice da
> Cantalice, *first of the Order of the* Franciscan Capuchins,
> *and afterwards profess'd a* Minorite; [1] *and St.* Catherine
> of Bononia, *of the Order of St. Clare. With all the*
> *Circumstances that occur'd before, at, and after it: And*
> *more particularly in the Consistory,* May the 22d. 1712,
> *held for that Solemnity: Perform'd by his Holiness Pope*
> Clement XI. *Dedicated to the High and Illustrious*
> *Senate of the City of* Bononia: By Luca Antonio Cracas.
> *Done from the Italian Manuscript at* Rome *into* High-
> Dutch, *and printed* at Frankfort *on the* Mayn, 1712.

It is pity we have no Account of the Thanks of the High
and Illustrious Senate of *Bononia,* to *Luca Antonio Cracas,*
for the Introduction of so many Saints, with whom they were
before unacquainted: And I do not doubt, but the Reader will
be highly satisfied, that he deserv'd at least something equivalent to the Honour of Knighthood amongst us, for the Importation into that their City, of so great Examples to the
Gentry, and at the same time Four New Holidays to the
Common People.

BUT my Author begins his Lofty Narration, [end of Intro-
duction]

. . . [concluding pages of Chap. I.] It is the known Practice
of the Church of *Rome,* to send into all Parts of the Habitable
World, Persons whom they call Missionaries, to propagate Her
Opinions and Doctrines. Over such Missionaries preside proper
Principals, to whom they are accountable. By this means his
Holiness is Master of the Secret of Foreign Princes and Poten-

tates: And I have receiv'd by a very Great Hand, out of a Learned Nobleman's Library, Minutes of the Cardinal *Gualtieri,* who, you must have heard, has been for some Time (by the Appointment of the *Pretender*) Guardian and Protector of the *British* Nation.

It is, it seems, the Ancient Usage, that just before the Great Acts of Canonization, the Provincials Principals (or whatever the Examinants of Missionaries are call'd) should make an Oration in *Camerâ Obscurâ,* that is to say, in the Secret Chamber, or Cabinet; setting forth the Progress, which the Diligence and Care of his Under-Officers have made in the Propagation of the Faith.

I have by me many Pieces, which regard all the several Nations and Countries of *Europe*; but having determin'd to pass my Life within the *British* Dominions, as long as they are wholesome for Honest Men, I have been Curious only in Secrets which concern'd the Place of my own Abode.

In the Evening before the above-mention'd Advancement of Saints, every Man having his Choir Cap in his Pocket, at a Cabinet Council of Cardinals, his Holiness present; the Cardinal *Gualtieri* having bless'd himself Three times, and been Once bless'd by the Pope, gave the following Account of the *British* Nation, and the Hopes he had conceiv'd of their Conversion, or rather Return to the Holy See.

May it please your Holiness,

As I have the Honour to be appointed by the Holy Ecclesiastical Chair, which you fill with Infallible Sanctity, and have such your Ecclesiastical Authority underwritten by my Master, who holds the same from your Holiness; Permit me, according to my Duty, to represent to your Holiness the State of Affairs in *Great-Britain.*

They are, as my Brother *Ottoboni*[a] has observ'd, extremely divided in their Affections and Interests; and give way to the Church of *Rome*, not out of any Zeal which they have for Her, but the intestine Jars and Dissentions under which they labour, divert their Minds from their Danger in general, and allow them to fear nothing, but from each other. I take upon me to

---

[a] Ottoboni *had spoken just before concerning the* English. [Steele's note]

say, that, tho' I cannot affirm I have introduc'd the *Roman-Catholick* Truth, I have gone some Length in Working up an Implicit Regard to the Word CHURCH, without affixing any certain Idea to it, and Pursuing it with the utmost Heat and Rage, without Examining into the Truth or Merit of the Cause before them.

To put this Matter in a proper and intelligible Light, we must look back upon the prevailing Humour amongst the *English* for many Years past, upon the happy Restoration of *Charles* II. to those his Dominions. The just Abhorrence which all good and sober Men of Rank and Condition had for the Sectaries and Enthusiasts, who had caused the Rebellion, transported the younger and more lively part of their Families and Dependancies, to a sort of Vanity of distinguishing themselves from such unaccountable Zealots, by a quite contrary Extreme. Thus because the Round-head, or *Puritan*, would pray in Publick, speak of God and a new Light on ordinary Occasions; in opposition to him, the *Cavalier* thought himself obliged to Swear as loud as he Canted; and to be as Loose and Prophane, as the other was Precise and Superstitious.

The libertine Humour and Example of the Court, gave such Encouragement to this natural Bent of the gayer Gentry, that the most Lewd and Abandon'd of both Sexes, provided they heartily hated a *Presbyterian*, were esteemed Professors and Patrons of Loyalty and Religion: They who drank deepest, talkt loudest, had least Charity, and most Fury, were the Men in Fashion. From this modish Contempt of Hypocrisie and Fanaticism, it came to pass, that the Drunkards and Debauchees, being very innocent of the other Imputations, brought the Mention of the Church into their Riots; and by the same prevailing force of Custom, into their very Passions and Sentiments. The Roundhead grew in the same manner extreamly apprehensive of what they called the Whore of *Babylon*, the Scarlet Whore, and the like bugbear Names, with which (forgive the Mention) their Sectaries scare their senseless Followers from the Holy See.

May it please your Holiness:

From these two sorts of People, the *Round-heads* and *Cavaliers*, are descended the Parties which are now call'd the *Whigs*

and the *Tories*: The Former, have their Mouths always full
with the Word, *Liberty*; and are in constant Apprehension for
their Civil Rights, without so frequent mention of their Religious, as is agreeable to good Policy. The Latter, recommend
themselves, by appearance of less interested Spirits, and seem
to place their Happiness and Glory in the Greatness of their
Prince, joining to it an inseparable Regard to the Church.

These Parties are at endless and irreconcilable Variance: The
Tory accuses the *Whig* of a Design to subvert the Monarchy
of ENGLAND; the *Whig* tells the *Tory*, his utmost Endeavour
is to introduce absolute and despotick Power in the Sovereign,
and destroy the Liberty of the Subject. Certain it is, that neither
of these Men aim directly at the Ills of which they accuse each
other, that is, they do not design the Abuse of those Sentiments
which they profess; for the *Whig* does not aim at *Republicanism,*
nor the *Tory* at *Slavery*; but it has been ever observed, that
from Aversion to each other, each shuns the opposite Character,
till he is reduced to an Absurdity in the prosecution of his own
Principles.

I would willingly, most Holy Father, be very clear in this
Point; I say therefore, the *Whig* pushes for Liberty, till he
stumbles upon Common-Wealth Principles; t'other for Monarchy, till he has almost courted Arbitrary Power. Neither, that
they affect the Abuse of their own Principles; but from their
Hatred to each other, they hurry to their undoing their own
Way, but grow Friends again when they have carried it to such
a Degree, as that they must be reconcil'd, or perish in good
earnest. . . .

. . . [concluding pages of Chap. II] At the Close of the
Evening, on the said *Friday* the 20th, their Eminences *Prioli,
Tomasi, Tolomei,* and *Cusani,* having now received the Cap,
were admitted to the Council in *Camerâ Obscurâ.* When his
Holiness, the Prelates, Archbishops, Bishops, and Cardinals were
assembled, and had taken their Places, the Clerk of the Council
march'd up in a solemn Manner to Cardinal *Gualtieri,* who
stood at the lower End of the Table, with his Eyes and Mouth
shut, according to the usual Form, when any Person is to make
a Speech before his Holiness and Cardinals, the said Cardinals

exceeding the Number of 14. The Clerk went up, as I was going to relate, and opened the Cardinal's Right Eye, who was then supposed to behold his Holiness, and to be astonished at his Refulgency; when the Clerk returned in a solemn Manner to his Holiness's Chair, and begg'd leave in the Name of Cardinal *Gualtieri*, that his other Eye might be opened. It was granted; and the Clerk severed his Lids accordingly.

GUALTIERI was now supposed to see the whole Company, and having made the most profound Obeisance to his Holiness, and made a Fraternal Salutation with a kind Smile and Gesture of his Hand to the Cardinals, he stood in the Action of a Person ready to speak, if permitted: When upon a Signal from his Holiness, the youngest Cardinal, according to his Duty, went up to the Orator, and seizing, according to the usual Form, with his Right Hand on his Nose, and Left on his Chin, opened his Mouth.

GUALTIERI with a most humble and submissive Gesture delivered himself as follows.

Most Holy Father,

I AM truly sensible that whatever I can relate to your sacred Ears, cannot be Matter of Instruction to your Holiness; and that I stand here not to inform you, but to acquit my self before you. The injured Prince my Master, who has your Holiness's Permission to recover the Possessions of his Dominions, by the Extirpation of Hereticks, who expell'd him an Infant, has given me his Orders to omit no Occasion of representing the State of those his Apostate Territories to your Holiness. When I had last the Honour to express my self before you, I gave you as intelligible an Account as I could, of the violent and outrageous Parties in *Great-Britain*; and represented that the hopeful Prospect of restoring your divine Authority amongst them was given us from their Aversion to each other, rather than the Inclinations of either Party to us. But as the particular Pursuits of each of them bears an Alliance to the Dissenters from each, in some particular Circumstances, they are followed and shunned respectively. All those who in their Sentiments are for an Absolute, Indefeasible, Hereditary Succession to the

Crown, follow those who are called *Tories*, for instance the Body of *Jacobites*, and *Non-Jurors*; and all Persons disappointed of Advancement in Fame or Wealth at the Revolution, or during the Reign of their King *William*, add themselves to this Body.

Those who wish for a Change in the Form of Government it self, those who are offended that they are only tolerated in the Exercise of Religion, and not Partners in Civil Power; in a word, all subordinate Sectaries to the grand Heresies of *England, Scotland,* and *Ireland,* think their Condition involved with that of the Whigs.

These Parties are also called by the Words *High-Church* and *Low-Church.* As to the former, they carry all Things before them by the skilful Application of the Word *Church* in Matters never so remote from Religion and Piety.

If You were to search from time to time into the Bottom of the Grievances of their Church, we shall find, that its utmost Oppression and Persecution ever is, that certain Lay and Ecclesiastical Brothers, who still Drink most heartily to its Prosperity, are left to ply their Bottles in the Country, without being sent for to Court, and made great Men.

The Characteristick of a true Churchman is apparently brought to this one Circumstance, to wish their own Friends only in Business, and to esteem a Discountenance of them at Court to be a declar'd Aversion to the Profession and Discipline of the Established Church. Let the contrary Party pay never so great a Deference to their Thirty Nine Articles, their Rubrick, their Canons, and their Homilies; let them frequent the Holy Sacraments, and all the Offices of Public Worship: In short, let them regulate their Lives according to the strictest Rules of Piety and Christianity, they are nevertheless far from being Orthodox; and their Religion is vain, unless they firmly and faithfully believe, that it is impossible for the Church of God to subsist in those Realms, if some very good Friend, or one they think such, is not in the most powerful Office in *Great-Britain.* This is the essential Article, the great Term of Communion, that admits them into, or shuts them out of the Pale of their Church: If they cannot receive, or if they fall from this Faith, they are *ipso facto* excommunicated, and in a word no better than *Dissenters, Republicans,* and *Fanaticks.*

If there be any of their own Clergy who never writ one Word
in Defence of their Faith, or whose Writings are forgotten;
who never Preached but when they were obliged to it, nor visited
the Sick if they could help it, and whose Lives are not fit to be
described; these you may depend upon it, are esteemed Pillars
of the *High-Church*: On the contrary, if there be any who adorn
their Stations with a suitable Conversation, and whose Studies
and Labours for the Advancement of true Religion are famous
in the Nation; These you will find are certainly against the
Church: Even as the present Archbishop, and most of the other
Bishops are called Enemies to their Church; and as Archbishop
Tillotson was before them; who, we must allow among our
selves, was the Living Ornament of his Profession, and whose
Works will always be read with Admiration, as long as Learning,
Reason, or Piety, shall remain in the World.

May it please your Holiness;

I have thus far let the Assembly, (your Holiness knowing
all things,) understand what I take to be the Disposition of
Men's Minds in my Master's Dominions.

Thus far we have already prevailed: That Nation is reduced
and perplexed into the Mistake of Words for THINGS, and
PERSONS for Opinions.

May it please your Holiness;

There remains no more but to keep up this Mistake; for
which there is abundant Occasion, from their own Hatred and
Animosity to each other; which the Assembly will be convinced
of, when I shall on the next Opportunity give a plain and ample
Relation of a Set of People lately become Powerful amongst
them, who like the *Jesuits* in our Church, find their Advantage
by cajoling and managing of each Side, having at Heart their
own Interest only; and who are called by one of their own
Poets, the *New Converts*. . . .

A Letter to a Member . . . Concerning the Bill for Preventing the Growth of Schism
(June, 1714)

The Tory Schism Act of June, 1714, had as its object the rooting out of Protestant dissent or schism in coming generations: it forbade dissenting parents to educate their children in their own schools and academies. The Act would make it illegal for anyone to teach without first qualifying by taking the sacrament in accord with the rites of the Established Church; and thus would be exterminated the dissenters' admirable educational system covering the whole field of primary, secondary, and higher education. The result aimed at was an educational monopoly for the Anglican Church and the barring of Protestant dissenters from liberal professions, as the Occasional Conformity Act (1711) barred them from municipal and state office. Fortunately, the Schism Act, which might have been, as it was intended to be, a severe blow to the Act of Toleration, was born dead. It came into force on the day of Queen Anne's death and, after being only laxly enforced for a few years, was formally repealed in 1718-19.

Without doubt Steele fully understood the two-fold political object of this reactionary legislation designed by Bolingbroke and the high church party, which was to destroy Oxford by undermining his moderation toward dissent and to unite the Tories by rousing the Hanover "whimsical" faction, led by such high churchmen as Hanmer and Nottingham. Without doubt, also, Steele by writing this tract was serving Whig ends. But he was opposed to the Bill on principle.

First he gives the substance of it and shows that it will revive repressive measures against dissenting Protestants in force during the Restoration but cancelled out by William's Act of Toleration. It will deprive dissenters of their natural, religious, and civil rights. Natural justice, which gives men as much right to means of knowledge as to means of life, will be violated. Religious justice will be violated by hindering a man of scrupulous conscience from serving God in his own way and educating his children in the same. Civil right will be violated when a law which men are possessed of to practice their religion is withdrawn. Steele believes that the Established Church will fail to realize any good or honor from a law which carries in it all the guilt of the Roman Catholic Church in using force to reduce schismatics. Not force but "Good will opens the way to Men's Hearts, and the Toleration has thinned Presbyterian Assemblies more than any rigid

237

Means could ever have done." He concludes with the inevitable question: What effect will this law have on the Succession? If the Catholic
Pretender should attempt a landing on English shores, would the half-
million antagonized dissenters lift a hand or employ a shilling to stop
him? But Steele saw the Bill for what it was—an attack on the Act
of Toleration—and he struck a blow against it for the cause of religious
liberty.

The anonymous member whom Steele is addressing has been con-
jectured—by the scholars Nichols and Aitken—to be Lord Finch. This
young Tory was the son of the Earl of Nottingham, high church leader
and a Tory power in the Lords, who was voting on principle with the
Whigs against this Bill. Such an address would be good tactics and also
further proof of Steele's gratitude to Finch, a mere acquaintance, for
a speech in his behalf at the Commons trial in March. The anonymity
might be explained on the ground that Steele had just dedicated another work to him on 25 May: *The Romish Ecclesiastical History of
Late Years.* Thus Nichols and Aitken probably reasoned. But it seems
to the present writer that a more plausible conjecture would be a Whig
member, prominent in the party councils of the Kit Cat and Hanover
Clubs, in which Steele was undoubtedly having a part at the moment
(See his letter to Mrs. Steele on 28 May), Walpole or Stanhope—very
likely Stanhope. The tone and phrasing in reference to Steele's expulsion suggests the banter of familiarity; and the reference at the very
end is to a seasoned, experienced political leader, as Lord Finch was not
and as Stanhope was. In the House debate on the Bill, especially that
on 1 June, Stanhope led the opposition; and it was he who, some years
later, introduced a bill for repeal, supported then as now by Steele
(*Correspondence of Steele,* ed. Blanchard, pp. 337, 339). Perhaps the
reason for not mentioning the name of Stanhope was that on the very
same day with the *Schism* tract, 3 June, appeared Steele's collected
Englishman dedicated to him. Textual notes on p. 642.

A
LETTER

TO A

Member of PARLIAMENT

Concerning the

BILL

FOR

Preventing the Growth of SCHISM.

By *RICHARD STEELE*, Efq;

LONDON:

Printed, and Sold by FERD. BURLEIGH
in *Amen-Corner.* 1714.

(Price Six-pence.)

239

A
LETTER
TO A
Member of PARLIAMENT.

London, May 28, 1714.

SIR,

THOUGH I have had the Misfortune to appear an unworthy Member of your House, and am expelled, accordingly, from my Seat in Parliament, I am not by that Vote (which was more important to the People of *England* than I shall at this Time explain) deprived of the common Benefits of Life, Liberty, or any other Enjoyment of a rational Being. And I do not think I can better bestow my Time, or employ these Advantages, than in doing all in my Power to preserve them to others as well as my self, and in asserting the Right of my Fellow-Subjects against any thing which I apprehend to be an Encroachment upon what they ought to enjoy as Men, and what they are legally possessed of as *Englishmen*, or, if you will, as *Britons*.

This, Sir, is all the Apology I shall make to you for addressing to you in this publick Manner my Thoughts concerning the Bill, now making its Way with all convenient Expedition through your House and the whole Legislature. I shall examine this Matter as well as Haste will allow me, and therefore must recite as distinctly as I can what you gave me in Discourse as the Substance of this intended Law, to wit,

" THAT whereas by an Act of Parliament, in the Thirteenth and Fourteenth Years of his late Majesty King *Charles* the Second, intituled, *An Act for the Uniformity of Publick Prayers, and the Administration of the Sacrament, and other Rites and Ceremonies; and for Establishing the Form of Making, Ordain-*

241

ing, and Consecrating Bishops, Priests and Deacons in the Church of England; it is among other Things enacted, that every School-Master keeping any Publick or Private School, and every Person Instructing and Teaching any Youth or Private Family, as a Tutor or School-Master, should subscribe before his or their Respective Bishop, or Archbishop, or Ordinary of the Diocess, a Declaration or Acknowledgment, in which among other Things is contained as follows,—*viz.* I, A. B. *do declare, that I will conform to the Liturgy of the Church of* England, *as it is now by Law Establish'd.*—*And if any School-Master or other Person instructing or teaching Youth in any Private School or Family as a Tutor or School-Master, before License obtained from the Respective Archbishop or Ordinary of the Diocess, according to the Laws and Statutes of this Realm, for which he should pay 12d. only, and before Subscription and Acknowledgment made as aforesaid; then every such School-Master or other instructing or teaching as aforesaid, should for the first Offence suffer Three Months Imprisonment without Bail, and for every second, and other such Offence, should suffer Three Months Imprisonment without Bail or Mainprize, and also forfeit to his Majesty the Sum of 5 l.*

" And whereas notwithstanding the said Act, sundry Papists and other Persons dissenting from the Church of *England*, have taken upon them to Instruct and Teach Youth as Tutors and School-Masters, and have set up Schools and Seminaries for the Education of several Persons, in Reading, Scholastick, Academical, or other Literature.—Whereby, if due and speedy Remedy be not had, great Danger might ensue to this Church and State. For the making the said recited Act more effectual, and for preventing the Danger aforesaid,

" Be it enacted by the Queen's most Excellent, &c. That every Person or Persons who shall from and after the   Day of   next ensuing, keep any Publick or Private School or Seminary, or Teach or Instruct any Youth or School-Master, or School-Mistress, in Reading, Scholastick, Academical, or other Literature, within that Part of *Great Britain* called *England*, the Dominion of *Wales*, or Town of *Berwick* upon *Tweed*, before such Person or Persons shall have Subscribed the Declaration or Acknowledgment before recited, and shall have had

and obtain'd a License from the Respective Archbishop or
Bishop, or Ordinary of the Place, under his Seal of Office, for
which the Party shall Pay   and no more; and in Case such
Person or Persons shall be thereof convicted by the Oath of
        or more credible Witness or Witnesses, before any
or more Justice or Justices of the Peace within any County,
Riding, City, or Town Corporate, where such Offence shall be
committed in that Part of *Great Britain* called *England*; which
Oath such Justice or Justices are hereby impowered and required
to Administer, and shall, and may. Provided always, and be it
hereby enacted, That no License shall be granted by any Arch-
bishop, Bishop, or Ordinary, unless the Person or Persons who
sue for the same, shall produce a Certificate of his, her, or
their having received the Sacrament according to the Usage of
the Church of *England*, in some Parish-Church within the Space
of   next before Grant of such License under the
Hand of   nor until such Person or Persons shall
have taken and subscribed the Oaths of Allegiance, and Supremacy, and Abjuration, as appointed by Law, before the said
Archbishop, or Ordinary; which said Oaths the said Archbishop,
Bishop, or Ordinary, are hereby impowered and required to
Administer. And be it further enacted by the Authority aforesaid, That any Person who shall have obtain'd a License and
subscribed the Declaration, and taken and subscribed the Oaths
above appointed, and should at any Time after, during the Time
of his, her, or their keeping any Publick or Private School or
Seminary, or instructing any Youth as Tutor or School-Master,
in Reading, Scholastick, Academical, or other Literature, know-
ing or willingly resort to, or be present at any Conventicle,
Assembly, or Meeting, within *England, Wales*, or Town of
Berwick on *Tweed*, for the Exercise of Religion in any other
Manner than according to the Liturgy and Practice of the Church
of *England*; or shall knowing or willingly be present at any
Meeting or Assembly for the Exercise of Religion, altho' the
Liturgy be there used, where Her Majesty (whom God long
Preserve) and the Princess *Sophia*, or such others as shall from
time to time be lawfully appointed to be pray'd for, shall not
there be pray'd for in express Words, according to the Liturgy
of the Church of *England*, shall

" Provided always, That any Person who shall find him or themselves aggrieved by any such Judgment of the said Justice or Justices, may appeal to the general Meeting of the Justices of the Peace of the next Quarter Sessions, to be held for the County, Riding, City, or Town Corporate, where the Offence shall have been committed; who are hereby impowered there and then finally to hear and determine the same, and no *Certiorari* shall be allowed to remove any Conviction, or other Proceeding for or Concerning any Matter or Thing in this Act contained, but the Justice of Peace shall proceed thereupon, any such Writ or Writs of *Certiorari* notwithstanding. And be it further Enacted by the Authority aforesaid, That if any Person licensed as aforesaid shall teach any other Catechism than the Catechism set forth in the Liturgy of the Church of *England*, or an Exposition thereof allowed, or hereafter to be allowed by the Bishop of the Diocess, the Licence of such Person shall from thenceforth be   and such Person shall be liable to   And be it Enacted by the Authority aforesaid, That it shall and may be lawful to and for the Bishop of the Diocess, or other proper Ordinary, to cite any Person or Persons whatsoever keeping Schools or Seminaries, or teaching without Licence as aforesaid, and proceed against and punish such Person or Persons by Ecclesiastical Censure, this Act or any other Law to the contrary notwithstanding. Provided always, That no Person offending against this Act shall be punished twice for the same Offence."

There has not, ever since this Bill was first talked of, any Definition or Description been made of what this same Schism is; nor has it been thought fit to explain whether the Word is to be taken in a Religious or a Political Sense: But as the Bill is proposed in a Parliament, and not a Convocation, we must receive it only in a Civil Consideration, and understand that the Schismaticks marked out in this Bill, are such as do not conform to the Church as it is established by Law, and not as they are Persons who live in an erroneous Way with Regard to Faith or Piety.

The first Thing that occurs to me on this Occasion, is, That by the Act of Union, the Churches of *England* and *Scotland* are equally exempted from any Innovation. The Schism seems to be too Geographical, for as the whole united Kingdom is equally under the Care of the Parliament, it seems a great Omission, that Dissenters in the North Part of *Britain* should not be as much discouraged as they are in the South: According to Justice, Episcopal Clergy should be under the same Disadvantages in *Scotland*, as Dissenting-Teachers are in *England*. But let us, according to the Bill, keep to Schism on this Side the *Tweed*.

By this Bill, without Regard to any thing done in favour of the Dissenters in the Reign of King *William*, (who by the Way was as much King of *England* as King *Charles*) this Act of King *Charles* the Second, of Pious Memory, is professedly supported, and certain Breaches against it urged as a Reason for bringing in this. In the first Year of King *William* and Queen *Mary*, of ever blessed and glorious Memory, an Act passed to exempt the Protestant Subjects dissenting from certain Laws; among which certain Laws, is recited this of the 13th and 14th of King *Charles* the Second.

This Act therefore, in a stealing and too artful a Manner, takes away the Toleration of Dissenters; for the Force of it is directed to take place in Confirmation of a Law which they are expressly defended against by the said Act of Toleration. Is this done like Neighbour to Neighbour? Like *Englishman* to *Englishman*? Give me leave to tell you, Sir, tho'[1] you Senators may do what you please to one another, may do what you please with the Persons of your own Members, we without Doors know you to be only our Attorneys, and that you are not sent thither to impose your Angers, Passions, or Prejudices, upon particular Persons or Parties, but to propose calmly and impartially, according to the Rules of natural and civil Right, Matters which may be for the Benefit of the whole Kingdom. Now, *Sir*, I say, if the Purpose of this Bill be to deprive the Dissenters of the Liberty of receiving Instructors into their Families, or publick School-masters or School-mistresses but under the above-mentioned Restrictions, this Bill is to deprive them of all Right, both Natural, Religious, and Civil.

It is inconsistent with the Natural and Original Right of Mankind; for it is an undoubted Truth, that Men have as much Right to the Means of Knowledge as to the Means of Life: To abridge Men (where there is no Guilt) of a Natural Right, by a small Penalty, is as unjust, tho' not as cruel, as to abridge them of such Right by a greater Penalty. And you may, with equal Justice, take away the Lives of the Dissenters, as punish the Dissenters in their Liberty or their Estates for instructing Children their own way.

This is a Step of the highest Degree of Violation, and there can be no Progress further but cutting their Throats; it is going much faster than our Neighbour Nation went in the like Design. By the Edict of *Nantes* in *France*, the *Hugonots* had Liberty of Conscience and Toleration; by that Edict they had Universities of their own, namely *Sedan* and *Saumur*. These subsisted till a little while before the Revocation of the Edict. Private Schools subsisted to the last. Protestants might breed their Children with Papists if they would, but Papists were discouraged if they sent their Children to Protestants; but still Protestants might educate their Children their own way; so if you please it may be here. It is enough for our Church to let Dissenters educate no Children but their own, and if they will send their Children to us for Education, they may be welcome; further to go is against all natural Justice.

As to Religious Right, our Blessed Saviour and his Apostles neither used or directed any other Means against Gain-sayers than Evidence; and we are often told from the Pulpit by our best Divines, that in the first Centuries, all Apologies for the Christian Religion constantly insisted on this as a Fundamental Truth, That it was unlawful to restrain Men from the Means of Instruction in the different Forms of Religion. It is against the Interest of the Church of *England*, as it is a Protestant Church in general; for it is the Characteristick of Protestant Churches to admit with all Candour the Liberty of studying the Scriptures, and consequently of teaching and being taught them. The Scriptures (by being open to Men who are not allowed to Commune with others upon them, and learn from whom they please with all Freedom) may serve only to aggravate their Guilt in conforming to what they in their Consciences may think Criminal. The Design of the Toleration Act was to give Ease to scrupulous Consciences; that supposes there are Men who think they cannot in Conscience Communicate with us, and this Disability (*of which the Dissenter himself is the only Judge*) is a sufficient Ground for Indulgence to him.

If a Man cannot in Conscience himself Communicate, he will think himself obliged to alarm his Son against our Errours. What a Man thinks the best way to Heaven, it would be monstrous not to shew his Child; and if he is debarred from that, he is persecuted in a Circumstance more grievous to him, than if he were to suffer in Reputation, Fortune, Limb or Life. The Question is not whether he is mistaken; he labours under that Mistake, and for his Sins in that (if he does not disturb the Publick Peace) he is accountable to God. But still it is his Belief.

The Government, as I said, if it thinks fit, may hinder him from propagating his Opinion among those who conform to the Church; but it cannot with Reason and Justice, and therefore cannot at all, hinder him from serving God his own way, and educating his Children in the same.

The *Mahometans* are as much persuaded of the Truth of what they profess, as Men can be; and yet, generally speaking, they suffer the *Greeks* and *Armenians* to breed their children their own Way. What Allowance God will give Erroneous Consciences, it is not our Business to enquire; but as an Erroneous may be a sincere Conscience, we should be Barbarous in pretending to Oppress or put Hardships upon it: The Welfare of their Children is as dear to the Dissenters, as their own; and if Men would make it their own Case, it would not require a moment's Thought to determine, in favour of this Unhappy, threatened People.

Now as to Civil Right. As *Englishmen*, they are possessed of a Law in their Favour, which indulges them in the Exercise of their Religion; and where there is a Right to a Benefit, there are supposed to go along with it, the necessary means of attaining that Right; These Means are intercepted, when Education towards enjoying this Right is prohibited. The plain and fair method of doing what is intended by this Act, had been to have numbered the Dissenters, and to have made a Law, that none should dissent from the Church, after the Decease of the Persons mentioned in a following List, and so to have named all the present Schismaticks; forbidding single Persons among them to Marry, 'till they had Conformed. This had been perhaps more Offensive at first View, but it had not been so Injurious as this Bill will appear, upon Reflection; For it is a much less Evil, to prevent the Encrease of Mankind, than to debar them of their Natural, Religious, and Civil Rights, after they are come into the World.

But let us consider this matter more closely, and examine this Bill, *First*, as it may affect the Tranquillity of the Nation in General: And *Secondly*, as it will affect the Prosperity of the Church of *England*, for the Safety and Benefit of which it is pretended to be calculated.

As to the Publick Peace, it will naturally bring that into the utmost Distraction, by alienating the Affections of Families, Neighbourhoods, and Corporations from each other, by Ten thousand little Incidents, which cannot be provided against, or described: Conversation throughout the Kingdom will turn upon this Subject; and this People, the Dissenters, as well as those who have any Compassion for them, will be marked out, to be the Scorn and Derision of those who are averse to them; and they, on the other side, will be filled with Rage and Indignation against such their Adversaries.

Men who are old enough to remember the manner of Executing the Laws formerly Enacted against the Dissenters, will inform you, that Constables attended by Guards, and Commission-Officers at the Head of Files of Armed Men, used to visit Meetings, and conduct the poor Wretches to Gaols, for calling upon and worshipping God their own way. Let any one read the Tryal of *Pen* and *Mead*, and he will see the Spirit of those Days: The whole Nation was made up of Criminals and Accusers, and both believed they were doing Service to God. But as this Bill is in it self to the last degree Cruel, even such as it is, it is not preserved so well against a Licentious Execution of it, as the Law directs in less Cases.

However well disposed Ministers and Officers may be, it is for the Good of Mankind, to put as many Checks against an Arbitrary Exercise of Power as possible; but this Bill puts the whole Body of Dissenters under such Persons, as may be pick'd out, by one Officer of State, to Exercise it in the most Summary and Passionate manner.

According to this Bill, if, in any future Reign, a Chancellor

should be an Enemy to that distressed People, he may bring a
Persecution upon them, by naming proper Sets of Justices of
the Peace, and himself sit well excused from their Irregularities;
for tho' he might know it in their Tempers to be violent, he is
not accountable for their Practice, nor are they themselves in
terrour of Appeals, for Arbitrary Conduct. There are Squires
enough in this Kingdom, ready to distress Presbyterians with
the utmost Rigour, tho' they know no more why they are angry
with a Presbyterian, than a Turkey-Cock why it raises its Crest
at a Man whistling at him. They are bred in a Prejudice against
them, and will fall upon them with as little Consideration, as
Beasts of Prey do on those Animals, which Instinct prompts
them to seize.

Such Judges as these this Bill would give a Court Power to
appoint, for pronouncing the last Decision in Cases of the
highest Consequence, tho' the Law gives an Appeal from them
in the lowest Disputes of Property!

Now let us consider how this Bill will affect the Church of
England. It will bring upon it great and unanswerable Scandal.
It will give Arguments to her Enemies, that she is conscious of
her Inability to defend her self by Reason and Truth, when she
flies to the Secular Power to take off her Dissenters. It will
carry in it all the Guilt which we object against the *Roman*
Catholicks, in founding her Power in the blind Obedience of
the People, and not in the Conviction of their Minds.

When we have done this, and used Force in our gaining
Proselytes, why should not the Church of *Rome*, which has more
Force, employ it all in reducing us, who are, they say, Schismaticks from them? Can any thing be juster than to make Us
suffer, what We in the same case impose on others? Add to
this, we shall prosecute them for omitting what our Church
cannot pronounce Necessary to Salvation; the *Roman* Catholicks
would assault Us for what they think Damnable, and what they
think they are obliged, in Conscience, to avenge and extirpate.

The Dissenters have a Law made in their Favour, since which
there has been also Care taken, by another Law, to prevent their
Capacity from any share of Power to give us Disturbance.
What have they done, to make it needful to take further Securities against them? If they have done nothing, it is the utmost

Barbarity to take any Right from Men, who have committed no Offence: Have our own Clergy remonstrated, that this is Necessary for their Interest or Safety? Do they say they are too busie in debauching their Flocks? Do our Universities say, their Academies breed Men too hard for them in Dispute? Do not Dissenters pay Dues and Tithes like the rest of their Congregations, tho' they maintain also Pastors in their own Way? Can we not believe them to act Conscienciously, when they are contented to have no part in the Honours and Profits from the Service of their Country, and put themselves also to double Expence to enjoy their Religion?

This is a most extraordinary Point, at this time of Day; When other Nations are plagued with Inquisitions and Ecclesiastical Tyranny, shall we from the Example of their Misery set up, or make a step towards such Tyrannies? Shall we at this time offer to make a Complement to the most Pure, Learned, and Apostolick Church in the World, of unjust Means to subdue their Opponents? Will you not at least have the Sense of the Convocation, now Sitting, before you take Measures to the Impeachment of their Reputation as Casuists?

But to use Force is not the way to subdue them; it is against Nature and common Sense to think they are to be gained by such Methods. Good-will opens the way to Men's Hearts, and the Toleration has thinned Presbyterian Assemblies more than any rigid Means could ever have done. No Man is persuaded by him who hates him, but all are easily prevailed upon by those who love 'em. The Dissenters are quite another kind of People, than they were before the Toleration. By this Indulgence to them, it is a known Observation, that they are brought into the Methods of Life in common with the best and most polite People, and Crowds of the Generations which have grown up under the Toleration have conformed to the Church, from the Humanity of that Law. The Fathers of Families have, perhaps, found some Pain in retracting their Errors, and in going into new Communities and Conversations; but we see thousands connive at the Conformity of their Children, the Parents have been secretly pleased at their Sliding into that Oeconomy, for which the Fear of the Imputation of Self-interest, or Apostacy prevented them in their own [2] Persons to declare.

And yet all of a sudden, without any manner of Provocation, a Million[?] of her Majesty's Subjects are to have the Law, by which they enjoy the dearest Blessings of Life, taken from them. An Act that will certainly gain to us all that are not worth having, and make those who are animated by Virtue and Piety more averse to us. They will have a juster Exception against us from this very Act than they had before. Kind Treatment every Day brought new Proselytes amongst us, and they were insensibly wrought into our Sentiments; but either as Men, or as Christians, they must abhor the thought of adhering to us out of Fear. This Motive is in it self a faulty one, for resigning not only any Tenet of Religion, but of common Obligation. Passive Obedience is said to be a Doctrine of the Church of *England*, but it is a terrible Article to be made the first in the Catechism, as it would be to those who are to come in upon Compulsion.

When we consider the putting this Law in Execution, there cannot be a more pleasant Image presented to the Imagination, than a poor Schismatick School-Mistress brought before a zealous angry Squire for transgressing this Act, and teaching one Presbyterian, yet little more than an Animal, in what the Letter *D* differed from the Letter *B*; maliciously insinuating to another Schismatick aged five Years old, without Licence from the Ordinary, that *O* is round; and not contenting her self with meerly showing to the said Schismaticks the Letters of a certain Book covered with Horn; but instructing the said Hereticks to put them together, and make Words of them; as appears by the Affidavit of one who heard one Infant Schismatick say, *o f, of,* another *o b, ob*—Prodigious! that a Church adorned with so many Excellent and Learned Members, supplied by two famous Universities, both endowed with ample Revenues, Immunities, and Jurisdictions, should be affronted with the offer of being reinforced with Penal Laws against the Combination of Women and Children! You might with the same Propriety provide against Schismatick Nurses.

This Act seems such a Violation of Natural Justice, that it may be made a Question whether it ought to oblige, after it is enacted. I am sure it is such, that if the Dissenters are to consider whether they will obey it, or fly into another Nation, they must chuse the latter; and Lands untenanted, or Tenants disabled by the loss of half a Million of People, will be sensibly felt by the Incumbents on small Livings. Now I have mentioned small Livings, Why does no Body represent, that in *Wales*, and some Parts of *England*, Men in Holy Orders are forced to subsist with an Income below that of Day-Labourers? Why do not you, while you are courting the Clergy, help this particular? If you go on in such Designs as these, will it not suffice? No: this would be nothing but Charity and Piety, and would carry no Point for those of the Clergy who affect Power and Grandeur, and lend the Word *Church* to promote Secular Ends, to the Disparagement of God's Holy Word of which they are unworthy Dispensers.

It is possible Bishops that are given to Preaching, and Ministers who are in earnest in their sacred Calling, would be enough obliged by such Acts in favour of their Indigent Brethren; but what would that do towards pulling down what they call *the Faction*? Godly Clergymen can't do that Service which is necessary; Self-denial, Meekness and Charity are too slow Instruments for men of Dispatch and Business.

But it is to be hoped the Fallacy of using the Pretence of the Church in Cases which are so far from promoting Religion, that they scandalize and disparage it, will be thoroughly understood, before such a destructive Bill, as this, can go through any Part of the Legislature; tho' if it shou'd, it is still to be hoped Her Majesty will confirm to her self the Love and Affection of all who have a true Sense of Religion, by rejecting a Bill so terrible to scrupulous Consciences, and which can be serviceable to none but such as have no Sense of Conscience at all, such as have so entirely forgotten what it is that they have no Notion of the Compunctions it may give others.

No Man can exert himself on a more worthy, or more important Occasion, than in Opposition to this Bill; and if it is at last rejected by Her Majesty, she will do as great a Service to true Piety, and the Interests of the Church, as Queen *Esther* did, when she averted the Extirpation of the *Jews*.

He that will in the least reflect, can have no room to believe, that the Interest of Religion can be advanced by this Bill. Therefore as it cannot truly concern the Church to have it take place, let us see a little how the passing of it into a Law would be Useful to the State.

The great Points to be considered at this Juncture in debating on any publick Circumstance, is how the Matter before us will regard the House of *Hanover*, or the Pretender.

It has been already observed, that this Proceeding against our Protestant Brethren may be a fatal Example to the *Roman* Catholick World, to join its whole Force to suppress Us.

If we look upon the Places distant from the Court: We have undoubted Intelligence, that there are Men carried away every Day out of *Ireland* for the Service of the Chevalier at *Bar-le-Duc*: That several of the Clans in *Scotland* seem to expect with impatience his Arrival in that Part of the Kingdom, in Hopes of Ravaging the Estates of Gentlemen, remarkable for their Zeal to the House of *Hanover*. If you please to consult the Members for that Part of *Britain*, they will not dissemble their Fears on this Occasion. This Pretender himself is still at *Bar-le-Duc*, notwithstanding the repeated Instances to remove him; and the King of *France*, his ancient Friend and Patron, is so little careful to manage it decently towards Us, that he does not only suffer him to stay at *Bar-le-Duc*, but in further Contempt of us, the Great Monarch is building an Harbour at *Mardyke*, to serve in the same stead that *Dunkirk* did heretofore.

Now when there are these melancholy Prospects before our Eyes; when no one of the Family of *Hanover*, tho' long expected, is yet arrived in this Kingdom; and when many Weak People are under strange Apprehensions, because the Proclamation for bringing the Pretender to Justice, in case he should land here, is put off; I say, when many things pass every Day on which *Jacobites* make Reflections to their own Advantage, and ordinary People, who cannot judge of Reasons of State, put all these things together, it creates in them a Chagrin and Uneasiness, which will be mightily encreased by the passing a Bill that may be to the Mortification of the meanest Persons in the Protestant Cause.

It is therefore no time to do a thing, which will take off the Hands and Purses of Half a Million of People, as Friends to the House of *Hanover*; Half a Million of People, as Enemies to the Pretender.

If this Bill passes, and the Pretender should come upon our Coast, I would fain know what could move a Dissenter to lift an Hand, or employ a Shilling against Him? He has at present no hopes of Preferment, and would by this Bill be under daily Apprehensions of the loss of the Toleration, as to himself, as well as being wholly bereft of it as to his Posterity. He would have certainly Promises from the Pretender of Liberty of Conscience, and he could but have those Promises broken, as in this Case he would have it to say they had been before, and must expect some Sweetnesses at a new Change for standing Neuter, or exerting himself for the Invader. Thus he would rather, according to his own Interest, wish an Invader Success than Disappointment; add to this, some Pleasure in the revengeful Hope of seeing us, who had Persecuted him, fall into the same Calamity.

This, dear Sir, is all I have to trouble you with on this Occasion; and tho' you accused me of being cast down with my Expulsion, you see I have not Dunn'd you to move, that the other Pamphlets may be examined, as well as the *Crisis* and the *Englishman*. Give my Service to poor *Tom* and *Ned*. I must confess they were the last I forgave, but I have forgiven them too now. I am thoroughly convinced, since this Bill, that I was not worthy: For now you have taken upon you Ecclesiastical Matters, and I should not have known how to behave my self among you as a Communion of Saints.

I doubt not, Sir, but your Voice and excellent Talents will be employed against this pernicious Bill: To oppose it strenuously, will be worthy that Resolution and Modesty for which you are so remarkably conspicuous; that Modesty which cannot incline you to bear hard against Persons or Things, when you happen to be with a Majority, and that Resolution which prompts you to assert what you think Truth, tho' under the Disadvantage of the most inconsiderable Minority.

I am, SIR,

Your most Obedient,

Obliged, Humble Servant,

Richard Steele.

The French Faith Represented in the Present State of Dunkirk (July, 1714)

In 1714 Dunkirk was still a symbol of Whig discontent with Tory foreign policy; and Steele, in accord with mercantile opinion, continued his propaganda against the delay in destroying the fort and particularly the harbor there. This, his third pamphlet on the subject, discloses France's method of procrastinating. While pretending to demolish Dunkirk, she had been constructing a new port at the neighboring Mardyk, insuring even more effective harbor facilities. Steele explains the unfavorable bearing of this fraud upon English trade, the disadvantages in the event of a surprise war with France, and the increased danger of the Pretender's movements toward English shores. He advocates a parliamentary vote denouncing the delay at Dunkirk in order to "fright our new Friend into common Honesty." Indeed Steele himself on 15 March of this year had introduced a motion—which was voted down—that the report of engineers and officers who had the demolition in charge be laid before the House.

The French continued this delay by one artifice and another until after the accession of George I. In August, 1716, Stanhope's treaty with France confirming other articles of the Treaty of Utrecht compelled her to destroy the fortifications and sluices of Dunkirk and Mardyk at last.

Steele had written two tracts on the subject in 1713 and had touched on it in others and in *The Englishman.* There were several answering tracts, some in agreement and others in disagreement. *The Examiner,* which Steele believed, if not written by Swift, to be under his direction, had kept up a running attack. Swift's tract *On the Importance of the Guardian Considered* (29-31 Oct. 1713), attacking him personally rather than his arguments, was deeply malicious. Textual notes on p. 643.

18

THE
FRENCH FAITH

Reprefented in the

Prefent State of DUNKIRK.

A

LETTER to the *EXAMINER,*

In Defence of Mr. S——le.

——*Summam vim effe in omnibus iis arbitriis, in qui-bus adderetur,* ex fide bona.   Tull.

LONDON,

Printed: And Sold by *Ferd. Burleigh,* in *Amen-Corner,* 1714.

THE

FRENCH FAITH

Represented in the

Present State of DUNKIRK.

SIR,

I Designed you this Trouble ever since the 24th of *May* last, in case all should not prove true in your Paper which came out that Day: You therein fall upon my mortified Friend *Dick Steele*, and endeavour to make an unfortunate Man ridiculous, by ending that your Paper with what you Inscribe,

A most humble Address or Memorial presented to R. S. *Esq*; *by the Sieur* Tugghe. You make *Tugghe* say, "I can now inform you, Sir, with Tears and a Heart full of Anguish, That *Dunkirk* is Demolish'd. Not only the Martial Works, that struck Terror on all the Beholders, and were thought Impregnable against all Valour, except *Your Mightiness's*, but the Mole, Dikes, Basons and Harbour, are all levelled and destroyed; a Spectacle full of Horror, and a lasting Moment of your Anger and Indignation, against the Inhabitants of a Town long since overwhelmed with Grief. So many Thousands, Mighty Sir! reduc'd to Want and Misery, might have pleaded for your Commiseration: But you were (pardon the Expression) Implacable; their Doom was gone out, and you would not Alter or Reverse it.

"Whither should so many wretched Families betake themselves? Could they look upon themselves devoted, by so great a Lover and Benefactor to Mankind as *Your Mightiness,* to utter Misery and Dispersion? Far be that Thought from our Hearts. But scarce had we made a small Settlement of some few Families at *Mardyke*, when the melancholy News reach'd our Ears, of the Umbrage taken against us at *Your Mightiness's* Court;

259

contrived by Evil-minded Men, the Enemies of Society; intending to make you Jealous of us, as if we were about to Fortifie and Erect another *Dunkirk* there; a Work, alas! as much unequal to our Circumstances, as it is distant from our Intentions; whereby we might once more become the deplorable Objects of your Vengeance.

"To prevent this Blow, we now lay our selves at *Your Mightiness's* Feet; intreating you to satisfie your Justice with our present Misery."

Here, Sir, is what you were pleased to say, or what Mr. *Tugghe* says, in your Paper. A Memorial was handed about the Publick Streets, praying that *Dunkirk* might not be Demolish'd, tho' the Memorialist acknowledged her Majesty had signified to him by her Secretary of State, the Lord *Bullingbroke,* that the Queen would have it demolished. Mr. *Steele,* to prevent the Poison which that Piece might disperse among the People, writ a Discourse against it, and exposed the specious Insinuations of Compassion to a devoted People, and the like, and defended the Queen's Resolution with so much Zeal and Warmth, that he drew upon himself the Anger of all the Courtly Writers, at the head of whom is deservedly placed your Eminence. He is a very unhappy Man, that could not speak against what was rejected at Court, without incurring the Displeasure of those who pretend to write for it. Supported by so good an Authority as the Queen and Her Minister, he thought it a good Action to convince all the World of the Necessity of Demolishing that Harbour, and that Necessity is very distinctly represented in the 26th Page of the Pamphlet called *The Importance of* Dunkirk *considered.*

"The Port of *London,* says the Author, is allowed to carry Two Parts in Three, or Six Parts in Nine, of the Foreign Trade of *England.* We may give one Ninth to the Ports on the *South* Coasts of this Island, which *South* Coast is opposite to the *North* Coast of *France*; the Sea between which is what we call the Channel.

"The *East* End of this, on our Side, is the *North* Foreland, which stands opposite to *Newport* in *France*; the *West* End, on our Side, is the Land's-End, over-against *Ushant,* or *Brest* in *France*; they allow one Ninth of the Trade to the *East* Coast washed by the *German* Ocean; and the other Ninth to the *West* Coast, which looks on the *Irish* Seas.

" *Dunkirk* is from the *South* Foreland about 13 Leagues, and the Coast from *Dunkirk* to the Foreland, *West, North-West,* to the Entrance of the River *Thames,* is *North-West* about 20 Leagues; so that any Easterly Wind, which carries our Ships down the Channel, at the same time brings those of *Dunkirk* to meet and intercept them: The *French* have very frequently this last War reaped the Advantage of this Situation, by surprising many rich Ships, and taking others as they lay at Anchor in the *Downs*; when the *French* are dispossessed of *Dunkirk,* the dread and danger of their Men of War, of any considerable Force, will be removed as far as *Brest,* which is a hundred and twenty Leagues, or three hundred and sixty Miles; and that of their Privateers, of any Consideration, as far as St. *Malo's,* which is 78 Leagues, or 234 Miles.

" *Brest* lies without the Channel, under this great Incapacity to hurt us, that the same Wind which carries our Trade down the Channel, prevents the Ships of *Brest* from coming into it.

" The *East* End of the Channel which is so much exposed to *Dunkirk* is but 7 Leagues broad, and gives an Enemy an Opportunity of seeing our Ships from Side to Side.

" The *West* End of the Channel, for which the greatest Fears are from *Brest,* is 28 Leagues broad, and of course there is at that End a greater Chance of escaping the Enemy.

" If Ships from *Brest* are appointed to Way-lay our Ships in the Channel, they must take the Opportunity of Westerly Winds, to come into it; and wait the coming of an Easterly Wind to carry our Ships down it; by this means they must all that time be at Sea, exposed to all Dangers for want of a Port in which to Harbour their Men of War, or return to *Brest,* which they cannot do with the Wind that brought them out.

" We must add to this, that if the *French* from *Brest* should be hovering to the Eastward of *Plimouth,* they are between two Fires, from those Ships in the *Downs,* and those from *Plimouth*; and our Ships from *Portsmouth* may chase them either Way, while they are way-laid at each End of the Channel by the others, not having the Port of *Dunkirk,* or any other in the Channel, to afford them Shelter. Thus, should they be chased up the

Channel by a too great Force, before they can return to *Brest,* they must either run into the *German* Ocean, and wait another Opportunity of coming down again, with the Hazard of meeting all our Men of War; or else sail *North* about *Great Britain,* which is at least 550 Leagues more than they need have sailed, with the Port of *Dunkirk* to fly to.

" This Want of *Dunkirk* will expose them to the same Inconvenience, to which the Fear of it often obliged our running Ships from the *South* Parts of the World, as well as our *East-India* Men, during the late War: To this Distress you are to add Wages, Provision, loss of Time, and the dangerous Navigation of the *North* Seas.

" From hence it plainly appears, that by the Demolition of *Dunkirk,* in case of a Rupture with *France,* Six Parts in Nine of our Trade, from the Port of *London,* is 330 Miles removed from the Hazards of the last War; and though part of this must be exposed when it passes through the *Chopps,* or Western Entrance of the Channel, it must be considered, that this it was also liable to before, besides the Terrors of *Dunkirk,* and that this is only the Southern Trade; and all that go to *Holland, Hamborough,* and other Northern Countries, will be quite out of Danger.

" The Ninth of our Trade on the *East* Coast would be still safer.

" From these distinct Considerations, you observe only one Ninth of the Trade on the *Irish* Seas and *Bristol* Channel, and part of the other Ninth in the Coast of the Channel (to come at which they are in danger from *Portsmouth* to *Plimouth*) is the whole of the *British* Trade, which after the Demolition of *Dunkirk* will lie open to the Assaults of the *French.* The Demolition of *Dunkirk* will in a great Measure secure seven Ninths of the Trade of *England,* from the Power of *France* at Sea, the *French* having no Port in the Channel but St. *Malo's,* which can harbour any great Ships, and that it self can receive none which exceeds 30 or 40 Guns. *Brest* lies 35 Leagues from the *Lizard* Point, which is the nearest Land of *England*; their Ships must have an Easterly Wind to come out, and that will serve them no farther than to the *Chopps* of the Channel, because it blows directly down it.

" The Course to go from *Brest* to cruise off the *Lizard* Point
in order to annoy Us, is first, *West* about 13 Leagues, and then
North or *North* and by *East* about 30 Leagues more, except
they run the Hazard of going within the Island of *Ushant* which
is not practised, and therefore may be supposed Impracticable.

" In the last Place, our Charge in defending our selves from
such Annoyance as we formerly had from *Dunkirk*, will decrease
in Proportion to the removal of the Danger.

" Such is the Importance of the Demolition of *Dunkirk*, with
regard to the Trade of *England* only; and in the present Conjuncture, I think we ought to have something more than the
Mercy of his Most Christian Majesty, to render the forbearing
such Demolition less Hazardous to our Religion and Liberty."

All that is of Consequence to us is, that *Dunkirk* should be
no longer a Receptacle for Ships, and the Demolition of it as
a Garrison is of much less Consideration, if not wholly insignificant to us.

Our Treaty of Peace provided for this, and demanded it to
be done in the first Place, and his most Christian Majesty consented it should be so. Mr. *Steele*, with his Name to what he
said, spoke of it as an *English* Subject, and your Eminence was
highly offended with him for doing so; you urged that it was
in the Queen's Hands, and therefore it was undutiful to raise
any Jealousies about it. This I thought had some Force in it,
and I had Reason to be confirmed in it, when you made Mr.
Tugghe in his Letter to *R. S.* say *the Harbour is destroyed*.

But now, *Sir*, I am quite of another Mind, and find that the
Man had too much Reason for his Apprehensions; for let me
tell you, Sir, I have certain Intelligence that it now is not in the
Queen's Hands, and that, if we take no Notice of the *French*
Proceedings, it will be before the Winter as good, if not a
better Harbour than it was before they began to make an Appearance of demolishing it. I have been so curious as to settle a
Correspondence in that Place, and I have had from thence the
enclosed Map of that Place and Neighborhood, as well as of
the New Projected Entrance to its Harbour for the future. For,
may it please your *Eminence*, there is nothing more intended,
nor is there any Disposition made for any thing more than
forming a New way for Ships to come into it. And his most

Christian Majesty has only put himself to a little present Cost and Charges, out of respect to the *English* Nation, to carry on a seeming Demolition, and improve his Harbour.

If your Eminence has leisure to cast your Eye on the Map, you will observe the most Frank and undissembled Fraud, that ever was put upon any People, by any but those who are Guilty of this. If you please to mark a Semi-circle in Scratchwork (which is the Character that represents Demolition) you will see at the End of that Semi-circle the *Scratchwork* continued to the Sea, which was the way by which Ships formerly came into *Dunkirk*; when you have done that, please to observe the Explanation of the Map, and you will easily perceive, that proper Channels are cut to make the same inland Rivers, which fell into that Harbour, serviceable to that which is now forming, and this is all we are like to have for our Satisfaction in this Particular.[1]

If your *Eminence* had been let into the Secret of this Design, I am confident *your Eminence* would not have said what you have, against those who were suspicious on this Occasion; for according to all the Rules of Honour and Justice, this is a most insufferable Violation, and pays no more Respect to our Understanding than it does to our Power; but the less we have exerted either of them, out of Confidence in our intended Ally, the more *intolerable is his Offence against us.*

If this Plan makes *Dunkirk* the Receptacle of as large Ships, as it could receive before the Demolition, consequently *Dunkirk* is the same Terror to *England*, which it was before.

This it is with Respect to us, in Case we and the *French* should ever become Enemies.

Dunkirk as it remains a Port, is our Rival in Time of Peace, by preserving the Stuff Manufactures at *Lille, Valenciennes* and *Doway*. The light Stuffs from those Towns are put on Board Ship at *Dunkirk*, and carry'd to the *West-Indies,* without which their Trade would be Lost, as effectually as the Traffick of *Antwerp* and *Southampton* is Transported to other Places.

Thus we have hinted how this Fraud may affect us in Peace and War; let us think a little, what use may be made of it, in case of a sudden Resolution in the *French* King, to start out of one into t'other; or, in plain *English*, to break the Peace

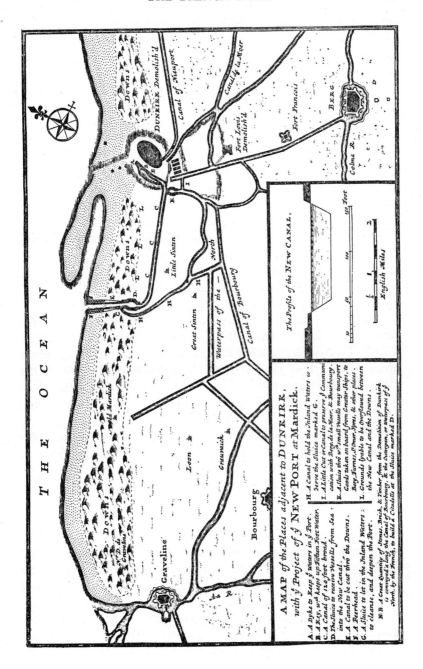

THE OCEAN

A MAP of the Places adjacent to DUNKIRK,
with ye Project of ye NEW PORT at Mardick.

A. A dyke to keep ye waters in ye Port.
B. A Key, wth keeps up fifteen foot Water.
C. A Canal of 120 foot broad.
D. The Sluice to receive Vessells from Sea:
    into the New Canal.
E. A Canal to be cut thro' the Downs.
F. A Rearhead.
G. A Sluice to let in the Inland Waters:
    to cleanse, and deepen the Port.

H. A Canal to hold the Inland Waters w
    serve the Sluice marked G.
I. A Little Cut or Canalto preserve ye Communi
    cation with Bergh, la Moer, & Bourbourg
K. A Sluice thro' wch small Vessells may transport
    Goods taken on board from Greater Ships, to
    Bergh, Furnes, S. Omer, Ipres, & other places.
L. Grounds lyable to be Overflowed between
    the New Canal and the Downs.

N.B. A Great Quantity of Stones, Brick, & Timber from the Demolition of Dunkirk
    is conveyed along the Canal of Bourbourg, & the Dorgean, or Surplus of ye
    North, by the French, to build a Citadelle at the Sluice marked D.

The Profile of the NEW CANAL.

English Miles

without Declaration of War, and surprize us at once. This very business (if there were no Examples of this Kind in History) gives room for such a Suspicion. There are now thirty Battalions at Work in that Place, and these are to be reinforced to forty.

The Proclamation of the other Day, giving a Price for the Pretender, represents that her Majesty's Instances for removing that Gentleman, who once already has invaded us, have been ineffectual. These Battalions may lie ready to receive him, and I know no better Reason, that the *French* King is pleased to pay for his Board at *Bar le Duc.*

I beg your Eminence's leave to say this is a dreadful Circumstance to which we lie exposed.

I profess sincerely to your Eminence, this is a very ungrateful Subject to me, and if I did not think this Remonstrance absolutely Necessary, I would not talk of a thing which cannot but reflect some Dishonour upon our selves, in being thus shamefully Deluded, or rather Insulted.

I do not remember to have read any where any thing like this Artifice (which is as pitiful as can be imagined) except in a little Treatise in *French,* called, *The History of False Promises since the Peace of the* Pyrenees. The Author tells us, that the *French* in a Treaty with *Spain*, obtained an Article, that whatsoever should be found within the Dominions of either State, at the time of the Ratification, shall belong to the respective Sovereign. The *French* Pillaged a Wood, and carried the Timber out of the bordering Territories of *Spain* into those of *France*, in order to *Profit, as they did, by this Article.*

This was a kind of Petty-Larceny in Politicks, but *there is nothing too mean for Ambition.*

When extent of Territory and Absolute Command are made the Objects of a Prince's Desire, Perfidiousness and a Degeneracy from every thing that is truly Good and Great, will be looked upon as things not to be imputed; but this is no more Greatness or Power, than Dropsie and Impostumation is Vigour and Strength.

Truth and Honesty are the Foundation of solid Greatness, and that which would be an ill thing in a Private Man, is much more so in a Nation or a Prince. Here are two Merchants, one lives at *Blackwall*, the other at *Deptford*; he at *Blackwall*, for valuable Considerations, Covenants with him of *Deptford* to destroy the Dock which brings in Ships to his own Door, and enables him to undersell him that Dwells over-against him. *Deptford* signs an Article, the Principal Intention of which is, that *Blackwall* shall hereafter be upon an equal Foot with *Deptford*, in that Point of lading and unlading Goods. After these Articles are signed, the Man of *Deptford* finds a Creek between *Greenwich* and *Deptford*, by which he can bring home his Goods, as well and as Cheaply as before, and that he can, with half the Cash he had from *Blackwall*, disappoint the Bargain he had lately made with it.

I appeal to your Eminence, whether he would not be a Cheat and a Knave for attempting it, and whether the Man who had paid him his Mony, not to take any Advantage of his Situation to out-trade him, would not have Just Cause of Complaint for such Usage.

The main End of the Bargain is always to be the Measure of our Actions in the Observation of it.

France has stipulated with us, that *Dunkirk* shall be no more an Harbour: They have made another sort of Harbour than it was before, but not a Jot less Commodious to themselves or less Terrible to us.

Your Eminence will observe by the Map, that the Ships in the Basin and Harbour of *Dunkirk* lie much safer from Attacks from the Sea-side, than before: You see the little *Scratchwork*, which was the former way of Entrance, ending over-against A, is not a fourth part so long as from the Peer-head F, to the said A. So that an Enemy would have so much more to do to fight his way into the Harbour of *Dunkirk* now, than he had before the Demolition.

In measuring any Iniquity, we are to consider the Person who commits it, and the Person against whom it is committed.

His most Christian Majesty lies under the Strongest Obligations imaginable to the *British* Nation. In his utmost Exigence and Distress, with an uncommon Generosity, we withdrew our Conquering Arms in his Favour: When he was reduced to be very near a Supplicant, we, according to outward Appearance, condescended to make Advances towards a Peace with him; and it is notoriously known, that a Secretary of State of *Great Britain* visited his Court to further the Negotiation.

If he can shew that he has been any way over-reached, or that the Address and Dexterity of any Minister of ours has surprized him into the Grant of too great an Equivalent for *Dunkirk*, there might possibly be some face of Justice by way of Reprisal, to make this fallacious Demolition. But when all the World must know, that we laid aside all Diffidence towards him, and in the midst of Conquest made an Halt of all the Powers of *Europe*, and continued that Suspension of all Hostilities 'till—

I have no manner of design to make this Confidence of ours odious, and mention it only as opposing it to the Falsehood and Ingratitude which we meet with in return to it.

I cannot tell in what Words to represent the Fact strongly enough to your Eminence, but if you will give me leave to repeat an admirable Simile or Illustration which your Eminence has brought out against the Whiggs, part of it will most excellently express what the *French* have done. Your Words are in the above-mentioned Number One of your Current Volume, speaking of those restless silly Rogues the Whiggs. *They have made no Discoveries; nor opened any new Sluices and Streams of Scandal; but yet like the Ingenious* Winstanley, *and other Masters in Hydrostaticks, they have laid their Pipes so well, and disposed their Wheels and Machines in such Order, that the same Mass and Body of Water, with good Husbandry and Management, circulates and comes round again at proper Periods, as they direct it.*

If you would be so good as to lead me, from the Words *they have laid their Pipes,* you will have the Mechanick part of this Affair in sublime Language, fit for expressing the Iniquity of so great a Prince.

But may it please your Eminence, whether we are Whiggs, Tories, or Jacobites, we should, methinks, have one common Indignation against this Usage, and I cannot have so little Charity as not to suppose, that how warmly soever any Party wishes for their own Scheme, they still retain Love enough for their Country, to wish it great and powerful under that Scheme. But in this Case the *French* have imposed upon us without Dissimulation, and in open Day-light are frustrating the main Article of the Treaty. It was principally the Concern of *England*, that the Harbour of *Dunkirk* should be Demolished; but so little Respect have they for us, that they have Dismantled it as a Fortification, and made it, for a time, less strong against States on the same Continent, but kept it in its full Power and Glory to insult us Islanders.

Your Eminence formerly said, of *Dunkirk* undemolished, *That it is a Bridle which the Queen has put into the Mouths of other Powers, besides the* French, *and is not therefore to be let go.* What can your Eminence say to it now? Our Garrison is marched, and they have left it a Bridle to no Nation in the World so much as to their own.

I cannot tell what the *French* will do, but I am sorry so much is in their Power.

The *French* attacked a Minor King of *Spain* in Profound Peace, 1677.

Their Emissaries made Medals for the *Dutch* against *France,* and made those inventions cause of Quarrel. Who has not read the Barbarous Invasion of the *Low Countries?* The *English* ought particularly to remember the Treatment of the *British* Troops recalled from the *French* Service after the abandoning of *Messina.*

The Surprize of *Luxemburgh* in time of Peace, is a good thing to set now before our Eyes.

The Surprize of *Strasburg.*

The Christian King's March of his Armies to the Frontiers of *Germany* in favour of the *Turk.*

The *French* Failure to their Allies the *Turks.*

All these Circumstances might be added to what has passed in our Days, to quicken our Apprehensions from an Ally who has ever formed his Greatness upon what is, with honest and sober Minds, the Disgrace and Degeneracy of Human Life, the Affectation of extending Power, without regard to the Means of doing it.

I fear, from this last Expression, I shall not be thought to speak like a Man of the World to your Eminence; but believe me, Sir, nothing but Justice can prevail for any duration of Time, and no State or Prince yet ever fell, but from the Practice of Injustice. To be Unjust, good Mr. *Examiner*, is to be against the Law of Nature, and nothing can be a Man's Interest which is not Just. But I will not go into abstracted Discourses, at a time when Men err against the Light of Reason, *when Men consciously offend and are not ashamed of it.*

I shall keep my Philosophy at this time to my self, only professing that nothing is Good or Evil, with me, Honourable or Dishonourable (by what Ideas interested Men pretend to affix to them) but as they stand in the Eye of Heaven, and before the Light of Nature.

For this Reason I address my self to you, Sir, under the Title of Eminence, because you Eminently are what you are, and what that is, will appear from your own Writings, not from mine; for which Reason I do not attempt to praise or blame you, but as the Fact it self does it.

I only say further, that it now plainly appears, we have been barbarously used with relation to *Dunkirk*; and I do not defend Mr. *Steele's* Writings against those of your Eminence, any further than it now is evident he had Reason to fear, and you no Reason to abuse him.

But now, Sir, I am to show what I hope from this Explanation of what is doing at *Dunkirk*; why, Sir, the Parliament is now sitting, and a Vote of theirs that we are Deceived and Affronted in the Demolition, and that the Continuation of that Port, or Erecting any other in the Channel, is an Infringement of the Article of the Demolition, would fright our new Friend into common Honesty.

I will be bold to say, Sir, it is our Charity for him, to which he owes his present Figure; and whenever we show a Resentment of his Artifice, ten thousand Dormant Evils will arise in his own Dominions, Dissatisfactions for Tyrannical Methods of bringing Men over to his Faith, insulting their Ancient Laws and Liberties, throwing away their Lives and Fortunes to purchase a vain Pomp and false Glory, will appear in an instant to distract a State which owes its Greatness to all the false Arts of Man, in Suppression of every thing which is instituted by God.

Alas! what signifies multiplying Words, look but upon this Map, and it is Demonstration that our Trade and our Liberty are, contrary to a Solemn Treaty, exposed to the Power of

France; and what remains, but that we implore Heaven that the Legislature would lay aside all Animosities, and exert themselves in Defence of their Deluded and Insulted Country.

I beg of your Eminence to pardon this Trouble, and as much as you are an *Englishman*,

I am, SIR,

Your Eminence's Most Humble Servant,

C. P.

P. S. *To the Examiner.*

Monday, June 28, 1714.

SIR,

YOUR Eminence's Paper which came out to Day is very full of that your usual kind of Argumentation which fills the Mouths of those who are for you, with more Words to vent their Passions and Prejudices, but affords no Reason to convince those who are against you.

As my above Paper is a professed Defence of Mr. *S—le,* I shall leave all you have raised so feebly on the side of those who opposed the Bill of Schism, which you say you foresaw, and come to the wonderful Things you could not foresee, which were objected by him for whom I plead.

You have it thus: *I could not foresee, that Mr.* Richard *S—le would be so unusually full of Reasons upon this Occasion. I could not foresee that modest Expression of his*: The Vote for my Expulsion, was more Important to the People of *England,* than I shall at this time explain.

I *Answer,* It is no breach of Modesty for the meanest Man upon Earth to say, his Case may be of ill Consequence to the Greatest Persons in the World, for all Humane Society is concerned in the Judgment upon the meanest of its Members.

I could not foresee, say you, *that he would call the* H—se of C—ns *the* People's Attorneys. *When he was One of them, he was* Accountable to no Man. *I am glad however, he calls them by a* Name *he has so much Reason to Dread.*

Mr. S—e must be understood, by the Words *Accountable to*

19

no Man, to have intended To no Man but to the House it self. As for the Commons being the People's Attorneys, every body knows they are so. Mr. S—e did not call them the People's Attorneys in what they Acted towards him. As for his dreading Attorneys, it does not lye before your Eminence.

But you again, *I could not foresee, that he would call it* a great Omission, that Dissenters in the North Part of *Britain* should not be as much Discourag'd as they are in the South. *The Fact is, They are not only* as much, *but* much more *Discourag'd; and in Nothing so much, as in this very Particular concerning* Education.

This is what they call *Gratis Dictum*, and merely Asserted, without giving Example or Argument for the Support of it.

I could not foresee, that he would call the Care of Dissenters Children *the* next thing to Cutting their Throats.

Mr. S—le Asserted no such thing; he might say, while this Act was in Agitation, that to take the Care of Children from their Parents was Cruelty next to Cutting their Throats.

You say, *I could not foresee, that he would call a* Church of *England* Education, *the way to encourage* blind Obedience in the People. I *Answer*, Imposing any thing of this kind but by Evidence is obliging to a Blind Obedience.

I could not foresee, that he would make it a Question, Whether the Bill ought to oblige, after it was Enacted. *Is he going to set up an Academy for* Sedition *and* Rebellion?

I am sure S—le loves the Universities, and has done them Service. But I will say nothing of what is passed into a Law, and I wonder your Eminence would mention that now.

I could not foresee, say you, *he would deny his Assent to the* Bill, *because the* Pretender *is still at* Bar-le-Duc, *and the* French *are about to Fortify* Mardyke. *He could not forbear the last invincible Argument, tho' the Fact happens to be false.*

I am now come to what is most Material to me at present. Your Eminence is strutting upon Ground which will Deceive, and Swallow you up. I maintain the Honesty of what he said, and if they have done worse than Fortifying *Mardyke*, you may forgive him if he said they were about doing it. According to the Representation which we at first had of the manner of eluding the Article of Demolition, it was to be by Fortifying

Mardyke; they have not put themselves to the trouble of removing their Harbour, but, with the most Impudent Insolence only cut through the *Downs* between *Mardyke* and *Dunkirk*, and kept the Identical Haven which we stipulated should be destroyed.

In what follows you are only Satyrical, and say Mr. S—le should not be against School-mistresses, since he wants to learn to Read. Why, you'll break the Man's Heart. But at present let us think of nothing but *Dunkirk* Undemolished. *I am,*

SIR,

Your Eminence's Gentle and Patient Reader,

C. P.

Mr. Steele's Apology for Himself and His Writings
(October, 1714)

On 19 February 1714, Defoe, secret agent in the employ of Lord Treasurer Oxford, reported of Steele: "If, my Lord, the virulent writings of this man may not be voted seditious, none ever may; and if thereupon he may be expelled it would suppress and discourage the party and break all their new measures." This was written three days after Steele took his seat as member for Stockbridge, Hants. An attempt to expel him on the illegality of his election proved inexpedient, and the alternative method was used. On 10 March Defoe laid before Oxford an analysis of the alleged sedition in Steele's writings on which an indictment could be based. And two days later formal complaint was made to the House by Thomas Foley, Oxford's kinsman, against parts of three pamphlets: *The Crisis* (19 Jan.) and *The Englishman* papers, Nos. 46 and 57 (19 Jan. and 15 Feb.), all published over Steele's name. On the 13th March the parts considered seditious were read and exceptions taken by Foley and Edward Harley, Oxford's brother. On the 18th the trial was held. It was voted that these writings are "scandalous and seditious Libels, containing many Expressions highly reflecting upon Her Majesty, and upon the Nobility, Gentry, Clergy, and Universities, maliciously insinuating that the Protestant Succession in the House of Hanover is in Danger under Her Majesty's Administration" . . . and that Steele be expelled the House. In the division, the majority against him was almost one hundred, a solid Tory party vote, including even the Hanover dissidents.

The Apology gives an account of the trial proceedings and of Steele's three-hour speech of defence. He had been more puzzled, he says, to know why he ought to defend his writings than how they ought to be defended: "Is a Man Seditious, who speaks in plain and open Terms against the Enemies of our Constitution and Country?" The accusation that "no private Man ought to take the Liberty of expressing his Thoughts as I have done in Matters relating to the Administration" he considers unjust. Preservation of personal freedom in politics under the law, a principle of the Revolution Settlement, he believed himself to be fighting for. If he had taken more liberty than was consistent with the laws of the land, let him be tried by those laws; the offending pamphlets were all published, he says, while he was a private subject, before taking his seat. Censure of a member for opposition to the Ministry was equally indefensible: "it is less the Part of the House of Commons, than any other Body of Men to be Inquisitors in Favour of them [the Ministry]. Their more graceful Province had been to

275

have encouraged what I had to say, if I had had Objections, rather than suppressed me." Walpole's speech in Steele's defence dwelt also on this fact that his prosecution struck at private and parliamentary rights.

The tone of Steele's exposition is impersonal except for strictures against Oxford, the Minister blamed for the policy of expulsion, and his placemen, Auditor Foley and Auditor Harley, managers of the trial. There is a touch of bitterness also in the references to the attacks upon his argument and his person by *The Examiner*, which Steele clearly believes to be instigated, at least, by Swift. These writings under public censure might even be considered, he says, as " a Paper War between two private Persons."

In commenting upon the several passages marked by the accusers, Steele led off with that eulogizing Marlborough's conduct of the late war and deploring his dismissal (labelled by Defoe "a fulsome Harangue"): "If it be a Crime to speak honourably of the Duke of *Marlborough*, it is a Crime that I must always be guilty of" was his defence. The passages relating to the Treaty of Utrecht concerned chiefly the menace of the House of Bourbon in Europe, the question of Dunkirk, and the case of the Catalans. As to Dunkirk, the French, he said, had artfully contrived to strengthen the harbor facilities (a recently-made map is included in this book as confirmation). In defence of his passionate account of England's betrayal and desertion of the Catalans, he merely said "Common Humanity will, I hope, be my Excuse." There was no retraction of the passages indicating danger signs in England and Europe to the Hanoverian Succession. Plain speaking now as then he believed to be justifiable: "I writ them in Behalf of the House of Hanover, and I own them with the same Unreservedness with which I abjured the Pretender." And, as we know, he continued during the summer before the Queen's death to write in similar vein.

The expulsion of Steele was only one sign of increasing uneasiness in Westminster. During April the question of the safety of the Succession under the present Ministry was aired in debates and divisions in both houses. The incident of "the Duke of Cambridge writ," a Whig plan to bring to England the young Duke to look after Hanoverian interests, failed, but had its effect. Defoe had forecast in February that "Mr. Steeele, the new champion of the party," was to move the question; and indeed Steele had printed the Preamble to the Duke's patent in *Englishman*, No. 56 (11 Feb.). Steele's offending tracts and his expulsion contributed largely to the cause he served. During the summer public leaders were on the alert, and plans were made carefully for the peaceful accession of George I. Textual notes on p. 643.

Mr. *STEELE*'s

APOLOGY

FOR

Himſelf and his Writings;

Occaſioned by his

EXPULSION

FROM THE

Houſe of COMMONS.

Fabula Quanta Fui !　　　　Hor.

LONDON,

Printed; and Sold by R. Burleigh in *Amen-Corner*. 1714.

277

Mr. *WALPOLE.*

SIR,

WHOEVER reads the following Apology, will easily allow me, that I am much less concerned for the Fame of a Writer than that of an honest Man. I have declared the Assistances I had in composing the Writings which are here defended; for the upright Purpose, the innocent Intention of them, is all which I am anxious to assert. In Defence of Truth I incurred popular Hatred and Contempt, with the Prospect of suffering the want even of the ordinary Conveniences of Life. The Probability of being undone I could not but form to my self when I took upon me what I did; but a Weight heavier than all this fell upon me, to wit, a Resolution of the Representative of my Country to my Dishonour. This indeed was a Blow unexpected; nor could it enter into my Imagination, that the Insolence of any Minister could run so high, as to demand of the House of Commons to punish one of its Members for being unacceptable to him. The Perusal of this Pamphlet will convince the Reader, there was not so much as the Appearance of any other Motive for my Expulsion. The Day of Debate was indeed a very memorable one, and the Persons concerned in it hugely worth suspending the Councils of a Nation. It was remarkable, however, that such was the Force of Truth, that the Member accused had not an harsh personal Expression used against him; and the Minister, in the Midst of all his Power, who brought on the Accusation, was treated in the Manner which all Mankind knows he deserves. As for my Part, I ever thought meanly of the Capacity, though not, till lately, of the Good-nature of that Demagogue, and saw very well his Audaciousness would one Day suffer by his Ignorance. It was visible, whatever became of his Country, which I believe had little Share in his Lordship's Cares, he would, with the Wand in his Hand, raise Powers which he would want Skill to command, and which consequently would tear him himself in Pieces.

But without dwelling upon the Contemplation of Mischiefs wrought by a cunning wicked Creature, placed in a Station proper only for a wise and virtuous Man, I am now to give you my Thanks for your generous Defence of me in this great Adversity. Your Behaviour was indeed equally noble during the whole *French* Administration, and your Eloquence was of publick Service to your Country, when the Prerogative was strained to the utmost, not to exalt our own Sovereign, but to compliment *France* with the Greatness and Interest of her and her People. The Intervention of Providence has given us a Stand against the imminent Destruction which such Iniquity and Folly had placed before our Eyes, and Men in great Employments can now be safe without depending upon *France.*

I have mentioned *Dunkirk* till I am sick, and there are not Words to represent the infamous Behaviour in a Ministry, to cover so great and pernicious an Imposture upon their Country, as the Improvement of that Port under the Pretence of the Demolition of it.

You have the Honour and Happiness to have eminently opposed all the Incursions which these guilty Men made upon the Greatness of the Crown and the Welfare of the Subject, by prostituting them both to their own selfish Designs, and destroying, as far as in them lay, the good Name of all Men of Virtue and Service.

They have indeed reaped this Good, that there can be nothing said of themselves, the worst Servants that ever Sovereign employed, but what they had caused to be laid to the Charge of those who were their Predecessors; Persons whose Abilities had raised their Country to such a Grandeur, that nothing but the unnatural Industry of her own Ministers could lower to the helpless Condition to which they had reduced it.

These Evils could not have been supported, had not the Demagogues, by the Abuse of Power, deafened many in the Legislature against Attention to the true Interest of themselves and their Country; while an inconsiderable Creature who had the Good-will of no Man, could manage Aversions skilfully enough to be suffered to destroy all, for fear of an Alteration of Affairs that might be grateful to an opposite Party.

Were the following Instance of the harsh and odious Disposition in Gentlemen to sit determined, before hearing, the Concern only of me and mine, it would not be worth troubling the World with so many Words on the Occasion; but neither what I now write, or what you much better spoke, is a Case of so little Consequence; and when you undertook it, you knew you were pleading for the Rights and Liberties of the Commons of *England*; and I will take upon me to say, that there never was a greater Insult on the Constitution than this, except one practised by the same Person without the least Deference to the Order of things, the common Sense of Mankind, the Honour of the Crown, or the Property of the Subject.

It needs not be said what this Impudence was, nor who had so little Grace as to be guilty of it: It was he who was born in our Days for the Chastisement and Dishonour of them, a Tool whose Insignificancy makes Sorrow, occasioned by him, the Subject of Laughter, takes all Dignity from Distress, and renders Calamity ridiculous.

As to my own Part under the fantastical Tyranny of the Demagogue's Administration, could what you said in the House be communicated to the Publick, I should have no need of this Defence; but since I have not here the Assistance of your Eloquence, I beg the Advantage of your Name and Character: For I know it will be an Argument with every honest Man that my Cause was good, that you so zealously espoused it; for that admirable Talent of speaking of which you are Master, has never been prostituted to serve dishonest Purposes; and you have too candid a Spirit not to esteem it a Praise, rather than Disparagement of your Eloquence, that the Cause for which you have at any Time pleaded needed no Art but from the Iniquity of its Opposers.

The happy Ability of explaining the most difficult Parts of Business to Men wholly unacquainted with Negociation, has been as useful to the Publick as honourable to your Self. As you have detected the Artful, so you have helped the Ignorant of your very Adversaries, according to their Intention to abuse or serve their Country.

It has been said, That the greatest Art is to hide Art; but you have a much better Instrument towards Persuasion, the having nothing to conceal; for *Truth is as certainly the greatest Eloquence, as Honesty is the best Policy.* Let those who speak or act against their Conscience, obtain their little Purposes and Applauses; be it ever your Commendation to despise Artifice and practise Uprightness. A long Course of suffering for your Zeal in an honest Cause, has gained you the Character of an *open honest English Gentleman*, with a Capacity which takes off the Imputation of Weakness from Simplicity of Manners, and adds the Dignity of Knowledge to the Beauty of Innocence.

As I never entered into Political Debates with ambitious Views, but have brought my Desires within the Necessaries and decent Conveniencies of Life, I am the more jealously tenacious of the little I expect of the World, which is only to accept of my Service to the best of my Ability, without loading me with unjust Reproach. In this reasonable Expectation Mr. *Walpole* generously lent me his Protection; and though he could not persuade my Judges to do me Justice, he convinced them I deserved a different Sentence from what they pronounced. But, alas, they had learn'd, by long Practice, to do shameful Things without being asham'd; and tho' your Arguments could command their Assent, it could not make them utter it in my Favour. You sent them away, I thank you, with the same Thoughts of themselves, which you had of them; and whatever Force and Oppression determined, in the Eye of Reason and Conscience the Judges were convict, and the accused Man found innocent.

I humbly thank you for your eminent Part in this Affair, and congratulate you on receiving the Favour of your Prince for your Service to your Country.

As doing Good to the Publick is the Motive of conferring Favours, it is, with such as you, the Rule in enjoying them. I wish you the Possession of all your frank Heart desires; and am, with great Respect,

  SIR,
   Your most Obliged,
    Most Obedient,
     And most Humble Servant,

      Richard Steele.

THE
PREFACE.

THIS Defence was printed before the Death of Her late Majesty; but upon that Accident the Publication was deferred, lest some Handle might be taken to interrupt the Business of the Nation, by an Offence given to Persons who were principally guilty of the Oppression here represented. They might possibly have attempted to borrow another Cast of Conscience in their Favour; and it was to be feared, that the same Tyranny which punished a Man for a thing in which he ought to have been encouraged and supported, would have gone on to condemn the least Murmur against its Determination. I have said Tyranny, because to resolve or act against Justice, Truth, or common Sense, is as much Tyranny in an Assembly as a single Person. But I must do the Majority of the House which expelled me the Justice to own, that they carried themselves as Men conscious they were doing wrong; and no one appeared active in it but professed Slaves and Hirelings, that is to say, such as I have called in the following Narrative the Messengers of the Treasury: Members of the House who were immediately dependent upon or related to a noble Lord whom I need not name, that sent Orders by his Kinsman to turn a Commoner of *England* out of Parliament, because it was not his Lordship's good Pleasure he should sit there any longer. When a Man is out of Power, it is usual to detract from the Fame of his high Talents and Qualifications: But I cannot be guilty of such Injustice to this great Man; for never was Minister since the Creation more thoroughly Master of that great Necessary in him who meditates vast Designs, the Choice of Instruments. *Machiavel*, in some Part of his precious Writings, advises against the Choice of raw Murderers, for such are apt to utter some soft Word flowing from Compassion, or other Weakness, for want of the Habit of Bloodshed, which might spoil the whole Design. Our Heroe cannot be accused of being injudicious this way; and I have a thousand times sate in deep Admiration of his Choice of Agents, who if they had been the least Grain more rich, more poor, more foolish, more wise, more tall, more short, more Knaves, or more Fools, had been unfit for the Work in hand. Had any Man against his Measures in either of the Assemblies more Eloquence, more Penetration, or more Credit than comes to a single Member's Share, let such a one open his Mouth, he should be attacked with one who had as much Right to speak as himself, with so firm Absurdity, and then seconded by One just one Degree worse than him, and a third Half-Fool pin up the Matter with an Assertion still wilder, to the utter Confusion of the Man in his Senses, whose noble Faculty of adorning the Cause of Truth should be immediately reduced to an Interjection of Sorrow, and down he must sit. Such was our Heroe's Manner of demolishing and frustrating all Persons against him. The same Genius in disappointing the Force of superior Talents ran through all Parts of Business.

The Writings hereafter spoken of were an apparent Vindication of the King's Title to the Crown, and an honest Representation of the dangerous State of the Nation. Now would any Man living believe, that it was in Nature this could be made an Accusation before an House of Commons? But so it was; and there appeared in it Fellows born and contrived by Nature for such a Work; Creatures that could vex, but not make you angry, such mean Instruments of Iniquity, that the Wickedness was disparaged by their managing it, and the Flagrancy and dangerous Consequence of what was doing, was hidden by the Inconsiderableness of the Agents. A Persecution from them was like being troubled with Vermin. Tho' I had too much at Stake to be in Humour enough to enjoy the Scene, there was, with all the Cruelty of it, something particularly Comick in the Affair. All the Men of Sense in the Majority of the House, tho' they did not design to deny a Friend a Vote, stood off, and left the whole Management to the Family and the Office.

The Onset was made in the poorest manner, and the Accusation laid with an insipid Action and cold Expression. The Accuser arraigned a Man for Sedition, with the same Indolence and Indifference as another Man pares his Nails: What was spoken appeared only a Rheum from the Mouth, and Mr. *Foley,* as well as do what he did, might have blown his Nose, and put the Question. But tho' the Choler of my Accusers was corrected by their Phlegm, insomuch that they were harmless with ill Will; yet had they Perseverance to go on, insensible of the Raillery of the contrary Party, and the Contempt of their own. The most lamentable thing of all to consider was, that tho' there was not one Man of Honour, who spoke on the side of the Ministry, but did it upon general Terms, wherein he apparently discovered his Disapprobation of the Work he was about, so many honest Gentlemen should join in a Vote of Expulsion!

It is possible some Gentlemen might think in their Consciences, it is an immoral Action for any private Man to animadvert upon the Administration of the Publick. God forbid I should say there were not some worthy Men who were thus perswaded in this Case; but if they were so, I know not why they should, as Members of the House of Commons, punish a Man for what he did before he came into the House, especially since that Thing would have been laudable in him to have done, if he had been in the House.

All I shall preface further is, that I thought the Circumstances of *Great Britain* and *Europe* were such as made it an honest and necessary Action to interrupt and oppose the Measures of the Ministry. When I thought it my Duty, I thank God, I had no further Consideration for my self than to do it in a lawful and proper Way, so as to give no Disparagement to a Glorious Cause from my Indiscretion or want of Judgment. A Work against them I was the rather enclined to undertake, because the Exceptions which were made against the Conduct of the Ministry seemed wild and calumnious, when written by nameless Authors; but when any Man with his Name asserted Things were amiss, it would behove the Persons concerned to prove it Calumny, or suffer under it; And I was willing to ripen the Question of the Succession upon my own Head. It soon appeared that there was so much Ground for what I said in the Papers I then printed, that it was thought much more proper to weaken the Validity of what I said by Invectives against me, which came out stitch'd, bound, and in loose Papers for some Months every Week, than gain-say what I asserted. In the midst of this Treatment the Conversation happened which gave Occasion to the CRISIS. The Gentleman mentioned in the following Defence, as giving the first Hint to the Design, I need no longer conceal; it was Mr. *Moor* of the *Inner-Temple,* a Man perfectly skilled in the History, the Laws, the Constitution, of this Kingdom, and, in my poor Opinion, as capable of doing eminent Service, where those Qualities are requisite, as any Man in *England* not already employed. All I have to say further concerning him is, that I hope the Mention of this his great Merit may prove to his Advantage; and it is not to be imputed to me if he feels no Effect of publick Favour, for starting so useful a Design as appeared in the *Crisis*.

When the *Crisis* was written Hand in Hand with this Gentleman, I, who was to answer for it with my All, would not venture upon our single Judgment, therefore I caused it to be printed, and left one Copy with Mr. *Addison*, another with Mr. *Lechmere*, another with Mr. *Minshull*, and another with Mr. *Hoadly*. I don't name Mr. *Hoadly* last because I honour or depended upon him least: For he has every good Quality, Talent, and Grace, that can adorn a Christian, a Gentleman, and a Divine; and whatever Prejudice may suggest, I think it a great Defence that the Work passed his Hand. From these corrected Copies (no one of these Gentlemen knowing till this Day that the other had seen it) the *Crisis* became the Piece it is.

When I was now fully convinced that what I said was justifiable in the Sight of God and Man, I thought I had an Opportunity of giving an Alarm to all honest Men, and disconcerting the Counsels of Men I thought ready to attempt any thing they could act with Impunity, and who cared not, so they carried on their own Game, though they did it by bringing on their native Country the Imputation of Falsehood and Treachery, accompanied with Slavery, Poverty, and Dishonour.

All this was plainly intimated in the *Crisis*, but expressed in such a manner as to be within the Law, against those who had the Administration of the Laws, and seemed to me to be undermining the Constitution. It was therefore reasonable to act within the Law as far as a Man could against those who made no Use of it, but to cover themselves in making Encroachments upon it and Transgressions against it.

Besides the Care of rescuing my own Name from a seeming Disgrace of a Vote of the Commons, I thought this Apology necessary to shew the arbitrary Use of Numbers in the most odious Colours, that Gentlemen may have a just Detestation of practising a Thing in it self unwarrantable, from the Support only of the insolent and unmanly Sanction of a Majority.[1]

A

LIST

OF THE

GENTLEMEN

Who voted against the Expulsion
of Mr. *STEELE.*

JOHN Harvey, *Esq*;
   John Cater, *Esq*;
Sir Thomas Lee, *Bar.*
Sir John Wittewrong, *Bar.*
Sir Roger Hill, *Kt.*
James Stanhope, *Esq*;
John Bromley, *Esq*;
Sam. Shepperd, *Esq*;
Peter Shakerly, *Esq*;
John Trelawny, *Esq*;
Sir Ch. Wager, *Kt.*
Hugh Boscawen, *Esq*;
James Craggs, *Esq*;
John Hopkins, *Esq*;
Edward Elliot, *Esq*;
John Knight, *Esq*;
Humphry Morrice, *Esq*;
James Lowther, *Esq*;
Gilfrid Lawson, *Esq*;
Tho. Stanwix, *Esq*;
Sir John Rogers, *Bar.*
Sir George Byng, *Kt.*
Richard Edgecomb, *Esq*;
George Treby, *Esq*;
Sir John Cope, *Kt.*

Roger Tuckfeild, *Esq*;
George Trenchard, *Esq*;
John Burridge, *Esq*;
Daniel Harvey, *Esq*;
John Baker, *Esq*;
James Littleton, *Esq*;
William Betts, *Esq*;
William Coventry, *Esq*;
Thomas Erle, *Esq*;
George Pit, *Esq*;
John Hedwith, *Esq*;
Sir Tho. Webster, *Bar.*
Sir Isaac Rebow, *Kt.*
Thomas Stevens, *Esq*;
William Dowdeswell, *Esq*;
Benjamin Bathurst, *Esq*;
William Grimston, *Esq*;
William Hale, *Esq*;
Sir Matthew Dudley.
Robert Piggot, *Esq*;
Lord Hinchinbrook.
The Hon. Sidney Wortley.
Sir Robert Marsham, *Bar.*
Sir Samuel Ongley, *Kt.*
Robert Heysham, *Esq*;

Sir Thomas Johnson, *Kt.*
Lord Willoughby.
Sir John Brownloe, *Bar.*
Sir John Thorold, *Bar.*
William Coatesworth, *Esq*;
John Morgan, *Esq*;
Sir Charles Turner, *Kt.*
Robert Walpole, *Esq*;
The Hon. William Feilding.
Horatio Walpole, *Esq*;
The Hon. John Fitzwilliams.
George Mountague, *Esq*;
The Hon. William Egerton.
Paul Methuen, *Esq*;
The Hon. Tho. Wentworth.
Earl of Hertford.
Sir John Jermayn, *Bar.*
Oley Douglass, *Esq*;
Richard Hambden, *Esq*;
Lord Sherrard.
Lord Newport.
William Whitmore, *Esq*;
John Weaver, *Esq*;
James Medlicot, *Esq*;
Norton Pawlet, *Esq*;
Tho. Broderick, *Esq*;
Lord William Pawlet.
Walter Chetwynd, *Esq*;
William Thompson, *Esq*;
Sir Harvey Elways, *Bar.*
Tho. Maynard, *Esq*;
Edward Hopkins, *Esq*;
The Hon. Carr Harvey.
Aubrey Porter, *Esq*;
Sir Richard Onslow, *Bar.*
George Evelyn, *Esq*;
Tho. Onslow, *Esq*;
James Cocks, *Esq*;
Paul Docminique, *Esq*;

The Hon. James Brudenell.
Tho. Pelham, *Esq*;
John Morley Trevor, *Esq*;
Nathaniel Gould, *Esq*;
Francis Chamberlayn, *Esq*;
The Hon. Spencer Compton.
Lord Thomond.
Lord Lumley.
Daniel Willson, *Esq*;
Sir Richard Sandford, *Bar.*
John London, *Esq*;
Tho. Pit, Jun. *Esq*;
John Eyres, *Esq*;
Reynolds Calthrop, *Esq*;
Edward Ash, *Esq*;
Price Acourt, *Esq*;
John Eyles, *Esq*;
Sir John Rushout, *Bar.*
Joseph Addison, *Esq*;
Sir Tho. Reade, *Bar.*
Tho. Pit Sen. *Esq*;
Tho. Wylde, *Esq*;
John Rudge, *Esq*;
Sir William Robinson, *Bar.*
Sir William St. Quintin, *Bar.*
Sir Charles Hotham.
Tho. York, *Esq*;
William Pulteney, *Esq*;
Hugh Cholmley, *Esq*;
Edward Dunch, *Esq*;
William Strickland, *Esq*;
Thomas Frankland, *Esq*;
Ralph Bell, *Esq*;
Henry Prater, *Esq*;
Leonard Smelt, *Esq*;
Archibald Hutchinson, *Esq*;
Philip Papillon, *Esq*;
The Hon. Edw. Watson.
Sir Robert Furnace, *Bar.*

Sir John Norris, *Kt.*
Philip Gibbon, *Esq*;
George Doddington, *Esq*;
Robert Bristow, *Esq*;
George Nayler, *Esq*;
Thomas Jones, *Esq*;
John Montgomery, *Esq*;
Sir James Campbell, *Bar.*
George Baylie, *Esq*;
Colonel John Campbell.
Charles Oliphant, *Esq*;
Sir William Johnstowne, *Bar.*
Sir James Stewart, *Bar.*

Alexander Grant, *Esq*;
William Steward, *Esq*;
Sir John Anstruther, *Bar.*
Henry Cunningham, *Esq*;
John Middleton, *Esq*;
John Cockburne, *Esq*;
Sir David Dalrymple, *Bar.*
John Steward, *Esq*;
Sir James Carmichael, *Bar.*
Tho. Smith, *Esq*;
Sir Gilbert Elliot, *Bar.*
Robert Monro, *Esq*;

Lord Fynch *was unfortunately shut out at the Division; but the noble Part he acted in the Debate will ever be remembered to his Honour.*

N. B. *The Honourable* John Campbell, *and* William Thompson *of* Scarborough, *Esq; were Omitted in the former Edition of this Book.*[2]

Mr. *STEELE*'s
APOLOGY, *&c.*

I Have waited with much Patience during the Session of
Parliament, without offering at any Thing in my Justification
against the Sentence which passed upon me on the 18th of
March last past; which Sentence, and the Motives to it, are
express'd in the two following Resolutions.

Resolved,

That a Printed Pamphlet, intituled, The ENGLISHMAN, *being
the Close of the Paper so called; and one other Pamphlet,
Entituled,* THE CRISIS, *written by* Richard Steele, *Esq; a Member of this House; are scandalous and seditious Libels, containing many Expressions highly reflecting upon Her Majesty,
and upon the Nobility, Gentry, Clergy, and Universities of this
Kingdom, maliciously insinuating, that the Protestant Succession
in the House of* Hanover *is in Danger under Her Majesty's
Administration, and tending to alienate the Affections of Her
Majesty's good Subjects, and to create Jealousies and Divisions
among them.*

Resolved,

That Richard Steele, *Esquire, for his Offence in Writing and
Publishing the said scandalous and seditious Libels, be expell'd
this House.*

I hoped every Day, during the Session, to have heard other
Writers called to an Account for their Errors as well as my
self, especially those who had provoked me to say what gave
so much Offence. In that Case I might perhaps have heard
something alleg'd, that would have made it appear necessary
in the Representative of the People, to censure as well those
who are imprudently zealous for them, as those who are against
them. But since they have punished only me, who, if I am
guilty at all, am guilty only of too forward Zeal in a good

Cause; I say, since the Commons, to show their Impartiality, have thought fit to distinguish only the Crimes of one of their own Members, by taking from him both his good Name and Seat in Parliament, while all other writers pass unmentioned; that Member thinks himself at Liberty to do what he can to weaken the Force of that Censure, by a Narrative of all that pass'd in their House relating to himself, as well as he can recollect it.

If the Reader will allow me the Liberty of speaking of my self sometimes as a third Person, to avoid the Word I, (which often repeated, even in a Justification, has an Offence in it) I will tell the Story very honestly.

It may, perhaps, appear undutiful to argue against what was acted by the Representative of one's Country: But in order to keep us within such Bounds, it is expedient, on their Side, to have a due Regard to the Lives and Honours of those whom they call before 'em, and not to expect that, when they have laid the heaviest Weight which they are able upon an Offender, he will be intimidated from disputing the Justice of their Sentence by the Terrors of their future Displeasure, which can have in Store nothing so terrible as what is already inflicted. The Resolution against Mr. *Steele* carries in it all the Infamy that can be joined to the Name of a Gentleman, and they have certainly made him desperate and regardless of what further they can determine to his Disadvantage.

In inflicting Punishments, especially where the Penalty is not prescribed, there should be always a Regard had to the Person who is to suffer; and whatever Sense any Body of Men may have of Good and Evil, they should still suppose there are some Men who prefer their Integrity to all other Considerations, not excepting those of Riches and Power.

Honour is the true Essence of a Man, and consists in the Consciousness of Innocence and Honesty. This, indeed, cannot be taken from him by the Outrage of Multitudes, or the Abuse of Power. But though such a Sense of Reproach is to be the private Rule of a Man's Conduct, and will certainly prove the best Support under all Disappointments and Adversities, it is too abstracted a Notion to carry him through the Business of the World, without having a due Regard to Reputation and

Fame. A Man's Reputation is the Dress of his Honour, and though tearing a Man's Cloaths cannot hurt his Life or his Limbs, yet if he'll allow them to be rent into Tatters, or patiently let Passengers throw Dirt upon them, he will be unfit to be received by the decent Part of Mankind in that Condition, from the Prejudice they cannot but have to his Habit and outward Appearance, and consequently he will be unable to perform the Offices of Life with Respect to others as well as himself. For these Reasons, in some Cases, a Man is necessitated to appeal to all the rest of Mankind, from the Judgment of those who have pronounced him guilty.

To convince the World that Mr. *Steele* did not deserve the Sentence before recited, I hope to shew that his whole Conduct as a Writer, in which Character only he has been charged in the House, has been full of Instances of a quite contrary Tenour to that of which they accuse him; as well as that the Passages themselves which were brought against him will not support their Accusation.

Anger, which is never wise, made a Man inconsiderable in himself of so much Consequence, that while he was in the House, People condescended (as if to lessen him was carrying a great Point) to brow-beat and disparage him. I know not how better to represent his Condition during that Time, than by saying he was the quite contrary to that Sort of Creature among 'em whom they call *a Favourite of the House.* A Favourite of the House, is one who says and does what he pleases, and is always acceptable, whatever he advances, because he is ridiculous. Mr. *Steele*, with a quite opposite Fate, was to do nothing but what should be dislik'd, because he was odious. This Disposition against him appeared the very first Day of the Session; what happened to him at that Time was the Entertainment every where for a whole Week, therefore I shall very circumstantially relate it.

After two or three Gentlemen had proposed Sir *Thomas Hanmer* for Speaker of the House of Commons, Mr. *Steele* took upon him to say he had the same honourable Sentiments of that Gentleman in the following Words:

Mr. Jodrell,

*A*T *the Close of the last Parliament, Her Majesty was graciously pleas'd to declare from the Throne, That the late
rejected Bill of Commerce between* Great Britain *and* France
*should be offer'd to this House. That Declaration was, certainly,
made, that every Gentleman, who should have the Honour to
be return'd hither, might make himself Master of that important
Question. It is Demonstration that was a most pernicious Bill,
and no Man can have a greater Merit to this House, than his by
whose Weight and Authority that pernicious Bill was thrown
out. I rise up to do him Honour, and distinguish my self by
giving him my Vote for that his inestimable Service to his
Country.*

It will be impossible for the Reader to conceive how this
Speech of his was receiv'd, except he has happen'd to have been
at a Cock Match, and has seen the Triumph and Exultation
which is raised when a Volatile whose Fall was some way
gainful to Part of the Company has been necked. At the mention of the Bill of Commerce, the Cry began; at calling it
Pernicious, it encreased; at the Words, Doing him Honour, it
grew insupportably loud: But having no Reason for being confounded for other People's Folly or Absurdity, Mr. *Steele* bore
the Insolence well enough to speak out what he intended. He
had Hardiness enough to do it, from a Resolution which he
had taken, to govern himself by, when he went into the House,
which was to prefer the Fame of an honest Man to that of an
Orator. I must confess I stand in some Amazement to find
where the Ridicule lay in the Words, *I rise up to do him
Honour*; the natural Meaning of which I take to be shewing
him Respect, and not implying that 'tis an Honour to him that
'tis I who do him that Respect: However, were it taken in the
latter Sense, in which Mr. *Steele* really did not intend it, I don't
see the Absurdity there would have been in it; he does not
deserve to sit in that House, who does not believe his Esteem
an Addition to the Person's Reputation on whom he bestows
it; for the good Opinion of an honest Man is an Honour to the
greatest Man living. At the same time Mr. *Steele* does not
attribute this particular Outrage to the House, any further than

that they ought to have suppress'd it, and severely observed upon it, by turning out the Offenders, who, 'tis supposed, were a Parcel of Rusticks who crowded in with the Members before the Election of the Speaker, from a received Error, that there is no Authority in the House till he is chosen. As he came out of the House, he could hear nothing but those loud Criticks talk to one another, *Oh! 'tis not so easy a Thing to speak in the House—He fancies, because he can scribble*—and the like deep Animadversions. But to the Matter it self.

On the 12th of *March*, 1713. a Complaint was made to the House against certain Paragraphs in three printed Pamphlets, one *Entituled*, The Englishman, *from* Saturday, Jan. 16. *to* Tuesday, Jan 19. 1713. *wherein is a printed Letter to the* Englishman, *to which is subscribed the Name* Richard Steele; *another, Entituled*, The Crisis, *in the Title Page whereof it is said, by* Richard Steele, *Esquire; and the other, Entituled*, The Englishman, being the Close of the Paper so called, *in the Title Page whereof it is also said, by* Richard Steele, *Esquire; as containing several Paragraphs tending to Sedition, highly reflecting upon Her Majesty, and arraigning Her Administration and Government.* Upon which the accused Member was ordered to attend in his Place the next Morning. He attended accordingly on *Saturday* the 13th, and heard the several Paragraphs, in the printed Pamphlet complained of, read. After which, at the proper Time, he stood up, and read a Paper containing the following Words:

Mr. Speaker,

I Have written and caused to be printed several Books and Papers with a sincere Zeal and good Intent to serve my Queen and Country, the present happy Establishment in Church and State, and particularly the Protestant Succession in the House of Hanover. But I submit it to the House, whether, in Justice to the Defence that is due to every Subject of this Kingdom, I ought to admit that either the Contents or Substance of the Papers laid upon your Table are the same I wrote and caused to be Printed, before I have perused and compared them; especially since every one knows it to be Fact, that false Editions of all Books, which sell, are published every Day.

Mr. Speaker,

*Though I was ordered to attend in my Place before any
particular Passages, if I am rightly informed, were read or
objected to in the House; yet now that I have heard what they
are, I trust to the Justice of this House, that I shall have a
reasonable Time to peruse and compare them, and if I find
them upon Perusal to be really the same which I wrote and
published, I shall ingenuously own them, and hope to make
such a Defence of them as will be satisfactory to the House;
for which, I doubt not but you will allow me sufficient Time.*

Since Time for comparing them was all Mr. *Steele* pretended
to, the *Monday* following was proposed for the Day of his
Defence; but that was easily got over, upon his urging that the
next Day was *Sunday.* After a proper Time to be allowed was
debated for some Moments, and that the desiring to collate the
Papers was said to be mentioned only as the most obvious
Circumstance absolutely necessary for the Member's Defence,
but that much more must be supposed as material, as that, for
his Justification, the House seemed in a very good Disposition,
which the accused Member did not think he abused in desiring
till the *Saturday* following. It was very faintly press'd that
this was too distant a Day, till a particular Orator stood up,
and endeavoured to warm the House into an Indignation of
treating, with so much Gentleness, so high an Offender. It cannot be expected that one can remember every Man's Name;
but the Man I mean was of an enormous Stature and Bulk, and
had the Appearance, if I may so speak, of a Dwarf-Giant. His
Complection Tawny, his Mein disturb'd, and the whole Man
something particularly unfamiliar, disingenuous, and shocking
to an *English* Constitution. I fancied, by his exotick Make and
Colour, he might be descended from a Moor, and was some
Purchase of our *African*, or other trading Company, which was
manumised. This Man, thought I, was certainly bred in Servitude, and being now out of it, exerts all that he knows of
Greatness in Insolence and Haughtiness. The untam'd Creature
stood up to turn off the merciful Inclination which he saw grow
towards the Member accused; and with well-chosen Words and
personated Vehemence, laid before the House, That he, forsooth, was glad to see the good Disposition Gentlemen appear'd

to be in, and applauded their Tenderness; but at the same Time he could not but remark, that the Drift of the Writings before them was to make the greater Number of the Gentlemen of *England* appear Jacobites and Enemies to their Country. I do not pretend to give exactly what he said to this unjust and cruel Purpose; but it prevailed very much towards the Effect he desired, and loosened all that was obtain'd on the Side of the Defendant in the preceding Part of the Debate, insomuch that Mr. *Steele* grew in fear he should have no Time at all allotted him; and therefore when the House was going to divide on the Question, Whether he should be allowed till *Saturday* or not, he stood up and begged till *Thursday*, in which Request Mr. *Pitt* of *Worcestershire* had the Humanity to second him, and the Affair was appointed for that Day without a Division.

On *Monday* following, the 15th of *March,* believing a great Part of the Ill-Will which he had brought upon himself was owing to what he had writ about *Dunkirk,* he thought it would make for his Defence to have what pass'd relating to the Collusive Demolition appear to the House before his Day came on. Mr. *Steele* therefore (upon the Suggestion of some Friend's Voice near him to be very humble) had the Folly to pretend to move their Pity, by a Comparison of the powerful Opposition against him from those who were numerously related in the House, and in such Circumstances as to draw all others to them; and representing his own Condition so particularly unallied and unassisted, that there was not one Man living of his Blood, nor he in Circumstances capable of engaging the Friendship of any Man there but from the Merit of his Cause. *I have,* said that facetious Person, *this to thank my Adversaries for, that their hard Prosecution has opened so good a way to the Breasts of* Englishmen *as Pity.* From this ill-judg'd quaint Harangue, which was received with much Coldness, he recovered himself as well as he could, by observing, That he never knew an unhappy Man speak *but just enough*; and therefore would not wander further, but hasten to the Question which he had prepared and held in his Hand, as of use to his ensuing Defence; which was, *That an humble Address be presented to Her Majesty, that she will be pleased to give Directions, that the several Representations of Her Majesty's Ingineers and Officers who have had the care and Inspection of the Demolition of* Dunkirk, *and all Orders and Instructions given thereupon, be laid before this House.* It passed in the Negative. And from that Moment Mr. *Steele* despaired of his Cause. He prepared his Mind as well as he could to meet with his Disgrace; and considered all that was to follow as a Farce, wherein heedless Men were to indulge their Curiosity, Mirth, or Cruelty, without any regard to Justice, or how far what they were doing would affect him or themselves. But *Thursday* the 18th is now come; and the Order of the Day for taking into Consideration the Printed Pamphlets complain'd of to the House being read, Mr. *Foley* the Accuser demanded that the Matter appointed for the Day might be entered upon, referring the Method of proceeding to the House. Mr. *Steele* chose to make his Appearance near the Bar of the House; and I will not forget to mention one Circumstance in this Scene that very much sweetened his Affliction, which was, that he had the Honour to stand between Mr. *Stanhope* and Mr. *Walpole*, who condescended to take upon them the Parts of his Advocates. The First Question proposed to divert the Company, was, Whether the Member accused owned the Writings or not? Upon which Mr. *Steele* stood up and said,

Mr. Speaker,

*W*HEN *I was called up the other Day upon the same Occasion, I suspended the utter Acknowledgment of the Papers laid on your Table against me. I was advised to do so. What has hitherto been insisted upon by me was meer Formality, in favour of other innocent Men who may hereafter fall into my Circumstances. I now frankly and ingenuously own all those Papers laid to my Charge to be Parts of my Writings. I writ them in Behalf of the House of Hanover, and I own them with the same Unreservedness with which I abjured the Pretender. I humbly submit my self to this honourable Assembly, and depend upon your Justice.*

This occasioned a long Debate, and in the Intervals between the speaking of particular Members, the House called out, Mr. *Steele*, Mr. *Steele*, to begin his Defence; but his Friends directed him to sit still. The Dispute in a little Time ripened into this

Question, Whether the Member accused should answer Paragraph by Paragraph, and hear what was urged against him to each, and thereupon answer; or that, now he knew upon what Heads he was charged, he should proceed to defend himself? It seems it is the Custom on such Occasions, that if the Member withdraws without speaking for himself in the way the House prescribes to him, he is to have no further Opportunity before the House proceeds to Censure: It was therefore intimated to him that now was his Time to stand up; and making use of his Papers he sometimes spoke, but chiefly read as follows:

Mr. Speaker,

YOU will easily believe I have not been in a very sedate Temper ever since I came into this House. When I composed those Writings of which I am accused, I studied carefully to avoid committing any Fault in them, and now on a Sudden I am to rack my Invention to find out Guilt in them. I have also been forced to apply my self to the making my Defence Paragraph by Paragraph, as well as according to this Method to which you have now been pleased to restrain me. From these Accidents, the different Opinions of Friends, being suspended between these Opinions, Want of Sleep, and being pressed in Point of Time, I am in a very ill Condition to make a Defence. But if you will forgive my Blundering and Stammering amidst an Huddle of Papers you see in my Hands, not read over since transcribed, and the References from some to others of them not fixed in my Mind, you shall have the Truth of my Heart in this Discomposure, which will I hope with generous Men do more for me, than what I could have produced with more Meditation. I must therefore, as well as I can, from Papers which, as I said, I have not so much as read over since transcribed, obey your Commands; and fall abruptly into the Particulars of my Defence, the Way to which I thought to make in a more gradual and unforced Manner, upon the Views I had before I came into the House.

I have not, I hope, written any thing with an improper Heat, tho' I have not shewn an Insensibility; and those who condemn what Heat I have shown, will at least approve the Ends to which it was directed.

If my Wishes for the Demolition of *Dunkirk*, and my Zeal
for that Succession which is the only Security under God of our
Laws, our Liberties, and our Religion, have betrayed me into
any Errors which I am not sensible of, I hope the Goodness of
these Motives which occasioned them, will be sufficient to
extenuate and cover them. I am sure there are several Writers
who have talked with as much Warmth and more Boldness for
a quite contrary End, without giving the same Offence to those
in whose Power it has been to punish them: I say, Sir, that
there are many who have written with as great a Zeal in a Cause
which is Condemned as Treasonable by our Acts of Parliament,
and yet have had the good Luck to escape the Notice of those who
have had either the making of Laws or the putting them in Execution. Besides, whilst I have thus preserv'd my Temper, it must
be allowed that no Man ever receiv'd greater Provocations. Those
Writers who declared themselves the professed Advocates of the
Ministry, and give themselves the Air of being in the Secrets of
the Administration, were the first Aggressors. They have loaded
me with groundless Calumnies, misrepresented me in every Part
of my Character, and have been as disingenuous and unchristian
in the Methods of publishing these false Reports, as they were
in the inventing of them. When I had the Honour to be returned
as a Member of Parliament, and was therefore presumed to be
such, instead of being thereby privileged from this infamous
Treatment, I was only the more expos'd to it. These Papers I
am now speaking of prejudged my Election, denounced to me
the Displeasure of Men in great Places, and foretold that Storm
which is now fallen upon me, unless it be averted by the Justice
and Honour of Gentlemen, who are the only Persons that can
interpose in this Case between an innocent Man and an offended
Minister. Such has been the cruel and ungenerous Usage which
I have met with from an Author who has several times professed himself a Champion for the Ministry, that no longer
since than last *Friday* he has fallen upon me with that Rage and
Malice, which is unbecoming a Scholar, a Gentleman, or a
Christian, at the same Time that so great a Misfortune befel me
as to be accused before this House. As if he did not think that
Weight heavy enough upon me, he makes his Court to his
Superiors by determining the Cause which lay before this

honourable Assembly, and represents me in such a Character as I hope is due to no Man living. I cannot but take Notice of his last Paper, which, if any Gentleman will be at the Pains of perusing, he will find, (by what strange Accident or concerted Measures I know not) that it is a Brief of the Charge against me before this House. It was in Answer to this Writer that I first employ'd my Pen, and, as I thought, for the Service of my Country. This Man has represented half of Her Majesty's Subjects as a Different People, who have forfeited the common Protection allowed them by the Constitution; but has never been called to account for it *as a Writer of Matters tending to Sedition.* He has treated the Fathers of our Church like the basest among the People, tore in Pieces the Reputation of the most eminent Names in *Great Britain,* marked out several Members in both Houses of Parliament, and endeavoured to render them odious to the Nation, when they have disagreed with him in Opinion, or rejected any Bill which the Ministry had seemed to promote. He has vilified those Persons which are in Friendship and Alliance with Her Majesty, and condemned Treaties which are still in Force. He has trifled upon so melancholy a Subject as that of Her Majesty's late Indisposition, and represented Her as actually dead, for the Sake of a poor Conceit which the greatest Part of his Readers were not able to take, and those who did could not but regard with Horrour. All this, Sir, the Author I am now mentioning has done, without being called to account for any Reflection *tending to Sedition, highly reflecting upon Her Majesty, and arraigning Her Administration and Government.* In the Opinion of the World he has not only done all this with Impunity, but with Encouragement. It is chiefly in Answer to this Author, that those Papers were written which are now upon your Table. I could not see without Indignation an Endeavour set on foot to confound Truth with Falsehood, and to turn the whole History of the present Times into a Lie. I thought I might act with the same Safety in vindicating, as he did in attacking the Reputation of several innocent Persons, who are unblemished every where but in his Papers; and of many honourable Persons, who by all Sides, are allowed to have deserved well of their Country. And now, Sir, let every *British* Gentleman lay his Hand upon his Heart, and ask himself, Whether it was possible for a Man of any Spirit to have received those private and personal Injuries which I have here mentioned, or for any honest Man to have seen others so barbarously treated, without giving some Loose to his Resentments. Sir, a good Name is as dear to me as it can be to the greatest Man in *England*; and whoever employs all his Artifices to make me appear vile and infamous, cannot be angry with me if I lay hold on what I think defective in his own Character and Behaviour, to expose it in the same Manner. I am sure no Man of Honour, and it is my Happiness that this Assembly is composed of no other, would make such a Sacrifice of himself to any, the most Powerful of his Fellow-Subjects. I know no Law of God or Man that requires this kind of Resignation or Self-Denial.

I have been the longer upon this Head, to shew Gentlemen that this great Affair which is now laid before them, has been hitherto, notwithstanding the many Insolencies I have now recited against the greatest Persons in Church and State, only a Paper War between two private Persons; and they must have but a mean Opinion of the Dignity of a *British* House of Commons, who think they will make themselves Parties in either Side of it. Besides, Sir, I have another Reason for opening my Defence in this Manner, because I find that the first Paragraph which is laid to my Charge, can accuse me of nothing else but of shewing a Disrespect to the *Examiner*. Here follows, as it is marked against me, what I say in the *Englishman*, Number 46.

" But there is still a Circumstance in the same Paper of the *Examiner's*, that may have a Consequence yet more immediately pernicious, and that is the last Sentence of it; *Since Her Majesty is to be the last, we hope they will be obliged to own Her for the greatest and wisest of the* Stuarts. I cannot but think this Expression uttered as lamenting in favour of a pretended *Stuart,* in whose Behalf he sighs, and says, *Since Her Majesty is to be the last.* The natural way of speaking his Sense, in a Man who was in the Interest of his Country, had been to say, *As Her Majesty without Issue is to be the last—* But whether his Inclinations be for the Pretender or not, I am sure he promotes his Service in a very great Degree, when he endeavours to villify that House of Commons which is now laying a Price upon his Head.

"But let the rest of the World do what they please, and delay their Protestations against these Evils as long as they think fit, I will postpone all else that is dear to me to the Love of my Country: And as this is, and I trust in Providence will be my strongest Passion to my Life's End, I will, while it is yet Day, profess and publish the Rules by which I govern my Judgment of Men and Things in the present Conjuncture.

"Does this Action bespeak such a one a wise Man if he is for the Pretender, a Madman if he is for the House of *Hanover*?

"Does this Position open a Way to the Pretender? Or, does it further secure the Protestant Succession?

"These are my Questions, which I make the Test of Men and Opinions; and if a Man does a thing that may advance the Interest of the Pretender or his Friends, and can no way do Good to the House of *Hanover*, he may swear to his last Breath that he is for that House, before he shall make me believe him. In like Manner, if People talk to me of hereditary Right, and then follow it with Professions for the House of *Hanover*, which can have no additional Security from the urging of hereditary Right, I shall no more believe them *Hanoverians*, than I should think a Man religious who should make a blasphemous Discourse, and close it with the Rehearsal of the Creed.

"I speak all this because I am much afraid of the Pretender; and my Fears are encreased, because many others laugh at the Danger. I presume to say, those who do laugh at it either do not think at all, or think it will be no Day of Danger to themselves. But I thus early let go my Fire against the Pretender's Friends, because I think my self a very good Judge of Men's Mein and Air, and see what they intend at a Distance. I own I have nothing to say for the Liberty I take now, or the Book I put out to Day, when no Body else talks in the same Stile, but what the Sailor did when he fired out of the Stage-Coach upon Highway-Men before they cried *Stand*; *Would you have me stay till they have boarded us?*"

My Adversaries must make the *Examiner* one of the Ministry, before they can bring the first of these Paragraphs within their Complaint. I cannot suppose that any *Englishman* can think me to blame for expressing my Love to my Country in the strongest Terms, as I have here done. As to the Rules by which I profess to govern my Judgment, they are, I suppose, what none will controvert, as being of the Nature of Maxims or first Principles, which can admit of no Dispute. The Paragraph that follows them is nothing else, but the Application of these general and undisputed Maxims to a particular Case. I cannot imagine why any Gentleman should mark it in particular, unless for the Sake of the Word *Hereditary*; a Word that teems with so many Disputes, and which, according to my Notion of it, is inconsistent with the Succession in the House of *Hanover*, which cannot be come at but by passing over many of those who are the next Heirs in Blood. But it happens that I have explained my self as to this Point in the *Englishman* Number 5, where I say,

" The unhappy Animosities which have reigned amongst us, have made each Side reduce it self to an Absurdity, from their Violence in opposing each other. While the one urges a Parliament Title, his Warmth betrays him into Expressions disrespectful to the Sovereignty; and his Opponent expresses his Indignation at Principles too near the Sentiments of Common-wealths-Men, with carrying too far the Terms Hereditary and Indefeasible. Let them both agree that the Queen is vested in all the Rights inherent in the Crown of *England*, and in Default of Issue, the same Titles devolved upon the House of *Hanover*. When we talk of Hereditary in general, all who can be perswaded that the Pretender is the Son of *James* II, may be insnared to conclude that his Title is superior to that of any other upon Earth: But when we allow that the Act of Settlement, and the other subsequent Acts, have well vested all possible Title in Her Majesty and the House of *Hanover*, the *Englishman* has but one View before him; and any Title of the Pretender, of whomsoever born, is as remote as that of the *Tudors* or *Plantagenets*, or any other extinct Family.

" In this plain Rule for the Direction of our Obedience, we have nothing to divert our Thoughts from pursuing the real Interest of our Queen and Country; and all, as one Man, will join in a common Indignation against those who would perplex our Obedience, as faithful Subjects and *Englishmen*."

21

The last Paragraph expresses my Fears of the Pretender, which I must still acknowledge; at least I can see nothing criminal in them, till such Time as it shall be made a Crime to say that the Protestant Succession is in Danger. I thought I had Reason to apprehend this Danger, from the Power of one who had declared himself the Friend and Patron of the Pretender, from his present Residence with a Prince, who has been ineffectually applied to for his Removal; from the Apprehensions of a whole House of Commons in another Kingdom, where Men have been actually listed for his Service; from Addresses sent out of *North Britain*; from Books written and published in Vindication of his Title. I thought my Fears were not too early, when the Danger appeared so imminent; and I believe every Gentleman will concur with me, that it is more for the Safety of the Publick we should, in this great Case, be affrighted with imaginary Danger, than lulled into imaginary Security.

I come now, Sir, to those Passages which are marked in the Dedication to the *CRISIS*. The first Paragraph runs thus:

"I will take the further Liberty to say, That if the Acts of Parliament mentioned in the following Treatise, had been from Time to Time put in a fair and clear Light, and had been carefully recommended to the Perusal of young Gentlemen in Colleges, with a Preference to all other Civil Institutions whatsoever, this Kingdom had not been in its present Condition, but the Constitution would have had, in every Member the Universities have sent into the World since the Revolution, an Advocate for our Rights and Liberties."

I suppose, Sir, those who have marked this Passage, would fetch an Innuendo out of it that I speak disrespectfully of the Universities; an Imputation which I thought could never be laid to my Charge, as may appear by innumerable Passages that may be drawn out of Books which I have published. It would take up the Time of this House too much, should I desire that all those Passages should be read; I shall therefore only beg Leave to make use of that Work which is intitled *The Englishman*, to vouch for me in this Particular. In the Paper of that Name, Number 12, I thus express my self:

"Our wholesome Laws, large Provisions, and the exemplary Characters of our Divines, place them above the Necessity of practising false Arts, to be in themselves, their Families, and their Posterity, the most happy as well as the most eminent of the People. If therefore they will at any Time separate themselves from the common Interest of their Country, such Errors in them must necessarily render them, in Instances which might be indifferent in others, to a Degree Schismaticks in the Church, and Rebels in the State." [a]

And I also say in the *Englishman* Number 34,

"I have ever been of Opinion, that our Universities, as they have been the strongest Support of our Church, will be no less zealous for the Defence of our Civil Liberties, whenever they shall see them openly attacked. One of those illustrious Societies cannot yet have forgot, when, by a most unexampled Piece of Cruelty, Six and twenty of her Members, for refusing to be guilty of direct Perjury, and bravely opposing an illegal Commission, were all of them deprived of their Fellowships, made incapable of any Ecclesiastical Dignity; and such of them as were not then in holy Orders, declared and adjudged incapable of being ever admitted into the same. I shall conclude with this Observation, *That these noble Foundations and Monuments of the Virtue of our Ancestors*, are in their very Nature directly opposite to Tyranny and unlimited Power; since as Ignorance is a natural Consequence of Slavery, *Arts* and *Sciences* may be properly called *the eldest Daughters of Liberty*." [b]

It appears by these, and many other Passages in my Writings, that I have retained the greatest Honour and Esteem for those learned Bodies; in one of which I received a Part of my Education, and where I can still boast of much personal Friendship and Acquaintance. But I believe, Sir, there are none among those learned Societies, who will think I derogate from them by any thing said in this Paragraph. They themselves bewail their Misfortune, that several Nonjurors are gone out from among them, and several still remain with them, who are the most able Defenders of that Cause, and who, if they had

[a] *Written by Mr.* Steele *himself.* [*Steele's* note]
[b] *Written by a Correspondent of Mr.* Steele. [Steele's note]

rightly studied our Constitution as settled by Acts of Parliament, might have been as able Advocates for our Rights and Liberties. Sir, I have Reason to esteem the Universities, as I had the Happiness to have had a Part of my Education in one of them: And it is for the like Reason that I shall always have a Veneration for the Clergy, as having been bred up from my Infancy (which I know not whether my Accuser was or not) in the Doctrine of the Church of *England*.

The Paragraph which follows in the Dedication of the *CRISIS* is this:

"There is one thing which deserves your most serious Consideration. You have bound your selves by the strongest Obligations that Religion can lay upon Men, to support that Succession which is the Subject of the Following Papers: You have tied down your Souls by an Oath to maintain it as it is settled in the House of *Hanover*: Nay, you have gone much further than is usual in Cases of this Nature, as you have personally abjured the Pretender to this Crown; and that expressly, without any Equivocations or mental Reservations whatsoever; that is, without any possible Escapes, by which the Subtlety of temporising Casuists might hope to elude the Force of these solemn Obligations. You know much better than I do, whether the calling God to witness to the Sincerity of our Intentions in these Cases; whether the swearing upon the holy Evangelists in the most solemn Manner; whether the taking of an Oath before Multitudes of our Fellow-Subjects and Fellow-Christians in our publick Courts of Justice, do not lay the greatest Obligations that can be laid on the Consciences of Men. This I am sure of, that if the Body of the Clergy, who considerately and voluntarily entered into these Engagements, should be made use of as Instruments and Examples to make the Nation break through them, not only the Succession to our Crown, but the very Essence of our Religion is in Danger. What a Triumph would it furnish to those evil Men among us, who are Enemies to your sacred Order? What Occasion would it administer to Atheists and Unbelievers to say, That Christianity is nothing else but an outward Show and Pretence among the most knowing of its Professors? What could we afterwards object to Jesuits? What would be the Scandal brought upon our holy Church,

which is at present the Glory and Bulwark of the Reformation?
How would our present Clergy appear in the Eyes of their
Posterity, and even to the Succession of their own Order, under
a Government introduced and established by a Conduct so
directly opposite to all the Rules of Honour, and Precepts of
Christianity?"

A Man may own he apprehends that Holy and Recluse men
may be misled by artful ones, without any Imputation to their
Characters of Weakness or Guilt. And I here only take the
Liberty of all Writers, to suppose a Case which is not likely to
happen; and by that Means to animate the Zeal of those to
whom I address my self, for that Cause; of the Justice of which
they are already perswaded. This is a way of arguing made use
of by every one who would bring over his Reader to a Zeal for
what he advances. What is more frequent than to hear from
the Pulpit it self, the Scandal that would be brought upon
Christianity, should the Professors of it deviate from those
Rules which it prescribes? And it would be as just to say, that
the Preacher does by this Method insinuate that his Hearers
are not Christians, as it would be to imply from that Paragraph
which I have now read, that our *English* Clergy are against the
Protestant Succession: Nay, I think, nothing can be so great an
Argument that I believe they are for it, as thus laying before
the Reader those solemn Engagements that this Holy Order of
Men have enter'd into for its Preservation. But to take off all
Possibility of an Innuendo in this Place, I have, in the Paragraph which immediately follows, disclaimed every such Implication; where I say,

"As I always speak and think of your Holy Order with the
utmost Deference and Respect, I do not insist upon this Subject
to insinuate that there is such a Disposition among your Venerable Body, but to shew how much your own Honour and the
Interest of Religion is concerned, that there should be no Cause
given for it."

It would be very unfair to separate my Words, and to pronounce a Meaning in them, which I have not expressed, when
that which I have expressed is a positive Denial of having
entertained any such Meaning.

Sir, I am afraid that those who stir up this Accusation against me, only make use of the Name of the Clergy to give it a more popular Turn, and to take off the Odium from themselves, by the Use of such Venerable Names. But I hope this Accusation will be thought to proceed from the real Cause of it; and if any Hardship should fall upon me, as I know there cannot, whilst I have the Honour and Happiness to be heard before this House, that it will rather be imputed to the Resentments of an angry Minister, than of an injured Clergy.

Sir, If I can arrogate to my self any little Merit from the Writings which I have published, it is chiefly this; That I have personally opposed such Authors as have endeavoured to ridicule Religion, and those Holy Professors of it. I have received several Approbations in Publick and in Private, from Men in Holy Orders, for my concurring with them, to the best of my poor Abilities, in the Advancement of Morality, and in beating down that unreasonable Humour which had prevailed with so many Writers to expose their Persons and Profession to the Derision of foolish and wicked Men. I must beg leave, on this Head, to produce some out of innumerable Passages which speak with the utmost Deference and Respect of their Holy Calling in general, and of some particular Persons in it, for whom, I believe, most of the Gentlemen of this House have a very great and just Esteem.

I shall first cite one or two very short Passages out of a Book called, *The Guardian*, which has been mentioned in this House; and which was published not long since. The first of which Passages is in the 13th, 14th, and 15th Pages of the 1st Volume, in the following Terms—

" I am diverted from the Account I was giving the Town of my particular Concerns, by casting my Eye upon a Treatise, which I could not overlook without an inexcusable Negligence, and want of Concern for all the Civil as well as Religious Interests of Mankind. This Piece has for its Title, *A Discourse of Free-Thinking, occasioned by the Rise and Growth of a Sect called Free-Thinkers*. The Author very methodically enters upon his Argument, and says, By Free-Thinking I mean the Use of the Understanding, in endeavouring to find out the Meaning of any Proposition whatsoever, in considering the

Nature of the Evidence for or against, and in judging of it according to the seeming Force or Weakness of the Evidence. As soon as he delivered this Definition, from which one would expect he did not design to shew a particular Inclination for or against any thing, before he had considered it; he gives up all Title to the Character of a Free-Thinker, with the most apparent Prejudice against a Body of Men, whom of all others a good Man would be most careful not to violate, I mean Men in holy Orders. Persons who have devoted themselves to the Service of God are venerable to all who fear him; and it is a certain Characteristick of a dissolute ungovern'd Mind, to rail or speak disrespectfully of them in general. It is certain that in so great a Crowd of Men, some will intrude who are of Tempers very unbecoming their Function. But because Ambition and Avarice are sometimes lodged in that Bosom, which ought to be the Dwelling of Sanctity and Devotion, must this unreasonable Author villify the whole Order? He has not taken the least Care to disguise his being an Enemy to the Persons against whom he writes, nor any where granted, that the Institution of religious Men to serve at the Altar, and instruct such who are not as wise as himself, is at all necessary or desirable; but proceeds without the least Apology to undermine their Credit, and frustrate their Labours. Whatever Clergymen, in Disputes against each other, have unguardedly uttered, is here recorded in such a Manner as to affect Religion it self, by wresting Concessions to its Disadvantage from its own Teachers. If this be true, as sure any Man that reads the Discourse must allow it is; and if Religion is the strongest Tye of Human Society; in what Manner are we to treat this our common Enemy?" [a]

I shall cite another Passage, Sir, which is taken out of the 245th and 246th Pages of the Second Volume of the same Work, and contains the following Words:

" But if to inform the Understanding, and regulate the Will, is the most lasting and diffusive Benefit, there will not be found so useful and excellent an Institution as that of the *Christian Priesthood*, which is now become the Scorn of Fools.

" That a numerous Order of Men should be consecrated to the Study of the most sublime and beneficial Truths, with a

---

[a] *Written by Mr.* Steele *himself.* [Steele's note]

Design to propagate them by their Discourses and Writings, to inform their Fellow-Creatures of the Being and Attributes of the Deity, to possess their Minds with the Sense of a future State, and not only to explain the Nature of every Virtue and Moral Duty, but likewise to perswade Mankind to the Practice of them by the most powerful and engaging Motives, is a thing so excellent and necessary to the Well-being of the World, that no Body but a modern Free-Thinker could have the Forehead or Folly to turn it into Ridicule.

" The Light in which these Points should be exposed to the View of one who is prejudiced against the Names *Religion, Church, Priest,* and the like, is, to consider the Clergy as so many Philosophers, the Churches as Schools, and their Sermons as Lectures for the Information and Improvement of the Audience. How would the Heart of *Socrates* or *Tully* have rejoyced, had they lived in a Nation where the Law had made Provision for Philosophers to read Lectures of Philosophy every seventh Day in several Thousand of Schools erected at the publick Charge throughout the whole Country, at which Lectures all Ranks and Sexes without Distinction were obliged to be present for their general Improvement? And what wicked Wretches would they think those Men, who should endeavour to defeat the Purpose of so Divine an Institution? " [a]

It ever was my Sentiment, before I could have formed to my self any Views of such Engagements as those I have since fallen into, that Respect to Clergymen and their Prosperity are essential to the Good of Society. Give me Leave, Mr. *Speaker,* on this Occasion, to read to you a Passage out of a little Tract called *The Christian Hero*; the 58th Page, speaking of the Enemies to the Christian Name, and Persons who envied the Clergy, runs thus:

" But alas! its State is as much Militant as ever; for there are earthly and narrow Souls as deeply scandall'd at the Prosperity the Professors and Teachers of this Sacred Faith enjoy, and object to them the Miseries and Necessities of the Primitive Believers. Light and superficial Men! not seeing that Riches is a much more dangerous Dispensation than that of Poverty.

[a] *This most reasonable and amiable Light in which the Clergy are here placed, comes from that modest and good Man the Rev. Mr.* Bartlett. [Steele's note]

This we oppose as a Foe, that we run to as a Friend; and an Enemy does his Business more successfully in an Embrace than a Blow. But since the Necessaries, Conveniencies, and Honours of Life which the Clergy enjoy, are so great an Offence to their Despisers, they are the more engaged to hold them dear; for they who envy a Man what he has, would certainly scorn him without it. When therefore they are both in good and bad Fortune irreconcileable to them, may they always offend with their Happiness: For it is not to be doubted, but that there are Bishops and Governours in the Church of *England*, whose decent Hospitality, Meekness, and Charity to their Brethren, will place them in the same Mansions with the most heroick Poor, convince the Mistake of their Enemies, and shew that the eternal Pastor has given his worldly Blessings into Hands by which he approves their Distribution; and still bestows upon us great and exemplary Spirits, that can conquer the Difficulties and Enchantments of Wealth it self."

I have carried this Inclination to the Advancement of Virtue so far, as to pursue it even in things the most indifferent, and which, perhaps, have been thought foreign to it. To give you an Instance of this, Sir, I must mention a comedy called *The Lying Lover*, which I writ some Years ago, the Preface to which says,

"Tho' it ought to be the Care of all Governments, that publick Representations should have nothing in them but what is agreeable to the Manners, Laws, Religion, and Policy of the Place or Nation wherein they are exhibited; yet it is the general Complaint of the more learned and virtuous amongst us, that the *English* Stage has extremely offended in this Kind. I thought therefore it would be an honest Ambition to attempt a Comedy, which might be no improper Entertainment in a Christian Common-wealth."

Mr. *Collier* had, about the Time wherein this was published, written against the Immorality of the Stage. I was (as far as I durst for fear of witty Men, upon whom he had been too severe) a great Admirer of his Work, and took it into my Head to write a Comedy in the Severity he required. In this Play I make the Spark or Heroe kill a Man in his Drink, and finding himself in Prison the next Morning, I give him the Contrition which he ought to have on that Occasion. 'Tis in Allusion to that Circumstance that the Preface further says as follows:

"*The Anguish he there expresses, and the mutual Sorrow between an only Child and a tender Father in that Distress, are perhaps an Injury to the Rules of Comedy, but I am sure they are a Justice to those of Morality: And Passages of such a Nature being so frequently applauded on the Stage, it is high Time that we should no longer draw Occasions of Mirth from those Images which the Religion of our Country tells us we ought to tremble at with Horrour.*

"*But Her most excellent Majesty has taken the Stage into Her Consideration; and we may hope, from her gracious Influence on the Muses, that Wit will recover from its Apostacy; and that by being encouraged in the Interests of Virtue, 'twill strip Vice of the gay Habit in which it has too long appeared, and cloath it in its native Dress of Shame, Contempt and Dishonour.*"

I can't tell, Sir, what they would have me do to prove me a Churchman; but I think I have appeared one even in so trifling a thing as a Comedy: And considering me as a Comick Poet, I have been a Martyr and Confessor for the Church; for this Play was damn'd for its Piety.

I shall in the last Place, Sir, with your Allowance, quote some Passages out of another Book, Intituled, *The Tatler*; the first of which is in the 37th Page of the first Volume, published in 1710, as follows.

Will's Coffee-House, April 20, 1709.

"THIS Week being Sacred to Holy Things, and no Publick Diversions allowed, there has been taken Notice of, even here, a little Treatise, called, *A Project for the Advancement of Religion*; dedicated to the Countess of Berkeley. The Title was so uncommon, and promis'd so peculiar a way of Thinking, that every Man here has read it, and as many as have done so have approved it. It is written with the Spirit of one who has seen the World enough to undervalue it with good Breeding. The Author must certainly be a Man of Wisdom as well as Piety, and have spent much time in the Exercise of both. The

Real Causes of the Decay of the Interest of Religion, are set forth in a clear and lively Manner, without unseasonable Passions; and the whole Air of the Book, as to the Language, the Sentiments and the Reasonings, show it was written by one whose Virtue sits easie about him, and to whom Vice is thoroughly contemptible. It was said by one of this Company, alluding to that Knowledge of the World the Author seems to have; The Man writes much like a Gentleman, and goes to Heaven with a very good Mien." [a]

The Gentleman I here intended was Dr. *Swift*; this kind of Man I thought him at that time: We have not met of late, but I hope he deserves this Character still.

The second Passage which I shall cite out of that Work, is in the 116th and 117th Pages of the second Volume, published the same Year 1710.

"The Dean, we heard the other Day together, is an Orator. He has so much regard to his Congregation, that he commits to his Memory what he is to say to them; and has so soft and graceful a Behaviour that it must attract your Attention. His Person, it is to be confessed, is no small Recommendation; but he is to be highly commended for not losing that Advantage, and adding to the Propriety of Speech (which might pass the Criticism of *Longinus*) an Action which would have been approved by *Demosthenes*. He has a peculiar Force in his way, and has many of his Audience, who could not be Intelligent Hearers of his Discourse, were there not Explanation as well as Grace in his Action. This Art of his is used with most Exact and Honest Skill. He never Attempts your Passions till he has convinc'd your Reason. All the Objections which he can form are laid open and dispersed, before he uses the least Vehemence in his Sermon: but when he thinks he has your Head, he very soon wins your Heart; and never pretends to show the Beauty of Holiness, till he hath convinced you of the Truth of it." [b]

The third Passage which I shall cite from that Work, is taken out of the 168th and 169th Pages of the same Volume—

[a] *Written by Mr.* Steele *himself*. [Steele's note]
[b] *Written by Mr.* Steele *himself*. [Steele's note]

"This Matter is too sacred for this Paper; but I can't see what Injury it would do any Clergyman, to have it in his Eye, and believe, all that are taken from him by his want of Industry, are to be demanded of him. I dare say, *Favonius* has very few of these Losses. *Favonius*, in the midst of a thousand impertinent Assailants of the Divine Truths, is an undisturbed Defender of 'em. He protects all under his Care, by the Clearness of his Understanding and the Example of his Life. He visits dying Men with the Air of a Man who hopes for his own Dissolution, and enforces in others a Contempt of this Life, by his own Expectation of the next. His Voice and Behaviour are the lively Images of a compos'd and well govern'd Zeal. None can leave him for the frivolous *Jargon* of the Ordinary Teachers among Dissenters, but such who cannot distinguish Vociferation from Eloquence, and Argument from Railing. He is so great a Judge of Mankind, and touches our Passions with so Superior a Command that he who deserts his Congregation must be a Stranger to the Dictates of Nature, as well as to those of Grace." [a]

In fine, Sir, the last Passage which I shall cite out of that Work, is taken from the Preface to the fourth Volume, published in 1711, where it is said,

"What a Man obtains from the good Opinion and Friendship of worthy Men, is a much greater Honour than he can possibly reap from any Accomplishments of his own. But all the Credit of Wit, which was given me by the Gentlemen abovementioned (with whom I have now Accounted) has not been able to Attone for the Exceptions made against me for some Raillery in behalf of that learned Advocate for the Episcopacy of the Church and Liberty of the People, Mr. *Hoadly*. I mention this only to defend my self against the Imputation of being moved rather by Party than Opinion; and think it is apparent I have with the utmost Frankness allowed Merit wherever I found it, though joined in Interests different from those for which I have declared my self. When my *Favonius* is acknowledged to be Dr. *Smalridge*, and the amiable Character of the Dean in the sixty-sixth *Tatler*, drawn for Dr. *Atterbury*, I hope I need say no more as to Impartiality."

[a] *Written by Mr.* Steele *himself*. [Steele's note]

Sir, I shall give you no more Instances on this Head, but shall beg that common Candour from Gentlemen, which is allow'd to every Body; that if my Intention should appear Doubtful or Suspicious in any one Passage, it may be explained by others which are more plainly and fully expressed. Sir, since I have touched upon the word *Religion*, I hope I may be indulged one Sentence more before I quit this Head, and if I speak as a Fool, that you will bear with me. I have in several of my Writings espoused the Interests of Virtue and Religion, and have Reason to hope I have been of some use to the Publick upon that account. Why may not these now plead for me? I wish those who have written against me, and have contributed their utmost to bring me into my present Misfortune, may in their Day of Adversity have the same Foundation for Support in themselves, and Claim to your Favour.

I now come, Sir, to the Passages marked in the first and second Pages of the *Crisis*.

" But since, by I know not what Fatality, we are of late grown Supine, and our Anxiety for It [a] is abated, in proportion to the Danger to which it is every Day more exposed, by the artful and open Attacks of the Enemies of our Constitution: It is a Seasonable and Honest Office to look into our Circumstances; and let the Enemies of our present Establishment behold the Securities which the Laws of the Country have given those who dare assert their Liberties, and the Terrors they have pronounced against those who dare undermine them. For, whatever is the Prospect before our Eyes, it is the business of every honest Man, to look up with a Spirit that becomes Honesty, and to do what in him lies for the Improvement of our present Condition, which nothing but our own Pusillanimity can make desperate.

" The most destructive Circumstance in our Affairs seems to be, that by the long and repeated Insinuations of our Enemies, many are worn into a kind of Doubt of their own Cause, and think with Patience of what is suggested in favour of contrary Pretensions. The most obvious Method of reviving the proper Sentiments in the Minds of Men, for what they ought to esteem most dear, is to shew, that our Cause has in it all the Sanctions

[a] *Speaking of Liberty* [Steele's note].

of Honour, Truth, and Justice; and that we are, by all the Laws
of God and Man, instated in a condition of enjoying Religion,
Life, Liberty and Property, rescued from the most imminent
Danger of having them all for ever depend upon the Arbitrary
Power of a Popish Prince."

I must here beg leave, Sir, to read the two or three following
Lines which are not marked, because they explain this latter
part of this last Paragraph, and show to whom these Words are
applied, where it is said, *That we are by all the Laws of God
and Man, instated in a Condition of enjoying Religion, Life,
Liberty, and Property, rescued from the most imminent Danger
of having them all for ever depend upon the Arbitrary Power
of a Popish Prince.* The following Paragraph, which determines
these words, runs thus,

"We shou'd have been chained down in this abject Con-
dition, in the Reign of the late King *James*, had not God
Almighty in Mercy given us the late happy Revolution, by that
*Glorious Instrument of his Providence the Great and Memorable
King* William."

And now, Sir, can any one say, that we were not instated in
a Condition of enjoying Religion, Life, Liberty, and Property,
by the late happy Revolution? Or that we were not before in
the most imminent Danger of having them all depend upon
the Arbitrary Power of a Popish Prince? I appeal to the Acts
of Parliament quoted in this Book; and might appeal, as I am
told, to a Report of the Grievances of this Kingdom, under the
Reign of King *James* II. made to this House by *Paul Foley*,
Esq; Father to the Gentleman who has so remarkably distinguish'd himself against me this Day. This Report, as I am told,
explains by a multitude of Instances, drawn up in the strongest
Terms, the several Particulars which I have here just touch'd
upon. If the House thinks fit that I should in this Place have
the Assistance of the Father against the Son, I will desire that
that Report may now be Read: Or, if that be not thought fit,
shall go on with my Defence.[a]

---

[a] *In this Mr.* Steele *was misinformed, for there did not upon Examination
appear any such Circumstance of* Paul Foley, *Esq; but he was a very Worthy
Man tho' Father to this Squire* Thomas. [Steele's note]

And here, Sir, I think I may save you a great deal of Time, by laying down a General Rule which every one will agree, ought to take place in the Perusal of any Writing. That which I shall insist on is this; that if an Author's Words, in the obvious and natural Interpretation of them, have a Meaning which is Innocent, they cannot without great Injustice be condemned of another Meaning which is Criminal. If the same Expression may be applied to different Persons, and according to such Application may be construed in my Favour or to my Prejudice, why should my Words be applied to hurt me, when they may more Naturally be applied in such a Manner as is not capable of incurring Censure? Thus, Sir, when I mention in the Paragraph I have just now read, *The Artful and open Attacks of the Enemies of our Constitution, the Enemies of our present Happy Establishment, The Terrors which are pronounc'd against those who dare undermine our Liberties*; why must all these and the like Expressions be applied to a Minister, when there are such Numbers of Popish Emissaries, Jacobites and Nonjurors, to whom these Expressions by a Natural and unforced Construction are very Applicable? Does not the Supposition of such an Innuendo reflect highly upon a Minister who has given no Occasion for it? Is a Man Seditious, who speaks in plain and open Terms against the Enemies of our Constitution and Country? or, is it impossible to make use of those words, without comprehending under them, Persons whom it is Criminal to attack? By this way of arguing, it is not in the Power of Words to be free from unwarrantable Hints and Innuendos. Thus, Sir, in the next Paragraph, where mention is made, of *indirect Arts and mean Subtleties practiced to weaken our Securities*—are not these Words as general as possible, applicable to Multitudes of open Enemies and disaffected Persons, both in Foreign Dominions and in her Majesty's Kingdoms? or will any one say that indirect Arts and mean Subtleties can be practiced only by one Man in the Kingdom? When there are two different Interpretations to be put upon any Expression, will any Gentleman of Candour and Humanity regard that only which carries Guilt in it? especially when the Interpretation which must render such Expression Criminal, is violent and forced, whereas the other that renders them Innocent is obvious and natural? I shall, after this, beg leave to read in this Light, the next Paragraph marked in the *Crisis*, page 2.

" I flatter my self that if the Passages which happened in those Days, the Resolutions of the Nation thereupon, and the just Provisions made from Time to Time, against our falling into the same Disasters, were fairly stated and laid in one View, all indirect Arts and mean Subtleties practised to weaken our Securities would be frustrated, and vanish before the glaring Light of Law and Reason."·

I cannot conceive why the other Paragraph that follows page 2d and 3d, should have been marked, since it is no Crime, nor any way tends to Sedition, to speak in Honour of Parliaments, or to quote Acts of Parliament. Here it is—

" I shall not govern my self on this Occasion, by the partial Relations of particular Persons or Parties, but by the Sense of the whole People, by the Sense of the Houses of Lords and Commons, the Representative Body of the whole Nation; in whose Resolutions, according to the different State of Things, the Condition of the Kingdom, by those who had the greatest Stakes in it, has been from Time to Time Plainly, Impartially and Pathetically expressed."

The next Passage is in the *Crisis*, page 27.

" And all this hath been done in so open a Manner, and in so Expressive and plain Terms, that one cannot but think that our Popish or Jacobite Party, who have been of late so bold, both in Writing and Speaking against the Settlement of the Crown of *Great Britain* in the Protestant Line, and cannot possibly plead Ignorance of these Things, must have some unaccountable Encouragement for their Support."

I here say that those who write or speak boldly and knowingly contrary to the Tenor of Acts of Parliament, which I have before cited, and which are now in Force, must have some Unaccountable Encouragement for their Support; and the Reason is very plain, because such a Person is declared liable to the most grievous Penalties who does act or speak after such a Manner; But whether this unaccountable Encouragment comes from the Pretender himself, the *French* Court, or the Dukes of *Lorrain*

or *Savoy*, whose Interest it may be to give them such Encouragement, I do not pretend to determine: And I hope it will not
be said that I do pretend to Account for such an Encouragement
which I do here plainly declare to be Unaccountable.

The two next Paragraphs are only a Narrative or Relation
of Matters of Fact, which I conceived I might set down with
that Liberty which is allowed to the most common News-Writer.
Here they follow.

" If the beating the Enemy in the Field, and being too vigilant
for their Councils in Foreign Courts, were effectual Means
towards ending the War, and reducing them to a Condition too
low for giving fresh Disturbance to *Europe*, the Duke of *Marlborough* took just Measures: But, however Unaccountable it
may appear to Posterity, that General was not permitted to
enjoy the Fruits of his Glorious Labours: But, as *France* chang'd
her Generals for want of Success in their Conduct; so *Britain*
changes hers, after an uninterrupted Series of Conquest. The
Minds of the People, against all Common Sense, are debauch'd
with Impressions of the Duke's Affectation of prolonging the
War for his own Glory; and his Adversaries attack a Reputation
which could not well be impaired, without sullying the Glory
of *Great Britain* it self. His Enemies were not to be softened
by that Consideration; he is dismiss'd, and soon after a Cessation
of Arms between *Great Britain* and *France* is publish'd at the
Head of the Armies. The *British*, in the midst of the Enemies
Garrisons, withdraw themselves from their Confederates. The
French, now no longer having the Britains, or their Great Leader
to fear, affect no more strong Garrisons and fortified Camps,
but attack and rout the Earl of *Albemarle* at *Denain*, and necessitate the brave Prince *Eugene* to abandon *Landrecy*, a Place
of such Importance that it gave Entrance into the Heart of
France. Of which the *French* King was so sensible, that before
he was recovered from his Fright, he acknowledg'd he owed
in a manner his Crown, to the Suspension of Arms between
him and *Great Britain*. The Suspension is follow'd by a Treaty
of Peace at *Utrecht*. The Peace is concluded between *Great
Britain* and *France*, and between *France* and the *States-General*.
The Emperor and the Empire continue the War! I shall not
presume to enter into an Examination of the Articles of Peace

between us and *France*; but there can be no Crime in affirming (if it be a Truth) that the House of *Bourbon* is at this Juncture become more formidable, and bids fairer for an universal Monarchy, and to engross the whole Trade of *Europe*, than it did before the War.

"All the World knows with what Frankness the *Dutch* have been treated to deliver up *Traerbach* to the *Imperialists,* as an Expedient for the *French* to besiege it; because forsooth it lies convenient for their Incursions upon the Empire. This Extravagant Demand must give a melancholy Prospect to other Nations."

If it be a Crime to speak honourably of the Duke of *Marlborough*, it is a Crime that I must always be guilty of, and is that which instead of denoting me a Stirrer up of Sedition, declares me to be *a Lover of my Country*. If I am rightly informed, that Great Man, when a Circumstance relating to him was under your Consideration during the last Session of Parliament, was mentioned in this Place, not only with Deference and Respect, but with the highest Encomiums by the most Eminent Members of this House. And I hope, the most private Man may take the liberty of expressing his Gratitude to the Duke of *Marlborough*, since there is no private Man in *England* who is not obliged to him. Those who are represented as his Adversaries and Enemies, are only those who will always be so; I mean such who are Friends to the Pretender and the *French* King, whose Hopes he hath often and gloriously defeated. If any one questions what I have said concerning the *French* King's letter, upon the raising of the Siege of *Landrecy*, let him read that Letter, and see what other Interpretation can be put upon it.

The last Sentence of this Paragraph I think defends it self, and is founded upon this Maxim, which I fancy no Gentleman will deny, That it is not a Crime to speak the Truth. Here is what follows in the 31st and 32d Pages of the *Crisis*.

"The most important Article between *France* and *England,* is the Demolition of *Dunkirk*; which they have begun contemptuously and Arbitrarily their own way. The Mole and Harbour, which only are dreadful to us, are yet untouch'd and just Suspicions given that they ever will be."

Sir, I always postpone my own private Safety to that of my Country; and therefore heartily wish that I lay open to the Censure of this House for what I have here advanced. I say, Sir, that I heartily wish, tho' I might have fared the worse for it at this time, that the Event did not Justifie those Apprehensions, which I have here, and in other Papers expressed, in relation to *Dunkirk*; I have regulated my Thoughts on that Subject, by the Treaty of Peace which has been published for the Perusal of her Majesty's Subjects. It was thereby Stipulated, that the Mole and Harbour should be first Demolished: But instead of this, the *French* (for it is there I lay the blame) have only demolished the Fortifications towards the Land; and thus, as I have said in another place, the Queen's Garrison is exposed, by levelling the Works, to the Mercy of the *French*; and the Mole and Harbour, which were first to be Demolished, stand as they did. Will any one say that this Proceeding of the *French,* so contrary to what was stipulated by the Articles of Peace, is not begun Contemptuously and Arbitrarily their own way? The Time stipulated by the same Treaty for the Demolition of the Mole and Harbour, is long since elapsed; and no longer since than a Week ago, as I can prove by incontestable Evidence, they were actually repairing that very Mole, which should have been long before this a heap of Ruins. These, and many other Reasons which I forbear insisting upon, will, I hope, explain what I have said in this Paragraph, to every Gentleman's Satisfaction. Here is that which follows marked in the *Crisis*, p. 32.

" *Landau* and *Fribourg* are taken, and in case there is no intermediate Peace, *which may still be more immediately fatal to us,* two hundred thousand *French* may be ready in the Spring to invade the Empire, and restore the Elector of *Bavaria* to his forfeited Dominions."

Will any one say there was no Danger to be apprehended from a Peace, which was treating, according to our publick Accounts, without her Majesty's Interposition? And when we had reason to fear that her Majesty's Ministers had no opportunity given them of promoting any thing in it for the Good of their Country, as not being let into the Secret? Have not our publick Prints told us, that *England* was not mentioned in the

Treaty? Do they not speak of private Articles, reciprocal Complaisances, and several other Particulars which prove, that the Apprehensions I here mention, were not altogether groundless?

The next Paragraph is only matter of Fact, and an Inference from it, which cannot be controverted. Here it is.

" These Incidents happen when the Capital of *Austria*, the Residence of his Imperial Majesty, is visited with the Plague. The Male Line of that House is likely to terminate in himself; and should it please God to take him off, and no King of the *Romans* chosen, a Prince of the House of *Bourbon* would [3] bid fair for the Imperial Dignity; after which Day, farewell Liberty, *Europe* would be *French*."

Here is the Paragraph that follows:

" But the Scene is not yet closed; *Portugal*, which during the War, supplied to us the place of *Spain*, by sending us vast Quanties of Gold in Exchange for our Woollen Manufactures, has only at present a Suspension of Arms for its Protection, which Suspension may possibly last no longer than 'till the *Catalonians* are reduc'd; and who knows but the old Pretensions of *Spain* to *Portugal*, may be then revived? I mention the *Catalonians*, but who can name the *Catalonians* without a Tear! Brave Unhappy People! Drawn into the War by the Encouragement of the Maritime Powers, from which only a Nation encompassed by Land by *France* and *Spain*, could hope for Relief and Protection, now abandoned and exposed to the Resentment of an enraged Prince, whose Person and Interest they have always opposed; and yet still so fond of their Ancient Liberties that tho' hemmed up in a Nook of Land by the Forces of the two Crowns, and closely besieged in *Barcelona*, they chuse rather, like their Countrymen, the famous *Saguntines* of old, to perish with their Wives and Children, than live in Slavery. Did the *French* King with a conquering Sword in his Hand, ever abandon the least and most inconsiderable of all his Allies? No. When these very *Catalonians* had assisted him against the King of *Spain*, he did not give up his Power of treating, 'till he had made the most honourable Conditions for them: Not a single Man amongst them was then hurt, either in his Person or Privileges; but now—Poor unhappy *Catalonians*, worthy of a better Fate! Good and gracious God! To whom shall be attributed the Loss of this brave People? Dreadful the Doom of those who shall in thy Sight be esteemed their Destroyers! "

I am at a loss with my self whether the Gentleman marked out this Paragraph for taking Pity on the poor *Catalonians*, or for having spoken honourably of the *French* King. Common Humanity will, I hope, be my Excuse for the first; and I shall trust to that Gentleman's known Good-Nature to pardon me for the latter.

But here the Gentleman finds another Innuendo, and has mark'd out a Seditious Blank: That is in reality, he is very angry with me, not for any thing I have said, but for something I have not said: Or rather, because I have not written what he would have had me write. But if he finds both my Silence and my Words Criminal, I must confess I don't know how to please him.

Sir, I am afraid I have tired out the Patience of this Honourable House, in explaining these Particulars, especially since I think they do sufficiently explain themselves to any impartial and unprejudiced Reader. As for the remaining part of the *Crisis* which has been marked, I have examined it very carefully, and am very much perplexed to find out the Passages in it which can have given any Manner of Offence. The greatest part of it consists of faithful Quotations out of History, that may give us an Abhorrence of Popery, and of a Popish Successor, with several Additional Arguments drawn from the Nature of the Roman Catholick Religion, which are the same which have ever been made use of against it since the Reformation. There are also several Considerations from the present Situation of Affairs in *Europe*, that may contribute to strengthen our Resolutions in the Defence of the Protestant Succession as established by our Laws. I have declared again and again in this Part of the Book, as well as in several of the foregoing Parts of it, that I wou'd inculcate nothing but a due Observance to the Laws of the Land, and a vigorous Exertion of our selves in the Defence and Preservation of them. Whatever Warmth or Spirit I have endeavoured to inspire my Readers with, I have declared over and over, that it is for the Maintenance of those Points which are established by Acts of Parliament and the Laws of their

Country. I must confess, Sir, that I am very much at a Loss, to imagine why my Accuser has laid his Finger upon these Passages which are so manifestly written in Favour of our Constitution, and in Opposition to Popery and the Pretender. He must have entertain'd a very mean Opinion of a *British* House of Commons, if he could think that such Passages would bring their Displeasure upon me: And I am verily perswaded that if Gentlemen will be pleased to hear them with Attention, they will be more apt to conceive an Indignation against that Person, who has charged them as Criminal, than against him who writ them. I shall only beg Leave to take Notice of one particular Passage in them, because it is a full Answer to an Insinuation made against me by one who spoke in a former Debate relating to this Subject. That Honourable Member was pleased to say, that I wou'd insinuate the Gentlemen of *England* were against the Protestant Succession in the House of *Hanover*. Were this my Thought, Sir, I wou'd give up that Cause as desperate. I say, Sir, if the Gentlemen of *England* were against it, all that he or any Body else could do for it, would be ineffectual. But, Sir, to show you that I could not be so weak and unjust as to make this wicked Suggestion, I beg Leave only to read these following Words—" As divided a People as we are, those who are for the House of *Hanover* are infinitely Superior in Number, Wealth, Courage, and all Arts Military and Civil, to those in the contrary Interest "—Will that honourable Person say, that the Gentlemen of *England* do not fall within this Description? Sir, my greatest Hope this Day is in the Gentlemen of *England*, who are above being prejudiced by any false Reports which are made of me, or by any sordid Motives that might have an Influence upon Men of base and mercenary Minds. But, Sir, I was going to read to you the remaining Part of the *Crisis*, as I find it marked upon your Table; but after having spoke thus much of it, I shall leave it to its own Justification.

" But to bring these several Facts and Circumstances home, we must observe, that the Person who seems to be the most favour'd by the *French* King in the late Treaties is the Duke of *Savoy*, who is made King of *Sicily*; and considering also the Enlargement of his Territories on the Continent, by Cession from the Emperor, is become the most powerful Prince in *Italy*.

This Prince put in his Claim to the Crown of *England*, in the Right of his Wife, a Daughter of the late Dutchess of Orleans, Sister of our late King *Charles* the Second, at the time of settling the Crown of *England* on the House of *Hanover*. This Prince, a Man of as great Address and Capacity as any now living, is supposed to have entered into a Secret and Strict Alliance with the House of *Bourbon*, and may therefore very well add to our Fears of a Popish Successor.

" Things standing thus, and the House of *Bourbon* being in the Actual Possession of *France* and *Spain*, bidding fair for the Conquest of *Germany*, or in Peace and good Understanding with it; what have *Great Britain* and *Holland* to hope from, but the Mercy of *France*? What else have we to prevent the Pretender's being imposed on us, when *France* shall think fit; nay, in failure of one Pretender, he has in his Quiver a Succession of them; the Dutchess of *Savoy*, or Her Sons, or the Dauphin Her Grandson. *The last named cannot be many Years from the Throne of* France.

" In the next Place how are we disposed at Home, for the Reception of such an Attempt? The Passions of many, which were raised so high by an Impudent Suggestion of the Church's Danger, seem to have subsided into a Lethargick Unconcern for every thing else; Harmless Men are ashamed to own, how grossly they have been imposed upon; and instead of resenting the Abuse, are willing to overlook it, with a certain Reluctance against being moved at any thing else; least they should fall into the Mortification of being misled a Second time. Many who are above being blinded by Popular Noise and Outcry, yet seem to think the Warmth and Zeal of a Publick Spirit to be little better than a Romantick Heat of Brain. Treasonable Books lately dispersed amongst us, that have apparently struck at the Protestant Succession in the House of *Hanover*, have passed almost without Observation from the Generality of the People; Subtile Queries have been Published, about the Birth of a certain Person, which certain Person every Body knows to be intended for the Pretender; The Author of the Conduct of the Allies has dared to drop Insinuations about altering the Succession; and a late Treasonable Book, on the Subject of *Hereditary Right*, has published the Will of King *Henry* the Eighth, which seems to be intended as a Pattern for the like Occasion.

" The Conversion of the *Pretender* to our Religion, has been occasionally Reported, and Contradicted, according to the Reception it met with among the soft Fools, who give that gross Story a hearing: The unhappy Prince, whose Son the Pretender calls himself, is a memorable Instance, how much such Conversions are to be depended upon. King *James*, when Duke of *York*, for a long time professed himself a Protestant; and even not long before his Accession to the Crown, several Persons had Actions brought against them for saying he was a Papist, and exorbitant Damages given and recovered; in a Word, from the Practice of all Papists, that have come to Protestant Thrones, upon Pretence of embracing the Reformed Religion, we have Reason to believe they have Dispensations from *Rome* to personate any thing, for the Service of that Church. A Popish Prince will never think himself obliged by the most Solemn, even the Coronation Oath, to his Protestant Subjects. All Oaths are as insignificant and as soon forgotten, as the Services done by such Protestant Subjects.

" King *James*, when Duke of *York*, was preserved from the Bill of Exclusion, by the Church of *England*, and particularly its Bishops; when he came to the Crown, the Church was soon insulted and outraged by him, and Her Prelates committed to the Tower.

" Has not a Neighbouring Prince cruelly Treated and Banished his Protestant Subjects, who preserved the Crown on his Head?

" Did not the Princess *Mary* promise the Men of *Suffolk*, who joined with Her against the Lady *Jane Grey*, that she would make no Alteration in the Religion Established by Her Brother, King *Edward* the Sixth? And yet as soon as she came to the Crown, by the Assistance even of *Suffolk* Men, she filled all *England*, and in a particular manner that County, with the Flames of Martyrs. The Cruelties of that Reign were such, that multitudes of Men, Women and Children were burnt for being Zealous Professors of the Gospel of the Lord Jesus. In short, nothing less than this can be expected from a Popish Prince; both Clergy and Laiety must share the same Fate, all universally must submit to the fiery Tryal, or renounce their Religion. Our

Bishops and Clergy must all lose their Spiritual Preferments, or submit to Antichristian Tyranny: And should they submit to every thing, they must notwithstanding part from their Wives and Children, which, according to the Church of *Rome*, are Harlots and Spurious. The Laiety, possessed of Lands that formerly belonged to the Roman Catholick Clergy, must resign their Estates, and perhaps be made accountable for the Profits received.

" What can be more moving, than to reflect upon the Barbarous Cruelties of Papists beyond all Example: And these not accidental, or the sudden Effects of Passion or Provocation, but the settled Result of their Religion and their Consciences.

" Above 100 000 Men, Women and Children were Murdered in the Massacre of *Ireland*. How hot and terrible were the late Persecutions of Protestants in *France* and *Savoy*? How frequent were the Massacres of the Protestants through the whole Kingdom of *France*, when they were under the Protection of the then Laws of that Country? How Barbarous, in a particular manner, was the Massacre of *Paris*, at the Marriage of the King of *Navarre*, the *French* King's Grand-father, a Protestant, with the Sister of *Charles* the Ninth, where the famous Admiral of *France*, the great *Coligny*, the glorious Asserter of the Protestant Interest, was inhumanly Murdered, and the Body of that Heroe dragged Naked about the Streets, and this by the Direction of the King himself, who had but just before most treacherously given him, from his own Mouth, Assurance of his Protection? Ten thousand Protestants, without distinction of Quality, Age or Sex, were put to the Sword at the same time; the King of *Navarre* himself narrowly escaped the Disaster, his Mother the Queen of *Navarre* having not long before been poysoned by the same Faction.

" These are some Instances of what must ever be expected. No Obligations on our side, no Humanity or Natural Probity on theirs, are of any weight; their very Religion forces them, upon Pain of Damnation, to forget and cancel the former, and to extinquish all remains of the latter. Good God! To what are they reserved, who have nothing to expect but what such a Religion can afford them? It cannot therefore be too often repeated. We should consider, over and over again, that should the Chain of the Protestant Succession be once broke in upon, though the Pretender should be laid aside, the next of the Blood Royal is the Dutchess of *Savoy*, after Her her two Sons; after them, the present Dauphin of *France*; the next in Succession to him, the Queen of *Spain*, and her Heirs; in Default of them, the Duke of *Orleans*, and his Heirs, and most of the other Princes of the Blood of *France*, all Papists, who may be enabled to demand Preference to the House of *Hanover*; so that besides the Probability of this Kingdom's being United to, and made a Province of *France*, the train of Popish Princes is so great, that if one should not compleat the utter Extirpation of our Religion, Laws and Liberties, the rest would certainly do it.

" And here I cannot but add what is still of more Importance, and ought to be the most prevalent of all Arguments, that should there be the least Hopes given to a Popish Successor, the Life of her Majesty will certainly be in most imminent Danger; for there will never be wanting bloody Zealots of that Perswasion, that will think it meritorious to take away her Majesty's Life, to hasten the Accession of such a Successor to her Throne.

" The only Preservation against these Terrors, are the Laws before-mentioned relating to the Settlement of the Imperial Crown of *Great Britain.* Thanks be to Heaven for that Settlement. The Princess *Sophia*, and the Heirs of her Body, being Protestants, are the Successors to her present Majesty, upon her Demise without Issue. The Way is plain before our Eyes, guarded on the Right Hand, and on the Left, by all the Sanctions of God and Man, and by all the Ties of *Law* and *Conscience.* Let those who act under the present Settlement, and yet pretend to dispute for an Absolute Hereditary Right, quiet *themselves* with the Arguments they have borrowed from Popery, and teach their own Consciences the Art of dispensing with the most solemn Oath to this Establishment, whilst they think them- selves bound only till Opportunity shall serve to introduce another. God be thanked, neither we, nor our Cause, stand in need of such detestable Prevarication. Our Cause is our Happi- ness. Our Oaths are our Judgment and Inclination. Honour and Affection call us, without the Solemnity of an Oath, to defend such an Establishment; but with it we have every Motive that can influence the Mind of Man. The Terrors of God, added to the Demands of our Country, oblige and constrain us to let our Hearts and our Hands follow our Wishes and our Consciences; and out of Regard to our Queen, our Religion, our Country, our Liberty and our Property, to maintain and assert the Protestant Succession in the Illustrious House of *Hanover*: It is no time to talk with Hints and Innuendos, but openly and honestly to profess our Sentiments, before our Enemies have compleated and put their Designs in Execution against us. As divided a People as we are, those who are for the House of *Hanover*, are infinitely superior in Number, Wealth, Courage, and all Arts Military and Civil, to those in the contrary Interest; besides which, we have *the Laws*, I say *the Laws* on our side. And those who by their Practices, whatever their Professions are, have discover'd themselves Enemies to the Constitution, and Friends to the Pretender, cannot make a Step farther without being guilty of Treason, without standing in broad Day-light, confessed Criminals against their injured Queen and Country.

" When the People were in a Ferment, when Faction ran high, with irresistible Prepossessions against every thing in its former Channel, sanguine Men might conceive Hopes of leading them their own Way. But the Building erected upon that Quicksand, the Favour of the Multitude, will sink, and be swallowed up by that treacherous Ground on which the Foundation was laid.

" It is easie to project the Subversion of a People, when Men see them unaccountably turned for their own Destruction; but not so easie to effect that Ruin, when they are come to themselves, and are sensibly and reasonably affected with Thoughts for their Preservation. We cannot help it, if so many Thousands of our brave Brethren, who laid down their Lives against the Power of *France*, have dyed in vain; but we may value our own Lives dearly, like honest Men. Whatever may befall the Glory and Wealth of *Great Britain*, let us struggle to the last Drop of our Blood for its Religion and Liberty. The Banner under which we are to enter this Conflict, whenever we are called to it, are the Laws mentioned in this Discourse; when we do not keep them in Sight, we have no Colours to fly to, no Discipline to preserve us, but are devoted, and have given our selves up to Slaughter and Confusion.

"While we act manfully under them, we have Reason to expect the Blessing and Assistance of Heaven on its own Cause, which it has so manifestly acknowledg'd to be such, by our many wonderful Deliverances, when all Human Assistances and ordinary Means of Succour seemed irrevocably removed. We have no Pretensions to the Divine Favour, but from our firm Adherence to that Settlement, which he has, by so many Wonders and Blessings, after such great Difficulties and Misfortunes, bestowed upon us, and which we have in his Sight, and with the Invocation of his Sacred Name, after preparing our Selves at his Altar, so frequently and solemnly Sworn to defend. This plain, unperplexed, unalterable Rule for our Conduct, is visibly the Work of his Hand to a favoured People. Her Majesty's Parliamentary Title, and the Succession in the Illustrious House of *Hanover*, is the Ark of God to *Great Britain*, and, like that of Old, carries Death to the profane Hand that shall dare to touch it." [a]

I come now to the Close of the *Englishman*, where I find the following Paragraph marked.

" But if God spares the good Queen's Life from such secret Attempts as we have too much Reason to fear, I doubt not but to see her judge rightly of such Pretences. Tho' Flattery carries Witchcraft, yet when she shall see that these Men, instead of supporting her Government with their Interest, cannot carry their Elections but by representing all others as under her Displeasure; when she shall see that they over-bear the Rights of Corporations by the impertinent Interposition of her Power and Name; when she shall see that those large Bodies of Men which the *Examiner* and others expose and exasperate, as Men whom the Queen hates, are so loth to be alienated from their Hope in her, that their being actually cast from all Preferments and Places, hath not made them guilty of one seditious, or even undutiful Action. When she shall see that those noisie Men who embarrass the Nation in every Question, with calling out *the Church*, are but like the Weather-Cocks and Clappers of

---

[a] *This is inserted because marked as Criminal but not defended, read or further spoken to by the accused Member.* [Steele's note. The quotation begins: "But to bring these several facts" p. 324.]

the Steeple; and that the sober, and laborious, and peaceable Church-men, are its real Support and Pillars. When a little more time shall bring out things that begin to appear pretty plain already; then the Queen will shew selfish Men that would ingross her Favour, that she will be the Mother of all her People; and as in Spite of these Men's studied Provocations, she hath their Hearts and Affections, so she will rule with equal Justice towards all. If the Nation will be so wise as to lay aside Parties and Party Quarrels, she will have no need to keep them up, but employ all Men according as the Law makes them qualified, and their Virtues and Parts make them fit. But if several Interests, and Opinions, and Humours shall still continue our Parties (as the *Examiner's* Violence and Partiality hath done more to sharpen them, than to take off the Edge) then she will let all see, that her Crown is not to be sunk down to be a Partizan of either side, so as to take these to be her Friends and the other Enemies; but that she is over both, and will use either in their Turns, according as they are fittest for the Service she hath for them at that time. And for those who shall dare to insult and exasperate the other as Enemies, they are Sycophants instead of Friends and rob her of her best Treasure, which is the Love of her People."

I have heard some Exceptions taken to the two or three Lines of this Paragraph where I say, " If God spares the good Queen's Life from such secret Attempts as we have too much Reason to fear ": But as to this Passage, I think it is sufficiently explained by a Paragraph which I shall beg Leave to read in the 35th Page of the *Crisis*.

" And here I cannot but add what is still of more Importance, and ought to be the most prevalent of all Arguments, that should there be the least Hopes given to a Popish Successor, the Life of her Majesty will certainly be in most Imminent Danger: For there will never be wanting bloody Zealots of that Persuasion, that will think it meritorious to take away her Life, to hasten the Accession of such a Successor to her Throne."

The remaining part of this Paragraph, is nothing else but the Picture of an excellent Princess, who notwithstanding the Suggestions of unreasonable Men, will still maintain in her the

Character of the best of Sovereigns, by shewing her self the Mother of all her People. If any Innuendo can possibly be found in this Paragraph, it can only affect those who would incline her Royal Heart, to make an unjust Distinction among her Subjects.

The next Paragraph is in the 6th Page of the Quarto Edition of the *Englishman*, in these Words:

" I insist the more upon these Revolution Principles, (as they are scornfully called now-a-days) not only because there never was more need of them than at this time, but because the best and greatest Part of the Clergy (especially those placed in eminent Stations) have in all Ages, so far as relates to our Nation, and as far as my small Reading informs me, been ready and hearty Assertors of the Privileges and Properties of the People; and why the whole Body should not be now, is past my Comprehension."

I suppose my Accuser would again insinuate by this Paragraph, for Reasons best known to himself, that I speak disrespectfully of the Clergy: But how he will be able to make this out, from an Eulogium which is given to their past Conduct, and a Presumption that their Future will be conformable to it, is past my Comprehension. I suppose he will not deny, notwithstanding his new and inexpressible Tenderness for the Clergy of the Church of *England*, that there are among them, some Nonjurors and Asserters of Hereditary Right, in Opposition to the Laws of their Country.

The following Paragraph in the 10th Page, concerning *Dunkirk*, has already receiv'd its Answer. Here it is.

"*Toby* is mistaken: At this Day it is in a more dangerous Condition as to *England*, than it was when I writ about the Importance of it. For I insisted upon the Demolition of the Mole and Harbour; and instead of that, they have, as exactly as if Mr. *Tugghe's* Memorial had been the Direction in this Case, demolished the Works, and left the Harbour, its Sluices, and all its Accesses that concern us, our Safety and our Trade, in good Condition. That is, they have destroy'd the Works in Possession of the *British* Garrison, to make that Garrison useless, and put off the Demolition of the Harbour 'till Time shall serve."

The three next Paragraphs are taken out of Page 17; and are only Matters of Fact, which may be proved out of several Books and Addresses, as well as from common Discourse, to which I dare say every Gentleman in this House has been a Witness. I shall therefore appeal from any little Sophistical Cavils which may be made against them, to the Honour and Veracity of those Gentlemen before whom I have now the Happiness to vindicate my self. I will only read them, and appeal to every Gentleman's own Conscience for the Truth of them.

"This is not all; for before this Run upon the Bank, a Man was thought to argue very well that would say, that for the better Consumption and Exportation of *British* Manufactures, it was absolutely necessary to give both *Spains* to the friendly House of *Bourbon*: But lest a great Monarch should be tempted by Ambition, to use that Trust for his own, rather than our Interest, it would be expedient to keep a Check upon him by dismissing all our Allies. For our further Security within our selves, and to prevent all Invasions on Liberty and Property, one might very lately have said, the Dignity and Authority of Parliaments could not be better strengthened, than by placing a despotick Power in the Sovereign.

"We have so little Publick Spirit amongst us, that these Things passed like Mathematical Truths, 'till each Man grew afraid for his own Pocket.

"A Man who was uneasie before this Accident, for the Publick Welfare; and has observed nothing since that puts us in a better Condition; a Man, I say, who from only hearing the News contradicted, that the Pretender was a coming, cannot infer that he may not still come, ought to be excused for writing as I have and do, to raise in his Fellow-Subjects, a just Concern for those Civil and Religious Rights, which they at present enjoy above all other Nations."

The next Paragraph is taken out of the 18th and 19th Pages of the same Book: And as it relates to *Dunkirk* has been already explained. Here it is.

"The Queen's Garrison is exposed by levelling the Works to

the Mercy of the *French*: And the Mole and Harbour, which were first to be demolished, stand as they did, *The Terror of the* British *Nation*. Thus, Sir, as the Interest of her Majesty and her People are inseparable, I think I have behaved my self like a dutiful Subject, in complaining of this open Violation of her Treaty in the most Important Article of it."   •

I am now come to the last Paragraph, in the 22d Page of the same Book, as follows.

" I wish Thirdly, That his Electoral Highness of *Hanover* would be so grateful as to signifie to all the World, the perfect good Understanding he has with the Court of *England*, in as plain Terms as her Majesty was pleased to declare she had with that House on her Part. This last Circumstance, Dear *Jack,* wou'd be very pleasing to all of us who are Churchmen, because if the Elector should be any way disobliged, I am confident her Majesty has given no Cause for it; and I cannot but attribute any Misunderstanding, if such there should be, to the Artifices of some new Converts, who, for ought I know, may still be Presbyterians in their Hearts."

I do not know whether I have been more troubled or surprized, to hear a Gentleman affirm that these Words, by an Innuendo, contradict what her Majesty had affirmed from the Throne. This Accusation may be put in such very hard Words, as may incline those to be displeased with me, who attend more to the Accusation it self, than to the Grounds I have given for it. The Gentleman who brought it against me, would artificially have stopped in the Middle of the Paragraph, had not he been put upon hearing the whole read out; wherein I positively assert that if the Elector should be any way disobliged, I am confident her Majesty has given no Cause for it. I say, Sir, I have positively asserted in the Words which immediately follow those which were objected to me, That if the Elector of *Hanover* should be any way disobliged, I am confident her Majesty has given no Occasion for it. And the Reason why I was so positive in this Assertion, is, because her Majesty, as I before said, was pleased to declare in plain Terms, that she had a perfect good Understanding with the House of *Hanover*.

And now, Sir, is there a Fault, after this, in wishing that his

Electoral Highness would be so grateful as to signifie to all the World, the perfect good Understanding he has with the Court of *England*. It is certain such a Declaration as this would quiet the Minds of all her Majesty's Subjects upon this important Article; and why should it be Criminal in me to wish for that, which would so manifestly redound to the Peace of our Country? Let every Gentleman ask his own Heart, whether he would not be glad that the Elector made such a Declaration as is here mentioned. And shall any Man be esteemed an Offender for wishing that which every Man would be glad of? If there be any Reflection in this Passage, it is plain that it does not fall upon her Majesty; and I question not but that in a Point of this Nature, Gentlemen will be so just as to keep my plain and express Words, and not to force a guilty Interpretation upon a Passage which has a natural Interpretation that is innocent.

I have now explained those several Paragraphs which have been laid to my Charge, and that in the shortest Manner I was able; reserving to my self the Liberty of producing any further Reasons, for the Defence of any particular Passage, as the Objections of my Accusers and my own Justification shall further require.

I must declare, Sir, that upon the Perusal of those Paragraphs which have been marked against me, I have been more puzzled to know why I ought to defend them, than how they ought to be defended. And I dare appeal to any Gentleman who is used to read Pamphlets, whether he has seen any of either side for some Years past, that have been written with more Caution, or more thoroughly guarded against giving any Occasion of just Offence.

Upon the whole Matter, I do humbly conceive that no Words which I have made use of can be censured as Criminal, in the Candid and natural Interpretation of them, and can only be construed as such by distant Implications and far-fetch'd Innuendoes. I shall therefore beg Leave to produce the Authority of a very great Man, with Reference to Accusations of this Nature: Since it is impossible for me to express my self with so much Judgment and Learning upon this Subject, as I find it already done to my Hand. The Passages I mention, are in the Speech of the now Lord Chancellor of *England*, as I find them in Doctor *Sacheverell's* Tryal, in the following Words.

23

" My Lords, if there be a double Sense, in either of which these Words are equally capable of being understood; if in one Sense the Doctor's Assertion be undeniably clear, but in the other some Doubt might arise whether his Words be Criminal or not, the Law of *England* is more merciful than to make any Man a Criminal, by construing his Words against the natural Import of them, in the worst Sense. This is the great Justice and Clemency of our Law in every Man's Case."

And a little lower.

" My Lords, if the Manner of this solemn Prosecution has not alter'd the Nature of Things, I hope I may insist, without putting in a Claim of Right in behalf of all the Factious and Seditious People in the Kingdom, to revile the Government at pleasure, that by the happy Constitution under which we live, a Subject of *England* is not to be made Criminal by a labour'd Construction of doubtful Words; or, when that cannot serve, by departing from his Words, and resorting to his Meaning. Too many Instances there were of this Nature, before the late happy Revolution; but that put an end to such Arbitrary Constructions."

After these Excellent Words of this Great Man, every thing I can say will appear very flat and low; for which Reason I shall give you but very little further Trouble. I have heard it said in this Place, that no private Man ought to take the Liberty of expressing his Thoughts as I have done, in Matters relating to the Administration. I do own, that no private Man ought to take a Liberty which is against the Laws of the Land. But, Sir, I presume that the Liberty I have taken, is a legal Liberty; and obnoxious to no Penalty in any Court of Justice. If it had, I cannot believe that this extraordinary Method would have been made use of, to distress me upon that Account. And why should I here suffer for having done that, which perhaps in a future Tryal, would not be judged Criminal by the Laws of the Land? Why should I see Persons, whose particular Province it is to prosecute Seditious Writers in the Courts of Justice, imploying their Eloquence against me in this Place? I think that I have not offended against any Law in Being: I think that I have taken no more Liberty than what is consistent with the Laws

of the Land: If I have, let me be tried by those Laws. Is not
the Executive Power sufficiently armed to inflict a proper Punishment on all kinds of Criminals? why then should one part of
the Legislative Power, take this Executive Power into its own
Hands? But, Sir, I throw my self upon the Honour of this
House, who are Able, as well as Obliged, to skreen any Commoner of *England* from the Wrath of the most powerful Man
in it; and who will never sacrifice a Member of their own
Body, to the Resentments of any single Minister.

Here I ended in the House. Most of what I said was put
into my Mouth by my Friends, whose Kindness and Discretion
prevented my adding to these forcible Arguments many honest
Truths, which they thought would Authorise a Severity from
the House to me, rather than secure me against their Resentment. I cannot, as an indifferent Man, dare to assert what I
would have done, under the Sanction of a Member of Parliament, speaking in Parliament. The Happiness of convincing
some honest Gentleman who were against me, was not to be
my Fate: But, (barring that I made the best and most respectful Obeysance I could to the Speaker) with a very awkward
and unwilling Air I withdrew; and the next News I heard was,
that I was Expelled.

It is Justice due to Human Nature, to signifie to an Offender
why he is punished. It is a Justice to inform the meanest Man
in Human Society, why he is distinguished from the rest to his
Disadvantage; it is a Christian Duty to give him the Contrition
he ought to have, and work in him a Repentance from Arguments towards his Conviction. But the House, without letting
me hear one Reason, or Shadow of an Argument to prove me
Seditious, have peremptorily pronounced me so.

To hear a Man speak, without being moved by what he says,
or controverting it before Sentence, is only to give Exercise to
an hard Heart; a ridiculous Candour, that is an Aggravation of
an Injury, by putting on the Face of Justice. I shall therefore,
as briefly as I can, consider the Matter yet further: For I am
now as much concerned to show why this Sentence should not
be a Reproach to me now it is passed, as I was before to speak
against its being pronounced.

It may be objected, that I am sure to come off, when I who am the Criminal, am also to be the Judge. I may make the same Objection against the Determination of the House, they who were the Judges, were also the Accusers. In the first place I aver, that if I had, as indeed I have not, been guilty of raising groundless Fears to the Disadvantage of the Ministry, it is less the Part of the House of Commons, than any other Body of Men, to be Inquisitors in Favour of them. Their more graceful Province had been to have encouraged what I had to say, if I had had Objections, rather than suppressed me for offering at it. It had been well, after such a Search, to have chastised or approved the Man accused, according to his Deserts. But my Fate is so Extraordinary, that I am punished by the House of Commons, (where Freedom of Speech is an essential Privilege) for saying what was Criminal no where else. Had what I have written been spoken in the House of Commons, no Man will pretend to say it had been Criminal: How then when it was Innocent in another Place, came it to be criminal by being produced there? I was safe, when in Circumstances that rendered me more accountable, and run into Danger by being privileg'd.

But I flatter my self that I shall convince all my Fellow-Subjects of my Innocence from the following Circumstances, allowed to be of Weight in all Tryals of this Nature. *From the general Character of the Offender, the Motive of his Offence, and the Character of the Persons who appear for him, opposed to those who are against him.* There are some Points to be allowed, which bear hard against the Prisoner at the Bar; and we must grant this by way of Confessing and Avoiding, and give it up, that the Defendant has been as great a Libertine as a Confessor. We will suppose then a Witness giving an Account of him, who, if he spoke true, would say as follows.

I have been long acquainted with Mr. *Steele*, who is accused as a malicious Writer; and can give an Account of him (from what he used to confess to us his private Friends) what was the chief Motive of his first appearing in Print. Besides this, I have read every thing he has writ or published. He first became an Author when an Ensign of the Guards, a way of Life exposed to much Irregularity; and being thoroughly convinced of many things, of which he often repented, and which he more

often repeated, he writ, for his own private Use, a little Book
called the *Christian Hero*, with a design principally to fix upon
his own Mind a strong Impression of Virtue and Religion, in
Opposition to a stronger Propensity towards unwarrantable
Pleasures. This secret Admonition was too weak; he therefore
Printed the Book with his Name, in hopes that a standing
Testimony against himself, and the Eyes of the World (that
is to say of his Acquaintance) upon him in a new Light, might
curb his Desires, and make him ashamed of understanding and
seeming to feel what was Virtuous, and living so quite contrary a Life. This had no other good Effect, but that from
being thought no undelightful Companion, he was soon reckoned a disagreeable Fellow. One or two of his Acquaintance
thought fit to misuse him, and try their Valour upon him; and
every Body he knew measured the least Levity in his Words
and Actions, with the Character of a Christian Heroe. Thus
he found himself slighted, instead of being encouraged, for his
Declarations as to Religion; and it was now incumbent upon
him to enliven his Character, for which Reason he writ the
Comedy called *The Funeral*, in which (tho' full of incidents
that move Laughter) Virtue and Vice appear just as they ought
to do. Nothing can make the Town so fond of a Man as a
successful Play, and this, with some Particulars enlarged upon
to his Advantage, (for Princes never hear Good or Evil in the
manner others do) obtained him the Notice of the King: And
his Name, to be provided for, was in the last Table-Book ever
worn by the Glorious and Immortal *William* the Third.

His next Appearance as a Writer was in the Quality of the
lowest Minister of State, to wit, in the Office of Gazetteer, where
he worked faithfully according to Order, without ever erring
against the Rule observed by all Ministries, to keep that Paper
very innocent and very insipid.

It is believed, it was to the Reproaches he heard every Gazette
Day against the Writer of it, that the Defendant owes the
Fortitude of being remarkably negligent of what People say,
which he does not deserve; Except in so great Cases as this now
before Us. His next Productions were still Plays, then the *Tatler*,
then the *Spectator*, then the *Guardian*, then the *Englishman*. And
now, tho' he has published, and scribled so very much, He may

defie any Man to find one Leaf in all these Writings which is not, in point, a Defence against this Imputation, to find one Leaf which does not mediately or immediately tend to the Honour of the Queen, or the Service of the Nobility and Gentry, or which is not particularly respectful to the Universities. Farther this Witness sayeth not.

When a Man is accused, it is allowable not only to say as much as will refute his Adversary, but if he can, he may assert Things of himself Praise-worthy, which ought not to be called Vanity in him, but Justice against his Opponent, by proving it is not only False what is said as to the Fault laid to his Charge, but also that he has exerted the contrary Virtue.

You may observe that the Votes of the 18th of *March* imply, that the Writings were under Consideration, as containing several Paragraphs *tending to Sedition, highly reflecting upon Her Majesty, and arraigning Her Majesty's Administration and Government.* There was not one Argument used to support this heavy Accusation against the Member; but I suppose, upon Consideration that his reflecting upon the Queen so directly, and arraigning Her Administration and Government, was just the quite contrary to what he had done, the Ill Behaviour towards Her Majesty is in the Resolution scattered among Her Subjects, and it was thought, since it was all equally true, it would be expedient to withdraw the Offence, and for the Amusement of the Vulgar, to say more diffusively, that the Pamphlets were Scandalous and Seditious *Libels,* containing *many Expressions highly reflecting upon* Her Majesty, *and upon the Nobility, Gentry, Clergy and Universities of this Kingdom, maliciously insinuating, that the Protestant Succession is in Danger under Her Majesty's* Administration, *and tending to alienate the Affections of Her Majesty's good Subjects, and to Create Jealousies and Divisions among them.*

This is a very pleasant Proceeding. The Indictment before them was, that the accused Member had reflected upon the Queen; ay marry has he, say they, and upon the Nobility and Gentry, Clergy and Universities, and he did this also with a malicious Intimation, that the Succession was in Danger under Her Majesty's Administration, and so forth. What need was there the Man should be Guilty of more than he was indicted for? Let this Resolve be taken out of its Formality, and it is just as if they had said, he has been Guilty of Treason, and also of ill Manners. But the huddle of Offences was only to make a Huy and Cry, and the Business was, that he should be marked; and as they well knew from the general Corruption and Meanness of the World, that if the Crimes did not distinctly hurt every sort of People, they would not be Zealous enough for the sake of the Queen only, to vilifie and distress the accused Man: But the Succession, say they, he says is in Danger *under Her Majesty's Administration*. This Phrase is Ambiguous and Evasive, it retains the Offence against the Queen, only to hide Ministers. This is a very thin Mask, for it is no help to them; if any Man should, in a proper Place, have anything to object to their Conduct; it would be no Answer to urge against such an Impeachment, that this was asserting ill things are done under Her Majesty's Administration. All manner of Crimes are committed under every Prince's Administration, but for that Reason are those Princes to be loaded with the Guilt? or would a Man that should complain of those Crimes, be supposed to intend Treasonably, or to assert that they are owing to his Prince's Administration? Should a Man be robbed, and when he asked for a Warrant against the Offender be answered by the Magistrate, 'tis arraigning Her Majesty's Administration to report any such thing? If any Epithets may be added to any Persons and Things, provided they add the Words, *under Her Majesty's Administration*, Approbation and Blame in those that use them will be both alike, and *Safe, Honourable*, or any other Adjectives will lose their Force, as well as the Words, *Seditious and Scandalous*. It is very possible the worst Designs imaginable may be laid, under Her Majesty's Administration, and Her Sacred Majesty's Honour no way impaired, as She (without Disparagement to Her Wisdom it may be supposed) may not be conscious of all that passes. Therefore on this Occasion, I repeat that the Phrase under *Her Majesty's Administration*, is only a feint way of coming up to my Indictment, and amusing the Populace with a show of what is not in Reality.

But to proceed with the Evidence on the side of the Offender. Taking the Words of the Resolution as they lye: It would be a Contradiction to all Mr. *Steele's* past Writings to speak to the

Disadvantage of the Nobility and Gentry. The War that the *Tatler* brought upon himself, for stigmatizing and expelling Sharpers out of their Company, is a Merit towards them, that will outweigh this Allegation, though it comes whence it does. That Gamesters, Knaves and Pickpockets are no longer the Men of Fashion, or mingled with so good an Air among People of Quality as formerly, is much owing to Mr. *Steele*; that a licentious Treatment of a Clergyman, as a Clergyman, is less practised, either on the Stage or in Common Conversation, is much owing to the Contempt and Ridicule of all such false and scandalous Pretensions to Wit, in the Writings which the Publick has had from Mr. *Steele*: That an University Education is reckoned a necessary Qualification to an *English* Gentleman, and the less Accomplishments without those Arts appear frivolous, though of great use with them, is more owing to Mr. *Steele* than to any other Author, Transcriber, or Publisher (or under whatever Class you Rank him) that ever made use of Pen and Ink: But it seems the Courtship in these Resolutions was to be made with no less a Resignation than that of all their Sense and Conscience.

All this is as clear and known as the Sun at Noon-day. But it may be answered, that though as to his former Writings this may be true; our Author or Publisher might grow Vain and Impertinent, and conceive new Thoughts of himself, from borrowed Excellencies of other Men, his Correspondents; and without Fear or good Manners run into the Crimes of which he here stands accused. I shall therefore give an account of the principal Thing laid to his Charge, which is the *Crisis*, and the occasion of its being written.

Mr. *Steele* happened one Day to make a Visit to a Gentleman of the Temple, who fell into Discourse on Publick Transactions; and complaining that dangerous Insinuations were every Day thrown among the People, ended his Discourse, by saying that he thought Mr. *Steele*, from the kind Reception the World gave to what he published, might be more Instrumental towards curing this Evil, than any private Man in *England*. After much Sollicitation, the Gentleman observ'd, the Evil seem'd only to flow from mere Inattention to the real Obligations under which we lie towards the House of *Hanover*; if therefore, continued he, the Laws to that Purpose were reprinted together with a warm Preface and a well urged Peroration, it is not to be imagined what good Effect it would have. Mr. *Steele* was immediately struck with the Thought, and told him, that he hoped so good a Design would repay his turning his Thoughts wholly to it for a Day or two, under Promise of half what the Sale of a Work, which would be every Body's Reading, should produce. This was agreed, and there is hardly a Sentiment or main Position in the Pamphlet, which that Gentleman did not put together, as lawful and warrantable to be said, and deliver into Mr. *Steele's* Hands to be published in the Dress and Manner he should think fit. But Mr. *Steele* was not content with writing the *Crisis* on this Plan, and Revising each Paragraph with this Gentleman only, but he also sent different Copies to Men of different Talents and Capacities; and with all their Corrections, according to the Authority of the Corrector, Mr. *Steele*, with his Council at his Elbow, put the last Hand to what he published under the Name of the *Crisis*. Very able Men passed and approved every Word of it. Mr. *Steele* therefore thought it a most necessary, seasonable and worthy Action to publish it.

The Care and Caution with which it was writ appears sufficiently in that it much offended, and the Author was not in the Courts of Justice brought to answer for the Offence. But alas! He was to suffer for it, where, of all Places in the World, he ought to have been encouraged and protected.

But I will hasten to a better Defence than all this, which is:

That the Gentlemen in the List at the Beginning of this Narrative, gave their Negative to the Votes against the Author.

That the Map at the End of this Book is the State of the Case of *Dunkirk*, and explains that the True Design of the *French*, was only to make *Dunkirk* stronger.

That there are these Words in Her Majesty's Proclamation of the first of last Month, concerning the *Pretender at Barleduc: Notwithstanding We have since insisted upon and renewed Our Instances in the most pressing Manner for that Purpose, Our Endeavours have not proved effectual, but he still continues and is entertain'd there.*

These Circumstances of *Dunkirk*, and the Stay of the *Pretender* at *Barleduc*, do strongly maintain the Grounds all Men ought to have for Suspicion of our being in imminent Danger; to improve that Suspicion has been the Chief Aim in all the Political Writings of this Author: That it was sincere in him, will appear from this Letter, wherein he resigned his Office to my Lord Treasurer.

To the Right Honourable the Lord High Treasurer of *Great Britain*

Bloomsbury Square, *June* 4, 1713.

My Lord,

I *presume to give your Lordship this Trouble, to acquaint you, that having an Ambition to serve in the ensuing Parliament, I humbly desire your Lordship will please to accept of my Resignation of my Office as Commissioner of the Stamp Revenue.*

I should have done this sooner, but that I heard the Commission was passing without my Name in it, and I would not be guilty of the Arrogance of resigning what I could not hold. But having heard this since contradicted, I am obliged to give it up, as with great Humility I do by this present Writing. Give me Leave on this Occasion to say something as to my late Conduct, with Relation to the late Men in Power, and to assure you whatever I have done, said or writ, has proceeded from no other Motive, but the Love of what I think Truth. For merely as to my own Affairs, I could not wish any Man in the Administration rather than your self, who favour those that become your Dependants, with a greater Liberality of Heart than any Man I have ever before observed. When I had the Honour of a short Conversation with you, you were pleased not only to signifie to me, That I should remain in this Office, but to add, that if I would name to you one of more Value, which would be more commodious to me, you would favour me in it. I am going out of any particular Dependance on your Lordship, and will tell you with the Freedom of an indifferent Man, that it is impossible for any Man who thinks and has any publick Spirit, not to tremble at seeing his Country, in its present Circumstances, in the Hands of so daring a Genius as yours. If Incidents should arise that should place your own Safety, and what ambitious Men call Greatness, in a Ballance against the

General Good, our All depends upon your Choice under such
a Temptation. You have my hearty and fervent Prayers to
Heaven, to avert all such Dangers from you. I thank your
Lordship for the Regard and Distinction which you have at
sundry times show'ed me, and wish you, with your Country's
Safety, all Happiness and Prosperity. Share, my Lord, your
good Fortune with whom you will; while it lasts, you will want
no Friends; but if any adverse Day happens to you, and I live
to see it, you will find I think my self obliged to be your Friend
and Advocate. This is talking in a strange Dialect from a pri-
vate Man to the first of a Nation; but to desire only a little,
exalts a Man's Condition to a level with those who want a
great deal. But I beg your Lordship's Pardon, and am with
great Respect,

> *My LORD,*
>
> > *Your Lordship's most Obedient,*
> >
> > > *and most Humble Servant,*
> > >
> > > > Richard Steele.

There is nothing here said like a Male-content, but like an
honest Man, who gave up everything to the Love of his Country;
where Obsequiousness interfered with that, he was ready to
force a Temper, the most unhappily ductile, to go through all
Oppositions and Discountenances in the Way to his Duty. It
has been frequently said in the Writings of this Publisher, that
all Merit consists in the Regulation of the Will, and that is the
only Merit pretended to in this Apology. The Wit, the Eloquence, the Learning in his Writings, the Town may as it
pleases give to others, but the Application of them all must be
ascribed to this Publisher; and I cannot but again and again
repeat, that there is no Man on whom a Censure, with *mali-*
ciously in it, could fall, from whose Character it could be more
remote. The Writings excepted against were sufficiently defended in the House, and nothing said in opposition to all that
was urged in favour of the accused Member. Therefore as those
accused Writings were Innocent, and all the drift of his other
Writings uncontestably Virtuous, What can any Gentleman
say to himself, or his Country, for joining in so unreasonable

a Vote against him? Let any Gentleman consider, if the Vote had been proposed to take away this Man's Life, with what Horror would the whole Assembly, except the Messengers of the Treasury, have rejected such a Motion? But let any Gentleman think on, and he will find, that this Resolution against Mr. *Steele's* Property in the House, and his good Name in the World, was only the same Injustice, in a less degree. Why then would they suspend their Good-nature and Generosity, as *Englishmen*, the natural bent of their Country, of running to the Aid of the Afflicted, to be made Tools, and form a *Posse,* to assist the Messengers of the Treasury against their Fellow Member?

No Man could help plainly seeing, that Mr. *Steele* in these Writings had gone as far as he could with any Safety to his Liberty or Life, and that he got into the House of Commons, for no Reason but to say more for the Good of his deluded Country: And must the House of Commons frustrate this Design?

There are many Instances of Punishments in the House for being too obsequious to the Court against the People; but Mr. Steele *is the first that fell there for being Audacious towards Ministers, in behalf of his Country.*

But be all that was done against him forgotten, and the Names of the Actors in it, except the Messengers themselves, never mentioned with this Circumstance of their Lives; but let those who were for an oppressed Gentleman, their Fellow-Citizen, against as high an Insolence as ever was offered to the Legislature, be had in everlasting Remembrance. Many of them have taken care of that for themselves, by illustrious Actions; many of them, with the Assistance of personal Accomplishments, as well as Youth, Birth, and Fortune, are blooming and growing in the Pursuits of Virtue, and Honour; the rest of them are Men of the greatest Fortunes in this Realm, who are come to the Evening of honourable Days, and have nobler Prospects in View, than to follow Mercenaries with their Vote against an *Impotent Patriot*; who attempted, from the irresistible Force of the Love he bears Mankind, with Poverty and Disgrace staring in his Face, to rouse his Country out of a Lethargy; a Lethargy from which she has awaked only to behold Her Danger, and upon seeing it too great has only sighed, folded her Arms, and returned to her Trance.

An Account of the State of the Roman-Catholick Religion
Throughout the World
(May, 1715)

This tract, published under the aegis of Steele, seems to be the sequel promised in *The Romish Ecclesiastical History* of May, 1714. During the year a Protestant Hanoverian had been safetly seated on the throne; but the need for this kind of propaganda was still felt. The long title is sufficiently explanatory of the contents, in the main an Italian document written for the use of Pope Innocent XI, which had been procured by Dr. Johann Heinrich Ott, Professor of Ecclesiastical History at Zurich (whom Steele later met at Dr. Woodward's in London), and translated by the French Huguenot, Michael de la Roche. The long satirical Dedication addressed to Pope Clement XI, although signed by Steele, was written by Dr. Benjamin Hoadly, distinguished low church clergyman, whom Steele had consulted on *The Crisis*. Through Hoadly's correspondence with Mrs. Clayton, Woman-of-the-Bedchamber in the household of Princess Caroline, we learn that the book was planned and approved at Leicester House.

Both Prefaces, that for the first edition and that for the second, which came out at the end of the year during the Jacobite rebellion, seem to have been written by Steele himself. Tradition has assigned them to Hoadly; however, in the absence of direct evidence that they are his and for the better reason that the views themselves and the expression of them are characteristically Steele's, the present editor has no hesitation in attributing them to him. As always, his objection to Romanism is on civil grounds. As in the *Romish History*, he affirms that the " Popery " to be feared as a threat to the Constitution and the Established Church is not any more that of Roman Catholics than that of Jacobite churchmen who " have begun the war anew and beat a fresh Allarm from their High Places." As in the tract on *Schism*, he finds it intolerable " that Protestants must be reduced to the Absurdity of renouncing Protestant as well as Christian principles, before they can pretend to make their Practices and their Professions consistent." He is as always careful of the feelings of such clergymen as have " acknowledged and asserted the Constitution, and Basis, of Our Government." Anti-papist propaganda with similar emphases was a main theme in Steele's periodical *The Englishman* (2nd series) running during the summer from 11 July to 21 November (See Nos. 6, 27-30, 35).

Whether or not it was justified, fear of papacy and of the disloyal

347

English Romanists, rather widespread during the last year of Anne, was heightened during these early months of 1715. The new Hanoverian dynasty was not popular. Riots were being promoted by Jacobite elements. It was suspected that plans were afoot on the continent for an invasion by James Stuart; and Louis XIV, who still lived, and the other Bourbon Powers favored his cause. There were unmistakable signs of a rebellion brewing in Scotland—which came to a head in September. It was believed, and with good reason, that once on the throne, James would do his utmost to restore the Catholic religion.

Such is the immediate background for this tract and several others within the twelve-month. Partizan propaganda, yes; but strong testimonial of Steele's belief in the principles of the Revolution—the right to personal and parliamentary liberty under a limited monarchy. Textual notes on p. 643.

AN
ACCOUNT
Of the STATE of the
Roman-Catholick RELIGION
Throughout the WORLD.

Written for the Ufe of P o p e *INNOCENT* XI.
by Monfieur *Cerri*, Secretary of the Congregation *de propaganda Fide*. Now firft tranflated from an Authentick *Italian* MS. never
Publifh'd.

To which is added,

A DISCOURSE concerning the State of RELIGION
in *ENGLAND*. Written in *French*, in the Time
of King *Charles* I. and now firft tranflated.

WITH

A Large *Dedication* to the Prefent POPE;
giving him a very particular Account of the
State of Religion amongft *PROTESTANTS*;
and of feveral other Matters of Importance
relating to *Great-Britain.*

By Sir RICHARD STEELE.

The Second Edition.

L O N D O N:

Printed for J. R O B E R T S, near the *Oxford-Arms*
in *Warwick-Lane*. M DCC XVI.

PREFACE.

[to the first edition]

I HAVE so unreservedly spoken my Thoughts to *His Holiness,* that I have but few Words left for any less sanctified *Reader.*

No one, who reads the following Account of the *Roman-Catholick* Religion, can doubt of its being *Genuine.* Many, it is probable, have seen the *Original Italian Manuscript,* in *Switzerland.* It was taken out of the Library of *St. Gall,* after the Defeat of the Abbot of that Name, by the United Troops of *Zurich* and *Berne,* and lodged afterwards in the Library at *Zurich.* An Authentick Copy was transmitted, by the Reverend and very Learned Mr. *Ott,* Principal Secretary of the *Zurichian* Library.

The *Translation* of it will be allowed, by all good Judges, to give Us the Sense of the Writer faithfully; when I inform them that it was done by the Learned Author of the *Memoirs of Literature*: A Work, of which I shall say no more, than that it well deserves a Place in the *Library* of Every Man who is a Friend to Learning and Good Sense; Being a Collection of many Compleat *Pieces,* very Curious and Uncommon; as well as a most Judicious *Epitome* of the very best Performances some of these last Years have produced in the *World* of *Learning.*

I must now say something, by Way of *Apology* to those who may be surprized, by the foregoing *Dedication,* at my being so deep in Points, which I never before pretended to meddle with.

I acknowledge it has been sometimes with *Me,* as it is with too many others, that a Sort of an Implicit *Religion* seemed the most easy, and most comfortable; and that a *Blind Veneration* for *I knew not what,* and *I knew not whom,* stood for every thing valuable, and important. I confess, I was not enough aware that this Implicitness of Conduct, is the great *Engine* of Popery, framed for the Destruction of *Good Nature,* as well as *Good Sense.* But my *Benevolence* to my *Fellow-Creatures,* I can truly say, is, and has been, always warm and inflexible: And *This* it is, that hath, at length, allarmed, and rouzed, my *Understanding*; which, *one* or *two* Accidental Shocks, have settled into the Order, wherein I now feel it.

I remember, that some time ago, I said, in Print, *That all Exorbitant Power in Clergymen was Popery*. What could be more General, or more Inoffensive, than to speak this, without determining at all, what is that *Exorbitant Power?* And yet it is incredible, what an *Outcry* there was made about this, as if it was the very Height of all Madness and Absurdity to say so. I know there are many of that *Reverend Body* who are disinterested Enough themselves, to Maintain such a Sentiment; but I soon found from the Resentment of *Others*, that no Power, let it be what it will in their Hands, can be esteemed by them to be *Exorbitant*: Or else, that that Part of *Popery* was not a thing they mightily abhorred. Upon this, I proceeded to think a little further of the Consequences and Tendencies of such Principles.

But the *Great Shock* of all that I ever received, was from the *Proceedings* about the late *Schism-Act*: which opened the *Scene* thoroughly. And this, I confess, was so great, as to move in me an Indignation not to be contained; to see the *Law* of *Nature*, and the Common *Rights* of Mankind, going to be sacrificed to *Fury* and *Bigottry*. I knew, indeed, very well, that the *Church*, was only a *Word*, made use of by those then at the *Helm*, who valued all Churches and all Religions equally, and that no farther than for the forwarding their own *Ruinous Projects*. But I saw by how great a *Party* the Design was warmly espoused; that their very Hearts were in it; and Crowds of Innocent People ensnared by them into the same Violence. This put Me upon more *Enquiries*; and led me to some *Thoughts*, of which I then gave the World a short Account.

It is upon that *Bottom*, I have govern'd my self ever since; till I am now brought, by the Natural Course of such Thoughts, to examine into the Conduct of *Christians*, and particularly of *Protestants*, of all Sorts. One Thing drew on another; And, as little Conversant as I have heretofore been in such Things, I quickly found that *Christianity* was neither *unintelligible*, nor *ill-natured*; That the Gospel does not invade the *Rights* of *Mankind*; nor invest any Men with Authority, destructive to *Society*; and, (what was the most melancholy Part of the

Whole) that *Protestants* must be reduced to the Absurdity of renouncing *Protestant*, as well as *Christian, Principles,* before they can pretend to make their *Practices* and their *Professions,* consistent. This I resolved to represent; and have done it, without regard to any one *Sort* of them, more than *another.*

I am more and more persuaded, every Day, that it is fitting, to understand Religion, as well as to praise it; and that it is the *Golden Rule* of *Proportion,* to give the highest Respect to *Those* only, who deserve it.

If I have used a Severity in some of the foregoing *Pages,* it flowed from the *Resentment* I have, at the Usage King GEORGE hath met with, from too many, of a *Body* of Men, who owe all their Security to *His* Accession. This Part of their Conduct admits of no *Apology.* I have given Them sufficient Proof of my Devotion to their Interest, when they do not divide it from that of their Country. But I thank God, my *Love* to the *Publick,* is above it: and I feel it true within, what the *Patriot,* and *Orator* of *Rome* said, *Omnes omnium charitates Patria una complexa est.* And therefore, since many of *Them* are not contented that the Glory of their past Conduct should be forgot, or buried in Silence; but have thought fit, by their renewed Assaults, to revive the *Remembrance* of their former Behaviour, when They engaged themselves in the *Cause* of a *Worthless Incendiary,* and taught the *People* by the *Cry* of the *Church,* (which hath deserved better *Usage* at their *Hands,*) to *Rebel* for *Passive Obedience,* and to *insult* the *Supream Authority* of the whole *Legislature,* out of *Loyalty:* Since, I say, *They* have begun the *War* a-new, and beat a fresh *Allarm* from their *High Places,* and, (unprovoked, and unmolested,) have given the *Best* of *Kings,* a reception, unworthy, I do not say of *Christians,* but of *Men*; it lies upon *Them* alone to answer for the *Consequences*; and upon all *Others,* to guard their *Country,* their *Laws,* and their *Prince,* from such Attempts; and to shew, by their Courage, and Constancy, that, in spite of all the Opportunities which such Men employ to the misleading of the *People,* We will not sacrifice, either our *Religion,* or our *Establishment,* or even the very *People* whom They mislead, out of any *Panick* Dread of their *Invectives,* or *Instigations.*

Indeed, whatever *Others* do, I think it *time* to let them see, that there are *those*, who are even passionately disposed to *love*, and almost *adore* them, who will not fear them. Whilst *They* show the World that they hate the *King*, it is my Humble Opinion, that *They* who *love* Him, do no better than make a *Sacrifice* of Him, whenever they show themselves afraid of such Men. As I am always *Romantick* enough to speak what I think; so, I am *weak* enough, to think, it has its Use.

All the World knows, with what a Tenderness of Affection, and what a Sincerity of Passion, I have espoused the Cause of the *Clergy*, and *Universities*; that they have been observed to be the Delight of my Tongue, and the Darling Subject of my Conversation; and that I have, with an Impetuousness of Warmth, *in Season and out of Season*, run into their *Defence*, and their *Panegyrick*. But what can I say? The *Cause*, the *Topick*, I delighted in, is torn from me; and left without any Support, but that of *Hope*, that the *Better Part*, (who have stood faithful, uncorrupted, and unwearied, amidst the *Throng*, of *Great Examples*, and against the Torrent of Violence and Reproach,) may be look'd upon, at present, as some *Atonement* for the *Contrary*; and their *Vertue*, (after the Season of *Mad Despair* is over,) spread its Influence: and create an Imitation, universal enough to raise again the *Sacred Character*, and make it once more shine in all that Brightness and Vigour of Glory, in which every Good Man wishes to see it.

And in the mean while, certainly it remains upon the Conscience, and Honour, of Every *True Britain*, to Employ all the Opportunities which can occur to Him, from His *Talents*, His *Station*, and His *Fortune*, in doing Honour and Service, to such Excellent Men in *Holy Orders*, as have, in the whole Bent of their Words and Actions, and upon all just Occasions, acknowledged and asserted the *Constitution*, and Basis, of Our Government. Happy *They*, who have the *Power*, and the *Will*, to do it!

Certainly, To Such *Clergy-Men*, *Esteem*, and *Regard*, are due, in proportion to the Excellence of their *Vertue*, and to that Course of Calumny, and Reproach, which They have suffered, both from their own *Order*, and from others, for their Candour and Honesty; in disdaining to exalt themselves, at the Expence of the Prosperity of their Brethren; and in labouring to shew themselves, the most *Generous Patriots*, in respect of this World, as well as the most *Faithful Stewards*, with respect to the *next*.

What I have to add, is, That, as I have taken sincere Pains to be rightly apprized of the *Facts*, which make up the *Foregoing Dedication*; so, whenever I am convinced of having been mistaken in any of them; I promise immediately to give his *Holiness* better Information, and to do Justice to all the World:

And, last of all, that, if there were occasion, I could call *God* to witness, that the Whole of this hath proceeded, not from any regard to *private Interest*, or the narrow *Spirit* of a *Party*; (which any one may see, at first View, who knows the World;) but from a *Principle* of *Benevolence*, and a dilated Zeal to serve the *Best* of *Princes*, and the *Best* of *Constitutions*: And particularly, to rescue the *Christian* and *Protestant* Name, and the *Church of England*, from all the Scandals of *Antichristianism, and Popery*.

PREFACE

TO THE

SECOND EDITION.

*T*HE *Rebellion*, which hath been begun, in favour of the *Popish Cause*, since the first *Publication* of this *Book*, makes it more seasonable to recommend the following *Account* of the *State* of *Popery* in the *World*, as what must certainly be of particular Use to all *Protestants* among us, at a Time, when it is Exerting all its Strength once more, to Enslave and Destroy us. For, tho' this Account of the State of *Popery* doth not come down so low, as might be wished; yet, it is as Authentick a Proof, and as Convincing a Demonstration, as possible, that the One Constant View of that *Religion* is, an Universal Empire over the *Bodies*, *Souls*, and especially the *Estates*, of all Mankind.

Whoever reads it, will see *Popery* recollected in its *Retirement*, and *Centre*; and from that *Centre* dispensing its Influences to the whole *Circumference* of *Europe*, *Asia*, *Africa*, and *America*. And no *Protestants* can read it, without considering the *Church* of *Rome*, as a sort of *Universal Spirit*, insinuating it self, as far as it can, into every Particle of the Universe; extending it self far and near; and even, where it seems most to lie dormant, and lifeless, always retaining the *Principles* of *Life*, ready to awake, and put all things around them, into Motion, upon every Occasion that offers it self.

When they see, what is here described at length, that no *Corner* of the *Earth* is out of the View of its Votaries; that in many Countries They reign without Controul; and that, in Places, where They lie under the greatest Discouragements, what would make any other Body of Men despair and sink, only serves to double and actuate their Diligence: When They see plainly set before their Eyes, the vast *Comprehensiveness* of their Design; (no less than the Conquest of the whole World;) their Regular *Oeconomy* in the ordering the several Parts of it; their Undaunted Zeal in executing it; and their Unwearied *Perseverance*, in pursuing it for ever: This alone, I should hope, as it is a Standing Monument of *Romish Policy*, must convince Them all, of how vast Importance it is, for Themselves to be *Watchful*, *Zealous*, and *United*, at this Time, against the Assaults of so *Formidable* an *Enemy*, which threatens *All* equally with *Persecution, Tyranny, Slavery,* and *Poverty.*

356

A Letter from the Earl of Mar to the King before His Majesty's Arrival in England (September, 1715)

The rising of 1715, during which on 22 December the Pretender, as James VIII of Scotland, landed at Peterhead, had started in September. On the 6th, the Earl of Mar raised the standard at Kirkmichael on the Braes of Mar. His Scotch forces at Sheriffmuir were defeated, although not decisively, by King George's army led by Argyle on 13 November, the same day that the English rebels capitulated at Preston. Early in February, 1716, when the Pretender returned to his exile in France, Mar was in the party. In March his army was finally broken up by Cadogan's forces; and by April the rebellion was under control.

John Erskine, 6th Earl of Mar (1675-1732) was among the Scotsmen who had supported the Union Treaty, 1705-7; and he had served Queen Anne in various ways, at the time of her death holding the Third Secretaryship for Scotland. As the letters printed in this tract indicate, until a few weeks before proclaiming himself a Jacobite rebel, he had professed to be a loyal supporter of King George.

Whatever the motives for Mar's treachery—ambition, opportunism, the pangs of conscience—Steele finds in his actions a chance to point a moral, to the Tories, on the binding obligation of oaths taken in abjuration of the Pretender and in allegiance to His Majesty King George. Non-jurors were at least above board; but " we have no Name for Men who act publickly under the same Government with us, and are constantly meditating our Ruine." Steele had been loathe to join in the vindictiveness of the Whig party, after George's accession, in discrediting the Tories as disloyal Jacobites, one and all. But Mar's avowal that he has been misrepresented to the King " upon Account of Party " brings up the question: " Is it then true what the Whigs intimated, and the more moderate of them would not believe, that Whig and Tory were at Bottom Jacobites and Hanoverians, the Promoters of Slavery and the Friends of Liberty? " Also, in another tract written a week earlier, *The Present Case of the British Subject Considered* (*Englishman*, No. 22, Sept. 23, circulated widely in a composite pamphlet called *The British Hero*), Steele, from a slightly different angle, had undertaken to defend the legality of George's title, now being contested by a group of English and Scots rebels. Textual notes on p. 644.

A
LETTER

FROM THE

Earl of MAR

TO THE

KING,

Before His MAJESTY's Arrival in *England*.

With some REMARKS on my Lord's subsequent Conduct.

By Sir *RICHARD STEELE*.

LONDON:

Printed for JACOB TONSON at *Shakespear's Head* over-against *Catherine-street* in the *Strand*. 1715.

A
LETTER
FROM THE
EARL of *MAR*
TO THE
KING, &c.

IT gives me a lively Sense of the Hardships of Civil War,
wherein all the sacred and most intimate Obligations between Man and Man are to be torn asunder, when I cannot
without Pain represent to my self the Behaviour of Lord *Mar,*
with whom I had not ever the Honour of any further Commerce than the Pleasure of passing some agreeable Hours at
different times in his Company: I say, when even such little
Incidents make it irksome to be in a state of War with those
with whom we have lived in any degree of Familiarity, how
terrible must the Image be of rending the Tyes of Blood, the
Sanctions of Affinity and Intermarriage, and the bringing Men,
who perhaps in a few Months before were to each other the
dearest of all Mankind, to meet on terms of giving Death to
each other at the same time that they had rather Embrace? I
am forced to reflect, that Lord *Mar* has already taken Measures
for bringing Brother against Brother, and Son against Father,
to do, with satisfaction to my self, the Duty which I think I
owe my King and my Country, of exposing to publick View his
present Behaviour. As this cannot be so fairly done by any
Method as by Vouchers under his own Hand, I shall produce
such, before I can acknowledge I have effaced out of my Mind
all remains of Good-Will or Pity towards a Man, whom to
serve I would very lately have hazarded a great deal: But as
Circumstances now stand between him and every Man who is
faithful to the King, his nearest Friend is obliged to blot out
all tender Considerations for him, which is not more hard to
do in any one that knew him than my self.

Repeating that this is a Test of the smarter Pain of Wounds in Domestick War, I must acquaint the Reader that the following is a true Copy of my Lord's Letter to the King, when His Majesty was in *Holland*. I have the Original in my Custody, where it may be perused by any one who has a Curiosity to see it.

Lord Mar *to the* KING.

SIR,

" HAVING the Happiness to be your Majesty's Subject, and also the Honour of being one of your Servants, as one of your Secretaries of State, I beg leave by this to Kiss your Majesty's Hand and Congratulate your happy Accession to the Throne, which I would have done my self the Honour of doing sooner, had I not hoped to have had the Honor of doing it personally e're now.

" I am afraid I may have had the Misfortune of being misrepresented to your Majesty, and my reason for thinking so is, because I was, I believe, the only one of the late Queen's Servants, who your Ministers here did not visit, which I mentioned to Mr. *Harley,* and the Earl of *Clarendon,* when they went from hence to wait on your Majesty, and your Ministers carrying so to me was the occasion of my receiving such Orders as deprived me of the Honour and Satisfaction of waiting on them, and being known to them.

" I suppose I had been misrepresented to them by some here upon Account of Party, or to ingratiate themselves by aspersing others, as our Parties here too often occasion; But I hope your Majesty will be so just as not to give Credit to such Misrepresentations.

" The part I acted in the bringing about and making of the Union, when the Succession to the Crown was settled for *Scotland* on your Majesty's Family, where I had the Honour to serve as Secretary of State for that Kingdom, doth, I hope, put my Sincerity and Faithfulness to your Majesty out of Dispute.

" My Family hath had the Honour for a great tract of Years to be faithful Servants to the Crown, and have had the care of the King's Children (when Kings of *Scotland*) intrusted to them. A predecessor of mine was honoured with the Care of Your Majesty's Grand-mother when young; and she was pleased afterwards to express some Concern for our Family in Letters which I still have under her own Hand.

"I have had the Honour to serve Her late Majesty in one Capacity or other ever since Her Accession to the Crown. I was happy in a good Mistress, and she was pleased to have some Confidence in me, and Regard for my Services: And since Your Majesty's happy Accession to the Crown, I hope You will find that I have not been wanting in my Duty in being instrumental in keeping Things quiet and peaceable in the Country to which I belong, and have some Interest in.

"Your Majesty shall ever find me as faithful and dutiful a Subject and Servant as ever any of my Family have been to the Crown, or as I have been to my late Mistress the Queen. And I beg Your Majesty may be so good not to believe any Misrepresentations of me, which nothing but Party Hatred and my Zeal for the Interest of the Crown doth occasion; and I hope I may presume to lay Claim to Your Royal Favour and Protection.

"As Your Accession to the Crown hath been quiet and peaceable, may Your Majesty's Reign be long and prosperous, and that Your People may soon have the Happiness and Satisfaction of Your Presence amongst them, is the earnest and fervent Wishes of him who is with the humblest Duty and Respect,"

SIR,

Your Majesty's most Faithful,

most Dutiful, and most Obedient

Subject and Servant,

Whitehall,, Aug. 30.   MAR.
O. S. 1714.

It is a very wide Step from this dutiful Letter to the following Declaration to all the World, and Order to his own Agent, which we have seen in the *Gazette* of the 24th Instant.

"OUR Rightful and Natural King *James* the 8th by the Grace of God, who is now coming to relieve us from our Oppressions, having been pleased to intrust us with the direction of his Affairs and the Command of his Forces in this his ancient kingdom of *Scotland*. And some of faithful Subjects and Servants met at *Aboyne, viz.* The Lord *Huntly,* the Lord *Tullibardine,* the Earl of Marischall, the Earl of *Southesk, Glingary* from the Clans, *Glenderule* from the Earl of *Broadalbine,* and *Gentlemen* of *Argyleshire,* Mr. *Patrick Lyon* of *Auchterhouse,* the Laird of *Auldbair,* Lieutenant-General *George Hamilton,* Major-General *Gordon* and my self, having taken into our Consideration his Majesty's last and late Orders to us, find that as this is now the time that he ordered us to appear openly in Arms for him, so it seems to us absolutely necessary for his Majesty's Service, and the relieving of our native Country from all its hardships, that all his faithful and loving Subjects and Lovers of their Countrey, should with all possible speed put themselves into Arms.

" These are therefore in his Majesty's Name and Authority, and by vertue of the power aforesaid, and by the King's special Order to me there'unt, to require and impower you forthwith to raise your fencible Men, with their best Arms, and you are immediately to March them to join me and some other of the Kings Forces at the *Invor* of *Bracmar,* on *Monday* next, in order to proceed in our March to attend the Kings Standart, with his other Forces.

The King intending that his Forces shall be paid from the time of their setting out, he expects, as he positively orders, that they behave themselves Civilly, and commit no Plundering nor other Disorders upon the highest penalties and his Dis- pleasure which is expected you'll see observed.

" Now is the time for all good Men to show their Zeal for his Majesty's Service, whose Cause is so deeply concern'd, and the releife of our native Country from Oppression and a foreign Yoke too heavy for us and our Posterity to bear, and to endeavour the restoring not only of our rightful and native King, but also our Country to its ancient, free and independent Constitution under him whose Ancestors have reigned over us for so many Generations.

" In so honourable, good and just a Cause, we cannot doubt of the Assistance, Direction and Blessing of Almighty God, who has so often rescued the Royal Family of *Stuart,* and our Country from sinking under Oppression.

" Your punctual observance of these Orders is expected, for

the doing of all which this shall be to you and all you employ
in the Execution of them a sufficient Warrant."

*To the Baillie and the
rest of the Gentle-
men of the Lordship
of* Kildrummy.

Given at
Bracmar the 9th
of Sept. 1715

Mar.

Invercauld, Sept. 9 at Night, 1715.

Jocke,

" YE was in the right not to come with the 100 Men ye sent
up to Night, when I expected four times the Number;
it is pretty thing, when all the Highlands of *Scotland* are now
rising upon their King and Countrys account, as I have accounts
from them since they were with me, and the Gentlemen of our
neighbouring Lowlands expecting us down to join them, that
my Men should be only refractory; is not this the thing we are
now about, which they have been wishing these 26 Years, and
now when it is come, and the King and Countrys Cause at
stake, will they for ever sit still and see all perish.

" I have used gentle means too long, and so I shall be forced
to put other Orders I have in execution, I have sent you enclosed
an Order for the Lordship of *Kildrummy*, which you are immediately to intimate to all my Vassals; if they give ready Obedience it will make some amends, and if not ye may tell them from
me, that it will not be in my power to save them (were I willing)
from being treated as Enemies by those who are ready soon to
joyn me, and they may depend on it that I will be the first to
propose and order their being so. Particularly let my own
Tenants in *Kildrummy* know, that if they come not forth with
their best Arms that I will send a Party immediately to burn
what they shall miss taking from them, and they may believe
this not only a Threat, but by all that's Sacred I'll put it in
execution, let my loss be what it will, that it may be example
to others, you are to tell the Gentlemen that I'll expect them in
their best Accoutrements on Horseback and no excuse to be
accepted of, go about this with all diligence, and come your

self and let me know your having done so, all this is not only as ye will be answerable to me, but to your King and Country."

Your assured Friend and Servant,

Sic Subscribitur Mar.

To John Forbes *of* Increrau,
Baillie of Kildrummie.

    This noble Lord, with the rest of the Nobility, took the Oaths to His Majesty King *George*, and did Homage to Him at His Coronation; both which Acts are but further Expressions, not more binding to a Man of Honour than what he had said before in his Letter. It appears prodigiously unaccountable how it is possible that Corruption should so far prevail, as that there does seem to arise among some Men very little Horror when this Obligation of an Oath is mentioned as broken in Political Occasions. If Man may upon Oath declare, *That the Person pretending to be Prince of* Wales, *and taking upon himself the Title of* James *the Third,* has not any Right or Title to the Crown of this Realm, or any other the Dominions thereunto belonging, and promise according to the same Oath he will defend King *George* to the utmost of his Power against all traiterous Conspiracies and Attempts whatsoever, and under the Shelter of the Security and Confidence reposed in such Obligation betray his Soveraign, there can be no such thing as any Band of Society. But Mens own private Interests and Ambition put their Conscience out of its Office, and make it obsequious to their Will, instead of being a Check upon it. Men who have brought themselves to this standing Inadvertency, have brought their Consciences to be very profitable Tools for the Improvement of their Fortunes; for it seems it can purchase for them, but it cannot alienate. If a Man has a mind to an Employment, he may take the Oaths to possess himself of it, but that Oath cannot detain him to the Allegiance of his Prince when he is turned out of his Office. My Lord has not given one Example of Injustice on the Part of the Government, which he can pretend diminish'd his Soveraign's Right to the Duty he subscribes in his Letter of the 30th of *August* 1714, and there--fore is as well in common Sense as Law a Traytor for his

Declaration that another is his rightful and natural King on the 9th of *September* 1715.

His Lordship in his Declaration speaks of Oppression for these twenty six Years past in general Terms; there is no one Instance wherein the King's is severed from the two preceding Reigns; so that the Reign of his Good Mistress was an Oppression, as well as this in which he rebels: But my Lord assigns the Reasons which sanctified her Power to him, *He had the Honour to serve Her in one Capacity or other ever since Her Accession to the Crown.*

But it has been long the Language of all the Conspirators, who have manifested themselves of late, to cover themselves by extolling the Queen whom they betrayed, and at the same time imputing their ill Conduct to Her Commands: My Lord, in the same Temper and Spirit with the rest, seems to impute his Disrespect to the *Hanover* Ministers to the Command of his Mistress. He tells the King his Ministers *carrying so to him,* occasioned that he had *such Orders* as deprived him of the Honour of being known to them.

My Lord supposes he has been misrepresented upon account of Party. I hope that Phrase will be utterly lost, or be spoken of another kind of Men than hitherto it has been understood to describe. Is it then true what the Whigs intimated, and the more moderate of them would not believe, that Whig and Tory were at the Bottom Jacobite and Hanoverian, the Promoters of Slavery and the Friends of Liberty? Poor *Jocke* in the Highlands has, for the fourth Part of a Century, known more than any of us in Town: The Lordship of *Kildrummy* was in the Secret all along. *Is not this* (says my Lord to them) *the thing we are now upon which they have been wishing these twenty six Years? It's a pretty thing,* as my Lord very well expresses himself, that none of those who meant this all along should shew themselves now, but have perjured themselves in vain for these three last Reigns, *to sit still and see all perish at last.*

A Leader who has so little Force at present, and is so little skilled in the Art of Persuasion, cannot, in himself, appear very formidable; but when the most solemn Tyes are of no manner of Force, who can avoid apprehending even from his next

Friend or Neighbour all the Miseries of War as Occasion shall offer? We have, with some Narrowness of Spirit, in many Cases, been very harsh upon poor Nonjurors, who have deny'd giving the Government the Security it required of them, and pretended to nothing but bare Protection, and Leave to live. But we have no Name for Men who act publickly under the same Government with us, and are constantly meditating our Ruine. These *Conjurors*, with whom we repeat the same Words at a Bar or a Table, and have gone on very lovingly after the Clerk, and begin all together with one Voice, *Do swear*, it seems have minded what they said no more than if it were a Matter of mere Form, like taking up or laying down a Mace, or bowing to an empty Chair, which is done only as an Overt Act, signifying that we are now going upon Business, or the like. We have all seen and heard the *Conjurors* speak very roundly out, (tho' now and then one repeats as if chawing Thistles) and indeed some have observed that they show'd little Relish to, or over-acted what they were doing; but I have always thought, till of late, that these Reflections were unmanly and uncharitable. But it is not growing insolent, to take notice from Events, there are every Day new Proofs, that what, in common Charity and Humanity, one would have thought the most cruel Aspersion, is not only true, but with greater Aggravations than their most violent Enemies could have supposed the *Conjurors* could have been guilty of. We have long had this kind of Imputation laid at the Door of the Church of *Rome*. They, it has been said, have had, for the Service of the Faith on particular Occasions, a Suspension of the Divine Vengeance from the Pope, by plenary Letters of Indulgence in that Behalf; But our *Conjurors*, whom we have looked upon, as to the generality of them, a mis-led, thoughtless, but far from a designing Set of Men, are, so far from wanting Dispensations, that they are void of all Sense of Conscience, when they betray, and use Perjury as a mere Expedient to do it with better Opportunities.

It is hard not to grow very grave on such an Occasion; but, without pretending to set up for much of the Divine or the Casuist, who is there that does not know that the Foundation of Moral Virtue is Justice? This is what respects the Community. One might desire these Gentlemen to recollect, that when a Man offends against Temperance and the like, he hurts only his individual self; but Society cannot subsist without the Practice of Justice. It is from this that nothing is more highly resented, or esteemed so odious as Breach of Promise; and notorious Neglect of this Kind always makes a Man, according to the respective Cases in which he trespasses, either detestable or inconsiderable. To guard against this loose Behaviour in Matters of Moment, and to secure humane Society against Breach of Faith, God is made a Witness in the Promises which Man makes to Men, on Pain of His Displeasure. We know he knows all we do, and in this Act call upon Him to observe what we do, and avenge himself in case of our Falsehood. What was before purely Morality, is by this Act become Religion. How great then is the Guilt of breaking through this solemn Appeal? Will our taking it lightly make it less sacred? If not, what is the Guilt of entering into this Obligation with no other View but to violate it?

It is certain that he who does not think a Government just ought not to swear to it; but when he has done so, there is no Consideration can absolve him of that Oath. As mutual Faith is the Support of Society, an Oath is the highest Obligation to keep that Faith inviolate. But this Question is excellently well considered in a little Pamphlet, called, *Advice to the Tories who have taken the Oaths*, to which I recommend my Reader. What I thought serviceable in publishing this Paper is to show that my Lord *Mar*, whatever the Guilt of professing to be in the King's Interest, and being at the same time in Measures against Him, has that Guilt upon him. The poor Vassals who follow him as their Leader, and a Man of Honour and Quality, that should know better than themselves what is the Duty of an honest Man, are not acquainted that he has violated all that is good and sacred; and all who may be in Inclination with him, may, from the Knowledge of his personal Behaviour to the King, either change their Minds, or at least not chuse to follow one who has been guilty of so solemn a Falsehood. It is not possible to have any Notion, consistent with Honour, to reconcile this Treachery. Perjury is not a Fault incurred by Surprize, by sudden Instigation of Desire, or Passion; it is no way to be accounted for by the Force which false Gallantry or

Mode of Life has upon our Actions: Perjury is a cool deliberate Crime, committed in Defiance of God, to do Violence to Man. How monstrous therefore must it appear, that a Man who barely to mend his own Affairs, or to gratify his Ambition, can meditate the disturbance of all the rest of the World, and at the Expence of the Lives and Fortunes of the best of a whole People, break through all that is Sacred, only to be himself a little more at Ease, and enjoy that silly Pleasure called Pomp?

In fine, the Earl of *Mar*, without any Provocation, or pretended Provocation to exasperate him as a Man, as a Subject, as a Gentleman, as a Nobleman, laying aside his private Faith given under his own Hand, as well as the publick Obligation of the most sacred Oaths, is now in Rebellion against a Sovereign, who had, at his humble Suit, consented to let him feel His Annual Bounty; to Introduce an Outlaw whom he had abjured, from no other Motive but Hopes of larger Supplies to his Avarice and Ambition.

His Ingratitude is not only that of a Subject, who had the Protection of his Prince in common with the rest, but that of a Man who stood justly suspected by the King; and after his Majesty's most generous Neglect of all that might be objected against him, was further engaged by the Receipt of undeserved, and therefore the more binding, Favour.

The OATH of ALLEGIANCE.

I A. B. do swear, That I will bear Faith and true Allegiance to His Majesty King *GEORGE*.

So help me GOD.

The OATH of ABJURATION.

I A. B. do truly and sincerely acknowledge, profess, testifie and declare in my Conscience before GOD and the World, That Our Sovereign Lord King *GEORGE* is Lawful and Rightful King of this REALM, and of all other His Majesty's Dominions and Countries thereunto belonging; and I do solemnly and sincerely declare, That I do believe in my Conscience, that the Person pretended to be Prince of *WALES* during the Life of the late King *James*, and since his Decease pretending to be, and taking upon himself the Stile and Title of King of *England*, by the Name of *James the Third*, hath not any Right or Title to the Crown of this Realm, or any other the Dominions thereunto belonging. And I do renounce, refuse and abjure any Allegiance or Obedience to him. And I do swear, That I will bear Faith and true Allegiance to His Majesty King *GEORGE*, and Him will defend to the utmost of my Power, against all Traiterous Conspiracies and Attempts whatsoever, which shall be made against His Person, Crown, or Dignity; And I will do my utmost endeavour to disclose and make known to His Majesty, and Successors, all Treasons and Traiterous Conspiracies which I shall know to be against Him, or any of them. And I do faithfully promise, to the utmost of my Power, to support, maintain and defend the Limitation and Succession of the Crown against him the said *James*, and all other Persons whatsoever, as the same by an Act, intitled, *An Act for the further Limitation of the Crown, and better securing the Rights and Liberties of the Subject*, is, and stands limited to the Princess *SOPHIA*, Electress and Dutchess Dowager of *HANOVER*, and the Heirs of Her Body, being PROTEST-ANTS. And all these Things I do plainly and sincerely acknowledge and swear, according to these express Words by me spoken, and according to the plain and common Sense and Understanding of the same Words, without any Equivocation, mental Evasion, or secret Reservation whatsoever. And I do make this Recognition, Acknowledgment, Abjuration, Renunciation and Promise, heartily, willingly and truly, upon the true Faith of a Christian.

So help me GOD.

FINIS.

Town Talk. In a Letter to a Lady in the Country
No. 5 (13 January 1716)

James Stuart's " Declaration," dated 25 October 1715, from his court at Commercy, Lorraine, and issued in the British Isles when he landed at Christmas time, was the subject of two tracts by Steele in January. " I have that in my Pockett which within a few days will be a great sum of money," he wrote to Lady Steele on 10th January. The first version appeared on the 13th in No. 5 of his weekly periodical *Town Talk*; on the 19th, the second appeared in the form of a folio half-sheet. On the 21st he assisted in drawing up the Commons' Address of Thanks for the King's speech on the Pretender.

During the Rebellion now in progress Steele had undertaken to be of service to the Hanoverian dynasty, " the common cause in which I am engaged to the end of my life." In both of these tracts his purpose is to justify the Revolution and defend King George's title. The design of both is the same—the text of the manifesto together with Steele's observations as " an Antidote to the Poison of it "; and the arguments are similar. The difference is one of tone. The paper in *Town Talk*, designed for an audience who did not care for political news, is somewhat sensational and gossipy; but there is no mistaking the seriousness of his purpose, to demonstrate that the Pretender's claim " moves upon Hinges which have long been rusty."

There are several satirical allusions to Bolingbroke, whose style Steele professes to see in the Pretender's manifesto—" your scribe Harry." During the impeachment proceedings against the late Ministry, Bolingbroke had escaped to France in April, 1715, and taken service with James Stuart as " Secretary of State." At home, his civil rights and his estates had been withdrawn by an Act of Attainder. In *The Englishman*, intended to publicize the impeachment, Steele had given the substance of the Articles against him (No. 19 on 12 Sept. 1715). Textual notes on p. 644.

Town-Talk.

IN A

LETTER

TO A

Lady in the Country.

To be publiſhed every FRIDAY.

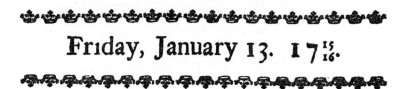

Friday, January 13. 17$\frac{15}{16}$.

LONDON,

Printed: And Sold by J. ROBERTS, near the *Oxford-Arms* in *Warwick-Lane*; J. GRAVES in St. *James's-Street*; and A. DODD, at the *Peacock* without *Temple-Bar*. Where Advertiſements are taken in.

[Price SIX PENCE.]

Town-Talk, &c. No. 5. Friday, January 13. 1716.

Madam,

Your Last admonishes me, that it is within the Orders you first sent me, that I should send you sometimes some Politick News; but I am very averse to these Subjects. However, it has so happened just now, that the Town is too busie for Pleasure or Speculation, and all the Chat is of the *Pretender*. I should never have heard of it, if all this had not been brought to Town, and made the whole Talk of it. You remember I told you, in my First, That *Covent-Garden* is the Heart of the Town, and by that Rule, the Playhouse is the Town-Hall. I must confess, my chief Intelligence is in that Neighbourhood. I happened to sit near Two Courtesans, in the First Gallery, the other Evening, who were warm in Politicks. One of them, who I perceived belonged to the Party of the *Whiggs*, said, the *Pretender* was ruined, for that his General, *Mar*, under Pretence of going to meet him at *Peterhead*, had left *Perth*, and taken an Opportunity to make his Escape. You are to know, Madam, that ever since Masks have been disallow'd, an open Confidence has done the same Thing, and the Wenches being impudent and meretriciously dress'd, are as well known as if they wore the former Signal.

A Lady of very great Fame for her Beauty, Impudence, and something like Wit, and from a Similitude in Merit and Manners, was particularly a Favourite of the late Secretary Bolingbroke, contradicted the News of the *Whigg* Libertine; and, indeed, with a Superior Air, gave her to understand, that her Friend had sent her a Token from *France*: There Hussy, said she, let any of your Queer Party answer that, if they can. It is well known that Statesman and Wit had writ more than Songs upon this Lady; and she had been his Desk to write upon in too notorious a Manner to describe to you. What she threw at her Sister proved to be the *Pretender*'s Declaration, which was conveyed from one Hand to another the whole Evening, till at last it was taken up and carryed to an Hand which I will not take upon me to name to you, but he has writ a long Answer to the *Manifesto*. This Letter has in it the Declaration at large, with an Antidote to the Poison of it; for which Reason, enclosing it, will entertain you a longer Time than any of my former have attempted.

To *the* Pretender.

Sir,

"A Discourse your Confessor, soon after my Expulsion from Parliament for the Crisis, had with a Friend of mine at *Paris,* gives me to understand you are not unacquainted with my Name and Character; and therefore you will not be surprized that I affect to do extraordinary Things, however ridiculous or odious I may appear to your Friends, provided that Irregularity draws an Attention to what makes for the common Cause, in which I am engaged to the End of my Life. I writ lately to the Pope about the State of Religion; and though I have Reason to fear I have not converted him, I still proceed in such Endeavours; and since you are now landed in Britain, I take the like Liberty with you, his Godson, in order to lay before you the true State of the Question between you and this Nation; whatever wild Notions have taken place amongst us, they have not prevailed so absolutely as to leave you any probable Grounds of Hope, either from Right or Force.

"There are, Sir, Thousands in *England*, that know, the Basis of all Government is the Good of the People governed; and that all Incidents of a State must be rectified by that single Rule, and no other; and that it is an impious and prophane Thought to believe any other Maxim to be consonant to the Goodness of the Creator; and that Law of Nature which he has implanted in the Mind of every Man living. According to this, the late King *James* was expelled *Scotland*, and himself, by his Crimes and Flight, abdicated *England*. He took you, it seems, with him at that Time, and bred you in the *Roman Catholick* Religion; from which Particular of your Faith, were I to admit that you are his Son, which I do not in the least regard whether you are or not, you would (besides all other Disadvantages from what has passed since) be, at best, in a worse Condition than he was, when the *Bill of Exclusion* against him was brought into Parliament. That Bill was offered when he was only suspected to be what you do not in the least deny yourself to be. His Conduct in the Throne, by no means gives us good Expectations [1] from you; and you cannot be surprized, that after this Experience, we do all in our Power to keep out you, who have no Pretence but that of being his Son, with a Profession of Faith that had like to have barred him himself, under whom you claim. Sir. you may depend upon it, we think our Lives in less Hazard with our Swords in our Hands against you, than if we should be at your Mercy from a Throne.

"Had the Gentleman who sent you to *France*, left you in safe Hands behind him; if you had appeared his Innocent Child, your Case had been, before the Nation, as an Object of Compassion, and Justice must have been unavoidably done on that Occasion; but your Patron either knew you to be none of his, or else was very indiscreet to carry you to be unqualified for the Prince of a Protestant People, when he knew he owed his own Crown to the Dissimulation of his Religion, and his loss of Empire to the Profession of it. *The Business of Mankind cannot stand still, if Princes by their unhappy Conduct render it unsafe for them to remain at the Head of their Subjects; and whatever has befallen you, you are to attribute to your Pretended Father, not his People, who, by his Flight with you, were under a Necessity to fly to the nearest Refuge.* You have not so much as pretended to be a Protestant, and, we very well know, that if you should pretend it, it would be only a Pretence; we know, that coming as you do, a professed Papist, you are bound in Conscience, under Pain of Damnation to propagate your Religion, not by all fair, but by all Possible Means, and consequently, that you will stand for ever Bound under the same Pain of Damnation which your Priests will constantly thunder in your Ears to take away, as fast as you can have Power so to do, not only the Estates and Liberties, but the Lives of all who will not become Papists, and that in the most cruel Manner, for an Example to others.

"The most solemn Promises and Oaths, which you would be so gracious as to make, will be in themselves, according to your Religion, unlawful and null. We have Examples of this in all Times and Places, you are not to depend on certain Persons, whom you think to swear against their Consciences to the present Establishment: They do not mean Popery for your Sake, but they would be contented to have it in themselves by your Means; as you would swear to them till you carry your Point, so they would swear to you to carry theirs. But when Popish Ministers of the Church of *England* should feel your Superstition, by displacing them for your downright *Roman Catholick* Priests, they would become, in an instant, entire Protestants, as they are now but Partially such, and abhor all unreasonable Doctrines and Impositions more heartily than ever *Luther* did, till they were reinstated in their Livings.

" This I tell you as a Truth you may depend upon; but least you should no more mind me than that graceless Wretch, the Pope, has, I must go on to tell you that we will take all possible Means to prevent your Power to hurt us. We have read of Inquisitions and Massacres, and are too lately escaped from the Danger of universal Slaughter, to trust to what we must expect from you. This we know to be our only Time to stand our Ground. When you come we know the Calamity will be final, but we have no Reason to fear it, but as a just Judgment upon those who call themselves Protestants, for their Thirst of Popish Power and Dominion over their Protestant Brethren. We know who shall be found opposing you,[2] won't be used like those who are now rebelling against King *George*: Those moderate Laws, which give every Criminal all possible Advantage to make whatever Defence their Case can admit, will cease when you conquer; and we shall be executed, nay, extirpated summarily without Justice or Form of Law. In the Time of King *James,* we saw Numbers who had been deceived into pleading Guilty, upon Promise of Pardon, were hanged up as soon as they had done what entitled them to that Pardon.

" While I was now writing, your Declaration has come into my Hands; the very first Paragraph discovers the Specious and Wordy Stile of our late Secretary, who foresaw he should be a Refugee; and a Refugee, without Religion, is a very proper Minister to a Bigot; for Infidelity, will, no Doubt, execute, without Remorse, the Dictates of Superstition. An old Friend of Mr. Secretary's shews it about as a Piece of Wit and Eloquence of her Gallant, and swears we are Blockheads if we are not converted by it. I shall recite it, least you should accuse me of Misrepresentation. . . ." [a]

[a] At this point, Steele gives the Pretender's Declaration. For the text, see pp. 393-96.

First, You declare you have the Goodness to be weary of depending on Foreign Princes, and are willing to be one yourself; and are further graciously disposed to relieve from *Miseries,* present, which we don't feel and you don't Name, and future Ones, which must be the Consequences of what you call an *Usurpation.*

Secondly, That during the Life of the Queen, whose Reign you allow was also an Usurpation; you rested contented, because you believed she would take Measures for your Enjoyment of the Crown, which you think she must know she did guiltily detain from you; and since a Plan, to which you intimate she was privy, of throwing yourself upon the People, is defeated by her Death, you are now under an Horror and Indignation at our present Circumstances and Prospect.

Thirdly, A Foreign Family is on the Throne, and Strangers even to our Language.

Fourthly, The Administration of the Government is in the Hands of the Worst, to the Oppression of the Best; that your Sister has been insulted in her Grave; A Parliament procured by unreasonable Influences; new Debts contracted; new Armies raised; *Dutch* Forces brought in, and the Accession of the Dutchy of *Bremen* to our King, is so Inconsiderable, that it will reduce us, to appertain to what is inconsiderable.

Fifthly, We have been Betrayed instead of being Rescued; and these Evils wholly owing to abandoning the Old Constitution, which many, who promoted the present Settlement, you believe, did not intend.

Sixthly, You observe the Generality are for you, and grow thankful for the Spirit which is miraculously raised in all Parts of your Kingdom: You are coming to Share the Dangers which your *Scotch* Subjects groan under from the unhappy Union: You place before your Eyes, your Grandfather who fell, and your Uncle who out-lived a Price upon his Head.

Seventhly, You talk in the Pompous Stile of Mr. Secretary, when he resolved to run for it; Let me, said the pious Churchman and heroick Patriot, be a Victim in *Smithfield* for the Cause for which I am proud to fall; and so got his Black Peruke and Whiskers ready, and went on in the same Noble

Stile in *France*; but I am going to Observations when I am only upon the Recital, and should only say, *Sic disputas Domine*. You do not make Promises, but use an Imperative; Let Consciences truly tender be indulged; Let Property, and Let an Act of Grace.

Eighthly, You absolutely Pardon all Faults to those who shall come in to you at your Landing, and are ready to concert with your Parliament upon all other Matters; and so very gravely you Sign from your Court at *Commercy*, the 25th Day of *October*, in the Fifteenth Year of your Reign.

The First Paragraph of this your Declaration, is unsupported with any Thing so much as Specious; for you roundly assert, what has been largely, and unanswerably denied by the most Knowing in our Constitution; and the Practice of all Mankind has been, and would not have been otherwise than to vary their Manner of Succession of Princes at such Exigences as that at the Revolution; and to all those Arguments I have added, that King *James* either knew you were not his Son, and therefore took you with him, that any Arguments for your being Supposititious, might have less Weight in your Exile; or was himself the primary Cause of your Fate, as you are pleased to call it.

In your Second Topick, you say, you bore with the Queen's Enjoyment of your Throne, because you expected she would contrive your Succession to it, and believe She secretly acknowledg'd, in her own Conscience, your Right to it; This is the most vile and barbarous Imputation that ever was laid upon any Prince, either dead or living. This is saying, she was an Imposter to her People, and was contented to be so for your Service: It is saying, her Religion, her Oaths, and her Royal State was one continued Scene of Idolatry towards God, and Artifice towards Man.

Your Third Observation, That the Family on the Throne are Strangers to our Language, is Scurrility; the Relation between a Prince and his People is not supported by Conversation, but the Distribution of Equity and Justice; And the King expresses an *Heart truly English*, when he declares the Constitution the Rule of his Government, and the Integrity of his great Mind has been evident in all his Actions, ever since he condescended to make us that Declaration.

Your Fourth Topick is, That the Administration is in the Hands of the Worst, to the Oppression of the Best. This is a quaint Expression your Secretary *Harry* has taken from *Tacitus,* or some other Writer, according to his Way of enriching his Speech with lively Expressions, and neglecting the Improvement of his Heart and Sentiments. This it was that made him a most excellent Reviler, while he was with us; and I find he keeps it for your Service, to which he indeed apply'd it while he was here. This Charge against the Ministers is base and groundless; for there is not one of them who has not distinguished himself before he came to his present Station, by brave Actions, seasonable Service in Negotiation, or laudable Eloquence in Assemblies, as well as that their Birth and Quality found them among the best of the People. I assure you I speak this very impartially; for whether you know it or no, I fear you won't believe, I am the modestest Man in *England*; I have desired only to be in as good Preferment as this Cause found me when I first commenced Grenadier for it, but that cannot, it seems, be, yet I forgive them for being Cold Friends to me, for being Warm Enemies to you. And you may please to tell your Scribe *Harry*, That they are diligent in the Administration of Publick Affairs, and have gone a great Way in rebuilding the Fabrick from the Ruins to which he and his wicked Accomplices had reduced it. You say, The Parliament was procured by unwarrantable Influences. It is confessed, it was not called by your Authority. What else you mean I cannot imagine; for there was not a Farthing of publick Money spent that Way; and if you mean great Private Expence was made, you see People had rather throw away half their Estates to keep you out, than part with the Whole by your coming: You shew your great Reach in Politicks in complaining, that we are running in Debt, and raising Armies. I believe you think they are both raised against you. You are offended the King has the Dutchy of *Bremen*: You perhaps, think it would be greater Generosity to take one that brings us nothing but a new Religion, than a Protestant Prince like ourselves, who is, at once, to this Nation, a Good and Gracious Prince, and a Rich and Powerful Ally.

Your Fifth Complaint, is, that we have been Betrayed, rather than Rescued, and that you are so gracious to believe the ill

26

Consequences were not intended. I do not understand this, it is General; and why you, say they, who made the Settlement did not expect the ill Consequences, which you intimate are those of not having you our Prince, is incomprehensible.

Your Sixth Assertion, That there is, in the Generality of the People, a Spirit raised miraculously for you. It is, indeed, wonderfully, but not miraculously; for they are known by their Fruit who brought forth our Calamities. A Ministry, that came into the Service of their Country engaged in a War against *France* and you, being resolved to raise that and bring in you, became, instead of Guardians of the People, their Betrayers; and with the Subserviency of impudent and apostate Clergy-men, laid the Seeds of the present Confusion and Rebellion. As for your Mention of *Charles* the First, and Second: The First lost his Life, he did so indeed, in a most barbarous and unjust Manner, in asserting the Constitution, and Illegality of the Proceedings against him; Which can never be your Case; for all Laws are against you. As to him you call Uncle, he escaped a Price on his Head; but it behoves you to reflect there is a greater on yours.

Your Seventh Paragraph, evades with a specious Skill any binding Promises to us, and instead of making them, you say, let them be made. This trick has been already practised by many of your Friends: People will make their Observations, that your Craft is of the same Kind. You must know there is a Cannon which directs our Clergy to Pray for the King in such and such Terms; instead of doing as they are bid, they bid others do it, and repeat the Order instead of paying obedience to it; instead of Praying themselves, they say to the People, you shall pray for King *George*; their *Bidding*, is as Loyal, as your *Letting* is Gracious.

Your Eighth Common-place is a General Amnesty to all that shall run to your Colours, and help you forwards upon your Arrival; After that, you and your Parliament will consider further: What we are to expect from thence give me leave to show you from—But before I go to that, having cast my Eye on your Date from *Commercy*, I must observe, that here, and in your Stile in the First Paragraph, you claim *France* too, for which I hope you will answer on that side of the Water, but I am glad to hear you act like an exasperated Man against his Royal Highness the Regent. I was going to show what we were to hope from you, and a Parliament of yours, by the Treatment the Protestants had from your Pretender Father, and his in Ireland. You are pleased to tell us, that if, upon your Arrival in these Realms we submit, you are disposed to receive us in your Equipage of Subjects, but if not, you in Parliament will proceed.

King *James* made a new Constitution of Corporations, to put in Creatures of his own; the manner of Election was, to send together, with a Writ for Election, a Letter or Recommendation whom to choose. A Parliament made in this manner set themselves to root out the whole Protestant Interest, by following a General Bill of Attainder against all absent from their Houses, whether in Arms or Employment against him or not, with an Act of Repeal, whereby the real Estates of all who *Dwelt or staid in any Place of the Three Kingdoms, which did not own King James's Power or correspond with any such as they term Rebels, or were any ways aiding, abetting or assisting to them from the First Day of August* 1688, *are declared to be forfeited and vested in his Majesty, and that without any Office or Inquisition found Thereof.* By which Clause almost every Protestant that could Write in the Kingdom, had forfeited his Estate; for the Packets went from *London* to *Dublin,* and back again, constantly, from *August* to *March,* 1688; and few had Friends in *England,* or in the North, but Corresponded with them by Letters, and every such Letter is made by this Clause a Forfeiture of Estate. There is a Book amongst us called " The State of the Protestants of *Ireland,* under the late King *James*'s Government," which gives us the most lively and faithful Idea of a Popish Prince over a Protestant People.

This whole Treatise is a Preservative against *Romish* Tyranny, and effectually explains King *James's* direct Intention to destroy his Protestant Subjects in their Persons, Religion, and Estates.

In a Word, Sir, the Time is come wherein it begins to be understood no Plea in Excuse of Treason, that what was done, was done under the Administration of a Lady, who was renowned for Goodness and Virtue: But you have said more on this Subject to us, than any of your Friends; you carry it so far as

to give us broad Hints, that she was privy to Designs in your
Favour: In Gratitude to her, if she was, you should have covered
this Circumstance otherwise: As I have above shown, you out-do
all who have attempted to bring her Name to Dishonour; in
Proportion that you are above your Followers, your Testimony
is a greater Injury than that of any of them. It is certain there
has not one Man appeared a manifest Traitor, but he took
Refuge under his Zeal for Her Majesty. One was accused for
betraying a Town; to which he gave as immediate and direct
an Answer as ever he did in his Life: The Queen, whom I
served, was the best of Women and of Sovereigns: What made
this the pleasanter, was, that she had before her Death discarded him, and her having turned him off seemed to turn her
Goodness, as well as Judgment, against him. If One so good
punish'd him, her Virtue certainly made more against him than
for him. This, Sir, was the Stile, this the Game of cross Purposes, which was used by all and every of your Friends, as far
as they have been surprized in their Iniquities. For all which
you have given us a Key; but really, Sir, I cannot think this
Step at all Politick in the Court of *Commercy*; for the Name
of the Queen was helpful only, but as from Her Character She
was believed incapable of betraying Her People and Her
Religion; and therefore Her Approbation of their Conduct was
a Cover to it: But if you should bring it to pass that She should
be universally thought in the Design, you will involve Her
in the Guilt, and consequently have no more Advantage from
Her Reputation to protect that Conduct which ripened it to
what it is.

Upon the whole, Sir, under Favour of the Counsellors of the
Court of *Commercy*, this Declaration is shallow and superficial;
it moves upon Hinges, which have long been rusty, and the
Prejudices are surmounted by Facts on our Side, against bare
Assertions on yours. In the Infancy of this Design, which the
wise and disinterested Earl of Godolphin saw, and spoke to
his Queen upon her first Intimation, that she was going into
Measures different from those which had raised her to the
Summit of Glory, on which she stood and could survey *Europe*
in Suspense, till it knew her Determination: I say, upon the
very first Step towards it, that memorable Minister told his

Sovereign what would necessarily, however she was disposed in it, follow from that Change of her Councils: To the endless Sorrow and Indignation of all Honest Men from that Moment she was exalted in Words and Protestations, but pulled down in Things and Facts in the Court of *England*; Cunning took the Place of Wisdom, Impudence of Ingenuity, and Sensuality of Pleasure, every Thing that was Praiseworthy was banished and discountenanced, and some monstrous Likeness of it set up to View in the Place where it used to appear. The setting up Idols and Images for the adorable Things which they ought to represent, from the Practice and Influence of the Court, grew the Fashion throughout the Nation, which was amuzed with Words to pursue the Destruction of what they understood these Words to signifie. Thus the Word *Church* giving naturally an Alarm to be ready in the Defence of Religion, and Loyalty to the Queen naturally implying the Love of our Country, which she had hitherto so well Governed and Protected, misled the People not only to suffer, but promote their Designs, who were gradually delivering up both Religion and Liberty into the Hands of your Worship. You may depend upon it, that the miraculous Spirit, which you boast is raised for you, is no other than a misguided Zeal against you; for which Reason, if I might advise, you should stick to your Kingdom of *France;* and therefore I can't believe you have removed the Court from *Commercy,* to *Peterhead,* or *Perth.*

You may be assur'd, I am not moved to the giving you this Trouble, from Passion, Avarice, or Ambition: As to Passion, I must own I never have received greater Civilities, or more frank and disinterested Offers of Kindness and Favour, than from Friends of yours now in Arms, or in Custody for your Cause; I wish them all, from my Soul, in Heaven; and have no more Personal Provocation to be against any one of them, than *Brutus* had to the stabbing of *Caesar.* But this is a Time, wherein there is no such Thing as a private Man, but all Offices of Life should give way to the Duties we owe to the Community; Father, Brother, Son, and Husband, must be laid aside, to exert the Citizen and the Subject.

As to Avarice and Ambition, when the Necessities of Life are provided, and conscious Honour well guarded, I can contemn both: To shew you that it is so, I can very frankly recommend you to the Cardinal's Cap, which the Provincial of the Jesuits proposes to have offered me, to avoid further unanswerable Objections to the Craft of Traders in Religion: Believe me, you would find a great Difference in sitting at your Ease inflaming others, and in being yourself, as they have now made you, a Mock-Hero in a *Holy War*: A tool to Sacerdotal Pride and Luxury.

In Hopes you will make the best Use of this Advice, I take Leave of your Eminence.

R. S.

The British Subject's Answer to the Pretender's Declaration (January, 1716)

This tract, the second treatment of the subject, was more compact in form and argument than that which had appeared in *Town Talk* during the preceding week. It was a folio half-sheet, the text of the " declaration " in numbered articles in one column and Steele's observations in the opposite. It was more dignified in tone than the first tract and unmistakably in a conciliatory vein. Steele sensed resentment against the Whigs' vindictiveness, by a minority, who still held out for the legality of James Stuart's title; he felt that these tenacious opponents to His Majesty's title—the Tory squirearchy, high-flying churchmen, and Scottish Jacobites—might be won over, in part, by more tactful methods. So out of respect to the scruples of conscience and the intellectual convictions of " our wavering and mistaken Fellow-Subjects," who have been " misled " and " ensnared," he would try with "Patience to consider the Assertions of the Pretender." This had also been his approach in *The Present Case of the British Subject Considered* (*Englishman,* No. 22, on 23 Sept. 1715), the word " British " used to gather in Scotsmen also. In both that and the present tract he attempts to use more reasoned and dispassionate methods to reach those who believed it was committing of sin to upset the divine hereditary succession. His statements about Charles I and Charles II are careful. He finds his defence in the Revolution Settlement: George's title is a combination of hereditary and parliamentary right. The claims of the Catholic Stuarts were made null and void by the flight of James II, whose tyrannies Steele brings to mind by recalling various articles in the Bill of Rights.

Also, in both Pretender tracts Steele had his say on a point raised in the " Declaration," which the minority were laboring in the pamphlet press: that Queen Anne favored the Stuart Succession and that the ministers who had attempted to carry out her orders were now being persecuted. This, Steele considers it treason to say. They were " wicked Men, who abused her late Majesty's Power when living, as they do Her Name now dead to give sanction to their Iniquities." The Tory ministers had been tried in 1715 on the charges of making a peace treaty traitorous to the interests of the nation and of plotting to overthrow the Protestant Succession. And the Whigs would not grant that her alleged authority was sufficient reason for acquitting them. This was one of the main themes treated in Steele's *Englishman* (1715). Textual notes on p. 645.

The British Subject's Answer, to the Pretender's Declaration.

By Sr. RICHARD STEELE.

DECLARATION.	ANSWER.
1. JAMES VIII. By the Grace of God, of Scotland, England, France, and Ireland, King, Defender of the Faith, &c. To all our Loving Subjects, or what Degree or Quality soever, Greeting. As we are firmly resolved never to omit any Opportunity of Asserting Our undoubted Title to the Imperial Crown of these Realms, and of endeavouring to put Ourself into the Possession of that Right, which is devolved upon Us by the Laws of God and Man; so must We, in Justice to the Sentiments of our Own Heart, Declare, That nothing in this World can give Us so great a Satisfaction, as to owe to the Endeavours of Our Loyal Subjects, both Our and their Restoration to that happy Settlement, which can alone deliver this Church and Nation from the Calamities which they lie at present under, and from those future Miseries, which must be the Consequences of the present Usurpation. During the Life of Our Dear Sister of Glorious Memory, the Happiness which Our People enjoyed, softned in some Degree the Hardship of Our own Fate: And we must further contess, That when We reflected on the Goodness of Her Nature, and Her Inclinations to Justice, We could not but persuade Ourself, That She intended to establish and perpetuate the Peace, which She had given to these Kingdoms, by destroying for ever all Competition to the Succession of the Crown, and by securing to Us at last the Enjoyment of that Inheritance, out of which We had been so long kept; which Her Conscience must inform	W HEREAS, our Forefathers, for the many and intolerable Acts of Tyranny committed by the late King James II. against the Churches and States of England and Scotland, now United into the Kingdom of Great Britain, did, in full Parliament, after the Flight of his said Majesty, pronounce the said King James to have Abdicated, and Forefaulted the Empire of the said Kingdoms; and for the Safety of themselves and of their Posterity placed in the said Thrones, William III. of Glorious Memory; which said King William, was succeeded by the late Queen Ann, under the same Title. And whereas, the Pretender to these Dominions has by an open Declaration set forth, That the said Queen had been reduced from the maternal Care and Protection of her People, which she had in the most solemn manner undertaken as our Queen and Sovereign Lady, to enter into Measures for favouring his the said Pretender's Succession to these Thrones. We, the Free Subjects of Great Britain, do utter Abhorrence of such a Design, ascribed to our Thrones, who had Reigned many Years over us in Just and Glory, surpassing any o Her Predecessors, &c. That we receiving with the utmost Horrour the insinuation of so cruel, monstrous and unnatural a Crime against a People, as Treason in the Throne of their Prince, Do, for the Honour of Humane Nature it self, as well as Regard to our own Rights and Liberties, turn away from such an

The British *Subject's* ANSWER, *to the* Pretender's Declaration.

By *Sir* RICHARD STEELE.

DECLARATION.

1. **J**AMES VIII. *By the Grace of God, o*f Scotland, England, France, *and* Ireland, *King, Defender of the Faith,* &c. To all our Loving Subjects, of what Degree or Quality soever, Greeting. As we are firmly resolved never to omit any Opportunity of Asserting Our undoubted Title to the Imperial Crown of these Realms, and of endeavouring to put Ourself into the Possession of that Right, which is devolved upon Us by the Laws of God and Man; so must We, in Justice to the Sentiments of our Own Heart, Declare, That nothing in this World can give Us so great Satisfaction, as to owe to the Endeavours of Our Loyal Subjects, both Our and their Restoration to that happy Settlement, which can alone deliver this Church and Nation from the Calamities which they lie at present under, and from those future Miseries, which must be the Consequences of the present Usurpation. During the Life of Our Dear Sister of Glorious Memory, the Happiness which Our People enjoyed, softned in some Degree the Hardship of Our own Fate: And we must further confess, That when We reflected on the Goodness of Her Nature, and Her Inclinations to Justice, We could not but perswade Ourself, That she intended to establish and perpetuate the Peace, which she had given to these Kingdoms, by destroying for ever all Competition to the Succession of the Crown, and by securing to Us at last the Enjoyment of that Inheritance, out of which We had been so long kept; which Her Conscience must inform Her was Our Due, and which Her Principles must lead Her to desire that We might obtain.

2. But since the Time when it pleased Almighty God to put a Period to Her Life, and not to suffer Us to throw Ourself, as We then fully purposed to have done, upon Our People, We have not been able to look on the present Condition of Our Kingdoms, or to consider their future Prospect, without

393

all the Horrour and Indignation, which ought to fill the Breast of every *Scotsman.*

3. We have beheld a Foreign Family, Aliens to our Country, distant in Blood, and Strangers even to Our Language, ascend the Throne.

4. We have seen the Reins of Government put into the Hands of a Faction, and that Authority, which was designed for the Protection of all, exercised by a few of the worst, to the Oppression of the best and greatest Number of Our Subjects: Our Sister has not been left at Rest in Her Grave; Her Name has been scurrilously abused; Her Glory, as far as in these People lay, insolently defaced; and Her Faithful Servants inhumanly persecuted: A Parliament has been procured by the most unwarrantable Influences, and by the grossest Corruption to serve the vilest Ends; and they, who ought to be the Guardians of the Liberties of the People, are become the Instruments of Tyranny. Whilst the principal Powers engaged in the late Wars. enjoy the Blessings of Peace, and are attentive to discharge their Debts and ease their People, *Great Britain*, in the midst of Peace, feels all the Load of a War; New Debts are contracted, new Armies are raised at Home, *Dutch* Forces are brought into these Kingdoms; And by taking Possession of the Dutchy of *Bremen*, in Violation of the Publick Faith, a Door is opened by the Usurper to let in an Inundation of Foreigners from Abroad, and to reduce these Nations to the State of a Province to one of the most inconsiderable Provinces of the Empire.

5. These are some few of the many real Evils, into which these Kingdoms have been betrayed, under Pretence of being Rescued and Secured from Dangers purely imaginary; And these are such Consequences of abandoning the Old Constitution, as We perswade Ourselves, very many of those, who promoted the present Unjust and Illegal Settlement, never intended.

6. We observe with the utmost Satisfaction, That the Generality of Our Subjects are awakened with a just Sense of their Danger, and that they show themselves disposed to take such Measures as may effectually rescue them from that Bondage, which has, by the Artifice of a few Designing Men, and by the Concurrence of many unhappy Causes, been brought upon them.

7. We Adore the Wisdom of the Divine Providence, which has opened a Way to Our Restoration, by the Success of those very Measures that were laid to disappoint Us for ever. And We most earnestly Conjure all Our loving Subjects, not to suffer that Spirit to faint or die away, which has been so miraculously rais'd in all Parts of the Kingdom; but to pursue, with all the Vigour and Hopes of Success which so just and righteous a Cause ought to inspire those Methods, which the Finger of God seems to point out to them.

8. We are come to take Our Part in all the Dangers and Difficulties to which any of Our Subjects, from the greatest down to the meanest, may be exposed on this important Occasion, to relieve Our Subjects of *Scotland* from the Hardships they groan under, on Account of the late unhappy Union; and to restore the Kingdom to its Antient, Free, and Independent State.

9. We have before Our Eyes, the Example of Our Royal Grandfather, who fell a Sacrifice to Rebellion; and of Our Royal Uncle, who, by a Train of Miracles, escaped the Rage of the barbarous and blood-thirsty Rebels, and lived to exercise His Clemency towards those who had waged War against His Father and Himself; who had driven him to seek Shelter in Foreign Lands, and who had even set a Price upon His Head.

10. We see the same Instances of Cruelty renewed against Us by Men of the same Principles, without any other Reason than the Consciousness of their own Guilt, and the implacable Malice of their own Hearts: For in the Account of such Men, it is Crime sufficient to be born their King. But God forbid that we should tread in these Steps, or that the Cause of a Lawful Prince and an injur'd People should be carried on like that of Usurpation and Tyranny, and we owe its Support to Assassins. We shall Copy after the Patterns above-mentioned, and be ready, with the Former of Our Royal Ancestors, to Seal the Cause of Our Country, if such be the Will of Heaven, with Our Blood: But we hope for better Things: We hope, with the Latter, to see Our just Rights, and those of the Church and People of *Scotland*, once more settled, in a Free Independent *Scots* Parliament, on their ancient Foundation: To such a Parliament [which We will immediately Call] shall We entirely refer

both Our and their Interests; being sensible that these Interests, rightly understood, are always the same: Let the Civil as well as Religious Rights of all Our Subjects Receive their Confirmation in such a Parliament; Let Consciences truly tender be indulged; Let Property of every Kind be better than ever secured; Let an Act of General Grace and Amnesty extinguish the Fears even of the most Guilty: If possible, Let the very Remembrance of all which have preceded this happy Moment be utterly blotted out, that Our Subjects may be united to Us, and to each other, in the strictest Bonds of Affection, as well as Interest.

11. And that nothing may be omitted which is in Our Power to Contribute to this desirable End, We do, by these Presents, absolutely and effectually, for Us, Our Heirs and Successors, Pardon, Remit, and Discharge all Crimes of High Treason, Misprision of Treason, and all other Crimes and Offences whatsoever, done or committed against Us, or Our Royal Father, of Blessed Memory, by any of Our Subjects, of what Degree or Quality soever, who shall, at, or after Our Landing, and before they engage in any Action against Us, or Our Forces from that Time, lay hold of Mercy, and return to that Duty and Allegiance which they owe to Us, their only Rightful and Lawful Sovereign.

By the joint Endeavours of Us and of Our Parliament, urged by these Motives, and directed to these Views, We may hope to see the Peace and flourishing Estate of this Kingdom in a short Time restored; and We shall be equally forward to concert with Our Parliament such further Measures, as may be thought necessary for leaving the same to future Generations.

And We hereby Require all Sheriffs of Shires, Stewarts of Stewartries, or their Deputies, and Magistrates of Burghs, to Publish this Our Declaration, immediately after it shall come to their Hands, in the usual Places and Manner, under Pain of being proceeded against for Failure thereof; and forfeiting the Benefit of Our General Pardon. Given under Our Sign Manual and Privy Signet, at our Court at *Commercy* the 25th Day of *October*, and in the Fifteenth Year of Our Reign.

ANSWER.

1. WHEREAS, our Forefathers, for the many and intolerable Acts of Tyranny committed by the late King *James* II. against the Churches and States of *England* and *Scotland*, now United into the Kingdom of *Great-Britain*, did, in full Parliament, after the Flight of his said Majesty, pronounce the said King *James* to have Abdicated, and Forefaulted the Empire of the said Kingdoms; and for the Safety of themselves and us their Posterity, placed in the said Thrones, *William* III. of Glorious Memory; which said King *William*, was succeeded by the late Queen *Anne*, under the same Title. And whereas, the Pretender to these Dominions has by an open Declaration set forth, That the said Queen had been seduced from the maternal Care and Protection of her People, which she had in the most solemn manner undertaken as our Queen and Sovereign Lady, to enter into Measures for favouring his, the said Pretender's Succession to these Thrones. We, the Free Subject of *Great-Britain*, do, with utter Abhorrence of such a Design, ascribed to a Princess who had Reigned many Years over us in Justice, Mercy and Glory, surpassing any of Her Predecessors, declare, That we receiving with the utmost Horrour the imputation of so cruel, monstrous and unnatural a Crime against a People, as Treason in the Throne of their Prince, Do, for the Honour of Humane Nature itself, as well as Regard to our own Rights and Liberties, turn away from such an Insinuation, but call all the Assistances with which we are blessed by the Light of our Religion, the Justice of our Laws, and the Possession of our Properties, to awaken a just Resentment against all those, who, by base Arts and Insinuations into our Late Sovereign's Favour and Councils, acted in direct Opposition to the Interests of Her their Queen, and us their Fellow Subjects, and gave Colour for this horrid Infamy cast upon the *British* Name by this Insolent Invader.

2. And since the said Pretender, at this Time openly avowing, that in Concert with Persons late in the Administration of this Kingdom, (for we will not impute ought to our Sovereign even Deceased) he was disappointed of a favourable Conjuncture

to throw himself upon us his People; having hitherto stood in suspense, and therefore not till now called us to his Obedience; we do with the highest disdain, abjure, disclaim, and contemn this groundless Allegation of Right: But in Consideration of many who may have been misled by wicked Favourers of the said Pretender, by Persons whose Character and Stations in Church and State require them to inculcate nothing contrary to Justice and Truth, and who, by that Authority gradually insinuated into the People Principles which naturally tended to revive such a Title as is now set up against all that is Sacred and Valuable amongst us: In tender Regard to our weak Brethren so insnared, we take the Patience to consider the Assertions of the Pretender, and set over against them Facts and Arguments, by which we confirm our own Minds, and endeavour to recall those of our wavering and mistaken Fellow Subjects. The Assertion of an undoubted Title, without Arguments for it, is a Reason to believe he is Conscious that 'tis doubtful, hid under the Disguise of its being taken for granted; his Pretence is, that he is Son of King *James*; if he were such, it does not follow that a Son is necessarily Heir to his Father. In many Nations the Eldest Son is not Heir to his Father's Estate, and no Man ever thought this a Breach of the Law of God; much less is it a Law of God to make a Man Successor to his Father's Office; and, to be a King, is to bear the highest Office in Humane Society. A Succession from Father to Son has been preserved from many Generations in no Country of the Universe. The Exigencies of respective Times and Places have not admitted it: Had such a Succession been unalterable, the Family, of which the Pretender boasts himself, had never ascended Our Throne. It was the Law of this Kingdom before, as well as since the Revolution, that the Limitation of the Crown is in the Parliament. According then, to Laws of our Country, we have sworn inviolable Allegiance to *George*, Our Sovereign Lord and King, the next capable Heir to the Throne of these Kingdoms; who governs us with Justice and Equity, and supports us by Our Laws, and preserves us in the possession of our Religion, against a Pretender, who is bred a Stranger and an Enemy both to our Constitution and our Faith; even they who disown the King's Government enjoy the Protection of it free from Hardship.

3, 4. The Reins of Government are put in the Hands of Ministers, who, by their Actions, Eloquence or Council, have strenuously oppos'd the Abuse of the late Authority of this Kingdom, exercised by wicked Men, who abused her late Majesty's Power when living, as they do her Name now dead, to give Sanction to their Iniquities. The Chief Officers, Civil and Military, in that fatal Distribution of Power, are either fled, in Arms, or in Custody for their Services to the Enemy of that Power and that Settlement to which they were sworn Servants. Our Sovereign has obtained (since his Accession) from his own Coffers, not by the Expence of our Blood, or that of the Subject of any other his Nations, new Dutchies, new Territories: We love, honour and obey him, not only as the most Gracious Sovereign, but also the most Powerful Ally of *Great-Britain.* We see new Armies raising, new Debts contracting, but we see it with Pleasure, since they both serve to support our King, and oppose the *Pretender* to his Dominions.

5. *These are some few of the many real Evils into which these Kingdoms were betray'd.* Such were the Dangers which our Forefathers did not think *imaginary*; Let us then recite the Reasons for which, according to the old Constitution, they made a new Legal Settlement; which Evils, we suppose, many of our Fellow Subjects have forgotten, or they would not at this Day of Peril be indifferent to the said Legal Settlement, when they put King *William* and Queen *Mary* into the Throne, which they said in the Act of Parliament for that Purpose, He had abdicated, by exercising a Power of dispensing with, and suspending Laws; by Committing and Prosecuting divers Prelates for petitioning against the said Power; by issuing, and causing to be executed, a Commission, called, *A Court of Commissioners for Ecclesiastical Causes*, by levying Money for the use of the Crown in other manner than was granted by Parliament; by keeping a Standing Army in this Kingdom in Time of Peace without Consent of Parliament, and Quartering Soldiers contrary to Law; by causing Protestant Subjects to be disarm'd, while Papists were Armed and Employed contrary to Law; by violating the Freedom of Election of Members to serve in Parliament. We perswade Our selves very many of those who promote the Repetition of the abovemention'd Calamities,

27

by their cool and indifferent Behaviour have forgot their Country was ever before exposed to them.

6. We observe, with the utmost Satisfaction, that the Generality of our Fellow-Subjects are awaken'd with a just Sence of imminent Danger, which they have escaped at a Conjuncture, wherein, after the Death of our Queen, the late *French* King had meditated to depute and impose a *Popish Tyrant* upon these Protestant Nations; and we have seen our abandoned Countrymen engaged in the Design.

7, 8. We thank and adore the Wisdom of the Divine Providence, which, by an Union of *England* and *Scotland*, makes the Protection and Care of the whole Island, at this Instant of Difficulty, less subject to Delays and Distractions. We observe, with Joy, the Enemy calls it an *Unhappy Union*: We slight the Rage which so terms it, without assigning an Instance wherein it is so; and rejoyce that he finds it, as he calls it, *Unhappy* to himself. We detest the Endeavours to dis-unite us, and think any one unworthy of the Blessing of being a Native of either Part of *Great-Britain*, who makes a Distinction in his good Will, from a Consideration of Birth in the *Northern* or *Southern* Parts of it. It is an Union of Protestants and Fellow-Subjects, fighting for their Civil and Religious Liberties: An Union that, we trust, will be ever hateful and terrible to the Friends of Slavery and Popery.

9. We remember, with Horror, the Rebellion which ended in the Murder of our Sovereign Lord *Charles* I. who fell a Sacrifice against the known Rule, which makes Ministers answerable for the Male-Administration of the State, and renders Princes, in their own Persons, sacred and inviolable. We detest also the Memory of that Rebellion from the Sufferings and Exile of our Sovereign Lord *Charles* II.—*We remember in him the Restoration of the Royal Family, after an Usurpation; as we do in King* William *the Restoration of the Constitution after a Tyranny.*

10. Lest we should see the Returns of such Tyrannies and Usurpations, we are to consider the Justice of our Cause. Law and Equity, are to contend against Invasion and Rapine; Honest and Faithful Subjects against Rebels and Assassins. Our Cap-

tains who have fought for the Cause of Liberty in foreign Nations, against Lawless Power, conduct our Armies in the Cause of Religion, against the Leaders of rude Multitudes, who have fled from our Altars and Sacraments, and in Violation of the Oaths there made, are endeavouring to cover their Native Country, with the Carnage and Bloodshed of their Friends, Relations, Fellow-Citizens and Brethren. We promise ourselves the Success due to so glorious a Cause, and presume upon the Iniquities more than the inferior Force of our Enemies. We abhor the ambiguous Term of the Church of *Scotland*; if the *Roman Catholick* Religion is meant, it is prevarication not to say so; if the Protestant Church, we know the *Pretender* bound in Conscience to destroy it: And, if he should do a prudential Act in her Favour, he would be oblig'd to rescind it. As to the Confirmation of Civil Rights, we have, before our Eyes, the Example of King *James* II. who, in Two Acts of Parliament in *Ireland*, destroy'd the whole Protestant Settlement, subjecting Old Age and Childhood, without Regard to their necessary Impotence to offend, to the Pains and Penalties inflicted by the Act of a Superstitious *Tyrant*, and his Mercenary Slaves, under the Name of a *Free Parliament*.

11. In Defiance therefore of an Outlaw, devoted for past Treasons with a Price on his Head, educated in Superstitious Hatred to our Religion, and urg'd by Revenge against Our Persons and Principles, and in Contempt of all his Abettors both publick and private, we will not suffer the *British* Spirit to faint and die away; but resolve, in Defence of Our King and Our Country, in the joint Cause of Heaven and Earth, to avenge us of our Enemies like Ministring Angels, or fall by their Hands like an Army of Martyrs.

A Letter to a Member &c concerning the Condemn'd Lords (March, 1716)

This tract is addressed to the Speaker of the House, the Honorable Spencer Compton, afterwards Earl of Wilmington, whose acquaintance with Steele was formed as early as 1709 in his capacity as Treasurer to the Prince of Denmark and Paymaster to Her Majesty's Pensioners. The occasion for it was an article criticizing Steele and other members for their opposition to the Ministry's prosecution of the rebel lords, leaders in the late rising. This offending article had appeared in a government organ, *The St. James's Post* of 2 March, and Steele assumed it to have been written at the instigation of the Ministry, even Walpole, himself, now First Lord of the Treasury and Chancellor of the Exchequer. Within a disguise of Polish names and places—Steele is called Cavaliero Risko Chalybeski—those who had advocated leniency, including Steele, are accused of having taken bribes from the Jacobite enemy. In this indignant reply made a few days later, Steele hints that he has grounds for a libel suit.

For several weeks the atmosphere had been tense. Seven Scottish and English rebel lords were impeached and tried in January; on 9th February they were sentenced to death; and on the 24th two were executed on Tower Hill—the Earl of Derwentwater and Viscount Kenmure. There had been a great outcry in both houses for reprieve, and during the month Steele seems to have exerted what pressure he could for mercy. On the 13th February the Countess of Derwentwater (Dorawotzki) had petitioned the king in person. On the 22nd Steele, among others, had presented petitions for friends of the prisoners and made a speech on their behalf. The opposition of both houses to Walpole's policy of severity had made it difficult for the Government to carry its measures; and punishment and purging were in order. For example, Nottingham, the veteran Tory, who had moved in the Lords the Address to the King for clemency, was soon relieved of his post as Lord President of the Council. Steele, who had seconded the move in the Commons and acted throughout as an opposition Whig, would inevitably suffer chastisement. His opposition was the more conspicuous because the Tory, William Shippen, supported him.

In the tract Steele reviews his position—which did appear inconsistent. No one had been more zealous than he while these men were " Authors and Leaders of the Rebellion " to track them down. But now when they are " Leaders of the Submission," he thinks the advantages of their submission should be wisely utilized. They had thrown themselves on the mercy of the King; and impeachment (unsuited, anyway, he believes, to this particular crime) had " hurt the Prerogative in its most amiable Instance, that of Forgiveness, and robb'd the Subject of the most valuable Effect of it, the receiving that Forgiveness." In this case the principle at stake, as he sees it, is the prerogative of the King rather than the rights and powers of parliament. And mercy, shown by both King and parliament, he believes, would be the most effective weapon against the King's enemies. Walpole was supported by Stanhope, Lechmere, and Boscawen (Walpeski, Stanoski, Lescamerino, Boscalli).

Indeed more than once in his political career Steele took his stand against ruthless punishment. In the Preface to the collected *Englishman* (2nd series) published about this time in the spring of 1716, he says, apropos the Tory leaders impeached in 1715, that it is no matter to him " whether they are ever punished for what they have done, according to their Deserts," since their infamy has been established. And apropos the rebel lords and his apparently inconsistent behavior, he makes a picturesque statement worth quoting:

. . . his Heart failed against submissive Criminals, though He has appeared determinate against Triumphant Wickedness. It ordinarily happens that the same Men who make an Attack very bravely upon Troops in good Order, do least Execution upon them, when they are put to Flight or ask Quarter. But I never heard it said that they were the less Zealous for the Cause, or that they were held Deserters from the Service, because they have been over-run, in pursuing a Defeat, by their Friends who were in the Rear at the Onset.

A Forfeited Estates Bill was an aftermath of the impeachment and attainder proceedings; and early in June Steele was elected by the Commons to the Commission for Forfeitures in Scotland, a post for which his conciliatory bearing might be a desirable qualification. This post, which took him to Scotland several times, he held until about 1722. Textual notes on p. 645.

A
LETTER

TO A

MEMBER, &c.

CONCERNING THE

Condemn'd Lords,

I N

Vindication of Gentlemen Calumniated in the St. *James's Post*
of Friday *March* the 2d.

LONDON,

Printed : And Sold by J. ROBERTS, near the *Oxford-Arms*
in *Warwick-Lane* ; J. GRAVES in St. *James's-Street* ;
and A. DODD, at the *Peacock* without *Temple-Bar.*

[Price THREE PENCE,]

A
LETTER
TO A
MEMBER, &c.

SIR,

I Presume to make this Address to you in Vindication of an Assembly, who, however they differ in other Particulars, agree in the most profound Respect for you: For which Reason, as well as that you preside in it, and are the Representative of it, I lay before you the insolent Treatment received without Doors from the *St. James's Post*, which was published on the 2d Instant. The Matter therein contained is of so nice a Nature, that I dare not, tho' a Person more immediately concerned, go into the Examination of it, except you will have the Good Nature to allow me a small Postulatum which this Author has taken, to wit, that we are now in *Poland*; for all the Disguise he puts on is, to date *Sendomir* instead of the Place in which we imagined our selves to have been in, at the Time the Things he talks of were transacted.

You are used to the Method of commending a Man's self at the Beginning of what he has to say, and therefore will not be surprized that in the Entrance of this Epistle I profess that I have long devoted my self to the Service of my Country, and am very much unconcerned at what possibly can be said of me, but as it may impair the little Ability I have to do that Service: And therefore, as I am in the most licentious Manner represented as a Malecontent, waging War with Men in Authority, and brib'd to defend our Enemies, I am oblig'd to stop, as well as I can, the Course of so malicious a Scandal. I beg of you again to remember we are in *Poland*, and with that Allowance admit me to say, I gave up, both in my Opinion and Discourse, the Condemn'd Persons, as Authors and Leaders of

407

the Rebellion, and consider'd 'em only as Leaders of the Submission, which is all I pretended to urge in their Behalf: But that the Advantage of this Submission shou'd be carry'd as far as it cou'd go, I thought it highly concern'd the Honour of His Majesty, and the Dignity of His Government.

"The Prisoners submitted to the King, at that Time undoubtedly capable of shewing them Mercy: When they were in Custody of the Government, they were Impeach'd by our Assembly: As no one ever imagin'd that Men, in their Circumstances, were the natural Objects of Impeachments, or such as were intended by the famous Act in that Behalf, so there was no Reason, but the Necessity of Affairs, which could move the House to take the Prosecution out of its ordinary Course: Now that Necessity is over, I thought it for the Honour of the King, that the Criminals should be capable of that Mercy to which they submitted; Otherwise our Enemies would have it to say, that the Prisoners were brought into their present Circumstances by an Artifice: Out of Hopes of the King's Mercy they submitted; but the Interposition of the Legislature made them incapable of that Mercy; so that this Circumstance of the Impeachment hurt the Prerogative in its most amiable Instance, that of Forgiveness, and robb'd the Subject of the most valuable Effect of it, the receiving that Forgiveness.——

"When the Enemy was put to Flight, and all those Reasons ceas'd, which induc'd the Legislature, for the common Safety, to make this Step, which so much concern'd the Prerogative of the Prince, and Liberty of the Subject, I thought it my Duty, in Regard to the highest and meanest of Mankind, to act as I did.

"These, Sir, were my true Motives for desiring, that something might be done to extricate unhappy Men who had nothing to plead, in Stay of Execution, but Submission and Acknowledgement of their Guilt. As inconsiderable as that Plea was, it was necessary and just that it should be made before a Power capable of admitting or rejecting it; till this was done, had the Prisoners more to offer, to merit the Favour of their King and Country, they could promise themselves no good Effect for that Service, since, according to some Men's Apprehension, there was no Power in being legally capable of rewarding it with

Mercy—This I thought an Interruption of Government itself: It is for these Thoughts, and these Sentiments, that I am publickly Calumniated, and suffer the same Usage for defending the Honour of the King and His Government, now he is on the Throne, as I did for doing my Part towards securing his Accession to it.——I have not enter'd into the Question, Whether the Prisoners are Objects of Mercy, or not: I have contended only, That, if they were, or should become Objects of Mercy, the King might have it in his Power, as well as I am sure it is in his Inclination, to bestow it, when deserv'd.

" It would have been an endless Reproach to have had such an Imperfection appear'd in our Government, As that there was an Instant wherein the Power of Punishing or Pardoning, for the Good of the Whole, was lodged no where; As the Thing stood in common Acceptation, The whole State was under a Difficulty and Incapacity of Action, as it should think fit for its own Good and Safety; and it was every Gentleman's Duty to observe and propose what he apprehended was for its Service in that Perplexity.

" But the Matter, from the Discussion of it among *Patricians* and *Plebeians*, has taken another Turn; and we have seen *Punishment and the Suspension of it*, upon the Condemned Lords, in this Exigence of Affairs, exerted by that Power, in which it was always lodg'd by the Constitution of the Realm; and whatever may be the future Construction of an Article in a certain Act, I am humbly of Opinion, That, in the present Conjuncture, if the Ministers see Cause, they may be well justified by their Care of the Whole, in advising the King to do what he shall think proper with the Prisoners.

" All that I aim'd at is come to pass; they now stand before a Power disposed to receive and reward their future Merit and past Submission: And I am so far from repenting the Part I had in this Affair, that I should have been a more unhappy Man, if I had done otherwise; for I should have had the secret Reproach in my own Bosom, That, for Fear of being mistaken by the Powerful, I had neglected my Duty to the Miserable.

" This, Sir, is the Sum of what I had to say, in order to state my Behaviour before my Countrymen, in a clear View; and whether what I have offered, had Weight in it or not, as to the

Matter then before us, it shows another Motive than that to
which my Behaviour is imputed in the News-Paper. Have your
usual Patience, and permit me to go on."

The *St. James's-Post* speaking of the *Six Condemn'd Nobles,*
and intimating that, *by distributing large Bribes to several Members, their Petitions were receiv'd both by the* Patricians *and*
Plebeians, goes on upon me in these Words: *Among the Latter,
a Doughty Knight, call'd* Cavaliero Risko Chalybeski, *who over-
rating his past Services to the* Saxon *Cause, has taken a Disgust
against the present Ministry, for not gratifying his craving
Ambition, made a Speech in Behalf of the Petitioners, and
exhausted the common Topicks of Clemency and Mercy: But
the Reputation this Gentleman had formerly gain'd by his Writings, being at a very low Ebb, not only because he had of late
made his Pen a common Prostitute, but also by Reason of his
own private Extravagances, at the same Time that he assumed
to himself the Character of a Publick Censor, no great Stress
was laid upon his Thredbare Oratory. On the other Hand,
Monsieur* Walpeski *rightly judging, that the new Friends the
condemn'd Lords appear'd to have in that Assembly, were procured by the same Methods which had been ineffectual with
himself, rose up and said*: " He was moved with Indignation,
to see that there should be such unworthy Members of that
great Body, who could, without Blushing, open their Mouths
in Favour of Rebels and Parricides, who, far from making the
least Advance towards deserving Favour, by an ingenious Discovery of the bottom of the present horrid Conspiracy, had rather
aggravated their Guilt, both by their sullen Silence, and pre-
varicating Answers: *Adding,* That the Count *Dorawotzki* pretended and affirmed, *That he went unprepared and unawares
into this Rebellion,* yet, to his certain Knowledge, he had been
tampering with several People, to persuade them to rise in
Favour of *Stanislaus,* Six Months before he appear'd in Arms."

Monsieur Walpeski *was seconded and backed by Seignior*
Boscalli, *Seignior* Lescamerino, *and General* Stanoski: *The last
said, among other Things,* " Twas with the most sensible Concern he observed, That the Rebels were grown more formidable,
since they were taken and disarmed at *Prestopoli,* than they
were before; for, it seems, they had gained Advocates even

among their Prosecutors, and they had found Means to divide an Assembly, which, hitherto, had acted with unparallelled Unanimity and Vigour for the Publick Welfare."

It is possible my Frankness in writing for a Cause, wherein they who should support me, traduce and villify my Endeavours, may make Disregard to my own Fame for the Sake of my Country, appear to the Vulgar, Prostitution. But if I have made my self Cheap, I am sure I have not made my self Mercenary: If I were so, I should desire no greater Reward than the Liberty for one Year, which the Post has taken for this Day. Give me but Leave to be at *Sendomir* when I please, without being called to an Account for what I say, in *Middlesex*, and it will soon appear whose *Oratory is most Threadbare*; that of those who have long used it, or those who have just began the Practice of it: Such an Indulgence would be an ample Fortune; and the Field is large enough to bring a Crop worth the Labour of the Husbandman: It would soon appear how much of a Man's Eloquence was owing to his Station or his Fortune, and how many Orators there are who think themselves well heard, while they owe their being uninterrupted to the Patience, not the Respect of their Hearers: It would appear that the Present State of Eloquence in *Poland* is at a very low Ebb, and that Warming the House is only Disturbing it: Orators would learn that it does not follow, that because they are in a Passion, other People must be so too: Tho' it is finely said by a Great Master, that *if you would have me weep, you must your self be in Grief*—— That will not do of other Passions, and particularly, it would be unfortunate to be angry, to make others fight for you.

Such a Licence would enable a Man to show empty Creatures, that all their Noise is owing to that Emptiness, and a little Admonition might rouse Men of Sense and Modesty to come into Debates, and exert their Reason in Defence of their Country. For certain it is, that in *Poland*, at this time, the Men of the best Sense are Dumb, and the shallowest Persons in the Assembly are most Talkative. Some are Silent from an Oppression under the Choice of a great Deal to say, and others are Eloquent from an Ignorance that what they say is nothing to the Purpose.

I am glad the *Post* has done so much Justice to the Honourable Persons he mentions in the recited Paragraph: I shall not quarrel with him for a great Opinion of Mens Abilities, whom I have endeavoured to celebrate before him; which I should have done perhaps as fortunately as he, if I had had so good Intelligence; for I acknowledge the best Way of applauding so great Orators, is to repeat their very Words. As to what he says of the Under Treasurer, I congratulate the fair Occasion that Great Officer took to refute the false Imputation of Corruption, against which I had always defended him: But I can say at the same time, that no one affronted me so much as with the Attempt to bribe me.

This News-Writer makes no Difficulty of accusing a Number of the Diet (which he acknowledges to be by Seven only less than all the rest of the Assembly) of being Enemies to the *Saxon* Line, of being bribed for their Votes, or being Followers of such as were. You know best what is to be done on such an Occasion; and if so slight an Artifice, as Altering the Scene by a Date of Place and Time, shall shelter a Man in Belying Men of Honour, who are doing their Duty in as nice a Circumstance as perhaps has ever happened, it will be impossible for those who do not comply with the Fashion, right or wrong, to be able to show their Faces, in their several Countries. As for me, I have frequently declared, That I take all Merit to consist in the Regulation of the Will; and I will not trouble my self so much as to mention what is said of me as a Writer at low Ebb, and the like. Whoever writes must be liable to whatever any Reader thinks fit to say of him; But the Case is alter'd when it comes to Facts within the Power of the Will, as in Matters of Justice and Integrity. It is not for me to say how I write, or speak; but it is for me to say, I do both honestly; and when I threw away some Fame for Letters and Politeness, to serve the nobler Ends of Justice and Government, I did not do it with a Design to be as negligent of what should be said of me, with relation to my Integrity in Support of those Ends. No; Wit and Humour are the Dress and Ornament of the Mind; but Honesty and Truth are the Soul it self, and the Difference in a Man's Care of his Reputation for one and the other is just in the Proportion that being Robb'd bears to being Murder'd.

I forbear saying any thing in Resentment against the Author

himself of this Paper, because I think he has heretofore pointed at me in a kind Way; but this Instance gives a strong Suspicion, that the present Licence he takes, is supported in some extraordinary Manner; and I humbly conceive, that for the Honour of Society, you will put us in some way to obviate this first Instance of Outrage in this kind, by making the Printer produce the Author, and the Author his Correspondent, or answer it himself. I presume, Sir, this is more particularly your Charge, because indeed the Offence is more immediately against you, than any other Person: The Paper takes upon it to give an Account of what passes in our House, which is the highest Offence without your Authority, and consequently a Trespass against your Authority.

There are those every Day in your Eye, who have no further Views than doing their Duty in the Place where they stand before you. They know it their Duty without Vanity, Discontent, or Peevishness, in all that is for the Common Good, to support those who have the Honour to serve their Country in Great Stations: But as they are always inclined to act in Concert with them, they are always free to act in Opposition to them. But, Honoured Sir, I beg of you to consider whether this equal Disposition is, possibly, to be maintained, if Men, who have no Hopes of Self-interest in their Actions, must meet with such cruel and false Representations from Writers, who attempt to recommend themselves to Persons in Authority, by Villifying Gentlemen who think it a Misfortune ever to differ from those very Men in Authority, whoever they are or shall be. Sir, Your great good Breeding and Civility in your Private Character, Your Justice and Equanimity in your Publick Station, will suggest much more to you than I can offer in Resentment of this Outrage. It would be an happy Day for your Country if there were more Men like you in great Employments, who can possess what they have with the same Air that they had when they were aiming at it, who can be composed enough to think of every Part of the Duty of their Stations in Preference to the Article of its Income, and acquit themselves to all the World before they think there is any thing due to themselves. This, Sir, I know by long Experience, to be your Temper and Mode of Action; and this will transmit you to Posterity with Honour and Reputation, with much greater Advantage than you could reap from the Distinction of your Birth, and the Superiority of your Understanding without this Moderation. You possess the greatest Station that your Country could bestow upon you; and when that ceases, I am so good a Patriot as to wish you the greatest that can be bestowed by your Prince.

But though I am interrupted with the strong Inclination I have to do Justice to you, you must not think I have done by having expressed Civilities towards the Gentleman I was writing to, as if I was at the End of my Letter; for I am called a doughty Knight, and must take Notice, according to the known Obligations of that Order, that *distressed Ladies* are as little spared as unhappy Men by this lawless Writer; The Errors in the Youth of some, and the Vertue and Complacency of others, are equally the Subject of his insipid Scurrility. I have only just mention'd this Circumstance to move your Indignation; but must lay before you a higher Offence, in a graver Tone, when I show you, that the Paper has assumed a Liberty of determining this Question on the Side of the *Pacta Conventa*, as he calls us according to his Gibberish, notwithstanding that the present Practice of those whom he commends is against that Notion. Speaking of the Sorrow of *Dorowatski*, he presumes to say as follows: " The King, who is the best natur'd Prince in the Universe, was touch'd with so moving a Sight, very kindly bid her rise, and said, *He was concern'd for her just Affliction*: But afterwards let her understand, That the *Pacta Conventa,* by which His Majesty was call'd to the Succession, was an *Invincible Bar* to his *natural Clemency*; and that the *Diet* having made this PROSECUTION their own, His Majesty did not think it proper for him to interpose in so nice an Affair; which he could not do neither, without shaking the very *Foundation* of his *Title* to the Crown."

There must be a Way found, if we would preserve any Thing that is valuable, to put an end to this Mixture of Arrogance, Indiscretion, and Ignorance. There is not much more in the Letter, except Personal and Domestick Reflections on me, which I have not observed to you, without it were worth while to take Notice, that he says I exhausted upon the Occasion the *common Topicks of Clemency and Mercy*; which last Assertion I deny with all my Might; for I never talked of Mercy and Clemency, but for the Sake of my King and Country, in whose Behalf I dare to say, That to be afraid to forgive, is as low as to be afraid to punish; and that all noble Geniuses in the Art of Government have less owed their Safety to Punishment and Terror, than Grace and Magnanimity. I will trouble you no further; I am satisfied as to myself with this Remonstrance, and doubt not but every Gentleman of those who inclined one Way, had as good Arguments against the Imputation of an unmanly Softness, as those disposed another had against that of an inhuman Cruelty. I have no Authority to adventure the Injury I may do them in the Repetition of what they offered, but submit what concerns them, as well as the Honour of our whole Proceedings, to your much wiser Consideration.

> *I am,*
>
> *S I R,*
>
> > *Your Sincere Admirer, and*
> >
> > *Devoted Humble Servant.*

Sir Richard Steele's Speech for Repealing of the Triennial Act (April, 1716)

Steele supported the party on the Septennial Bill, which was introduced early in April and became a law on 7 May 1716. Under the Triennial Act of 1694, the existing parliament would be soon dissolved and a general election held early in 1718. The Septennial Bill proposed to extend this and subsequent parliaments from three to seven years. Such a measure, the Whig government maintained, would stabilize domestic conditions, which were still disturbed by Jacobite threats, and benefit foreign affairs by ensuring continuity which could be trusted abroad. It would not only meet a temporary need but would eventually strengthen the independence and authority of the Commons. Opponents of the Bill regarded it as unconstitutional: as illegal for members elected for three years only to vote themselves in for a longer period. They denounced it as a purely political and a corrupt measure designed to perpetuate Whig supremacy.

At first Steele seems to have been among the opponents. As there had recently been friction between him and the party leaders on the question of punishing the rebel lords, he was in a mood of asserting his freedom to vote against party leaders and to dissent in opinion from his friends. A draft manuscript is extant of an article begun (never printed?) by Steele as a rejoinder to one of the *Freeholders* (No. 25, on 17th March), in which Addison advocated the Septennial measure. This "one change more" to the constitution Steele feared would be a play into the hands of its enemies (The substance of the article is given by Aitken, *Life*, II, 82-3). His opinion, however, was altered in the course of the debate.

He argues in his speech that the seven-year plan will be more efficient; that under the three-year plan little can be accomplished. The work of the first year is impeded by recriminations following the election; of the second, by the spirit of contradicting the preceding parliament; of the third, by apprehension of the coming election. To those who feared the changing of the constitution, he answered that laws must be altered as well as safe-guarded if public good is to be served. To those who feared arbitrary power of the Ministry, he answered that they will continue to be responsible to parliament for their actions. The law proved useful and was in effect until 1911. Since February, 1715, Steele had been a member for Boroughbridge, Yorkshire. Textual note on p. 645.

Sir Richard Steel's Speech for Repealing of the Triennial Act and His Reasons for the Septennial Bill as it was Spoken in the House of Commons.

SIR,

After the very material Quotation which that Gentleman [a] in the Gallery has produced, it is evident that new chosen Annual Parliaments were never the Custom or Right of this Kingdom: It remains therefore only to consider, (that now there is a Law, which makes Parliaments meet, as of Course, at such a Stated Time) whether the Period of Three Years answer'd the Purposes intended by it? The Preamble to the Triennial Act expresses, that it was introduc'd into the Constitution for the better *Union and Agreement of the King and his People*; but it has had a quite contrary Effect; and Experience has verified, what a Wise Man [b] said of it when it was enacted, *That it had made a Triennial King, a Triennial Ministry, a Triennial Alliance.* We feel this in all Occurrences of State; And they who look upon us from Abroad behold the Struggle in which we are necessarily engag'd from Time to Time under this Law. Ever since it has been enacted, the Nation has been in a Series of Contention: The first Year of a Triennial Parliament has been spent in vindictive Decisions and Animosities about the late Elections; the Second Session has enter'd into Business, but rather with a Spirit of Contradiction to what the prevailing Set of Men in former Parliaments had brought to pass, than of a disinterested Zeal for the Common Good; the Third Session languished in the Pursuit of what little was intended to be done in the Second; and the Approach of an ensuing Election terrified the Members into a Servile Management, according as their respective Principles were disposed towards the Question before them in the House. Thus the State of *England* has been like that of a Vessel in Distress at Sea: The Pilot and Mariners have been wholly employ'd in keeping the the Ship from Sinking: The Art of Navigation was useless; and

[a] Mr. Craggs, Jun. [the annalist's note].
[b] The late E. of Sunderland [the annalist's note].

they never pretended to make Sail. It is objected, *that the Alteration propos'd is a Breach of Trust*: The Trust, Sir, repos'd in us, is that of the Publick Good; the King, Lords, and Commons are the Parties who exercise this Trust, and when the King, Lords, and Commons exercise this Trust, by the Measure of the Common Good, they discharge themselves as well in the altering and repealing as in the making or confirming Laws. The Period of Time, in this Case, is a subordinate Consideration; and those Gentlemen who are against the Alteration, speak in too pompous a Stile, when they tell us *We are breaking into the Constitution.* It has been further objected, that all this is only giving great Power to the *Ministers, who may make an Arbitrary Use of it*: The Ministers are indeed, like other Men, from the Infirmity of Humane Nature, liable to be made worse by Power and Authority; But this Act gives no addition to that Authority it self, tho' it may, possibly, prolong the Exercise of it in them. They are nevertheless responsible for their Actions to a Parliament: and the Mode of Enjoyning their Offices is exactly the same. Now when the Thing is thus, and that the Period of Three Years is found, from infallible Experience it self, a Period that can afford us no Good, where shall we rest? The Ills that are to be done against Single Persons or Communities are done by Surprize, and on a Sudden; but good things are slow in their Progress and must wait Occasion: Destruction is done with a Blow; But Reformation is brought about by leisurely Advances. All the Mischiefs which can be wrought under the Septennial Act, can be perpetrated under the Triennial; but all the Good which may be compassed under the Septennial, cannot be hoped for under the Triennial. We may fear that the Ministers may do us Harm, but that is no Reason why we should continue them under a Disability of doing us good. For these Considerations, I am unreservedly for the Bill.[1]

An Account of the Fish Pool (November, 1718)

Steele well knew that he was including himself when he spoke of
"Men of undertaking Complexions." Of his many undertakings—
journalistic, financial, theatrical—none was more characteristic or conceived with more altruism for the welfare of the public than the Fish
Pool project. And running through the lot—the journals from *Tatler*
to *Theatre*, the Censorium, the Multiplication Table, a Nation a Family,
etc.—we see that none, unless it was the experiment in alchemy,
required so costly a stake in time, money, and energy. This Fish Pool
project was characteristic not only of Steele but also of his age: the
invention was intended to be a practical application of experimental
philosophy, and the joint-stock company projecting it was modelled on
the South Sea Bubble.

The idea was an improvement on the well-boat. In an ordinary well-
boat the water and air remained unchanged, and fish were transported
to the market in a state of putrefaction. "In this Invention the Air and
Water flow together, come into the Ship horizontally, and pass thro'
it in a constant Succession, yielding fresh Air and Fresh Water," Steele
wrote. Fish caught at any distance away could be brought in the Fish
Pool vessel to the market, alive and in good condition. He hoped that
this invention would be the means of introducing a new and profitable
course of trade, whereby commerce and navigation would be advanced.

From 1713 to 1722, Steele was more or less occupied with the project.
His interest began on his seeing some experiments with an air-pump. In
the early stages he was assisted by William Benson, an hydraulic engineer of sorts and a man of wealth (successor in 1718 to Sir Christopher
Wren as Surveyor of the Works), and in the later stages by one Joseph
Gillmore, a mathematician. By 1717 " the machine " was finished and
" with great success," Steele thought, as it had the interest of Sir Isaac
Newton (Letter to Lady Steele, 22 April). Letters patent for the
invention were secured, and the Fish Pool sloop, embodying its principles, was constructed by builders at Rotherhithe. After the initial voyage
of the sloop down the Thames to the Tower in September, 1718, with
the inspection and approval of " Gentlemen of Learning and Curiosity,"
this tract was published. In the next three or four years there followed
demonstrations, trial fishing trips in the sloop, and—during the summer
of 1720 when the gambling of the South Sea Bubble was at fever
pitch—the organization of the project into a joint-stock company.
Despite increasing difficulty in finance and organization, four sloops
were launched in the spring of 1721. But whatever the cause—inept
management, pressure of competition, lack of capital, legal restrictions,

419

or the worthlessness of the invention—the failure was decisive by
November, 1722. Throughout the difficulties, Steele faced cheerfully
the ill-will of the fishing industry, the merry-making of the wits, and
scepticism on all sides. Several well-known names besides Newton's
appear in the annals of the Fish Pool: those of Dr. J. T. Desaguliers,
the scientist; the wealthy Duke of Chandos; Francis Hauksbee, the
inventor; Robert Knight, treasurer of the South Sea Company; and
even John Law.

The *Account* gives the history of the project and a journal of the
experiments up to the launching of the first sloop. The original idea
of the invention was Steele's. Gillmore applied the idea and directed
the experiments in " the contriving of a vessel to carry no Lading but
Water and Fish, whereby Fish might live commodiously, and such
Water be admitted, and made to pass thro' at Will, and nevertheless
the Ship to sail with Safety." The tract describes the various steps: the
projection from which the machine was modelled; the miniature model
sloop; the technical problems in lading, sailing, steering; and finally the
construction of the sloop and of the land carriage. The technical
aspects of the tract Gillmore was doubtless responsible for, but Steele's
hand can be seen in the writing and editing. And no empiric could
have taken more pleasure and pride than he in the calculations, diagrams, and scientific data. The project was supported, he said, " by
Reason and the Laws of Mechanism "; and he submitted " the whole
Matter, with great Humility, to the Consideration of the Publick."
Textual notes on p. 646.

AN
ACCOUNT
OF THE
FISH-POOL:

Confifting of

A DESCRIPTION of the VESSEL fo call'd, lately invented and built for the Importation of Fifh alive, and in good Health, from Parts however diftant.

A PROOF of the Imperfection of the *Well-Boat* hitherto ufed in the FISHING TRADE.

The true REASONS why Ships become ftiff or crank in Sailing ; with other Improvements, very ufeful to all Perfons concern'd in Trade and Navigation.

Likewife,

A DESCRIPTION of the Carriage intended for the Conveyance of Fifh by Land, in the fame good Condition as in the *Fifh-Pool* by Sea.

By Sir *RICHARD STEELE*, and Mr. *JOSEPH GILLMORE*, Mathematician.

LONDON:

Printed and fold by *H. Meere* at the *Black Fryer* in *Black-Fryers*, *J. Pemberton* at the *Buck and Sun* in *Fleet-ftreet*, and *J. Roberts* in *Warwick-lane*. 1718.
Price One Shilling.

To the Honourable

Sir *John Ward*, Kt.

Lord Mayor of LONDON.

My LORD,

A S I think it manifest that the Design, explain'd in the following Account, will introduce a new and profitable Course of Trade; I presume to address this Narration to the Greatest Magistrate of the Greatest Commercial City.

Your personal eminent Qualities, as a good Citizen, and Man of Business, which I have frequently heard you exert, where you, with great Ability, represent the same City in another honourable Character, entitle you also to the Veneration and Esteem which determine me in my present Application.

The Arts and Sciences (in which I pretend to no accurate Skill) should always be employ'd in Enquiries that may tend to the general Advantage; and they must lose the Name of Liberal, when the Professors of them seclude themselves from Society; or live in it, without applying their Abilities to the Service of it. For it is by the joint Force of Men of different Talents, that useful Purposes are best accomplish'd; and a certain Felicity of Invention in one, join'd to the Experience and practical Skill of another, may bring Works to Perfection, which would be so far from Growth, that they would not so much as have had Birth, but from the good Intelligence between Persons of unlike Abilities, whose Good Will towards each other united their Endeavours.

I dare promise your Lordship, that the Correspondence between the Undertakers of this Design, will produce to the World many other Operations, which will create more Wonder, that they were not perform'd before, than that they are now brought into Use. For it is certain, that great and worthy Works are every Day lost, by the Distance which is kept between Men, from the very Reason which should make them seek each other in their different Way of Life and Education.

Among the Employments of human Life, that of the Merchant (whose Good is the Good of all Men) should by all be held in the first Esteem: It is he, who enlarges the Interests of his Country; it is he, who, by his Credit, makes his Fellow-Citizen every where at Home, and extends the Offices, Advantages, and Civilities of Acquaintance and Neighbourhood, to all Parts of the habitable World.

The following Invention is propos'd to be carry'd on with a superior Regard to the Laws and Rights of Commerce, which oblige every Man to think of himself but in the second Place, or to make his first Intentions, at least, strictly agreeable to the Good of his Country, and that of all his Fellow-Citizens; and therefore, the Account of it may be a Present not unworthy a Gentleman of your free and disinterested Character; and I flatter myself it will have the Influence of your Lordship in the Prosecution of it. I need not say how great that Influence must needs be, where you act for them in the greatest Capacities your Fellow-Citizens have to bestow.

I congratulate both them and you, that a Person of such known Equanimity is vested with the double Capacity of asserting and protecting their Privileges; whose Candour and Benignity naturally tend to abate Animosity, encourage Industry, promote Peace, prevent Disorder, secure Wealth, and relieve Poverty: In all which noble Ends and Cares I wish you a prosperous and memorable Mayoralty; and again humbly desiring, that if this Design shall in the least Degree appear serviceable in any of these generous Respects, it may have your Protection,

I remain,

My LORD,

Your Lordship's most obedient

And most humble Servant,

RICHARD STEELE.

THE
FISH-POOL, &c.

THERE has much Calumny been utter'd, and many impertinent Observations made upon one of the Undertakers of this Work which I am now going to describe; but as he formerly declar'd in Print, that while he was pursuing what he believ'd might conduce to the common Good, he gave the Syllables *Richard Steele* to the Publick, to be used and treated as they should think fit, he must go on in the same Indifference, and allow the Town their usual Liberty with his Name, which I find they think they have much more Room to sport with than formerly, as it is lengthen'd with the Monosyllable *Sir.*

But tho' I am not solicitous for what they say of Sir *Richard Steele,* merely as it regards the Matter of his Fame or Reputation, which is too large to be unexceptionably good or bad, but must necessarily share the Fate which attends Men of undertaking Complexions, who are the Entertainment and Discourse of idle People, that insensibly, for Want of other Employment, hate the Persons of those they never saw, and oppose Designs into which they never examine. I say, let one of the Undertakers be considerable or inconsiderable, according to the Temper of the Company wherein he is mention'd, I cannot let a Great and Good Work, which may be a Benefit to all the World, be lost and run down, because, perhaps, his Part in it may have been only a mere Suggestion, or a lucky Start, that owes its Progress to the being communicated to a more capable Man, that ripen'd it into Practice, and qualify'd it for the Service of Society.

If this were the Case, as I know it is, and that with great Inconvenience to himself, any Man, from a restless good Spirit, has attempted (not to say accomplish'd) a most extraordinary Work, for the Advantage of the whole Species, especially the poorer Sort, all Men are oblig'd, in Justice and Gratitude, at least to give the Matter a fair Hearing.

The Reader is desir'd, on this Foundation only, as it regards himself and all other Men, as well as the Undertakers, to approve or condemn the Design of the FISH-POOL, and to hear the Relation of the several Steps and Degrees by which it was brought to its present Perfection.

It is now about five Years since Sir *Richard Steele*, upon seeing certain Experiments of an Air-Pump, consulted a Gentleman of known Experience and Ability, concerning a Design to form a Vessel which should preserve dead Fish from Corruption a longer Time than usual; but the Gentleman so consulted, convinc'd him of the Impossibility of performing that Matter in the Manner he suppos'd it practicable, and discourag'd him from farther Enquiry that Way.

But the Matter did not end there; that Disappointment only gave his Thoughts another Cast; and much Reflection on that Subject ended in an Imagination, that tho' dead Fish could not be preserv'd from Putrefaction by what he had suggested, live Fish might, by new Methods, be convey'd better than they had been by the Means already practis'd, which would end in the same Advantage.

About this Time Mr. *Steele* had the good Fortune to become acquainted with Mr. *Gillmore*; and falling by Degrees into great Familiarity, frequently hinted to him, that he could not but think it practicable, that a Vessel might be contriv'd so as to bring Fish alive much better that at present; and took frequent Occasions to solicit him, whom he knew very well skill'd in Navigation and other Parts of the Mathematicks, to turn his Thoughts on that Subject. Mr. *Gillmore* could not be brought to apply himself to this Proposal, 'till about a Twelvemonth ago he was urg'd, by a Letter from Sir *Richard Steele*, to comply with his former Request, now he (Mr. *Gillmore*) was at Leisure, at his Place of Abode at *Nettleton* in *Wiltshire*.

The Thing that dwelt upon the Imagination of the Inventor was, That since it was notorious, that Ships, without sinking, frequently admitted many Tuns of Water, besides their proper Lading; a Vessel, by a good Artist, who knew the Reason, Nature, Philosophy, Principles, and Laws of Mechanism, might be contrived to carry no Lading but Water and Fish, whereby Fish might live commodiously, and such Water be admitted, and made to pass thro' at Will, and nevertheless the Ship to sail with Safety.

Mr. *Gillmore* began now to listen, and return'd for Answer, he would immediately take the Matter into Consideration, and in a few Days after, sent his Friend the Projection from which the FISH-POOL was modell'd, and built 16 inches by the Keel; which 16 Inches was divided into 40 equal Parts, and made into a Scale call'd Feet, and by it projected the FISH-POOL, 40 Foot by the Keel, 16 Foot broad in the Midship, and 6 Foot deep between the Kelson and Deck on which she swims; with Grates 'fore and aft', Air-Pipes, Well into the Hold through both Decks, Masts, Yards, Rigging, and Hatchway to go down between-Decks, and other Conveniencies, all in Proportion.

From this Model, by a lesser Scale, was made an Hull of very small Dimensions, as 10 Inches by the Keel, 5 Inches broad in the Midship, 2 Inches and a Quarter deep in the Hold, with a proportionable Well, and a little Glass deck, on which it was to swim.

We carry'd our Vessel over Land to a Place near the Village of *Hackney*, call'd *Temple-Mills*, which is the Spot that divides *Middlesex* from *Essex*, near an Island which we nam'd, from its Bigness, *Tresacre* Island.

After we had put into our Vessel a *Flounder* and six *Gudgeons*, (on which latter Word we allow all *Small Wits* to make merry) we plac'd her in the Current of the second Trough of a Logwood Mill, and moor'd her very safely, where, from Hour to Hour we visited her, and thro' her Glass Deck saw her Passengers very merry, which made us not a whit less contented. After we had remain'd in the House adjacent as long as we thought convenient, we left a Young Man to attend the Vessel, and keep a Journal of what pass'd, as to the Consumption of the Food of the Fish and the like.

The Ignorant are naturally malicious to any Thing they see out of the common Road, and we found the Weight of it in our first Essay; for a Servant of the Mill, tho' desir'd and brib'd to give Warning, when he should have Occasion to raise the Flood-gate, imagining he was able to do Mischief, open'd it upon our Vessel, which tore her from her Moorings; but she, tho' her proper Lading is but about one Pound, rid the Storm; and our trusty Pilate jump'd into the River, and took her up, where she was driven on the North of the Island of *Tresacre*, without having receiv'd the least Damage in her Hull or Cargo, from a greater Storm and Stress of Weather than any Ship can possibly meet with at Sea.

Tho' this appear'd very satisfactory, Mr. *Gillmore* comply'd with his Partner, to give him more than Ocular Demonstration, by going thro' the proper Experiments, which should make him as clearly understand the Causes, as he saw the Effects; without which, it was impossible to enjoy Quiet under so great an Expence, as the Building a Vessel for Use must necessarily require.

For this End we resolv'd to go from one Circumstance to another, and consider the Nature of the Elements and Parts of Matter with which we were to deal, and from thence form Conclusions that might make us easy and confident in our future Proceedings. [Fig. 1]

The first Experiment was thus; we exhausted the Air out of a Cylinder 12 Inches diameter, and 2 Foot deep, as P, whose Superficies on the Top is 113.1428, by an Air-Pump, as B, being 1 Inch diameter, whose Superficies on the Top is .78571, and found the Weight C to be 12 Pounds 9 Ounces; then, if the Superficies on the Top of the Air-Pump be .78571, and the Weight of the Atmosphere pressing on the Air-Pump 12.57 Pounds, the Weight of Air on the Cylinder B, at a Foot diameter, will be 1810.2848 Pounds: So, by Consequence, on every Inch square is 16 Pounds in the Summer; and every Foot square, or 144 Inches, the Weight pressing on it is 2304 Pounds, or 20 hundred 2 Quarters and 8 Pounds *Averdupois*. From which Experiment, and the Reflection that the Parts of Water are globular, we concluded, that the Air being press'd into the Water by the Weight of the Atmosphere, is thereby convey'd to all living Creatures under Water; and that if this Air is not put in Motion, it must soon corrupt; for, a Breeze is no more than a Body of Air broken, or forc'd by something more solid than itself: Note also, that Water is impell'd by the same Means; for, force Air or Water horizontally, like Springs, they will yield and fly before you while nothing more weighty drives back; but force them downward, and the Earth, by being more weighty, will resist it, and make it spread horizontally.

By the Rule of this Philosophy, before we proceeded farther, we took into Consideration the only Engine hitherto employ'd for carrying Fish alive, to wit, *The* WELL-BOAT. [Fig.]

Since all that has been hitherto attempted of this Kind, has been by a *Well-Boat*; and that it is known, that from the Moment Fish are put into that Vehicle, they sicken, foam, and froth at the Mouth, fall into Convulsions, and in a small Time die; it behov'd us to examine the Reason of this, and found that it cannot happen otherwise, as appears from *Fig.* 1, which shows, that they cannot receive in that Machine what are absolutely necessary to their Being, *viz.* fresh Air and fresh Water; because the Pillar of Air A, presses down upon the *Well-Boat* B, which *Well-Boat* is supported by Pillar of Water C, and surrounded by the like Trapezium of Water d e f g h i, by which Means, and the Bulk-heads OO, all fresh Air and Water are excluded.

This is farther prov'd by *Fig.* 2. L is a Cylinder well clos'd and without the least Hole or Crack, in the Middle of which a Candle was plac'd, and in few Minutes went out; but when a lighted Candle was again fix'd, as before, and in a small Space of Time was in the same Manner going out, a little Vent or Hole was made in the Side, on which it reviv'd; and will still do so more, in Proportion to the Greatness of the Hole; by which we concluded, that the Cylinder being full of Air, and pressed by the Pillar above it, the Flame of the Candle could not subsist; but when the Pillar of Air was broken in the Cylinder, by means of the Vent-Hole, we apprehended the Matter of the Candle to be put (or rather continu'd) in Motion and therefore it reviv'd: From either of which Circumstances the Confinement of only a certain Quantity of Water in a *Well-Boat*, or Air in any such Vessel, equally appears.

Now, that the Fish in this new-invented Vessel are constantly supply'd with fresh Air and fresh Water will appear from *Fig.* 3.

It is to be understood that this Vessel is to have no other Lading than Water and Fish; *i. e.* this Vessel is to carry as much Weight of Water and Fish, as another would of dry Goods, to make her sink low enough down into the Water, so as to be fit for sailing; and that the Fish and Water are to fill all the Hold of the Vessel.

A B is the lower Deck, on which she swims; she is supported by the Pillar of Water A B F G, and encompass'd all round by the Trapezium of Water E R G F pressing against it.

Hitherto the *new Vessel* is but in the Condition of all other Boats, and even of the *Well-Boat* itself.

But whereas the Imperfection of the *Well-Boat* consists, in that the Water and Air are constantly the same, and constrain'd to be such by a perpendicular Weight of both, and an horizontal Pressure on all Sides; from which the Fish are reliev'd only by the Motion of their own Struggling, and the Tacking of the Vessel, without which they could not live 24 Hours after they are in the Boat.

In this Invention the Air and Water flow together, come into the Ship horizontally, and pass thro' it in a constant Succession, yielding fresh Air and fresh Water, to the Relief, Sustenance, and Delight of the Fish; which great Advantage is effected by large Grates at the Head and Stern, or each End of the Vessel, at P [R] and M, and by the Vents which open into 4 large Pipes before, and 2 abaft, and in the Midships, the Well is cover'd with Gratings, as O. There are also other Conveniences, to-wit, the Main-mast, and Sluice-pipe, all which yield a free Discharge, and form an uninterrupted Passage for the Air.

After the Projectors were satisfy'd of the Use and Benefit of the Air and Water, in which they were to work, as far as it concern'd their Design, the next Thing was to consider how their intended Vessel would receive Advantage from them in its sailing and working; which brought on the third Experiment, that is demonstrated by *Fig.* A. which shews the Form of a Parallelopepidon, 12 Foot long, 9 Inches broad, and 6 Inches deep, as a b c d: This Trough was fill'd with fine clear Water, which done, there was put into it a small Model of the Hull of our Sloop, 12 Inches long, 4 broad, and 3 deep, with Grates 'fore and aft', and a Glass Deck, to render all that pass'd thro' her visible, as B. Into the Well P, we put a deep red Liquor, and found that by the Motion of the Vessel thro' the Water, the Distance 20 Times her Length, she would discharge all her said red Water.

Now, the Fish-Vessel design'd being 40 Foot by the Keel,

if you divide 5280, the Feet in a Mile, by 800 Foot, 20 Times her Length, the Quotient sheweth she discharges herself of all her old Water six Times and six Tenths in a Mile, or 33 Times every 5 Miles.

From which it appears by Demonstration, that the whole Mass of the Parts of Water are mov'd more or less, by the Motion of any of them, in Proportion to the Magnitude and Velocity of the Bodies which press upon them, and the Succession of fresh Air and Water in the Vessel to be accordingly: So that the whole Body of Water contain'd in such a Vessel will be chang'd, as aforesaid, in 20 Times its Length; and the more swift the Motion of the Vessel is, the more rapid the Current will be thro' her, as in *Fig.* 4. where A B C D represent the Iron Gratings 'fore and aft', thro' which the Water passeth, forming the Currents A C and B D; whose Motion is nearly equal, tho' in a contrary Direction to that of the Ship.

In the Hold are put Stops, to throw some Part of the Water into Eddies, as L L L; that the Fish may not be hurt by its Velocity, but swim and play as easy as in the free and open Sea.

The last Experiment was by the aforesaid Vessel with the Glass Deck, whose Hold had Gratings 'fore and aft', and was full of Holes on the Sides; the Length of it was 12 Inches, and Breadth 4, which makes 16 Inches for the Height of the Main-mast; but we made it 20 Inches long; and when it floated on the Water, we found it truly boyant, and neither too *crank* nor too *stiff*.

Then we stopp'd up the said Gratings and Holes in her Sides, and sunk her 'till she drew as much Water as before; which we effected by loading her with dry Gravel, and found her then somewhat *more stiff*; because, by so much as the Gravel is heavier than Water of the same Magnitude, it must lie farther from the *Center of Motion*, and make her too stiff. This proves Water to be the truest Lading, and was still a Confirmation of this *new Invention*.

Thus far we have prov'd the Capacity, the Aptness, the Power, and Commodiousness of our Vessel; after all which, we may still fail, if we do not understand the Nature of Lading, which Experience and Wisdom has brought to Light and Practice among men.

29

To avoid any Error from Inadvertency this Way, it was well debated and consider'd, that there is a great Difference between a Shipwright's and Merchant's Way of calculating the Tunnage of a Ship; and finding this Difficulty, made us think it proper to examine, from the Nature of the Thing itself, how many Tuns *Averdupois* Weight a Ship will carry.

The Shipwright's Way is to multiply the Length of the Keel by the middle Breadth, and that Product by half the Breadth, and then they divide the last Product by 94, and the Quotient is the Tunnage.

The *Fish-Pool Sloop* is 40 Foot by the Keel, and 17 Foot Broad in the Midships, which by their customary Rule measures 61.5 Tuns.

To find how many Tuns Weight a Ship will carry.

The *Fish-Pool Sloop* being Inched according to common Gauging, the mean Length in the Hold is 42 Feet, mean Breadth is 13.687 Feet, and the Depth 6 Feet, which multiply'd together is 3449.124 Cubick Feet of Water; each Foot of Salt Sea Water, by the nicest Experiments, weighing 64.25 Pounds,* and a Cubick Foot of clear fresh Water weighs but 62.5 [1] Pounds, which is the very Reason why a Ship is more boyant in salt Water than in fresh: Now if the Cubick Feet of salt Water in the Hold be multiply'd by 64.25 Pounds, (the true Weight of a Cubick Foot of Sea Water) it will be 221606 Pounds *Averdupois* Weight, or 98 Tuns, 18 Hundred, 2 Quarters, and 14 Pounds; and so much Weight of any Sort of dry Goods must be in the Hold of a Ship of her Burthen, to make her neither too crank nor too stiff; and this Weight is no more than what is commonly allow'd by Merchants themselves, of Box, Bale, or Case Goods, by allowing 66 Cubick Feet to a Tun in Bulk. Suppose you have 6 Bales of Goods, 6 Foot long, 2 Foot broad, and 2 deep; multiply the Length, Breadth, and Depth, one into the other, the Product is 24 Cubick Feet for one Bale; and that multiply'd by 6, is 144 Cubick Feet in the 6 Bales; the whole divided by 66, the Quotient is 2.182 Tuns. We will suppose this 2.182 Tuns to be Red Wine, of which a Cubick

* See Ward's *Tables*. [Steele's note]

Foot weighs 62.06 Pounds *Averdupois*, the Goods before-mention'd measure 144 Cubick Feet, which multiply'd by 62.06, the Product is its true Weight, *viz.* 3 Tuns, 19 Hundred, 3 Quarters, and 4 Pounds; or suppose it be Oyl Olive, of which 57.06 Pounds is a Cubick Foot, then the aforesaid 2.182 Tuns, or 144 Cubick Feet of Oyl Olive will weigh 3 Tuns, 13 Hundred, 1 Quarter, and 12 Pounds; and the Quantity of the *Fish-Pool*'s Hold, as before-mention'd, is 3449 Cubick Feet, divided by 66 Cubick Feet, the Quotient is 52.25 Tuns of Merchants Tunnage; which said 3449 Cubick Feet, or 52.25 Tuns, we will proportion to the several Weights of Liquids following, *viz.* that 1 Cubick Foot of salt Water weighs 64.25 Pounds, of clear fresh Water 62.5 Pounds, Red Wine 62.06 Pounds, and Oyl Olive 57.06 Pounds *Averdupois Weight*. If so,

Then 66 Cubick Feet, or 1 Tun of Merchants Allowance will weigh,

	hun.	*qu.*	*p.*
If Salt Water..............	37	3	12
Clear Fresh Water.......	36	3	9
Red Wine..............	36	1	26
Oyl Olive..............	33	2	14

It is plain that different Solids and Liquids have different Weights, and, by Consequence, all different Cargoes must vary the same, as appears by the Table following.

That a Hold measuring 3449 Cubick Feet

	Tun	*hun.*	*qu.*	*p.*
Of Salt Water is.....	98	18	2	14
Clear Fresh Water.	96	4	2	18
Red Wine........	95	11	0	13
Oyl Olive........	87	17	0	16

This Account is purely to satisfy those that are not acquainted with the Nature of these Things, that so much Goods ought to be in the Hold, as is equal to such a Weight of Water as would fill the Hold, and will bring the Ship down so far into the Water as is limited; for the Weight of Goods presses out no more Water than would fill the Hold; and if the Goods are lighter or heavier than Water of the same Magnitude, the Ship will be either *too stiff* or *too crank*, as will be demonstrated in its proper Place.

The next Thing we consider'd was, how much all the Timber, that bounds the Hold from the Floating-Deck to the Keel, is lighter than Water of the same Magnitude.

The Keel, Floor-Timbers, Kelson, Stem, Stern-Post, dead Wood 'fore and aft', and Step of the Mast, were exactly measur'd, and found to be 649.5 Cubick Feet. By the best Experiments that have been made,* a Cubick Foot of sound dry Oak will weigh 58 Pounds, by which multiply the said 649.5 Feet, the Product is 37671 Pounds *Averdupois* Weight,

	Tun	hun.	qu.	p.
Or,	16	16	1	10
Iron Bolts, Gratings, &c. .	01	00	0	00
Clay abaft.	02	00	0	00
Total	19	16	1	10

649.5

	Tun	hun.	qu.	p.
649.5 Cubick Feet of Sea Water, of the same Magnitude of the Timber, at 64.25 Pounds each Foot.	18	12	2	10
Two Tuns of Clay abaft, being twice as heavy as Water of the same Magnitude, and therefore takes up but half the Room of Water, the ½ is.	01	00	0	00
Total	19	12	2	10
From	19	16	1	10
Take	19	12	2	10
Remains	00	03	3	00

Which is over and above the Weight of Water.

The specifick Gravity of Bodies of the same Magnitude will

* *According to* Ward's *Book*. [Steele's note]

press them downward, if heavier than Liquids; and the Liquids will press them upward, if lighter.

	Tun	hun.	qu.	p.
Add the Water in the Hold	98	18	2	14
To the Weight over and above the Weight of Water	00	03	3	00
The Total	99	02	1	04

Is the whole Weight under the Floating-Deck, or the true Weight a Ship for this Purpose ought to have; and, to be sure, a great deal of Care must be taken, that there is but a small matter of Weight added more to the Timber, Iron, &c. than the Weight of Water of the same Magnitude of the Timber.

The next Thing we consider'd, was the Weight of every Thing above the Floating-Deck, the Weight the Sloop will carry between Decks, and by Consequence, how many Inches the Floating-Deck will sink under the Superficies of the Water on the Outside of the Sloop, and from thence, how much Water she will bear between-Decks, before she will sink.

First, The Timber, Necessaries, &c. as the Floating-Deck, Beams, Knees, Timbers in the Sides, Timbers in the upper Deck, Windless and Cheeks, Paulbits, Cattheads, Capston, Stem, Masts, Yards, Rigging, Necessaries, &c. were all exactly measur'd and weigh'd.

	Tun	hun.	qu.	p.
All the Timbers measur'd 966.5 [2] Cubick Feet, at 58 Pounds *per* Foot, is..	25	00	2	04
Cordage, Anchors, Iron Bolts, Meat, Drink, Coal, six Men, &c. Weight....	06	00	0	00
Weight in all	31	00	2	04

2dly, *What Weight she will carry between Decks, and how many Inches the Floating-Deck will sink under the Superficies of the Water on the Outside.*

Length of the Deck E D 50 Foot, mean Breadth 16 Foot, and Depth 6 Foot, which, multiply'd one by the other, is 4800 Cubick Feet, and multiply'd by 64.25 Pounds, the Weight of a

Cubick Foot of Water, the Product is 308400 Pounds *Averdupois,* or 137 Tuns, 13 Hundred, 2 Quarters, and 8 Pounds, between-Decks E N P D. [Fig. 5]

3dly, *To Find how many Inches the Floating-Deck E D will sink under the Superficies of the Water on the Outside.*

Having before found, that between-Decks she measures 4800 Cubick Feet of salt Water, at 6 Foot deep; then every Inch deep must contain 66,666 Cubick Feet of salt Water, allowing 64.25 Pounds to a Cubick Foot, as before, the Weight is 38 Hundred, and 27 Pounds on every Inch deep; now, if 38 Hundred and 27 Pounds sink the Floating-Deck 1 Inch, then all the Timbers, Cordage, Anchorage, &c. being 31 Tuns and 60 Pounds, as before-mention'd, will sink it 16.227 Inches under the Superficies of the Water on the Outside of the Middle-Deck; that is, the Floating-Deck E D in *Fig.* 5. will be 16.227 Inches under Water, as E A or D B.

The aforesaid E A or D B is 16.227 Inches; the Depth of the Arch of the Deck thwartships is 4 Inches; the ½ is 2 Inches, which 2 Inches added to 16.227, makes 18.227 Inches, the Depth of the Water in the Well, as L C; then take 18.277 Inches, as L C, from 6 Foot as L H, the Remainder is almost 54 Inches, or 4 Foot 6 Inches, as C H equal to B P, or A N, free Board.

Now, (as we prov'd before, that the Hold measur'd 3449 Cubick Feet, allowing 66 Cubick Feet to a Tun, Merchants Tunnage) the *Fish-Pool Sloop* is not quite 53 Tuns; and where is any Ship of her Burthen more than 4 Foot 6 Inches free Board when loaden, besides the Thickness of her upper Deck Plank, and 2 Inches more to the Scupper-Holes?

4thly, *How much Water the* Fish-Pool Sloop *must take in between-Decks, to make her sink, and consequently, whether this* Fish-Vessel *is as safe as a Merchant-Man, or less dangerous than a common* Well-Boat?

In order thereunto, we must find how much Water she must ship between-Decks to make her sink.

We have calculated before, that between-Decks E N D P measures 4800 Cubick Feet, and allow'd 64.25 Pounds to a Foot of salt Water, the Weight is 137 Tuns, 13 Hundred, 2

Quarters, and 8 Pounds; We have likewise before calculated that 38 Hundred, and 27 Pounds Weight of Water will sink her but 1 Inch, then, if 1 Inch requires 38 Hundred and 27 Pounds to sink it, then 4 Foot 4 Inches, the Remains of the 6 Foot between-Decks, as B P or A N, will require 99 Tuns, 8 Hundred, 2 Quarters, and 4 Pounds; so, by Consequence, she must ship so much Water before she can sink; and if by God's Blessing, we can keep all things Close in a Storm, she is a great deal safer than any other Vessel; because, if you spring a Lake in a Merchant-Man, she must sink, if you cannot keep her free with the Pumps; but in this *Fish-Vessel*, the Floating-Deck being under your Feet, the Lake may be seen, and stopp'd immediately.

Farther, we are much safer than a *Well-Boat*, because all our Water is confin'd, like Water in a Bottle, as *Fig.* 5. E D N P is all dry between Decks; the Vessel is sunk to A and B on the Outside of the Ship; and if so, by Consequence the Water in the well will rise to C. Now considering how the Deck she swims on E L D is press'd down into the Water as deep as E A or D B, how is it possible, under such a Confinement, the Water should be toss'd by the Sallies of the Vessel (occasion'd by the Surges of the Sea) from one Side to the other, like a common *Well-Boat*?

Again, how can it be, but that there must ensue a constant Succession and fresh Supplies of Water, since she hath large Gratings before, containing 360 square Inches, to let the Water in; and abaft, Gratings of 740 square Inches, to let the Water out; and the Conveniencies of large Blow-Pipes, to vent what Air shall happen to be forc'd in by the Risings of the Vessel in head Seas.

But the *Well-Boat* is of a Different Nature, as in *Fig.* 6, which represents an *English Well-Boat*, A, the Mouth of the Well, B, the whole Body to contain the Fish, P P, two Bulkheads, or Ends of the Well, running athwartships; so Part of the two Sides, and the two Bulk-heads or Ends, make the Well; C D, all Cavity between the Bulk-heads and the two extreme Ends of the Boat, to make her boyant.

It is impossible such a form'd Vessel as this should approve itself to the Examination of those in this Great City, who understand the Nature and Reason of Things, and whose Business it is, on a diligent Enquiry, either to correct, approve, or reject it. Which proves it was never calculated by Art, but brought to what it is by the long and dear Cost and Experience of some poor publick-spirited Fishermen.

For, 1*st*, no manner of Provision was made for the Conveyance of Air, without which no Creature can live.

2*dly*, On every Sally of the Boat, the Water in the Well must shift its Place; and in violent Seas it sometimes hath forced the Hatches open which cover the Well, and sometimes breaks thro' the Bulk-heads.

Besides this, how uneasy must the Fish be in such violent Motions, to be batter'd against the Sides of the Well; and if a Calm happen, the Water having no Motion, the Fish must in a little Time be suffocated: And at the very best, they have no Relief by fresh Supplies of Water, but by the Vessel's tacking about; and then, perhaps, the Fishes Motion, and struggling for Life, may press out some filthy Slime, thro' the Holes in the sides of the Well, and so make their Situation a little more healthful.

The next Thing we are to prove is, That Water is as good, or indeed, better Lading than any dry Goods whatsoever.

Suppose, (so far as the Ship sinks in the Water) an imaginary Line to go from Stem to Stern; in that Line lies the *Center of Motion* of the Ship; and the *Center of Gravity* not being in the *Center of Motion*, it will descend 'till it comes under the *Center of Motion*; and the farther it is distant from the *Center of Motion*, the more will its Weight be, and the nearer, the less, so as to render her accordingly more stiff or more crank.

The *Fish-Pool Sloop* will carry in her Hold 99 Tuns Weight, or 52 Tuns of Merchants Allowance, reckoning 66 Cubick Feet to a Tun, as hath been before prov'd.

Fig. 7. *Suppose a Ship laden with 99 Tun Weight of Lead, and that should lie in the Bottom of the Hold, to the Height B C, and equal to the whole Weight of Water that would fill the Hold D E C.*

It is plain here, that A is the Center of Motion, on which the whole Body moves; and every Man, concern'd in Sea

Affairs, knows by Experience, (and that sometimes dearly bought too) that there is a Necessity of raising the Weight of Lead nearer the Center of Motion A, by dividing the Weight, and laying several Ranges of Billet-Wood between the like Ranges of Lead; or else the Ship would lie so stiff in the Sea, that she could not yield to the Wind; by which Opposition, all the Masts would be blown down, or brought by the Board, and the Seas would make a high Road over her Decks. Which proves, that by so much as the Cargo is heavier than Water of the same Magnitude, by so much the Ship will be stiffer than she ought to be, and move the heavier upon the Center of Motion A towards D or E; because, the Quantity of the Lead B C, in the Bottom of the Hold is 99 Tuns, and that of Sea Water of the same Magnitude B C, would be but a little above 11 Tuns; for, a Cubick Foot of Lead is 707 Pounds and 13 Ounces, and a Cubick Foot of salt Water 64 Pounds and 4 Ounces.

Fig. 8. *Suppose a Ship laden with 99 Tuns of Sugar as deep as* a b, *and which Loading lies nearer the Center of Motion A than the former Cargo of Lead did.*

By so much as the Cargo of Sugar a b D, is heavier than Sea Water of the same Magnitude, by so much she is too stiff; because, the Magnitude of Sugar a b D is 99 Tuns Weight, and Water of the same Magnitude is but 80 Tuns Weight; therefore the Ship must be too stiff, and moves the heavier upon the Center of Motion A towards B or C.

Fig. 9. *Suppose a Ship be laden with 99 Tuns Weight of lighter Goods, where a great Part of it must be stow'd between-Decks, or above the* Center of Motion A, *as high as* L N.

Now, by so much Weight as is between-Decks A L N, on every Sally of the Ship, so much is the Weight in the Hold A P R lessen'd: For by so much as the Cargo is lighter than Water of the same Magnitude, by so much the Ship must be cranker, and be conseqeuently more in Danger to overset: For, all the light Goods that will fill the Hold and between-Decks, will weigh but 99 Tuns, which is her real Cargo; and Water of the same Magnitude (that is, were the Hold and between-

Decks full of Water) would weigh 198 Tuns; which plainly
proves she hath 99 Tuns Weight to assist the Wind to overset
her. But if the Cargo be lighter than Water of the same Magnitude, and under the Center of Motion, Balast must be used
to sink her down to the Center of Motion; but then she will
be too stiff, by so much as the Balast is heavier than Water of
the same Magnitude; as would be the Case, were she loaded
with Tobacco, or other such light Goods.

Fig. 10. But if a Ship hath 99 Tuns Weight of salt Water
in the Hold B A C D, and that Water be stopp'd down, (as
is the Case of our FISH-POOL) it must needs lie there more
equal and uniform than any Cargo of Goods can possibly do;
for it will lie, with Regard to the Motion and Sallies of the
Ship, just as if it were congeal'd into a solid Body of Ice of the
same Weight and Magnitude. And it is impossible, that any
Kind of dry Goods (not even Corn itself, were her Hold full
of it, and well caulk'd down) can be stow'd so commodiously;
neither can such a Ship, thus moving upon the Center of Motion
A, be either *too crank* or *too stiff*.

What hath been said about the Weight in the Hold of a
Ship, may be demonstrated by a Balance, and needs not any
large Explication, the Properties of the *Libra*, or Balance, being
so well known; but, for Illustration, be pleas'd to observe, that
if the Weights at the Ends be equal, and at equal Distances
from the Center of Motion, it will cause an Equilibrium, and
the Center of Gravity will be in the Center of Motion, as *Fig.*
11, A is the Center; suppose B and C equally distant from the
Center A, it is plain the Beam will be horizontal; but if the
Weight C be slipp'd to D, the Beam must of Necessity decline;
because A D being double the Distance of A B, half the Weight
at D will balance B; and if the Weight be mov'd to E, being
three Times the Distance A B, one Third will balance the
Weight B; that is, were the Weight B 30 Pounds, 10 at E would
bring the Beam to a Balance; that is, the Power at E must be
of the same Proportion to the Weight B, as the Distance A B
is to the Distance A E.

The following Demonstrations will farther prove what hath
been said of the Ponderosity of a Ship's Cargo being nearer or
farther off from the Center of Motion.

Fig. 12.   B represents the Materials above the Floating-Deck, L the Weight of the said Materials 6 Tuns, C the Lead in the Hold, P the Weight of the said Lead 99 Tuns, and A the Center of Motion: Now, so far as the Weight P (being the Center of Magnitude to C) is remov'd from the true Center of Magnitude *h*, (if the Hold was full of Water) by so much the Ship must be too stiff; for the Weight P, being four Times and a Half distant, more than L, from the Center of Motion A, the Weight L must be 445 Tuns, 10 Hundred, to poize the Weight P; and how is it possible such a Vessel should yield to the Wind, to move 445.5 Tuns, but all the Masts must be blown by the Board. To prevent which, the Lead C must be broken into Parts, and by Billet-Wood, or some such light Thing, between, rais'd to the Center A, as a b c, as aforesaid.

Fig. 13.   B represents the Materials, as aforesaid, L the Weight of the said Materials, T the Sugar in the Hold, P the Weight of the said Sugar, and A the Center of Motion: The Weight P being 99 Tuns, and three Times farther from the Center of Motion A than L, the Weight L must be 297 Tuns, to balance the Weight P of 99 Tuns, and must be rais'd gradually from Q to the Center of Motion A, to make her truly boyant: Therefore, so far as the Weight P, (being the Center of Magnitude to the Sugar T) is remov'd from the Center of Magnitude *h*, if the Hold was full of Water, by so much she must be too stiff, and ought likewise to be rais'd to the Center of Motion A.

Fig. 14.   *Suppose a Ship of 99 Tun Weight to be laden with light Goods, that you are forc'd to stow some of her Cargo between-Decks.*

Let V be light Goods in the Hold, and B Part of the light Goods between-Decks, L the Weight of the Goods between-Decks, *viz.* 30 Tuns, and likewise the Weight of the Materials above the Floating-Deck, *viz.* 6 Tuns, which added, makes 36 Tuns, and P the Weight of the Goods in the Hold, *viz.* 69 Tuns: Now, so far as the Weight P is drawn towards the Center of Motion A, from the Center of Gravity of the Goods that should be in the Hold, *viz.* d, by so much the Weight of Goods between-Decks must be added over and above to the Weight L, and makes the Ship too crank; for which Reason, Balast must be in the Bottom of the Hold, to make her stiffer.

Fig. 15. B Represents the Materials above the Floating-Deck, L the Weight of the Materials 6 Tuns, W the Water in the Hold, P the Weight of the Water in the Hold 99 Tuns; this proves that the Weight P, lying under the Center of Gravity or Magnitude e, or between the Center of Motion A, and the End of the Beam or Kelson of the Ship R, the Vessel must be truly boyant, if you pitch your Deck in a true Height from the Kelson, otherwise she must be too stiff or too crank. This proves, as before-mention'd, that the Water in the Hold will divide itself naturally into such equal Parts, from R to the Center of Motion A, as no dry Goods can be made conform to. Therefore Water is the most proper Cargo to make a Ship truly boyant; and in all other Lading the Goods will be either above or below the Center of Motion A.

Now, when the Reader comes to be convinc'd by Demonstration, that what has been above deliver'd is Matter of Fact, I hope there will be no Room for any farther Objections.

I shall in the next Place represent this Vessel in as great Stress of Weather as I hope she ever will be, and demonstrate that she is then as safe as any Ship whatsoever.

Fig. 16. A B the Upper-Deck, D F the Floating-Deck, L K equal with the Superficies of the Water on which she swims when upright, in which is the Center of Motion ⊙; E B equal with the Superficies of the Water on which she now swims, heeling down to the Scupper-Holes of the Upper-Deck, and passing thro' the Center of Motion ⊙ as before; therefore, so deep as the Floating-Deck is sunk down under Water by the Weight of Timber, Iron, Rigging, &c. as D L or F K, so deep is the Water in the Well, as G ⊙. Observe, altho' all between Decks, as A B D F is Cavity and dry, and holds 137 Tuns, 13 Hundred, 2 Quarters, and 8 Pounds; yet nevertheless, the whole Vessel being sunk to L K, and supported on the Outside by a Trapesium of Water, as before shew'd, the real Cavity between-Decks, as L A, K B, measures but 99 Tuns, 8 Hundred, 2 Quarters, and 4 Pounds.

Now, considering how the Vessel is born down on one Side,

by the Sails on the Mast C, in a violent Storm, the Point K being the Height of the Water on the Outside when upright, will be press'd under Water as deep as B, and forms a new horizontal Line E ⊙ B, on which she now swims; and by Consequence must form the Triangle ⊙ B K, whose Base ⊙ K is 8 Foot, (the ½ of L K thwartships) and the Perpendicular K B, the Depth between-Decks, from the Superficies of the Water to the Upper-Deck, is 4 Foot 6 Inches, whose Superficies ⊙ K B is 18 Foot; the Length of the Sloop from Stem to Stern is 50 Foot, which multiply'd by the Superficies ⊙ K B 18 Foot, makes 900 Feet; which said 900 Feet multiply'd by 64.25, the Weight of a Cubick Foot of Salt Water, the Product is 57825 Pounds, or 25 Tuns, 16 Hundred, 1 Quarter, and 5 Pounds. Now let any Sea-faring Man judge how great such a Storm must be, to heel a Vessel of her Burden up to her Scupper-Holes, when there is almost 26 Tuns of Cavity, equal in Weight to salt Water of the same Magnitude, to press down to B, besides her Weight in the Hold. All the Water (by such a Heel) that is empty'd out of the Hold, is comprehended in the Triangle E H D; which is so inconsiderable, that it is not worth taking Notice of; because what Air is taken in at such a Time, will be forced out at the Air-Pipes, when the Vessel rightens again. So considering the Condition of this Vessel, and of another laden with dry Goods, we are as safe as any Ship whatsoever; for all Ships can but move upon the Center of Motion; and when she is forc'd by the Wind on one Side, she can press no greater Weight of Water than the Cavity (that is pressed down under Water) will hold.

The next Thing incumbent on us is to prove, that such a Vessel, freighted with Water and Fish, and a Current running thro' her at Command, will feel her Helm, and steer as well as any Vessel whatsoever, if her Rudder be made in Proportion to her Burthen, and properly fix'd. This becomes necessary from a receiv'd Notion, that this Vessel, whose Lading is only Water and Fish, will neither steer nor sail.

To obviate this Objection, it must be well understood, that no Ship will steer, but in a Current in a contrary Direction to that of the Ship; that is to say, the Helm must oppose or press against the Body of Water in which the Vessel works, to make her alter her Way or Course.

We will consider this, 1*st*, in a standing Water; 2*dly*, against a Current; and 3*dly*, with a Current.

Fig. 17. Suppose D H to be a standing Water, and the Vessel makes her Way from D towards H: Now the Vessel's Motion presses the Rudder B against the Body of Water D, by which Means the Vessel is thrust round at the Stern on the Center A.

2*dly*, If she sails against a Current, as, suppose the Current runs from H towards D, and the Vessel sails from D towards H, if she makes any or no Way through the Current, or falls a-stern, yet if her Head be to the Current, she will steer; because the Rudder B presses against the Current H D at D, and turns the Vessel in the same Manner as aforesaid.

3*dly*, Suppose a Vessel sails with a Current, as from D towards H; if she hath not more Way than the Current, she cannot steer, because the Motion of the Ship is slower than the Current of Water, which makes it impossible the Rudder B should press any Weight of Water before it to make the Vessel steer. But if the Ship's Motion be faster than the Current, the Rudder B, by its moving faster than the Current D H, will collect a Weight of Water at D, and steer as before.

I think it will be proper to take the Sloop (as at *Fig.* 17.) out of the Water, and examine where her Imperfections can be, that she will not (as reported) sail and steer, as well as any other Vessel. First, I think it proper to enquire into the Reason, according to Nature and Philosophy, why any Ship, Sloop, or other Vessel, ought to be built broader at the Bows than at the Stern, and likewise cleaner abaft than before, if you intend she shall steer or sail well.

Suppose *Fig.* 18, to be the Hull of a Ship or Sloop: The Triangle A is the most Part of it dead Wood, that is work'd and fill'd up with solid Timbers, and no thicker than the Stern-Post, on which the Rudder hangs; but from thence (being skinn'd over with Plank) it grows wider and wider, to the whole Breadth of the Bulge at C, which they call a clean Tail; and from the Stem at E it is somewhat clean'd off underneath; that by the Ship's pressing forward, her broad Bows at E will contract the Water, like a Current, to the clean Tale at A, and cause the Rudder B to press against it, which is the Cause of her Steering. This is the Case of all Ships whatsoever.

Now, in our Sloop, the Water running through her in a contrary Direction to that of the Sloop, vents itself on each Side of the Stern-Post; which said Current, if the Rudder B is on the Starboard or Larboard Tack, must strike the said Rudder; and by so much as the Weight and Force of Water press out of the Hold, and are stopp'd by the Rudder, by so much the quicker she will answer her Helm.

But supposing (tho' far from granting) that she will not steer so well with the Current running through her, we can (upon a Lee Shore, or any other Occasion) immediately stop all the Sluices 'fore and aft', and make her a whole Vessel, as of the ordinary Form. And again, by opening the Sluices, in the Space of half a Minute, we can relieve our Fish with a full fresh Supply of Water: We say, were it so (as we assert it is not) it would be great Injury to value this Vessel like a *Well-Boat*, wherein Fish cannot have fresh Supplies of Water, perhaps, in a Month or six Weeks together; and which is no other than a Vehicle to bring Fish wasting alive, and to be deliver'd sick and decay'd, instead of (what is much better) fresh and just dead.

Now farther, as to her sailing so well as another Ship; the Nature of the Cargo (Water and Fish) hath been sufficiently explain'd already, and (made appear) are in the Hold, in Regard to the Ship, better than dry Goods; and if a Fish Vessel of this Kind is built in its true Proportion, she will sail as well as any Merchant-Man whatsoever; but Mistakes and Inadvertencies often happen to Vessels, for want of knowing the true Reason of Things; and particularly, why a Vessel ought to be broader before than abaft, which is demonstrated in *Fig.* 18. Suppose D and F to be two Pyramids, by 2 Lines at the Ends, force them equally, the Pyramid D will move faster than F; because the great End moves or forces but little Weight of Water more than the Cube of the Square at the End doth contain: But the Pyramid F moves with the Point forward, like a Wedge, pressing as much Water as its own solid Body contains.

This proves how cautious Persons ought to be how they pinch in a Vessel Before, and leave her Too broad Abaft; for certainly nothing can be more hurtful to the Sailing of a Ship, than a Neglect in this Particular.

Thus, we hope to have fully clear'd the Suspicion, which is grounded only on the Circumstance of the Water passing thro' her Hold, that she will not steer or sail: For she has, you see, an Advantage in the Current passing thro' her, for feeling her Helm quicker, and consequently, as we have just now shewn, is more likely to steer readily than any other Ship; if it be now remember'd also, that we have before prov'd, that Water is a better and safer Lading than dry Goods, we need only add concerning the Steerage of our Sloop, that whether our skilful and ingenious Builders, Mr. *French* and Mr. *Williamson*, or any other, shall build a Vessel of the common Structure, they will be as unable to answer for her steering or sailing better or worse than any other Vessel that shall be nam'd, as they must be as to one of this Sort. From all which it appears, that there is nothing particularly disadvantageous in our Sloop, as to her Capacity for steering or sailing.

The last Thing we consider'd was, how to supply the Fish with constant fresh Air and Water; and to limit the Water, so that the Currents thro' the Hold shall be no stronger at one Time than at another, by which Means the Fish will be as easy in a Storm as in a Calm. This is effected by Sluices in the Hold, that stop and let go the Water thro' it, to the 10th Part of an Inch. But because this is to be done by the Run of the Sloop, measur'd by a Log-Line, we think it proper, in the first Place, to inform you what the Log-Line is, that measures the Distances run at Sea, and how the Knots are knit at their true Distances, by which we regulate the Flux of Water into the Hold.

Note, That the Equator is divided into 360 Degrees, and each Degree into 60 Parts call'd Miles: And the Distance on any Meridian is divided likewise into the same equal Parts as the Equator, *viz.* 60 Miles or Parts to a Degree: This does not answer our *English* Measure, but is nearest the *Italian* of 5000 *English* Feet to a Mile, and 60 such Miles to a Degree. But since it hath been found by Mr. *Norwood*, by an Observation made between *London* and *York*, and measur'd by a Chain between those two Places, found it to be 69 Miles, a Half, and 14 Foot to a Degree of Latitude, therefore the same must be a

Degree of Longitude on the Equator. Neither could this be true, if the Angles of the Roads were not exactly taken by an Instrument, and by the said Angles and Distances, find the Difference of Latitude, and East and West Meridian-Distances of the two Places, in the Nature of a Ship's Traverse.

Now it is believ'd by most, that Mr. *Norwood*'s Computation is the best and truest that ever was made; yet, notwithstanding all this, most divide the Log-Line in such Proportion as before-mention'd, that 5000 *English* Feet make $\frac{1}{60}$ Part, or a Mile on the Equator: But Mr. *Norwood* makes it to be 6116 *English* Feet to $\frac{1}{60}$ Part, or a Mile, on any Meridian, or the Equator.

Now considering the Log-Line to be measur'd by a Half-Minute Glass, which is the $\frac{1}{120}$ Part of an Hour; divide Mr. *Norwood*'s Mile, viz. 6116 Feet by 120, the Quotient is almost 51 Feet between Knot and Knot on the Line; but if you divide the old Calculation, *viz.* 5000, by 120, the Quotient is but 41.66 Feet between Knot and Knot; but they commonly knit 42, which must be very false, or else the famous Mr. *Norwood* was out in his Observations, which could not well be, if he had good Instruments to take his Angles, an exact Chain to measure the Distances, and a Quadrant of a large Radius for an Observation.

It is by this Log-Line we govern the Current, or the Course of the Water thro' this Sloop, according to the Ship's Way; for, by so much as she will run faster or slower, by so much is the Current in the Hold faster or slower.

Fig. 19, represents a Circle divided into 8 Parts; 3, 4, 5, 6, 7, 8, 9, 10, are the Knots the Ship runs; A, the Hand, to move to those Knots. This Circle is fix'd between-Decks, over the Sluices before. At 10 Knots the Sluices are quite Close, and will not admit of a Gallon of Water into the Hold in six Hours; but move the Hand A backward from 10 to 10, the Sluices are quite open, and let in the whole Current of Water: If the Ship runs 3, 4, 5, &c. Knots, or 3¼, 3½, or any of the rest; move the Hand A to the Knots, Halves, or Quarters, it opens or shuts the Sluices with immediate Readiness, and is manag'd with the same Ease as the Hand of a Clock; without which Contrivance, the Fish must have had perpetual Disturbance, and been driven all together, as in a Net, and stifled for want of Air. The Sluices abaft are likewise closed or open'd at Pleasure, as we shall see convenient.

We must desire the World to excuse us from discovering how this Contrivance in the Hold is fram'd; for we are constrain'd by prudential Reasons, to conceal it for some Time.

It is now our Business to proceed to an Explanation of an Engine for carrying Fish alive by Land, and describe the Contrivance of it, which we conceive to be as well supported by Reason and the Laws of Mechanism, as that for the Conveyance of Fish by Sea. [Fig. 20]

The Description *of a Carriage to convey Fish alive to any Part by Land, keeping a constant Current of Water thro' it.*

A, the Cistern to hold the Fish, being 4 Foot 6 Inches long, 2 Foot 9 Inches broad, and the whole Depth 2 Foot 3 Inches, but in Water 1 Foot 6 Inches. It will hold 138.8 Gallons, Weight 1160 Pounds, or 10 Hundred 1 Quarter and 12 Pounds *Averdupois* Weight; F, the Fountain to supply the Cistern with Water, as fast as it is pump'd up by the Wheel of the Carriage, being 2 Foot 9 Inches long, 1 Foot 3 Inches broad, and 1 Foot 3 Inches deep, measures 32.14 Gallons, Wine Measure, Weight 268 Pounds, or 2 Hundred 1 Quarter and 16 Pounds *Averdupois* Weight; D, the Pump fix'd in the Cistern; E, the Nozel of the Pump; C, an Iron Bar, fasten'd to the Rod of the Pump, which said Rod is forc'd up by 3 Tappets, fasten'd to the Stock of the Wheel, as P, Q, &c. and B, a large Tap, to draw out all the old Water, when an Opportunity serves to fill with fresh.

Now it is plain, as the Carriage is drawn along, the Motion of the Wheels must pump the Water out of the Cistern A, which contains the Fish, into the Fountain F, which, by so much as the said Fountain is higher than the Cistern, by so much the Weight of Water must press thro' the small Holes out of the Bottom of the Fountain F, into the Cistern A, which must of Necessity keep the Water always in Motion, to the Relief of the Fish; but at all Opportunities on the Road, we shall draw out, at the Tap B, all the stale Water, and fill the Fountain and Cistern with fresh River or running Water. This Carriage hath been prov'd by a Carriage made in the like Form, wherein was put small Fishes, and kept there seven Weeks; but when

we stopp'd the Current for some Time, we found them to grow
sick, and one or two die; but when the Water was put in
Motion, we could perceive those still living to revive and grow
brisk. By this we concluded, that according to the Number of
Fishes in the Carriage, the Water would sooner or later corrupt;
which likewise proves our Assertion in the *Fish-Pool* Sloop.

We have gone through the Illustration and Proof of our
Design, as to the Reasonableness of it; it remains only that we
say something concerning its Usefulness; upon which Subject,
it is neither graceful or necessary to say much, but the Thing
speaks itself; and when we consider what Injury is receiv'd by
tormenting Land-Animals, and how the Corruption of their
Bodies is hasten'd by chasing and driving them, we may easily
conceive, that the miserable and painful Way, in which Fish,
for a much longer Time, is convey'd in *Well-Boats*, must have
suitable unhealthy Effects: That so delicious a Food as that of
Sea-Animals, brought alive and in Health to our very Kitchins,
wherever we reside, cannot but be as welcome and beneficial
to all Mankind, as well as fortunate to the Undertakers, as any
Invention that has been brought into Practice for many Ages.

Neither can this Design have any ill Consequences upon the
FISHING TRADE in general; since all Men, upon very easy
Terms, may be admitted into the Use of this Machine, in such
a Manner, as that the Persons already engag'd in it, may have
no Reason to complain, and all the rest of the World have very
great and unexpected Benefit by it.

The lowering the Price of Fish will abundantly make up to
the Sellers of it, by the much greater Number of Purchasers;
and if a Man gets ten Pound by selling what cost him five, to
twenty People, he will be in a better Condition, than when he
made seven Pounds of five, by selling the Commodity which
cost him that Sum, to fifteen, ten, or five Persons: For it is certain, that when a better Commodity can be had for a lower
Price, the Number of new Purchasers will more than make up
for the Abatement of the Price formerly given by a few.

But notwithstanding the plain Proof of the Reasonableness
of this Design, which has been here made in Theory, and the
Practice of it in little Experiments; we must not expect the
World will be fully convinc'd of the Truth and Usefulness of

it, 'till we have actually presented them with Fish imported in great Quantities this Way: But we thought it incumbent upon us to explain our selves, before we expos'd Men to the Hazard of the Seas on so new a Projection: For should it so happen, (which God forbid) that this Vessel should come to any Disaster in Circumstances, which would be equally dangerous to any Vessel of the ordinary Structure; it would be attributed to the Novelty of her Make, and never acknowledg'd that any other Ship in that Situation would have equally suffer'd.

But it is Time to fear, that we are falling into the natural Infirmity of being too fond of our own Productions; we therefore (begging Leave to annex the Patent, which his Majesty has been graciously pleas'd to give for the Use of this Invention for the ordinary Term in such Cases) submit the whole Matter, with great Humility, to the Consideration of the Publick.[3]

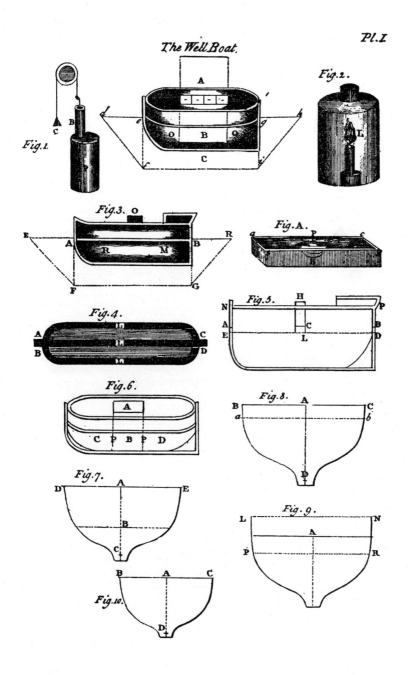

Pl. I

The Well Boat.

Fig. 1.

Fig. 2.

Fig. 3.

Fig. A.

Fig. 4.

Fig. 5.

Fig. 6.

Fig. 7.

Fig. 8.

Fig. 9.

Fig. 10.

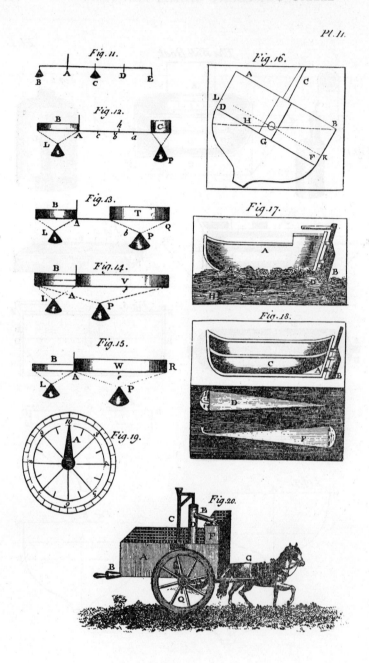

Pl. II.

Fig. 11.

Fig. 12.

Fig. 13.

Fig. 14.

Fig. 15.

Fig. 16.

Fig. 17.

Fig. 18.

Fig. 19.

Fig. 20.

The Plebeian. To be Continued Weekly . . . By a Member of the House of Commons Nos. I-IV
(March and April, 1719)

Steele made a considerable contribution to the discussion of the Peerage Bill, the issues of which were before the public during the year of 1719. It was a ministerial measure, brought up in February in the first session, at once finding favor in the Lords. On 2 March the King agreed to it in principle, and on the 14th it was read in the Commons. On that day Steele's *Plebeian*, No. I, appeared. Between that time and the end of the session, about the first of May, he contributed three more numbers of the periodical and *The Joint and Humble Address* to the steadily growing opposition. The Ministry considered it ill-advised, for the time being, to press the measure; but in November at the beginning of the second session, the Bill was again introduced, with alterations, and it passed the Lords on the 23rd. On the morning of 8 December, when it had the second reading in Commons, Steele's *Letter to Oxford* was published; and in the memorable eight-hour debate of the afternoon, he delivered his speech, together with other opposition speakers under the leadership of Walpole. At the division the vote stood 177 for the Ministry and 269 for the opposition.

This Bill provided that not more than six beyond the existing number of 178 English peers could ever be created, the King's peer-creating prerogative to be limited to the filling of vacancies caused by extinct peerages. And the 16 representative Scots peers elected for each parliament from the peerage of Scotland (according to the terms of the Union Treaty) were to be permanently replaced by 25 hereditary Scots peers. The effect would be to make the Lords, already powerful in wealth and prestige, a closed body of increased power. The Commons—and the electorate—would be overshadowed. The Royal prerogative would be greatly limited. The Lords would become a dominating oligarchy.

The underlying purpose of the Bill was to provide further for the Whig supremacy by ensuring a permanent Whig majority in the Lords. Creation by the King of new peers inimical to the Whig ministry was not feared; but this use of the prerogative by his successor, the Prince of Wales, mainstay of the opposition, was feared. The King agreed to the arbitrary measure as a blow at the Prince, against whom he had a grievance. The scheme seems to have originated with Lord Sunderland, first Lord of the Treasury, whom the Prince disliked; but it was supported by Stanhope and Craggs, Jr., Secretaries for the Northern and Southern Departments; Aislabie, Chancellor of the Exchequer; Newcastle, Lord Chamberlain; and Addison, late Secretary for the Southern Department. The opposition came from the Tories of the House, led by Shippen and Wyndham, and from the dissident Whigs. Steele was quite independent, not taking sides in the party rift; but his principles and convictions on this issue put him on the side of Walpole and progressive Whiggism. The price he paid for his active politics against the Ministry was removal in January, 1720 from the governorship of Drury Lane Theatre.

In *Plebeian* No. I, Steele outlines what he considers the weaknesses of the Bill, which he declares is " Neither a Whig nor a Tory point but a Scheme that might hereafter set up some nobles above the Crown and Commons both." His main arguments against it are that it threatens the alteration of the constitution, a breach of the Union Treaty with Scotland, and an encroachment upon the Royal prerogative. As an additional objection he mentions the closing thereby of peerages to the commoner: " a discouragement to virtuous actions, to learning, and industry." All his arguments, however, are brought to bear on one central point: that the equilibrium of power among Crown, Commons, and Lords as determined by the constitution, at the Revolution, will be destroyed and that the limited monarchy will be replaced by an aristocracy.

In answer to *Plebeian* No. I, the first number of Addison's *Old Whig* came out anonymously on 19 March. *Plebeian* No. II on the 23rd was the rejoinder. Steele answers the *Old Whig's* criticisms and examines his position: " I am afraid he is so *old a Whig* that he has quite *forgot his Principles.*" Addison's main point (Steele thinks) is that the Royal prerogative, unwisely used, may become a menace—that is to the freedom of the Ministry; curtailing it, Addison argues, will be a safe method of holding the Lords in check, so that the incident of 1711 can never be repeated, and will, moreover, tend to strengthen the Commons. Steele maintains that the power of the Commons—the plebeians—will inevitably be diminished in the event of a curtailed Royal prerogative as the Lords will be, " a limited, fix'd, hereditary Body." (He speaks of 235 peers: that is, 178 English, 25 Scots, 26 Bishops, 6 additional).

No. III is short, consisting of the reprint of a rather feeble speech on behalf of the Bill by an nonentity, presented, Steele says ironically, with " great Strength of Reason." It was addressed to a government official, Martin Bladen, Comptroller of the Mint, who was Chairman of the Committee on the Peerage Bill.

No. IV is in part addressed to Addison's *Old Whig*, No. II (the last) of 2 April; and there is a brief reference also to *The Patrician*, a periodical of four numbers which ran concurrently with *The Plebeian*. The controversy between Addison and Steele is not advanced by new arguments. Although there are several personal gibes—and, it must be admitted, at least one inscrutable reference—the spirit is by no means as acrimonious as has sometimes been made out; and the ending is on a friendly note. The main point of No. IV, as announced in the title, is the Scots affair. A main purpose of the Bill, according to its preamble, was to remedy a provision in the Union Treaty of 1707 which was alleged to be unfair to Scotland. Steele maintained that to replace the 16 elective Scots peers by 25 who were to be hereditary and permanent would be a breach of the Treaty. He was sensitive to Scottish interests, being at the time on the Commission for Forfeitures in Scotland. Textual notes on p. 646.

THE

PLEBEIAN.

****

To be continued Weekly.

****

Nº I.
Considerations upon the Reports relating to THE PEERAGE.

Quifquis erit vitæ fcribam color.   Horat.

By a Member of the Houfe of COMMONS.

LONDON:

Printed for S. POPPING at the *Black Raven* in *Paternofter-Row.* 1719. (Price 6 d.)
Where Letters are taken in, directed for the *Plebeian.*

Considerations upon the Reports relating to the Peerage.

—Hoc miserae Plebi—commune Sepulchrum. Hor.

ALL Men in high Stations have their Enemies, who are ready to suggest on every Occasion, whatever may tend to lessen their Credit, and make them odious to the Publick. The Persons at present in great Authority have been pursued by this Evil Spirit; but it would be unjust to give too easy a Belief to the Insinuations of malicious People. At the beginning of this Session it was reported with much Assurance, that a wonderful Discovery was made, that all the Charters of *England* were forfeited into the Hands of the Crown; and this happy Incident, as they call'd it, was to afford an Opportunity of introducing a Law much for the publick Service: But this was so far from being true, that the Bill which came down from the House of Peers was a Confirmation of the Charters, without so much as a Declaration of any Forfeiture. Perhaps it might have been true, that some little Lawyer had found out some mean Chicane in Law, worthy enough of the Pursuit of such a Person, in a private Corporation-Squabble; but such a Project, in order to a universal Forfeiture, could never have Weight with any judicious Man whatever. Nobody could be so very a Novice in Business, or so extravagant in Politicks, as to put his Majesty upon an Undertaking, which contributed more towards the Ruin of King *James*, than any one thing, or perhaps than every thing else besides. When this Report was blown over, the next thing insinuated to the Publick was a Design of making a Jest of what Justice has been accidentally done to the Nation, by repealing the Attainder of one of the greatest Offenders of the late Reign. 'Tis very certain no such attempt will be now made: There has been a just Indignation shewn already at the bare mention of it, and it is unfair to charge any particular Person with having had any such Intention; much less should a scandalous Discourse gain Credit, that any great Officer belonging to his Majesty would correspond abroad with an attainted Fugitive, intercede for him at home, and even prostitute the Character of an Ambassador so low, as to become the Messenger of a Traitor. These [1] two unjust Accusations were laid at the door of some Great People, at the beginning, and towards the middle of this Session; and now at the End of it, the Publick is alarmed with the Report of another Design, of a more dangerous Nature than either of those already mentioned. But as those former reports have not prov'd true, so I doubt not but this will likewise vanish in the same manner. However, as I was ready to have appear'd in Publick on either of the former Occasions, if there had been a necessity for it; so, if I am a little more forward in the present Affair, I hope the importance of it will justify me: and if I should lose my labour, I shall however shew that good Intention for the Service of my Sovereign and my Fellow-Subjects, with which I have always expos'd my self at a dangerous Crisis.

IT is affirm'd by some People, that a bill will be offer'd to the House of Commons, in which the present Sixteen Peers of *Scotland* are to be made Hereditary, to the Exclusion of their Electors, and Nine more added upon the same foot; and Six more are to be added to the number of *English* Peers; and then the Crown is to be restrain'd from making any new Lords, but upon the Extinction of Families.

AT first sight, this Proposal must appear very shocking: it carries with it so [2] great an Alteration of the Constitution; it implies so direct a Breach of the Union, and of natural Justice; and encroaches so much upon the Prerogative of the Crown.

AS to what relates to the *Scottish* Peerage, I must confess I am at a loss to say any thing to it. If the most solemn Contract betwixt two Nations is to be violated; if Persons are to be depriv'd of their Right without being heard, and without any pretence of Forfeiture; if those who have a power intrusted to them by their Principals only for a few Years, can seize it to themselves and their Posterity for ever; what use will be made of Power so acquir'd, I leave every one to judge.

THE shutting up the Door of the House of Lords in the manner talk'd of, cannot but prove a great Discouragement to virtuous Actions, to Learning and Industry, and very detrimental to the House of Peers itself, by preventing such frequent

Supplies from going into it, as the Nature of such a Body requires; for want of which, it may in time become corrupt and offensive, like a stagnated Pool, which hitherto has been preserv'd wholesome and pure by the fresh Streams that pass continually into it.

I AM not unaware that it will be said, *That the frequent Extinctions of Families will solve this Inconvenience, and make room for the rewarding of Merit.* But this Expedient, I fear, is not much to be depended on; for the Uncertainty of the Time when the Crown will have any such Power, will make it much the same as if it was never to have it at all. Besides, it is to be consider'd, that the Patrons of this Proposal argue vehemently for it, *on account, that this will be a means to ease the Crown from the great Importunity of Pretenders to Peerage.* If so, it is certain in what manner they will proceed in all Vacancies, which will be by filling them up instantly; or else the Inconvenience wou'd be increas'd as to Importunity, and not diminish'd. This being the Case, it is very evident by what sort of People those Vacancies will be supply'd; undoubtedly by the Creatures and Relations of those Peers who have at that time the greatest Influence in the House, and whose Requests to the Throne will very much resemble Demands: and this Honour, in all probability, will only be thought proper for their own Families. An instance of this we have in the Distinction of the Garter. At the first Institution of that Order, and till of late Years, several Commoners had the Honour (as the Reward of Merit) to be of that Noble Body: But at present, it would be look'd upon as a high Presumption in any Commoner to pretend to it, let his Services be never so great.

BUT another Consequence, of a much higher nature, attending the Limitation of the Number of Peers, is the Danger there will be of changing the Constitution by this means into an Aristocracy: And this may at any time in such case be effected by the Confederacy of two or three great Families, which wou'd form such a Body amongst the Lords, as the Crown wou'd not be able to controul. That this kind of government is one of the worst sorts of Slavery,[3] is too well known to be disputed. In a Democracy a great many different Persons may come to have a Share of Power by several Incidents; but in the other State it is Birth only that entitles to Superiority: and the Milk such Nobles are nursed up with, is Hatred and Contempt for every Human Creature, but those of their own imaginary Dignity.

THESE being some of the Inconveniences and Hazards which naturally occur upon this Proposal, let us see what are the Advantages which on the other hand, it is said, will flow from it.

First, "THAT this will be a Bar upon the Crown, and prevent the King upon the Throne from flinging in a great Number of Lords on a sudden, only to answer a present Purpose, as the late Queen once did."

Secondly, "THAT it will be a means to keep Property or great Estates in the House of Commons, from whence they are generally drawn out into the House of Peers."

THESE are said to be such plain Whig-Points, as no Whig can oppose.

WHIGGISM, if I understand it aright, is a Desire of Liberty, and a Spirit of Opposition to all Exorbitant Power in any part of the Constitution. Formerly the Danger on this account was from the Crown; but since the *Habeas Corpus* Act, and the many *Restraints* laid upon the Crown in King *William's* Time, and the great and numerous *Limitations* of the *Succession Acts,* the *Prerogative* of the Crown is reduc'd so low, that it is not at all dangerous to the Commons. Besides, the Crown has frequent occasions for the Assistance of the Commons; but the Lords never. The Lords are judges of the Property of the Commons in the last Resort; and even in Cases where they themselves are concern'd, they have their actions *de Scandalis Magnatum*, and exercise a Power of imprisoning, not confin'd within any very certain boundaries. And therefore the chief Circumspection of the Commons ought to be employ'd at present, that those who have so much Power already, do not get more than the Commons will be able to withstand in any manner. I confess the making a great Number of Lords on a sudden has one Inconvenience: It may prevent some Good to the Publick, but cannot do any great Hurt, and is more grievous in its Consequences to the Crown than to the People. The increasing the Number of Peers is always to be wish'd for by the Commons, because the greater their Number, the less considerable they become, and the less within the Influence of Court Favours;

by which means alone Ministers are kept in awe, and remain in a Situation of being called to account for their Actions. Were it otherwise, they wou'd be out of the reach of any Accusation: They wou'd know exactly by whom they were to be try'd, and their Judges might be their Accomplices. And shou'd this once come to be the Case, what might they not attempt with Impunity?

ON the other hand, if their Lordships complain of the great Number of Peers as a Grievance to themselves, why are they desirous any more shou'd be made? If twelve at once was so bad a Precedent, what is fifteen, taking it in one Light? What is thirty-one, if you take it in another?

IF at the Union, sixteen *Scottish* Noblemen were found to be a just Proportion to represent their whole Nobility, what has happen'd since, to give reason to increase their Number to twenty five? Why may they not as well a few Years hence, especially if the Head of a Clan is to be taken in, who may not like the Set of Nobles at that time, demand to be made fifty, to give his Followers the Majority; and so from time to time continue to play the Game into each other's Hands, as long as there is one Nobleman left in *Scotland,* or any Civil List in *England?* If the Commoners of *England* are to be excluded from the House of Lords, why are they not excluded forthwith? It cannot be suppos'd that Titles *in petto* are kept on purpose to bribe Persons of Consequence in the House of Commons, to drive such a Bill through that part of the Legislature.

UPON the foot the Constitution has subsisted many Years, the Crown, in all great Emergencies relating immediately to it self, has been able to fence against the Lords by adding to their Number, and against the Commons by Dissolutions; and in like manner in Cases of Difference betwixt the two Houses. But if such a Law as is mentioned above shou'd be made, and any Difference happen hereafter betwixt the Crown and the House of Peers, or betwixt the Two Houses of Parliament, the Crown may not have it in its power to influence the Lords in relation to it self or in relation to the Commons. And therefore it must be the inevitable Consequence of such a Misfortune that both the Crown and the Commons must submit to the Lords. In former times, the greatest Art and Care of the Crown and

31

Ministers us'd to be the Preventing of Jealousies and Differences betwixt the two Houses. This Proposal, I fear, would be raising an implacable Animosity and Hatred, scarce ever to be reconciled.

THE great Advantage that the Number of their Body cannot be increas'd, is at present the most valuable Privilege of the Commons, and the only thing that makes them considerable. The Lords are possess'd of many great Privileges, that they will not permit the Commons to share with them; and therefore the Commons would be highly wanting to themselves, if they shou'd add this Advantage likewise to the Lords, which is the only one that they enjoy distinct from them.

IT has been used as an Argument, by some People, for the increasing the Number of the Lords, "That the Crown formerly increased the Number of the Commons, in particular in Queen *Elizabeth*'s reign." But I desire it may be understood, that the sending Members to Parliament at that time was not desir'd as a Favour, but impos'd as a Burden. Queen *Elizabeth* erected several new Corporations; but then the Reason for it was, she reliev'd several ancient and decayed ones from sending any Members at all. And how little this resembles the present Case, is easily perceiv'd.

THE other Advantage, which 'tis said will accrue from this Proposal, is, "That it will be a means to keep Property amongst the Commons."

I cannot see that there is occasion for so extraordinary a Step as this is, and accompany'd with so many Evils, to procure us this Assurance. Property or Wealth in every Age flows faster back to the Commons by the extinction of Families, but much more by the want of Oeconomy in the Peers, than it is drawn from them by the Promotions of the Crown. Besides, we see Estates are often extinct before Families; and Property is very rarely increas'd in the House of Peers. Indeed, if a Restraining Bill shou'd pass, I do not doubt but it wou'd be soon follow'd with a Bill to prevent Lords from alienating their Estates, for which many plausible Reasons are to be produc'd: And then, without all dispute, the Balance of Property wou'd be soon turn'd on the side of their Lordships.

THESE are all the Arguments I have heard for this supposed Bill; which is neither a Whig nor a Tory point, but wou'd be

a Scheme that might hereafter set up some Nobles above the
Crown and the Commons both. For as to what is commonly
said, That the Lords would get nothing, no new Power would
be added to them by this means; I beg leave to state this Matter
in a proper Light. Suppose the Balance to be now *even* betwixt
the Lords and the Crown, as it certainly is, or else the Constitution wou'd not subsist in quiet; is it not plain to the most
common Capacity, that when two Scales are upon an equal
Poise, if you take any Weight out of one of them, you give the
Advantage to the other, without putting any thing into it?

HOW dangerous it may prove to vary the Balance of Power
in a limited Monarchy, we may learn from the Ruin of one of
the best-founded Governments amongst the Antients. The
original Power, the *Ephori*, in the *Lacedæmonian* State, were
invested with, besides that of being part of the Legislature, was
chieflly the determining Law-Matters relating to private Contracts, and such-like Business. In the Absence of their Kings
they compos'd the Regency: *Regum absentum vicarii erant*, is
the Expression made use of by *Crags, De Rep. Lac. p.* 76. But
afterwards, upon the Diminution of the Regal Authority (which
indeed was voluntarily comply'd with by their King, as I shall
shew by and by) their Power grew immense; *Eorum potestas
in immensum aucta est.* Crags, ibid.

THEY administer'd every Thing of consequence: they dispos'd of the publick Treasure: They influenc'd the Assembly
of the People, and made them vote for Peace or War, as they
thought fit; *Concionem populi Regebant; Bellum pacemque
Concionis suffragiis sciscebant.* Ub, Em. des Re. la, Gr. p. 293.
They made or broke Treaties; They rais'd or disbanded the
Army. In fine, they *had* or *usurp'd* the Right of rewarding or
punishing whom and when they pleas'd. At last they took upon
them to dethrone, or imprison, or execute their Kings themselves. *Theopompus*, King of *Sparta*, was advis'd against giving
way to the *Diminution* of the Royal Dignity, by which the
Power of those Magistrates grew so great: But he declar'd he
did it, to settle *the Government by that means upon a more
lasting Foundation: Ut diuturniorem potestatem relinqueret.*
Crags, p. 74.

THIS unwary Step prov'd fatal both to the Crown and the

People, and ended in the Ruin of the Constitution. *Theopompus* was one of the most virtuous, most moderate, and most gracious Princes amongst all the *Spartan* Kings. It appear'd evidently by this very Instance of his Willingness to part with the Power of the Crown for the Good of his People: But for that very Reason the People shou'd not have suffered the Authority of the Crown to have been weaken'd, but should rather have added to it, since Power could not be lodg'd any where else so much for their Safety and Advantage. When the Prince had no longer Force enough to restrain the many-headed Sovereignty, it bore down all that *stood in its way*, as we have heard; and in the end grew so insupportable, that the People, to be deliver'd from so vile a Slavery, submitted to the Usurpation of a *private Person*, who, to the Satisfaction of revenging them upon their *Oppressors*, added this single Act of Grace: [He wip'd off all the publick Debts at once.] *Ut Plebem demulseret, Æs alienum universum delevit.* Em. p. 349. *Et respublica in Tyrannidem conversa est.* Crags, p. 72.

THOSE who are desirous to consult the Author himself, whom I have chiefly quoted on this occasion, must have recourse to his Book of the *Lacedemonian* Government, printed 1593, *apud Petrum Santandreanum.* It appears by the Dedication of this Treatise, that he was a Follower of the first Minister of the Court of *Denmark,* upon whom he solely depended to make his Fortune, *tuo patrocinio salus mea constituta,* Ep. D. The character *Ubbo Emmius,* a great Lawyer of that Age (who was a sort of Rival to my Author) gives of *Crags,* is, That he was a person of great Boldness and Industry, *ausu & industria,* Pref. to Des Re. Graec. but not so happy in his Judgment. But begging pardon for this Digression, which is only intended for the Curious, and to return to my Subject: There are other and more modern Instances, and living Historians of our own, who can satisfy us, that too great a Power in the hands of the Nobility, has brought on the Ruin of many free Nations. This was the Case of *Sweden* a few Years ago, as appears plainly from the very ingenious Labours of a venerable Prelate of the present House of Peers. This was the Case of *Denmark,* of which a very accurate Account has been given by a Noble Lord of a neighbouring Kingdom, a Member of the House of Com-

mons. Nothing can be better writ, or more instructive to any
one that values Liberty, than the Narrative of that Tragedy in
that excellent Treatise. I wish Gentlemen would see there, how
Commoners were treated by the Nobility when they had the
power over them. This Noble Lord will inform them, That
" they laid heavy Impositions on the Commons at Pleasure;
which Weight they themselves would not touch with one of
their Fingers." And when the Commons presum'd to complain,
tho they were just come " from saving, from a Foreign Yoke,
not only the capital City of their Country, but the whole Kingdom, the Royal Family, nay those very Nobles that dealt so
hardly by them": I say, when the Commons ventur'd to complain, let any *Englishman* but hear the answer that was given
them: "A principal Senator," *says his Lordship*, " stood up,
and in great Anger told the President of the City, That the
Commons neither understood nor considered the Privileges of
the Nobility, nor the true Condition of themselves, who were no
other than *Slaves*." The Commons, fir'd with Indignation at
this Treatment, and resolving, if they were to be *Slaves*, to be
Slaves to their Prince, rather than *Slaves* to their Fellow-Subjects,
instantly surrender'd all their Liberties to their King; and the
Lords were forc'd to follow their example with so much haste,
that " in four days time that Kingdom was chang'd," *says my
noble and honest Author*, " to as absolute a Monarchy as any
in the whole World."

IN short, it has been for our antient Constitution that we have
struggled with so much Vigour for many Years together: 'tis
for That we have pour'd out a River of *English* Blood, and a
Treasure unheard of in any former Age. This Constitution may
have its Imperfections; but, faulty as it is, our Ancestors have
convey'd down Liberty to us thro that Channel: and we ought
to continue it on, as well as we can, to our Posterity, and not
give way to the new-modelling Schemes of every *extraordinary*
Genius. It would certainly be new-modelling the Constitution
in a great measure, to take a considerable part of what Power
is left to the Crown from the Crown, and by that means add
very much to the Power of the Lords.

BESIDES, it is to be remember'd, that the Evil, which may be
brought upon the Commons by this means, will be irretrievable.

Those Persons deceive themselves, who think, that if such a Law should prove destructive, it may be annull'd, *nothing being more usual than for one Parliament to repeal the Acts of another.* This is true in common Cases, because almost all Laws relate to every part of the Legislature, and any Inconvenience is felt in some measure by each of them: But this will be a Law which will relate chiefly, nay solely, to the Lords; and whatever Injury the Crown or the Commons may receive by it, their Lordships will be very sensible of the Advantage of it to themselves: and nothing can be more vain, than to imagine, that the Commons will be ever able to shake off any Exorbitant Power that the Lords shall be once possess'd of, unless it be by an universal Destruction, like those just mentioned, which will swallow Lords and Commons, and all Estates together. For which Reasons, this Project, if it should ever be offer'd to the Commons, is not only to be opposed with all the Zeal imaginable, but every Step, every Attempt towards it, is to be detested. *He that gives the Power of Blood, is a Murderer; and he that gives the Power of Tyranny, is a Tyrant.* I shall add but one word more: The greatest *Traytor* to Civil Society that ever yet appear'd, will be the Man, if such a one can be found, who shall contend for such a Bill, should it be propos'd amongst the Commons, with the Assurance in his Pocket of being a Peer as soon as the Bill passes: And should he succeed, which God forbid, that Honour which is to be the reward of so base a Treachery, will be a lasting Mark of Infamy to the Family that bears it, whilst any Notion of Honesty remains amongst Mankind.

[*The Plebeian.* No. II. Monday, March 23, 1719.]

Considerations upon the Reports relating to the PEERAGE continu'd.

THOSE who are not particularly acquainted with the Vocation of Pamphlet-Writing, have very much wonder'd that a Matter of so great Consequence, as the Affair of the PEERAGE, and espous'd by such Persons as are very well known to be its Patrons, cou'd have been so long a while upon the Stage, and

no Champion appear for it: but others, who are more vers'd
in this kind of Business, know, there cou'd not be wanting
Persons enough to make their Court, by producing their Lucu-
brations on this Head. But as it is a Subject that will not very
well bear debating, their Masters, without doubt, were of
opinion, that the best way was, to let all manner of Writing
alone, and keep all that cou'd be said on the Subject, for the
Time and Place where it was absolutely necessary to say something.

THE Agitators for the bill assur'd themselves, that nobody
wou'd be so bold as to attack first; and consequently judg'd
themselves out of all danger. But the PLEBEIAN [1] starting forth
unexpectedly, they were forc'd, like People in a Surprize, or on
an Invasion, to march immediately any Troops they had: and
indeed, these are some of the most tatter'd I ever saw.

THE first Champion that appear'd for this Bill, was a Person
who exhibited himself in the *St. James's-Post*, of Wednesday,
March 18, in this Advertisement: *Some Considerations relating
to the Peerage of* Great Britain. *Wherein the Arguments for
the Reasonableness and Expediency of a Bill, said to be depending, are stated* Pro *and Con.*

THIS Performance I have not been able to venture upon;
for He that can state Arguments *for* the Bill, both *Pro* and *Con,*
is too slippery a Person for any body to lay hold of.

THE next that enter'd the Lists, on the same side of the
Question, having been more fortunate than to *discover himself
beforehand,* I have perus'd his Labours. The Account he gives
of himself, is, " That he is a *Member of the House of Commons,*
who has a Friend with whom he uses to talk over in *private* all
Arguments and Considerations which concern any thing of
moment, as far as they could collect and remember them: and
they having both agreed, that this was a Matter of a very extraordinary Nature, the one entreated the other to put his Thoughts
about it in Writing, that he might be better able to judge of
them all together. And in order to continue the Privacy of this
Correspondence, those Thoughts came out, printed for *J. Roberts*
in *Warwick-Lane.*"

THIS notable Introduction was very near having the same
effect upon me, as to this Pamphlet, as the Advertisement just

mention'd had to the former; but with much ado I went thro the
Performance. All I can learn from it, is, That this Gentleman
was present at the Debates of the House of Lords; where he
does not seem to have been mightily enlighten'd as to the true
State of the Case, the Debate having in all probability run
pretty much one way.[a]

THE next that follows these two Combatants for this Bill, is
somebody or other that is us'd to Masquerading, as I suppose;
and indeed he is so well disguis'd, that 'tis impossible to know
him. When I first read the Title, *The Old Whig*, I expected
no less than the utmost Wrath and Indignation against the
House of Lords. I could not help thinking but he would have
been for *Voting them useless* at least, as his Ancestors did
formerly: But I was extremely surpriz'd to find just the contrary; that he is for giving them such a Power, as would soon
make the *House of Commons useless*; and therefore he might
as well have taken any other Title in the World, as *The Old
Whig*. I am afraid he is so *old a Whig*, that he has quite
forgot his Principles.

BUT I shall shew now more plainly, what is said in the
former PLEBEIAN, that this is neither a *Whig* nor a *Tory* point,
but is a Jumble, a Hodge-Podge, a Confusion of all Parties and
all Persons together; and must inevitably in its Consequences
destroy first *Whig* and *Tory*, and afterwards *Crown* and *People*.
As all sorts of People unite for it, so ought all Sorts, and of
every Denomination, that have any value for their Constitution,
to unite against it.

THIS Pamphlet, by the Marks it appears with, being in all
probability the best Performance that is to come from that
Quarter, the PLEBEIAN will consider it thoroughly: and in order
to proceed more methodically, for this Author's Satisfaction,

First, I WILL answer the Objections made to the last
PLEBEIAN.

Secondly, I WILL consider the Argument, as the *Old Whig*
states it himself.

THE first Objection the Author of the Remarks makes to the
PLEBEIAN, is page 12. where he says, "That the *Introduction*,

---

[a] P. 8. [Steele's note]

the Digression upon the *Ephori*, and the *Conclusion*, are all Arguments *ad conflandam invidiam.*" He who says that Arguments drawn from History, which can only shew what has happen'd in former times, are Arguments *ad conflandam invidiam*, gives up the Matter in dispute, and lets the World know, by passing them so slightly over, that he feels their force: for it is a tacit admission, that in all probability the like Disasters will happen from the Alterations now projected in our Constitution: which History informs us were the real Consequences of Alterations of the like nature in other Countries; otherwise those Arguments could not now contribute to make Persons invidious. Besides, I always thought that bringing Examples from History was look'd upon as the most impartial and unexceptionable Method of arguing, as it is abstracted from the Passions and Interests of the present Times: for what is the use of Learning, and History, if it be not to draw inferences of what may happen, from what has happen'd?

AS to the Digression upon the *Ephori*, the PLEBEIAN was very careful to avoid giving Offence. Amongst the many extraordinary Powers exercis'd by those Magistrates, there was one of a very uncommon nature; which was, That as they took upon themselves the sole Inspection of the Youth, they were particularly curious of the Persons of the *Boys*. They employ'd every tenth Day in examining the *Youths of about Fifteen, stark naked, Oportebat Ephebos decimo quoque die Ephoris se sistere sine veste*, Ubbo Emmius, des Re. La. p. 235. with whom *Crags* agrees almost in the same words, in the Treatise mention'd in the former PLEBEIAN, p. 78. What an ill Use was made of this Power, we may see in Emmius, p. 236. where speaking of the manner how [2] the *Ephori* liv'd with *those young Men they lik'd best*, he says, *Iis* (Ephebis) *assiduo fere adhaerebant*. Which Words, for fear of offending the PLEBEIAN Ladies, I am not at liberty to translate. However, it is very plain all this was omitted to avoid the least Appearance of personal Reflection.

THE first Argument of the PLEBEIAN, which the *Old Whig* objects to, is p. 12. " That tho the *Plebeian* declares against the propos'd Bill, because it will make so great an Alteration in our Constitution, yet he produces an eminent Instance of a great

Alteration of our Constitution in the Lower House under the Reign of Queen *Elizabeth*, when the Crown erected several new Corporations, and relieved several ancient decay'd ones from sending any Members at all."

THIS, the Remarker says, was as great an Alteration in one Branch of our Legislature, as is now propos'd to be made in another. The Remarker quite mistakes this Point; for, instead of being an alteration of so great consequence to the Constitution of the Commons, as this new proposal is of that of the Lords, it was an Alteration of no consequence at all. Suppose the Towns of *Watchet* and *Dunster*, two Sea-Ports in *Somersetshire*, to have been destroy'd in the Wars with Ireland in Queen *Elizabeth's* Time. The Inhabitants, on account of poverty, apply to the Crown to be exempted from the Charge of paying four Members to represent them in Parliament. The Crown some time after grants Charters to two neighbouring Towns in flourishing Circumstances, and directs the Writs to a following Summons of a Parliament to be sent to *Tiverton* and *Honiton,* instead of *Watchet* and *Dunster*. Let any body judge if this Alteration can be of any consequence to the House of Commons. Here is nothing else but the Places changed; and four Members from *Tiverton* and *Honiton* are the same thing as four from *Watchet* and *Dunster*: But to state this Matter with Nicety would require much more Labour and Time than I am able to allow it.

ANOTHER Argument, which the Remarker says the PLEBEIAN furnishes against himself, is, " That he owns the Prerogative has been retrench'd in several Instances; because without such Retrenchment the Power of it appear'd exorbitant and dangerous to the Commons." But these Retrenchments being now made, the Question at present is, Whether the Commons ought to go on stripping the Crown of every Jewel, till it becomes less resplendent than a Doge of *Venice's* Coronet, or less comfortable than the Sword-bearer's Cap of Maintenance; and, what is of the greatest Moment to the Commons, less able to protect them against the Power of a House of Lords, if ever their Lordships should be disposed to claim a larger Share of Authority than belongs to them.

AS to the Complaint the Remarker makes, That the PLEBEIAN

applies to Mens Passions, and not their Reasons; and declaims, instead of arguing. What must be said in answer to this is, That people must make use of what Arms they have. On the one Side, it is evident there can be nothing but arguing and reasoning, and declaiming and exemplifying; but, on the other, the PLEBEIAN is afraid there are more irresistible Arts of applying to the *Passions*, rather than to the *Reasons* of Men, or else he would not have one Minute's Pain for the Issue of this Question.

THE Manner in which the *Remarker* states the PLEBEIAN's Argument, relating to the *shutting up the Door of the House of Lords*, shews he either wilfully or ignorantly mistakes that part of the Controversy: For, after having cited the words of the PLEBEIAN, he asks, "if it can be detrimental to the House of Lords, and at the same time throw into their Hands all the Places and Honours that the Crown can confer upon them? Will that Body of Men, which wou'd become mean and despicable, and offensive as a stagnated Pool, by the means of this Alteration, be rais'd by the same Means to be the most formidable and most honoured Part of the Constitution? Or would they be able, without numerous Recruits of Wealth, Learning and Industry, to oppose any thing for the Good of the Community?" To this I answer, It will not be detrimental to them in point of Power, but will be detrimental on account of those Talents that ought to accompany Power; the want of which the Commons will feel in their *Judicature*,[3] and in many more Particulars. They will be *offensive* to others, but not perceive it themselves; they will be *formidable*, but not *honour'd*. These are natural *Effects* that all *Exorbitant Power produces*. As to Wealth, they will take it, 'tis to be feared, where they can find it; and Learning and Industry will be as useless Baubles to their Lordships, as *Dangling Peerages* (as my Author describes them excellently well) are to Men of Sense amongst the Commons.

THE next Objection of the *Old Whig* to the PLEBEIAN is, "That he avers the Uncertainty of the Extinction of Families will leave so little Opportunity for the Crown to reward Merit by PATRICIAN Honours, that it will be much the same thing as if the Crown were never to have any such Power at all." *Whereas* (says he) *there will be two Titles extinct every year, according to the Calculation generally received.*

BY the *Calculation generally received*, I suppose the *Remarker* means the List publish'd by way of prelude to this Project. Whether it be true or false, if some Heralds know any thing of this Matter, would take more time to examine into, than, I dare say, the Constitution it is intended to introduce wou'd subsist. But supposing, for Argument sake, that that Calculation is right, and that in one hundred and sixteen Years there have been one hundred and fifty four Extinctions, there will be found wanting seventy eight to make up his Number of two a Year: So that the Extinctions have not been during that Term quite so many as after the Rate of one *Lord and a half* per *Annum*. But besides this Error in Arithmetick, there is another Error of an *odd Nature* in this *Computation*; which, unless some Method is proposed to ascertain it, will reduce the Extinctions to fewer than even one a Year. And if so, those who expect to have their Services rewarded by Reversions so uncertainly computed, may have Time enough to try all their Patience, and at last find that instead of advancing themselves to Dignity, they have been forging their own Chains. In the *Computations of the Titles extinct*, all those are comprehended who have been extinguished by the *Edge of the Law, for Treason, Rebellion, and other Capital Offences*: and who, without the Spirit of Prophecy, can foretell what *Vacancies* may happen by such Means for the future? But if, in favour of this *Scheme*, it be admitted that in all probability there may be as many and as great *Criminals* hereafter in that Noble Body, as there have been for the Time past, is it not to be fear'd that the *Path to justice may be more difficult, after this narrowing the Way up to the House of Peers, than it has been formerly*?

AS to what the *Remarker* has objected to the Arguments of the PLEBEIAN, which prove, " That the Limitation of the Number of the Lords will run the Constitution into an Aristocracy"; this Matter shall be fully considered presently, when I come to examine the *Old Whig's* State of the Case.

IN a following Paragraph, where the *Remarker* takes notice of what the PLEBEIAN urges on the Side of the King and Commons, *viz.* " That an ill Minister might be skreen'd against them both, if this Law should take place, by reason that in such case he wou'd know exactly his Judges (who might likewise be his Accomplices), and so act with Impunity"; the *Remarker* argues, "That if this Bill does not pass, an innocent Minister cannot be secure, nor a guilty one punish'd, if the Crown should add to the House of Peers a sufficient Number of the Enemies of the one, or of the Friends of the other." [4] In either of which Cases the utmost Iniquity must be suppos'd in the Crown, which, I confess, I cannot bring myself to do, and therefore my Argument remains entire. And it would grieve me to the Heart, if I could think there were any *innocent Ministers*, who ought to be embolden'd by the Consciousness of their Integrity, and yet should have greater Apprehensions from honest Actions, than have [5] been hitherto shown by Men of the most guilty Consciences, thro the many Ages that this Constitution has subsisted, without the Alteration now desir'd.

THE *Remarker* thinks it wonderful how the PLEBEIAN cou'd advance, "That the Number of the House of Commons not being subject to an Increase, is the only Advantage that they enjoy distinct from the House of Lords"; and alledges, that *all their Lordships Privileges together are not equal to that one of commanding the Purse of the Community*. Were it true, that the Commoners enjoy'd this Privilege of *commanding the Purse of the Community*, distinct from The House of Lords, they would be very easy as to the increasing, or diminishing, or fixing, their Number, or as to any thing else that might belong to that Noble Assembly. But, alas! this is not the Case; for their Lordships' Concurrence is as necessary to a Money-Bill as to any other Bill: nay, whether a Money-Bill may not originally take its Rise in their House, is a Point never yet clearly given up by their Lordships, if I am not very much misinform'd; and whether they may not be more inclinable to dispute this Matter, if ever their Door comes to be shut in the manner now propos'd, may deserve very serious [6] Reflection.

THUS having answer'd every Objection made to the former PLEBEIAN by the *Old Whig*, except such as will occur in considering this Argument, as he states it himself; I shall now proceed to that Point which I propos'd at first setting out.

I AGREE with our Author, "That the best kind of Government is that which is compos'd of these three Branches, the *Regal*,[7] the *Noble*, and the *Plebeian*." This is at present our happy Constitution: "But then," says this Author, "we have one Imperfection or Defect in it, which wants to be remedy'd, and that is, the Crown has too great a power over one Branch of this Constitution, namely, the Noble; in that the Crown can, whenever it pleases, add so many to their Number as to Influence their Actions." And this Author likewise assures us, p. 4. "That the Crown has power enough also to gain a House of Commons of what Complexion it pleases." From whence I observe, First, That if it be a fault in the Constitution, that the Crown has so great power over one Branch of the Constitution, the *Noble*, as this Author affirms, it is as great an Imperfection that the Crown has so great a Power, as he also affirms it has, over the PLEBEIAN. And therefore this Author should have propos'd some Method to have remedied this Defect in the latter, as well as in the former Branch; or else that Perfection in the Constitution he seems to be desirous of, cannot be arriv'd at. He contends, that it is absolutely necessary the *Lords should be entirely independent of the Crown*: An impartial Friend to the *whole Body of the People,* and to sound Reason, would have said as much for the Commons; then these two Estates would have been upon a Level. But even by such an Alteration, which is the only equal one, our Constitution would not be mended, but made much worse; for if both Lords and Commons were as independent of the Crown as this Author desires the Lords may be, the unhappy Consequence that must ensue wou'd be, that if any Discord shou'd arise betwixt them, and each remain inflexibly resolv'd, here the Constitution wou'd certainly want a casting Power; and the only way of ending the Dispute must be like a *Polish* Dyet, *by getting up on horseback.* And therefore this Power now in the Crown, and which has been in it for so many Ages, is necessary for the Good of the whole Community, to prevent the greatest Confusion, which might otherwise arise from the Passions of Men.

THE Crown once parted with this Power out of its hands to the Commons; and that Concession produc'd the Ruin of the Monarchy, and of the Peerage. If the Crown shou'd part with the Power now to the Lords, that it has over them, why may it not be very reasonably apprehended, that the same fatal Consequence may ensue to the King and the Commons?

IF it be necessary, as it has been plainly shewn, that the Power now in the Crown should remain there, for the Good of the People in general; it is as necessary for the Defence and Advantage of the Crown itself. The Lords (by the Power the Crown has of adding to their Number) are a fluctuating uncertain Body. This is all that gives the Crown any influence over them, and prevents Combinations, Cabals, and Factions against the Crown: But if the Door comes once to be shut, so that the Crown cannot make any considerable Addition to their Number in any Exigencies whatever, what a Door is open'd at the same time to form a Power superior to that of the Crown, and superior to all human Controul! Then they will become a fix'd certain Body: And should three or four ambitious bold Men combine together hereafter, of the greatest Families, and the greatest Estates, where wou'd the Difficulty be of getting a Majority of two hundred thirty five? And, if once obtain'd, what Remedy cou'd be provided in so desperate a Case? Whilst they act in the common Methods of Government, they would command all *Favours*; and, shou'd they ever act in an *arbitrary* Manner, Necessity and Self-defense wou'd make the Union amongst them the stronger.

I WILL now examine what the Author of the *Old Whig* calls the *Great Point*, and which ought to carry the chief Weight with us in this Case; which is, " That the Alteration now propos'd will give such a mighty Power to the Bulk of the *English* Commons, as can never be counter-balanc'd by the Body of the Nobility. Shou'd we suppose two hundred thirty five Peers possess'd one with another of 5000 *l. per Annum*, this wou'd amount to no more than 1,175,000 *l. per Annum*. And what is such a Property, and the Power arising out of it, compar'd with the Power arising out of the Property of those many Millions possess'd by the Commons?"

BY this State of the Case, we are to suppose on the one hand a certain, limited, fix'd, Hereditary Body, of two hundred thirty five Peers, enjoying great privileges above the Commons, and possess'd of an annual Revenue amounting to 1,175,000 l. which they have entirely in their own power; and this Estate not so equally divided as 5000 l. *per Ann.* to every Individual, but to some the Command of 50,000 l. a Year apiece, others not

500 l. a Year. On the other hand, you must suppose a Body
of above twice the Number fluctuating, unfix'd, in the power
of their Prince every Moment, at furthest not able to subsist
above a few Years, and possess'd of not near half the Estate
before-mention'd; is it not too evident which of these two Bodies
must destroy the other, if once this should come to be really
the Case? The Lords are Principals, and act entirely for themselves: The Commoners are no farther Principals, than as to
the Estates they possess themselves. As our Author has stated
this Matter, in order to magnify the Power of the Wealth of
the Commons, tho he is all along speaking of the aggregate
Body, yet he wou'd insinuate as if they had as great Command
over the universal Body of the People, as the Lords have over
themselves. This is as much as to say, that the four Members
of the city of *London* have as absolute Command over the
Estates of all the Inhabitants of that great *Metropolis*, as any four
Lords have over their Tenants. Indeed, if the Commons had
a Power of laying Taxes upon the estates of all those they
represent, that wou'd be the same thing in this Case, provided
they had it abstractedly from the Lords. But this Fallacy, which
is often insinuated in this Pamphlet, has been already detected.
The Commons have no more power over their Fellow-Subjects
estates than the Lords: They cannot lay any Tax without their
Lordships Concurrence. And all that is peculiar to the Commons in this matter is, That they have hitherto been allow'd
to chuse what Tax they judg'd easiest for the People: But every
Day's Experience shews us, that, if the Lords differ in Opinion
from the Commons, their Power is at an end. The better to
illustrate this *Great Point*, as our Author properly calls it; as
he has computed the Value of the Wealth of the Body of Peers,
I will take the liberty to compute the Value of the Wealth of
the Body of the Commons. Supposing them to be worth, one
with another, 800 l. *per Ann.* including personal Estates, which
I am certain is not disparaging this, or any other House of Commons that has sat in a British *Parliament*; the annual Income of
five hundred fifty eight Commoners will amount to 446,400 l.;
which is so insignificant a Sum, in proportion to the Value of
the Property of the Lords, that I will beg leave to compute his
Majesty's whole Civil List with the Property of the Commons,

both Sums together making but one Million forty six thousand four hundred Pounds; and there will still remain a Balance on their Lordships side of one hundred twenty eight thousand six hundred pounds *per Annum.* *Therefore, if it is an uncontested Maxim, That Power follows Property* (*Old Whig* p. 7); here is Power, here is Property; and let the Body that possesses both in such a degree be but once made so independent as is propos'd, would not the Crown, would not the Commons, be absolutely under the Dominion of the Lords, according to this Author's own way of Reasoning?

I AM satisfy'd the Controversy is ended here: But I will suppose my Author not to have been mistaken so very grossly, and examine his Argument upon an Imagination, that the Property of the House of Commons was ten times superior to that of the Lords, whereas the Property of the Lords is near three times as much as theirs; yet even in this Case, the Lords would have the advantage of them; because an united constant Body of Men, always acting for the same Interest and Grandeur, and pursuing a continued Scheme, must be an Over-match for so transitory a Body, and made up of persons of such different Views and Interests as the House of Commons is. To bring an example on this Head. Let us imagine the Stock of the Bank of *England* to be of the Value of One Million, and the Stock or Cash of all the Bankers, Scriveners, Goldsmiths, and Dealers in Money throughout *London,* to be four times or eight times that Sum; is there any body who does not believe the Bank, incorporated and well compacted in all respects for its own private Interest, will not have a greater Power, greater Credit and Authority, than all those particular Proprietors of a much larger Capital, who cannot possibly be ever put into any Posture, so as to act with that weight for their Interest, as the Bank will do for itself in the Circumstances above-mentioned? The great Power of all such fix'd Bodies is chiefly owing to the Circumstance, that two or three Persons always govern the rest; and it is as well the common Interest of the Society that they should be so govern'd, as the particular Interest of the Governors. In this their Strength chiefly consists; and for this reason five or six hundred Lords (if any body can be so wild as to suppose the Crown will ever increase their number to such a degree)

32

will not be so terrible to the Crown or the People, as two hundred thirty-five, or any such fix'd number. For to suppose that the Majority of two hundred thirty-five Lords, were they so fix'd, would not be entirely directed and influenced by three or four amongst them of the greatest Wealth, Abilities, and Resolution, is as absurd and improbable to common Reason and constant Experience, as any thing that can be thought of.

IF it be allow'd then, as it certainly must be, that the Weight of so great Power, and of such disproportionable Property, may by this means come into a very few hands, what Havock may it not make of the Dignity of the Crown, and of the Liberty of the People?

THUS I have shewn the certain destructive Consequences of this Project, as stated by the PLEBEIAN, and even as stated by the *Old Whig* himself. I must confess, I do not believe that the Authors of this Scheme were apprehensive how far it would go; but since it is now so plain, that *he who runs may read,* I hope they themselves will desist from so desperate an Undertaking.

I CANNOT help observing, that his Majesty is treated with great Indignity by the Author before me, in several passages of his Pamphlet. In one place, he says, *Whilst the Door of the House of Lords is always open, People of overflowing Fortunes may find no great difficulty in procuring an Entrance.* In another, he insinuates, That *there is another kind of Merit besides what arises from virtuous Actions, Learning, and Industry, that has been often rewarded with Peerage.* I am satisfy'd his Majesty has us'd this Prerogative as he has every other Prerogative of the Crown, with the greatest Discernment, and therefore I am willing to trust it still in his hands. The House of Lords is treated by this Author still more *en Cavalier* than his Majesty. His words are these: "If the *English* Commonalty should (by this Bill) gain only this single Advantage, I think it a very considerable one, That it will hinder the Nation from being over-run with Lords. We know, that in the Sale of an Estate, it is no small Recommendation to the Buyer, that there is no Lord within so many Miles of it; and the distance of such a Borderer is often look'd upon as an Equivalent to a Year's Purchase. But who can be secure from such a Neighbour, whilst the Species is so apt to increase and multiply? I shall not insist upon paying of Debts, which is looked upon as a moral Duty amongst Commoners, who cannot but be sorry to see any Additions to an Order of Men that are shelter'd by Privileges from the Demands of their honest and industrious Creditors. To which many Considerations of the like nature might be added, were they not obvious to the Private Reflection of every Reader."

I CANNOT very well account for it, how this Author comes to take so great a liberty as he has done here; even so far, as to endeavour to make it believ'd, that the Lords are sheltered from their just Debts; whereas every one knows, a Lord's Goods and Effects are liable to the Pursuit of his Creditors, tho his Person is always protected. This Author and I differ on every account, as to what relates to this Branch of the Legislature. They seem to me to have been for many Years, and to be at present, a just and honourable Body. This, I think, is owing to the Frame of that Body, and the Situation it is in. I am against altering either, for fear [8] lest they should become Tyrannical and Odious. The *Old Whig* represents them to be at present a Species of such a nature, as I dare not venture to repeat, but must refer to his own words; and yet contends to vest them with much greater Powers than they now have.

I HAVE but one Remark more to make upon this Author, which is indeed in a Matter of the last Consequence, and which cannot be thoroughly consider'd till the next Paper. The Author of the *Old Whig* has very truly stated the Power of the Crown, as it relates to the Legislature, in these words:

" The CROWN, as a Branch of the Legislature, cannot desire a greater Prerogative, than that of a negative in the passing of a Law: and as it ought not to influence either House in their Debates, what can a good King desire more, than the Power of approving or rejecting any such Bill as cannot pass into a Law without the Royal Assent?"

AS I readily admit of all that is here advanc'd, That the Regal part of the Legislature is to wait for the Advice of its Great Council, both Houses of Parliament, and to give its Negative to what it does not approve; that doing otherwise would be influencing the Debates of one or both Houses, and turning the Constitution quite upside-down: As I sincerely allow a good King cannot desire any more than the Approving or Rejecting any Bill offered him; and as I believe from the bottom of my Heart, that we never had so good a King as we have now: what Credit can I give to what this Author asserts, that *his Majesty has already signify'd his Consent on this Point,* of so great Consequence to Himself, and to the very Being of his FAITHFUL COMMONS, before he has so much as once heard their Opinion? Our Author calls this *an Act of unparallel'd Goodness.* But what I have to say upon this Subject, I shall reserve to another Opportunity, if what this Author seems to be assur'd of, should prove true.

[*The Plebeian.* No. III. Monday, March 30, 1719.]

Farther Considerations upon the Reports relating to the PEERAGE.

The PLEBEIAN expected before now to have heard again from the *Old Whig,* expecially as to his making good the last Particular taken notice of in the Paper, *Numb.* II. which relates to the Part he was pleas'd to affirm his Majesty had already taken in this Affair; and for which there does not seem to be any Foundation. However, as *Age is apt to be slow,* the PLEBEIAN is willing to wait some time longer to be satisfied in that point. In the mean while, to shew with how much Candor he proceeds in this Dispute, he will not decline publishing in this Paper, a Speech made in a kind of a Private-publick Company for the Bill; in which all the Arguments on that side the Question are urg'd with that great Strength of Reason, and with all that Advantage of Oratory, for which the Hon—able Person who made it is so deservedly admired.

The FORM in which it was sent to the PLEBEIAN is as follows.

A SPEECH in the Long Room at the COMP——LER'S.
Optat Ephippia BOS—— Hor. Epist. 14.

" Mr. Bla——n,

THO the worthy Gentleman that spoke last has represented
the B—l that occasions this Meeting as destructive of all that
ought to be dear to every one that values his Country, yet I
am not asham'd to appear for it *with all the little Zeal I am
Master of.* According to the *way that I have the Honour of
thinking of this Matter,* this seems to me to be the best B—l
that ever was offered us; and therefore I *shall be for it to the
last Drop of my Breath.* I wish any Gentleman would lay his
Hand upon his Heart, and answer me whether the making
twelve L—s at once in a late Reign, was not the wickedest Thing
that ever was heard of: And such a Thing I am certain may be
attempted again, if we do not shew them *a New Game,* and
give them *one and thirty* of our own Friends, to prevent any
such Practice for the future. The Worthy Gentleman was pleas'd
to say, That the Noble L—— who was the Author of that
Advice might in some measure be excus'd, if that Matter is
compared with what is now propos'd.

" THAT L—— says, he plainly shew'd that he thought what
he did was a justifiable Action, because he left the Door open
for himself to be call'd to account for it, in the same manner
as all other Ministers had done before him; and did not endeavour to put himself out of all reach, by fixing those Persons
to be his Judges, who concurr'd with him in what he did. Sir,
I must tell that worthy Gentleman, That tho it has often happen'd that wicked Men have been infatuated, and slipt their
Opportunity; yet that should not prevent honest Gentlemen
from providing for their own Safety upon the like Occasion.
In all these Cases, that worthy Person added, that we ought to
consider *Quo Animo* a Man acts. I have already given my
Judgment in another place as to those Words, and I shall give
the same Opinion here again. The Gentleman, he thinks that
this is a very bad B—l; that is his *Quo Animo.* I think it a
very good one; that is my *Quo Animo.* As to what he said
about the S—— L——ds, That this would be invading their
Property, and taking away their Birthright, out of a pretence of

curing a publick Inconvenience; and that in the same way of
arguing, the P———t may as well take away the Fu—ds;
nothing being more inconvenient to the Publick, than paying
such great and endless Taxes: I hope the Gentleman will allow
there is a great deal of difference between what is done by
Friends, and what is done by Enemies. If we do take away their
Property, I hope there is nobody here that imagines that we do
it out of Ill-will; and the World must allow, that what is done
is rather out of Kindness to ourselves, than out of Malice to
them. Besides, I have been inform'd by a very *Honourable
Gentleman, That three of them are Boys at School*; and I hope
nobody can imagine at this time of day, that any of those Gentlemen, for whom I own I have the greatest Esteem, would be so
barbarous, *as to hurt young Boys, out of an Aversion to their
Persons*. As for those of *Riper Years*, there are several of
them *Jaco—es*, as the same *Honourable Person* has assur'd me;
and I hope no such sort of People will meet with any Encouragement here. Gentlemen are pleas'd to dwell much upon the
S— No———y in this case, as if their Re—— intended to take
their Property from them; whereas it is very plain, they intend
to make a Pr—y of them: And is not that the same thing to
the whole Nation, so long as it is all amongst their *own Countrymen*? And therefore I cannot imagine how any body can be so
absurd, as to look upon this as a Breach of the Un—: And I
hope we shall hear no more of that matter.

"THERE has been one thing often insinuated in this Debate,
as if some Gentlemen were influenced to come into this Proposal by *Assurance of Peer—s*, as if *they had Warrants in their
Pockets*, and I do not know what. For my part, Sir, I act
according to the best of my *Understanding*, and none of those
mean Considerations can have any weight with me. As for all
their Titles and Honours, *I cast them all behind my back, like
Chaff before the Wind*. For all which Reasons, I shall be
heartily for the B—l."

THE
PLEBEIANS.

By a Member of the House of COMMONS.

The SIXTH EDITION.

LONDON,

Printed for S. POPPING at the *Black Raven* in
Paternoster-Row. M.DCC.XIX.

(Price One Shilling.)

485

Considerations upon the Reports about the
PEERAGE, continued.

THE PLEBEIAN has been oblig'd to object to the *Old Whig*
one of the *Infirmities of Age*, viz. *Slowness*; and he must now
take notice of another, tho he does it with great reluctance, that
is, *Want of Memory*: for the *Old Gentleman* seems to have
forgot, that at his first Appearance he promis'd the Publick a
particular Treatise on the Subject of the *Peerage*, as it relates
to *Scotland*; Pag. 22.

THERE is at present very little probability that he will be
so good as his word, and therefore I shall not delay any longer
publishing something that is come to my hands on that Head,
which in my opinion may be of use in this Controversy. Indeed,
I am informed, that it has already been produced in a weekly
Pamphlet, which very few People, I fear, ever read, called *The
Honest Gentleman*; and therefore I hope at least to be excus'd
in making it more publick, and in using this worthy Person as
an Ally in this Quarrel, since I have so strong a Confederacy
against me. What I am speaking of, is a *Letter from a Nobleman of* Scotland *to a Gentleman of* England. When I mention
a *Scottish* Nobleman, I would not have it understood to be one
of the *Elect*, but one of the *Outcasts*: and as the Case of those
unfortunate Persons will be, if possible, more abject and deplorable than that of the Commons of *England*, it is not strange
that the PLEBEIAN should endeavour to do them what Service
he can.

The Letter is as Follows.

" SIR,

IF the Pleasure of doing Good be indeed its own Reward,
you will easily excuse the Trouble of this Letter. Nothing is so
talkative as Misfortune: But they surely may be allow'd to
speak for themselves, who, as they find to their great Surprize,
have none to speak for 'em.

" I WAS born a Peer of *Scotland*, formerly a Character of
some Importance, but at present (I'm afraid) degenerating into

so little Significancy, that perhaps this is the last Time there will be any Reputation to me in owning it.

"EVERY one that is acquainted with our History sees very well how much we gain'd, and what we lost, by the Union: We lost our Senate and our Senators; we lost the Service of many of our Great Men, and they seem to have lost—I know not what. But yet it might be remember'd by your free and generous Nation, that when we resign'd our selves to that Union, we intended at least to have retain'd the Rights of Men and Subjects, without the least Suspicion of any Encroachments upon us, which you have ever so bravely rejected from your selves. And even at this Union, there were some Articles agreed to, which seem to make for our Country, and which it would be very proper for the Party in the present Design to consult; and if after that they can deliberately give us up, they merit all the reproaches that the Injuries of a betray'd ruin'd People can extort from 'em. We justly call our selves a ruin'd People: for if at present we are any thing short of it, what may we not expect from those, if any such there are, who shall dare to assume a Power which we never gave 'em; and that not to be used for our Advantage, but to the Injury of the Nation they represent, and the Peerage of which they are part? 'Tis certain, a Principle that can at any time prevail above the Love of one's Country, may engage 'em at some time or other in any Designs, to the very Extinction of it.

"NEXT to the Pleasure that flows from the conscious Innocence of an honest Heart and a good Meaning, the Art of disguising and palliating a bad one gives the greatest, though the falsest Satisfaction. Thus I have heard it has been alledg'd by some who have been too advantageously engag'd on one side of the Question, that there is a very ingenious Distinction to be made between absolutely violating such and such Articles, and a commodious Deviation from 'em, for certain Reasons; though a plain Man would not immediately find out the real difference.

"I HAVE read in very old Books, that Justice was once the End of Power, and that the Great were such as were meritorious and useful. But if this Bill should pass, it wou'd seem that those Errors are to be exploded by this Bill; and yet many of

the most antient Families among us believe, that they and their
Descendants are thereby to be made unhappy and uneasy to
themselves, and useless to their Country: They think the Title
of a Lord is the most insignificant Part of his Character; but
when it is worn to adorn the Merit and Services of a truly
great Man, it exposes Virtue in the most amiable Light to universal Emulation.—How irksome will it be to many a great
Spirit to be thought a mere Lord, to reflect on the Worth of
his great Ancestors, and to inherit only their Title; to have every
Talent of being useful, but the Power; to hear his Fathers call'd
good, and great, and wise, and himself his Lordship?—May
we not expect that if great Men should find themselves thus
manag'd out of their Birthrights, they will not easily resign
themselves to a Life of Indolence and Supineness, but still hope
that some Occasion or other may court 'em to Action elsewhere:
God forbid it should be against that Country which shall have
so injuriously render'd them supernumerary to its Happiness,
and which wou'd then perhaps too late find 'em fatal to it.

" IN such case they will, no doubt, pretend in their Justification, that by having been thus divested of their Birthright, in
representing themselves, or the Right at least of electing their
Representatives; that they apprehended they were implicitly
disclaim'd by the Government, and reduc'd to the Condition
of Outlaws, and thereby discharg'd from the Obligations and
Laws of Society.

" BUT as the Injuries which we fear may be done us by this
Bill, do not so nearly affect you, I might give several Reasons,
why as *Englishmen* you shou'd reject it; and shew you, that at
the same time that it will be the greatest Discouragement to the
Merit of the Commonalty, it may end in equal Dishonour to
the Peerage.

" AS to the Commonalty, 'tis apparent that almost every great
Genius has for a long time been produc'd among them, and all
the Posts of Service have been fill'd by such who were born
Commoners, while the Offices of mere Favour and Show have
been supply'd from elsewhere. The Reason of this is evident:
A Commoner finds a great deal of Merit necessary to his
Character, as an *Equivalent* for the want of Quality; while the
young Lord, infinitely satisfy'd with the Adulations of his

Creatures and Dependants, with ease believes what is their Interest to tell him, and so aims no higher. But, shou'd this Bill pass, a Commoner will have as little Incitement to great Actions as a Peer, and be as far below the Possibility of rising, as a Lord is often above it.

" AS to the Peerage, if we look into their Assembly, and compare the many that sit there by Right of Descent, with the Characters of those who were first created to those Honours, and consider the modern Education by which they are usually form'd to their future Greatness, how much Looseness, Flattery, and false Politeness they affect from their first Entrance into Life; we shall be able to form some Notion of what sort of Geniuses that Assembly will be compos'd twenty Years hence, in case this Bill should pass, which is ever to be our Supreme Court of Judicature, but will be incapable of receiving into it even the most conspicuous Merit of the Age: I fancy it will very little resemble the body of antient Barons of this Kingdom, whose Actions supply such an illustrious Part of our History. On the contrary, we may expect, that as they have before been voted *Useless*, they will be in danger of being really so; and if that is ever the Case, tho now and then a Family should be extinct, and thereby an Obstacle to vertuous Actions be remov'd, it will be in vain to endeavour to retrieve their Honour, by thinking to supply the Extinction with a Man of Worth and Merit, who will not be over-fond of making one in so indifferent an Assembly. So that this Project, which pretends to do so much for the Honour of the House, may prove as injurious to it, as to every one that is excluded from it.

" A COMMONER should not too carelessly reply to this Objection, That the more insignificant that House appears, the greater Weight is in the Representatives of the People; for the Commons are the Guardians of the Constitution in general, as well as the private Rights of their Electors in particular; besides, it does not seem upon just Reflection so expedient, that that Court, which is the *dernier Resort* of Justice, should ever be fill'd with such Judges as they might despair or disdain to apply to for Relief.

" BUT, in fine, if public Justice is as obligatory as private; if what is so injurious to our Country may be as fatal to yours;

if such a Bill would be the greatest Provocation to Disaffection and Uneasiness to a powerful Body among us, and the greatest Discouragement to Merit both to you and us; if it would prove prejudicial to the Reputation of the Peerage, though not to their Power, which is worst of all, for at the same time it would lay the foundation of a most wretched Aristocracy; if the Notions of Faith and Honour are not obliterated; if the most solemn Engagements are any more than Words; if we ought not to violate the Rights of Nations for mere private Convenience; this Bill will be rejected with the Detestation with which all true *Britons* will treat every Encroachment on the Rights of Mankind, or their Fellow-Subjects. I *am, SIR,* &c."

I CANNOT but think that what this Noble *Briton* has here said on the Proposal for turning sixteen Scottish Elective Peers into twenty five Hereditary ones, to the Exclusion of all the rest of their Principals, must make great Impression upon every one that thoroughly considers it. I have not yet troubled the Publick throughout the whole Course of this affair, with my Thoughts on this Point. For my part, I am so far from being of opinion that this *precarious Situation* of the *Scotch* Peers is an *Evil* in the Body of the House of Lords that wants to be remedied, that it seems to me to be a very *fortunate Circumstance, and the best Remedy that can be provided for the Ill that both the Lords and Commons complain of.* Indeed, if the Lords can be satisfy'd with nothing less than being made *absolutely Independent,* which, as it has been plainly shewn, is entirely destroying the Constitution; I must confess this will not answer their purpose: But if it be reasonable they should be under some Influence of the Crown, as the other branch of the Legislature is, and, however, may be desirous that their *Dignity be not debased, nor their Weight diminish'd* by the frequent Additions of Peers, which the Necessities of Affairs may require to be made to their Body; is it not in this Case *a desirable Circumstance,* that the Crown can change once in three or four, or a few years more at farthest, so many of their Members, as may answer the Intentions of the Government, and not add to their Number? And in like manner, if the Commons are apprehensive that the frequent Draughts out of their Body, to make an Over-balance in the House of Peers, are detrimental to their Power, in point of Property, by taking so many considerable Estates from them; are they to be instrumental in changing that precarious Situation of so many Members of the Upper House, as leaves it in the power of the Crown to make such Alterations in that House, from time to time, as the Crown may think expedient, *without taking one Member from the Commons?*

BESIDES, there is a Reason of another nature why the Commons, in my poor Judgment, ought to rest very well satisfy'd that the Crown has this Power over so many Members of the other House; because it is just the same kind of Power as the Crown has over the Commons themselves. And in some Circumstances, this may prove even such a Check upon the Crown as the Commons may reap Advantage from, and prevent the putting such sudden Periods to their Being, as have been known formerly. Nay, I very much suspect, that if the proposed Alteration shou'd be made, the Effect of it wou'd be very soon felt; and if so, I beg Gentlemen wou'd consider with themselves, what Reception they may in all probability meet with from the general Body of the Commons of *England*, immediately after their having given such Power to the House of Peers, as no one ever ventur'd to mention to their Ancestors. How this Matter is understood in the Country, we hear from all Parts already; and this is indeed an *Advantage from the late Recess* on the side of those who are against the Bill.

BUT to return from this Digression: How little soever what has been said may relish with some of those of another Body, I am speaking here as a Commoner of *England*; as one that has no ambitious Desire of *being a Lord*, but very great Apprehensions of *being a Vassal*. As the House of Lords now stands, there are several Members of it in the same Circumstances with my self; what reason have I to consent to any thing that shall put any of them into a more independent State than I found them? Is there any one of their Lordships that would not laugh at a Proposal for making any Numbers of the Commons *hereditary*, who are now *all elective*, (tho it might be done with the same Justice as to their Principals.) Their Lordships would all say, *That is the Constitution of the House of* Commons, *and there we will leave it.* And has not this been the Constitution of the House of Lords ever since the *British* Nation was united?

IT is allow'd that, according to the Treaties between the two Kingdoms, confirm'd by the most solemn Acts of Parliament, this is true: But then, say they, other Things were promis'd, without which they would never have consented to the Union. For my part I have as bad an Opinion of *Oral Tradition in Politicks, as in Religion*; and therefore nothing of this kind can weigh at all with me. But supposing that there is some Inconvenience, in the present Situation of the Peerage, to the House of Lords, that Difficulties may happen in relation to the Seats of some Noblemen amongst them; are not those difficulties arisen entirely from themselves? And is it not an odd compliment to the Commons, that if the Lords *feel a thorn in their feet, they should desire the Commons to take it out, to put it into their own?* Surely they will never be brought to do this; much less to endanger their utter Ruin for the Convenience of another Body of Men.

THERE is one thing more which I think not improper to take notice of on this Head.[1] It is said, That by the Bill, which perhaps may be propos'd to the Commons, his Majesty is to have the naming the twenty five hereditary *Scottish* Peers; that they are all to be named before the next Session: But that if it shou'd happen that any of the present sixteen shou'd not be of the Number of those nam'd by his Majesty, in such case the present temporary Peers are to remain Lords of Parliament so long as this Parliament subsists, and their hereditary Successors are during that Term to be withheld from what, it is probable, they may be more than a little desirous of, *viz. a Seat in the House of Peers.* If this is to be the Case, I beg leave to ask these two Questions: The first is, Whether any of those Lords, who at present are of the House of Peers, will continue to be *very easy Company,* when they shall find themselves excluded at the end of this Parliament? For that some of them are to be excluded, seems to be indisputable, if what is mention'd above is a right State of the Case; for otherwise the sixteen might have been all declar'd hereditary, and his Majesty only left to add nine to the *Scots,* as he is six to the *English.*

THE next Question I would ask, is, Whether it is not very

natural to think, that those *Scottish* Peers who are to be the Hereditary Successors of the present Elective ones, will not be very pressing to be put in possession? Should both these Points be allow'd, as I believe they must, and likewise that the Patrons of this Project do not wish for any thing so much as to be in the full enjoyment of this Salutary Scheme; then I will venture to affirm, that there is no one Expedient to gratify the ardent Desires of those Gentlemen, to deliver them from the *Disquietude* of those that *are in*, and from the *Importunity* of those that are *to come in*, but the Diss—n of this P——t. On the other hand, if this Bill should not be offer'd to the House of Commons, or if offer'd, should not pass, I leave every one to judge whether the present Sixteen *Scottish* Peers will not be very sollicitous of sitting out the remainder of the Septennial Term, to wear off the Impressions which it is to be fear'd such an Attempt as is talk'd of may have made upon the Minds of their Electors.

WHILST I am writing this, the *Old Whig*, Numb. II. is come to my Hands. I really thought he had been *departed*; and whether it be *himself*, or his *Ghost* that walks, I am not thoroughly satisfy'd.

THE first *Old Whig*, I must confess, had stated his Argument, and was going on very regularly, if he had not been disturb'd in his progress; but this *second* is as inconsistent as possible. In the first Paragraph of the Performance before me, he treats the PLEBEIAN as a *Grubstreet*-Writer; but in the last, and several other Paragraphs, as a very *able shrewd Fellow*.

AS to his Remarks on the PLEBEIAN, Numb. II. he owns himself, " That he was very unwilling to have been concerned any farther in the Dispute, and *nothing could have engag'd him to have given himself or the Publick any more trouble*, had he not been so peremptorily call'd to it by the last PLEBEIAN, *p.* 15."

BUT as to what that PLEBEIAN calls upon him for, which was to make good what he had asserted in relation *to his Majesty's Concession*, he does not say one word about it. Indeed, in his *Motto* he hints at it, and a *Fellow-Labourer* of this Author has spoke out something more plainly on this Subject. Upon the whole, it is very extraordinary. Here is at present the greatest Favour or Bounty, call it which you will, offer'd to the Com-

mons, that ever was known, and the like it is probable will
never be made to them again; and yet I do not know how it
happens, they are so blind, or so perverse, that they will not
see what is *so prodigiously for their Good*; nay, one can hardly
tell how to get them into it *by any means whatever*. The
Patrician says, " It is an affront of the highest Nature to the
Crown, and a petty kind of Rebellion to refuse this Offer."
And the *Old Whig* seems to be of opinion, that they deserve
to have their Ears box'd for it. As to the rest of his *Motto, Nil
ultra quaero Plebeius*. Hor. But whether this Project was chiefly
intended for the Benefit of the Commons, I leave every one to
judge from both these Authors, one of which plainly discovers,
" That he has a prodigious concern for Innocent Ministers,
and trembles for what may happen to them from Kings who are
yet unborn." [a] But the *Patrician* has two Paragraphs, which I
shall transcribe without any Commentary. " The general Clamour, &c. As if the Design of limiting the Number of Peers, and
restraining the Prerogative of the Crown, was at first projected
with a view of insulting the Prince of *Wales*, who by this
Proceeding will be debarr'd the Liberty of creating Peers as his
Predecessors have done; is so low a Reflection on the present
Ministry, that I should not have regarded it, but that I find it a
popular one.[b]
   " IN short, we never know into whose hands the Reins of
Government may devolve. It therefore behoves us to secure
our Privileges, that we may not fall the Victims of any aspiring
Prince's enraged Dispositions." [c]
   BUT to return to the *Old Whig*: I confess, I am uncapable
to answer what he calls his Remarks, or his Objections. When
I talk'd to him last, it was, as to the Commons, upon a foot as
he had stated it himself, That the Crown could have a House
of Commons of what Complexion it pleas'd; which are his own
words. As to the Lords, That they had a very considerable
Property of One Million one Hundred and Seventy-five Thousand
Pounds *per annum*: But now he says all that was only in *Jest*.
And as to the Commons, the Crown has no power at all over

[a] *Old Whig,* No. II. *p.* 7. [Steele's note]
[b] *Patrician,* No. II *p.* 8. [Steele's note]
[c] *Pag.* 12. [Steele's note]

them; and as for the Lords, he pleads Poverty in their behalf. And he behaves in the same evasive contradictory manner, on every other Point in dispute between us. But what is worst of all, he very frequently, for want of any the least shadow of an Argument, has recourse to telling *old Stories*, as if they were things that happen'd but yesterday; which I confess, is another of the *Defects of Age.* And if he will not continue to be *Testy,* I shall admonish him, that he has *every where* prov'd himself *Old,* but *no where a Whig.* As to what he seems to insinuate in relation to what is said in the second PLEBEIAN concerning the *Ephori,* the PLEBEIAN can maintain it by the best authority. *Crags* is the Man I have all along depended upon on this Head, and he says, *they led the most abandon'd dissolute Lives*; and certainly he ought to know. His words are these, *Quamvis ipsi* Ephori *viverent indulgentius & dissolutius*; p. 78.

THE rest of this Paragraph is very mean; and this Author's Menaces in this place are as vain, as his Compassion in another part of his Pamphlet is insolent.

I SHALL take notice but of one thing more in this Pamphlet, which is the last Paragraph, in these words:

"I MUST own, however, that the Writer of the PLEBEIAN has made the best of a weak Cause; and do believe, that a good one would shine in his Hands; for which reason I shall advise him as a Friend, if he goes on in his new Vocation, to take care that he be as happy in the Choice of his Subject, as he is in the Talents of a Pamphleteer."

AUTHORS in these Cases are nam'd upon *Suspicion*; and if it is right as to the *Old Whig,* I leave the World to judge of *this Cause* by comparison of this Performance to his *other Writings.* And I shall say no more of what is writ in *Support of Vassalage,* but end this Paper, by firing every free Breast with that noble Exhortation of the Tragedian:

> *Remember, O my Friends, the Laws, the Rights,*
> *The gen'rous Plan of Power, deliver'd down*
> *From Age to Age by your renown'd Fore-fathers,*
> *(So dearly bought, the Price of so much Blood.)*
> *O let it never perish in your Hands!*
> *But piously transmit it to your Children.*

Mr. *Addison's* Cato.

The Joint and Humble Address of the Tories and Whigs Concerning the Bill of Peerage (May, 1719)

This tract, addressed to King George, was written and published at the end of the first session in 1719, when, because of a general public clamor against the measure, it had been temporarily withdrawn by the Ministry. Steele takes occasion to emphasize two points which he had made in *The Plebeian*: that the issues involved are above mere party politics and that criticism of a measure concerning the Royal prerogative, to which the King has assented, should not be construed as disloyalty.

The professed purpose of the Whig Peerage Bill was to prevent a repetition of the 1711 incident, when Queen Anne had created twelve peers overnight to ensure a majority for Tory measures. Moderates in both parties, Steele believes, deplore such an abuse of the peer-making prerogative at the importunity of party; but the curtailing of it will not dispose of the more subtle danger involved in this scheme of "our Common Enemies, who pretend to Correct the Crimes of their Predecessors, by practising the same Thing in an higher Degree; and can find no better expedient to Secure the Constitution from Wounds, than that of putting it to Death."

Steele speaks tactfully of the King's grace in resigning his power, but points out the danger to a balanced system of government of changing certain protection for possible oppression: "The Crown is ever to Act by his Ministers, but an unchangeable House of Peers might Act unaccountably for themselves." England now possesses, Steele says loyally, "the only Prince who was ever sollicited to be more Potent than he desir'd." Textual notes on p. 648.

The Joint and Humble [1] Address of the Tories and Whigs Concerning the [2] Bill of Peerage.

We Your M——y's Faithful Subjects the Tories and Whigs in P——t Represented, beg leave to Congratulate your M——y on the late Escape of your M——y and your Faithful C——ns, from the Designs lately carry'd on at Home, when we were Threatened with an Invasion from Abroad. We do not so much Felicitate your M——y upon the dispersion of our late Enemies, whom we despised, as upon the disappointment of our late Friends, whom we feared.

We look back with Pleasure and Amazement at your M——y's Goodness is resigning [3] your Prerogative, but with Contempt and Hatred on those who Solicited you to it, and prevailed upon your Noble Nature to part with what is so Essential to our Safety and your Grandeur.

The Persons who have discovered themselves and Betrayed you, as far as in them lay in this Attempt, had no recommendation to your People, but from your Majesty's regard of them: [4] and now no Safety, but in that Prerogative which they would have given up. It is not doubted by your Good People, but what was to have been obtain'd by T——y [5] to their Prince, and Usurpation upon their Fellow Subjects, would have been used with Disloyalty to your M——y, and Tyranny over us.

We find it therefore necessary to declare, we shall always be ready to oppose the Designs of such Audacious and Wicked Men, who Acknowledge [6] they are determin'd to Attempt the same Violation [7] on another occasion, and shall not ever think our Representatives to behave themselves as such, except they shall Chastise the Insolence of such Men; should they provoke, by a repeated Attempt, the Injured Patience [8] of their Fellow Citizens.

We the Whigs and Tories, who mean honestly the General Good, tho we Pursue it by different means, shall hereafter be Watchful over these Projectors of our Ruin, who mean nothing but to Enrich and Aggrandise themselves, without regard to Justice, but occasionally [9] Agree and Disagree with each other under our Names for their own Ends. Those of both Sides who pretend to be at the Head of our Parties, have let us see at long run, that they will never Manifest any Love to their Prince, but by Heaping up his Coin, or to their Country, but by getting as much of the Land of it as they can, for their own use. This Accident of Common Danger has buried our Mutual Aversions, and we hope will turn upon our Common Enemies, who pretend to Correct the Crimes [10] of their Predecessors, by practising the same Thing in an higher Degree; and can find no better expedient to Secure the Constitution from Wounds, than that of putting it to Death. We the well meaning Tories and Whigs cannot enough Felicitate each other, that the Bill of Peerage never came before our Representatives, from the Dread [11] we have of what some [12] would have asked of your M——y, in Favour of the Commons. And we the well meaning Whigs and Tories take as much Pleasure in reflecting how far [13] the Violent Tories [14] would have asked an Addition of Power to the Crown in Favour of the Lords.

We apparently see the general [15] danger in which we have all been involved, and are willing to impute it to the Inadvertency and hasty Zeal of well meaning Persons; but now we observe their profess'd Obstinacy to persevere in the like Designs, we are resolved to animate each other into a Common Resolution for Common Safety. We have long seen that Powerful Men have no true Resentment or Passion, but Revenge and Fear; and therefore know that honest Men have no way to deal with them but by Jealousy and Courage.

With Hearts full of Loyalty we thus Congratulate your M——y that you have escaped the Dangerous Importunity of both Houses after the most generous Concession for greater Power to be hereafter in them both.

We have sent to your M——y's Assistance and Service in P——t Members who never did, and who we believe never will, oppose your M——y, but when you are Inclin'd to Lessen your own Power. It has been heretofore our Complaint, that our Princes affected to be Arbitrary, but we bewail that your M——y is restraining your Will: We know that is confin'd to the Common Good, and we implore your M——y that you would never let it be farther confin'd. To give [16] any part of your present Power to any other Persons would be to transfer [17] that Safety which we have in your Royal Breast, to the Breasts of others whose Inclinations you cannot know. Let us not, Dread Sir, change certain Protection [18] for possible Oppression. [19] The Crown is ever to Act by his Ministers, but an unchangeable House of Peers might [20] Act unaccountably for themselves. There is no reason alledg'd against the Violation [21] of the Union, and the Rights of Peers of Scotland under it; but in convenience to their House, the Rights of us all might [22] in Time stand equally in the Way of their Ambition, their Avarice, or any of their other desires. They have none that can hurt their Neighbours at present, but such is the infirmity of Human Nature that new Appetites arise in the new Opportunities;

Men's wishes [23] have never yet been known to be check'd by an Impunity for Indulging them.

We fear we have offended your Sacred M——y in this long Address, but cannot but conceive delight in that we have the only Prince who was ever sollicited to be more Potent than he desir'd; and in order that this may be always your M——y's Condition, we shall, according to the Liturgy of our Church (however that Blessing may have been wasted by our Sins) pray that Heaven would Grant your Counsellors Wisdom.

Advertisement

Within few Days will be publish'd a short Treatise of the Art of Short Hand whereby the longest Words are express'd by two Letters and Monosyllables by one Letter, as P——t Parliament, R——e Representative, T——y Treachery, T—s, Tories, W— Whigs, S— State, M——y Majesty, P— Peers, P——e Peerage.

The Antidote in a Letter to the Free-Thinker (June, 1719)
The Antidote No. II (June, 1719)

This pair of tracts were written partly for a personal reason, partly for a principle or two, partly because Steele would be unable to abstain from joining in the fray. It was a paper war among the London physicians. Dr. John Woodward, antiquary and natural philosopher, Professor of Physick at Gresham College, had recently published his medical theories in *The State of Physick and of Diseases* (1718), which was itself a reply to a book by Dr. John Freind. Other physicians took sides, and finally the wits and fun-makers had made it a free-for-all ridiculing Woodward. Steele's first motive seems to have been defence of his family physician, Dr. Woodward. His point in *Antidote* No. I, however, is that the attack is not directed fairly at Woodward's theories, but maliciously at his person and character. Moreover, the subject itself is not one for mirth. Two recent humorous tracts Steele uses as illustrations of what he considers unfair and unsuitable satire: *A Letter to the Learned Dr. Woodward by Dr. Byfield*, which, it seems, was written by Dr. Freind himself; and *A Letter from the Facetious Dr. Andrew Tripe at Bath, To His Loving Brother the Profound Greshamite*, at the time laid at Dr. Richard Mead's door, but since attributed to Dr. William Wagstaffe or to Dr. John Arbuthnot. The Tripe pseudonym had been used in 1714 in a tract ridiculing Steele. The mock-opera mentioned by Steele as an example of the excessive satire upon Woodward was *Harlequin-Hydaspes: or the Greshamite*, performed, very recently, on 27 May.

The occasion for *Antidote No. II* was a duel, fought a few days prior to its appearance, between Dr. Woodward and Dr. Mead. Steele says that if Dr. Woodward and his friends intend to show their faces hereafter among gentlemen, the Town must have the real facts. And to correct misstatements in the newspapers, he prints a statement from Dr. Woodward giving his version. It could not be expected that one who had been a publicist against duelling for nearly twenty years would miss this opportunity for a little sermon. " In a Nation where *Forgiveness of Injuries* is taught as the greatest Perfection to which the Soul of Man can arrive it is ridiculous and absurd to make it [Honour] consist in a profess'd *Impatience of them*." In defence of Woodward, he can only say that the attack upon him was made without notice, " that secret Injuries or unexpected Blows " are the more detestable.

Steele seems to have thought the *Free-Thinker* (March 1718-June 1721) a suitable periodical to make disinterested comment and to have consulted with the editor, his friend Ambrose Philips. The *Free-Thinker* of Friday, June 5 (No. 126), written while Steele's first tract was in the press, is on the subject. Steele's note to Philips on 12 June asking for an appointment is probably related to *Antidote No. II*, dated the 13th.

These pamphlets were published anonymously and never acknowledged. Aitken, Steele's biographer, was the first to identify them, and on the strength of good external evidence: the Bodleian has a volume of the tracts on the controversy, which Dr. Woodward himself presented, and Steele's name is written on the title page of No. I in Woodward's handwriting. (*Life*, II, 202, n.) The note to Philips, which has turned up since Aitken's time, seems to be corroboration. Textual notes on p. 649.

THE
ANTIDOTE,
IN A
LETTER
TO THE
Free --Thinker,

Occafion'd by the Management of the Prefent Difpute between Dr. *Woodward* and certain other Phyficians.

- - - - - *Quod Medicorum eft*
Promittunt Medici - - - - Hor.

LONDON:

Printed for J. ROBERTS near the *Oxford-Arms* in *Warwick-Lane.* 1719. Price Six Pence.

The Antidote,

IN A

LETTER

TO THE

Free-Thinker.

SIR,

THE Generous Part, which you have undertaken, of instructing the Publick in the Pursuit of what is worthy of being
follow'd, or giving Rules how to escape what it is our Duty to
avoid, encourages me to hope you will receive this Epistle with
Candour.

I do not here pretend to lay before you Matter of so high a
Nature as what usually engages you, who are a Philosopher, to
wit, the Considerations of Good and Evil, but presume to
trouble you with Things of much less Moment, and which concern only Life and Death, abstracted from the Regards of
Virtue or Vice.

You must, I doubt not, have read the Pamphlets which certain Members of the College of Physicians have prescrib'd to
the Town; wherein they have mutually admonish'd us against
taking each other, as very bad for us in all manner of Distempers. This has, by no means, been carry'd on like a Controversy among Men of Breeding and Learning; but the Subject-
matter in Debate, tho' it regards our very Being, has been wholly
neglected, in order to turn the Person who gave Rise to it, into
Contempt and Ridicule, and to suppress his Doctrine by destroying his Character. Upon this Occasion I take the Liberty to
appeal to you, and hope you will interpose in Behalf of the
Publick; lest a good and useful Design may be lost to the
World by your being diverted from the Consideration of it,
thro the Artifice of those, whose Interest it may be to draw our
Attention another Way.

See then how this Dispute lies. Dr. *Woodward*, who heretofore published *The Natural History of the Earth, with an
Account of the Deluge,* as also, *The History of Vegetation,*
(which Works are had in great Esteem among the Learned all
over *Europe*) has finally, turn'd his Thoughts to the Improvement of Physick. In order to this most useful Purpose, he has
made Dissections of various Animals, and search'd into the
Body of Man, with an inexpressible Diligence and Care, as well
knowing from the Failures of others who had gone before, that
there was no Safety or certain Reliance, but on the Foundation
of Nature herself; and that she was only to be understood by
Experiments and Observations: By the Help of these he has
made Discoveries not only new, but also of the highest Moment;
and his attempt has been no less than that of Rescuing Physick
out of the Mystery and Obscurity wherein it has hitherto lain,
and reducing it into the Form of a Science, by which means it
may be render'd so intelligible, that every Man may understand
his own Case, and know whether his Physician treats him in a
Rational Manner or not. As to the Medicines, he has taken
them under strict Examination, and shewn, that there are several
in common Use which are of no Effect, and others that are really
hurtful: He has given the *Idea* of the Body of Man in Health,
and also under Diseases, assigning the Causes and Remedies of
each in a Method that is Natural and Mechanical. In a Word,
Dr. *Woodward* attempts to settle a Rational Test in Physick;
and in the Course of this Labour he could not avoid taking
Notice, that the Practice of some very eminent Physicians would
be of great Weight and Authority against him, which made it
necessary to examine their Conduct, but at the same Time,
confines Himself strictly to Nature and such Arguments as arise
from it; nay, he treats them with that Candour, that he takes
the Representations of their Practice from their own Words,
by all which it appears, that it was necessary for him for the
Sake of the Rest of Mankind to take Care lest the Tenderness
towards the Character of a Few, might endanger the Lives of
a great Many. If Dr. *Woodward* is less Received by the Town,
than those whom he answers; in that Proportion it became the
more excusable in him to discover their Errors; or his Antidote
must have been egregiously unequal to their Poison. If there

be a Case in Nature wherein one Man is allowed to censure the Conduct of another, it certainly is where he professes to save his Neighbour, whom the Person he opposes, is going to destroy.

It is with this Support that Dr. *Woodward* has brought certain other Physicians to the Test of Nature. What do they on this Occasion? They do not pretend either to question the Truth or the Importance of his Discoveries. They, no where, alledge that he has represented or quoted them unfairly. The World therefore might very reasonably have expected, that these Gentlemen should, for the Common Good, have enter'd upon Arguments, offer'd Reasons, or endeavour'd to falsify the Facts which he produces, especially since he has observed the greatest Respect and Civility to their Persons, in all that he has written against their Practice: But instead of this, we find them sitting down under a plain and direct Condemnation of their Practice, and contenting themselves with attacking him only in his Person and Character, industriously omitting whatever concerns the Reasons of his Practice. This Endeavour to render him contemptible has been carry'd on with so great a Spirit and Eagerness, that it has produc'd a quite contrary Effect upon reasonable People, and alarm'd impartial and indifferent Men into a Suspicion, that so much Rage could not be provok'd by the meer contrary Opinion of so frivolous a Man as they would represent Dr. *Woodward*. A Revenge above the Provocation has rais'd the Curiosity of those, who are Strangers to the Doctor, to enquire into this Matter, and it appears that there is much further Cause of Anger against Him than has been represented in Print, for He has cured those whom his Antagonists have given over, and frequently found easie Remedies for the Recovery of such, whom they had for a *Series* of Time tortur'd into a Despair of Life, and Impatience of Being.

Since this is the real Fact and State of the Case, I cannot but desire of you *Sir*, in Vindication of a Truth of this Importance, to admonish these Gentlemen, that it is required of them, to say something in Refutation of His Doctrine, more than that there is one Dr. *Byfield*, who is learned enough to transcribe the Words *Depredations* of the *Bile*, the Adjectives *Nervous* and *Elegant*, or the Terms *Saccharine Vitriolick*, or *Ammoniack*. Please to inform these Writers, that it is no Argument that

Dr. *Woodward* wants Understanding that they have made Dr. *Byfield* use his Phrases and talk Nonsense.

It would be worthy of you to let these witty Gentlemen know, that it is expected of them to do something more than this, before they can prevail upon Us to believe ill of a Man, who attempts to do us good Offices at the Hazard of the Scandal he could not but foresee He should meet with from censuring Persons, he believ'd had nothing to bring against Him but Reproaches and Invectives foreign to the Matter in Debate: But because it is seldom seen, that Men are out of Countenance while they support the Reputation of their Parts, however they misapply them, it may be necessary for you who lead us in our Taste of Politeness, to examine whether Dr. *Woodward* has been, after all, really expos'd with Wit and Humour, or whether he did not deserve those Qualities should rather have been employ'd in His Favour and Defence.

As for my Part, I cannot see how Men are justify'd in using the Talents of their Minds, any more than the Strength of their Hands against innocent Men. At the same Time that I say this, I do not accuse the Writers against Dr. *Woodward* of any more than a Will to hurt Him, and am really of Opinion that those Gentlemen are Guilty of much more Evil than they have committed. For Dr. *Woodward* is in good Health, and Safe, out of the Hands of those who *Murder'd* and *Dissected* Him for Alarming the Town against their being assassin'd by them in *their real Persons*, as he himself has, since, been in *Effigie*.

The Dispute is about the Life of Man, and it is a melancholy Consideration that Nothing is answer'd but in profest Mirth.

What then, *Sir*, will you instruct us to do on this Occasion, who are indifferent in the Quarrel, I should rather say who are unprejudic'd, but cannot be indifferent. For it is the *Cause of Mankind which these Men, harden'd and habituated to the Sighs, Lamentations and Groans of the Sick-bed*, treat with this abandon'd and merciless Levity. Such awkward and unseasonable Pretenders to be witty, should be made to understand how far they fall short of their Aim: They should be terrify'd from making themselves thus mean and contemptible, which is always the Consequence of Mens endeavouring to be what Nature never design'd them. Be pleas'd therefore to convince the Town, by declaring what you very well know, that the Letter from Dr. *Byfield* to Dr. *Woodward* is not a Piece of Wit or Humour, either in the Contrivance of it, or the manner of conducting the Thing contriv'd. For without dwelling upon the Scurrility of drawing in an innocent Man's Name for the Abuse of another only to serve a Jest, it is silly [1] to the last Degree, and against all Propriety, to make Him, who is introduc'd for a Creature, full of Vanity and Self-Conceit, speaking of Himself, as he does, Things that must render Him contemptible. The Letter, under the feign'd Name of Dr. *Andrew Tripe*, you will say, is full of the same Want of Circumspection, and without Sense of Character. It is too insipid even to give Offence, except where it is nauseous and deals in Allusions that expose the Infirmities of human Nature it self, rather than those of any individual man.

When you shall be pleas'd to take this Matter into your serious Consideration, you will cast your Eye upon the *Mock-Opera of Hydaspes*, and there you will observe that it concerns Dr. *Woodward* no otherwise than that the Title of *Greshamite* says where he lives, and the Satyr goes no farther than to declare (what very many owe their Health to the Knowledge) That Dr. *Woodward* lives [2] in *Gresham-College*. The World may also see, that this Gentleman passes his Time there in Contemplation and constant Attention on the Cases of the Sick and Diseas'd, and that he is far from pretending to perform Cures *Extempore*, but ever meditating on the Torments and Sorrows of those in Pain, when he is not at their Bedsides or Couches, observing the Administration or Operation of his Medicines, and abating and enlarging them as Events and Symptoms declare the momentary Condition of his Patients. If this Care, Assiduity and Attention to one Thing, and that Human Life it self, in Hazard and Distress, appears in a Man's very Gesture and Countenance, it is by no means among virtuous and intelligent Men, a Cause of Reproach and Ridicule, but any Singularity arising from so generous a Cause, should inspire Respect and Kindness wherever it is observ'd. Haughtiness and Arrogance in Men who are constantly conversant with the lowest State of human Nature argue an Insensibility worthy the Reproof of the Stage, and I doubt not, if Men will not recollect themselves and consider their own Persons and Behaviour, but they will be Part of our Winter's Diversion there. For it will be a virtuous Action in whoever shall undertake it, to make a Jest of merry Homicides.

In the mean Time these Men have, with all their Might, done no more against Mr. *Woodward,* than what has been done in all Ages against the best of Men, by Persons envious of Great and Laudable Undertakings. And you know, *Sir, Socrates* himself met with the like Treatment; and the two greatest Philosophers of the last Age, Dr. *Harvey* and Monsieur *Descartes* with a much worse; nay, our own Time has seen a Gentleman not only of a noble Family, but celebrated also over the whole World for his great Discoveries, made the Subject of a Comedy.

I hope, Sir, when you consider this great and populous City, subject at every Season of the Year to the Rage of Distempers, and these Epidemical, a Question concerning the Health of Men, offer'd with Learning and Discretion against the apparent Interest of him that advances the Novelty shall not be overlook'd, but have the Honour of your Examination. All that is demanded is, that the Persons concern'd may be inform'd, that Dr. *Woodward* has a just Pretence to the Respect of Mankind for his Attempt, and that the Falsity of his Assertions is to be prov'd, before his Friends and Patients will decline supporting Him by all just and honourable Methods. For if such Proceedings as those against this Gentleman are to be tolerated, there will be still fewer who will hereafter sacrifice Their Ease, Their Time and Their Fortune to the Service of Their Country.

I am, *Sir,*

Your most Obedient

Humble Servant.

THE
ANTIDOTE.

NUMBER II.

IN A

LETTER

TO THE

Free-Thinker.

Occasion'd by later Actions between Dr. *Woodward* and Dr.
Mead.

- - - - - - - *Quippe minuti,*
Semper et infirmi eſt animi, exiguique voluptas
Ultio. - - - - - - - Juvenal.

LONDON:

Printed for J. ROBERTS near the *Oxford-Arms* in
Warwick-Lane, 1719.

THE
ANTIDOTE.
IN A
LETTER
TO THE
Free-Thinker.

SIR,

WHILE my former Letter was in the Press, your own Humanity prompted you to interpose in the present Quarrel among certain Physicians; but the good Sense which you express'd in that Paper concerning it, had not the Effect on them which one would have thought must have been a natural Consequence of it; for the Affair has been prosecuted with much greater Rage than before, as you will find by the Representation of a late Encounter, subscrib'd by Dr. *Woodward,* which shall be plac'd at the End of this Epistle.

The licentious Way of treating this Gentleman, in the publick Papers, makes it necessary for him and his Friends (if they intend ever to shew their Faces hereafter among Gentlemen) to give the Town, fairly and honestly, the Particulars of what is unjustly represented in those Papers.

The *Whitehall Evening-Post* of Thursday last, gives the following Account.

"We hear, that an Experiment was last Night made, in *Gresham-College* Yard, of a new Method of Duelling, with Sword and Cane, instead of Sword and Pistol, between two eminent Physicians, who had been engag'd for some Time in a Paper-War. Both these Engagements were equally ridiculous, the former producing no Blood, and the latter no Argument."

The Paper call'd the *Post-Boy,* publish'd this Day, being *June* the 13th, in the Article from *London,* says thus:

" We hear, that on Tuesday last in the Evening, an Eminent Physician, who had been maliciously and scandalously abused in several Pamphlets by another of the Faculty, meeting him accidentally near *Gresham* College, took Occasion to Cane him for his villainous Usage; whereupon both drew their Swords, and in the Rencounter the latter was disarm'd, but his Adversary contented himself only with breaking his Sword, and generously gave him his Life."

The *Evening Post* of the same Date, has it as follows, *viz.*

" Last Tuesday a Duel happen'd between an Eminent Physician and another of the Faculty, in *Gresham* College; the latter was wounded in the Hand, and disarm'd."

The *Weekly Journal,* or *Saturday's Post,* has the two following Paragraphs.

" Last Week Dr. *Mead* and Dr. *Woodward,* both belonging to *Gresham-College,* in walking down *Bishopsgate-street,* quarrell'd and can'd one another; and when they came into the Square of the College, they drew and fought; the latter was wounded in several Places, and making another Pass, Dr. *Woodward* fell down backwards, and the other gave him his Life.

" The Quarrel between Dr. *Mead* and Dr. *Woodward* we have told another Way, *viz.* That the latter having maliciously and scandalously abused Dr. *Mead* in several Pamphlets, and meeting with him accidentally going into his Lodgings in *Gresham-College,* took Occasion to cane him; thereupon both drew their Swords, and in the Re-encounter the latter was disarm'd; but his Adversary contented himself with only breaking his Sword, and generously gave him his Life."

These Historians have had the Account of this Matter from some that knew nothing of it, and have been much impos'd upon, or certainly Persons who have been notorious for the great Care they take against publishing disadvantageous Characters of those whom they treat of, would never have given us the quite contrary to what is the Truth.

A nameless Author, as I am, is not to say harsh Things of Gentlemen who are known to set forth these Memorials from Time to Time. Should I, who am unknown, write against one who is known, as to his personal Character, I should fall into the Crime of which I am going to complain, to wit, of striking another, when I my self stand safe against a Return for it.

The Gentleman who subscribes the Narrative of this Quarrel, is answerable for the Truth of it, and the rest of the World are in Justice to believe him, 'till Evidence of the contrary is produc'd by the Person whom he mentions to have treated him with so great Inhumanity.

I shall presume only to desire of you to take this Occasion to treat *of Resentment of Injuries* in general; for I cannot but think the Way now pursu'd amongst us, from the Force of Custom, on Occasion of Distaste or Dislike, is not only unwarrantable, but in the highest Degree criminal, and ought to be, for that Reason, shameful.

The Honour of a Man living in Society, must have an Analogy to the Nature and Religion of the Government under which he lives. For I take Honour to be the Term which fashionable Men use for what they would have understood to be their Religion, or Rule of Life: And in a Nation where *Forgiveness of Injuries* is taught as the greatest Perfection to which the Soul of Man can arrive, it is ridiculous and absurd to make it consist in a profess'd *Impatience of them.*

What then shall we say, when even a Jealousy of an Affront, and searching for an ill Interpretation of doubtful Expressions, instead of taking the kinder one, is become the affected and distinguishing Character of a Man of Spirit? However, that Part which is hardest to perform, will always be, among reasonable Men, the most laudable to perform; and the Difficulty of an Atchievement must be the highest Circumstance of Praise to him who shall accomplish it.

It is therefore to be distinguish'd, that Forbearance of returning an Injury, is not, in it self, a great Act in the Mind; no, it is stupid not to resent, but it is great not to prosecute Resentment. To forbear Vengeance, for Fear of the Person who does you an Injury, is poor and base; but to suppress Resentment, for the Sake of Virtue, and conquering a strong Impulse to revenge, because a Man knows it is his Duty so to do, is heroick.

From this it appears, that as the Desire of Vengeance is, of all others, the hardest, in a great Spirit, to master, so it is the most laudable of all Affections to conquer. If this be true, what are we to think of those who resent Injuries in a Manner whereby it is manifest that Fear had a greater Part in the Affair than Indignation? Such is the Case, when the Onset is made without giving Notice to the Person attack'd, when the Declaration is made by a first Blow, design'd for above half the Battle, and the Enemy puts the Man he assails in the Condition he wishes him, before he is alarm'd to begin the Contention.

Hence we may learn to measure the Quality of Offenders, and judge of the Degrees, downward, from the State of Honour and Virtue: And tho' the Highway-man and Foot-pad are both lawless Persons, he who bids you stand, is more excusable than he who knocks you down without that Ceremony. The yet more mischievous and unmanly Injuries of Calumny and Slander, are, in a like Degree, more abominable than what is said of a Man before his Face. This is it that makes it so shocking to revile the Dead, as Somebody says, because the Dead are for ever absent, and out of a Possibility of doing themselves Justice.

But, for the Honour of the *British* Nation be it spoken, base Blows are seldom given amongst us. Our very Malefactors are such, with a better Grace than is observ'd elsewhere. The *English* generally challenge those who have done them the most secret Injury, and bring the Lurker in Iniquity into broad Daylight; it is common when they account with them, to see a fair and open Breast oppos'd by him who demands Satisfaction for the most close and wicked Wrong, which could be perform'd only by a Friend, and a Man entrusted with Secrets, which have been divulg'd to defame or dishonour, or kept to cheat or betray the Challenger.

As the Colours and Qualities of Mens Actions are to be consider'd as they regard themselves, and as they regard their Neighbours, there are always some seeming Remains of something like Virtue in those who do even a wrong Thing, without too much Regard to their own Persons; and the Man who openly (and exposing himself at the same Time to the Fury of his

Adversary) makes an Assault, has not lost all Sense of Honour; but he who does it with Safety to himself, certainly has bid adieu to it. Secret Injuries, or unexpected Blows, are detestable in the Eye of common Sense; but much more odious among Men of liberal and acquir'd Abilities.

The next Thing, to conquering the Desire of Revenge, is to demand it in an undisguis'd Way; but to avenge what is said or done, in an open Dispute, by indirect, unexpected, or secret Methods of taking Satisfaction, is doing an Injury, instead of demanding Satisfaction for one.

These, and the like loose Reflections, you will in a better Manner communicate to the Town for the respective Use of your Readers, who shall peruse the following Advertisement; and we expect that your Part in it, be only that of a *Free-Thinker*, who governs your self by Facts and Arguments, which will more fully appear, when you are, as we desire, as impartial in any Applications that may be made to you from those of the other Side of this important Question; which concerns the whole Town, nay, the whole Race of Mankind, both as to the Matter in Dispute, and the Manner of carrying it on, as much as any Point that could be started to employ Speculation. It is not of so abstracted a Nature as to be the Entertainment only of Thinking Men. Even those who come as near Animals as to have Affection to nothing but Eating, Drinking, and Sleeping, will be most considerate and thoughtful Readers on a Subject wherein the Stomach and the Heart are equally concern'd.

I am,

SIR,

Your most obedient

Humble Servant.

June 13, 1719.

Postscript.

Whereas it has been inserted in the *publick Papers*, That an *eminent Physician, and another of the Faculty,* had a Rencounter, the former of whom is said to have *caned* the other, in order to insinuate that Dr. *Woodward* caned Dr. *Mead*; this is to certify, that Dr. *Woodward* had no *Cane* in his *Hand*.

Finis

ADVERTISEMENT

" There having been spread several false Reports of what lately happen'd between Dr. *Mead* and me, at *Gresham College,* I think my self oblig'd to give the Publick an Account of the Matter of Fact.

" On the 10th Instant, about eight in the Evening, passing, on Foot, without a Servant, by the *Royal Exchange*, I there saw Dr. *Mead*'s Chariot, with him in it, and heard him bid his Footman open the Door. But Dr. *Mead* made no Sign to speak with me, nor did I in the least suspect that he would follow me. I walked so gently, that had he intended to have come up with me, he might have done that in less than twenty Paces. When I came to the College-Gate, which stood wide open, just as I turn'd to enter it, I received a Blow, grazing on the Side of my Head, (which was then uncover'd) and lighting on my Shoulder. As soon as I felt the Blow, I look'd back, and saw Dr. *Mead*, who made a second Blow at me, and said, *I had abused him*. I told him, *That was false*, stepp'd back, and drew my Sword at the Instant; but offer'd to make no Pass at him 'till he had drawn; in doing which he was very slow. At the Moment that I saw he was ready, I made a Pass at him; upon which he retreated back about four Foot. I immediately made a Second, and retired as before. I still pressed on, making two or three more Passes; he constantly retiring, and keeping out of the Reach of my Sword; nor did he ever attempt to make so much as one single Pass at me. I had by this Time drove him from the Street quite through the Gateway, almost to the Middle of the College-Yard; when, making another Pass, my right Foot was stopp'd by some Accident, so that I fell down flat on my Breast. In an Instant I felt Mr. *Mead*, with his whole Weight, upon me. 'Twas then easy for him to wrest my Sword out of my Hand, as he did; and after that, gave me very abusive Language, and bid me *ask my Life*. I told him, *I scorn'd to ask it of One who, through this whole Affair, had acted so like a Coward and a Scoundril*; and, at the same Time, endeavour'd to lay hold of his Sword, but could not reach it. He again bid me *ask my Life.* I reply'd, as before, *I scorn'd to do that*; adding Terms of Reproach suitable to his Behaviour. By this Time some Persons coming in, interpos'd and parted us. As I was getting up, I heard Dr. *Mead*, amidst a Crowd of People, now got together, exclaiming loudly against me for *refusing to ask my Life.* I told him, in Answer, *he had shewn himself a Coward; and 'twas owing wholly to Chance, and not to any Act of his, that I happen'd to be in his Power.* I added, that *had he been to have given me any of his Physick, I would, rather than take it, have ask'd my Life of him; but for his Sword, it was very harmless; and I was ever far from being in any the least Apprehension of it.*"

J. WOODWARD.

Gresham-College,
June 13, 1719.

A Letter to the Earl of O----d concerning the Bill of Peerage (December, 1719)

Steele had had an understanding with Lord Treasurer Oxford in 1711-12 and had held a minor post under the Tory Ministry; but he had blamed Oxford for his expulsion from the Commons in 1714 and had publicly criticized him more than once (*The Lover*, Nos. 11 and 14; Dedication of *The Apology*; and *The Englishman*, 2nd series). Steele, however, never held a grudge very long for personal or political injuries; hence during the recent impeachment proceedings against Oxford, his attitude had been at the worst one of indifference. Genuine admiration for the abilities of the great statesman can be seen in his letter resigning the Stamp Commission in 1713 and also in this tract, expressed in self-respecting independence: "I transgressed, my Lord, against you when you could make twelve Peers in a Day; I ask your Pardon when you are a private Nobleman; and as I told you when I resign'd the Stamp-Office, I wish'd you all Prosperity, consistent with the publick Good." Steele's only motive in addressing Oxford now was to gain publicity for opposition arguments against the Peerage Bill. Oxford had been conspicuous in the Lords for his opposition, although what seems to have been his main argument (as was Walpole's in the Commons), Steele only mentions, and not with any special emphasis in any of his tracts against the Bill. That argument was that the Royal peer-making prerogative would prevent the award, for public service, of peerages to Commoners.

In this really momentous debate, Steele took a position which brings out the thread of unity in his political thinking: adherence to the doctrines derived from the Revolution. At this juncture he continues to work toward establishing the Hanover dynasty and the Revolution system. He acts, from all appearances, on the side of the dissident Whigs, but nevertheless independently in what he believes to be the true Whig tradition: "Whiggism, if I understand it aright, is a desire of Liberty and a Spirit of Opposition to all Exorbitant Power in any part of the Constitution" (*Plebeian* No. I). And in this tract to Oxford as in his others on the Bill, his arguments center on the oligarchical effect of a closed body of such prestige, wealth, and power as the House of Lords. If enacted, the Bill, he fears, "may change this free State into the worst of all Tyrannies, that of an Aristocracy." The three-part system of Crown, Lords, and Commons with "their vigilant Checks upon each other, equally unconfin'd, but by Reason and Justice" would be destroyed in giving any one of the three permanent, disproportionate power. It is seen, however, that he is less fearful of the King than of the Lords.

521

The Lords was already a highly influential body, its members belonging to an exclusive caste of landed wealth and social prestige and capable of exerting considerable influence on the electorate. In addition to having deliberative and legislative functions, it was the highest court in the land; and it already claimed other privileges above those of the Commons. The Peerage Bill would increase these powers and by legal enactment, power over the Crown. Steele envisages the far-reaching effects of the Bill—" a Hundred Years hence,"—and urges disinterested consideration of it, apart from " the little Quarrels and Animosities of our Time " (party strife and the quarrel in the Royal family) and apart from temporary issues.

For a general discussion of the Peerage Bill and Steele's tracts on it, see the Introduction to the *Plebeians*, p. 453. Textual notes on p. 649.

A
LETTER

TO THE

Earl of O—d,

CONCERNING THE

BILL of PEERAGE.

---

*Rarus enim ferme Senſus communis in illa
Fortuna* —— Juv.

By Sir *R*—*d S*—*le.*

LONDON:

Printed for J. ROBERTS in *Warwick-Lane.* 1719. Price 6 *d.*

A
LETTER

TO THE

Earl of *O—d.*

MY LORD,

I AM very glad of an Occasion, wherein I have the good
Fortune to think the same Way with your Lordship, because
I have very long suffer'd a great deal of Pain in reflecting upon
a certain Virulence, with which my Zeal has, heretofore, transported me to treat your Lordship's Person and Character. I do
protest to you, excepting in the first Smart of my Disgrace, and
Expulsion out of the House of Commons, I never writ any
thing that ought to displease you, but with a reluctant Heart,
and in Opposition to much Good-will and Esteem for your
many great and uncommon Talents: And I take the Liberty to
say thus publickly to yourself what I have often said to others,
on the Subject of my Behaviour to you. I never had any other
Reason to lessen my Lord of *O——d* than that which *Brutus*
had to stab *Caesar*, the Love of my Country. Your Lordship
will, I hope, believe there cannot be a more voluntary, uncon-
strain'd Reparation made to a Man, than that I now make to
you, in begging your Pardon thus publickly for every thing I
have spoken or written to your Disadvantage, foreign to the
Argument and Cause which I was then labouring to support.
You will please to believe I could not have been so insensible
as not to be touch'd with the Generosity of part of your Conduct
towards me, or have omitted to acknowledge it accordingly, if
I had not thought that your very Virtue was dangerous; and
that it was (as the World then stood) absolutely necessary to
depreciate so adventurous a Genius surrounded with so much
Power as your Lordship then had. I transgress'd, my Lord,
against you when you could make twelve Peers in a Day; I ask
your Pardon, when you are a private Nobleman; and as I told

you, when I resign'd the Stamp-Office, I wish'd you all Prosperity, consistent with the publick Good; so I now congratulate you upon the Pleasure you must needs have, in looking back upon the true Fortitude with which you have pass'd through the Dangers arising from the Rage of the People, and the Envy of the rest of the World. If to have rightly judg'd of Mens Passions and Prejudices, Vices and Virtues, Interests and Inclinations, and to have waited with Skill and Courage for proper Seasons and Incidents to make use of them, for a Man's Safety and Honour, can administer Pleasure to a Man of Sense and Spirit, your Lordship has abundant cause of Satisfaction.

In Confidence that you will accept of my Sorrow and Repentance for the unprovok'd Liberties I have taken in my former Writings, I make you my Patron in this present Discourse on the greatest Occasion that has, perhaps, ever happen'd in *England*: Your Lordship will see I write in haste, and the necessity of pressing forward to be time enough to be of any use, will excuse the Failures in Stile and Expression. I shall therefore immediately fall into the Matter of the Bill, which I fear may change this free State into the worst of all Tyrannies, that of an Aristocracy: I shall support my Reasons for that Terror, by running thro' the several Parts of it, and making it appear that this is more likely than any other Consequence that can be suppos'd will attend such a Law as this would be: The whole Tenor of it is very unfortunately put together, if any thing but an Addition of Power to the Peers is intended by it. I believe, my Lord, all Mankind will allow that the only plausible Reason for this Law, is what your Lordship remembers as well as I; but the Preamble assigns no such Reason, but says that sixteen Peers of *Scotland*, by reason of many new Creations since the Union, are not a sufficient and proportionable Representative of that Nobility, and therefore they shall hereafter not be represented at all, but a thing *much more suitable to the Peerage of* Scotland ought to be done for them, to wit, *that twenty-five of them should, at all times hereafter, have hereditary Seats in Parliament*. I always imagin'd no one was Judge of what was suitable to a Man but himself; and I see no manner of Comfort that it can possibly be to one who has any thing taken from him, that the Possession of it is more suitably plac'd:

How is it suitable to the Peerage of *Scotland*, that instead of having a Representative of sixteen sitting by their Election, they are hereafter to be favour'd with having five and twenty there instead of them, and not one there in their behalf? It is, my Lord, very much below Noblemen to use Cunning and Artifice; and it must be allow'd that the Peers of *Scotland* cannot complain of any thing like being trick'd, but their potential Seats in Parliament are barr'd and taken from them, not by Collusion and double Dealing, but the most unreserv'd and candid Usurpation imaginable. But tho' this is done with so much Ease, and no Reason given but that they who do it are pleas'd to say *it is most suitable*, it is to be presum'd those whose Consent is necessary for the divesting innocent Men of their Liberty and Honour, will desire some better Account of the Matter before they deprive their Fellow-Subjects; I cannot but from a natural Detestation of Injustice say, that it is the highest Wrong done to the *Indulgence* mention'd a little after in the Preamble, to expect it will be granted in Favour of any Men, in Wrong of any other: And I will not doubt but the faithful Commons will alarm that Benignity from being employ'd to the Destruction of it self, or Oppression of others. I hope the best Man, and best Prince in the World will be Gracious, so as to have it *always in His Power to be Gracious.* I am sure He will never give His People any Reason to complain but of His too Great Goodness: Happy the Sovereign, and happy the People, when Excessive Grace is all that is to be fear'd from Him: Dr. *Burnet* Compliments King *William, Non Te fortem Dicimus, sed Querimur.* This Nation may say at this Time the same thing to Her Monarch. We do not only acknowledge, but bewail that he is so Gracious.

But to come close to the Point. The Peers of *Scotland* have an Indefeasible Right by the Act of Union to be Elected, and to serve in Parliament as Peers of *Great-Britain,* in the Manner therein stipulated; and it would be but more cruel, not more unjust, to take from them their Lives and Fortunes, as this Honour and Privilege which their Ancestors purchas'd by the frequent Hazard of theirs. The Terms of this Union are Plain and Absolute; nor can there be any Privilege, Liberty, or Property, secur'd by it to the meanest Subject of either Nation,

35

violated or alter'd against his Will, and no Satisfactory Reparation done him, without Infringement of the whole Act, and
leaving the Persons so injur'd, at large as Innocent Outlaws,
at Liberty to avenge by Force, what was done by Force; for
Protection and Obedience are reciprocal, and the withdrawing
the one, discharges the other. What then is the Condition of
these unhappy Men, who are to be divested of their Rights, and
Privileges of Subjects, and yet no doubt to be deem'd Traitors,
should they fly to any Foreign Power, or Invader of that Nation,
which has in the dearest and greatest Considerations, (those
of Honour and Distinction) made them Foreigners? But I will
argue this Point from the Nature of Power in General.

Power as it is to be exerted by Men over Men, must be directed
according to Nature, Justice and Reason; the first obvious Step
from Confusion and Anarchy towards such a Power, is Submission to the Will of one Great Good Man; but such is the
Weakness and Insufficiency of the Greatest and Best for such a
Charge, that every Abatement, Limitation, and Division of that
Power which was at first Despotick, are so many Improvements
of Government. The Legislature of these Kingdoms, in spight
of many Convulsions, has rested in three States; but neither this,
or any other Form, can preserve it self, but according to the
Rules of Justice and Honour; Power separated from them is
Brute-Force, and becomes Violence, which is inconsistent with
Reason and Nature, according to which, it is as just a Maxim
to say, The Legislature can do no Wrong, as to say, The King
can do no Wrong; for to do Wrong, is not to do as becometh
a Legislature, or becometh a King, and therefore not in the
Power of either.

If we should suppose the State to commit Injustice, it would
in that Act be as destructive of it self, as of the Persons violated;
for it would cease to be a Congregation of Men living under
Laws, and begin to be a Collection of Robbers and Pirates,
supporting themselves by Force and Strength; it is therefore
certain that it is impossible and against the very Nature of the
Thing, the Legislature should do Injustice.

The Terms of the Union cannot be revok'd without disuniting
the Kingdoms; for after that is done, they are no longer held
together by Law, but by Force, and the Power which keeps us

together must be Arbitrary, and not Legal; or if Legal, not Righteous; for a Law not supported by Justice, is in it self Null and Void; nor are the Makers of it Legislators, but Oppressors.

Thus then it appears, without any possible Contradiction, that the Parliament of *Great Britain* cannot exclude the Peers of *Scotland* from the Benefit of the Twenty-third Article in the Act for the Union, without becoming an Arbitrary Power, acting with an Indifference to Good and Evil, on the Foundation of Might only.

Now, as Men are attempting what is not in their Power to do, according to Honesty, and therefore not in their Power to do at all, one would think this were enough to say against it; but the World is so corrupt, that an Argument that a thing is inconvenient, is more forcible than Reasons to prove a thing unjust.

I shall go on then to urge that We are safer under the Prerogative in the King. than we can be under an Aristocracy.

The Prerogative is a Power in the Sovereign, not express'd or described by the Laws, but to be exerted in the Preservation of them, by the Rule of the general Good. And if you could prove, that the Business of the Twelve Gentlemen was done purely to save the Nation, and that it was done for the Good of the Whole, the Statesman, who advis'd it, would deserve the Thanks of all Mankind for exposing himself to the Misinterpretation and Resentment of future Parliaments for the Good of his Fellow-Subjects. I say, Sir, the Fault is not in the Power, but the Misapplication of it: And in judging of this Matter we are to carry our Thoughts beyond the Age we live in, and abstract ourselves from the little Quarrels and Animosities of our Time, and consider, if this Power may not be proper to be lodg'd in the Chief Magistrate of this Kingdom a Hundred Years hence. The Magistracy of the King of *England* will be disabled if this Power is taken away; and we are to expect Protection, as well as fear Oppression from it. And, my Lord, had I time, I am confident I could cite you as many Instances of Preservation from the Prerogative in good Princes, as of Violation from arbitrary ones. I believe it will puzzle all the Civilians in the World to account for the Behaviour of the S—x—n L—ds on this Occasion. For though a Deputy or Repre-

sentative has indeed full Right to act for his Principal or Constituent in as ample and effectual Manner as if it were such
his Principal himself, who did all which he the Representative
acts; at the same time, it is, from Reason and Equity, understood,
that these Acts should be for his Constituent's Good and Interest,
and never can be construed to extend to the taking all the Constituent's Property, and converting his Authority to act for him,
into a Power to act against him; much less for vesting in himself,
the *Representative*, the Right intrusted by the Principal.

I will not pretend to doubt but that those noble Personages
have under the Hands and Seals of all, and every of their
Electors, the Peers of *Scotland*, full Power and Authority for
this Alteration; without which Authority this Proceeding cannot be reconciled to common Honesty. But I will aver, that if
the thirty odd, who are to be enobled by this Bill, are to be
made up by present Members of the House of Commons, such
Members are to climb to Honour through Infamy. Nor can
I imagine what Comfort reasonable Creatures can take in an
Advancement so purchased, but that of hiding the Sirnames of
their Families (which they shall have made detestable) under
the Covering of Titles.

This is not, my Lord, talking passionately, but plainly and
honestly; and I do not do such Men, if there are such, Injury;
but they do me, and every Commoner of *England* Injury, by
treacherously attempting to facilitate the Passage of this dreadful Bill into a Law, that may enslave their present Equals, and
contriving to partake of the Tyranny over them obtain'd by such
their Perfidiousness.

My Lord, what I promis'd to maintain, was, that the Bill is
made for an Aristocracy, and, indeed, it seems to me calculated
for nothing else; nay, it has not so much as the Appearance of
any thing else; for tho' a Man of Honour, that is to say, a
Man of conscious Integrity, knows that he is a Peer for the
sake of his fellow Subjects, and that this Right is vested in him
and his Family for the sake of Society, not for himself and
Successors only; yet is there no part of Society consider'd in
this Bill, but merely the Peers and Nobles. Your Lordship, who
has declar'd against it, has observ'd this with proper Care of
the Prerogative; give me leave to declare the same, not only

in behalf of the Prerogative, but also that of the People. The Lords exercise a Power in the last Resource of Justice; and an Appeal, they say, lies to them from the Courts of *Westminster-Hall* for determining all the Property of *Great-Britain*; and yet they are willing to have a Law, which must necessarily disable them from being a Court of Justice, that is, a capable Court of Justice for the future. The Bill even provides for their Insufficiency as to this purpose; and there is a Clause, which, instead of looking out for great and knowing Men, is very careful to leave Power in the King to give Titles, in case of Extinctions, to Minors. But such at the same time is the Partiality of the Bill that Females are to be excluded from their future Right, as if a Lady of good Sense were not as capable of bringing into the World a Man of Sense, as a Boy under Age is of becoming a Man of Justice and Honour from the mere Recommendation of his Fortune; for it is not to be doubted but that would be his best Pretension; but Lords have thought it more eligible to have in view the providing rich Husbands for their Daughters from among the Commons, than leaving it to their Female Heirs to make Lords of the Descendants of meritorious Commoners.

Thus, my Lord, you see the Aristocracy is already set out by this Bill, for all the Provisions and Limitations of it regard only the Titles and Honours of the Peers, and a prodigious Care is taken that no one should suffer from possible Contingencies and distant Incidents among themselves, but no regard had to the known immediate present Rights of those who do not sit in their House, but have title of Election into it; there is no difficulty of destroying those whom they know to have Titles, but they are prodigious tender of hurting who may have Titles of which they do not know. And we Commoners are suppos'd not to have Eyesight enough to see through this noble Subtlety. The Lords will be Judges, and give and admit to whom they please incidental Claims, but Extinctions are to be supplied only by the King, and he might possibly give them to Persons they should not like.

The worthiest Circumstance in the Bill, is the Favour and Notice taken of the Title in the Dutchess of Bucclugh, and if good Sense, Virtue, and all manner of Merit are Reasons for honouring any Persons in their Descendants, the Heirs of that illustrious Lady have indisputable Pretensions, and I hope the King will never want the Assistance of his Legislature for conferring it upon them, without the Assistance of such a Bill as this is.

To conclude, My Lord, the Restraint of the Peers to a certain Number will render the House useless, because it is well known that the great Business is always carry'd on by Men created first in their own Persons; and if all such were now to be excluded, I need not say what would be the Ability of the House.

When they are confin'd to a Number, the most Powerful of them will have the rest under their Direction, and all the Property disputed before them will be bestowed not by Judgment, but by Vote and Humour, or Worse. Judges so made by the blind Order of Birth, will be capable of no other way of Decision. It is said that Power attends Property, it is as true that Power will command Property; and I am at Liberty to say, that according to the Degeneracy of Humane Nature, the Lords may as well grow corrupt as other Men; and if they should do so, how will this be amended but by the Consent of those who shall become so corrupt? What shall we then say? Shall We expose Our selves to probable Evils, with the Prospect of impossible Remedies against them?

I will not insinuate any thing from the Suspicions or Dangers that may very well be expected will arise from the Impatience of those new Nobles, who are not to be seated in the House till another Session of Parliament; but am at liberty to suppose that Session would not be very far off after this Bill should become a Law. It is hardly to be read seriously, when the Bill in a grave Stile and sober Contradiction has these Words, *The twenty-five Peers on the Part of the Peerage of* Scotland, as if they who were made instead of the Peers of *Scotland*, could without a Banter, be called Peers on the Part of the Peerage of *Scotland*. The true Description of them is Peers made, when the Peers of *Scotland* were no more to be Peers; for the Titles resting in their Families, without Hopes of Succession in the Peerage and Legislature, is only a Bar against any Participation of Power and Interest in their Country. It is putting them into the Condition of Papists Convict, as to what ought to be most dear to them, their Honour and Reputation.

It is held by true Politicians a most dangerous thing to give the meanest of the People just Cause of Provocation, much more to enrage Men of Spirit and Distinction, and that with downright Injuries.

We may flatter our selves that Property is always the Source of Power; but Earl *Mar,* who led and commanded Men of much greater Property than himself, is an Instance that Property, like all other Possessions, has its Effects according to the Talents and Abilities of the Owner: And as it is allow'd that Learning and Courage are very common Qualities in that Nation, I should think it not very advisable to provoke the greatest, and for ought we can tell, the best Men amongst them.

Thus we are barr'd from making this Law by prudential Rules, as well as from the inviolable Rule of Justice and common Right with relation to the *Scotch* Peers; but if we consider the Matter, with regard to the King's Prerogative, this Law would diminish it to an irreparable Degree; And it is a strange time to take away Power, when it is in the Possession of a Prince who uses it with so much Moderation, that he is willing to resign it: But we are to consider the Prerogative as part of the Estate of the Crown, and not consent to the taking it out of the Crown, till we see just Occasion for it.

His Majesty's Indulgence makes it safe in his Royal Breast, and we know of nothing any other of the Family has done to alter it for fear of him. If others have just Apprehensions, from whencesoever they arise, they shall speak them, and prove them just, before they have any honest Man's Vote for altering the Estate in the Crown. The Prerogative can do no hurt when Ministers do their Duty, but a settled Number of Peers may abuse their Power, when no Man is answerable for them, or can call them to an Account for their Encroachments.

I know it is said, and that very truly, the manner of their Power will be the same as now, but then the Application of it may be altered when they are an unchangeable Body. Schemes of Grandeur and Oppression can be form'd to invade the Property, as well as Liberty of their Fellow-Subjects; which would, according to the present Establishment, be vain to undertake, when they are subject to Alteration before their Projects could be ripen'd into Practice and Usurpation.

As for any sudden and surprizing Way of Creation, that lies before the Legislature for Censure, and the great Diminution which all Creations bring upon the King's Authority, is a sufficient Defence against the abusive Employment of that Authority this Way. For when the King makes Peers, he makes perpetual Opponents of his Will and Power, if they shall think fit; which one Consideration cannot but render frequent Creations terrible to the Crown.

This Constitution has subsisted in Spight of Convulsions and Factions, without restraining or expressing the Extent of the Legislative Powers; nor is it possible for any Man, or Assembly of Men, to circumscribe their distinct Authorities: No, they are to be left eternally at large, and Safety of each Part, and the Good of the Whole, are to be the Rules of their Conduct. And as 'tis impossible to foresee all the Circumstances which must arise before them, there is no other safe Way, but leaving them at large, as vigilant Checks upon each other, equally unconfin'd, but by Reason and Justice.

Hence it is, my Lord, that I have always asserted, that if there was any Outrage committed in the Case of the Twelve Gentlemen, the Peers should have then withstood the receiving of them, or done what they thought fit at another Season for their Satisfaction, and not when it is too late, instead of asserting their Liberties, meditate their future Security in unreasonable Concessions from the Crown, and Discouragements upon the Merit of the Commons.

I have, my Lord, lain under unjust Imputations of turning the Persons and Characters of Men in present Power into ridicule; but as I abhor to do any thing but what I think I may defend, I neither have nor will presume to take such a Licence, but leave it to Gentlemens own Modesty and Reflection, to consider whether they can reasonably think the Consummation of the *English* Glory and Merit is to close and rest in their Persons.

After the Bill has sufficiently provided for the Aristocracy over these Dominions, it goes into a kind of Oeconomy and Order among themselves, which relates to their Nobility and not to their Peerage; we plain Men and Commoners will not dispute about any thing which we know to be merely trifling

and ornamental; and if they will be satisfied with a Power in
them as Peers, they shall be Dukes, Marquesses, Earls, or whatever other Words they please, without our Envy or Opposition.
But when we come seriously to consider what we are going to
do, we must take the Liberty to be very jealous, as the last time
that it may be in our power to make a Stand for ourselves and
our Posterity; and Noblemen cannot blame Commoners, who
are as shy in bestowing, as they are importunate in urging the
Grant of such a Power in themselves, which can be of no Use
or Advantage but to themselves; at the same time one cannot
resist observing to them, that, with respect to the Prerogative,
the Peerage of *Scotland*, and the Rights of the whole Body of
the People of *Great Britain*, they cannot be more exorbitant in
the use of this Bill, should it become a Law, than in the Circumstances under which they send it to us for our Concurrence;
and 'tis not Thirst of Power, but Moderation in the Demands
made of it, can recommend Men to further Trust; and we cannot apprehend but that which would be founded on Usurpation,
would be exerted in Tyranny. But, my Lord, it is to be hop'd
this unreasonable Bill will be entirely rejected, when no one
can pretend to amend what is in its very Nature incorrigible,
for it would be in vain to attempt a Superstructure, which ought
to be approv'd, upon a Foundation which deserves nothing but
Indignation and Contempt. It is a melancholy Consideration,
that under the Pressure of Debts, the Necessities of a War, the
Perplexities of Trade, and the Calamities of the Poor, the
Legislature should thus be taken up and employ'd in Schemes
for the Advancement of the Power, Pride and Luxury of the
Rich and Noble: I speak not this, my Lord, to spread Discon-
tents or sow Divisions, but to compose and heal them; I speak
it in Charity to all Men, and address it to one, towards whom
of all others my Behaviour has been most exceptionable. Thus
far, my Lord, have I treated this Affair in a most solemn manner,
by reason of the awful Authority from whence it comes; but we
must not, on such great Occasions, be opprest by outward things,
but look to the Bottom of the Matter before us, divested
of every thing that should divert us from seeing the true Reason
of what passes, and the Pretensions to what is ask'd; if this Bill
is requir'd for preventing the Creation of occasional Peers, why,

at the same time, are five and twenty *Scotch*, and eight *English* to be now made? Is not this the same thing as to say, If you will let us make so many this one Time, under the Sanction of a Law, we will make no more, for we shall have no Occasion for any more.

Accusat Catalina Cethegum.

It appears indeed very unlikely any more should be wanted; if all that is wanted is to prevent the sudden and occasional Increase of Peers, a more easy Method for that purpose is obvious, to wit, a Prohibition to sit and vote in Parliament, till after a convenient Distance of Time after their Creation. I speak not this as I approve even such a Remedy, for every Power of Parliament (as is already observ'd) has from the Reason of the thing, and their distinct Safety, proper Limitations, as well as Privileges; but I name that Expedient only to show that more is ask'd than is wanted; and when more is asked than is wanted, it cannot be thought unfair to suspect much more is to be done with the superfluous Power than is acknowledg'd; the former Conduct of the House of Peers, of admitting or opposing Creations of the Crown, shows that they well know they have a Power of so doing, when the Reason of the thing gives them Authority for it, much more when Reason dictates that their very Existence, as a House of Parliament, is struck at, as in the Case of pouring in new Members in the midst of their Debates.

The latter End of the Bill seems to have some Compassion towards the Prerogative, and enacts something Gracious towards the Descendants of the Sovereign before the Commencement of the Aristocracy. *Provided always nevertheless, That nothing in this Act contained shall be taken, or construed to lay any Restraint upon the King's Majesty, his Heirs or Successors, from advancing or promoting any Peer, having Vote and Seat in Parliament, to any higher Rank or Degree of Dignity or Nobility; nor from creating or making any of the Princes of the Blood Peers of Great Britain, or Lords of Parliament; and such Princes of the Blood, so created, shall not be esteemed to be any Part of the Number, to which the Peers of Great Britain are by this Act restrain'd.*

You see, my Lord, the Grace and Favour which (as soon as all their own Posterity, and Accidents that could befall them, are provided for) is most bounteously bestowed upon the Children of the Royal Family; as this Goodness is confer'd on those of it who are not yet entitled to that Honour, it is to be presum'd, in spight of all groundless Insinuations that are spread abroad, nothing vested in others of them will be assaulted; but that whatever becomes of this Bill, their present Estates, their then remaining Estates will be still inviolable. I am confident none will deserve any other; and as all humane Nature is subject to Infirmities, those are most excusable which grow upon the Dignity of our Nature. I will dwell no more upon this tender Place, but say with the Tragedian:

Pyrrhus *is violent, but he's sincere.*

To conclude, my Lord, I will not doubt but Mens Spirits will be sufficiently rais'd, in a Cause which so nearly concerns the Subject, from the highest to the lowest; and that since the House has given this Affair such proper Usage, as to call a full Assembly to be present at the Debate, it will infallibly end according to Justice; for I can never think the Liberty of *England* in danger at such a Meeting. Rancors, Animosities, and private Hates vanish in common Danger; and I doubt not but the Zeal that demanded a Hearing before this full Assembly, will be doubled at it. I cannot leave off till I have done Justice to a noble and generous Youth, who pleaded for the more distant Day, and wish I could represent him in the amiable Figure which he bears in my Imagination, to all the rest of his fellow Subjects. The *Roman*, the *English* Virtue is not lost, while a young Nobleman is contending against a Power as a Patriot, which he has so near a Pretense to as a Son; filial Piety to his Country and to his Family had no Struggle, but work'd together to break thro' a Modesty which long withheld him from taking a leading Part in this glorious Contention: Many, who are nearer to him in Interest and Fortune, will, I hope, on the approaching Occasion, emulate his Virtue; none who have the Honour to sit in the Legislature should be indifferent in it, but exert themselves according to the Interest they have in these Dominions, the only remaining Seats of Liberty: As for me, a poor *Plebeian*, who, from Love of Justice and Virtue, have at the Entrance into old Age, but just lifted my Head out of Obscurity into Noise, Clamour and Envy, be it enough to applaud and celebrate their noble Qualities, be it enough for me to be permitted and forgiven.

I am,

MY LORD,

Your Lordship's most Obedient,

AND

Most Humble Servant,

R——d S——le.

Sir Richard Steele's Speech against Committing the Peerage Bill (December, 1719)

The debate against committing the Peerage Bill was one of the most important in the Commons during the reign of George I. A full assembly was present for the second reading, and several distinguished speeches were made during the afternoon and evening of 8 December 1719, that by Walpole, leader of the opposition, being one of the most effective he ever made. Steele's speech, as it has come down to us, seems to have been made from notes taken from his *Letter to Oxford*, which had been published in the forenoon. Steele had been a member for Boroughbridge, Yorkshire, since 1715. The division was made late in the evening, and the Bill was defeated by a large majority. For further comment on the Peerage Bill, see the Introduction to the *Plebeians*. Textual notes on p. 649.

Sir Richard Steele's Speech against Committing the Peerage Bill

Sir Richard Steele spoke first against committing the Bill as follows: Mr. Speaker: I am against the Bill, because I fear it may change this free state into the worst of tyrannies, that of an aristocracy, which is the most likely to attend such a law as this would be: the whole tenor of the Bill is very unfortunately put together; if anything, but an addition of power to the peers, is intended by it. All mankind must allow, that the only plausible reason for this law, was what happened in the last reign, when twelve peers were made in one day; but the Preamble assigns no such reason, but says, "That sixteen peers of Scotland, by reason of many new creations since the Union, are not a sufficient and proportionable representative of that nobility. And therefore they shall hereafter not be represented at all: but, a thing much more suitable to the peerage of Scotland ought to be done for them, to wit, that twenty-five of them should, at all times hereafter, have hereditary seats in parliament."

I have always imagined that no man could judge what was suitable to him but himself; and that it could be no manner of

539

comfort to one who has any thing taken from him, that the possession of it is more suitably placed in another. How is it suitable to the peerage of Scotland, that instead of having a representative of sixteen sitting by their election, they are hereafter to be favoured with having five and twenty there instead of them, and not one there in their behalf? It must be confessed, that the peers of Scotland cannot complain of any thing like being tricked; but their potential seats in parliament are barred and taken from them, not by collusion and double dealing, but by the most unreserved and candid usurpation imaginable: but though this is done with so much ease, and no reason given but that they who do it, are pleased to say it is most suitable; it is to be presumed, that those, whose consent is necessary for the divesting innocent men of their liberty and honour, will desire some better account of the matter, before they deprive their fellow-subjects of their undoubted rights. I cannot but, from a natural detestation of injustice, say, that it is the highest wrong done to the indulgence mentioned in the preamble, to expect it will be granted in favour of any men in wrong of any other; and I doubt not but that this House will alarm that benignity from being employed to the destruction of itself, or oppression of others.

I hope that the best man and best prince in the world, will be gracious so as to have it always in his power to be gracious: I am sure he will never give his people any reason to complain, but of his too great goodness: happy the sovereign and happy the people, when excessive grace is all that can be feared of him.

The peers of Scotland have an indefeasible right, by the Act of Union, to be elected and serve in parliament as peers of Great Britain, in the manner therein stipulated and it would be more cruel, not more unjust, to take from them their lives and fortunes, than this honour and privilege, which their ancestors purchased by the frequent hazard of theirs: the terms of the Union are plain and absolute; nor can any privilege, liberty, or property secured by it to the meanest subject of either nation, be violated or altered against his will, and no satisfactory reparation done him, without infringement of the whole act, and leaving the persons so injured, at liberty to avenge by force what was done by it: for protection and obedience are reciprocal, and withdrawing the one, discharges the other. What then is the condition of these unhappy men, who are to be divested of their rights and privileges of subjects, and yet, no doubt, to be deemed traitors should they fly to any foreign power, or invader of that nation, which has in the dearest and greatest considerations, those of honour and distinction, made them foreigners? The terms of the Union cannot be revoked without disuniting the kingdoms: for when that it done they are no longer held together by that law, but by force; and the power which then keeps us together must be arbitrary not legal; or if legal, not righteous; for a law, not supported by justice, is in itself null and void; nor are the makers of it legislators, but oppressors. It appears, without any possible contradiction, that the parliament of Great Britain cannot exclude the peers of Scotland, from the benefit of the 23d Article in the Act of Union, without becoming an arbitrary power, acting with an indifference to good and evil, on the foundation of might only.

We are safer under the prerogative in the King, than we can be under an aristocracy. The prerogative is a power in the sovereign, not expressed or described in the laws, but to be exercised in the preservation of them by the rule of the general good: and if it could be proved, that the business of the twelve gentlemen, [meaning the twelve lords created by Queen Anne in the time of the Earl of Oxford's ministry] was purely done to save the nation, and that it was done for the good of the whole, the statesman who advised it would deserve the thanks of all mankind, for exposing himself to the misrepresentation and resentment of future parliaments, for the good of his fellow-subjects.

I will not pretend to doubt but those noble personages have, under the hands and seals of all and every of their electors, the peers of Scotland, full power and authority for this alteration, without which their proceeding could not be reconciled to common honour: and if the thirty odd, who are to be ennobled by this Bill, are to be made up by present members of the House of Commons, such members are to climb to honour through infamy.

The Bill seems to me to be calculated for nothing but an aristocracy, and indeed, has not so much as the appearance of any thing else; for though a man of honour and conscious integrity knows, that he is a peer for the sake of his fellow-subjects, and that this right is vested in him and his family for the sake of society not for himself and successors only, yet is there no part of society considered in this Bill, but merely the peers and nobles. The Lords exercise a power in the last resource: and an appeal lies to them from all the courts of Westminster-hall, for determining all the property of Great Britain, and yet they are willing to have a law, which must necessarily disable them from being a capable court of justice for the future; for the Bill even provides for their insufficiency as to this purpose; and there is a clause, which, instead of looking out for great and knowing men, is careful to leave the power in the king to give titles, in case of extinction, to minors: much of the same stamp is the partiality of the Bill, that females are excluded from their future right; as if a lady of good sense were not as capable of bringing into the world a man of sense as a boy, under age, is of becoming a man of justice and honour from the mere recommendation of his fortune; for it is not to be doubted but that would be his best pretensions; but lords have thought it more eligible to have in view the providing rich husbands for their daughters from among the Commons, than the leaving it to their female heirs, to make Lords of the descendants of meritorious commoners.

Thus the aristocracy is set out by this Bill; for all the provisions and limitations of it regard only the titles and honours of the peers, and prodigious care is taken, that no one should suffer from possible contingencies and distant incidents among themselves, but no regard had to the known immediate present rights of those who do not sit in their House, but have title of election into it: there is no difficulty of destroying those whom they know to have titles, but they are prodigious tender of hurting those who may have titles, of which they do not know; the lords will be judges, and give and admit to whom they please incident claims: but extinctions are to be supplied only by the King, and he might possibly give them to persons they should not like. The restraint of the peers to a certain number will make the most powerful of them have the rest under their direction; and all the property disposed before them will be bestowed, not by judgment, but by vote and humour, or worse. Judges so made by the blind order of birth will be capable of no other way of decision.

It is said that power attends property; but it is as true, that power will command property; and according to the degeneracy of human nature, the Lords may as well grow corrupt as other men; and if they should do so, how will this be amended, but by the consent of those, who shall become so corrupt? What shall we say then? Shall be expose ourselves to probable evils, with the foresight of impossible remedies against them?

It is hardly to be read seriously, when the Bill in a grave stile and sober contradiction has these words, viz. " the twenty-five peers on the part of the peerage of Scotland "; as if they who were made instead of the peers of Scotland, could, without a banter be called peers on the part of the peerage of Scotland; the true description of them is, peers made when the peers of Scotland were no more to be peers; for the title resting in their families, without hopes of succession in the peerage and legislature is only a bar against any participation of power and interest in their country; it is putting them into the condition of papists convict, as to what ought to be most dear to them, their honour and reputation. It is held by true politicians a most dangerous thing to give the meanest of the people just cause of provocation; much more to enrage men of spirit and distinction, and that too with downright injuries.

We may flatter ourselves, that property is always the source of power; but property, like all other possessions, has its effects according to the talents and abilities of the owner; and as it is allowed, that courage and learning are very common qualities in that nation, it seems not very advisable to provoke the greatest, and for ought we can tell, the best men among them. Thus we are barred from making this law by prudential reasons, as well as from the inviolable rule of justice and common right, with relation to the Scots Peers.

If we consider the matter, with regard to the king's prerogative, this law will diminish it to an irreparable degree; and it is a strange time to take away power, when it is in the possession of a prince, who uses it with so much moderation, that he is willing to resign it; but we are to consider the pre-

36

rogative as part of the estate of the crown, and not consent to the taking it out of the crown, till we see just occasion for it. His majesty's indulgence makes it safe in his royal breast; and we know of nothing any other of the family has done, to alter it for fear of him.

The prerogative can do no hurt, when ministers do their duty; but a settled number of peers may abuse their power, when no man is answerable for them, or can call them to an account for their incroachments. It is said, and truly too, that the manner of their power will be the same as now; but then the application of it may be altered, when they are an unchangeable body: schemes of grandeur and oppression can be formed to invade the property, as well as liberty of their fellow-subjects; which would according to the present establishment, be vain to undertake, when they are subject to an alteration, before their project could be ripened into practice and usurpation.

As for any sudden and surprising way of creation, that lies before the legislature for censure; and the great diminution which all creations bring upon the king's authority, is a sufficient defence against the abusive employment of that authority this way; for when the king makes peers, he makes perpetual opponents of his will and power, if they shall think fit; which one consideration cannot but render frequent creations terrible to the crown. This Constitution has subsisted in spite of convulsions and factions without restraining or repressing the extent of the legislative powers; nor is it possible for any man, or assembly of men to circumscribe their distinct authorities; no they are to be left eternally at large; and the safety of each part, and the good of the whole, are to be the rules of their conduct: And as it is impossible to foresee all the circumstances which must arise before them, there is no other safe way but leaving them at large, as vigilant checks upon each other, equally unconfined, but by reason and justice.

If there was any outrage committed in the case of the twelve gentlemen, the peers should have then withstood the receiving of them, or done what they thought fit at another season for their satisfaction; and not, when it is too late, instead of asserting their liberties mediate their future security in unreasonable concessions from the crown, and discouragements upon the merits of the Commons: and can the gentlemen in present power, reasonably think, that the consummation of the English glory and merit, is to close and rest in their persons?

After the Bill has sufficiently provided for the aristocracy over these dominions, it goes with a kind of oeconomy and order among themselves, which relates to their nobility and not to their peerage. We plain men and Commoners will not dispute about any thing which we know to be merely trifling and ornamental; and if they will be satisfied with a power in them as peers, they shall be dukes, marquises, earls, or whatever other words they please, without our envy or opposition: But when we come seriously to consider what we are going to do, we must take the liberty to be very jealous, at the last time, that it may be in our power to make a stand for ourselves and our posterity; and noblemen cannot blame commoners, who are as shy in bestowing, as they are importunate in urging, the grant of such a power in themselves, which can be of no use or advantage, but to ourselves: at the same time one cannot resist observing to them, that, with respect to the prerogative, the peerage of Scotland, and the rights of the whole body of the people of Great Britain, they cannot be more exorbitant in the use of this Bill, should it become a law, than in the circumstances under which they send it to us for concurrence; and it is not thirst of power, but moderation in the demands made of it, which can recommend men to farther trust; and I cannot but apprehend that what is founded on usurpation, will be exerted in tyranny.

It is to be hoped, that this unreasonable Bill will be entirely rejected, since none can pretend to amend what is in its very nature incorrigible; for it would be in vain to attempt a good superstructure which ought to be approved upon a foundation which deserves nothing but indignation and contempt.

It is a melancholy consideration, that under the pressure of debts, the necessities of a war, the perplexities of trade and the calamities of the poor, the legislature should thus be taken up and employed in schemes for the advancement of the power, pride, and luxury, of the rich and noble. It is true, this affair ought to be treated in a most solemn manner, by reason of the awful authority from whence it comes; but we must not, on such occasions, be oppressed by outward things, but look to the bottom of the matter before us, divested of everything that can divert us from seeing the true reason of what passes, and the pretensions to what is asked.

If this Bill is required for presenting the creation of occasional peers, why, at the same time are five and twenty Scots and eight English, to be now made? Is not this the same thing, as to say if you will let us make so many this one time, under the sanction of a law, we will make no more, for we shall have no occasion for any more? The latter end of this Bill seems to have some compassion towards the prerogative, and enacts something gracious towards the descendants of the sovereign, before the commencement of the Aristocracy, viz. " Provided always nevertheless that nothing in this act contained, shall be taken or construed to lay any restraint upon the king's majesty, his heirs or successors, from advancing or promoting any peer having vote and seat in parliament, to any higher rank or degree of dignity or nobility; nor from creating or making any of the princes of the blood peers of Great Britain or Lords of Parliament; and such princes of the blood, so created, shall not be esteemed to be any part of the number to which the peers of Great Britain are by this act restrained." This is the grace and favour, which, as soon as all their own posterity and accidents that could befall them, are provided for, is most bounteously bestowed on the children of the royal family; as this goodness is conferred on those of it, who are not yet intitled to that honour, it is to be presumed, in spite of all groundless insinuations that are spread abroad, that nothing vested in others of them will be assaulted; but that whatever becomes of this Bill, their present estates, their then remaining estates, will be still inviolable.

Since there is so full a House at this debate, I doubt not but it will infallibly end according to justice; for I can never think the liberty of Great Britain in danger at such a meeting; but for my part, I am against committing of this bill, because I think it would be committing of sin.

The Spinster: In Defence of the Woollen Manufactures
(December, 1719)

This pamphlet is evidence of Steele's perennial interest in trade, manufacturers, merchants, and shippers. The comment is that of a publicist,
useful chiefly in putting an issue before the public and stirring up
controversy. In this case women are addressed and urged to buy their
clothes and house furnishings with more thought to the trade advantages
of their country.

Steele's emphasis seems to be the defence of domestic manufactures,
presumably woollen goods, against foreign imports, mainly French and
Italian silks. But his argument is related to a problem of internal
competition, at the time under debate in Parliament. It was a conflict
between the woollen manufactures and the Spitalfields silk industry on
the one hand and the rapidly expanding cotton manufactures, at Man-
chester (for example), on the other. At first the clamor had been
against imported cottons—Indian printed and " painted calicoes "; and
legislation of about 1700, prohibited their importation. But of late the
popularity of English-made printed cotton, in imitation of the foreign
product, had raised alarm, particularly among the Spitalfields silk
weavers, whose rioting and demonstrations in the winter of 1719, when
Steele's tract was written, forced parliamentary action. An Act passed
in 1720, to take effect in 1722, extended the prohibition as well to the
purchase or use of domestic printed cottons.

Steele shows that the fine lady is dressed from the skin out in foreign
silks (only her maid is in calico), and then raises the questions: may
it not be foreign silk rather than domestic cotton which is injuring the
trade of British wool and silk dealers? And, may it not be possible
for the home calico industry to prove that their business brings more
revenue to England than is lost by foreign luxury imports?

As always he is emphasizing the Whig principle of protectionism,
especially against the old enemy France:

Foreigners sell this Lady to the Value of a thousand Pounds, where the English
sell her to the Value of five; and I believe any Company, or Person, Trade,
or Trader, on the *British* side of the Channel, will find it hard to ballance this
loss to our Country by what they sell of *English* Cloathing to Foreigners.

But it is only foreign trade with a balance to the disadvantage of
England which he deplores. Lest his real position on the interchange
of goods be misunderstood, he prefaces a quotation from Addison's
eulogy of the merchant in *Spectator* No. 69 with the statement: " This

is not at all said to disparage Trade in general, but to make us more circumspect in maintaining the Balance of it on our own Side."

Steele probably intended in future issues of the periodical to discuss further the domestic problem of silk and wool versus printed cotton, but aside from *Theatre*, Nos. 3 and 11 (9 Jan. and 6 Feb.), he did not return to the subject. The authorship of *The Spinster* seems not to have been directly acknowledged by Steele, but that it was known at the time to be his is seen in the pamphlets written in reply. John Nichols, at the end of the century, included it among Steele's writings. Textual notes on p. 649.

T H E
SPINSTER:
I N
DEFENCE
OF THE
Woollen Manufactures.

To be continued Occaſionally.

N U M B. I.

Cætera, ni Catia eſt, demiſſa veſte tegentis. **Hor.**

L O N D O N:

Printed for J. Roᴮᴇʀᴛs in *Warwick-Lane.* 1719. Price 3 *d.*

The Spinster. No. 1. December 19, 1719.

This Discourse is written in Behalf of the Needy and Distress'd, in Opposition to the Wealthy and Powerful; who, I fear, may conspire for their own Ends, to leave the Afflictions and Complaints of their miserable Fellow-Subjects and Fellow-Creatures neglected, and unreliev'd; I shall continue it from time to time, during the Dispute between the Dealers concern'd in the Woollen and Callico Manufactures.

But tho' my present Opinion is clearly on the Side of the Cloathing made from our own Wool, I shall not be deaf to Callico.

And if any Gentlewoman, dating herself at the present Writing and Time of Year in *England*, and in Callico, shall write her Thoughts to *Rebecca Woolpack*, Spinster, at Mr. *Roberts's,* in *Warwick-lane*, Post-paid, (for the Woollen-Manufacture cannot at present bear Postage), she shall have a fair and candid Answer.

I write my self Spinster, because the Laws of my Country call me so, and I think that Name, us'd in all Writings and Instruments as the Addition and Distinction of a Maiden or single Woman of this Island, denotes to us, that the general Expectation of our Lawgivers was, that the Industry of female Manufacturers would be most laudably employ'd this way, and therefore they gave the Office of the Spinner as a Title to the Gentlewoman.

It might be further urg'd, that this Word intimates that a Woman's chief Praise consists in Domestic Industry, and in Simplicity, rather than Variety of Dress.

In order to come at the true State of Trade, and the Interest of this Island, with relation to the Habits now worn, I shall take the modern *English* Lady at eleven a-clock in the Forenoon, which is her break of Day, and allowing her to twelve for private Devotion, suppose she has call'd to be dress'd, and from the Parcels of her Dress, observing what she wears of *English,* and what of foreign Product, with the Prices of each part of her Habit, make my Inferences accordingly.

None amongst those whom we call People of Condition can

be at Home, or Abroad, visit, or receive Visits, without having several Dresses, with several suitable Undresses, according to the following List, of absolute Necessaries for a fine Lady. She has now nothing on but her Slippers, and her Maid in Callico cloathes her with the Productions of the whole Earth, as under-written:

	l.	s.	d.
A Smock of Cambrick Holland, about three Ells and a half, at 12s. *per* Ell	2	02	00
Marseilles quilted Petticoat, three Yards wide and a Yard long	3	06	00
An Hoop-Petticoat cover'd with Tabby	2	15	00
A *French* or *Italian* Silk quilted Petticoat, one Yard and a quarter deep, and six Yards wide	10	00	00
A Mantua and Petticoat of *French* Brocade, 26 Yards, at three Pounds *per* Yard	78	00	00
A *French* Point or *Flanders* lac'd Head, Ruffles and Tucker	80	00	00
Stays covered with Tabby, *English*	3	00	00
A *French* necklace	1	05	00
A *Flanders* lac'd Handkerchief	10	00	00
French or *Italian* Flowers for the Hair	2	00	00
An *Italian* Fan	5	00	00
Silk Stockings, *English*	1	00	00
Shoes, *English*	2	10	00
A Girdle, *French*	0	15	00
A Cambrick Pocket Handkerchief	0	10	00
French Kid Gloves	0	02	06
A black *French* Silk Alamode Hood	0	15	00
A black *French* lac'd Hood	5	05	00
Imbroider'd Knot and Bosom Knot, *French*	2	02	00
	210	07	06

This is the necessary Demand upon every Gentleman, who would live in Fashion and in Quiet, for one Dress for his Lady; and as it would be scandalous, (as his Wife, anxious for his Reputation, according to her Duty, admonishes him) for her to be known by her Cloathes, she cannot but have five Suits at least, and even with that she must stay at Home one Day in the Week; but she is willing to do anything for her Children and Family, and would not appear abroad every Day, like that flaring Busybody her Neighbour Mrs. *Blank*.

According to this Rule, Foreigners sell this Lady to the Value of a thousand Pounds, where the English sell her to the Value of five; and I believe any Company, or Person, Trade, or Trader, on the *British* side of the Channel, will find it hard to ballance this Loss to our Country by what they sell of *English* Cloathing to Foreigners: I shall not therefore press the Advantage further in the Argument, so far as to mention that her Garters are *French*, and cost one Pound five; that she has a Pair of Pockets of *Marseilles* quilting, which is another one Pound five: Nor need I observe that her Stay-Buckles, and Buckles for her Shoes, cannot be any other than *Brilliant*, the Price of which alters according to the Price which others of our Acquaintance, whom we love or envy, have purchas'd theirs. But I wonder I forgot that whatever Part of the Town the Lady lives in, she must have a Muff of five Pounds five Shillings; and if she lives in the City, she will catch Cold if she has not a Sable Tippet worth fifteen Pounds.

I had like to have concluded without taking notice, that the Lining of her Gown and Petticoat was *Italian* Lutestring, cheap at eight Pounds; but on the *English* side of the Account, which I forgot, when about her Legs, it must be added that she had Thread Stockings worth ten Shillings.

In an Affair of this Nature, wherein a great Demand of things of small Price rises to great Profit, it must not be forgotten that the Cap on which her Head is dresst is foreign Silk, and so is the Lace that ties it, as well as the Lace for the Stays. But for our Encouragement at Home, we supply her with Pins, Patches, Powder, and Wire. Patches may perhaps make a Fraction in the Account, therefore it must be consider'd that it is *English* labour upon *Italian* Silk. I am dressing her for a Visit; and as she is going out, she calls for her *Turkey* Handkerchief, for which she gave five Pounds five Shillings; but she is now ready to move, and has call'd for either her Coach or her Chair; but as the Maid is going, she bids her call both, lest she should alter her Mind before she comes to the Door, and then 'tis time enough to chuse which of the Vehicles she pleases.

Whether we are taller this Age than we were formerly, I

cannot determine; but am divided in my Conjectures whence
it is that our Women dress their Heads lower, and the Ceilings
of our Rooms are rais'd higher than in former Times; but be
that as it will, the Apartments thro' which I am to conduct this
Lady are hung with foreign Silks, and the Chairs cover'd with
the same. But she is come to the Door, and takes her Chair
lined with Velvet, as dear as the Silk with which herself is
cloathed, and bids her Coach (the inside of which is of Velvet
also, but of a Colour less suitable to her Complexion) put off.

This is the State of the Case, and it behoves all on the Callico
Side of this Question to make out, as is above demanded of
them, that they bring to *England*, by Sale of the Product of
these Kingdoms, more than the Luxury and Charge in Dress,
describ'd in the Instance of one Lady, reduces us to the Necessity
of supplying our selves with from other Nations.

The Legislature, before which this Question now lies, will
certainly consider whether the Manufacturers of Wool, which
is as much a Produce of the Land as are Corn and Grass, shall,
instead of working those Fleeces, and gaining to themselves a
comfortable Livelihood, and raising the Rents of their Land-
lord, become immoveable Incumbrances upon that Land, and
live in the Poors-rate, to the Ruin of them both.

It is not proper to dictate to Law-givers; but we may give
them Information. I have read in the *Lives of Plutarch*, that the
wise *Lycurgus*, in order to maintain the Commonwealth in its
Simplicity, forbade the Use of certain Dresses to Women; and
to deter them from appearing in them, allow'd them no Remedy
against Abuse of their Persons in those Habits.

As I am talking to the Female World, whose Apparel is the
cause of this Evil, and speaking of *Lycurgus*, let me recommend
the Imitation of the *Spartan Dame*, now represented on the
Stage, where they will find the Duty of a Lady not restrain'd
to domestick Life, but enlarging the Concern for her Family
into that of her Country. When a Woman of Honour and
Understanding takes this Matter seriously into her Thoughts,
she will consider how far her Fortune and Person may influence
or support a Fashion, destructive to the Society of which she is
a Member; she will then, in Justice as well as Compassion, be
fearful of putting on an Ornament, which, if generally worn,

may respectively expose, according to their Sex, Crowds of her
Fellow-Subjects to Shame or death.

It is not to be imagin'd, nor perhaps desir'd, that we should
return to the Manners of the first Ages of the World; but it is
to be watchfully guarded that we admit of no Refinements that
may be prejudicial instead of being advantageous: an *English*
Lady will therefore be such, not only in her own Person, but
also in her Children and Servants. There needs no greater Skill
for coming at the truth of this Debate, than what every ordinary
Mistress of a Family must be capable of. *No one will make and
provide at home* what will hinder a Family from doing what
would purchase a great deal more than what would *buy the
same thing* from abroad; and, on the contrary, no one will go
abroad for what they can have for less Cost and Labour at
home. This is, perhaps, the main principle, which, observed
or neglected, makes Men rich or poor, a Nation great or
contemptible.

But I shall transgress the Design and Limits of this first
Discourse, which I intended shou'd go no further than just
alarming the innocent Causes of this Evil, the Ladies, against
ruining their Country; their great Grandmothers, who for Ornament and Dress painted their own Bodies, would be astonish'd
at the Callico *Picts*, their degenerate Children, and fly from
their own Offspring, as putting themselves in Masquerade only
to reduce themselves to their primitive poverty and Nakedness:
This is not at all said to disparage Trade in general, but to
make us more circumspect in maintaining the Balance of it on
our own Side: No, it is very far from that, and I very much
admire that excellent Eulogium in the sixty-ninth *Spectator,*
first Volume. That judicious, delightful, and memorable Writer,
after having celebrated, with greatest variety of Eloquence, Wit,
and Humour, our Happiness as a trading People, has it thus:
" There are not, says he, more useful members in a Common-
wealth than Merchants. They knit mankind together in a
mutual Intercourse of good Offices, distribute the Gifts of
Nature, find Work for the Poor, and Wealth to the Rich, and
Magnificence to the Great. Our *English* Merchant converts the
Tin of his own Country into Gold, and exchanges his Wool for
Rubies. The *Mahometans* are cloathed in our *British* Manu-

facture, and the Inhabitants of the frozen Zone warm'd with the fleeces of our Sheep.

" When I have been upon the *Change*, I have often fancied one of our old Kings standing in Person, where he is represented in Effigy, and looking down upon the wealthy Concourse of People with which the Place is every Day fill'd. In this Case, how would he be surpriz'd to hear all the Languages of *Europe* spoken in this little Spot of his former Dominions, and to see so many private Men, who in his Time would have been the Vassals of some powerful Baron, negotiating like Princes for greater Sums of Money than were formerly to be met with in the Royal Treasury! Trade, without enlarging the *British* Territories, has given us a kind of additional Empire: it has multiplied the Number of the Rich, made our landed Estates infinitely more valuable than they were formerly, and added to them an Accession of other Estates as valuable as the Lands themselves."

If it should appear that there are particular Collections or Bodies of Merchants, or particularly over-grown Traders, who act and deal with a direct contrary View to that of this general Prosperity of Trade, I will at present say no more of them, but that they have no Pretension to any part of this Panegyrick. Upon the whole, we are undone, if, in the present Posture of the World, something is not *resolv'd* for the Improvement and immediate Preservation of our Trade; for as it now stands, I think it may be comprehended in what one *Indian* Boy, talking to another one Day as they waited for their Masters at the great House in *Leadenhall-street*, said to his Comrade. The poor *Indian*, governing himself by outward Appearances, and what he observed wherever he went, was overheard to say, *I cannot see,* Pompey, *in what the people of this Country excell those of ours, except it be that they are govern'd by their* Wives; *they go to our Country to bring home to their Women fine Dresses from Head to Foot, only to Purchase of them their Hair for Periwigs.*

The Crisis of Property (February, 1720)

Steele held independent views on public finance which he expressed fearlessly and vigorously. *The Crisis of Property* and its sequel were written in opposition to the South Sea Bill, then in passage through parliament.

The Public Debt was a growing encumbrance, which Walpole's Sinking Fund of 1717—a provision for borrowing cheaper money to pay off liabilities bearing a high rate of interest—had only partially lightened. Now the South Sea Company proposed to take over into its capital the government debts—which were in the form of redeemable and irredeemable annuities—and to redeem them by means of their joint-stock machinery. The redeemables were to be paid off at once and the irredeemables, after a period of progressively diminished interest—payment, at least in part, to be in shares of stock. The Company would pay well for its bargain and would receive remuneration from the government for its expenses in managing the debt in addition to receiving a trade monopoly. Success for the plan was to be ensured by an inflation of the Company's stock to induce the public to buy.

Steele no doubt foresaw some of the pit-falls ahead, but he did not here undertake to point out fallacies in the financing procedure; his objection to the proposed disposal of the annuities was on ethical grounds. The government, he maintained, had no moral right to turn over the annuitants to the mercy of a private company. Because the estates of these creditors were now worth and would bring more money than they cost was no reason for treating them like usurers and extortioners by an Act of Parliament. The money was loaned by patriots (about 1700) to their country " lately rescued from imminent Danger . . . of arbitrary Power, divided in itself by Factions at Home and engaged in a War with a much more powerful Enemy." Justice demanded that the state stand by its bargain. " The Annuitants have nothing but what they have purchased for valuable Considerations, and their Property lent with Hazard and Uncertainty." Money is not saved, Steele reminds, by a violation of public faith and credit. Nothing dishonorable to a Commonwealth can be gainful to it.

Steele had taken this same position towards the management of the annuities in 1717, when Walpole's plan was proposed. He had even then spoken in opposition, because " I did not think the Way of doing it Just " (Letter to Lady Steele, 19 March 1717). But the expediency of some such plan he had recognized: " I believe the Scheme will take place, and, if it does, Walpole must be a very great man."

In this pamphlet Steele's point of departure is dissent from Archibald

Hutcheson's pronouncements. As a "Novice in these Things" Steele defers to Hutcheson's authority in finance, nevertheless deprecating this particular plan as "a notion against Faith and Justice." The day the pamphlet was published, a committee of the whole House resolved that the proposals of the South Sea Company should be accepted. Although there is no record of Steele's speech on that occasion, we know that he was ready to support his argument "*Viva Voce* against all Gain-sayers" and that his thesis (of a piece with all his thinking) was to be that power should always be supported "by humane and social Qualities, soft Steps, or skilful Insinuations" and not by "downright brutal Force and Violence." For further comment on the South Sea Bubble, see the Introduction to the next tract. Textual notes on p. 650.

THE
CRISIS

OF

PROPERTY:

A N

ARGUMENT

PROVING

That the ANNUITANTS for ninety-
nine Years, as such, are not in the Condition of other Subjects of *Great Britain*, but
by Compact with the LEGISLATURE
are exempt from any new Direction relating
to the said *Estates*.

By Sir *RICHARD STEELE*, Knt. Member of Parliament, and GOVERNOR of
the Royal Company of *Comedians*, &c.

------ *Aliena Negotia curat*
Excussus propriis ------ Hor.

LONDON: Printed for *W. Chetwood*, under *Tom's Coffeehouse* in *Covent-Garden* ; *J. Roberts*, near the *Oxford-Arms*
in *Warwick-lane* ; *J. Brotherton*, at the *Black Bull* in *Cornhill*; and *Charles Lillie*, at the Corner of *Beaufort-Buildings* in
the *Strand*. 1720. Price 6 d.

THE

CRISIS

OF

PROPERTY.

H AVING advertis'd this Work as soon as it was resolv'd
upon, and that Resolution being taken against an Occasion
very near approaching, I shall not, as I have seen People now
and then do, make Prefaces and lose Time, because I am in
haste, and have none to spare.

Mr Hutchinson, the most celebrated modern Writer, concerning the publick Funds, in his Remarks says thus:

" As to the 99 Years Annuities which were granted in and
before 1694, if the Grantees and their Assigns were to account
in Chancery, as for Mortgages redeemable on the Repayment of
the principal Money, with the Interest of 6 £. *per Cent per
Annum*, they would be found at this time to be over-paid about
30 £. *per Cent.* and would have that Sum to repay, instead of
receiving any thing: And therefore, if, besides this Advantage,
they can now sell for 1900 £. or 2000 £. what originally cost
them but 1100, 1150, or 1200 £., they have not made a disad-
vantagious Bargain, since they hereby gain above *Cent. per Cent.*
But those surely, who manag'd thus for the Publick, were far
from being good Stewards in this Particular. It was certainly
very ill judg'd to incumber the Nation with any Debt, that was
not made redeemable by express Condition, and the longer the
Retrieving this imprudent Step is delay'd, it will be worse in all
Probability for the Publick; for to the End of the Queen's Reign,
the current Price of these Funds did not exceed 155,964 £. the
Money which was originally advanc'd; and in *February* 1716-17,
(the 99 Years Annuities being then 16 Years Purchase) the
current Price of these Funds, one with another, did not exceed

1,067,642 £. the Money originally advanc'd; and in *March* following, when the Scheme for Redemption of the publick Funds was first open'd, the 99 Years Annuities being at 17 Years Purchase, the Value of the said Funds was then 1,951,648 £. more than the Money originally advanc'd; but the Time being then let slip for getting them subscrib'd, these Funds are become an Incumbrance on the Nation of above two Millions more; and if an Act of Parliament, which was attempted last Sessions, be obtain'd for reducing the National Interest to 4 £. *per Cent. per Annum*, before the said Annuities are re-purchas'd by the Publick, or an Agreement made for the Re-purchase of the same, their Value will be increased the further Sum of 3,582,500 £. and then the same would be worth 7,997,689 £. more than the Money originally advanc'd, which would swell the Value of these Funds to the Sum of 20,557,558 £. But if the Parliament shall not be of Opinion to repurchase these Funds, then there will be no need to make mention of them in any future State of the publick Debts, and the Nation is then to rest contented with the Burden of those Duties which are appropriated for raising the annual Sum of 911,678 £. until the Expiration of the long Term of Years for which the same were granted."

If the Majority of that Honourable House, whereof the Author is a Member, were of this Opinion, and should act accordingly; farewell the Wealth and Honour of *Great Britain*.

The general Notion of Mankind is, that the Borrower is a Servant to the Lender; but this Gentleman goes upon a Supposition, that the Borrower is the Master of the Lender; else would he not publish a Notion against common Faith and Justice, without being aware that he proposes, as he does in plain Terms, an Expedient of depriving the Friends of the Government, of the Property which they have purchas'd of the Legislature, and the Interest, which is due to them for their Money, which they have lent for its Support.

It is necessary, before we go any further, to consider a little the Nature of Power, as it is exerted, that is to say, ought to be exerted amongst Men, when we talk of a Capacity of doing what this Proposer intimates, for it would be far from lawful, to do every thing which there is no Law against doing. Altho' the last Decision of a Matter is made to rest upon one, or many appointed for that End; yet the Person or Persons so appointed, are nevertheless bound to do only what is Honest, Just, and Reasonable. Thus Power, in the last Resort of it, is far from being Arbitrary Power, that is to say, Arbitrary with an Indifference to Good and Evil; but such Persons so appointed, are the more engag'd to walk by the Rules of Humanity, good Sense, and Justice, from the Consideration that their Judgment is to be decisive; it is therefore something rash to imagine that even a Legislature is to be justified in all it should do, were it to act against the known Sense of Mankind, and against the Nature of Things. Good and Evil are in themselves unchangeable, nor can Time, Place, Person, or any other Circumstance, alter the Nature of 'em; for tho' never so great a Crowd, never so solemn or awful an Assembly should pronounce a thing, in itself *Unrighteous*, to be just and equitable, it would still retain its natural Deformity, and be exactly what it was, before it receiv'd the vain Sanction of their Formalities.

The Author says, if the Grantees and their Assigns were to account in Chancery, as for Mortgages redeemable on the Repayment of principal Money, they would be found to be over-paid. This is a very unapt Similitude! Relief in Chancery is always founded upon an Artifice, a Breach of Faith, an involuntary Act, Incapacity of Acting, or some Instance of Falsehood, or Cruelty complain'd of by the Plaintiff against the Defendant; but a Legislature cannot be suppos'd to be surpriz'd into what it does, by the Artifice, by the Power, or any other Superiority of its own Subjects to ensnare, or circumvent it; it is therefore strange want of Reflection to suppose, or imagine, that Men, when they borrow, shall be credited like just Senators, and able Legislators; but when they are to repay, are to be reliev'd like circumvented Bubbles, or foolish Children. The seeming popular and plausible Argument for supporting Men, who think no further than this is, that the Estates of these Creditors are now worth, and will bring more Money than they cost, and therefore the Possessors of them are to be consider'd, and treated like Usurers and Extortioners: Tho' this is fully answer'd already, in only saying, as we have just now, that this Bargain was made by a greater, wiser, and more powerful Party with an inferior, invited into the Contract by the said Party, and consequently, that there can be none of those Pretensions which intitle to an Equity of Redemption from the said Bargain: I say, tho' the very Mention of this Circumstance of the respective Persons engaged, is enough to destroy all Thoughts of a Repeal; yet we will have the Patience to proceed to further Arguments.

To make a Man come under the odious Imputations of Usury and Extortion, it is necessary to prove, that, without any Hazard to himself, he demanded from his Debtor more than the lawful Interest for his Money; but in this Case the Interest could not be unlawful, for the Bargain was made with Law-givers, his Money could not be secure, for it was lent to the State itself in Danger of Ruin.

The Case was thus: The State of *England*, lately rescu'd from imminent Danger of falling under lawless and arbitrary Power, divided in itself by Factions at Home, and engaged in a War with a much more powerful Enemy, than itself would be, tho' united, abroad, in the utmost Distraction and Terror from the Opposition made by its own Subjects, to the necessary Means of Defence, and the increasing Hazards from the Preparations of its foreign Foes, enacts by its Legislature, that such, who will lend Money under these Disadvantages, shall have such and such Terms for the Loan of it.

These Lenders saw the Condition of the Borrowers, knew they had not Security, but from the Hopes that the Debtors Condition would grow better by their Money, and from the Zeal and Affection to such Borrowers, parted with their Fortunes.

Shall then these Men or their Assigns, the Members of that Parliament, or their Successors in this, have to do with one another upon any other Terms, than to ratify the Friendship between them, and for an Example to all succeeding Generations, secure the Right of the Benefactors, with all the Power, Interest, and Fortune, of those who receiv'd the Benefit?

It is a known Case, that in the Insurance of a Vessel from the common Hazards of the Sea, the Owners can pretend to no Remedy, against whatever they may have contracted to give above the common Interest of Money, upon the Return of the Ship into Port: It would in such a Case be frivolous and unjust to dispute the Payment, upon Account of fair Weather, sailing before the Wind with a most prosperous Gale, and the Premisses insured having met with no manner of Danger or Difficulty thro' the whole Voyage. For the Insurers would answer: Who could foresee this? Had you sunk, we must have lost our Money; and because it has happen'd just as you gave Money to be sure it should happen, you have the Modesty to desire your Money again, because they, who were to bear all your Adversity, demand to have some Share in your Prosperity.

I defy any Man breathing to make the Case of those who purchased these Annuities less Meritorious than the Insurers of a Vessel going to Sea, who are to lose all, if the Ship is cast away, and receive but the Share which they agreed for, in case of a safe Return.

These Men are not Usurers, are not Extortioners, they are good Citizens, they are Patriots, they lent their Country Money, because they lov'd their Country; they stept out of the Ranks as the *Forlorn Hope of Property*, in Defence of the Land of *England* and its Owners, which Owners had been safe and secure in their Possessions, whatever had befallen these generous Insurers, whose Fortunes fought for 'em. But it is urg'd, that in such a Year they were worth so much, in such a Year so much, and now worth more than they gave for 'em, tho' so many Years, in which they have enjoy'd 'em, are run out.

If this be a Plea against an absolute Bargain, let the Buildings all around us, erected upon late Wastes and Pastures, stand still. He who makes more of his Estate than the Person did who sold it him, shall account in Chancery for all above the legal Interest of the Purchase Money.

At the first Sight it appears, from the very Nature of Credit, that it is utterly destroy'd, when the Borrower pretends to inter-meddle with what is lent, but by the Command or Application of the Lender; and if the Borrower pretends to make himself Judge of what is proper for the Lender to receive when he has enough, or in any degree *Modify, Manage, Abate* or *Alter the Terms* upon which he has it, he becomes Master, that is, Posses-sor and *Usurper* of such the Property of the Lender. This is certainly the Practice, the common Sense, the obvious Rule and Measure of Life wherever there is humane Nature; and Calcu-lations, Remarks and Proposals of entire Discharges of National Debts and Incumbrances, against this plain Law of Reason, are only Chimeras, Crudities and Extravagancies.

Can a Man be supposed to have placed his Money safely, or to be ready to lend it to the Hands that publickly and shamelessly profess themselves not bound to their Articles, proposed, drawn, sign'd, and executed by themselves?

No! Reason and Justice are ever the same, and, in spight of Passions, Changes and Animosities, are fearless and impassive; and whoever does the Injury, it is still an Injury aggravated when it comes from them that should be Guardians against it.

But some will say, shall any part of the Subject of *England* be exempt and excluded from her Laws? shall any Estates, any *manner of Tenure, cease to be under the Guidance of the Legislature?* Yes, all that the Legislature has stipulated to be so. This is far from Disparagement done to that awful Power, it is Respect, it is Religion towards it; and, if I may compare that to what only it is below, I can say it, without Diminution to its Power, when I can say in the same Breath, that the Omnipotent can do no Evil.

An Argument of this kind, wherein the very Being, Honour and Safety of one's Country is concern'd, raises Indignation above what wou'd naturally arise from an unwary well meant Assertion; but the Circumstance of Place, as nearer or farther off the Center of Power, makes a Thing considerable or inconsiderable: Where a Man has a Right of being heard among Lawgivers, Experience shows, that such a Right, exerted with Spirit, tho' with less Force than this Generation can give it, has prevail'd to a fatal Degree in the greatest Concerns.

This Attempt of unsettling what has been made irrevocable and absolute, will appear to every Man's Observation, in the colour it ought, from a late Circumstance, wherein the Sanction is as sacred and immutable, from the Right of the Thing, as if it had been done by the *British* Legislature: The thing, of which I wou'd remind my Reader in this Place, is the Loan given to the Emperor of *Germany*, under a great Distress of his Affairs, upon the Lands of *Silesia.*

Will any Man say, that when the Emperor had rescu'd himself from the Difficulties he was in, when he borrowed this Money, he was then at Liberty to lower the Advantages arising from their common Success, owing to the zealous and voluntary Hazard of the Lenders?

If it be true, that the Emperor was still as much obliged as before, tho' to whom he had no Relation, but as Lenders, how much more must a Government be tied down to a Bargain made with these, who have a Right to Protection in their Property, as well with that Regard as all other Considerations? If the Emperor is indispensably obliged to protect and pay the Creditors, as much as if there was the Relation between 'em of Sovereign and Subject, and to pay *Englishmen*, as punctually as he ought to have *Silesians*, by the same force of Reason, a Nation that borrows of its own Subjects, as to the Circumstance of Debtor and Creditor, has thrown off the Sovereignty, and the Parliament of *England* has no other Power over these Annuitants, than if the Purchase had been made by the People of *Silesia*.

The Owners therefore of this Property, who stept out of the Rank of common Subjects, with their Fortunes in their Hands, and gave them to the Faith of the Legislature, are exempt from any Act of Legislature, by all the Rules of Honour, Justice, and Equity, but as they are our Friends and Allies. If Men say that all other Professions of Property in these Realms sigh under large and heavy Debt; the Answer is obvious, that their Creditors have, during a long and expensive War, been in a worse Condition to render such Proprietors safe, in whatever they have wherewith to pay 'em.

If I talk reasonably in this, the Proposal favour'd by some unskillful Patriots, amounts to this; that we are to save Money by the loss of the Nation; and this Attempt, were it to be brought into an Act, might with the same Justice affect any other of the Subjects of these Realms, nay a whole Nation, which not many Years ago united it self to us. Any thing given in equivalent to *Scotland*, for resigning its separate Constitution, may as well be stopt and deny'd to them, as new Terms impos'd upon these Annuitants; but 'tis not to be doubted, but that the Legislature will be full as tender of Trespassing against the Right of these Annuitants, as they have been of Titles derivative only from the Royal Favour; since, with all other the most prevalent Reasons, they have also that which saved the *English* Grants, the Consideration of Families, who claim under them, to secure 'em from Revocation. Those Grantees had a Right founded on meer Grace and Favour, not always obtain'd by Merit or Service; the Annuitants have nothing but what they have purchased for valuable Considerations, and their Property lent with Hazard and Uncertainty.

Thus the Injustice of this Attempt appears from the Nature of Things, and I think it is easy to prove also the Folly of it. For, according to my Notion of Credit, whatever Power gives occasion of Distrust of Safety to the Creditor, must of Necessity become Bankrupt; and who can raise a greater Cause of Suspicion, than they who assert, that the Right and Disposal of any part of what they have borrowed, is yet in themselves?

After this Declaration, who cou'd be confident that their Money is as safe with such Dealers, as in their own Pockets? And when it is otherwise, there is an end of Credit.

That plain word Credit carries with it every thing that is valuable amongst Men; the Nations all around us have lost it, but let us open our Eyes, and extend a little our Faculties from the Prejudice, which particular Education and Circumstances of Life may have wrought up in us, and we shall find, that not only Ease, Conveniency, Safety, but Pomp, Glory and all the Distinctions of Life are wrapt up in it, and when this is lost, the Landed Man will be impoverished, and the Soldier disarm'd, as certainly as the Merchant is beggar'd.

But I shall trouble my Great, Learned and Powerful Adversaries on this Head no longer, but change their Opponent from a poor, cheap (but not mercenary) Scribbler, to that of the most renowned of Authors. It is in vain to oppose Authority but with as great Authority; and I forget all this is supported by a Novice in these Things against a Writer that has long made the Consideration of Credit his Business. Let therefore the Success of this Dispute concerning Credit turn upon the Personal Characters of *Archibald Hutchinson* Esq; Member for *Hasting*, and that of Sir *Richard Steele,* Kt. Member for *Burrowbrig.* But let the latter call to his Assistance a more suitable Adversary, and lay it upon the Reputations of *Archibald Hutchinson*, Member for *Hasting*, and *Marcus Tullius Cicero*, Consul of *Rome.* The last nam'd of these three great Men arguing, that no Advantage imaginable can be an Equivalent for Loss of Publick Credit, and, like an able and true Statesman, above

Shifts and Managements, maintaining that nothing which is dishonourable to a Common-wealth, can be gainful to it, mentions a stupid, and impudent Expedient for raising Money to the Publick, by breaking a Contract made by one of their Generals. The Passage is in the Third Book of his *Offices*, which, by the way, if I had never read, I had been at this Hour what they call a Plumb.

If, says he, *Money is gotten without regard to the Means of doing it, the Publick will find themselves in the End no Gainers, for nothing can be Profit that's purchas'd with Infamy. What then shall we say of the Project of* Lucius Philippus, *who mov'd in the Senate, that those Cities, who had bought Roman Liberty from* Sylla, *should still be tributary without returning them their Money, with which they had purchas'd it? The Senate, to the Shame of all Government, consented to the Expedient, the natural Consequence of which was, that they lost their Credit, and the Faith of Pyrates was from that Moment more to be depended upon, than that of the Senate of* Rome.

All this I argue against the Remarks of my worthy Fellow-Labourer, Mr. *Hutchinson*, who aims at the same End by different means; and I cannot but declare at the same time I believe that Gentleman as disinterestedly zealous for the publick Good, as any Man in *England*; and I must own further, that I know he has of his Side as eminent Men as any in this Kingdom; and yet, after all, I must presume to say, with great Deference to him and them, that in Cases of this sort, I acknowledge no Authority but that of Reason and Justice.

Reason and Justice, it will be answer'd, will still be done to these Annuitants, because there is nothing expected from them but what is voluntary; but when a superior Power talks to an inferior, even in the Stile of Invitation, it has the Air and Effect, in common Acceptation, of a Command, but the readiest way of coming at the true Nature of this Affair, is to read over the enacting Words, by which these Estates for this Term, were vested in the Purchasers by Parliament. They import, "That for the Consideration-Money (*which is the very Term used in this Law*) either Natives or Foreigners, may contribute and pay into the Exchequer any Sum, or Sums of Money, for purchasing Annuities for ninety-nine Years, commencing from the 25th

Day of *March* 1704, and that they shall be paid out of the Excise."

This is as absolute a Purchase as can be made, and the Matter is involved for the common Security of Natives and Foreigners; for *quoad hoc*, Foreigners become Natives, and Natives Foreigners. And, if you offer to meddle with them, you will be ask'd by Natives, if we were to be affected in this Possession any way hereafter, but by your becoming Bankrupt; *Why, did you not tell us, when you took our Money, we lent it because we lov'd our Country, and were willing to hazard with you?* Foreigners will answer, *We were Strangers, and had no Ties of Friendship, but thought of honest Gain from honest Men.*

I repeat it, that these Persons are Purchasers for a valuable Consideration, and that in the most absolute Terms imaginable; for which Reason I have and do aver, that the Parliament has no further to do with them, than if the Purchasers were of another Nation. It is the Essence of a Contract, that the Contracters should keep the Agreement without Fraud or Force. And, in this Case, as in all others, the Borrower is a Dependant on the Lender, and not the Lender on the Borrower. Thus the greater Power that the one Party has in other Circumstances, the more is that Party obliged to keep the Obligation inviolable; because the Weaker, who puts himself in the Power of the Stronger, has Justice more forcibly on his Side, from the Merit of that Confidence. In a Word, two Contracters always understand each other to be, and covenant to be, Equals, and never to use any Advantages for Evasion; and I appeal to all the World, whether they think these Annuitants would have purchas'd under a Reservation, that forty Years after, the Publick should have an Equity of Redemption; but the Purchasers should refuse what should then be call'd full Satisfaction, or keep their Estates in their own Hands. The mention of this at the time of making of this Sale would have broke the Bargain, and therefore it is not supportable by the Rules of Honesty to mention it now, and to subject their Fortunes to the same imaginary and changeable Condition, which Moneyers put upon the intrinsick Value of the Money lent on the rest of the publick Securities: For tho' the Annuitants may keep their Yearly Income, notwithstanding the Noise and Importunity about them, yet from this

Clamour, the Sale of an Annuity will be at an higher or lower Value, if the Circumstances of the Owner should require him to sell it.

I shall forbear many Assertions, which I hope to have Opportunity to speak to upon another Occasion, or in this Way again. But I fear a Fit of the Gout, caus'd by open Oppression, and rigid Justice from certain *Wanton, and Forgetful Men call'd Courtiers*, will disable me, if I do not discontinue my present Attention. If I can suffer with Resolution a little longer out of a sick Bed, I'll shew some half Politicians, that they know nothing of what they are doing; and tho', according to my Duty, and the Liturgy of the Church, I am bound to pray, to give them Understanding, I shall not neglect to use also all Humane means, to inform them, that the best Friends of the Government are not to be mark'd out for Punishment and Disgrace, or Ruin; because unexperienc'd Men do not know how to support Power by humane and social Qualities, soft Steps, or skilful Insinuations, but by downright brutal Force and Violence. Whenever their Fortune shall be changed, I shall pity 'em, as well knowing, Disgrace is a hard Suffering even *with* Integrity. I shall continue in the mean time to endeavour to prevent their hurting their Master with other Innocent and Zealous Men who love him, who may not have the Moderation to distinguish and consider, that none are Acts of the King, but Acts of Favour. These slight Creatures, with their usual Insensibility, may call this Plain-dealing with them Folly and Extravagance, as indeed it would be, if I thought it would reform them; no, I mean only to explain, and admonish them. They are to me wicked Men, but that must not transport me, to say they are to the rest of the World, any other than only weak ones, so shall end this Argument, which I am ready to support, *Viva Voce*, against all Gain-sayers, that the Annuitants are no Objects of the Legislative Power of *Great Britain*, but for their Protection, in order to be well and faithfully paid the Income of the Money which *Great Britain* has receiv'd of them, and is a Rent-Charge on the Revenues of the Kingdom. They who think otherwise on this Subject, I shall have an Opportunity of proving, to think like Cashiers and Stockjobbers, and not like Wisemen and Politicians.

FINIS

A Nation a Family (February, 1720)

In this pamphlet, a fortnight after the appearance of *The Crisis of Property*, Steele offered somewhat more concrete criticism of the proposal made by the South Sea Company. The advantages for which it offered to pay so dearly boded, he thought, something destructive of the public good: by "Art and Dexterity in the turning of Stocks and Money" it would deceive the annuitants and thus taint parliamentary credit; and by engrossing trade it would cause wide-spread suffering. Nevertheless, he sought the good will of the Company and of its Sub-Governor, Sir John Fellows. "Fair Traders," he said, "are in my Opinion, the most honourable, because the most useful of Men to this State."

He was concrete also in making a counterproposal—a kind of actuarial or lottery scheme—which he acknowledged had not received favorable attention from those "who can make it practicable" but which he considered it his duty to give more publicity.

His plan was to convert the public debt into life annuities, and it, also, turned upon cooperation between the Company and the government. It provided for raising four millions sterling by 40,000 persons, to be turned into the capital of the South Sea Company, these annuitants to be paid by the Company at a good rate of interest. A table of figures is given to demonstrate the possibilities. Thus the annuitants now threatened would not be forced to action by law; the Company would be supplied with a reasonable and safe profit for trading; the national debt would be paid off within a term of years. This plan he calls "A Nation a Family," as the entire nation, through its individual family investors, would be strengthened; and the King, the father, would be made more popular, great, and safe. All this may have harked back to the "Multiplication Table" of June, 1712, a lottery, which Steele planned to be worked in connection with the State Lottery and which he had to drop, when such private schemes were declared illegal. At this time in 1720, Steele was developing his Fish Pool Project; and during the following summer, when the Bubble excitement was greatest, he floated his own joint-stock company. Whatever the merit of any of these schemes, their motivation, although he was not averse to making money, was, to a large extent, a desire to serve the public interest.

From now on to the enactment of the South Sea Bill in April, Steele continued in active opposition to it (as shown by *Theatre*, Nos. 17, 20, 22, 23, 24, 25, 27, and a speech in the Commons on 23 March), even to the point of a threatened expulsion from the House. And there is no record of his having been among the public figures who accepted stock as bribes or of his having speculated privately. During the financial panic following the bursting of the Bubble, he advocated a full investigation into the proceedings of the Company; but when it was over, he fell in with Walpole's policy of moderation in dealing with the implicated Ministers and also with his scheme for restoring public credit. And it is not surprising to find that, even though such a position stirred up the charge of inconsistency and worse insinuations, he stood out against vindictive punishment of the South Sea directors. Textual notes on p. 650.

A Nation a Family:

BEING THE

SEQUEL

OF THE

CRISIS

OF

PROPERTY:

OR, A

PLAN

For the IMPROVEMENT of the

South-Sea PROPOSAL.

By Sir *RICHARD STEELE*, Knt. Member of Parliament.

LONDON: Printed for *W. Chetwood*, under *Tom's Coffeehouse* in *Covent-Garden* ; *J. Roberts*, near the *Oxford-Arms* in *Warwick-lane* ; *J. Brotherton*, at the *Black Bull* in *Cornhill*; and *Charles Lillie*, at the Corner of *Beaufort-Buildings* in the *Strand*. 1720. Price 6d.

T O

Sir *John Fellows,*

S U B-G O V E R N O R of the

South-Sea Company.

SIR,

I Presume to offer you the following Treatise, tho' it is written in some sort of Opposition to the Proposal of the Sub-Governor, Deputy-Governor and Company trading to the *South-Seas*, since, at the same time, it is a Defence of the Governor of the said Company, and all the People under his Dominions. I depend therefore upon it, that your Excellency will be so gracious as to allow me to offer to you, what I humbly conceive is more gainful and more proper for you to have than what you ask. If I make this out, it will be for your Service; if I do not, it will only be for your Diversion. I assure you, it is writ with a true Zeal and Spirit of good Will to all fair Traders, who are, in my Opinion, the most honourable, because the most useful of Men to this State. Without them, we are confin'd within a narrow Tract, productive only of Necessaries; with them, the whole Earth, and all its Fruits, are within our Reach, for the Supply of our Pleasures, as well as our Wants: If this Plan should be approv'd, you will find I *write in* to you more than you offer the Government for your Bargain, without any other Hopes than that of manifesting myself a true Lover of my Country, on which Merit you'll allow me the Honour of being,

SIR,

Your most Obedient, and

Most Humble Servant,

RICHARD STEELE.

THE
SEQUEL
OF THE
CRISIS
OF
PROPERTY.

WHAT has been already said, was offer'd in Support of an Assertion, That the Annuitants for Terms of Years, are Purchasers from, not Creditors to, the Publick: The Legislature has absolutely sold to them those Estates for those Terms; and the Parliament has nothing further to do in this Case, but to protect the Owners, and pay them punctually and honestly. The Annuitants, it is said, are not to be forc'd to part with their Estates; but there are indeed Persons who will give Millions, if they may be allowed to purchase them: Nay, if they should not succeed in the Solicitation, or Invitation of such Owners, they will pay a certain Sum of Money; that is, several hundred thousand Pounds for the Convenience and Allowance of making the Attempt: But all this while the Annuitants are to do nothing but what they shall think fit, and are to be wholly Volunteers in this Action: If they are to be such, and no Compulsion put upon them, to what End do the Proposers to purchase apply to the Legislature? Their Power, it seems, is to have no Effect towards making the Bargain cheaper; if so, why do they not purchase of these Men now, that can do what they please with their own, without the Intervention of Parliament, which Parliament is still to leave them to do what they please with their own.

Are not Men willing to do what they please with their own, till they are permitted to be willing by the Act and Will of the

Parliament? We have heard, that in former Times Men were
sent to by Messengers to be willing, or else to be *forced* to
voluntary Contribution; but I think there was one Mr. *Hampden*,
in *Buckinghamshire*, declared, He was not willing to do any
thing against his Will, and by that Means preserv'd every Man's
Property to be dispos'd according to his own Will.

But I take the Liberty to say, that when the Parliament has
done this (I speak it before it has done so) they will have given
up their own Credit, and sold it, according to my poor Understanding, for a Sum of Money, to those whom they shall have
encouraged to be Purchasers. And I am, if not humbly, yet
from the Force of Truth and right Reason, boldly of Opinion,
that such a Step would hurt this Kingdom, as it is a Kingdom,
a Nation, a Commonwealth, much more in its true Interest and
Credit, than the Price of all the Annuities would balance and
make up to us. Will any Man living look stedfastly at another,
and affirm, that he believes, after this is done, Parliamentary
Credit will be to all Intents and Purposes as good as it was
before? If Men in a Prosperous Condition, and in reasonable
Expectation of the Continuance of it, shall show an Uneasiness,
that those who contributed to such their Success, and must have
been undone, if it had happen'd otherwise, should have, in proportion, a superior Share in the publick Good, they must never
expect more to be supply'd in their Exigence. If you, in your
Wants, will make a Bargain for a Supply, and when you are at
Ease dispute, or haggle, to change the Conditions for your
further Ease, take care to want no more, or be contented to want
for ever. But we are amused by Words, and, according as meer
Sounds strike the Imagination, we are carried into most destructive Resolutions; we play with the Words *Redeemable*, and
Irredeemable, when we should understand the quite contrary
of what we do by those Terms.

That is call'd Irredeemable, from which we are in some
Degree relieved, while we are yet speaking, and know when it
must certainly end. That is call'd Redeemable, which, till
Measures are taken to discharge, can never be redeem'd. Time
releases one as fast as it passes away; the other, till put into a
way of Satisfaction, must last till Time shall be no more.

Is not that Family in a better Condition, a part of whose

Estate is charge'd with an Annuity for twenty Years to come, after which that part is to revert to the Father, and his Heirs, than the House who owes such a Debt, but lives paying the Interest, and at the End of twenty Years has the whole Principal to pay? Would not a young Gentleman be in a better Condition, whose Mother should keep a Jointure from him five and twenty Years, of 500 *l.* a Year, than if his Estate was charged with 10000 *l.* and he were to pay Interest, instead of the Jointure, for the 10000 *l.* for twenty-five Years, and then should have the Whole to pay? Prejudices run too strongly to admit me the Liberty of saying what a Gentleman at the *Chop-House* said t'other-Day, That the Irredeemables are so far from being a Grievance, that it would be the cheapest Way, and best Management, to turn all the Debts into Annuities for certain Terms of Years. I readily consented to him; for, thought I, when *Time* is the Paymaster, the Weight grows less, according to the Force and Duration of the Body incumber'd. The Body Politick is supposed immortal, and consequently the Point of Time, as it affects that, and a single Person, bears not the Proportion of an Hour to a Year. The Crowds, who think another way, headed by eminent Persons, who think this way, but won't act accordingly, will be too impatient, at this very Hint, to bear any more to be said upon it. They won't give me leave to show how apparently it is the Interest of a State, which is to live for ever, and may possibly find Safety and Convenience from having easy Creditors depend upon it. I say, they will not endure, under their present Prepossessions, so much as the mention of such an Expedient; and therefore I shall not now offer to reason further from the Difference between the Case of the publick and that of a private Person, That giving Ten *per Cent.* by the Community, Principal and Interest, to end at almost any distant Time, is a better Bargain than five given, and Principal and Interest stand out a Debt till repaid.

When I have repeated, that *Time* is the best Pay-Master from the State, I shall go on to explain a Scheme of my own, which turns upon the Lives of Individuals, and makes the Mortality and Decay of Particulars, the Foundation of new Life and Strength to the whole: And this is the mutual Advantage of the Private and Publick, but the greater Good to the latter.

This Scheme has already been spoken of, where I would not knowingly offer improper Things.

I go on to communicate it, as having already suffer'd the worst I can on that Account, in having it hitherto passed unconsider'd by those only who can make it practicable. I shall adventure it this way to further Notice, and whatever becomes of it, I have done my Duty.

What I do, and have offer'd, is in the following Form, but with the Addition of a Calculation made upon it.

A Nation a Family.

True Policy requires that the Government should be rich, the People in moderate, safe, and comfortable Circumstances: This is far from being our Condition; for the Publick is loaded with Debts, and the generality of the People extremely necessitious, while private Persons, to the Disadvantage of the whole Community, are immoderately Rich, and every Day growing richer by artificial Rumors, whereby self-interested Men affect the publick Funds, and act upon the Hopes and Fears of the People, for their own Gain, tho' to the apparent Hazard of their Country. In order, therefore, to make the King the Father of his People, and unite their Interests by an Inseparable Advantage, and that mutual, let it be provided, that the publick Debts be converted into Annuities for Life, equally advantagious to every individual Person, and to all Persons of what Degree, or Quality, or Circumstance soever; to wit, that the Purchasers be divided into Classes of ten Persons in a Class; and, upon Payment of the Consideration Money, receive Indentures or Tickets, promising the Payment of an Annuity of ten *per Cent.* to each Annuitant, and their Nine Successors, being themselves the same Persons, each leading, ending and nam'd, in each Part of one or other Ticket; by which Means each ten Pounds will Purchase the annual Value at ten *per Cent.* and possibly, by Survivorship, ten Pounds a Year for Life. To make this evident to the meanest Capacity, ten such Indentures, with the Names diversified according to this Design, are as follow:

In consideration of the Sums received from each of the underwritten Persons.

This First Ticket *entitles* First, Second, Third, Fourth, Fifth, Sixth, Seventh, Eighth, Ninth, and Tenth, to the annual Sum of   according to the Order in which they are nam'd, and the Rule of Survivorship, till the Death of the longest Liver of them.

This Second Ticket *entitles* Second, Third, Fourth, Fifth, Sixth, Seventh, Eighth, Ninth, Tenth, and First to, *&c.*

This Third Ticket *entitles* Third, Fourth, Fifth, Sixth, Seventh, Eighth, Ninth, Tenth, First and Second to, *&c.*

This Fourth Ticket *entitles* Fourth, Fifth, Sixth, Seventh, Eighth, Ninth, Tenth, First, Second, and Third to, *&c.*

This Fifth Ticket *entitles* Fifth, Sixth, Seventh, Eighth, Ninth, Tenth, First, Second, Third, and Fourth to, *&c.*

This Sixth Ticket *entitles* Sixth, Seventh, Eighth, Ninth, Tenth, First, Second, Third, Fourth and Fifth to, *&c.*

This Seventh Ticket *entitles* Seventh, Eighth, Ninth, Tenth, First, Second, Third, Fourth, Fifth and Sixth to, *&c.*

This Eighth Ticket *entitles* Eighth, Ninth, Tenth, First, Second, Third, Fourth, Fifth, Sixth and Seventh to, *&c.*

This Ninth Ticket *entitles* Ninth, Tenth, First, Second, Third, Fourth, Fifth, Sixth, Seventh and Eighth to, *&c.*

This Tenth Ticket *entitles* Tenth, First, Second, Third, Fourth, Fifth, Sixth, Seventh, Eighth, and Ninth to, *&c.*

To explain it further, I shall call it a SCHEME to raise four Millions Sterling by forty thousand Persons, at one hundred Pounds each; these Persons to be joined or united into distinct Classes, of ten in a Class, which will be four thousand Classes, each Class raising one thousand Pounds.

Secondly, This Sum to be paid either in Tallies, Lottery-Tickets, or any Debts or Annuities, Parliamentary Funds, or in Money itself, in order to add the said four Millions, as Principal or Capital to the Stock of the South-Sea Company. These four Millions shall be repaid in the Manner and Form following:

Each Class (as above) consisting of ten Persons, Proprietors in one thousand Pounds Share in the Stock, shall receive annually

ten Pounds *per Cent.* of the Company, which is one hundred
Pounds yearly, during the Lives of these ten Persons, the
thousand Pounds being sunk in the said Company; but with this
Restriction, that on the Death of any Person in a Class, Notice
shall be given to the said Company, who shall not that Year pay
the hundred Pounds to the Survivors, but reserve it for the Use
and Advantage of the Company; but the next Year the hundred
Pounds shall be paid to the surviving nine, and so on as they
die: on the Death of each one that Year shall be a Stop to the
Payment, but the Year after, the Survivors shall receive the
whole hundred Pounds, to divide amongst them; so that at last
the longest Liver shall receive, during Life, one hundred Pounds
per Annum, for his hundred Pounds in the Class. A Profit
greater than can be any other Way gain'd by Money out of
Trade, and calculated to fall in with the Circumstances, (as to
Part of their Substance) of all Owners of Property.

The Advantage to the Company will be this: They will be
supplied with Money to trade with; the Ten Pounds *per Cent.*
can never be fully paid, by reason of the Deaths of single
Persons, which will yearly occasion several Abatements; for as in
the several Classes there will be forty thousand People, of which
we may rationally suppose that but few, if any, will be alive
sixty Years hence, and should all die in that Time, their Payments will wholly cease; and should all die in sixty Years, then
proportionably to forty thousand in sixty Years, it is six hundred
sixty-six each Year of the sixty, and forty remain alive at the
sixty Years end.

Accordingly for the Classes being extinct; four thousand
Classes to be extinct in sixty Years, if they die proportionably
one Year with another, then there will be sixty-six Classes every
Year extinct, and forty Classes remain to survive the sixty
Years; if it so happen, then there will be yearly, on the Deaths
of single People, six hundred sixty-six Pounds paid less than
the ten Pounds *per Cent.* and on the Extinction of Classes each
Year, there will be sixty-six, that is, so many hundred Pounds
of the Principal paid off, thus continuing till the whole is clear'd.

Before we enter on the Advantage this Scheme will be to the
Nation, in order to the clearing its Debts, let us first calculate
the whole as Debtor and Creditor, in order to its being demonstrated more plainly.

And here I must take for granted, that the South-Sea Company doth employ these four Millions in Trade, and the Profit of this Trade must be at least seven *per Cent.* or otherwise they could not support the Proposal they have made the House of Commons; therefore I shall calculate the four Millions in a Way of Trade to bring in yearly two hundred and eighty thousand Pounds.

THE CALCULATION.

The Tax annexed to those Funds which are annexed to the four Millions propos'd:

Is now, at five *per Cent,*	200,000	Due to four Millions at 10 *per Cent*	400,000
		Deduct by Deaths and Ext. of Classes	7,266
		Really paid but————	392,734
The Profit of Trading	280,000	Deduct by Death of single Persons	666
	————	Deduct by Classes extinct	6,600
	480,000		
Really paid————	392,734		
		Total	7,266
First Year, Stock increased to————	87,266	Second Year abated of the ————	400,000
To which add Tax and Profit————	480,000	By Extinct of Classes and Death of Persons	13,866
Total	567,266		
Really paid but————	386,134	Really paid but————	386,134
Second Year, Stock increased to————	181,132	Third Year abated by Deaths and Classes extinct	400,000
			20,466
To which add yearly Tax and Profit————	480,000	Really paid but————	379,534
Total	661,132		
What really paid————	379,534		

Third Year, Stock in-) creased to————-} 281,598

To which add yearly) Tax and Profit————} 480,000

Total 761,598
Deduct what really) paid ————————————} 372,934

Fourth Year, Stock) increased to ————-} 388,664

Tax and Profit added 480,000

Total 968,664

Deduct what really) paid ————————————} 366,334

Fifth Year, Stock in-) creased to————-} 602,330

Tax and Profit Added} 480,000

Total 1,082,330
Deduct what really) paid ————————————} 359,734

Sixth Year, Stock in) creased ————————} 622,596
Taxes and Profit———— 480,000

Total 1,102,596
Deduct what paid———— 353,134

Seventh Year in Stock 749,462
Taxes and Profit———— 480,000

Total 1,229,462
Deduct what paid———— 346,534

Fourth Year deduct)
Deaths and Classes} 400,000
extinct ————————-} 27,066

Really paid ———————— 372,934

Fifth Year deduct)
Deaths and Classes} 400,000
Extinct ————————-} 33,666

Really paid ———————— 366,334

Sixth Year deduct)
Deaths and extinct} 400,000
Classes ————————-} 40,266

Really paid———————— 359,734

Seventh Year deduct,) 400,000
&c. ————————————} 46,866

Really paid———————— 353,134

Eighth Year deduct,) 400,000
&c. ————————————} 53,466

346,534

Eighth Year in Stock	882,928		Ninth Year deduct, }	400,000	
Tax and Profit added—	480,000		&c. ————————{	60,066	
Total	1,362,928		Really paid ————	339,934	
Deduct what paid	339,934				
Ninth Year in Stock	1,022,994		Tenth Year deduct, }	400,000	
Add Tax and Profit	480,000		&c. ————————{	66,666	
Total	1,502,994		Really paid ————	333,334	
Deduct what paid—	333,334				
Tenth Year in Stock	1,169,660		Eleventh Year deduct, }	400,000	
Add Tax and Profit	480,000		&c. ————————{	73,266	
Total	1,649,660		Really paid————	326,734	
Deduct what paid—	326,734				
Eleventh Year in Stock	1,322,926		Twelfth Year deduct, }	400,000	
Add Tax and Profit	480,000		&c. ————————{	79,866	
Total	1,802,926		Really paid————	320,134	
Deduct what paid	320,134				
Twelfth Year in Stock	1,482,792		Thirteenth Year deduct, }	400,000	
Add Tax and Profit	480,000		&c. ————————{	86,466	
Total	1,962,792		Really paid ————	313,534	
Deduct what paid—	313,534				
Thirteenth Year in Stock	1,649,258		Fourteenth Year deduct, }	400,000	
By Tax and Profit add	480,000		&c. ————————{	93,066	
Total	2,129,258		Really paid ————	306,934	
Deduct what paid—	306,934				
Fourteenth Year in Stock	1,822,324				
To which add prin- }					
cipal Stock————{	4,000,000				
Total	5,822,324				

Should the Company say they cannot be sure to make seven *per Cent.* Profit by Trade, I then repeat they are not able to perform what they have offer'd to the Honourable House of Commons; therefore it is reasonable to suppose that is the least Profit they propose to make. Which if so,

Then as their Stock is increas'd to near half, and their Payments abated near one Quarter, surely then those Taxes which now are appropriated to pay the five *per Cent.* Interest for this four Millions, may very well cease; for if trading with four Millions, and the two hundred thousand Pounds yearly, can pay ten *per Cent.* for four Millions, as it is apparent by this they can; then certainly trading with five Millions, eight hundred and twenty-two Thousand, three hundred and twenty-four Pounds, can pay the Interest of three Millions at ten *per Cent.* especially since the Stock yearly increases, and the Payments yearly lessen.

Should any object that it is probable, the Persons may neither die so fast, or the Classes be extinct so fast as I have computed: I answer, It is more likely they should die faster, and the Classes be extinct faster than slower; for it is more rational to suppose that six hundred sixty-six People should die in one Year, out of forty thousand, than out of half that Number, and sixty-six Classes be extinct out of four thousand, than out of two thousand.

Which if so, then their Payments will lessen faster than I have supposed, and of Consequence the better for the Company.

As to the *national* Advantage this Way, if four Millions are so raised yearly, and so paid, eight Years time will bring all in, and in sixty-eight Years all will be paid, both Principal and Interest, and at fourteen Years end the Taxes for four Millions will cease, and fifteen Years for four Millions more, and in less than twenty-four Years all our present Taxes settled to pay the Interest of thirty two Millions will be wholly at an End, whereas by the now Proposals of the *South-Sea* Company our Debts are only transferred, and not paid, only after 1724 the Interest of all will be but three Pounds *per Cent.*

To conclude, It would be entirely needless for the Parliament to interfere with the Annuitants future Bargain with the *South-Sea*, if they are to be altogether in the same Condition, after the Bill passes, in which they now are, and not to receive the least Disadvantage from any distant Influence of the intended Act.

The *South-Sea* must design some Advantage to themselves by their Proposal to the Parliament, otherwise they would not be at such an *expensive Zeal* in soliciting its Acceptance. And if they aim at Profit to themselves by it, whence must it arise? Must it not proceed from such Art and Dexterity in the turning of Stocks and Money, as may deceive the present national Creditors, the Annuitants, and deprive them in some Measure of the Advantage of their Bargain? If this be not their View, what else can it be? Do they grasp at something more terrible, the Monopoly of Trade, and Impoverishment of the Nation? If they have in View neither of these Designs, *viz.* to injure some who are Wards of the Government, and by that Means taint Parliamentary Credit, or to ruin and starve the Bulk of the Nation by engrossing Trade, or to build their proposed Advantage upon any Scheme destructive of the publick Good, we must allow, according to a late Author, they will shew more Virtue and Integrity than those, who shall put such Designs in their Power to execute, shall discover Wisdom or Prudence. Let me add, If they can afford the great Sums they offer, without any indirect Design, much more able will they be, by fair Trading, to execute what we propose. According to our Scheme, their Trade will advance by safe, and as expeditious Steps, as the Nature of the Thing will allow; according to their Way of taking all at once, it is impossible to dispose of their Stock in Trade alone, which is the only fair Way by which they can comply with their Bargain. Besides this, let it be well consider'd also, that in their Way they part with vast Sums of ready Money, when they take upon them this prodigious and sudden Enterprize.

Whoever shall duly attend to this Discourse, will find, that with all its Incorrectness and Imperfections (much of which may be owing to many other Avocations and Cares) it answers its Title of *A Nation a Family.* Considering a Nation as such, the great Bargain of ten Years Purchase, for the Lives of ten thus ally'd, is like a careful Provision for the elder Children, and the whole House made stronger and wealthier, while any one of them lives, by the Loss of any of its Kindred.

It will make the Father of the Family still more powerful; and to explain that Word yet further, the Sovereign more Popular, more Great and more Safe; and that Popularity, Greatness, and Safety, incorporated with the Happiness of his People, and conducing to it.

It preserves the Superintendency, Guardianship, and by Consequence the Credit of the Legislature, and ties the whole People, their Lawgivers and Governors, by a Band (which only can join the great and little, good and bad Men together) their common Interest. I had quite forgot to intimate that I propose these future Annuitants are to be paid by the Company, in Correspondence with the *Exchequer.*

I hope People will consider this Matter without Prejudice, and (forgetting that *Isaac Bickerstaffe*, the ridiculous Censor, says it) seriously enquire whether any Sum can be given for the Loss of the Opinion in Mankind, that a *Parliamentary Engagement is unalterable.*

Believe, (tho' it be only *Nestor Ironside*, the imaginary Guardian, who tells you so) that no Price can ballance the Loss of a Belief, *that what the Parliament has sold, can never be redeem'd, but at the Request of the Owner.*

Believe (since you have it from *Marmaduke Myrtle, the true and faithful Lover*) that *the Price of the Lady* Carona Credit *is far above Rubies.*

FINIS

The State of the Case (March, 1720)

This tract was Steele's public statement of affairs at the playhouse in March, 1720, at the height of his troubles with the Lord Chamberlain, the young Duke of Newcastle, which began when Newcastle took office in 1717, culminated in January, 1720, with Steele's expulsion as Governor, and finally ended in a truce, at least, with his reinstatement in the spring of 1721. The difficulty was in part a matter of politics and in part a conflict in authority. Should the players be under the jurisdiction of the Chamberlain of the King's Household or of the Drury Lane Governor? Steele based his legal rights on a license issued by the King in 1714 and a patent issued in 1715, valid for his lifetime and three years beyond. His authority, however, had been challenged in various ways, Newcastle's summary dismissal of a player, Colley Cibber, Steele's friend and co-worker, bringing things to a head. When at this juncture Steele had petitioned the King, Newcastle had secured a revocation of the license (not the patent) on the ground of " Great misbehaviours of our Company of Comedians . . . for want of a Regular Management . . . and from the neglect of a due Subordination and Submission to the Authority of our Chamberlain." So, now for two months, Steele had had no standing at Drury Lane, his powers as Governor were withdrawn, and his salary was suspended.

In the pamphlet he is setting forth his legal position as patentee. He quotes the patent in full and compares it with those formerly granted by Charles to Davenant and Killigrew. He has looked into the judgments of certain well-known legal authorities—Sir Francis Pemberton, Sir Edward Northey, and Sir Thomas Parker, now Lord Chancellor—on the validity of the earlier patents and gives these judgments as evidence that the "Authority of Licencing Players in this manner is just." These patents, he is careful to say, in no way impair or oppose a Chamberlain's authority or injure his office. Nevertheless he asserts his rights as patentee and maintains stoutly that he has been deprived illegally of what amounts to a freehold by an arbitrary application of the Sign Manual.

This difficulty had political complications. In the first place Steele owed his seat in parliament (Boroughbridge, Yorks, 1715) to Newcastle and was sincerely grateful to him for patronage. And then, Steele was just now in the bad graces of the Whig Ministry for his active opposition both to the Peerage Bill of the preceding year and to the South Sea Bill now being debated. In both measures he was, by conviction, on the same side with Walpole; and when Walpole came into power in the spring of 1721, Steele was reinstated at Drury Lane by a warrant—issued by Newcastle—ordering the management to account to him for his share of the profits, past and present.

It seemed to require all of Steele's courage to issue this particular pamphlet. He was ill; public attacks were being made upon him and public defences of Newcastle (for there were two sides to the question) ; there was talk of his expulsion from the House for the second time. "Disgrace is a hard suffering even with Integrity," was his comment on the situation (*Crisis of Property*). And he is frankly appealing for moral support in this argument for his legal rights. That "Whig, Tory, Roman-Catholick, Dissenter, Native, and Foreigner" are in his debt for good offices endeavored towards them in their civil rights is not an exaggerated claim, as can be seen by examining his record as a publicist and as a member. Textual notes on p. 650.

THE
STATE
OF THE
CASE

Between the

Lord-Chamberlain

OF

His M A J E S T Y's Houſhold,

AND THE

GOVERNOR

OF THE

Royal Company of Comedians.

WITH

The OPINIONS of *Pemberton*, *Northey*,
and *Parker*, concerning the Theatre.

By Sir *RICHARD STEELE.*

L O N D O N:

Printed for *W. Chetwood*, under *Tom's Coffee-houſe*
in *Covent-Garden* ; *J.* *Roberts*, near the *Oxford-*
Arms in *Warwick-lane* ; *J.* *Graves*, near *White's*
Chocolate-houſe in St. *James's-ſtreet* ; and *Charles*
Lillie, at the Corner of *Beaufort-Buildings* in the
Strand. 1720. Price 6 d.

593

THE
STATE
OF THE
CASE.

AS there cannot happen a greater Distress, than a Necessity of appealing to Mankind against Hardships impos'd by those with whom a Man has liv'd in Friendship; the Injury which I have receiv'd, great as it is, has nothing in it so painful, as that it comes from whence it does. When I complain'd of it in a private Letter to the Chamberlain, he was pleased to send his Secretary to me, with a Message to forbid me writing, speaking, corresponding, or applying to him in any manner whatever. Since he has been pleased to send an *English* Gentleman a Banishment from his Person and Councils, in a Stile thus Royal, I doubt not but the Reader will justify me in the Method I take to explain this Matter to the Town. I am sure there is no Man living more obsequious to his Friends than I am; and I hope to show my Enemies, all my Life, that I certainly have Courage enough to defend my self against Wrongs, as well as to forgive them, according as the Circumstances require one or the other, in the respective Characters of a Christian, and an honest Man.

My Lord Chamberlain has, contrary to Law and Justice, dispossessed me of my Freehold in a manner as injurious to the King his Master, as to me his Fellow-Subject. But though I had a Right to dispute even a legal Disturbance of me in my Partners, Tenants, and Servants, as the whole Company of Actors (in their different Qualities) are to me in the Eye of the Law: I say, though I might very justly have insisted upon Privilege of Parliament in the Case, I told my Lord, in my Letter to him, that I had not Confidence to urge, even against Oppression from him, a Right which my Electors gave me, upon no other Motive but their Knowledge of the kind Opinion he had of me at the time when they chose me. No: I could not plead what I owed to his Favour against his Change of Mind, but have waited, as I promised, till he had cancelled his good Offices by Injuries, which I am to show he has already done. In order to this, I must recite my Patent, as follows.

"*GEORGE*, by the Grace of God, of *Great Britain, France* and *Ireland*, King, Defender of the Faith, *&c.* To all to whom these Presents shall come, Greeting. We having inform'd Ourselves, since Our Accession to Our Crown, of the State of Our Theatre; and finding, to our Sorrow, that, thro' the Neglect and ill Management thereof, the true and only End of its Institution is greatly perverted; and, instead of exhibiting such Representations of Humane Life as may tend to the Encouragement and Honour of Religion and Virtue, and Discountenancing Vice, the *English* Stage hath been the Complaint of the Sober, Intelligent and Religious Part of Our People; and, by indecent and immodest Expressions, by prophane Allusion to Holy Scripture, by abusive and scurrilous Representations of the Clergy, and by the Success and Applause bestowed on Libertine Characters, it hath given great and insufferable Scandal to Religion and good Manners. And, in the Representations of Civil Government, care has not been taken to create, in the Minds of Our good Subjects, just and dutiful Ideas of the Power and Authority of Magistrates, as well as to preserve a due Sense of the Rights of our People; and through many other Abuses, that, which under a wise Direction, and due Regulation, would be useful and honourable, has proved, and, if not reformed, will continue a Reproach to Government, and Dishonour to Religion. And it being Our pious Resolution, which, with the Blessing of Almighty God, We will steadily pursue, through the whole Course of Our Reign, not only by Our own Example, but by all other Means possible, to promote the Honour of Religion and Virtue; and, on every Occasion, to encourage good Literature, and to endeavour the Establishment of good Manners and Discipline among all Our Loving Subjects, in all Stations and Ranks of Men whatsoever; these being, in Our Opinion, the proper Means to render Our Kingdoms happy and flourishing. We having seriously revolved on the Premises, and being well satisfied of the Ability, and good Disposition of Our Trusty and Well-beloved *Richard Steele* Esq; for the promoting these Our Royal Purposes, not only from his publick Services to Religion and Virtue, but his steady Adherence to the true Interest of his Country. Know ye, That We, out of Our especial Grace, certain Knowledge, and meer Motion, and in Consideration of the good and faithful Services, which the said *Richard Steele* hath done Us, and doth intend to do, for the future, have Given and Granted, and by these Presents, for Us and Our Heirs, and Successors, do Give and Grant unto him the said *Richard Steele,* his Executors, Administrators, and Assigns, for and during the Term of his Natural Life, and for and during the full End and Term of Three Years, to be computed next and immediately after the Decease of him the said *Richard Steele*, full Power, Licence, and Authority, to Gather together, Form, Entertain, Govern, Privilege, and keep a Company of Comedians for Our Service, to Exercise and Act Tragedies, Plays, Operas, and other Performances of the Stage, within the House in *Drury-lane,* wherein the same are now exercised, by Vertue of a Licence Granted by Us to him the said *Richard Steele, Robert Wilks, Colley Cibber, Thomas Dogget*, and *Barton Booth*, or within any other House built, or to be built, where he or they can best be fitted for that Purpose, within Our Cities of *London* and *Westminster*, or the Suburbs thereof; such House or Houses so to be built (if Occasion shall require) to be Assigned, Allotted out by the Surveyor of Our Works for a Theatre or Playhouse, with necessary Tiring and Retiring Rooms, and other Places convenient, of such Extent and Dimension, as the said *Richard Steele*, his Executors, Administrators or Assigns, shall think fitting; wherein Tragedies, Comedies, Plays, Operas, Musick-Scenes, and all other Entertainments of the Stage whatsoever, may be shewed and presented. Which said Company shall be Our Servants, and be stiled *The Royal Company of Comedians,* and shall consist of such Numbers as the said *Richard Steele,* his Executors, Administrators, or Assigns, shall from Time to Time think meet. And we do hereby, for Us, Our Heirs and Successors, Grant unto the said *Richard Steele*, his Executors, Administrators or Assigns, full Power, Licence, and Authority to Permit such Persons, at and during the Pleasure of the said

Richard Steele, his Executors, Administrators or Assigns, from Time to Time, to act Plays and Entertainments of the Stage of all sorts, peaceably and quietly, *without the Impeachment or Impediment of any Person or Persons whatsoever*, for the honest Recreation of such as shall desire to see the same; nevertheless under the Regulations herein after-mention'd, and such other as the said *Richard Steele*, from Time to Time, in his Direction, shall find reasonable and necessary for Our Service. And We do for Ourselves, Our Heirs and Successors, further Grant to him the said *Richard Steele*, his Executors, Administrators and Assigns, as aforesaid, That it shall and may be lawful, to and for the said *Richard Steele*, his Executors, Administrators and Assigns, to Take and Receive of such Our Subjects as shall resort to see or hear any such Plays, Scenes and Entertainments whatsoever, such Sum or Sums of Money, as either have accustomably been given and taken in the like kind, or as shall be thought reasonable by him or them, in regard of the great Expences of Scenes, Musick, and such new Decorations as have not been formerly used. And further, for Us, Our Heirs, and Successors, We do hereby Give and Grant unto the said *Richard Steele*, his Executors, Administrators and Assigns, full Power to make such Allowances out of that which he shall so receive by the Acting of Plays and Entertainments of the Stage, as aforesaid, to the Actors, and other Persons employed in Acting, Representing, or in any Quality whatsoever, about the said Theatre, as he or they shall think fit. And, that the said Company shall be under the *sole* Government and Authority of the said *Richard Steele*, his Executors, Administrators, or Assigns: And all scandalous and mutinous Persons shall, from time to time, by him and them be Ejected and Disabled from Playing in the said Theatre. And for the better attaining Our Royal Purposes in this Behalf, We have thought fit hereby to declare, that henceforth no Representations be admitted on the Stage by Vertue, or under Colour, of these Our Letters Patents, whereby the Christian Religion in general, or the Church of *England* may, in any manner, suffer Reproach, strictly inhibiting every Degree of Abuse, or Misrepresentation of sacred Characters, tending to expose Religion itself, and to bring it into Contempt; and that no such Character be otherwise introduced, or placed in other Light, than such as may enhance the just Esteem of those who truly answer the End of their sacred Function. We further enjoin the strictest Regard to such Representations, as any way concern Civil Policy, or the Constitution of Our Government, that these may contribute to the Support of Our sacred Authority, and the Preservation of Order and good Government. And it being Our Royal Desire, that, for the future, Our Theatre may be Instrumental to the Promotion of Virtue, and instructive to humane Life, We do hereby Command and Enjoin, That no New Play, or any Old or Revived Play be Acted under the Authority hereby Granted, containing any Passages or Expressions offensive to Piety and good Manners, until the same be Corrected and Purged by the said Governor from all such offensive and scandalous Passages and Expressions. And these Our Letters Patents, or the Inrollment thereof, shall be, in all Things, good and effectual in the *Law*, according to the true Intent and Meaning of the same, any Thing in these Presents contained, or any Law, Statute, Act, Ordinance, Proclamation, Provision, or Restriction, or any other Matter, Cause, or Thing whatsoever to the contrary, in any wise notwithstanding. In Witness whereof, We have caused These Our Letters to be made Patents."

Witness Our Self at Westminster, *the Nineteenth Day of* January *in the First Year of Our Reign.*

By Writ of Privy Seal.

COCKS.

When Mr. *Steele* was dispatch'd by the then Solicitor-General Mr. *Lechmere*, the Learned Gentleman used this Expression: *Sir, the King has here given you a Free-Hold; and if from it you can prove you receive Six Hundred Pounds a Year, you are qualified to be Knight of any Shire in* England. When this Patent was passing, the Patentee was inform'd, that this Grant would be an Infringement upon those under which Mr. *Rich* claimed. Upon which, in Justice to His Majesty, and Abhorrence of encroaching upon other Men, the Patentee went to the Secretary's Office, and obtain'd the Reference, before address'd to the Attorney, *or* Solicitor-General, should be directed to the

Attorney *and* Solicitor-General. In this he acted with his known Zeal for His Majesty's Honour and Service, which would not admit him to desire any Favour to the Injury of any other of His Subjects. The Terms of this Patent were settled by the joint Consent of Sir *Edward Northey* and Mr. *Lechmere*, Names illustrious in the Law, and no way inclin'd, or capable of being awed into a Concurrence from Deference to each others Opinion. They agreed the King could grant this, and I shall take care to assert my Right to what he has granted. The Patentee carried his Self-denial still further; and though he could have had this Patent, as well as Sir *William Davenant* and Mr. *Killigrew* had before him, to himself and his Heirs for ever, he asked it but for his Life, and three Years after his Death; which three Years he thought necessary to be in his Executors, to make an End of any Account between his Family and the Theatre upon his Death. The Patent itself, as to the Powers in it, is exactly the same with those others formerly granted, and no way opposes or impairs any Authority of a Chamberlain, any more than those did: Neither is there any the least Pretension, or Colour of Pretension, for disputing this Authority, without those who dispute it will assert, that King *George* is not, to all Intents and Purposes, as much King of *England* as King *Charles* the Second. But however other Men, for their own Humour, or Vanity, attempt to diminish, frustrate, or invade this Act of their Master, I will, to their Teeth, defend it; and make them understand, that there are Men who are not to be teiz'd, vex'd, worried, calumniated, or Brow-beaten out of the Laws of *England*.

But some have been pleas'd to say, in common Conversation, that Actors, as such, are not within the Rules of the rest of the World; as if they were among Men, like the *Ferae Natura* among Animals; and that it is against our Laws to tolerate the Profession in itself. If this were so, they would (except within the Verge of the Court) be no more under a legal Dispensation or Constitution, when directed by the Lord-Chamberlain, than they would when governed by any other Man; and, by the way, he has not taken this Power to destroy it as unwarrantable, but to exercise it, be it what it will, himself. This Matter will appear as it ought to do, by the Opinions of *Pemberton, Northey,* and *Parker,* who have been consulted by the Successors of

Davenant and *Killigrew*. I shall give them in the Order I have named them, and as the Questions were stated to those great men.

Quere 1. " Whether the Grant of a Power to *A. B.* his Heirs and Assigns, by the Letters Patents, to erect a Theatre, and to act Plays &c. be a good Grant in Fee, and Assignable, or shall determine with King *Charles* the Second's Death?

Quere. "About the Words, To be Servants to the King and Queen, and to be Servants to the Duke of *York* ? "

1. *I do not see, that to act Plays, or Interludes, or Operas, is unlawful in it self, either by the Common Law, or by any Statute. It's true, to wander about from Country to Country, as Stage-Players, is forbid* by 39 El. c. 4. *But not the acting of Plays, &c. which may be used (for ought I see) as an innocent Recreation.*

2. *I think the King's Patent may be available, to give the better Countenance to the Entertainments, and so may be Transfer'd from Ancestor to Heir, or Assign'd for that Purpose.*

3. *For that Purpose, to give a Countenance or Reputation to these Play-houses, I think it may be effectual, after the Death of King* Charles II. *and that Operation I think did not dye.*

Quere 2. " Whether the King's Agreement, that no Company shall be permitted in *London, Westminster,* or the *Suburbs,* shall hinder all others from acting within that Circuit, unless authorized under the Letters Patents? "

Taking this to be an Imployment permitted, or not prohibited by Law, (as I take this to be) I do not think the King's Concession in his Letters Patents, that no one shall be permitted to act Stage Plays, or Interludes, &c. in London, *or* Westminster, *will be effectual to hinder others from acting there. However, I think, such a Prohibition will last no longer than the King who grants it lives.*

Quere 3. " Whether the Lord Chamberlain, as such, or any other except the King, can Grant a Licence to Actors, in regard it is not (as suppos'd) a Lawful Calling, but only for the King's Pleasure? The Lord-Chamberlain hath lately sworn several Actors to be the King's Servants, to save them from being molested? "

If the acting of Plays were unlawful in its Nature, and Malum in se, *(which I do not take it to be) I do not see how the Lord-Chamberlain, or any other Officer, or the King himself, could give a Licence to any to act Plays, &c. But taking the Imployment not to be unlawful in itself, I conceive the Lord-Chamberlain, or Master of the Revels (with the King's Allowance) may authorize any Persons to act, or forbid and hinder them from acting in any of the King's Houses or Palaces. And their Grants to any to act in other Places may be us'd to countenance or give a Popular Reputation to the Comedies or Plays that they act. But I know of no other Effect that they can have. And I conceive they cannot prohibit any to act in any Place out of the King's Palaces, so long as they behave themselves modestly and decently.*

F. PEMBERTON.

Sir *Edward Northey* is consulted, and delivers his Opinion as follows:

"Whether the Grants by Letters Patents from King *Charles* the 2d to Sir *William Davenant*, his Heirs and Assigns, to purchase Lands, and to build a Theatre thereon to act Plays, be not a good Grant in Fee, and assignable? Or whether the same be determinable upon the Death of King *Charles* II. they having laid out to the Value of 8000*l.* in purchasing Land, and building Theatres, and other necessary Buildings and Decorations, for the more commodious Representation of Operas and other Plays by Virtue of the Letters Patents?"

I am of Opinion, the Letters Patents were a good Licence to Sir William Davenant, *his Heirs and Assigns, to build a Theatre, and therein to cause Plays to be acted; and if he, his Heirs or Assigns, do not abuse such Licence, they may continue the Plays, notwithstanding the Death of King* Charles II.

24th Feb.   EDWARD NORTHEY.
1702-3

I shall conclude my Authorities by the Opinion of Sir *Thomas Parker*, now Lord High Chancellor of *Great Britain*.

Quere, "Whether the Grant by Letters Patents from King

Charles II. to Sir *William Davenant*, his Heirs and Assigns, to Purchase Lands, and to build a Theatre thereon to act Plays, &c. and a like Grant to *Tho. Killigrew*, Esq; to build another Theatre, &c. be not good Grants in Fee, and Assignable? Or whether the same be not determinable upon the Death of King *Charles* II. They having laid out to the Value of 8000*l.* in Purchasing Lands, and Building two Theatres, and other necessary Buildings, Scenes and Decorations for the more commodious Representation of Operas, Plays, and Entertainments of the Stage, under the Authority of the said Patents? "

Answ. *The Letters Patents are both express, That the King Grants for him, his Heirs and Successors; and I think the Assigns of Sir* William Davenant *and Mr.* Killigrew, *and their Heirs, may still continue their Plays, and Theatrical Entertainments in the House built under the Authority of those Letters Patents, as well as Sir* William Davenant *and Mr.* Killigrew *themselves could have done if they were now alive, or as they could do in the Life-time of King Charles II. who made those Grants.*

Nov. 10.   THO. PARKER.
1705

Hence it appears, that the Authority of Licencing Players in this manner, is just, and well supported from the Reason of the Thing itself, and this Authority is given to Mr. *Steele*, in no other manner, than it was before given, and differs only in Circumstances, that plead for *Steele*. The Grant to *Steele* for Life, and three Years after, is given upon stronger Motives, than those alledged for granting to *Davenant* and *Killigrew* for ever: K. *Charles's* Grants were Acts of meer Favour and Motion; that of King *George*, for worthy Services expressly recited, and has a Merit above them (I mean only as to the Force of the Patents, not the Characters of the Patentees) as much, as voluntary Acts are more valid in Law, than those given for valuable Considerations. This is the Title by which Sir *Richard Steele* is Governor of the Royal Company of Comedians. We are now to consider the manner of his being deprived of that Right.

The Reader will observe, that my Patent describes very largely the Uses and Purposes of it, as well as the Limitations, and

Restrictions under which it ought to be enjoy'd; and there is no Power which can make it void or ought to frustrate it, except the Patentee, or his Assigns, shall be prov'd to transgress, or go beyond the Limits prescrib'd; in such Case, there is a plain Method of bringing the Offenders before Courts of Justice, and the Patentee, or those claiming under him, are there to stand upon the Defensive; But I have been deprived of my Property by Violence, under the Conduct of Craft, but that Violence has been as open, and that Craft as shallow and as little disguis'd, as follows: Without any Cause assign'd, or Preface declaring by what Authority, a noble Lord sends a Message, directed to Sir *Richard Steele,* Mr. *Wilks,* and Mr. *Booth,* to dismiss Mr. *Cibber,* who for some time submitted to a Disability of appearing on the Stage, during the Pleasure of one that had nothing to do with it. When this lawless Will and Pleasure was chang'd, a very frank Declaration was made, that all the Mortification put upon Mr. *Cibber,* was intended only as a remote beginning of Evils, which were to affect the Patentee, with some broad Intimations, that the Force of the Patent itself should very soon be made ineffectual by a Sign Manual: Under an Amazement at this audacious Proceeding against the Validity of a Patent from the King on the Throne, and taking myself as a Parliamentary Commissioner, to be of Quality to write to Ministers of State, especially when it was only to implore their Assistance and Protection, in order to avert this intended Outrage upon the King's Authority, and the Subjects Property, I writ to two great Ministers to that Purpose. But so great is the Rage conceiv'd against me, that the Consideration that the Dignity of the King is offended in his Grant, could not protect me, from being ruin'd against his Laws, or procure the least notice of my Remonstrance. However, on *Friday, Jan.* 22. I presented, in the Presence of my Lord-Chamberlain, the following Petition to the King.

TO THE

KING'S

Most Excellent Majesty.

The Humble Petition of Sir RICHARD
STEELE,

Sheweth,

THAT *Your Petitioner is possessed, by Letters Patents, of the sole Government and Authority of keeping a Company of Comedians, under the Title of* The Royal Company of Comedians.

THAT *the Lord-Chamberlain of Your Majesty's Household has, by a written Order, intimidated a principal Comedian from Acting; and, by Promises, does encourage other Actors to disturb Your Petitioner's said Government, to the great Prejudice of his Fortune and Property.*

THAT *Your Petitioner is further threaten'd with an extraordinary Use of Your Majesty's Power, to the Disappointment and Frustrating his said Authority.*

THAT *Your Petitioner humbly conceives, that he has fully answered all the Designs of Your Majesty's Grant, to the great Improvement of the Theatre.*

Your Petitioner therefore most humbly prays he may not be any way molested but by due Course of Law.

And Your Petitioner shall ever Pray, &c.

It was my ill Fate to find no other Effect of this Petition, but the following Order the next Day.

" Whereas by Our Royal Licence, bearing Date the 18th Day of *October*, 1714, We did give and grant unto *Richard Steele* Esq; now Sir *Richard Steele* Knight, Mr. *Robert Wilks*, Mr. *Colley Cibber*, Mr. *Thomas Dogget*, and Mr. *Barton Booth*, full Power, Licence and Authority, to form, constitute and establish a Company of Comedians. And having received Information of great Misbehaviours committed by our Company of Comedians, now acting at the Theatre in *Drury-lane*. Therefore, for reforming the Comedians, and for establishing the just and antient Authority of the Officers of our Household, and more especially of our Chamberlain: We have thought fit to revoke the above-mentioned Licence. And we do farther, (as much as in us lies, *and as by Law we may*) revoke and make void all other Licences, Powers and Authorities whatsoever, and at any time heretofore given by us to the said Sir *Richard Steele, Robert Wilks, Colley Cibber, Thomas Dogget,* and *Barton Booth,* or to *any of them severally.*"

I must here acknowledge, that the Sense of the Chamberlain's former Patronage made me write him a Letter in the *Theatre*, much below the Justice of my Cause, and that Manhood which Right and Equity ought to have supported me in, against Injury and Oppression.

In the Allegory of a Bee-hive, and its Owner, I have represented myself and Company destroy'd by the Precipitancy which sometimes attends the most generous Natures. But since this was received as it was, I shall study no more Types, Shadows, or Similies, to inform this Lord of, and prove to him the Wrong he has done me; but will seek Redress by Application to the King in Council, or by due Course of Law. The Reader will observe, that the Order mentions Licences, Powers and Authorities, to the Persons nam'd therein, and then obliquely aims at the Patentee in the Words, *or to any of them severally*, but not a Word of Grant or Patent, which was vested only in *Steele*, and would not have agreed well with the just and gracious Words, *as much as in us lies, and as by Law we may.*

Under this thin Disguise, and by misleading the King by the Words of Reserve against any unlawful Molestation to be done me, the Lord-Chamberlain took upon him immediately after, to send the following Order to the Managers of the Play-house, with which they were intimidated, to forbear to act any longer under my Jurisdiction, or pay me any Money for the future, in Contempt of our former Contracts and Agreements.

Whereas His Majesty has thought fit, by his Letters of Revocation, bearing Date the twenty third Day of January 1719, *(for divers weighty Reasons therein contain'd) to revoke his Royal Licence. For the effectual Prevention of any future Misbehaviour, in Obedience to His Majesty's Commands, I do, by Vertue of my Office of Chamberlain of His Majesty's Household, hereby discharge you the said Managers and Comedians at the said Theatre in* Drury-lane *in* Covent-Garden, *from farther Acting. Given under my Hand and Seal this 25th Day of* January 1719.

To the Gentlemen managing the Company of Comedians at the Theatre in *Drury-lane* in Covent-Garden, and to all the Comedians and Actors there.

The Loss I have hereby sustain'd, I value as follows.

	l.	s.	d.
Six hundred a Year, for Life, is moderately valued at	6000	00	00
The Three Years after my Life———	1800	00	00
My Share in the Scenes, Stock, &c.———	1000	00	00
The Profit of acting my own Plays already writ, or I may write———	1000	00	00
	9800	00	00

The thing itself is but a Shop to work in, and received nothing from the Crown. And if a Man shall hazard his All for the Publick, and expect no more but what his own Skill and Labour, in Conjunction with his Assigns, shall bring him, such a one should be the last Man that ought to suffer Molestation. If I had been Laceman, Saddler, or Shoemaker to the Crown by Patent, I could not have been disposses'd but by due Course of Law, and according to the Prices I should have set upon my Goods: And shall the noble Ends and Purposes, set forth in this Charter, be overlook'd and suppress'd in a summary Way, and no Redress?

But it is apparent the King is grossly and shamelessly injur'd against his gracious Precaution in the Order by *Sign Manual.* The Chamberlain has done the same Favour to other Gentlemen, with regard to Parliament, which he has done for me, and they have acted their own Way as well as I, and he has not yet enter'd upon their Estates.

40

I never did one Act to provoke this Attempt; nor does the Chamberlain pretend to assign any direct Reason of Forfeiture, but openly and wittingly declares he will ruin *Steele*; which is, in a Man in his Circumstances against one in mine, as great as the Humour of *Malagene* in the Comedy, who valued himself upon his Activity for tripping up Cripples. All this is done against a Man, to whom Whig, Tory, Roman-Catholick, Dissenter, Native, and Foreigner, owe Zeal and Good-will for good Offices endeavour'd towards every one of them in their Civil Rights, and their kind Wishes to him are but a just Return. But what ought to weigh most with his Lordship, the Chamberlain, is my Zeal for his Master; of which I shall at present say no more, than that his Lordship, and many others, may perhaps have done more for the House of *Hanover* than I have; *But I am the only Man in His Majesty's Dominions who did all he could.*

FINIS

Pasquin

No. 46 (9 July 1723) No. 51 (26 July 1723).

These two papers were written for a Whig periodical defending the government during the Jacobite intrigue at the beginning of Walpole's régime. The first confidential information of another plot to restore James Stuart was received by Walpole in April, 1722, and almost immediately he called upon Steele for some sort of journalistic service (inference from Steele's letter to him on 20 May 1722). There had been a good understanding between them since the spring of 1721; and, of course, Steele had given able service as a publicist during the rising of '15. Nothing has been identified from his pen in the year 1722, when the thing came to a head. But in the spring of 1723, in the aftermath, he was actively engaged in related parliamentary committee business (*Journals of the Commons,* XX, 167); and in July there are these *Pasquin* papers, defending Walpole and the Bishops and denouncing Bishop Atterbury.

Francis Atterbury, Bishop of Rochester and Dean of Westminster, had been for a decade England's outstanding sympathizer of Stuart claims and was unquestionably involved in these intrigues. He had been arrested for high treason in August, 1722; and in May, 1723, the sentence was passed depriving him of his high preferments and banishing him to life-long exile. The press was full of excited discussion for and against the learned, witty, and able prelate—evidence or lack of evidence of his complicity and the justice or injustice of his sentence. To some, he may have appeared a martyr; but strong Hanoverians saw only his impiety and guilt. *The True Briton*, a periodical in his defence, was started in June by the young, notorious Philip, Duke of Wharton; and Steele's *Pasquin* papers are answers to recent numbers of this periodical.

The main details of the plot, personages, and events, and the drift of the correspondence with its fictitious names were common knowledge. Christopher Layer, one of the chief conspirators, was executed in May, 1723; George Kelly, a non-juring clergyman, was Atterbury's secretary; Illington was the fictitious name for Atterbury. Steele refers to Walpole as "the Great Man" and "the Comptroller." Probably "Jeronimo" is Lord Finch. The gibe at Walpole's state speeches Steele takes particular note of: "He can speak extremely well, and certainly does it with a great deal of Art and Skill or he had not been the Man he is."

These papers were anonymous and were never acknowledged; the evidence for Steele's authorship, however, is quite acceptable. In the *Pasquin* file of the Burney Collection at the British Museum, which belonged to Isaac Reed, Nos. 46 and 51 are marked as being by Steele, as is No. 46 in the Bodleian file (No. 51 wanting) ; and there is a corroborative contemporary statement that he wrote some of the *Pasquins*. John Nichols first included them in his writings.

Ill-health and preoccupation with his play *The Conscious Lovers,* produced in December, may have prevented Steele's writing for the cause in 1722; but his health was improved by mid-summer, 1723 (Letter to Elizabeth, 15 July), and it is unlikely that he could keep entirely silent in this crisis. It seems fitting that his last public writing to be identified should bear, if somewhat indirectly, on the Revolution Settlement and the Protestant Succession, about which he once declared passionately that it was "a Cause, in which I am engaged to the End of my Life" (*Letter to the Pretender* in *Town Talk,* No. 5). Textual notes on p. 650.

Pasquin. No. XLVI.
Tuesday, July 9, 1723.

Noctem Peccatis & fraudibus objice nubem.

I shall not make any Apology for inserting a Letter which comes from so famous a Name as *Illington,* to one who so zealously pursues Renown as the *True Briton*; but give it the Reader just as it comes to my Hands: solemnly protesting that I had it not from any of the Clerks of the Post-Office, nor does it need passing through the Hands of Decypherers.

To the TRUE BRITON

Your unexpected Zeal for me has infinitely oblig'd me, and demands all the Returns of good Offices that are in my Power. There is a Spirit in your Style, which is worthy the Party you have now chose; but has a little of Youth and Inconsideration, which I fear may hurt you, and consequently hurt the Cause. You stand loose, indeed, and free from Attachments, or Prejudices, or Fears, or Hopes; but give me leave to advise you to a little more Circumspection, which is necessary in all great Designs, which are not to be carried on without Method and a Preservation of Appearances. *Machiavel,* in his excellent *Book of Ethicks for Great Men,* says, It is necessary to seem pious, but an Offence to be so. This admirable Rule, my dear Lord, you are too young, and have too much Fire in your Temper, to keep to; for tho' you may dispense with your self as to all the Maxims the Lower World are govern'd by, and not let them at all affect you, or your Life; yet you are to consider, when you are to make Impressions upon Men, that you are to seem moved by the same Principles as move them: Thus tho' an abandon'd Man may have all the Arguments which are used by a good Man, they will not be so useful, because of the Imperfection of his Character. And therefore I would advise your Lordship to put into your Character Hypocrisy; for 'tis a very great Mistake to imagine, that because you can speak readily upon any Argument, that therefore you shall prevail; nay, you will find it by certain Experience, that the World minds more who says a thing, than what is said: For which Reason, I take the Liberty to advise, that if you wou'd have what you say regarded, you should not be so sincerely wicked. I cannot but excessively applaud your Insinuation, of *Tiberius* at *Caprea*; I mean, I applaud it, as a bold Stroke: But then it wants every other Requisite to make it fix where you mean it; for *Cato* and *Catiline* can never be alike, only because they are both gone out of Town, and agree in nothing else but that Circumstance. Now you did not consider when you said this, any thing else but your own Temper, and the exerting your Anger without Guard, which made you do it without Effect. For this Reason, I would inculcate to you to be less sincere.

There is another Art, which a Man who would succeed in the World must be master of, which is the Art of Prevarication; that is, a Way of seeming to speak the Truth, but keeping a Reserve in your own Heart, as if you had said nothing: But this may be more easily explained to you by Example, than deliver'd by Precept. I put the last Confidence in you, when I give you an Instance of this from my own Works. You know 'twas my Affair to erace out of the Opinion of the Audience all Suspicion of Guilt, which I did after the following Manner:

But, my Lords, there is still a Way allow'd of vindicating my self: It is generally Negative; that is, by protesting and declaring my Innocence to your Lordships, in the most deliberate, serious and solemn Manner; and appealing to God, the Searcher of Hearts, as to the Truth of what I say, as I do it in what follows:

I am charg'd in the Report with directing a Correspondence to Mr. Kelly; but I solemnly deny that I ever, directly or indirectly, saw a single line of any of their Letters, till I met with them in Print: Nor was the Contents of any of them communicated to me. I do, in the next Place, deny that I was ever privy to any Memorial to be drawn up to be deliver'd to the Regent: Nor was I ever acquainted with any Account to be made on the King's going to Hanover, or at the Time of the Election: Nor did I hear the least Rumour of the Plot to take Place after the breaking up of the Camp, till some Time after Mr. Layer's Commitment. I do, with the same Solemnity, declare, that I never collected, remitted, received, or ask'd any Money of any Man to facilitate those Designs; nor was I ever acquainted with, or had any Remittances whatsoever from any of those Persons: That I never remitted or drew any Declaration, Minutes, or Paper, in the Name of the Pretender, as is expressly charged upon me. And that I never knew of any Commission issued, Preparations of Arms, Officers, or Soldiers, or the Methods taken to procure any in order to raise an Insurrection in these Kingdoms. All this I declare to be true, and will so declare to the last Gasp of my Breath.

Now you are to observe the Words, *deliberate, serious and solemn Manner, appealing to the Searcher of all Hearts*; and then again, *directly or indirectly*, are terms which amaze and amuse the Hearers, and divert them from observing the Illusion; wherein I say, I never SAW a single Line of those Letters, till I saw them in Print. The immediate and plain Answer had been, I never directly or indirectly dictated any Letter to Mr. *Kelly*; but I took care never to see them after I had dictated them, and therefore was able to say what I have there said. It is certainly just the same thing as to Point of Conscience; for there the Truth is to be utter'd, and every thing that does not make for the right Information of the Audience, is equally Criminal with a plain Lie: This I say, lest you shou'd think I did not know the Force of what I utter'd; and is a thing to be said but between you and me, to whom the Reputation of Understanding is preferable to that of Integrity: And therefore I ended with this, *All this I declare to be true, and will so declare to the last Gasp of my Breath.*

Declaring *to the last Gasp of my Breath*, has in it a Solemnity that mightly affects Fools, who are frighted with Bugbears; and has an incredible influence when it comes from a Clergyman: a Character which is held indelible; insomuch, that now they have turn'd me out of my Revenue, they still allow me a Bishop of the Universal Church! Which, I may say *inter nos*, is allowing that ill Actions may incapacitate a Man for any Office, but that which requires his being the best of Men. For this Reason I wish I could have your Company for one Fortnight, because I would Ordain you; and then you might do as I have done before you, Squabble, Debate, Bully, Cant, or Live just as you do, and do no hurt to your Character; at least so as to destroy it.

I am extremely obliged to you for the advantageous Character you have given me in your Writings; but you should not have fallen upon a certain Great Man in the same Paper, for you may be sure he will rejoice in an Invective from that Hand, that gives me a Panegyrick. In your *True Briton*, Numb. V. pointing at him, you say, *In C. 64. he carries his Insinuations much higher, and suggests that even the Great Man, who chuses to deserve Honours rather than receive them, would give little Opposition to the Pretender's Measures; but this is so foreign to Truth, and so contrary to the whole Series of that Gentleman's Life, that it were taking up the Time of my Readers unnecessarily to expose the Falsehood and Villainy of such an Assertion.* The Villainy of such an Assertion, was an Expression a little too strong; for tho' you very well don't care a Farthing for what People think of you, while you can enjoy the Comfort of no Conscience, yet you should regard Appearances; for to as many as think you inserted that Paragraph, to suggest the Great Man would in such Case give little Opposition to the Pretender's Measures, you unguardedly call your self what you know your self to be, the Enemy will say, for making so improbable an Insinuation. But all these Things might do, if I had you with me to give you the indelible Character; for with that, my *Fornication* with *Moll Paulin* when a young Student was as consistent, as *High Treason* against King *George* when a Prelate. You have indeed an excellent Talent for the Gown, that is to say, as the Gown is a Covering to what the Lower World call Offences. But, my dear Son, let me beg of you, if it is not already too late, to avoid that meek Text, with which I ended my Banter to the Lords, *Naked I came out of my Mother's Womb, and naked I shall return*: I can assure you, this had been a very uncomfortable Text, if it had not been for some Ladies; to whom pray give my most humble Service. I am

Yours

ILLINGTON.

Pasquin. No. LI.
Friday, July 26, 1723.

Est modus in rebus, sunt certi denique; fines,
Quos ultra, citraq; nequit consistere rectum.

I shall not at present talk with the TRUE-BRITON in the Style of *Pasquin,* nor concern my self whether he is a man of this or the other Quality; but take leave to aver, that if he is at all a Subject of *England,* he has injudiciously and outragiously offended against every Person in the Kingdom, in his last Paper. *The Liberty of the Press is the Preservation of the Liberty of the State*; but it is not to be used with such a Licence, as to trample upon all Orders of Men; and thereby not only lose all Benefit by it, but be exposed to all it should guard us against. The honest Use of it, is the best Security from any Encroachments of Courts and Ministers: Therefore, lest this Writer's Insolence and Inadvertency may be an Argument against it, I chuse this Way to chastise his Offences against the Press, by the Press, that his notorious Injuries may not turn to the Prejudice of Printing itself.

He begins his imagin'd Ridicule upon the whole Bench of Bishops, whom he calls *the Surprize of other Nations, and Curiosities of our own*; and goes on to say of them with the same Force of Genius, " Many of their Predecessors equall'd them in Composure, but all impartial Criticks concur, that none of them had Talents half so well adapted to *Translation*: Whilst He, whose Company they a little while ago, with so much Prudence as well as Justice, rejected, was confessedly *not upon a Level* with them in either." As sawcily as this Author speaks of the Bishops in general, the whole Nation are highly satisfied with their Learning, their Piety, and good Sense; and know them to be an excellent Body of Protestant Divines, who are more regardful of the Rights and Privileges of their Fellow Subjects, than any Pre-eminence of their own; nor is there any Part of Learning they want by the Absence of the Bishop of Rochester, except that now he is gone, they could not write so good an Epigram, if it were put upon them to produce one. For it was the peculiar Excellence of that Prelate, to keep alive in himself the kind of Learning we are admired for when Boys, and play it against his Adversaries in his ripe or declining Age; from which he would with great Readiness, no matter what Decency, skip to a Text of Scripture, and enjoy the Advantage of the Bishop, and the Vivacity and Pertness of the School-Boy, at the same time. Such a prompt and ready Excellence join'd with a consummate Hypocrisy and glaring Impudence, which my Lord had to a great Perfection, could not fail of gaining almost as many Admirers as he saw Men; for it requir'd deep Penetration to understand him to be any other than a very fine Person: since he could thus retire from the Man of Wit, in which he was somebody, to the Pious Divine, in which he was no body. But now his Character is so thoroughly understood, that I agree with the *TRUE BRITON*, " The Unanimity of the Nation is such as it was hardly ever blessed with before! For since the Departure of the late Bishop of *Rochester* into Exile, it is universally agreed on, That there is One Man now abroad, whom no Man desires to see come back again."

The Author goes on; and with his prodigious Wit and Contrivance, turns the Invective against Churchmen into a singular Purpose of making it under the Cover of what he had met with in a Library in *Spain*: *He thinks he had it in the* Franciscan *Library* at Madrid. "A little before, and about the time that the Light of the Reformation began to dawn, there was not such a Pack of abject Wretches in the World, as the Ecclesiasticks of most Countries. To confirm this, I shall oblige the Curious with Part of a Manuscript I pick'd up in my Travels into *Spain*. It had no Date, but it is plain it could not be writ many *Centuries* ago."

With the deep Design of having finish'd all he had to say of State Affairs, he *comes to Church and* Churchmen, *with that*

Openness and Freedom as becomes a candid Historian: But here he levels his whole Invective against *Don Ferdinando*, who was Comptroller of the *Finances*, for whom he makes a very silly Speech about *Quadrupeds having four Legs*. He had done with Churchmen before, and call'd 'em plainly enough *abject Wretches*; so that now his Wit is to fall only on the Comptroller: But he should have consider'd whom he had undertook to mimick, and made an Harangue accordingly; for this Speech has nothing in it but the daring to point out a Great Man in a High Employment, after a ridiculous Manner; and then making the Bishops also out of all Character talk prophanely, and solemnly affirming that *Two and two make Fifteen—So help us G—d—Demonstration by G—d—*and *Crucify him, Crucify him,*—All which is so mean, so silly, and so wicked, that it will scarce bear so much as to be repeated. This writer puts me in mind of the *Tale of a Tub*, where there is a great deal of Humour mixt with an equal Negligence of every thing solemn. But the wretched Imitator, as it is ordinary with common Swearers, has no Spirit but what is raised from his Impiety: He cannot ridicule a great Officer, but he must prophane the Name of Heaven to come at him; and represents the whole Bench of Bishops as his *Ringwoods* and *Jowlers*.

It is of no Consequence who this Great Wit, this Worthy Author is; it is certain he has a little more to do than to make up with a Minister of State. But I must not grow too serious with this facetious Gentleman; but shall give him a Letter of Advice how to mingle his Thoughts and Sentiments, if he would have them pass upon the World for any thing.

To the TRUE BRITON.

Sir,

As you have lately done Justice to a Great Man in disowning your self to be Him, we are not to take you for any Body; but consider you as an Enemy to us all, and tearing about you, without keeping any Terms with Persons or Things; but labouring for something that is smart, that is bold, that is witty, or some way surprizing, to keep our Attention close to you, and engage us either by our Curiosity, our Spleen, our Malice, or our Envy. But you are, it seems, a *Country Gentleman*; and as such you should have consider'd, that the Comptroller can be when he pleases an Equal to a Country Gentleman, tho' 'tis not so easy for a Country Gentleman, to be equal to the Comptroller: He can speak extremely well, and certainly does it with a great deal of Art and Skill, or he had not been the Man he is; for in our Government, a Person must have Talents, or it is impossible for him to possess great Power. But you have fallen upon him, as envying his good Fortune only; and have not at all shewn that he does not deserve it, or that he misapplies it. Then there are some things which a Man should not be endur'd to touch upon; as your cruel Usage of him you call *Jeronimo*, who has offended no One, and can deserve your Envy only for being the Son of an illustrious Man, who devolves the Effect of his Labours upon him, whilst he himself is still wrestling and contending with the Enemies of his Country, with great Capacity and Application. You should have learnt to distinguish Things a little before you commenced Writer; for it is not the Countryman that is fit for these things. *Rusticus ab normis sapius* will never be able to talk of Ministers and their Designs; and barely to hate a great Man because he is so, will do nothing but expose the Weakness of your Head, and the Malignity of your Heart.

I am, &c.

N. B. *The promis'd Preamble to Friend Stratter's Patent will be inserted next* Tuesday.

The APPENDIX

[Greatness Among the Moderns]
To Lord ——
(1705-1707?)

Clues within this manuscript letter, as to its purpose, date, and addressee are almost indiscernible, if indeed there are any. On the surface it seems to be a bid for political patronage at a time when Steele was himself hoping to enter public life. But nothing is known of the purpose it served or was intended to serve in this or a revised form. The date is also a matter of conjecture. We know that in the period between 1699 and 1701 Steele was meditating the elements of greatness and was contrasting the ancients and the moderns—to the advantage of the moderns— as he presented the case for Christianity: *An Argument Proving that no Principles but Those of Religion are Sufficient to Make a Great Man.* In the present essay the advantage lies with the ancients; and the Stoic ideal of greatness, as outlined by Cicero, he praises as the standard of excellence.

It is only an impression, we must admit, that this letter on *Greatness Among the Moderns* was written not at the turn of the century, when Steele was pursuing a military career, but later, within the years 1705 to 1707, when he deliberately sought a place for himself in government service. In 1705, he was at a juncture in his affairs. Early in the year, he retired from the army, and during the summer he married. His self-confidence was doubtless heightened at the public acclaim for his third play, *The Tender Husband,* produced successfully in April. Now in his middle thirties, he was settling down to a steady course; and possibly in emulation of admired personal friends, Addison and Maynwaring, he hoped to engage in active government work. A statement in a letter dated August, 1705, has a significant ring: "I believe I shall soon be very well employed." The patronage given to Whig friends during that year must have seemed impressive: In October, Maynwaring was made Auditor of Imprests; in December, Congreve was given a minor sinecure as commissioner for wines; Addison, already in the Commission of Appeals, was appointed in July an undersecretary of state. Stirring things were in the air in 1705, a year of political agitation and change. Parliament was dissolved in April on a note of fierce controversy; by midsummer, the general election had demonstrated that high Toryism was eclipsed and that the Ministry would go along with the Whig lords in the great and impending tasks of war and peace. But although this was a year of decision for Steele, his affairs moved slowly. Not until August, 1706, did he get the first and minor post—that of Gentleman-Usher to Prince George of Denmark—and it was May, 1707, when he became editor of *The Gazette*. If this letter is connected with his entrance into civil employments, it might have been drafted at any time during the interval 1705 to 1707. One wonders whether later than this period, Steele would be likely to address those in a position to dispense patronage with the remark: "I am not in the least acquainted with you."

It is not possible, moreover, to identitfy the addressee, "My Lord," with certainty. Marlborough, Steele's life-long hero, seems out of the question, as neither military preferment is being sought nor military greatness celebrated. Is it one of the Whig lords of the Junto—Halifax, Wharton, Sunderland, Somers—whose assistance was later publicly acknowledged in Steele's dedications? If the date of the letter is 1705-7, Halifax may possibly be ruled out, as he would be known in some degree by that time to a close friend of Addison. Wharton, the Whigs' astute politcal manager and a leader in the Lords, might qualify; but then he was a man of great wealth, and the addressee, Steele says, is not rich in land and money. The young Sunderland does not fit; although by 1705, he was a power in the Lords and the Marlborough circle and in 1706 a secretary of state, he had not yet become—if ever he did—the assured political leader whom Steele is describing. If the date were earlier—during William's reign—Lord Chancellor Somers might be identified as Steele's great man; and it is true that, although this scholar-statesman had not been in the Ministry since 1702, he was, during these years out of office, a man of immense power, the accepted leader of the Junto, whose favor was worth bidding for, as is seen by Swift's dedication to him in 1704 of *Tale of a Tub* and Addison's in 1705 of *Remarks on Italy*. But it may be that Steele was seeking outside the Junto for patronage. In what respects does Cowper fit the portrait? One remembers that after laying his gifts of *Tatler* I and II at the feet of personal friends—Maynwaring and Wortley Montagu—and even before thanking Halifax (in IV), Steele dedicated *Tatler* III in 1711 to Cowper, frankly signing his own name to the acknowledgments for favors received. In 1705-6, Cowper was winning plaudits on all sides. He was the first Whig to be given an eminent post in the new Ministry in October, 1705—Lord Keeper of the Great Seal—with promises of more honors, which materialized as a peerage in 1706 and the Lord Chancellorship in 1707. And Cowper's original and independent action in 1706, which multiplied both enemies and friends, his refusing to accept " New Years' gifts " from the counsellors at law,—that was the kind of integrity which would elicit Steele's praise for " introducing into the World things extraordinary."

From this distance, however, only one person would appear to measure up in 1705-7 to every specification of the portrait drawn by Steele, and that is Lord High Treasurer Godolphin, who was at the head of the government from 1702 to 1710. And Steele's phrase, " the first man now in being, according to the prevailing notion of Pre-eminence," can be interpreted to mean just that—the " prime minister "— great, he goes on to say, not only because of his high rank but also by virtue of his conduct and example. The implication is that his lordship is a self-made statesman, one whose first motive in accepting responsibility and power always has been to serve his country and not to accumulate land and money. There come to mind Godolphin's humble beginnings, his long public service under three sovereigns, his scrupulous and incorruptible honesty where public finances were concerned—and finance was usually his province—and his retirement, finally, in comparative poverty. Godolphin would certainly know to within twenty shillings " the price of every considerable man's integrity in England." He had known through years of government service what it was not only to accept public employments but also to resign them or to be turned out, as calm of temper and free from perturbation and ambition withal, as was Steele's wise man. Godolphin, himself a moderate in politics, hardly a party man at all, had always handled conflicting political elements with adroitness. Perhaps Steele is thinking of recent violent Tory opposition in the Ministry as he exclaims, " With this reluctant train of Followers what Great things have you done! and to what Height did you raise your Personal Greatness at the Head of a Crowd of men differing from each other in every other Circumstance, but that of Hating and Obeying your Lordship." It may be significant that this letter is not written in a spirit of faction, nor with any reference to purely Whig principles.

Whomever Steele is addressing, until we know more definitely to the contrary, we can only say it might well be Lord Treasurer Godolphin. Other suppliants wrote odes to Godolphin (Congreve, for one, in 1706) ; Steele, with little skill in verse, would prefer the prose epistle. What is known of their relations in later years? They at least became personally acquainted, as we see from a Steele letter in 1710 which mentions their being in company together. When the Godolphin Ministry was dissolved in 1710, Steele held the *Gazette* post and a commissionership of stamps and appeared to stand well in ministerial circles. He never made a dedication to Godolphin. But we find in *The Guardian, The Englishman,* and elsewhere, his intrepid praise of the late Ministry, and after Godolphin's death and Marlborough's exile, more than one gallant defence of the two statesmen against Tory onslaughts.

It is his beloved Tully whom Steele draws upon for the ancients' ideal of greatness, the third and fourth paragraphs of the letter being a close translation of *De Officiis* I. xx. 66-69. Steele's development of his theme—contrast of Tully's standard, to which "his lordship" measures up, with the want of rectitude found in modern leadership— is not full and complete. But even in this draft form, there are original, lively, spirited strokes which are Steele at his best. As far as is known, the letter has not been published before. Textual notes on p. 651.

[*Greatness Among the Moderns*]

My Lord

As Your Lordship is a gentleman who has always been pleased with introducing into the World things extraordinary, I will make no Apology for being of the same tast and writing to [1] Your L[sp] tho I am not, in the least acquainted with You; [2] Especially since [3] I am to entertain You on the Subject [4] of Greatnesse among the moderns, and that the examination of this Grandeur will naturally show,[5] that Your Lordship is [6] the first man now in being, according to the prevailing notion of Pre-eminence, and not only so but that Your conduct and Example have principally [7] made the sense of Greatnesse to be [8] what it is at present among Us.

Before I enter upon any Observations concerning that state to which Your Lordship and others [9] have attained, Forgive me that [10] I show, and for fear of Offence and Scandal [11] I will [12] be very brief, in what the Antients Thought the Greatness of man to consist. I won't be such a Pedant as to name Greek and Latin Writers,[13] but from one of the Greatest of them give the sum of what they have to say, or have said on this [14] old fashioned Subject.

A great mind, says my Author, is chiefly distinguish'd by two things. The one by a contempt of Exterior Considerations, as when a man is verily persuaded, that He ought [15] not to admire, wish, or pursue any thing but Honesty and Truth, and that He ought not to [16] accommodate Himself to the Will of any other men, to give way to any perturbation of Spirit, or [17] be affected

with any accident of Fortune. The second indication of Greatnesse is when a man who [18] is master of His Temper, as thus
describ'd, enters upon Publick businesse with [19] a design of
serving His Country in the most important and difficult affairs,
with the prospect [20] before Him, of undergoing [21] the greatest
Toils and [22] hazard of all that [23] makes life agreeable to [24]
ordinary men, nay with [25] the danger to life it self.

All the Dignity Grandeur pleasure and profit that can touch
a Great mind results from the latter of these considerations,
but [26] that which [27] constitutes and forms Great men is the
former. In this dwels that which makes the mind excell, and
which begets a contempt of Humane affairs.[28] From hence you
think nothing but what is Honourable good, and [29] within
this persuasion you possesse your [30] soul and are free from all
molestation from without. For to [31] have a mean opinion of
what [32] most men [33] esteem Great and Honourable, and with
firmnesse and fortitude to contemn them accordingly is an Act
of true magnanimity.[34] At the same time to bear with indifference the various turns of fortune, and be easy under what [35]
others think [36] calamitous, so as to [37] follow reason and Nature
is a token of Equall Constancy. He that appears a Stranger to
fear, must be as able to resist Lawlesse [38] desire, and the man
who is patient of Fatigue, must be as insencible to pleasure.
Above all this, care must be taken to avoid the Love of Money,
for as there is nothing more mean than to make money ye God,
when you have it not, so there is nothing more great than to
use it with Liberality and Magnificence if you have it. We
must [39] be cautious how We entertain ev'n the Love of Glory,
for this passion may endanger the Liberty of the Soul, which
is essentiall to its Greatnesse.[40] Under all this it is not understood but that Great Employments are to be desired, that is to
say accepted, and sometimes [41] resigned. But on such Occasions,
the Soul is to be free from all perturbations,[42] from Ambition,
fear, discontent, pleasure or anger, that Her Tranquillity and
Security in Her self may be preserved, without which [43] Her
Constancy and Dignity vanish and disappear.

Such, My Lord, is the State of mind requisite to form a Great
man according to the Old Way of thinking and a noble indifference with relation to man's own life or fortune, in the Service

of the Publick, was [44] anciently of absolute necessity to the
denomination of Great among men, but the New Way is to
think of the Publick in the second place, or not at all [45] and
with a very few maxims much more easy [46] and much more
profitable the moderns grow up to their desired [47] eminence.
This Subject is of [48] high consequence and ought to be treated
with the most carefull perspicuity. Your Lordship will therefore allow me to divide the *Greatnesse* which is now in fashion
and made the Object of our Wishes into

Personall
Domestick and
Genealogicall

Personall Greatness consists in maintaining [49] Supporting [50] and
Gratifying Self Love, with all the outward shows of esteem and
Benevolence that can be given by those who converse with or
approach us. If this outward show is made by one who mortally
hates [51] and contemns the man to whome he pays it, He exalts
that despis'd person still the more, and when two Courtiours
are dealing Civilities to each other, He who hates [52] the more
Heartily pays the [53] Greater Homage. For as good Breeding is
the *Art of Hiding ill Will* [54] *and expressing good will* [55] a man
who understands the World, is much more pleas'd with the
respect paid Him by a man who is not sincere in it, than by a
man who [56] is. The latter indeed does Him a pleasure, but the
former affords Him a Triumph. Complacency and Mutuall
affection are ingredients of delight among Low People, Good
Neighbours, and Agreeable Companions, but Ambition considers these affections are the effect of Saucinesse and Freedome,
which [57] destroys the delight the man of the world takes in
reflecting that His Spirit is too Awfull to let another's be disengag'd and capable of its own [58] operations when in his Lordships presence. [59] From Hence it appears that personall Greatnesse consists in [60] being indifferent whether We are Lov'd or
Hated by others while We are too Powerfull [61] in [62] the way
to [63] our own desires. These desires in former days tended,
when not governed according [to] the strict old rule above
mentioned, to Vain Glory & Popularity: [64]
But inordinate riches have now taken another Bent, and are

41

all comprehended in the [65] single passion [66] for Growing rich. Love of mankind and the publick does not now, My Lord, subsist even in the affection and Hypocrisy of it, But Self interest as necessarily weighs down all Spirits as Gravity does all bodies. The Center of a Great man is Himself. He Shows his Love of His Prince by getting as many Pictures of Him as He can on His Coin, and His Love of His Countrey by purchasing as many Acres of it as He can for His own Use. The King is beloved by the Guinnea, and the Countrey by the Furlong. It is indeed very true that Y[r] Lordship made, that We Know of but very little progresse in this Kind of Greatnesse, and Wealth seemed to be in y[r] view but as a consequent of [67] successes in another Kind, and not as your first motive. But it must be allowed that your L[p] has enjoy'd as much of the other parts of Grandeur, particularly that of the Homage of those who hated You, as any man living ever did. Your Lordship knows within ten or Twenty shillings the Price of Every [68] considerable man's integrity in England,[69] and by that Knowledge have had the Satisfaction of making the Haughty servile, the [70] Affected Patriot sell His Countrey, the Church Zealot take laws from a Fanatick, and Youths of Wit and Pleasure grow Knaves and Politicians: With this reluctant train of Followers what Great things have you done! and to what Height did you raise your Personall Greatnesse at the Head of a Crowd of men differing [71] from each other in every other Circumstance, but that of Hating and Obeying Your Lordship: To Conclude this Topick, I cannot tell whether Your Lordship despised or ——[?] being rich. But sure I am that all y[r] designs terminated in Your own advantage, whether you placed it in Wealth or in Power:

The second division of Greatnesse among the Moderns is [72] Domestick, and that is the endeavour to make our Own the first of the Children of Men. In order to this We are to breake through all Freindships,[73] Engagements, and familiarities to [74] adorn our Wives with Jewels,[75] bestow our Daughters into Great estates, and make our sons Shine in Equipage and Luxury.

The third partition is Greatnesse Genealogicall, which, when our own immediate House is provided for, [is] to grow publick spirited and Extend our thoughts to our next relations. To Smugg up all the faces that own our Blood into new aspects of

Joy and insolence, and on all occasions to prefer them to the rest of the species, to think in Military discipline it is no injury to prefer a Fresh whole man for King's Service, before a Veteran [76] with one Legg or one Arm, that is sawcy for His Services and can't appear in a Withdrawing to grace the Court of his master, in a Word to [77] examine the merits of all pretenders to [78] preferrment Ecclesiasticall, Military, or Civil with this plain proverbiall Question *What's He akin to Me.*

Thus, My Lord, you observe that to be Great, is only to take great care of Your self, and whatever you do to provide for your self and family the care of the nation, you know, my Lord, must necessarily follow. For that indeed is every bodye's duty to take care of and therefore great men need not trouble Themselves about it; It will do, as it has from time to time of it self; It is, My Lord a most [79] frightfull task to attempt the amendment or better Government of the World. It is certainly as much as ought to be expected from any Man of Power to Keep it from Breaking to pieces, while He is cutting a large share of it's conveniences to Himself, and after that [80] consign it to other hands till they also have allotted and divided to themselves as reasonable a Portion. Your Lordship knows what vast [81] Blessings attend a man that's true to Himself and attends his own businesse with an Obstinate and careful negative to the rest of the World. A Man shall get money, by only Loving, and the mere reckoning of money with an unfeigned Love towards it, will make you master of a great share of it, and no man living the Worse. You may have known a Clerk of an Hundred [a] year, in [82] seven years save [83] as much of it, as if He had lived upon half of it, to the Age of Methuselah. The Shortnesse of our days is made up to us in the Extent of Our Capacities and since Gain is the purpose of life, He among us that has lived fifty Year and sav'd fifty-thousand pounds has fought a better fight, than an Antediluvian, who liv'd five hundred year and When the Deluge came, was drowned in it not worth a Groat.

Isaack Bickerstaffe Esq. to Pasquin (1711?)

The manuscript is not intact, and a completely satisfactory interpretation of the pamphlet without the missing leaves cannot be made. Nevertheless, as it stands, it is an interesting statement, the earliest, of Steele's Whiggism. There is no record of its having been published.

The particular background is two provocative letters of political coloring, anonymous of course, introduced into *The Tatler* in 1710— No. 129 on 4 February and No. 187 on 20 June—from "Pasquin of Rome to Isaac Bickerstaff of Great Britain." Steele had printed the letters without comment except to indicate his satisfaction at the correspondence and to explain the name Pasquin (in No. 130). That he refrained from answering them in *The Tatler* was probably due, in part, to remonstrance from several quarters against the intrusion of politics in his periodical, for example the blunt letter signed Aminadab in No. 190 on 27 June and that signed Orontes, dated 6 July (published later in Lillie's *Original and Genuine Letters*, I, 56-7). Steele admits in the tract that printing the Pasquin letters had damaged the circulation of *The Tatler* to the amount of several pounds and had alienated some of his friends "whom separated from the business of your correspondence I cannot but love." Prudence also must have deterred him: for he was holding two government posts, editorship of *The Gazette* and a place on the Stamp Commission, and his patrons were relinquishing their power— Sunderland, Secretary for the Southern Department, in June; Godolphin, Lord Treasurer, in August; Henry Boyle, Secretary for the Northern, and Cowper, Lord Chancellor, in September,

The general background for it was, apparently, the somewhat tumultuous first session of the new Tory parliament (25 November 1710 to 4 June 1711), which followed upon the Sacheverell trial in the spring, the fall of the Whig ministry, the general election of the autumn. For months the Sacheverell motif continued strong. The church was at the height of power; and the Tory Commons, dominated by the high church party, seemed to have been returned only to carry out its interests.

Steele addresses himself chiefly in the tract to two of Pasquin's queries. In the first letter Pasquin had asked for "an account of those two religious orders . . . the Whigs and the Tories"; in the second— what makes it possible for a criminal (Sacheverell) to "pass through your towns with acclamations, etc." The answers to these questions constitute a downright and plain expression of Steele's Whiggism, the earliest direct testimony that the main root of his political creed was in Revolution principles. But whereas the question of the dynasty most often engaged him in later tracts, in this it is the Act of Toleration for

Protestant Dissenters. And on points at issue in relation to church and state, we have here a basic statement of his position as a moderate.

Before defining the Low Churchman—the type of Whig with whom inferentially he identifies himself—Steele, to forestall criticism, affirms his belief in the Established Church, as an integral part of "Our Government and Constitution which We cannot resign but with the whole," and in the clergy, whose interests are "interwoven with the State." The Low Churchman, he says, is a product of the Revolution and the reign of William, who holds the creed that religion should be esteemed according to its effect on a man's actions. Moderation and tolerance are the Low Churchman's first tenets. Their beneficent effect on the fanatical Puritan, in contrast to the mistaken method of persecution in the seventeenth century, has been to bring many dissenters into the Established Church and to make good citizens of them all, even the zealous Roundhead. This same tolerance is now being shown the new type of zealot, at the other extreme, more dangerous because more subtle, the High Churchman, whose every action is motivated by the cry of danger to the church. An example of this moderation, Steele asserts, was the restraint shown toward the armed mobs escorting and meeting Dr. Sacheverell, the impeached High Tory, in his triumphant journey across the country to his new benefice. Such restraint was a demonstration that the low church is "steady in its measures" and gives "the new Phanatics the same toleration which they did to the old ones." In this time of real peril to church and state—the war with Roman Catholic France—the chief aim of the Low Churchman, according to Steele, is to keep the old and the new fanatic from tearing each other to pieces.

The date of the tract cannot be fixed precisely. It was written, of course, after Pasquin's second letter, 20 June 1710 (alluded to as "your last"), but not too long afterward, as popular interest is assumed in the Pasquin letters and the name Bickerstaff. If the reference to "the Bille, which we have all liberty to read," means what it appears to mean, then parliament was in session; and therefore the months from June to November 1710 during the recess are ruled out. Up to Christmas 1710, the new parliament was engaged only with routine business relating to controverted elections and the conduct of the war, with no bills introduced bearing on the church. In the early months of 1711, therefore, the date of the tract should lie. That would be about the time when Steele made his contribution to *The Medley*. Steele's last *Tatler* paper came out on 2 January 1711 (followed by Harrison's continuation); but the collected volume, No. III, widely circulated, which contained the Pasquin letters, was not published until 17 April.

There is another topical allusion in the tract—to Abel Roper the Tory *Post Boy*—which is not helpful in establishing the date. The piece by Roper Steele refers to may possibly be one which has been ascribed to him: *Impartial Relation of What Has Happened the Most Remarkable in Last Session of Parliament in Case of Sacheverell,* 1710 (See Morgan, *Bibliography of British History* II, 170).

But the only clue to the date worth considering is Steele's casual mention of a church bill, which was doubtless amplified at some point in the missing leaves of the manuscript. And although conjecture may be fruitless, a description of the bills which lie in the realm of possibility will at least show the kind of political manoeuvering which would give a handle to Steele's tract.

Such bills as the Placeholding Bill (January), the Qualification Bill (February), the Resumption Bill (April), which were before parliament from January to the end of the session in June, 1711, can be ruled out as not pertinent. Two others, however, of high church origin and coloring are more likely, although it must be admitted that neither precisely fits Steele's implication that the bill he speaks of is not avowedly high church legislation but is warped to that end or is aligned with the cry of danger to the church: [the present state of fanaticism] "which consists in carrying the interest of the Church above what the Bille, which we have all Liberty to read, ever intended it should arrive." The first of these church bills was one intended to repeal the Act for Naturalizing Foreign Protestants; it was under consideration for only a short time in the Commons, from 15 to 31 January, was passed, and was sent to the Lords, where it was rejected on 10 February at the first reading. The second, a bill for the building of fifty new churches in greater London on a grant of public funds, was formulated in March and passed by both houses in April.

The Bill to repeal the Act for Naturalizing Foreign Protestants was a blow aimed at the toleration for dissent, the very thing that Steele is pleading for in this tract. The Act to be repealed was a Whig law passed in 1709 (incidentally, it had been introduced by Steele's friend, Wortley Montagu) and designed to give the benefits of naturalization to the colony of French Huguenots living in England. The Act had always been unpopular with High Churchmen, and they now professed to believe that it was directly responsible for the influx of Protestant refugees from the German Palatinate in 1709-10, who had become a public charge. The late Whig ministry was accused of having harbored a design against the church by increasing the number of dissenters; and Sunderland (Steele's patron), who as Secretary of State had tried to arrange for the care of the " Palatines," was now censured by Commons. Steele himself spoke several times in *The Tatler* of his sympathy for "these unhappy strangers" and later (1715) did what he could for the Palatinate colony settled in Ireland. It will be seen that this bill

Fanaticus error et Iracunda Diana

Isaack Bickerstaffe Esq To Pasquin.

If I were to regard my own
private interest ~~~~ I protest to You I ~~~~ may say it
were better for me by severall
pounds that I had never corresponded with You, ~~~~
~~~~ my Works being set at
an halfpenny a piece at first
hand ~~~ the Fanaticks ~~~~

^ care so little to hear of Rome that ~~~
~~~~ ^ Severall
of them ~~~~
R[h]emes are ~~~ made Wast
for containing what comes from   paper ~~~~
thence.   ~~~~ greater, ~~~~
~~~~ which is that I am
for what I have published of
yours hated by some men ^ whom
^ separated from the business of Your   I Love and reviled by ~~~~
correspondence I ~~~ not but   ^ you know
whom I honour. But, We are in
the popularity of Opinions, ~~~
~~~~ to take ~~~~
interest ~~~~
no notice of the interpretations
of our Actions if we are
^ both have   right in the design of them.
Surceasing, therefore ~~~~   Your first Letter ~~~~
~~~ proceeds from mistake   ~~~~ concerning the benefits
I shall go on to satisfye yr demands.

might well incite him to write a pamphlet. The bill for the erection of fifty new churches in greater London was undeniably high church political manoeuvering to identify the state with the church. The plan originated in the high-flying Lower House of Convocation, of which Bishop Atterbury was prolocutor, and was hailed by the Tory Commons as a method of fighting schism and dissent. But even though the project grew amazingly from the small beginnings of assistance in repairs for one parish church (Greenwich) to the building of fifty new churches at an expenditure of £350,000 of public money, it seemed to Whigs and Low Churchmen, and presumably to Steele, a more acceptable means of showing favor to the church than repealing the naturalization rights of French Protestants.

Either one of these high church bills before parliament in the period from January to April 1711 may have roused Steele to action. Casting about for a pamphlet design, he would remember the unanswered Pasquin letters. Here was one providing at least partial anonymity, and in it he could use the effctive device of explaining English politics to a foreigner (an idea he later used in *The Romish Ecclesiastical History of Late Years*). The probability is that the date is early 1711. The next striking piece of high church legislation was the Occasional Conformity Act of December 1711, too late, it would seem, for an effective appeal of the " Bickerstaff to Pasquin " theme. Textual notes on p. 653.

Isaack Bickerstaffe Esq. to Pasquin

Fanaticus error et Iracunda Diana. Hor:

Isaack Bickerstaffe Esq, To Pasquin.

If I were to regard my own private interest [1] I protest to You I may [2] say it were better for Me by several pounds that I had never corresponded with You; For tho' my Words are sold at an halfpenny a peice at first hand the Fanaticks care so little to hear of Rome [3] that severall Rhemes of them are made [4] Wast paper for containing what comes from thence. There is another matter of yet greater greif to me [5] which is that I am for what I have published of Yours hated by some men whome separated from the businesse of Your correspondence I can not but Love, and that I am reviled by others [6] whome I honour. But you know We are in the perplexity of Opinions and interests of this World to take no notice of the interpretations of our Actions if we are right in the design of them. Overlooking therefore both love and hatred for and against when it proceeds from mistake I shall go on to satisfye yͬ demands. Your first letter asks me to be particular in Explaining the tenets and merits of the two Sects ⁷ among Us called the Whigs and the Toryes. In order to [do] this ⁸ I must look back into a series of time past.

When this Nation after a long and Bloody War had at last made a sort of Stand in a seeming fall ⁹ of Government during the Usurpation of Oliver Cromwell, Whose great successe and reputation for Military atcheivements preserved that Tyranny for His own life, I say during His Mock-reign and the little time after till the restoration of King Charles the Second, the Nation had felt such Severe instances of their folly in deviating from the old and happy constitution, that nothing could be had in more Just and irreconcilable detestation than those Principles which produced such ¹⁰ convulsions. A Young Prince returning from Exile the Joy and Expectation of an happy people Just restored from the Miseryes which were brought upon them by Enthusiasm, Anarchy and Distraction, could not Himself look more Graceful, or His People more Loyall than by showing the livelyest sense of their present ¹¹ [page 3 missing] [?] rule of their own, as a Contra . . . tion to each other. If the Round-head thought fitt to fast and Pray, the Cavalier believed Himself obliged to Swear and Drink. The Streets were the Scenes both of Riot and Enthusiasm, and the businesse of Heaven and Hell were both professed ¹² in Publick. When the first transports of the restoration were over the Cavaliers began to go into regular Schemes for the Suppression of Fanaticism for the future. The Mistaken method towards this was Persecution, which in cases of Religion always propagates the dissensions ¹³ by turning delusion and obstinacy into Grace and perseverance in the Eye of the Sufferer. This lasted till the Death of that King and His Brother ascended His Throne. [This] Prince was in himself mild, affable, and Just ¹⁴ but by the force of His Religion was prevailed upon ¹⁵ to lay aside the Naturall disposition of His mind and Use the Regall Authority to the Destruction of all our Religious Rights.¹⁶ This introduced the Revolution of which William the third of Glorious Memory was the happy Instrument. It was naturall to a Deliverer to Use ¹⁷ a Fatherly Tendernesse and Impartiall benevolence to Men of All orders and

opinions among His People. This produced the Toleration to
all our Protestant dissenters and had so good an effect that
Crowds of them are come over to the Worship of the Church
of England, and all in Generall to an indifferent behaviour in
common life; the puritan no longer is Bawling in the Streets
for the Iniquities of Israel, but the remains of that sect of People
among Us are orderly in [their] behaviour, and the condescen-
sions used to Dissenters has [sic] made them in the mode and
Practise of ordinary things follow their Occupations with [18]
Peace and Order. The Reign of the Abovementioned Hero
Produced a new Species of men among Us called the Low
Church. These are they [19] who esteem men's Religion [20] according to their Practise and behaviour, and thinke the Church a
Part of Our Government and Constitution which We cannot
resign [21] but with the whole. But at the same time they know
that She Teaches to Love even our Enemies as our Selves, therefore they begin at home when they say abate their pride and
assuage their malice, they Humbly take care to extirpate out of
their own bosomes all that they desire should be removed from
their opposers. These Low Churchmen, Mr. Pasquin, have
brought the Roundhead [22] to act like a reasonable man, to forget
the rebellious Principles of His Father, and to Know that the
words New light, Righteousnesse, the Inward Man and a
thousand others have nothing to do with the ordinary commerce
of Life, but that the right understanding and application of them
must [23] make Him the more obedient to the Civill Magistrate
and to Venture His life for His Prince. This Moderation has
made very many examine [24] whether when their Minister is a
Low Church man, they are not at a needlesse expence in Paying
to a Conventicle when they can hear one, who Loves them quite
as well as any other they can go to. This Low Temper of mind
is the naturall effect of a True Sense of Religion, and as to
their regard of the Ministers of it, these Men are glad that the
interests of spirituall men are so blended and interwoven with
the State that nothing can shake their Secular Advantages.
Their Bishops are Peers of the Realm, and their Exemplary lives
make them such apparent [25] Successors of the Apostles, that
whether their order is derivative from them or not is an insignificant Question.

This, Mr. Pasquin, is a Sketch of our British affairs with relation to religion, but tho this Low party has brought the dissenting Fanatick to reason, We are at present infested with a Spirit of Fanaticism, where it was least Expected which consists in carrying the interest of the Church above what the Bille, which we have all Liberty to read, ever intended it should arrive, and the New Zealots at a time when both She and Her [dissenters?] go hand in hand in the common cause against Her Enemies are apt to be seized with fear for Her in Her Highest prosperity. As the Old Fanatick used to talk of Sanctity regeneration and so forth without any manner of provocation to it, the New ones fall into the same delirium; and whatever Men are treating of they Cry out the Church. The Low people, who really are the Church of England, are ever upon their Guard to keep these two Fanaticks [26] from tearing each other to peices. The Present Fanaticks are in the more dangerous way towards Hurting themselves and others, in that their madnesse is more subtle. They are many of them persons of sense except in the Use of that monosyllable the Church, and a few other Larger Words as Antimonarchiall, Unlimited Passive Obedience, Republican, and Schismaticall and so forth, which are applyed by the new Phanatick as much out of Place as the Tenets of Scripture were brought out in the ravings of the old ones. Thus it is that the Sober part of mankind take a man that drinks night and day and Hussa's for the Church to be as much a Phanatick as He that fasts and prays and talks against all powers and Principalities of the Earth for a Kingdome of Saints. I find by yr last Letter You know at Rome as well as We at London, that a Phanatic Preacher was moved to Abuse all the World from His Pulpit in the Cheif City of Great Brittain, and that because He was generally Known to be what We, here, call a merry Honest Fellow and of all[?] the least inclined to an Enthusiastick one was called to an account thereupon. I do not Know whether you have heard yt He was pronounced Guilty of what was Charged against Him, but I am sure you have that He was very Gently punished. Tho no man pretends to insinuate [27] yt it was too much Learning that made Him Mad, He is a Doctor in Divinity. Soon after this Great Catastrophe of the Tryall of this Casuist, it seemed but necessary to Him in His Way to a

Benefice at the other end of the Island to Visit the Churches. They of Banbury received great consolation from His presence, and all the Brethren there were Comforted on yt occasion with what even that opulent town could afford. The Phanaticks of Warwick and Coventrey were not wanting in Administring to Him also; But you are to remark that as Devout persons according to the Customs of yr Church [28] travell meekly clad [29] and make Pilgrimages, with Us who are a warlike People, they march like faithfull Souldiours and Sergeants [30] in Rank and file Horse and Foot. You Wondered, I warrant You, how it should be that two thousand [31] well appointed Saints should meet this persecuted Brother in one place and three thousand in another in Hostile Habiliments and no one man of them be taken up. You are therefore to understand that this was the Policy of the Low Church, who are Steady in their Measures, and gave [32] the new Phanaticks the same toleration which they did [33] to the old ones. As for the Doctrines of these Enthusiasts [34] I enclose to you a volume of the Ecclesiastical History of them Written by my Learned Contemporary Mr. Abell Roper called the Postboy. As for Antimonarchiall Schismaticall and Republican, these are words wch in their ravings are uttered against [35] the Low Church. But you know by being abroad that it is by their means that the Church of England is in greater purity [?] of Worship [36] than any other, that the Subject has greater liberty than in any Republick, and the Monarchy [of England an Higher Glory than]. . . .

Pamphlets and Papers Attributed to Steele

This list does not pretend to include all of the pamphlets and papers which at one time or another have been attributed to Steele's pen, and lack of space prevents annotation explaining precisely why these were selected for inclusion here. Suffice it to say the titles given are those to which his name—with or without justification—has clung and still clings in library catalogues, book lists, and elsewhere with the most persistency. Doubtless they will all bear further study. It should be borne in mind that the list includes several having very little about them to suggest his handiwork, several that have already been convincingly assigned to other writers, and several that he may conceivably have written in whole or in part.

The Critical Specimen. Ipsa ingens arbos, faciemque simillima lauro: Et si non Alium late jactaret odorem, Laurus erat.— Virg. London: Printed in the Year, 1711.

> 8vo, 16 pp. Pub. late summer(?), 1711. Copy at Texas. The pamphlet is a pretended advertisement for a work to be printed by subscription: *The Mirror of Criticisme: or The History of the Renown'd Rinaldo Furioso, Critick of the Woful Countenance.* (Assigned to Pope.)

Two Letters Concerning the Author of the Examiner. London. Printed and Sold by A. Baldwin. 1713.

> 4to size, 21 pp. Pub. Nov. 1713. Copies at Harvard and Texas. Letter, No. 1: from a country gentleman to his friend in town, dated York, 1 Nov. 1713. Letter, No. 2: from a gentleman in town in answer, dated London, 7 Nov. The tract was reprinted by Abel Boyer in *The Political State of Great Britain* for Nov., 1713.

The Case of Richard Steele, Esq; Being an Impartial Account of the Proceedings against Him. In a Letter to a Friend. London, J. Roberts. 1714.

> 8vo size, 35 pp. Pub. 24 March 1714. Copy at Texas. Translation: *La Cause de Mr. Steele, ou Relation des Procedures qu'on a faites contre lui . . . dans une Lettre a un Ami* (in *Œuvres Diverses de Mr. Richard Steele*. . . . Amsterdam, David Mortier. 1715). Copies at Texas and in Professor Sherburn's collection.

A Full Account of the Proceedings in the Last Session of Parliament against Richard Steele, Esq; With a Defence of His Writings. In a Letter to His Excellency the Earl of N—tt—m. London, J. Roberts. 1714.

> 8vo size, 35 pp. Pub. August, 1714. Copy at Texas. With the exception of the opening paragraph, this tract is like the item immediately above.

The Protestant Packet. Containing the Freshest and Most Faithful Account of All Occurrences Foreign and Domestic. Nos. 1-4. 21 Jan.–11 Feb. 1716. London. [?Roberts]

> Folio. Copies of the four numbers in the Bodleian Library. One paper or more contributed by Steele?

The Layman's Letter to the Bishop of Bangor, or an Examination of His Lordship's Preservative against the Non-jurors . . . London. Roberts, Graves, and Dodd. 1716.

> 4to, 44 p. Pub. April or May, 1716. (Assigned to John Shute Barrington.)

The Tea Table. Nos. 1-3. February and March 1716. London. [J. Baker?]

> No copies known. Three numbers were advertised under the description of a pamphlet to be published fortnightly, No. 1 appearing on 2 Feb. (*St. James's Post,* 6 and 10 Feb. and 2 March). Papers contributed by Steele?

A Vindication of Sir Richard Steele against a Pamphlet entituled A Letter to the Right Worshipful Sir R. S. concerning his Remarks on the Pretender's Declaration. London. J. Roberts. [1716].

> 8vo. Pub. 20 Feb. 1716.

Chit-Chat. In a Letter to a Lady in the Country. By Humphrey Philroye. Nos. 1-3. London, R. Burleigh. 3(?), 10, and 16 March 1716.

> sm. 4to. Copies of Nos. 2 and 3 in the Bodleian Library. One paper or more contributed by Steele?

The Whigg. London. W. Chetwood [publisher? editor?]. 1718.

> No copies known. Weekly(?) periodical. First issue 3 Sept.(?) 1718. One paper or more by Steele?

The D[ean] of W[orceste]r Still the Same; or His New Defence of the Lord Bishop of Bangor's Sermon, &c, Considered as the Performance of a Great Critick, A Man of Sense and a Man of Probity. By an Impartial Hand. London. J. Knapton. 1720.

> 112 pp. Pub. April, 1720. Copy at the University of Chicago. (Assigned to Dr. Benjamin Hoadly.)

A Proposal Humbly Offered to the Consideration of Both Houses of Parliament for Encouraging and Improving Trade in General. London. J. Roberts. 1721.

The TEXTUAL NOTES

THE CHRISTIAN HERO (p. 1)

The Christian Hero, 1701. 8vo, xvi, 95 pp. Pub. April (15-17 Apr., *Post Boy*). Copies at Texas, Harvard, Yale, British Museum, and Huntington Library. Second ed., 1701. 8vo, x, 102 pp. Pub. July (17-19 July, *Post Boy*). Copies at Texas, Yale, British Museum.
Third ed., 1710. 8vo, x, 93 pp. Pub. Nov. (7-9 Nov. *London Gazette*). Copies at *Chicago, Texas, British Museum.
Other numbered edns. published by Tonson: in 1711 (2), 1712, 1722, 1727, 1741.
Edns. published in Dublin: 1725. 8vo, x, 55 pp., copy at Columbia; 1737. 8vo, 64 pp., copy at Texas.
Other edns.: London, 1737, 1755, 1764, 1766 (2), 1776; Whitehaven, 1756; Berwick, 1792; Oxford, 1802; Worcester, Mass., 1802; Philadelphia, 1807; Bungay, 1820. Copies at Texas.
Translation: *Le Heros Chrétien Par le Chevalier R. Steele. Traduit de l'Anglois Par M. A. De Beaumarchais, Et Les Vertus Paiennes Par le Traducteur,* A La Haye, 1729. Copy at the Library of Congress.
For a more detailed bibliography, see *The Christian Hero,* Ed. Rae Blanchard (Oxford University Press, 1932).

The text is that of the third edition (1710). That this one contains Steele's final revisions is shown by a collation of the eight numbered editions published during his lifetime. The second (July 1701) had also contained revisions, corrections, and additions. The variant readings listed below indicate the stylistic alterations of the original text as first issued, for which Steele was undoubtedly responsible, and indicate also the edition, second or third, which first incorporated them. A few obvious misprints in the text of the third edition as given here are silently corrected, usually on the authority of at least one of the earlier editions. In the Preface, the italic and roman print are reversed. A more thorough study of the text will be found in my edition of *The Christian Hero,* pp. xxxi-ii.

[1] Receiv'd : Imbib'd (1st ed.)
[2] they come (added, 2nd ed.)
[3] Real Immortality : real and sensible Immortality (1st ed.)
[4] stamp'd . . . Vices, and (added 2nd ed.)
[5] Essay : discourse (1st ed.)
[6] For ill Habits of the Mind, no more than those of the Body, : For Intellectual ill habits no more than Physical (1st ed.)
[7] For (however they are dis-esteem'd . . . Stab without Hatred. (This paragraph was added, 2nd ed.)
[8] But Virtuous Principles . . . great Attempts, : And such Principles must infallibly be better than any other we can Embrace, not only to warm us to great Attempts (1st ed.)
[9] For as nothing . . . than Innocence : For what can be thought more daring than Truth, more chearful than Innocence (1st ed.)
[10] Happiness is not . . . place it : Happiness is only to be found where I at present place it (1st ed.)

[11] inform'd where only . . . to be had : told where only I should find it 1st ed.)

[12] a melancholy Prospect : Melancholy prospects (1st ed.)

[13] (as some Men would persuade us) (added, 2nd ed.)

[14] engag'd (added, 2nd ed.)

[15] even (added, 2nd ed.)

[16] they arriv'd : arriv'd they (1st ed.)

[17] which he design'd should be his last, : he design'd his last (1st and 2nd edns.)

[18] the Ocean, : Oceans (1st ed.)

[19] admit : easily admit (1st ed.)

[20] having : having through (1st ed.)

[21] the : of the (1st ed.)

[22] for the Extirpation of it : for it's extirpation (1st ed.)

[23] that (added, 3rd ed.)

[24] believ'd 'twas : believ'd that 'twas (1st and 2nd edns.)

[25] it is : 'tis (1st ed.)   it 'tis (2nd ed.)

[26] as (added, 2nd ed.)

[27] and (added, 3rd ed.)

[28] to the taking away : to taking (1st ed.)

[29] it is : 'tis (1st ed.)   it 'tis (2nd ed.)

[30] any farther than it is necessary : but as it is necessary (1st and 2nd edns.)

[31] which (added, 3rd ed.)

[32] and : which (1st and 2nd edns.)

[33] Retreated : had Retreated (1st and 2nd edns.)

[34] after having express'd : after he had expressed (1st and 2nd edns.)

[35] *Brutus* his : Brutus's (1st and 2nd edns.)

[36] *Cassius* his : Cassius's (1st and 2nd edns.)

[37] from the Greatness . . . Philosophy (added, 2nd ed.)

[38] of a (added, 3rd ed.)

[39] Soul : Soul too (1st and 2nd edns.)

[40] Imperceptibly : Imperceptibly to it (1st and 2nd edns.)

[41] Intelligent : Intelligible (1st ed.)

[42] the : a (1st and 2nd edns.)

[43] conscious : nobler (1st ed.)

[44] who : which (1st and 2nd edns.)

[45] to whom : which (1st and 2nd edns.)

[46] Conceptions : Thoughts (1st and 2nd edns.)

[47] whom : which (1st and 2nd edns.)

[48] with whom : on which (1st and 2nd edns.)

[49] did (added, 3rd ed.)

[50] who : who as such (1st ed.)

[51] Crime : cause (1st ed.)

[52] to be (added, 3rd ed.)

[53] in a manner (added, 2nd ed.)

[54] Stones : Stones near him (1st and 2nd edns.)

[55] him : him in (1st and 2nd edns.)

[56] and which : and those themselves (1st ed.)   and those (2nd ed.)

[57] self (added, 3rd ed.)

[58] so strictly apart : to be so strictly apart (1st and 2nd edns.)

[59] who (added, 2nd ed.)

[60] was (added, 2nd ed.)

[61] in that Place (added, 3rd ed.)
[62] longer : longer there (1st and 2nd edns.)
[63] having : as having (1st and 2nd edns.)
[64] such (added, 3rd ed.)
[65] in (added, 2nd ed.)
[66] from (added, 2nd ed.)
[67] but (added, 2nd ed.)
[68] an (added, 2nd ed.)
[69] hath (added, 3rd ed.)
[70] (I say) (added, 3rd ed.)
[71] ones self (added, 3rd ed.)
[72] that such a Person : that Person (1st ed.)   that that Person (2nd ed.)
[73] and (added, 3rd ed.)
[74] you've also : and you've (1st and 2nd edns.)
[75] tight : right (1st ed.)
[76] a certain Beauty : an Harmony (1st ed.)
[77] covers : drowns (1st ed.)
[78] disagreeableness : Incapacities (1st ed.)
[79] who (added, 2nd ed.)
[80] in some measure (added, 2nd ed.)
[81] insuperable : Insupportable (1st ed.)
[82] to : in (1st and 2nd edns.)
[83] drag'd him as Dead : as Dead drag'd him (1st and 2nd edns.)
[84] even (added, 3rd ed.)
[85] a (added, 3rd ed.)
[86] nothing but (added, 2nd ed.)
[87] is : there is (1st ed.)
[88] not the less : nevertheless (1st and 2nd edns.)
[89] the : their (1st and 2nd edns.)
[90] that : he saw (1st and 2nd edns.)
[91] to : into (1st and 2nd edns.)
[92] His : But his (1st and 2nd edns.)
[93] Judgment : Abstinence (1st ed.)
[94] to be (added, 2nd ed.)
[95] Passages : passage (1st ed.)
[96] and (added, 3rd ed.)
[97] This is *Seneca's* very Spirit, Opinion and Genius : This is his very Spirit, Opinion and Genius express'd in better Words than ever he was Master of (1st and 2nd edns.)
[98] as (added, 2nd ed.)
[99] adapted : apt (1st and 2nd edns.)
[100] of : for (1st and 2nd edns.)
[101] the Embraces : that Embrace (1st ed.)   the Embrace (2nd ed.)
[102] absurdly : so absurdly (1st and 2nd edns.)
[103] are (added, 2nd ed.)
[104] but : but that (1st and 2nd edns.)
[105] But since we have hitherto . . . this World can attack it. (This passage of about fifteen paragraphs was added, 2nd ed.)
[106] from : in (2nd ed.)
[107] seldom : seldom ever (2nd ed.)
[108] the (added, 3rd ed.)
[109] Love : Love of it (2nd ed.)

[110] a (added, 3rd ed.)
[111] or the like : and so forth (2nd ed.)
[112] hath (added, 3rd ed.)
[113] manner : kind (2nd ed.)
[114] This point marks the end of the passage beginning with Chap. IV, which was added, 2nd ed.
[115] is : is now (1st and 2nd edns.)
[116] of : under (1st and 2nd edns.)
[117] to (added, 3rd ed.)
[118] though : but (1st ed.)
[119] doth always see : always sees (1st and 2nd edns.)
[120] in (added, 2nd ed.)
[121] is : would be (1st ed.)

THE MEDLEY. No. 23 (p. 63)

The Medley. First series: 5 Oct. 1710-6 Aug. 1711. Weekly, single sheet folio. Nos. 1-45. London, Printed and sold by A. Baldwin. Contributors: Maynwaring, Oldmixon, Addison, et al.

No. 23. Monday, 26 Feb.-5 March 1711. Anon. First part by Steele. *A copy of the folio at Texas.

Reprinted: (1) *The Medleys for the Year 1711. To which are prefix'd The Five Whig-Examiners.* London, Printed by John Darby and sold by Egbert Sanger: 1712. 12mo. Copy at Indiana University. (2) *The Lover and the Reader; To which are prefix'd The Whig-Examiner and a Selection from the Medley . . . A New Edition with Notes and Illustrations.* Printed by and for John Nichols, London, 1789.

The text is that of the original issue in folio, which was not altered in any particular in the collected *Medleys for the Year 1711* (1712). The final section of No. 23 is not reproduced here. It is " A Comparison between the Examiner and His Brother Abel," not written by Steele.

THE ENGLISHMAN'S THANKS (p. 66)

The Englishman's Thanks to the Duke of Marlborough, 1712. Anon. Size, 6.3 by 8 inches, 5 pp. Pub. 4 Jan. (*Daily Courant*). Copies in the British Museum and at Yale.

Reprinted: **The Political Writings of Sir Richard Steele,* 1715.

The text is that of Steele's reprint in his *Political Writings,* which shows only a few minor alterations from the first edition in spelling and capitalization, such as Councils (first), Counsels; Countrey (first), Country; Easy Mien (first), Easie Mein.

A LETTER TO SIR M. W. (p. 72)

A Letter to Sir M.[iles] W.[arton] Concerning Occasional Peers, 1713. Anon. Single sheet folio, two columns on one side. Dated 5 March 1713. Publisher and publication date not known. Copy in the British Museum.

Reprinted: **The Political Writings of Sir Richard Steele,* 1715. The separate

42

title for the tract in this collected edition reads: *A Letter to Sir Miles Wharton, Concerning Occasional Peers. Written in the Year 1713.*

The text used is that reprinted by Steele in his *Political Writings.* Collation of this with the text of the first edition indicates no changes except in spelling and capitalization, and a very few of these: such as, shewn (first), shown; Half Dozen (first), half dozen; outlives (first), out-lives.

GUARDIAN No. 128 (p. 79)

The Guardian of August the 7th, 1713 (No. 128). Anon., folio, London, Printed for J. Tonson and Sold by A. Baldwin. This seems not to have been issued except in the folio-sheet format of the *Guardian* papers, but Steele did include it as a separate item in his *Political Writings* of 1715, pp. 15-19.

Translation: *Raisons pour la Demolition de Dunkerque Du 7 Août 1713,* Amsterdam, David Mortier, 1714 (in *Oeuvres diverses de Mr. Richard Steele,* Amsterdam, 1715). Copies at Texas and in Professor Sherburn's collection.

The complete text is given here as a part of the tract, *The Importance of Dunkirk Consider'd: in Defence of the Guardian of August the 7th. . . .* See pp. 94-97 of this volume.

THE IMPORTANCE OF DUNKIRK (p. 83)

The Importance of Dunkirk Consider'd, 1713. 4to, 63 pp. (Some copies have the folding map designed for *The French Faith . . . in Dunkirk,* 1714). Pub. 22 Sept. (*Guardian* No. 167). Copies at Texas, Goucher College, and elsewhere.

Second ed., 1713. 8vo, 40 pp. Pub. 26 Sept. ("with a small letter" *Guardian* No. 171). Copy at Harvard.

Third ed., 1713. 8vo, 40 pp. Pub. 29 Sept. (*Guardian* No. 173). Copies at Texas and at McGill University.

Fourth ed., 1713. 8vo, 40 pp. Copies at Chicago and Texas.

Other edns.: "4to, 1 shilling and 8vo, 6 pence for J. Roberts" (*Englishman* No. 27, 5 Dec. 1713).

Another ed., Printed by R. Reily, London, 1730. Copy at Harvard.

Translations: (1) *Réflexions sur l'importance de Dunkerque.* Trad. de l'anglois. Londres., 12mo (Aitken's record). (2) *Reflexions sur l'importance de Dunkerque et sur l'état present de cette place . . . Par Mr. Richard Steele.* Traduit de l'Anglois. Amsterdam, David Mortier, Libraire, 1715 (in *Oeuvres diverses,* Amsterdam, 1715). Copy at Texas.

Reprinted: *The Political Writings of Sir Richard Steele,* 1715.

The text is that of Steele's reprint in his *Political Writings* (1715). Collation of this text with that of the first edition shows that in addition to the few verbal changes given below, there are a good many variations in capitals, punctuation, and spelling, none of any significance. A few obvious misprints in the text of *Political Writings* are silently corrected in the present text, usually on the authority of the first edition.

¹ The Latin motto for this *Guardian* paper in the original issue is *Delenda est Carthago.* Except for this omission, it is printed here verbatim.

² to them : them (first edition).

³ two : three (In the original *Guardian* paper, but corrected in the first
edition of *The Importance* and in the *Guardian* text of *Political Writings*.
In *Guardian*, No. 131, Steele himself, in another letter signed " English
Tory," called for this correction.)

⁴ their (omitted in the collected edition).

⁵ Advertisement : Admonition (first edition; the correction was indicated in
an *erratum* at the end and was silently made in subsequent editions).

THE CRISIS (p. 125)

The Crisis, 1714 (Some copies dated 1713, i. e. Old Style). 4to, vii, 37 pp.
Pub. 19 Jan. (*Englishman,* No. 46). Copies at the Library of Congress, British
Museum, Texas, Goucher College, and elsewhere.

Second ed., London, 1714. 8vo size, vii, 38 pp. Copies at Harvard and in
the collection of A. E. Case.

Pirated ed., London, 1714. 21 cm., 24 pp. Printed by J. Read. Pub. 25 Jan.
(" very imperfect and erroneous," *Englishman,* No. 49). Copy at Texas.

Another ed., Edinburgh, 1714. 8vo, 58 pp. [Printed and sold at Mrs. Ogston's
shop or David Scot's]. Copies at Texas, Chicago, and McGill University.

Another ed., Dublin, 1714. 8vo, xvi, 70 pp. Reprinted by A. Rhames. Copy
at Texas.

Another ed., Philadelphia, 1725. Printed by Samuel Keimer. (Reported by
Evans: *American Bibliography*).

Translations: (1) *La Crise ou discours où l'on démontre par les actes les
plus authentiques les justes causes de l'heureuse revolution . . . Traduit de
l'Anglois par Mr.* [Abel] *Boyer.* 4to, xv, 52 pp. Imprimé pour Ferd. Burleigh,
A Londres. Pub. 1 Feb. 1714 (*Englishman,* Nos. 49 and 51). Copy in the
collection of A. E. Case. (2) *La Crise ou discours où l'on démontre par les
actes les plus authentiques les justes causes de l'heureuse revolution. . . .
Traduit de l'Anglois de Mr. Richard Steele.* Amsterdam, David Mortier, 1714
(in *Oeuvres diverses de Mr. Richard Steele,* Amsterdam, 1715. Copy at Texas).
(3) *Des Herrn Richard Steele Crisis,* Hamburg, 1714. 4to (Aitken).
Reprinted: **The Political Writings of Sir Richard Steele,* 1715.

The text is that of *Political Writings,* which shows only four verbal alterations
of the first edition. There are, however, a number of variations in spelling,
capitalization, and punctuation. Several obvious misprints of the first edition are
corrected; and several new ones creep in, which are silently corrected in this
present edition.

¹ and : or (first edition).
² another : one other (first edition).
³ judged : adjudged (first edition).
⁴ Succession : Accession (first edition).

THE ENGLISHMAN No. 57 (p. 183)

The Englishman: Being the Close of the Paper So Called (No. 57), 15 Feb.
1714. 4to, 22 pp. Copies at Texas, British Museum, Goucher College.

Second ed., 17 Feb. (*Daily Courant*). 4to, 22 pp. Copy at Texas.

Translation: *L'Anglois pour servir de Clôture aux Feuilles volantes qui ont
paru sous ce titre: Le dernier Anglois de Mr. Steele du* $\frac{15}{26}$ *Fevrier 1714,*
Amsterdam, David Mortier, 1714 (in *Oeuvres diverses de Mr. Richard Steele,*
Amsterdam, 1715). Copy at Texas.

Reprinted: *The Englishman: Being the Sequel of the Guardian [coll. edn., 12mo]. London, Sam. Buckley, 1714. Pub. 3 June 1714.

The text is that of the collected edition of The Englishman, which varies only in a few details of punctuation and capitalization from that of the pamphlet, first edition.

MR. STEELE'S SPEECH (p. 213)

Mr. Steele's Speech upon the Proposal of Sir Thomas Hanmer for Speaker of the House of Commons. London, 1714. 4to size, 5 pp. *Copy in the British Museum. Speech delivered 16 Feb. 1714 and presumably printed at once. Reprinted: Mr. Steele's Apology for Himself and His Writings, p. 25.

The text used is that of the small separate tract in the British Museum, which was doubtless unauthorized by Steele and the phrasing of which probably not so near the text of his speech as that given in The Apology. See p. 293.

THE ROMISH ECCLESIASTICAL HISTORY (p. 215)

The Romish Ecclesiastical History of Late Years, 1714. 8vo, [xiv], xii, vi, 168 pp. Pub. 25 May (Daily Courant, 21 and 26 May). But see The Lover, No. 19, April 8, 1714, where it is advertised for "This Day." Some copies lack leaf F 8, pp. 79-80. Copies in the British Museum, at Chicago, Texas, Library of Congress, *Goucher College.
Another ed.(?) Pub. by Tonson (advertised in Addison's Spectator, No. 565, 9 July 1714).
Translation: L'Histoire ecclesiastique de Rome, A. H. de Sallengre (Aitken's record, not confirmed).

The parts of the text which are reproduced are thought by the present editor certainly to be Steele's: the Dedication, the Preface, the introductory paragraphs, pp. 1-4, Chap. I, pp. 20-26, Chap. II, pp. 38-44. The long translated manuscript, the framework of the tract, constitutes the remainder, with the exception of a final interpolation in Chap. III, pp. 82-101, which seems to be the work of a collaborator. In the Preface as printed here, the italic and roman forms of the original are reversed. Only one point in the long list of errata applies to the portion written by Steele.
[1] profess'd a Minorite : a Profess'd Minorite (first ed.).

A LETTER TO A MEMBER (p. 237)

A Letter to a Member . . . Concerning the Bill for Preventing the Growth of Schism, 1714. 4to, 23 pp. Pub. 3 June (Daily Courant). Copies at Texas, British Museum, Chicago, Goucher College.
Second ed., 1714. 4to, 23 pp. Pub. 4 or 5 June (Daily Courant). Copies at Texas, Library of Congress, and McGill University.
Another ed. (?), 1714. 4to, 23 pp. (differing from the first and second in details on the title and the half-title and in the arrangement of signatures and lacking the advertisement at the end). Copy at Texas: WK St 32 714 1c.
Another ed., Dublin, Reprinted by Eliza Dickinson on Cork Hill, 1714. 4to, 24 pp. (listed by Aitken and Morgan).
Another ed., Edinburgh, Reprinted in the Year 1714. sm. 8vo, 31 pp. Copy at the Huntington Library.

Translation: *Lettre de Mr. Steele à un Member du Parlement sur le Bill qu'on destine à prévenir l'accroissement de schisme,* Amsterdam, chez David Mortier, 1714 (in *Oeuvres diverses de Mr. Richard Steele,* Amsterdam, 1715). Copy at Texas.

Reprinted: *The Political Writings of Sir Richard Steele,* 1715.

The text is that of *Political Writings* (1715), which indicates only minor alterations from the first edition.

[1] tho' (first edition; but omitted, by oversight, in the collected form).
[2] own (first edition; omitted in the collected form).

THE FRENCH FAITH (p. 255)

The French Faith Represented in the Present State of Dunkirk, 1714. Anon. 4to, 20 pp. With a folding map. Pub. 2 July (Addison's *Spectator,* No. 562). Copies at Texas, Newberry Library, and the Library of Congress.

Translation: *Reflexions sur l'importance de Dunkerque et sur l'état present de cette place. Avec une carte de nouveau port a Mardick & le plan des anciens ouvrages de Dunkerque. Par Mr. Richard Steele. Traduit de l'Anglois.* Amsterdam, Chez David Mortier, 1715 (in *Oeuvres diverses de Mr. Richard Steele,* Amsterdam, 1715—copy at Texas).

Reprinted: *The Political Writings of Sir Richard Steele,* 1715.

The text used is that of the reprint in *Political Writings,* which shows only a few alterations from the first edition and those in italics, punctuation, and the like.

[1] Steele's note at this point in the first edition: "A Map of the Places adjacent to Dunkirk. With ye Project of ye New Port at Mardick." In *Political Writings* the direction is given: "The Map to be inserted between Page 88 and 89." The same map was inserted in *Mr. Steele's Apology* (1714), and we find it in some copies of *The Importance of Dunkirk.* It is reproduced in this volume on p. 265.

MR. STEELE'S APOLOGY (p. 275)

Mr. Steele's Apology for Himself and His Writings, 1714. 4to, 88 pp. With a folding map. Pub. 22 Oct. (*Daily Courant*). Copies at Texas, British Museum, Library of Congress, Goucher College.

Reprinted: *The Political Writings of Sir Richard Steele,* 1715.

The text is that of *Political Writings.* Collation with the first edition shows many alterations in minor details of italics, capitals, and punctuation but nothing of consequence.

[1] The entire Preface is printed in italics in *Political Writings.*
[2] The note beginning "N. B." was added to the text in *Political Writings.*
[3] probably (omitted in the collected edition).

AN ACCOUNT OF THE ROMAN–CATHOLICK RELIGION (p. 347)

An Account of the State of the Roman-Catholick Religion, 1715. 8vo, lxxviii, viii, 198 pp. Pub. 13 May (*Daily Courant,* 12 May; *Post Boy,* 14 May). Copies at *Texas, British Museum, and elsewhere.

Second ed., 1716. 12mo, iv, lxx, viii, 202, ix pp. Pub. Nov. or Dec., 1715 (*Daily Courant,* 9 Dec. 1715). Copies at *Texas, Chicago, and elsewhere.

Translations of the entire tract: (1) *L'etat présent de l'Eglise Romaine dans toutes les parties du monde, ecrit . . . par Urbano Cerri, traduit de l'anglois par Jean Remond.* Amsterdam, 1716, 8vo. (Aitken). (2) *Etat présent de l'Eglise . . .* [trans. A. H. de Sallengre], 1716, 8vo (Michaud, *Biographie Universelle, sub.* Sallengre).

Translation of the dedication (Dedication written by Bishop Hoadly, signed by Steele): (1) *Epître dédicatoire du Chev. R. Steele au pape Clement XI . . . tra. de l'Anglois par A. Boyer,* London, Baldwin, 1715, 4to. Pub. May or June ("Just published" *Daily Courant,* 4 June). (2) *Epître dédicatoire au Pope Clement XI. Par Mr. le Chevalier Steele. Traduite de l'Anglois pour la troisieme fois, avec son approbation.* Londres, 1717, 8vo. (3) *Mr. Pillonniere's* [Francis de la] *Preface, notes, and additions to his French translation of Sir Richard Steele's Epistle Dedicatory to Pope Clement XI . . . Done into* English [London?], 1717, 8vo.

The text of Preface No. 1 is that of the first edition and the text of No. 2 is that of the second edition; in both prefaces as given here the italic and roman print have been reversed.

A LETTER FROM THE EARL OF MAR (p. 357)

A Letter from the Earl of Mar to the King, 1715. 8vo size, 19 pp. Pub. 30 Sept. (*Daily Courant*). Copies at Texas, British Museum, Newberry Library, and *Goucher College.

Another ed., London, 1715. 8vo, 32 pp. (Morgan).
Another ed., Edinburgh, 1715. 12mo, 24 pp. Copy at Yale.
Another ed., Glasgow, 1715. 8vo. (Aitken).
Another ed., London, 1752. 4to. (Morgan).
Translation: *Lettre de My Lord Mar au roi de la Grande Bretagne &c avec des remarques par M. le Chevalier Steele. Traduit de l'Anglois* [n. d.]. Copy at the Library of Congress.
Reprinted (1) at the end of some copies of *The Englishman,* Vol. II, 1716, 1737. (2) *Somers' Tracts,* 4th Coll., 1751, IV, 426-32. (3) *The Town Talk, The Fish Pool, The Plebeian . . . First Collected in 1789; With Notes and Illustrations. A New Edition.* London, Printed by and for John Nichols, 1790, pp. 130-45.

The text used is that of the first edition, except for the corrections, silently made, of several misprints chiefly in spelling, which are corrected also in the text printed at the back of the collected *Englishman* (2nd series, 1716). The Oaths of Abjurgation and Allegiance are omitted from the latter text.

TOWN TALK. No. 5 (p. 373)

Town-Talk. In a Letter to a Lady in the Country. (9 Nos., 17 Dec. 1715 to 13 Feb. 1716). No. 5. 13 Jan. 1716. Signed: R. S. 4to (8$\frac{3}{16}$ by 5$\frac{3}{4}$ inches), paging 51-67. *Copy at Texas.

Second ed. (?). Third ed., 1716, copies in the British Museum and at Texas. Fourth ed., 1716, copy at Harvard. Fifth ed., 1716, copy in the British Museum.

Reprinted: *The Town Talk, The Fish Pool, The Plebeian . . . Now First Collected: With Notes and Illustrations,* London, Printed by and for John Nichols, 1789, 1790.

The text used is that of the first edition with the corrections as indicated in the *Errata*.

[1] Expectations: Exceptions (first edition)

[2] you: (its omission was noted in the *Errata* of the first edition and the correction was made in the third edition)

THE BRITISH SUBJECT'S ANSWER (p. 389)

The British Subject's Answer to the Pretender's Declaration, London, J. Roberts, J. Graves, and A. Dodd, 1716 (2 pence). Single folio half-sheet, 12⅝ by 7¾ inches, two columns on both sides. Pub. 17-19 Jan. (*Evening Post*). Copies in the British Museum and the *Collection of Professor Sherburn.
Reprinted: *Somers' Tracts*, 4th Coll., 1751, IV, 190-6.

The text used is that of the folio half-sheet.

A LETTER TO A MEMBER (p. 403)

A Letter to a Member . . . Concerning the Condemn'd Lords, n. d., Anon. 4to, 12 pp. Pub. 6 March 1716 (*Postman*). Copy in the British Museum; *photostat at Goucher College.
Reprinted: *The Town Talk, The Fish Pool, The Plebeian . . . Now First Collected; With Notes and Illustrations*, London, Printed by and for John Nichols, 1789, pp. 165-181; 1790, pp. 167-183.

The text used is that of the first edition.

SIR RICHARD STEELE'S SPEECH (p. 416)

Sir Richard Steel's Speech for Repealing of the Triennial Act and His Reasons for the Septennial Bill. As it was Spoken in the House of Commons. In Answer to Several Speeches made against it: the 24th of April 1716. London Printed and Reprinted in Dublin, C. C., 1716. The pamphlet examined with this title page contains also the annalist's notes on the procedure and the speeches of Mr. Lydall, Mr. Hampden, and Mr. Tuffnel. It is inferred, however, from the arrangement of the pamphlet that Steele's speech was first printed separately with this title page. And other records seem to indicate that another title page including the names of the other speakers was used for some copies of the same pamphlet. See Morgan, *Bibliography of British History*, II, No. S 414. Without doubt, the publication was unauthorized by Steele, the text probably being taken from Boyer's *Political State*, XI, 471-3. The pamphlet consists of 12 pages consecutively numbered. *Copy at Trinity College, Dublin.
Reprinted: (1) *The Town Talk, The Fish Pool, The Plebeian . . . Now First Collected; With Notes and Illustrations*. London, Printed by and for John Nichols, 1789, pp. 182-4; 1790, pp. 183-6. (2) William Cobbett, *Parliamentary History*, VII, 325-6.

The text is that of the copy in the library at Trinity College, Dublin, which has been collated with the text of what was probably its source, *Political State*, XI, 471-3, and also with that of *Historical Register*, I, 364-6.

[1] At this point there follows an account of the procedure in the House, of other speeches, and of the division at 11 o'clock at night, with the date, 25 April. Then " Finis," followed by the statement that speeches of Mr. Lydall, Mr. Hampden, and Mr. Tufnell will be printed " with all Expedition."

THE FISH POOL (p. 419)

An Account of the Fish-Pool, 1718. 8vo size, vii, 60 pp. Pub. 19 Nov. (*Daily Courant*). Copies in the British Museum, at Texas, Chicago, *Goucher College, and elsewhere.

Reprinted: *The Town Talk, The Fish Pool, The Plebeian, The Old Whig, The Spinster . . . Now First Collected; With Notes and Illustrations,* London, Printed by and for John Nichols, 1789, pp. 193-250; 1790, pp. 187-236.

A new edition of the *Account* was announced on 13 March 1721 (*Daily Post*), but no copy of it is known.

A second tract was advertised on 13 July 1719 (" In a few Days will be published," *Daily Courant*) of which there is no further record: *A Postscript to a Pamphlet call'd The Fish Pool. Being an Account of the Accomplishments and Success of that Useful Design.*

The text is that of the first edition except that two corrections called for in Steele's *errata* at the end of the pamphlet are incorporated.

[1] 62.5 : 62.75 (first edition).

[2] 966.5 : 982 (first edition).

[3] At this point, before "Finis," Steele gives in full the Royal Letters Patent issued to him by King George on 10 June 1718. The gist of this lengthy, repetitive document is that Sir Richard Steele, his Executors, Administrators, and Assigns shall have the sole use and benefit of this invention called the Fish Pool for a term of fourteen years. The patent is given for the reasons that Sir Richard Steele has represented in his petition (of February): " that he has for some Years last past, turn'd the Intention and Bent of his Thoughts and Studies to the Good and Services of the Publick; that he has from much Search, Enquiry and Conversation, among sundry Artists, Artificers, and Persons of Learning, at great Expence, invented a certain Vessel, which, by the Structure thereof, can bring Fish where-ever caught, to any distant Place, alive and in Health; that the said invention will greatly contribute to the general Good of all our Subjects. . . ."

N. B. The illustrative diagrams scattered through Steele's original tract were assembled on two plates by Nichols for use in his reprint (1789). These plates are reproduced in the present volume, following p. 450.

THE PLEBEIAN (p. 453)

The Plebeian. To be Continued Weekly . . . By a Member of the House of Commons. Anon. Nos. I-IV.

No. I. 14 March 1719. 4to, 16 pp., five " editions." Copy of the first at Texas. Copies of the second in the British Museum and in Professor Sherburn's collection. Copy of the third not found. Copy of the fourth in the British Museum. Copies of the fifth in Professor Sherburn's collection and at Texas. These seem to be new editions only by designation on the title page. A list of *errata,* however, is given on p. 16 of the second and the corrections called for are made in the fifth (The third and fourth were not available for checking).

No. II. 23 March 1719. 4to., 18 pp., number of " editions " ? Copies of the first in Professor Sherburn's collection and at Texas. Copies of the second in Professor Sherburn's collection and in the British Museum. Copy of the fourth at Texas. The title page of the second contains an addition to the Latin motto, but the body of the tract, in the copy examined, is exactly like that of the first with none of the corrections called for in the *errata* of the first.

No. III. 30 March 1719. 4to, 10 pp., four "editions." Copies of the first in Professor Sherburn's collection and at Texas. Copies of the second and third not found. Copy of the fourth at Texas.

No. IV. 6 April 1719. 4to, 20 pp., four "editions" (Aitken's record). Copies of the first in the collection of Professor Sherburn and in the British Museum. Copy of the second in the collection of Professor Sherburn. Copies of the third and fourth not found.

The Plebeians. 6th ed. [collected ed.], 1719. 4to, 68 pp. Pub. 9-12 May (*Post Boy*). Copies in the British Museum and at *Texas.

The title page of this collected edition and of No. I, first edition, are reproduced in facsimile in this book. Transcripts of the title pages of Nos. II, III, and IV are given below.

Reprinted: (1) *The Town Talk, The Fish Pool, The Plebeian . . . Now First Collected; With Notes and Illustrations,* London, Printed by and for John Nichols, 1789, 1790. (2) *The Works of Joseph Addison* (ed. Bohn), V, 236 ff.

The / Plebeian./ No. II. / *Considerations upon the Reports relating / to the* Peerage *continued; and / Remarks upon the Pamphlets that have / been writ for the supposed* Bill. / By a Member of the House of Commons. / *Quis enim jam non intelligat Artes. / Patricias?* [1] / *London*: / Printed for S. Popping at the *Black Raven* in *Paternoster- / Row.* 1719. (Price 6 d.) / Where Letters are taken in, directed for the *Plebeian.* /
[1] In the title of the second and subsequent editions is inserted: Juv. Sat. 4.

The / Plebeian. / No. III. / By a Member of the House of Commons. / *London*: / Printed for S. Popping at the *Black Raven* in *Paternoster- / Row.* 1719. (Price 3 d.) / Where Letters are taken in, directed for the *Plebeian*: / And where may also be had the Fourth Edition of No. I. and II. /

The / Plebeian. / No. IV. / *Considerations upon the Reports about the* / Peerage, *continued; in particular, / with relation to the* Scots Nobility / *With Remarks on the* Patrician, No. II. / *and the* Old Whig, No. II. / By a Member of the House of Commons. / *—Quorum melior sententia menti. / —Pelago Danaum insidias, suspectaq; dona / Praecipitare jubent.—*Virg. / *London*: / Printed for S. Popping at the *Black Raven* in *Paternoster- / Row.* 1719. (Price 6 d.) / Where may be had the Three former Numbers. /

The text of the four numbers of *The Plebeian* used here is that of the sixth edition, collected.

No. I. Collation of the final text of No. I with the earlier editions available— first, second, and fifth—indicates a few minor changes in spelling, punctuation, and capitalization. The corrections called for on p. 16 of the second edition are made as follows:
[1] these : then (first)
[2] so : too (first)
[3] Slavery : Knavery (first)

No. II. The final text incorporates all but one of the corrections which were called for in the *errata*, placed at the end in some copies of the first edition (p. 18):
[1] PLEBEIAN to be printed in small capitals and *Old Whig* in italics. (direction).
[2] how (to be added).

[3] Judicature (to be italicized; but the direction is not followed in the coll. ed.).
[4] " that if . . . the other " (to be enclosed in turned commas).
[5] have (to replace) has.
[6] serious (to replace) curious.
[7] *Regal* (to replace) *Royal.*
[8] for fear (to be deleted, but it remains in the coll. ed.).

No. III. Only minor changes are made in spelling, punctuation, etc. in the final form.

No. IV. A change in arrangement at the end is made as follows:

1. In the first and second editions of No. IV, the passage beginning, " It is said, That by the Bill " and ending, " the Minds of their Electors," is given at the end after the quotation from *Cato,* as a postscript (so labelled). The opening sentence of the postscript, " I beg pardon for giving my Reader this irregular trouble, having omitted something of consequence in this affair," is dropped out in the final text and replaced by—" There is one thing more which I think not improper to take notice of on this Head."

THE JOINT AND HUMBLE ADDRESS (p. 497)

The Joint and Humble Address of the Tories and Whigs Concerning the Bill of Peerage. Printed for J. W. and sold by Sam. Briscoe at the Bell Sauvage, Ludgate Hill. [1719]. Anon. Pub. 30 Apr.-2 May 1719 (*Postman*). These facts about the tract are given by Aitken, *Life,* II, 218 n. No copy is known; but a draft of the text in Steele's handwriting is preserved among the MSS at Blenheim Palace, and a copy of this manuscript indicating Steele's own deletions and additions, made by Aitken, is among the Steele Papers at the University of Texas.

Reprinted: *Abel Boyer, *The Political State of Great Britain,* May, 1719, XVII, 490-93.

Collation of Boyer's text, which is used here, with Steele's manuscript indicates that this manuscript draft was the final version printed, that is, assuming that Boyer used Steele's pamphlet. The readings discarded by Steele are indicaed below. The Advertisement at the end is not in the manuscript.

[1] Humble *deleted*; Joint *substituted.*
[2] Intended *inserted.* That is, in the draft copy, the title reads: *The Joint Address of the Tories and Whiggs Concerning the Intended Bill of Peerage.*
[3] resigning : offering
[4] regard of them : choice
[5] T———y : Treachery *spelled out.*
[6] Acknowledge : professedly declare
[7] Violation : insolence
[8] Patience : mercy
[9] occasionally *added*
[10] Crimes : errors
[11] from the Dread : dreading *deleted*; out of dread *deleted.*
[12] some : violent Whigs
[13] far : high
[14] Violent Tories : some
[15] general : common
[16] give : muster
[17] transfer : take

[18] Protection : Safety
[19] Oppression : Tyranny
[20] Peers might : Power would
[21] Violation : Infringement of
[22] Might : May
[23] wishes : appetites

THE ANTIDOTE I AND II (p. 501)

The Antidote, In a Letter to the Free-Thinker, 1719. Anon. 4to, 18 pp. Pub. late in May or early in June. Copy in the British Museum; *photostat at Goucher College.

The Antidote. No. II. In a Letter to the Free-Thinker. 1719. Anon. 4to, 18 pp. Pub. 15 June (*Daily Courant*). Copy at the British Museum, and at Chicago; *photostat of the former at Goucher College.

The text of each tract is that of the first and only edition published. Two alterations are made in *The Antidote,* according to directions given in the *Errata* appended to *The Antidote* No. II.

[1] silly : Pity (original tract)
[2] lives : lies (original tract)

A LETTER TO OXFORD (p. 521)

A Letter to the Earl of Oxford, 1719. 8vo, 32 pp. Pub. 8 Dec. (*Daily Courant*). Copies at Texas, *Goucher College, and elsewhere.

Second ed., 1719. 8vo, 32 pp. Copies at Texas and in the British Museum.

Third ed., 1719. 8vo, 32 pp. Copies at Texas, in the British Museum, and at McGill University.

Third ed., Dublin, 1719, sm. 8vo, 16 pp. Copy at Harvard.

Another ed., London, 1719, 19cm, 24 pp. Copy at the Library of Congress.

Reprinted: (1) *The Orphan Revived or Powell's Weekly Journal,* London, 26 Dec. 1719 to 23 Jan. 1720; (2) *The Town Talk, The Fish Pool, The Plebeian . . . Now First Collected; With Notes and Illustrations,* London, Printed by and for John Nichols, 1789, pp. 381-404, 1790, pp. 371-392.

The text is that of the first edition, which was not altered in the second and third " editions."

SPEECH ON THE PEERAGE BILL (p. 539)

Steele's Speech Against Committing the Bill of Peerage. Delivered in the House of Commons on 8 Dec. 1719. Printed versions: *Historical Register,* 1720, V, No. XVII, pp. 7-14; William Cobbett, *Parliamentary History,* VII, 609-616.

The text is that of Cobbett's *Parliamentary History,* derived, it appears, from the *Historical Register.*

THE SPINSTER (p. 547)

The Spinster: In Defence of the Woollen Manufactures, 1719. Anon. 8vo size, 16 pp. Pub. 19 Dec. (*Postman*). Copies at Chicago, the British Museum, and *Texas.

Reprinted: *The Town Talk, The Fish Pool, The Plebeian . . . Now First*

Collected; With Notes and Illustrations, London, Printed by and for John Nichols, 1789, pp. 415-426; 1790, pp. 413-423.

The text is that of the only edition of the pamphlet published.

THE CRISIS OF PROPERTY (p. 557)

The Crisis of Property, 1720. 8vo size, 30 pp. Pub. 1 Feb. (*Evening Post* and *Theatre* No. 9). Copies at Texas, Chicago, Newberry Library, *Goucher College, and in the British Museum.

Second ed., 1720. 8vo. Pub. 4-6 Feb. (*Evening Post*). The editor has not seen this edition, but a copy was advertised by McLeish, London, in *Catalogue* No. 133, December, 1942.

Reprinted: *The Theatre by Sir Richard Steele; to which are added The Anti-Theatre; the Characters of Sir John Edgar; Steele's Case with the Lord Chamberlain . . . Illustrated with Literary and Historical Anecdotes by John Nichols,* London, 1791, pp. 530-548.

The text used is that of the first edition.

A NATION A FAMILY (p. 573)

A Nation a Family . . . 1720. 8vo, 32 pp. Pub. 26 or 27 Feb. (*Daily Courant*). Copies at Johns Hopkins, *Goucher College, Chicago, Harvard, British Museum, Newberry Library. Reprinted: *The Theatre by Sir Richard Steele; to which are added The Anti-Theatre; the Characters of Sir John Edgar; Steele's Case with the Lord Chamberlain; . . . Illustrated with Literary and Historical Anecdotes by John Nichols,* London, 1791.

The text used is that of the only edition published.

THE STATE OF THE CASE (p. 591)

The State of the Case . . . 1720. 8vo size, 31 pp. Pub. 29 March (*The Theatre* No. 26). Copies at Texas, *Goucher College, and in the British Museum.

Second ed., 8vo size, 31 pp. Pub. early in April 1720. Copies at Harvard and McGill University.

Reprinted: *The Theatre by Sir Richard Steele; to which are added The Anti-Theatre; the Characters of Sir John Edgar; Steele's Case with the Lord Chamberlain . . . Illustrated with Literary and Historical Anecdotes by John Nichols,* London, 1791, pp. 447-467.

The text used here is that of the first edition (which has not been collated with that of the second).

PASQUIN (p. 609)

Pasquin. Nos. 1-120. 28 Nov. 1722–26 March 1724. Folio. [Ed. by George Duckett and Nicholas Amhurst]. Sold by J. Peele in Pater-noster Row.

No. 46. 9 July 1723, Tuesday. By Steele. *Copy at Yale.

No. 51. 26 July 1723, Friday. By Steele. *Copy at the Folger Library.

Reprinted: *The Theatre by Sir Richard Steele to which are added The Anti-Theatre; the Characters of Sir John Edgar; Steele's Case with the Lord Chamber-*

lain . . . Illustrated with Literary and Historical Anecdotes by John Nichols,
London, 1791, pp. 568-580.

The text of each paper is that of the original folio issue.

GREATNESS AMONG THE MODERNS (p. 618)

In 1938, this manuscript of 9¼ folio leaves in Steele's hand was in London in
the possession of Maggs Brothers. Originally it came from the collection of
Steele papers at Blenheim Palace, having been sold by Sotheby (property of
the Duke of Marlborough, Lot 36) and bought by Maggs on 1 July 1920.
Several times since that date it has been advertised by Messrs Maggs as an
autograph draft letter from Steele to Lord Sunderland, with an excerpt and a
one-page facsimile reproduction given (see for example, *Catalogue* No. 449,
1924, Item 398, and Pl. XCIX). In the summer of 1938, the present editor was
permitted to examine, but not to transcribe the autograph manuscript. There is
nothing written on it which would indicate that it was addressed by Steele to
Lord Sunderland, the ascription in the Maggs *Catalogue* apparently being a
surmisal based on its provenience in the Blenheim archives. The source of the
text given here is a copy of the original manuscript made by George A. Aitken
in the 1880's, when he had access to the Blenheim collection, this copy being
preserved with the Aitken papers at the University of Texas, where in 1941 it
was made available to the editor. Aitken's transcription was so carefully made,
with every deletion, interlinear addition, even every smudge and blot so faithfully
reproduced, that it is possible to record below the alterations made by Steele in
the process of composition.

[1] the Greatest first person in the Age   *deleted*
[2] Him   *deleted*
[3] my whole dissertation is to be   *deleted*
[4] which I shall Treat with much freedome   *deleted*
[5] as even the Words of a Text divide themselves into severall parts,   *deleted*
[6] not only the Greatest person   *deleted*
[7] principally   *added*
[8] settled as   *deleted*
[9] your Lordship and others of lesse degree in the sort of superiority to which
    yᵣ Lordship has   *deleted*
[10] I lay before you for   *deleted*
[11] and Scandal   *added*
[12] do in the shortest Manner   *deleted*
[13] Authors   *deleted*
[14] Thredbare   *deleted*
[15] warily earnestly to pursue nothing but what   *deleted*
[16] to be concerned   *deleted*
[17] yield to   *deleted*
[18] is possessed   *deleted*
[19] a prospect of meeting therein   *deleted*
[20] no other but Labour and Danger   *deleted*
[21] labour   *deleted*
[22] danger of life itself   *deleted*
[23] usually   *deleted*
[24] other   *deleted*
[25] to   *deleted*

[26] indeed   *deleted*
[27] properly   *deleted*
[28] This again consists in this limitation, that   *deleted*
[29] that in   *deleted*
[30] self   *deleted*
[31] slight   *deleted*
[32] other   *deleted*
[33] think Honourable and   *deleted*
[34] and on the other hand   *deleted*
[35] they   *deleted*
[36] grevious   *deleted*
[37] maintain the power   *deleted*
[38] Lawlesse   *added*
[39] even   *deleted*
[40] and for which all Consider—Magnanimous men are always to Labour   *deleted*
[41] laid down   *deleted*
[42] of   *deleted*
[43] she loses   *deleted*
[44] then   *deleted*
[45] or not at all   *added*
[46] and to flesh and Blood   *deleted*
[47] their desired   *added*
[48] great   *deleted*
[49] and   *deleted*
[50] and gratifying   *added*
[51] despises   *deleted*
[52] most   *deleted*
[53] most respect   *deleted*
[54] gracefully   *deleted*
[55] gracefully   *deleted*
[56] really approves Him   *deleted*
[57] take from   *deleted*
[58] free   *deleted*
[59] Personal Greatnesse   *deleted*
[60] allowing persons below others to Love us, and   *deleted*
[61] for their resentments, and carrying on or being interrupted by them   *deleted*
[62] our   *deleted*
[63] We Riches [be Rich?]   *deleted*
[64] And   *deleted*
[65] one   *deleted*
[66] of   *deleted*
[67] other   *deleted*
[68] considerable   *added*
[69] who is willing to part with it on valuable considerations at all   *deleted*
[70] land   *deleted*
[71] among   *deleted*
[72] the   *deleted*
[73] and   *deleted*
[74] make   *deleted*
[75] endow   *deleted*
[76] without a   *deleted*
[77] answer   *deleted*

[78] all *deleted*
[79] unseasonable *deleted*
[80] after that *deleted*
[81] an Height *deleted*
[82] few *deleted*
[83] out of it *deleted*

ISAACK BICKERSTAFFE ESQ. TO PASQUIN (p. 626)

This manuscript, which has been since 1929 in the Library of Harvard University, was originally in the possession of Lieutenant-Colonel Edward James Tickell, D. S. O., J. P., of Carnalway, County Kildare. It is written in Steele's hand and consists of ten numbered foolscap pages 12 by 7⅝ inches in size. Page 3 is missing, and the subject matter is abruptly interrupted at the bottom of page 11. The arrangement of the pages shows Steele's way of composing: one half of each page at the left, from top to bottom, is used as a wide margin for additions and corrections (See illustration, p. 629). Like the manuscript of the *Joint and Humble Address of the Tories and Whigs* and that of *Greatness Among the Moderns*, this one is of interest and value in showing Steele at work in the act of composing. His deleted phrasings which are legible are given below as variant readings. The motto is from *Ars Poetica*, line 454.

[1] and safety (deleted)
[2] may : should
[3] care so little to hear of Rome : having a mortall aversion to anything which comes from Rome
[4] made : become
[5] greif to me : consequence
[6] others : those
[7] Vid : Tatl : (deleted from the margin opposite)
[8] In order to [do] this : It would be too long
[9] fall : sort
[10] such : these
[11] change (deleted)
[12] professed : carried on
[13] dissensions : distrust
[14] Just : merciful
[15] prevailed upon : (1) obliged (2) easily persuaded
[16] all our Religious Rights : the Church to whose loyalty He owed His Crown
[17] Use : place
[18] with : in
[19] they : men
[20] esteem Men's Religion : Measure Religion
[21] resign : put off
[22] Roundhead : Fanatical Roundhead
[23] must : will
[24] examine : consider
[25] apparent : indisputable
[26] Fanaticks : Phrenzys
[27] pretends to insinuate : thinks
[28] which is supremely powerfull (deleted)
[29] travell meekly : go alone

30 faithful Souldiours and Sergeants : Warriours
31 two thousand : so many thousand
32 gave : will Baffle . . . by
33 did : used
34 Enthusiasts : Lunaticks
35 uttered against : Levelled at
36 is in greater [purity] of Worship : Enjoys its present Worship

The INDEX

The INDEX

657